Charles Knight

The Pictorial Edition Of The Works of Shakspeare

Charles Knight

The Pictorial Edition Of The Works of Shakspeare

ISBN/EAN: 9783743603219

Manufactured in Europe, USA, Canada, Australia, Japa

Cover: Foto ©Thomas Meinert / pixelio.de

Manufactured and distributed by brebook publishing software (www.brebook.com)

Charles Knight

The Pictorial Edition Of The Works of Shakspeare

THE
PICTORIAL EDITION
OF THE WORKS OF
SHAKSPERE.

EDITED BY
CHARLES KNIGHT.

COMEDIES.—VOL. I.

NEW YORK:
P. F. COLLIER.

CONTENTS.

	PAGE
TWO GENTLEMEN OF VERONA	1
LOVE'S LABOUR'S LOST	73
THE MERRY WIVES OF WINDSOR	155
COMEDY OF ERRORS	200
TAMING OF THE SHREW	361
A MIDSUMMER-NIGHT'S DREAM	329
THE MERCHANT OF VENICE	385

ILLUSTRATIONS TO VOL. I.

COMEDIES.

FRONTISPIECE.

Various Portraits of Shakspere.

TITLE-PAGE TO VOLUME.

Flaxman's Thalia. The Clowns and Fools of the Old Comedy in the Background, their Insignia being cast down at the base of the Statue of Legitimate Comedy. W. DICKS.

TWO GENTLEMEN OF VERONA.

	PAGE
Title-page—Group embodying the final Scene, an original design by W. HARVEY	1

INTRODUCTORY NOTICE.

Autograph of Shakspere, from his copy of Florio's Montaigne, now in the British Museum	3
Costume of Italian Gentleman (after Vecellio)	15
Costume of Italian Nobleman (after Hoghenburg)	15
Ditto, second example, ditto	16
Costume of Italian Lady (after Vecellio)	17

DRAMATIS PERSONÆ.

Border of Flowers (after Domenichino)	18

ACT I.

Open Place in Verona, including the Piazza Della Bra (from an old Print)	19
Verona—View on the Adige (from an old Print)	24

ILLUSTRATIONS OF ACT I.

A Beadsman	25
Torture of the Boot (from Millæus)	26
Silver Ducat of Venice	27
Gold Ducat of Venice	27
Tester—Shilling of Henry VIII	28

ACT II.

Room in the Ducal Palace at Milan. A Composition	30
Street in Milan (from Aspari)	38

ILLUSTRATIONS OF ACT II.

Groves	39
Beggar-man and Woman (from the Romau de la Rose)	39
Table-book (from Gesner)	40

	PAGE
ACT II.	
Costume of Page (after Paul Veronese)	41
True-love Knots (from Boissard and a Print of the 16th century)	41
ACT III.	
General View of Milan	42

ILLUSTRATION OF ACT III.

Queen Elizabeth's Salt-cellar (from Nichols's Progresses)	48

ACT IV.

Forest, with Outlaws (after Salvator Rosa)	49
Court of the Duke's Palace at Milan. A Composition	55

ILLUSTRATIONS OF ACT IV.

Friar Tuck (from Mr. Tollett's Window)	56
St. Winifred's Well (from an old Print)	56
The Stocks (from Fox's Acts, &c.)	57
The Pillory (from ditto)	57

ACT V.

The Abbey of St. Ambrosio at Milan (from an original Sketch)	58
Triumph at Milan. Composition after Hoghenburg	62

ILLUSTRATION OF ACT V.

Pageant. Designed from Sharp's Dissertation on Coventry Pageants	64

SUPPLEMENTARY NOTICE.

Ornamental Head. The Comic Muse (Cipriani)	65
Shakspere's House at Stratford (from a Drawing by W. H. PYNE)	72

LOVE'S LABOUR'S LOST.

Title-page—Group from Act V.; design by W. HARVEY	73

INTRODUCTORY NOTICE.

Thalia, from an original Drawing by Cipriani	75
Costume of a Spanish Gentleman and a French Lady, from Vecellio	79

DRAMATIS PERSONÆ.

Border, and a View in Navarre, near Pampeluna	80

ACT I

Dull, Costard, and Jaquenetta; design by R. W. BUSS	81
Knotted Garden	87

v

ILLUSTRATIONS TO VOL. I.—COMEDIES.

ACT II.

Pavilions in Park: the meeting of the Princess of France and the King of Navarre, and their attendant Ladies and Nobles: design by G. F. SARGENT........ 89

ACT III.

The Palace and Park—Biron and Costard: design by G. F. SARGENT 93
The Inamorato, from Burton's Anatomie of Melancholy 96

ILLUSTRATIONS OF ACT III.

The Brawl: design by R. W. BUSS 97
The Hobby Horse: design by R. W. BUSS 99
The Tumbler's Hoop: design by R. W. BUSS 100

ACT IV.

Don Armado and Moth: design by R. W. BUSS 101

ACT V.

Holofernes as Judas Maccabæus, and Moth as Hercules: design by R. W. BUSS 112
Song of Winter: design by R. W. BUSS 126

ILLUSTRATIONS OF ACT V.

Costume of Muscovites, from Vecellio 127
Statute Caps 128
Bowls: design by R. W. BUSS 128
Quarter-staff: design by R. W. BUSS 129

SUPPLEMENTARY NOTICE.

Chimney Corner of Shakspere's Kitchen, from an original Drawing by EDRIDGE 140
Love's Labour's Lost acted before Queen Elizabeth. Composition by R. W. BUSS 156

THE MERRY WIVES OF WINDSOR.

Title-page. From a design by W. HARVEY 137

INTRODUCTORY NOTICE.

Part of Windsor Castle, built in the time of Elizabeth 139
Insignia of the Order of the Garter 149

DRAMATIS PERSONÆ.

Border, from a design by W. HARVEY 150

ACT I.

Garden Front of Page's House.—'I pray you, sir, walk in.' From a design by T. CRESWICK 151

ILLUSTRATIONS OF ACT I.

Master of Fence. From a design by R. W. BUSS 159
Mill Sixpence 160
Autograph and Seal of Sir Thomas Lucy 160
Bear-baiting.—'Sackerson loose.' R. W. BUSS 161
Winchester Tower, Windsor Castle. T. CRESWICK 162

ACT II.

Street Front of Page's House. T. CRESWICK 163
Farm-house Porch.—'At a farm-house, a feasting.' T. CRESWICK 170

ILLUSTRATIONS OF ACT II.

Silver Penny of Elizabeth 172
State Procession of Elizabeth to Nonsuch House 173
Beech. T. CRESWICK 174

ACT III.

Street, Windsor. T. CRESWICK 176

Datchet Mead.—'The rogues slighted me into the river.' T. CRESWICK 183

ILLUSTRATIONS OF ACT III.

Bucklersbury, with Woolchurch. From Aggas's Map, 1578. F. FAIRHOLT 185
Old Bridge at Windsor. T. CRESWICK 186

ACT IV.

Ford's House, Windsor.—'Out of my door, you witch.' T. CRESWICK 187
Scene in Windsor Forest. T. CRESWICK 193

ILLUSTRATIONS OF ACT IV.

Mufflers 195
Standing Bed and Truckle Bed 195
Eton. T. CRESWICK 196

ACT V.

'Herne's Oak.' From an old Sketch 197

ILLUSTRATIONS OF ACT V.

Oak and Avenue of Elms, Windsor Home Park T. CRESWICK 201
Oak, near the site of Herne's Oak. T. CRESWICK 205

SUPPLEMENTARY NOTICE.

Windsor, 1859. T. CRESWICK 206
Runnemede, with a distant View of Windsor Castle. From a Design by T. CRESWICK 208

THE COMEDY OF ERRORS.

Title page, from an original design by W. HARVEY 209

INTRODUCTORY NOTICE.

Restoration of the Second Temple of Diana, at Ephesus. S. SLY 211
Medal of Ephesus 219

DRAMATIS PERSONÆ.

Border; Group of Ruins at Ephesus. H. ANELAY 220

ACT I.

Ephesus 221
'We were encounter'd by a mighty Rock.' W. DIGGS 224

ACT II.

Remains of Gate at Ephesus 226
Remains of Aqueduct at Ephesus 231

ACT III.

Syracuse. G. F. SARGENT 233
'Sing, Siren.' FLAXMAN 236

ACT IV.

Remains of the Gymnasium, Ephesus 240
'Far from her nest, the Lapwing cries.' L. WELLS 246

ACT V.

Remains of the Amphitheatre at Ephesus 247
Corinth 253

SUPPLEMENTARY NOTICE.

Thalia 255
Coin of Ephesus 260

ILLUSTRATIONS TO VOL. I.—COMEDIES.

TAMING OF THE SHREW.

Title-page. W. HARVEY................................. 261

INTRODUCTORY NOTICE.

Noble Huntsmen. From the Frontispiece to the
  'Noble Art of Venerie or Hunting.' 16 1....... 265
King James I. and Attendants, hawking 268
English Lady and Hostess. From a Painting by
  M. Gerrard, and a Print by Strutt.................. 269

INDUCTION.

Wincot. From a Drawing by S. SLY................... 271
Barton-on-the-Heath. F. FAIRHOLT.................. 273

ILLUSTRATIONS OF THE INDUCTION.

Abu-l-Hasan 276
Abu l-Hasan awakening in the Palace 280

DRAMATIS PERSONÆ.

Border: Composed from an original Drawing of a
Room in the Doge's Palace, Venice; and Articles from the Antique. Cellini, &c. &c. 282

ACT I.

Town-house, Padua. From a Plate in 'Storia
  Dimostrazione della Citta di Padova,' 1767...... 285
Ladies of Padua. From Prints by Vecellio and
  Weigul 290

ACT II.

Pisa—showing the Baptistery, Campo Santo,
  Church, and Leaning Tower. From a Print
  by Franciscus of Milan, 1705....................... 293

ACT III.

Church of St. Ghustinia, Padua. From Plate in
  'Storia Dimostrazione della Citta di Padova,'
  1769... 300
'Hark, hark! I hear the Minstrels play.' Designed from Prints by Schopper, 1568 304

ACT IV.

Prato della Valle, Padua.—Print by Piranesi, 1786 306
Mountain-road near Arqua.—An original Sketch
  by H. ANELAY 315

ACT V.

Gymnasium, Padua.—From an old Print in the
  King's Library, British Museum 319

ILLUSTRATIONS OF ACT V.

Sly at the Ale-house Door.—Design by H. MELVILLE 324

SUPPLEMENTARY NOTICE.

Itinerant Players in a Country Hall.—Design by
  H. ANELAY 325
'The pleasant garden of great Italy.' View between Padua and the Coast.—Design by H.
  ANELAY 328

A MIDSUMMER NIGHT'S DREAM.

Title-page. W. HARVEY.................................. 329

INTRODUCTORY NOTICE.

Battle of the Amazons. From a Sarcophagus in
  the Imperial Cabinet at Vienna 331
Athenian Costume. From the Elgin Marbles...... 333
  Ditto   ditto 334
  Ditto   ditto 334
An Amazon. From a Statue in the Vatican 335

DRAMATIS PERSONÆ.

Border. From a design by W. HARVEY............... 336

ACT I.

Hermia and Helena. W. HARVEY.
  'And in the wood, where often you and I
  Upon faint primrose beds were wont to lie.'..... 337
Bottom. W. HARVEY.
  'I will roar you as 't were any nightingale'...... 342

ILLUSTRATIONS OF ACT I.

Bringing in the May-pole 344
Chorægus instructing the Actors. From a Mosaic
  found at Pompeii..................................... 345

ACT II.

Fairies.—Scenes I. and II. W. HARVEY............. 346
Oberon enchanting Titania. Ditto.
  'What thou seest, when thou dost wake,
  Do it for thy true-love take.'....................... 352

ACT III.

Bottom. W. HARVEY. 'I will walk up and down
  here, and I will sing, that they shall hear I am
  not afraid'.. 355
Puck. W. HARVEY.
  'Up and down, up and down;
  I will lead them up and down '................... 363

ILLUSTRATIONS OF ACT III.

Group of Birds,—'The woosel-cock, so black of hue' 364
Mount Taurus... 366

ACT IV.

'When in a wood of Crete they bay'd the bear.' W
  HARVEY... 367
Bottom awaking. W. HARVEY......................... 371

ACT V.

Palace of Theseus. W. HARVEY.
  'Now, until the break of day,
  Through this house each fairy stray '............ 373
Puck. W. HARVEY.
  'I am sent, with broom, before,
  To sweep the dust behind the door'............. 378

ILLUSTRATION OF ACT V.

Theseus and the Centaurs. From the Elgin Marbles 379

SUPPLEMENTARY NOTICE.

Love in Idleness... 381
Group of Fairies. W. HARVEY........................ 384

ILLUSTRATIONS TO VOL. I.—COMEDIES.

THE MERCHANT OF VENICE.

	PAGE
Title-page. From a design by W. HARVEY	385

INTRODUCTORY NOTICE.

Venice, from the Lagunes. From a Print of the commencement of the 18th century	387
Doge of Venice. From Vecellio's 'Habite Antichi'	394
Venetian Nobleman Do.	395
Venetian Gentleman—The Young Lover Do.	395
Venetian Doctor of Laws Do.	396
Venetian Lady Do.	396

DRAMATIS PERSONÆ.

Border. The Doge's State Gallery, the Bucentaur, passing one of the Red Columns of the Piazzetta. From Prints in 'Vedute di Venezia, designata da Antonio Canale and Antonio Visentini' 400

ACT I.

St. Mark's Place. W. H. PRIOR	401
Venetian Ships of the 16th century.—'Argosies of portly sail'	407

ILLUSTRATIONS OF ACT I.

Two-headed Janus. From an antique engraved in Montfaucon	408
Jester. From the 'Triumphs of Maximilian'	408

ACT II.

Canal in Venice. G. F. SARGENT	410
Place for hiring Gondolas. From Canaletti	410

ILLUSTRATIONS OF ACT II.

	PAGE
Hand—shewing the principal lines and points used in Palmistry. From Indagine's Treatise	420
Terminal Figure of Pan. From Townley Collection in British Museum	421
Gold Angel of Queen Elizabeth	422

ACT III.

Rialto Bridge. W. H. PRIOR	423

ILLUSTRATION OF ACT III.

The Goodwin Sands during a Storm. From a Sketch by S. SLY	433

ACT IV.

Court of the Ducal Palace. W. H. PRIOR	434
Piazzetta di San Marco. W. H. PRIOR	440

ILLUSTRATION OF ACT IV.

Bagpipes. From a Sculpture in Cirencester Church, temp. Henry VII	441

ACT V.

Avenue to Portia's House. G. F. SARGENT	442
'That light we see is burning in my hall.' G. F. SARGENT	448

SUPPLEMENTARY NOTICE.

Caskets. From Titian and the Antique	449
Italian Crosses in Lombardy. From original Sketches	456

* The above autograph of "WILLM. SHAKSPERE" is copied from his undoubted signature in the volume of Montaigno's Essays, by John Florio, which was purchased, for a large sum, by the Trustees of the British Museum.

NOTICE OF THE ORIGINAL EDITIONS OF THE PLAYS.

We propose here to give a very brief account of the Original Copies, upon which the Text of every edition of our author must be founded. We reserve a more detailed notice for a General Preface, when this new impression of the 'Pictorial Shakspere,' with large corrections and additions, is more advanced.

"Mr. William Shakspeare's Comedies, Histories, and Tragedies, published according to the True Originall Copies," is the title of this first collection of our poet's plays. This volume is "printed by Isaac Iaggard and Ed. Blount;" but the Dedication bears the signatures of "John Heminge, Henry Condell." That Blount and Jaggard had become the proprietors of this edition we learn from an entry in the Stationers' registers, under date November 8, 1623; in which they claim "Mr. William Shakspeere's Comedyes, Histories, and Tragedyes, soe many of the said copies as are not formerly entered to other men."

Most of the plays "formerly entered to other men" had been previously published—some in several editions—at dates extending from 1597 to 1622. These are what are commonly spoken of as *the quarto editions*.

John Heminge and Henry Condell were amongst the "principal actors" of the plays of Shakspere, according to a list prefixed to their edition. In 1608 they were shareholders with Shakspere in the Blackfriars Theatre. In his will, in 1616, they are honourably recognized in the following bequest—"To my fellows, John Hemynge, Richard Burbage, and Henry Condell, twenty-six shillings eight-pence apiece, to buy them rings." In 1619, after the death of Shakspere and Burbage, they were at the head of their remaining "fellows."

NOTICE OF THE ORIGINAL EDITIONS OF THE PLAYS.

This first folio edition is dedicated to the Earl of Pembroke and the Earl of Montgomery. The two friends and fellows of Shakspere, in an Address "to the great variety of readers," use very remarkable words:—"It had been a thing, we confess, worthy to have been wished, that the author himself had lived to have set forth and overseen his own writings. But since it hath been ordained otherwise, and he, by death, departed from that right, we pray you do not envy his friends the office of their care and pain to have collected and published them; and so to have published them, as where, before, you were abused with divers stolen and surreptitious copies, maimed and deformed by the frauds and stealths of injurious impostors that exposed them,—even those are now offered to your view cured, and perfect of their limbs; and all the rest, absolute in their numbers, as he conceived them; who, as he was a happy imitator of Nature, was a most gentle expresser of it. *His mind and hand went together; and what he thought, he uttered with that easiness that we have scarce received from him a blot in his papers.*"

That the editors of Shakspere were held to perform an acceptable service to the world by this publication, we may judge from some of the verses prefixed to the edition. Ben Jonson's celebrated poem, "To the Memory of my beloved the Author, Mr. William Shakespeare: and what he hath left us," follows the preface, and it concludes with these lines :—

> "Shine forth, thou star of poets, and with rage,
> Or influence, chide, or cheer, the drooping stage;
> Which, since thy flight from hence, hath mourn'd like night,
> And despairs day, *but for thy volume's light.*"

Another poem in the same volume, by Leonard Digges is in the same tone :—

> "Shake-speare, at length thy *pious fellows* give
> The world thy works; thy works by which outlive
> Thy tomb thy name must. When that stone is rent,
> And time dissolves thy Stratford monument,
> Here we alive shall view thee still. *This book,*
> When brass and marble fade, shall make thee look
> Fresh to all ages."

The edition of 1623 secured from a probable destruction, entire or partial, some of the noblest monuments of Shakspere's genius. The poet had been dead seven years when this edition was printed. Some of the plays which it preserved, through the medium of the press, had been written a considerable period before his death. We have not a single manuscript line in existence, written, or supposed to be written, by Shakspere. If, from any notions of exclusive advantage as the managers of a company, Heminge and Condell had not printed this edition of Shakspere,—if the publication had been suspended for ten, or at most for fifteen, years, till the civil wars broke out, and the predominance of the puritanical spirit had shut up the theatres,—the probability is that all Shakspere's manuscripts would have perished. What then should we have lost, which will now remain when "brass and marble fade!" We will give the list of

NOTICE OF THE ORIGINAL EDITIONS OF THE PLAYS.

those plays which, as far as any edition is known, were printed for the first time in the folio of 1623:—

COMEDIES . . {
The Tempest.
The Two Gentlemen of Verona.
Measure for Measure.
The Comedy of Errors.
As You Like it.
The Taming of the Shrew.
All's Well that Ends Well.
Twelfth Night.
The Winter's Tale.

HISTORIES . . {
King John.
Henry VI., Part I.
Henry VIII.

TRAGEDIES . . {
Coriolanus.
Timon of Athens.
Julius Cæsar.
Macbeth.
Antony and Cleopatra.
Cymbeline.

In addition to the eighteen plays thus recited, which were first printed in the folio, there were four other plays there first printed in a perfect shape. Of the fourteen Comedies, nine first appeared in that edition. Between the quarto editions of the four Comedies,—"Love's Labour's Lost," "A Midsummer Night's Dream," "The Merchant of Venice," "Much Ado about Nothing,"—and the folio of 1623, the variations are exceedingly few; and these have probably, for the most part, been created by the printer. "The Merry Wives of Windsor"—of the quarto edition of which, in 1602 and in 1619, we shall give a more particular account in our notice of that play—is a very incomplete sketch of the Comedy which first appeared in a perfect shape in the edition of 1623.

The second edition of 1632 was held up as an authority by Steevens, because, in some degree, it appeared to fall in with his notions of versification. We doubt if it had an editor properly so called; for the most obvious typographical errors are repeated without change. The printer, probably, of this edition occasionally pieced out what he considered an imperfect line, and altered a word here and there that had grown obsolete during the changes in our language since Shakspere first wrote. But, beyond this, we have no help in the second edition; and none whatever in the subsequent ones. For eighteen plays, therefore, the folio of 1623 must be received as the only accredited copy —standing in the same relation to the text as the one manuscript of an ancient author. For four other plays it must be received as the only accredited complete copy.

The folio of 1623 contains thirty-six plays: of these, thirteen were published in the author's lifetime, with such internal evidences of authenticity, and under such circumstances, as warrant us in receiving them as authentic copies. These copies are, therefore, entitled to a very high respect in the settlement of the author's text. But they do not demand an exclusive respect; for the evidence, in several instances, is most decided, that the author's posthumous copies in manuscript were distinguished from the printed copies by verbal alterations, by additions, by omissions not arbitrarily made, by a more correct metrical arrangement. To refer these differences to alterations made by the players, has been a favourite theory with some of Shakspere's editors; but it is manifestly an absurd one. We see, in numerous cases, the minute but most effective touches

NOTICE OF THE ORIGINAL EDITIONS OF THE PLAYS.

of the skilful artist; and a careful examination of this matter in the plays where the alterations are most numerous, is quite sufficient to satisfy us of the jealous care with which Shakspere watched over the more important of these productions, so as to leave with his "fellows" more complete and accurate copies than had been preserved by the press.

The order in which the Comedies are presented in the folio of 1623 is as follows:—

The Tempest.	Midsummer Night's Dream.
The Two Gentlemen of Verona.	The Merchant of Venice.
The Merry Wives of Windsor.	As You Like It.
Measure for Measure.	The Taming of the Shrew.
The Comedy of Errors.	All 's Well that Ends Well.
Much Ado about Nothing.	Twelfth Night, or What You Will.
Love's Labour 's Lost.	The Winter's Tale.

In the 'Pictorial Edition' we have endeavoured, to the best of our judgment, to arrange the Comedies and Tragedies according to the evidence of the dates of their composition. The Histories follow the Chronology of the several Reigns.

We subjoin a Chronological Table of Shakspere's Plays, which we have constructed with some care, showing the *positive* facts which determine dates *previous* to which they were produced.

CHRONOLOGICAL TABLE OF SHAKSPERE'S PLAYS.

Henry VI. Part I.	Alluded to by Nash, in 'Pierce Pennilesse,'	1592
Henry VI. Part II.	Printed as the 'First Part of the Contention'	1594
Henry VI. Part III.	Printed as 'The True Tragedy of Richard, Duke of York'	1595
Richard II.	Printed	1597
Richard III.	Printed	1597
Romeo and Juliet	Printed	1597
Love's Labour 's Lost	Printed	1598
Henry IV. Part I.	Printed	1598
Henry IV. Part II.	Printed	1600
Henry V.	Printed	1600
Merchant of Venice	Printed 1600. Mentioned by Meres	1598
Midsummer Night's Dream	Printed 1600. Mentioned by Meres	1598
Much Ado about Nothing	Printed	1600
As You Like It	Entered at Stationer's Hall	1600
All 's Well that Ends Well	Held to be mentioned by Meres as 'Love's Labour 's Won'	1598
Two Gentlemen of Verona	Mentioned by Meres	1598
Comedy of Errors	Mentioned by Meres	1598
King John	Mentioned by Meres	1598
Titus Andronicus	Printed	1600
Merry Wives of Windsor	Printed	1602
Hamlet	Printed	1603
Twelfth Night	Acted in the Middle Temple Hall	1602
Othello	Acted at Harefield	1602
Measure for Measure	Acted at Whitehall	1604
Lear	Printed 1608. Acted at Whitehall	1607
Taming of the Shrew	Supposed to have been acted at Henslowe's Theatre, 1593. Entered at Stationer's Hall	1607
Troilus and Cressida	Printed 1609. Previously acted at Court	1609
Pericles	Printed	1609
The Tempest	Acted at Whitehall	1611
The Winter's Tale	Acted at Whitehall	1611
Henry VIII.	Acted as a new play when the Globe was burned	1613

Out of the thirty-seven Plays of Shakspere the dates of thirty-one are thus to some extent fixed in epochs. These dates are, of course, to be modified by other circumstances. There are only six plays remaining, whose dates are not thus limited by publication, by the notice of contemporaries, or by the record of their performances; and these certainly belong to the poet's latter period. They are:—

Macbeth.	Julius Cæsar.
Cymbeline.	Antony and Cleopatra.
Timon of Athens.	Coriolanus.

INTRODUCTORY NOTICE.

STATE OF THE TEXT, AND CHRONOLOGY, OF THE TWO GENTLEMEN OF VERONA.

We have seen, from the list previously given, that this comedy was originally printed in the first folio. The text is singularly correct.

In the edition of 1623, the Two Gentlemen of Verona appears the second in the collection of "Comedies." The Tempest, which it can scarcely be doubted was one of Shakspere's latest plays, precedes it. The arrangement of that edition, except in the three divisions of "Comedies, Histories, and Tragedies," and in the order of events in the "Histories," is quite arbitrary. It is extremely difficult, if not impossible, to fix a precise date to many of Shakspere's plays; and the reasons which Malone, Chalmers, and Drake have given for the determining of an exact chronological order (in which they each differ), are, to our minds, in most instances, unsatisfactory. In the instance before us, Malone originally ascribed the play to the year 1595, because the lines which we shall have occasion afterwards to notice,—

> "Some, to the wars, to try their **fortunes there**
> Some, to discover islands far away;"—

he thought had reference to Elizabeth's military aid to Henry IV., and to Raleigh's expedition to Guiana. He has subsequently fixed the date of its being written as 1591, because there was an expedition to France under Essex in that year. The truth is, as we shall shew, that the excitements of military adventure, and of maritime discovery, had become the most familiar objects of ambition, from the period of Shakspere's first arrival in London to nearly the end of the century. The other arguments of Malone for placing the date of this play in 1591, appear to us as little to be regarded. They are, that the incident of Valentine joining the outlaws has a resemblance to a passage in Sidney's Arcadia, which was not published till 1590;—that there are two allusions to the story of Hero and Leander, which he thinks were suggested by Marlowe's poem on that subject; and that there is also an allusion to the story of Phaeton, which Steevens thinks Shakspere derived from the old play of King John, printed in 1591. All this is really very feeble conjecture, and it is absolutely all that is brought to shew an exact date for this play. The incident of Valentine is scarcely a coincidence, compared with the story in the Arcadia;—and if Shakspere knew nothing of the classical fables from direct sources (which it is always the delight of the commentators to suppose), every palace and mansion was filled with *Tapestry*, in which the subjects of Hero and Leander, and of Phaeton, were constantly to be found. Malone, for these and for no other reasons, thinks the Two Gentlemen of Verona was produced in 1591, when its author was twenty-seven years of age. But he thinks, at the same time, that it was Shakspere's first play.

SUPPOSED SOURCE OF THE PLOT.

A charge which has been urged against Shakspere, with singular complacency on the part of the accusers, is, that he did not invent his plots. A recent writer, who in these later days has thought that to disparage Shakspere would be a commendable task, says, "If Shakspere had little of what the world calls learning, he had less of *invention*, so far as regards the fable of his plays For every one of them he was, in some degree, indebted to a preceding piece."* We do not mention this writer as attaching any value to his opinions; but simply because he has contrived to put in a small compass all that could be raked together, in depreciation of Shakspere as a poet and as a man. The assertion that the most inventive of poets was without invention "as far as regards the fable of his plays," is as absurd as to say that Scott did not invent the fable of Kenilworth, because the sad tale of Amy

* Life of Shakspere in Lardner's Cyclopædia.

INTRODUCTORY NOTICE.

[Ro]bsart is found in Mickle's beautiful ballad of "Cumnor Hall." The truth is, that no one can properly appreciate the extent as well as the subtlety of Shakspere's invention—its absorbing and purifying power—who has not traced him to his sources. It will be our duty, in many cases, to direct especial attention to the material upon which Shakspere worked, to shew how the rough ore became, under his hands, pure and resplendent—converted into something above all price by the unapproachable skill of the artist. It is not the workman polishing the diamond, but converting, by his wonderful alchemy, something of small value into the diamond. It is, in a word, precisely the same process by which the unhewn block of marble is fabricated into the perfect statue: the statue is within the marble, but the Phidias calls it forth. The student of Shakspere will understand that we here more particularly allude to the great plays which are founded on previous imaginative works, such as Romeo and Juliet, and Lear; and not to those in which, like the Two Gentlemen of Verona, a few incidents are borrowed from the romance writers.

"But what shall we do?" said the barber in Don Quixote, when, with the priest, the housekeeper, and the niece, he was engaged in making bonfire of the knight's library—"what shall we do with these little books that remain?" "These," said the priest, "are probably not books of chivalry, but of poetry." And opening one, he found it was the Diana of George Montemayor, and said (believing all the rest of the same kind), "These do not deserve to be burnt like the rest, for they cannot do the mischief that those of chivalry have done: they are works of genius and fancy, and do nobody any hurt." Such was the criticism of Cervantes upon the Diana of Montemayor. The romance was the most popular which had appeared in Spain since the days of Amadis de Gaul;[*] and it was translated into English by Bartholomew Yong, and published in 1598. The story involves a perpetual confusion of modern manners and ancient mythology; and Ceres, Minerva, and Venus, as well as the saints, constitute the machinery. The one part which Shakspere has borrowed, or is supposed to have borrowed, is the story of the shepherdess Felismena, which is thus translated by Mr. Dunlop:—"The first part of the threats of Venus was speedily accomplished; and, my father having early followed my mother to the tomb, I was left an orphan. Henceforth I resided at the house of a distant relative; and, having attained my seventeenth year, became the victim of the offended goddess, by falling in love with Don Felix, a young nobleman of the province in which I lived. The object of my affections felt a reciprocal passion; but his father, having learned the attachment which subsisted between us, sent his son to court, with a view to prevent our union. Soon after his departure, I followed him in the disguise of a page, and discovered on the night of my arrival at the capital, by a serenade I heard him give, that Don Felix had already disposed of his affections. Without being recognised by him, I was admitted into his service, and was engaged by my former lover to conduct his correspondence with the mistress who, since our separation, had supplanted me in his heart."

This species of incident, it is truly observed by Steevens, and afterwards by Dunlop, is found in many of the ancient novels. In Twelfth Night, where Shakspere is supposed to have copied Bandello, the same adventure occurs; but in that delightful comedy, the lady to whom the page in disguise is sent, falls in love with him. Such is the story of Felismena. It is, however, clear that Shakspere must have known this part of the Romance of Montemayor, although the translation of Yong was not published till 1598; for the pretty dialogue between Julia and Lucetta, in the first act, where Julia upbraids her servant for bringing the letter of Proteus, corresponds, even to some turns of expression, with a similar description by Felismena, of her love's history. We give a passage from the old translation by Bartholomew Yong, which will enable our readers to compare the romance writer and the dramatist:—

"Yet to try, if by giving her some occasion I might prevaile, I aside unto her—And is it so, Rosina, that Don Felix, without any regard to mine honour, dares write unto me? These are things, mistresse (saide she demurely to me againe), that are commonly incident to love, wherefore, I beseech you, pardon me; for if I had thought to have angered you with it, I would have first pulled out the bals of mine eies. How cold my hart was at that blow, God knowes; yet did I dissemble the matter, and suffer myself to remain that night only with my desire, and with occasion of little sleepe."—(p. 55.)

Those who are curious to trace this subject further, may find all that Shakspere is supposed to have borrowed from Montemayor, in the third volume of "Shakspeare Illustrated," by Mrs

---

[*] Dunlop's History of Fiction.

TWO GENTLEMEN OF VERONA.

Lenox. We have compared this lady's translation of the passages with that of Bartholomew Yong. The substance is correctly given, though her verbal alterations are not improvements of the quaint prose of the times of Elizabeth.

The writer in Lardner's Cyclopædia, whom we have been already compelled to mention, says, "The Two Gentlemen of Verona (a very poor drama), is indebted for many of its incidents to two works—the Arcadia of Sidney, and the Diana of Montemayor." This writer had neither taken the trouble to examine for himself, nor to report correctly what others had said who had examined. The single incident in Sidney's Arcadia which bears the slightest resemblance to the story of the Two Gentlemen of Verona, is where Pyrocles, one of the two heroes of the Arcadia, is compelled to become the captain of a band of people called Helots, who had revolted from the Lacedemonians; and this is supposed to have given origin to the thoroughly Italian incident of Valentine being compelled to become the captain of the outlaws. The English travellers in Italy, in the time of Shakspere, were perfectly familiar with banditti, often headed by daring adventurers of good family. Fynes Moryson, who travelled between Rome and Naples in 1594, has described a band headed by "the nephew of the Cardinal Cajetano." We may, therefore, fairly leave the uninventive Shakspere to have found his outlaws in other narratives than that of the Arcadia. With regard to the Diana of Montemayor, we have stated the entire amount of what the author of the Two Gentlemen of Verona is supposed to have borrowed from it.

Period of the Action, and Manners.

Amongst the objections which Dr. Johnson, in the discharge of his critical office, appears to have thought it his duty to raise against every play of Shakspere, he says, with regard to the plot of this play, "he places the emperor at Milan, and sends his young men to attend him, but never mentions him more." As the emperor had nothing whatever to do with the story of the Two Gentlemen of Verona, it was quite unnecessary that Shakspere should mention him more; and the mention of him at all was only demanded by a poetical law, which Shakspere well understood, by which the introduction of a few definite circumstances, either of time or place, is sought for, to take the conduct of a story, in ever so small a degree, out of the region of generalization, and, by so doing, invest it with some of the attributes of reality. The poetical value of this single line—

"Attends the emperor in his royal court,"*

can only be felt by those who desire to attach precise images to the descriptions which poetry seeks to put before the mind, and, above all, to the incidents which dramatic poetry endeavours to group and embody. Had this line not occurred in the play before us, we should have had a very vague idea of the scenes which are here presented to us; and, as it is, the poet has left just such an amount of vagueness as is quite compatible with the free conduct of his plot. He is not here dramatizing history. He does not undertake to bring before us the fierce struggles for the real sovereignty of the Milanese between Francis I. and the Emperor Charles V., while Francesco Sforza, the Duke of Milan, held a precarious and disputed authority. He does not pretend to tell us of the dire calamities, the subtle intrigues, and the wonderful reverses which preceded the complete subjection of Italy to the conqueror at Pavia. He does not shew us the unhappy condition of Milan, in 1529, when, according to Guicciardini, the poor people who could not buy provisions at the exorbitant prices demanded by the governor died in the streets,—when the greater number of the nobility fled from the city, and those who remained were miserably poor,—and when the most frequented places were overgrown with grass, nettles, and brambles. He gives us a peaceful period, when courtiers talked lively jests in the duke's saloons, and serenaded their mistresses in the duke's courts. This state of things might have existed during the short period between the treaty of Cambray, in 1529 (when Francis I. gave up all claims to Milan, and it became a fief of the empire under Charles V.), and the death of Francesco Sforza in 1535; or it might have existed at an earlier

* Act I. Scene III.

period in the life of Sforza, when, after the battle of Pavia, he was restored to the dukedom of Milan; or when, in 1525, he received a formal investiture of his dignity. All that Shakspere attempted to define was *some* period when there was a Duke of Milan holding his authority in a greater or less degree under the emperor. That period might have been before the time of Francesco Sforza. It could not have been after it, because, upon the death of that prince, the contest for the sovereignty of the Milanese was renewed between Francis I. and Charles V., till, in 1540, Charles invested his son Philip (afterwards husband of Mary of England) with the title, and the separate honours of a Duke of Milan became merged in the imperial family.

The one historical fact, then, mentioned in this play, is that of the emperor holding his court at Milan, which was under the government of a duke, who was a vassal of the empire. Assuming that this fact prescribes a limit to the period of the action, we must necessarily place that period at least half a century before the date of the composition of this drama. Such a period may, or may not, have been in Shakspere's mind. It was scarcely necessary for him to have defined the period for the purpose of making his play more intelligible to his audience. That was all the purpose he had to accomplish. He was not, as we have said before, teaching history, in which he had to aim at all the exactness that was compatible with the exercise of his dramatic art. He had here, as in many other cases, to tell a purely romantic story; and all that he had to provide for with reference to what is called costume, in the largest sense of that word, was that he should not put his characters in any positions, or conduct his story through any details, which should run counter to the actual knowledge, or even to the conventional opinions of his audience. That this was the theory upon which he worked as an artist we have little doubt; and that he carried this theory even into wilful anachronisms we are quite willing to believe. He saw, and we think correctly, that there was not less real impropriety in making the ancient Greeks speak English than in making the same Greeks describe the maiden "in shady cloister mew'd," by the modern name of a nun.* He had to translate the images of the Greeks, as well as their language, into forms of words that an uncritical English audience would apprehend. Keeping this principle in view, whenever we meet with a commentator lifting up his eyes in astonishment at the prodigious ignorance of Shakspere, with regard to geography, and chronology, and a thousand other proprieties, to which the empire of poetry has been subjected by the inroads of modern accuracy, we picture to ourselves a far different being from the rude workman which their pedantic demonstrations have figured as the *beau idéal* of the greatest of poets. We see the most skilful artist employing his materials in the precise mode in which he intended to employ them; displaying as much knowledge as he intended to display; and, after all, committing fewer positive blunders, and incurring fewer violations of accuracy, than any equally prolific poet before or after him. If we compare, for example, the violations of historical truth on the part of Shakspere, who lived in an age when all history came dim and dreamy before the popular eye, and on the part of Sir Walter Scott, who lived in an age when all history was reduced to a tabular exactness—if we compare the great dramatist and the great novelist in this one point alone, we shall find that the man who belongs to the age of accuracy is many degrees more inaccurate than the man who belongs to the age of fable. There is, in truth, a philosophical point of view in which we must seek for the solution of those contradictions of what is real and probable, which, in Shakspere, his self-complacent critics are always delighted to refer to his ignorance. One of their greatest discoveries of his geographical ignorance is furnished in this play:—Proteus and his servant go to Milan by water. It is perfectly true that Verona is inland, and that even the river Adige, which waters Verona, does not take its course by Milan. Shakspere, therefore, was most ignorant of geography! In Shakspere's days countries were not so exactly mapped out as in our own, and therefore he may, from lack of knowledge, have made a boat sail from Verona, and have given Bohemia a sea-board. But let it be borne in mind that, in numberless other instances, Shakspere has displayed the most exact acquaintance with what we call geography—an acquaintance not only with the territorial boundaries, and the physical features of particular countries, but with a thousand nice peculiarities connected with their government and customs, which nothing but the most diligent reading and inquiry could furnish. Is there not, therefore, another solution of the ship at Verona, and the sea-board of Bohemia, than Shakspere's ignorance? Might not his knowledge have been in

* Midsummer Night's Dream.

TWO GENTLEMEN OF VERONA.

subjection to what he required, or fancied he required, for the conduct of his dramatic incidents? Why does Scott make the murder of a Bishop of Liege, by William de la Marck, the great cause of the quarrel between Charles the Bold and Louis XI., to revenge which murder the combined forces of Burgundy and France stormed the city of Liege,—when, at the period of the insurrection of the Liegeois described in Quentin Durward, no William de la Marck was upon the real scene, and the murder of a Bishop of Liege by him took place fourteen years afterwards? No one, we suppose, imputes this inaccuracy to historical ignorance in Scott. He was writing a romance, we say, and he therefore thought fit to sacrifice historical truth. The real question, in all these cases, to be asked, is, Has the writer of imagination gained by the violation of propriety a full equivalent for what he has lost? In the case of Shakspere we are not to determine this question by a reference to the actual state of popular knowledge in our time. What startles us as a violation of propriety was received by the audience of Shakspere as a fact,—or, what was nearer the poet's mind, the fact was held by the audience to be in subjection to the fable which he sought to present;—the world of reality lived in a larger world of art;—art divested the real of its formal shapes, and made its hard masses plastic. In our own days we have lost the power of surrendering our understanding, spell-bound, to the witchery of the dramatic poet. We cannot sit for two hours enchained to the one scene which equally represents Verona or Milan, Rome or London, and ask no aid to our senses beyond what the poet supplies us in his dialogue. We must now have changing scenes, which carry us to new localities; and pauses to enable us to comprehend the time which has elapsed in the progress of the action; and appropriate dresses, that we may at once distinguish a king from a peasant, and a Roman from a Greek. None of these aids had our ancestors;—but they had what we have not—a thorough love of the dramatic art in its highest range, and an appreciation of its legitimate authority. Wherever the wand of the enchanter waved, there were they ready to come within his circle and to be mute. They did not ask, as we have been accustomed to ask, for happy Lears and unmetaphysical Hamlets. They were content to weep scalding tears with the old king, when his "poor fool was hanged," and to speculate with the unresolving prince even to the extremest depths of his subtlety. They did not require tragedy to become a blustering melodrame, or comedy a pert farce. They could endure poetry and wit—they understood the alternations of movement and repose. We have, in our character of audience, become degraded even by our advance in many appliances of civilization with regard to which the audiences of Shakspere were wholly ignorant. We know many small things exactly, which they were content to leave unstudied; but we have lost the perception of many grand and beautiful things which they received instinctively and without effort. They had great artists working for them, who knew that the range of their art would carry them far beyond the hard, dry, literal copying of every-day Nature which we call Art; and they laid down their shreds and patches of accurate knowledge as a tribute to the conquerors who came to subdue them to the dominion of imagination. What cared they, then, if a ship set sail from Verona to Milan, when Valentine and his man ought to have departed in a carriage;—or what mattered it if Hamlet went "to school at Wittemberg," when the real Hamlet was in being five centuries before the university of Wittemberg was founded? If Shakspere had lived in this age, he might have looked more carefully into his maps and his encyclopædias. We might have gained something, but what should we not have lost!

We have been somewhat wandering from the immediate subject before us; but we considered it right, upon the threshold of our enterprise, to make a profession of faith with regard to what many are accustomed to consider irredeemable violations of propriety in Shakspere. We believe the time is passed when it can afford any satisfaction to an Englishman to hear the greatest of our poets perpetually held up to ridicule as a sort of inspired barbarian, who worked without method, and wholly without learning. But before Shakspere can be properly understood, the popular mind must be led in an opposite direction; and we must all learn to regard him, as he really was, as the most consummate of artists, who had a complete and absolute control over all the materials and instruments of his art, without any subordination to mere impulses and caprices,—with entire self-possession and perfect knowledge.

"Shakspere," says Malone, "is fond of alluding to events occurring at the time when he wrote;"* and Johnson observes that many passages in his works evidently shew that "he often took advantage of the facts then recent, and the passions then in motion."† This was a part of the method of

---

* *Life*, vol. ii. p. 331, edit. 1821. † Note on King John.

INTRODUCTORY NOTICE.

Shakspere, by which he fixed the attention of his audience. The Nurse in Romeo and Juliet, says, "It is now since the earthquake eleven years." Dame Quickly, in the Merry Wives of Windsor, talks of her "knights, and lords, and gentlemen, with their coaches. I warrant you, coach after coach." Coaches came into general use about 1605. "Banks's horse," which was exhibited in London in 1589, is mentioned in Love's Labour's Lost. These, amongst many other instances which we shall have occasion to notice, are not to be regarded as determining the period of the dramatic action; and, indeed, they are, in many cases, decided anachronisms. In the Two Gentlemen of Verona, there are several very curious and interesting passages which have distinct reference to the times of Elizabeth, and which, if Milan had then been under a separate ducal government, would have warranted us in placing the action of this play about half a century later than we have done. As it is, the passages are remarkable examples of Shakspere's close attention to "facts then recent;" and they shew us that the spirit of enterprise, and the intellectual activity which distinguished the period when Shakspere first began to write for the stage, found a reflection in the allusions of this accurate observer. We have noted these circumstances more particularly in our Illustrations; but a rapid enumeration of them may not be unprofitable.

In the scene between Antonio and Panthino, where the father is recommended to "put forth" his son "to seek preferment," we have a brief but most accurate recapitulation of the stirring objects that called forth the energies of the master-spirits of the court of Elizabeth :—

> "Some, to the wars, to try their fortune there;
> Some, to discover islands far away;
> Some, to the studious universities"

Here, in three lines, we have a recital of the great principles that, either separately, or more frequently in combination, gave their impulses to the ambition of an Essex, a Sidney, a Raleigh, and a Drake :—War, still conducted in a chivalrous spirit, though with especial reference to the "preferment" of the soldier ;—Discovery, impelled by the rapid development of the commercial resources of the nation, and carried on in a temper of enthusiasm which was prompted by extraordinary success and extravagant hope ;—and Knowledge, a thirst for which had been excited throughout Europe by the progress of the Reformation and the invention of printing, which opened the stores of learning freely to all men. These pursuits had succeeded to the fierce and demoralizing passions of our long civil wars, and the more terrible contentions that had accompanied the great change in the national religion. The nation had at length what, by comparison, was a settled Government. It could scarcely be said to be at war; for the assistance which Elizabeth afforded to the Hugonots in France, and to those who fought for freedom of conscience and for independence of Spanish dominion in the Netherlands, gave a healthy stimulus to the soldiers of fortune who drew their swords for Henry of Navarre and Maurice of Nassau ;—and though the English people might occasionally lament the fate of some brave and accomplished leader, as they wept for the death of Sidney at Zutphen, there was little of general suffering that might make them look upon those wars as anything more to be dreaded than some well-fought tournament. Shakspere, indeed, has not forgotten the connexion between the fields where honour and fortune were to be won by wounds, and the knightly lists where the game of mimic war was still played upon a magnificent scale; where the courtier might, without personal danger,

> "Practise tilts and tournaments,"

before his queen, who sat in her "fortress of perfect beauty," to witness the exploits of the "foster-children of desire," amidst the sounds of cannon "fired with perfumed powder," and "moving mounts and costly chariots, and other devices."*

There was another circumstance which marked the active and inquiring character of these days, which Shakspere has noticed—

> "Home keeping youths have ever homely wits,"

exclaims Valentine; and Panthino says of Proteus, it

> "Would be great impeachment to his age
> In having known no travel in his youth"

* See Illustrations to Act I.

TWO GENTLEMEN OF VERONA.

Travelling was the passion of Shakspere's times—the excitement of those who did not specially devote themselves to war, or discovery, or learning. The general practice of travelling supplies one amongst many proofs, that the nation was growing commercial and rich, and that a spirit of inquiry was spread amongst the higher classes, which made it "impeachment" to their age not to have looked upon foreign lands in their season of youth and activity.

The allusions which we thus find in this comedy to the pursuits of the gallant spirits of the court of Elizabeth are very marked. The incidental notices of the general condition of the people are less decided; but a few passages that have reference to popular manners may be pointed out.

The boyhood of Shakspere was passed in a country town where the practices of the Catholic church had not been wholly eradicted either by severity or reason. We have one or two passing notices of these. Proteus, in the first scene, says,

"I will be thy Beadsman, Valentine."

Shakspere had, doubtless, seen the rosary still worn, and the "beads bidden," perhaps even in his own house. Julia compares the strength of her affection to the unwearied steps of "the true-devoted pilgrim." Shakspere had, perhaps, heard the tale of some ancient denizen of a ruined abbey, who had made the pilgrimage to the shrine of our Lady at Loretto, or had even visited the sacred tomb at Jerusalem. Thurio and Proteus are to meet at "Saint Gregory's well." This is the only instance in Shakspere in which a holy well is mentioned; but how often must he have seen the country people, in the early summer morning, or after their daily labour, resorting to the fountain which had been hallowed from the Saxon times as under the guardian influence of some venerated saint. These wells were closed and neglected in London when Stowe wrote; but at the beginning of the last century, the custom of making journeys to them, according to Bourne, still existed among the people of the North; and he considers it to be "the remains of that superstitious practice of the Papists of paying adoration to wells and fountains." This play contains several indications of the prevailing taste for music, and exhibits an audience proficient in its technical terms; for Shakspere never addressed words to his hearers which they could not understand. This taste was a distinguishing characteristic of the age of Elizabeth; it was not extinct in those of the first Charles; but it was lost amidst the puritanism of the Commonwealth and the profligacy of the Restoration, and has yet to be born again amongst us. There is one allusion in this play to the games of the people—"bid the base,"—which shews us that the social sport which the school-boy and school-girl still enjoy,—that of prison base, or prison bars,—and which still make the village green vocal with their mirth on some fine evening of spring, was a game of Shakspere's days. In the long winter nights the farmer's hearth was made cheerful by the well-known ballads of Robin Hood; and to "Robin Hood's fat friar" Shakspere makes his Italian outlaws allude. But with music, and sports, and ales, and old wife's stories, there was still much misery in the land. "The beggar" not only spake "puling" "at Hallowmas," but his importunities or his threats were heard at all seasons. The disease of the country was vagrancy; and to this deep-rooted evil there were only applied the surface remedies to which Launce alludes, "the stocks" and "the pillory." The whole nation was still in a state of transition from semi-barbarism to civilization; but the foundations of modern society had been laid. The labourers had ceased to be vassals; the middle class had been created; the power of the aristocracy had been humbled, and the nobles had clustered round the sovereign, having cast aside the low tastes which had belonged to their fierce condition of independent chieftains. This was a state in which literature might, without degradation, be adapted to the wants of the general people; and "the best public instructor" then, was the drama. Shakspere found the taste created; but it was for him, most especially, to purify and exalt it.

It is scarcely necessary, perhaps, to caution our readers against imagining that because Shakspere in this, as in all his plays, has some reference to the manners of his own country and times, he has given a false representation of the manners of the persons whom he brings upon his scene. The tone of the Two Gentlemen of Verona is, perhaps, not so thoroughly Italian as some of his later plays—the Merchant of Venice, for example; but we all along feel that his characters are not English. The allusions to home customs which we have pointed out, although curious and important as illustrations of the age of Shakspere, are so slight that they scarcely amount to any

INTRODUCTORY NOTICE.

violation of the most scrupulous propriety; and regarded upon that principle which holds that in a work of art the exact should be in subordination to the higher claims of the imaginative, they are no violations of propriety at all.

SCENES AND COSTUME.

In the folio of 1623, there are no indications of the localities of the several SCENES. The notices, such as "An open Place in Verona, The Garden of Julia's House, A Room in the Duke's Palace, A Forest near Mantua," are additions that have been usefully made, from time to time. The text, either specially or by allusion, of course furnishes the authority for these directions.

The scenes which we have illustrated are the following; and we shall mention in this, as in all other cases, the authorities upon which we have founded our designs.

1. *An open Place in Verona.* In this view is seen the "Piazza della Bra" of Palladio, which was erected about the time of Shakspere; and, of course, somewhat later than the period we have assigned to the dramatic action. An old print in the British Museum has been here copied.

2. *Room in the Duke's Palace at Milan.* This is after a composition by Mr. A. Poynter, strictly in accordance with the architecture of the period. The apartment is supposed to open upon a loggia, with a balcony looking over a garden.

3. *Street in Milan.* The authorities for this view are, Aspar Veduta di Milano, and Veduta dell Ospitale Maggiore, 1456. The hospital is the large building shewn on the left of the design.

4. *General View of Milan.* Braun's Civitates Orbis Terrarum, a very curious work, in six folio volumes, first printed in 1523, contains a plan of Milan; and an old print in the King's Library has been partly copied, with some slight picturesque adaptations.

5. *Forest near Mantua.* A well-known print after Salvator Rosa has furnished this scene.

6. *Court of the Palace, Milan.* This is also after a composition by Mr. A. Poynter, in which he has endeavoured to exemplify the Lombard architecture of the sixteenth century.

7. *Abbey at Milan.* This is a view of the Cloister of Saint Ambrosio, in that city, a building existing at the period of the play. It is drawn from an original sketch.

The period at which the incidents of this play are supposed to have taken place, has been our guide in the selection of its COSTUME. It is fixed, as we have previously noticed, by the mention of the Emperor holding "his Royal Court" at Milan, while there was a sovereign prince of that particular duchy. We have therefore chosen our pictorial illustrations from authorities of the commencement of the sixteenth century; as, after the death of Francesco Sforza, in 1535, the duchy of Milan became an appanage of the Crown of Spain, and, as such, formed part of the dominions of Philip II., husband of our Queen Mary.

Cesare Vecellio, the brother of Titian, in his curious work, "Habiti Antiche e Moderni di tutto il mondo," completed in 1589, presents us with the general costume of the noblemen and gentlemen of Italy at the period we have mentioned, which has been made familiar to us by the well-known portraits of the contemporary monarchs, Francis I. and our own Henry VIII. He tells us they wore a sort of diadem surmounted by a turban-like cap of gold tissue, or embroidered silk, a plaited shirt low in the neck with a small band or ruff, a coat or cassock of the German fashion, short in the waist and reaching to the knee, having sleeves down to the elbow, and from thence shewing the arm covered only by the shirt with wristbands or ruffles. The cassock was ornamented with stripes or borders of cloth, silk, *or velvet* of different colours, or of gold lace or embroidery, according to the wealth or taste of the wearer. With this dress they sometimes wore doublets and stomachers, or *placcards*, as they were called, of different colours, their shoes being of

TWO GENTLEMEN OF VERONA.

velvet, like those of the Germans, that is, very broad at the toes. Over these cassocks again were occasionally worn cloaks or mantles of silk, velvet, or cloth of gold, with ample turn-over collars

of fur or velvet, having large arm holes through which the full puffed sleeves of the cassock passed, and sometimes loose hanging sleeves of their own, which could either be worn over the others or thrown behind at pleasure.

INTRODUCTORY NOTICE.

Nicholas Hoghenberg, in his curious series of prints exhibiting the triumphal processions and other ceremonies attending the entry of Charles V. into Bologna, A.D. 1530, affords us some fine specimens of the costume at this period, worn by the German and Italian nobles in the train of the Emperor. Some are in the cassocks described by Vecellio, others in doublets with slashed hose; confined both above and below knee by garters of silk or gold. The turban head-dress is worn by the principal herald; but the nobles generally have caps or bonnets of cloth or velvet placed on the side of the head, sometimes over a caul of gold, and ornamented with feathers, in some instances profusely. These are most probably the Milan caps or bonnets of which we hear so much in wardrobe accounts and other records of the time. They were sometimes slashed and puffed round the edges, and adorned with "points" or "aglets" i.e. tags or aiguillettes. The feathers in them, also, were occasionally ornamented with drops or spangles of gold, and jewelled up the quills.

Milan was likewise celebrated for its silk hose. In the inventory of the wardrobe of Henry VIII., Harleian MSS., Nos. 1419 and 1420, mention is made of "a pair of hose of purple silk, and Venice gold, woven like unto a caul, lined with blue silver sarcenet, edged with a passemain of purple silk and gold, wrought at Milan, and one pair of hose of white silk and gold knits, bought of Christopher Millener." Our readers need scarcely be told that the present term milliner is derived from Milan, in consequence of the reputation of that city for its fabrication as well "of weeds of peace" as of "harness for war;" but it may be necessary to inform them that by hose at this period is invariably meant breeches or upper stocks, the *stockings*, or *nether stocks*, beginning now to form a separate portion of male attire.

The ladies, we learn from Vecellio, wore the same sort of turbaned head-dress as the men, resplendent with various colours, and embroidered with gold and silk in the form of rose leaves, and other devices. Their neck chains and girdles were of gold, and of great value. To the latter were

TWO GENTLEMEN OF VERONA.

attached fans of feathers with richly ornamented gold handles. Instead of a veil they wore a sort of collar or neckerchief (Bavaro) of lawn or cambric, pinched or plaited. The skirts of their gowns were usually of damask, either crimson or purple, with a border lace or trimming round the bottom, a quarter of a yard in depth. The sleeves were of velvet or other stuff, large and slashed, so as to shew the lining or under garment, terminating with a small band or ruffle like that round the edge of the collar. The body of the dress was of gold stuff or embroidery. Some of the dresses were made with trains which were either held up by the hand when walking, or attached to the girdle. The head-dress of gold brocade given in one of the plates of Vecellio, is not unlike the beretta of the Doge of Venice; and caps very similar in form and material are still worn in the neighbourhood of Linz in Upper Austria.

The Milan bonnet was also worn by ladies as well as men at this period. Hall, the chronicler, speaks of some who wore "Myllain bonnets of crymosyne sattin drawn through (i.e. slashed and puffed) with cloth of gold;" and in the roll of provisions for the marriage of the daughters of Sir John Nevil, *tempore* Henry VIII., the price of "a Millan bonnet, dressed with aglets," is marked as 11s.

PERSONS REPRESENTED.

DUKE, *father to Silvia.*
VALENTINE, } *The two Gentlemen.*
PROTEUS,
ANTONIO, *father to Proteus.*
THURIO, *a foolish rival to Valentine.*
EGLAMOUR, *agent for Silvia, in her escape.*
SPEED, *a clownish servant to Valentine.*
LAUNCE, *the like to Proteus.*
PANTHINO, *servant to Antonio.*
HOST, *where Julia lodges.*
OUT-LAWS *with Valentine.*

JULIA, *a lady of Verona, beloved of Proteus.*
SILVIA, *the Duke's daughter, beloved of Valentine.*
LUCETTA, *waiting-woman to Julia.*

Servants, Musicians.

*** In the original, *Proteus* is invariably spelt *Protheus.*

THE TOMB OF THE SCALIGERS AT VERONA.

Two Gentlemen of Verona. Act I. sc. 1.

ACT I.

SCENE I.—*An open place in* Verona.

Enter VALENTINE *and* PROTEUS.

Val. Cease to persuade, my loving Proteus;
Home-keeping youth have ever homely wits;
Wer't not affection chains thy tender days
To the sweet glances of thy honour'd love,
I rather would entreat thy company,
To see the wonders of the world abroad,
Than, living dully sluggardiz'd at home,
Wear out thy youth with shapeless idleness.
But, since thou lov'st, love still, and thrive
  therein,
Even as I would, when I to love begin.
  Pro. Wilt thou be gone? Sweet Valentine,
  adieu!
Think on thy Proteus, when thou, haply, seest
Some rare note-worthy object in thy travel:
Wish me partaker in thy happiness,
When thou dost meet good hap; and in thy
  danger,
If ever danger do environ thee,
Commend thy grievance to my holy prayers,
For I will be thy bead's-man, Valentine.
  Val. And on a love-book pray for my success?
  Pro. Upon some book I love, I'll pray for
  thee.
  Val. That's on some shallow story of deep
  love,
How young Leander cross'd the Hellespont.

Pro. That's a deep story of a deeper love;
For he was more than over boots in love.
  Val. 'T is true; for you are over boots in love,
And yet you never swom the Hellespont.
  Pro. Over the boots? nay, give me not the
  boots.[a]
  Val. No, I will not, for it boots thee not.
  Pro. What?
  Val. To be in love, where scorn is bought
    with groans;
Coy looks with heart-sore sighs; one fading
    moment's mirth,
With twenty watchful, weary, tedious nights:
If haply won, perhaps a hapless gain;
If lost, why then a grievous labour won;
However,[b] but a folly bought with wit,
Or else a wit by folly vanquished.
  Pro. So, by your circumstance, you call me
    fool.

---

[a] Steevens gives the passage thus:—
  Val. No, I'll not, for it boots thee not.
  Pro. What?
  Val. To be
In love, where scorn is bought with groans; coy looks
With heart-sore sighs; one fading moment's mirth, &c.
By this reading, the Alexandrine in the line beginning with "coy looks" is avoided;—but the force and harmony of the entire passage are weakened. Our reading is that of the edit. of 1623. We mention this deviation from the reading of the common octavo edition here; but we shall not often repeat this sort of notice. Steevens having a notion of metre which placed its highest excellence in monotonous regularity, has unsparingly maimed the text, or stuck something upon it, to satisfy his "finger-counting ear." We shall silently restore the text, as Malone has in many cases done.

[b] *However.* In whatsoever way, "haply won," or "lost."

Val. So, by your circumstance,[a] I fear, you'll prove.
Pro. 'T is love you cavil at; I am not love.
Val. Love is your master, for he masters you:
And he that is so yoked by a fool,
Methinks should not be chronicled for wise.
Pro. Yet writers say, as in the sweetest bud
The eating canker dwells,[a] so eating love
Inhabits in the finest wits of all.
Val. And writers say, as the most forward bud
Is eaten by the canker ere it blow,
Even so by love the young and tender wit
Is turn'd to folly; blasting in the bud,
Losing his[b] verdure even in the prime,
And all the fair effects of future hopes.
But wherefore waste I time to counsel thee,
That art a votary to fond desire?
Once more adieu: my father at the road
Expects my coming, there to see me shipp'd.
Pro. And thither will I bring thee, Valentine.
Val. Sweet Proteus, no; now let us take our leave.
To Milan let me hear from thee by letters,[c]
Of thy success in love, and what news else
Betideth here in absence of thy friend;
And I likewise will visit thee with mine.
Pro. All happiness bechance to thee in Milan!
Val. As much to you at home! and so, farewell. [*Exit* VALENTINE
Pro. He after honour hunts, I after love:
He leaves his friends to dignify them more;
I leave myself,[d] my friends, and all for love.
Thou, Julia, thou hast metamorphos'd me;
Made me neglect my studies, lose my time,
War with good counsel, set the world at nought;
Made wit with musing weak, heart sick with thought.

Enter SPEED.

Speed. Sir Proteus, save you: Saw you my master?
Pro. But now he parted hence, to embark for Milan.
Speed. Twenty to one then he is shipp'd already;
And I have played the sheep, in losing him.

Pro. Indeed a sheep doth very often stray,
An if the shepherd be awhile away.
Speed. You conclude that my master is a shepherd then, and I a sheep?
Pro. I do.
Speed. Why then my horns are his horns, whether I wake or sleep.
Pro. A silly answer, and fitting well a sheep.
Speed. This proves me still a sheep.
Pro. True; and thy master a shepherd.
Speed. Nay, that I can deny by a circumstance.
Pro. It shall go hard, but I'll prove it by another.
Speed. The shepherd seeks the sheep, and not the sheep the shepherd; but I seek my master, and my master seeks not me: therefore, I am no sheep.
Pro. The sheep for fodder follow the shepherd, the shepherd for food follows not the sheep; thou for wages followest thy master, thy master for wages follows not thee: therefore, thou art a sheep.
Speed. Such another proof will make me cry baa.
Pro. But dost thou hear? gav'st thou my letter to Julia?
Speed. Ay, sir; I, a lost mutton, gave your letter to her, a laced mutton;[b] and she, a laced mutton, gave me, a lost mutton, nothing for my labour!
Pro. Here's too small a pasture for such store of muttons.
Speed. If the ground be overcharged, you were best stick her.
Pro. Nay, in that you are astray;[b] 't were best pound you.
Speed. Nay, sir, less than a pound shall serve me for carrying your letter.
Pro. You mistake; I mean the pound, a pinfold.
Speed. From a pound to a pin? fold it over and over,
'T is threefold too little for carrying a letter to your lover.
Pro. But what said she? did she nod?[c]
[SPEED *nods*.

---

[a] *Circumstance.* The word is used by the two speakers in different senses. Proteus employs it in the meaning of *circumstantial deduction*:—Valentine in that of *position*.
[b] According to modern construction, in his valuable "Philological Commentary on Julius Cæsar," he has clearly shown that "*His* was formerly neuter as well as masculine, or the genitive of *it* as well as of *He*."
[c] *To Milan.* Let me hear from thee by letters, *addressed to Milan.* This is the reading of the first folio, and has been restored by Malone.
[d] The original copy reads, "I love myself."

---

[a] *A laced mutton.* The commentators have much doubtful learning on this passage. They maintain that the epithet "laced" was a very uncomplimentary epithet of Shakspere's time; and that the words taken together apply to a female of loose character. This is probable; but then the insolent application, by Speed, of the term to Julia is received by Proteus very patiently. The original meaning of the verb lace is to catch—to hold (see Tooke's Diversions &c. part ii. ch. 4); from which the noun lace,—any thing which catches or holds. Speed might, therefore, without an insult to the mistress of Proteus, say—I, a lost sheep, gave your letter to her, a caught sheep.
[b] *Astray.* The adjective here should be read "a *stray*"—a stray sheep.
[c] *Did she nod?* These words, not in the original text, were introduced by Theobald. The stage-direction, "Speed nods," is also modern.

Speed. I.[a]
Pro. Nod, I; why, that's noddy.
Speed. You mistook, sir; I say, she did nod: and you ask me, if she did nod; and I say, I.
Pro. And that set together, is—noddy.
Speed. Now you have taken the pains to set it together, take it for your pains.
Pro. No, no, you shall have it for bearing the letter.
Speed. Well, I perceive, I must be fain to bear with you.
Pro. Why, sir, how do you bear with me?
Speed. Marry, sir, the letter very orderly; having nothing but the word, noddy, for my pains.
Pro. Beshrew me, but you have a quick wit.
Speed. And yet it cannot overtake your slow purse.
Pro. Come, come, open the matter in brief: What said she?
Speed. Open your purse, that the money, and the matter, may be both at once delivered.
Pro. Well, sir, here is for your pains: What said she?
Speed. Truly, sir, I think you'll hardly win her.
Pro. Why? Could'st thou perceive so much from her?
Speed. Sir, I could perceive nothing at all from her; no, not so much as a ducat[d] for delivering your letter: And being so hard to me that brought your mind, I fear, she'll prove as hard to you in telling your mind.[b] Give her no token but stones; for she's as hard as steel.
Pro. What said she,—nothing?
Speed. No, not so much as—*take this for thy pains.* To testify your bounty, I thank you, you have testern'd[e] me; in requital whereof, henceforth carry your letters yourself: and so, sir, I'll commend you to my master.
Pro. Go, go, be gone, to save your ship from wrack;
Which cannot perish, having thee aboard,
Being destined to a drier death on shore:[c]—
I must go send some better messenger;
I fear my Julia would not deign my lines,
Receiving them from such a worthless post.
    [*Exeunt.*

[a] *I.* The old spelling of the affirmative particle *Ay.*
[b] The second folio changes the passage to "*her* mind." The first gives it "*your* mind." Speed says,—she was hard to me than *brought* your mind, by letter;—she will be as hard to you in *telling* it, in person.
[c] The same allusion to the proverb, "**He that is born to be** hanged," &c., occurs in the Tempest.

SCENE II.—*The same. Garden of Julia's House.*
Enter JULIA *and* LUCETTA.

Jul. But say, Lucetta, now we are alone,
Would'st thou then counsel me to fall in love?
Luc. Ay, madam, so you stumble not unheedfully.
Jul. Of all the fair resort of gentlemen,
That every day with parle[a] encounter me,
In thy opinion, which is worthiest love?
Luc. Please you, repeat their names, I'll shew my mind
According to my shallow simple skill.
Jul. What think'st thou of the fair sir Eglamour?
Luc. As of a knight well-spoken, neat and fine;
But, were I you, he never should be mine.
Jul. What think'st thou of the rich Mercatio?
Luc. Well of his wealth; but of himself, so, so.
Jul. What think'st thou of the gentle Proteus?
Luc. Lord, lord! to see what folly reigns in us!
Jul. How now! what means this passion at his name?
Luc. Pardon, dear madam; 'tis a passing shame,
That I, unworthy body as I am,
Should censure[b] thus on lovely gentlemen.
Jul. Why not on Proteus, as of all the rest?
Luc. Then thus,——of many good I think him best.
Jul. Your reason?
Luc. I have no other but a woman's reason;
I think him so, because I think him so.
Jul. And would'st thou have me cast my love on him?
Luc. Ay, if you thought your love not cast away.
Jul. Why, he of all the rest hath never mov'd me.
Luc. Yet he of all the rest, I think, best loves ye.
Jul. His little speaking shews his love but small.
Luc. Fire[c] that's closest kept burns most of all.
Jul. They do not love that do not shew their love.

[a] *Parle.* Speech. The first folio spells it par'le, which shews the abbreviation of the original French *parole.*
[b] *Censure.* Give an opinion—a meaning which repeatedly occurs.
[c] *Fire* is here used as a dissyllable. Steevens, whose ear received it as a monosyllable, corrupted the reading. In Act II. Sc. VII., we have this line—

"But qualify **the fire's extreme** rage."

See Walker, on "Shakespeare's Versification," § xviii. The present play furnishes other examples, such as,

"Trenched in ice, which with **an** hour's heat."

When the reader has a key to the reading of such words—*fi-er, how-er-er*—he may dispense with the notes that he will perpetually find on these matters in the pages of Steevens.

Luc. O, they love least that let men know
   their love.
Jul. I would I knew his mind.
Luc.   Peruse this paper, madam.
Jul. To *Julia*,—Say, from whom?
Luc.   That the contents will shew.
Jul. Say, say; who gave it thee?
Luc. Sir Valentine's page; and sent, I think,
   from Proteus:
He would have given it you, but I, being in the
      way,
Did in your name receive it; pardon the fault,
   I pray.
Jul. Now, by my modesty, a goodly broker!
Dare you presume to harbour wanton lines?
To whisper and conspire against my youth?
Now, trust me, 't is an office of great worth,
And you an officer fit for the place.
There, take the paper, see it be return'd;
Or else return no more into my sight.
Luc. To plead for love deserves more fee than
      hate.
Jul. Will you be gone?
Luc.   That you may ruminate. [*Exit.*
Jul. And yet, I would I had o'erlook'd the
      letter.
It were a shame to call her back again,
And pray her to a fault for which I chid her.
What[a] fool is she, that knows I am a maid,—
And would not force the letter to my view!
Since maids, in modesty, say *No*, to that
Which they would have the profferer construe *Ay*.
Fie, fie! how wayward is this foolish love,
That, like a testy babe, will scratch the nurse,
And presently, all humbled, kiss the rod!.
How churlishly I chid Lucetta hence,
When willingly I would have had her here!
How angerly[b] I taught my brow to frown,
When inward joy enforc'd my heart to smile!
My penance is, to call Lucetta back,
And ask remission for my folly past :—
What ho! Lucetta?

     Re-enter LUCETTA.

Luc.   What would your ladyship?
Jul. Is 't near dinner time?
Luc.   I would it were;
That you might kill your stomach on your meat,
And not upon your maid.
Jul.   What is 't you took up
So gingerly?
Luc. Nothing.
Jul.   Why didst thou stoop then?
Luc. To take a paper up that I let fall.

[a] What[a] fool (for what a fool). *Dyce.*
[b] *Angerly*, not angrily, as many modern editions have it, was the adverb used in Shakspere's time.

Jul. And is that paper nothing?
Luc.   Nothing concerning me.
Jul. Then let it lie for those that it concerns.
Luc. Madam, it will not lie where it concerns,
Unless it have a false interpreter.
Jul. Some love of yours hath writ to you in
      rhyme.
Luc. That I might sing it, madam, to a tune·
Give me a note: your ladyship can set.[a]
Jul. As little by such toys as may be possible
Best sing it to the tune of *Light o' love.*[b]
Luc. It is too heavy for so light a tune.
Jul. Heavy? belike, it hath some burden then.
Luc. Ay; and melodious were it, would you
      sing it.
Jul. And why not you?
Luc.   I cannot reach so high.
Jul. Let's see your song;—How now, minion?
Luc. Keep tune there still, so you will sing it
      out:
And yet, methinks, I do not like this tune.
Jul. You do not?
Luc. No, madam; 't is too sharp. .
Jul. You, minion, are too saucy.
Luc. Nay, now you are too flat,
And mar the concord with too harsh a descant:[b]
There wanteth but a mean[c] to fill your song.
Jul. The mean is drown'd with you, unruly
      base.[d]
Luc. Indeed, I bid the base[e] for Proteus.
Jul. This babble shall not henceforth trouble
      me.
Here is a coil with protestation!—[*Tears the letter.*
Go, get you gone; and let the papers lie:
You would be fingering them, to anger me.
Luc. She makes it strange; but she would be
      best pleas'd
To be so anger'd with another letter.   [*Exit.*
Jul. Nay, would I were so anger'd with the
      same!
O hateful hands, to tear such loving words!
Injurious wasps! to feed on such sweet honey,
And kill the bees, that yield it, with your stings!
I 'll kiss each several paper for amends.
Look, here is writ—*kind Julia*;—unkind Julia!
As in revenge of thy ingratitude,
I throw thy name against the bruising stones,

[a] *Set.* Compare. Julia plays upon the word, in the next line, in a different sense,—to " set by," being to make account of.
[b] *Descant.* The simple air, in music, was called the " Plain song," or ground. The " descant " was what we now call a " variation."
[c] *Mean.* The tenor. The whole of the musical allusions in this passage shew that the terms of the art were familiar to a popular audience.
[d] You in the ordinary reading is " your unruly base."
[e] The quibbling Lucetta here turns the allusion to the country game of base, or prison-base, in which one runs and challenges another to pursue.

Trampling contemptuously on thy disdain.
And, here is writ—*love-wounded Proteus*:—
Poor wounded name! my bosom, as a bed,
Shall lodge thee, till thy wound be throughly
 heal'd;
And thus I search it with a sovereign kiss.
But twice, or thrice, was Proteus written down:
Be calm, good wind, blow not a word away,
Till I have found each letter in the letter,
Except mine own name: *that* some whirlwind
 bear
Unto a ragged, fearful-hanging rock,[a]
And throw it thence into the raging sea!
Lo, here in one line is his name twice writ,—
Poor forlorn Proteus, passionate Proteus.
To the sweet Julia; that I'll tear away;
And yet I will not, sith so prettily
He couples it to his complaining names;
Thus will I fold them one upon another;
Now kiss, embrace, contend, do what you will.

Re-enter LUCETTA.

Luc. Madam, dinner is ready, and your father
 stays.
Jul. Well, let us go.
Luc. What, shall these papers lie like tell-tales
 here?
Jul. If you respect them, best to take them up.
Luc. Nay, I was taken up for laying them
 down:
Yet here they shall not lie, for catching cold.[b]
Jul. I see you have a mouth's mind to them.[c]
Luc. Ay, madam, you may say what sights you
 see;
I see things too, although you judge I wink.
Jul. Come, come, will please you go.
 [*Ex.*

SCENE III.—*The same. A room in* Antonio's
 House.

Enter ANTONIO *and* PANTHINO.

Ant. Tell me, Panthino, what sad[d] talk was that,
Wherewith my brother held you in the cloister?
Pan. 'T was of his nephew Proteus, your son.
Ant. Why, what of him?
Pan. He wonder'd, that your lordship

[a] *Fearful-hanging* adopted from Delius, in Camb edit. 1863.
[b] *For catching cold.* Lest they should catch cold.
[c] *The month's mind,* in one form of the expression, referred to the solemn mass, or other obsequies directed to be performed for the repose of the soul, under the will of a deceased person. The strong desire with which this ceremony was regarded in Catholic times might have rendered "the general expression "month's mind" equivalent to an eager longing, in which sense it is generally thought to be here used. But we are not quite sure that it means a strong and abiding desire: two lines in Hudibras would seem to make the "month's mind" only a passing inclination:—
 "For if a trumpet sound, or drum beat,
  Who hath not a month's mind to combat."
[d] *Sad.* Serious.

Would suffer him to spend his youth at home;
While other men, of slender reputation,
Put forth their sons to seek preferment out:
Some, to the wars, to try their fortune there;
Some, to discover islands far away;
Some, to the studious universities[a]
For any, or for all these exercises,
He said, that Proteus, your son, was meet:
And did request me, to importune you,
To let him spend his time no more at home,
Which would be great impeachment to his age,
In having known no travel in his youth.'
 Ant. Nor need'st thou much importune me to
  that
Whereon this month I have been hammering.
I have considered well his loss of time;
And how he cannot be a perfect man,
Not being try'd, and tutored in the world:
Experience is by industry achiev'd,
And perfected by the swift course of time:
Then, tell me, whither were I best to send him?
 Pan. I think, your lordship is not ignorant,
How his companion, youthful Valentine,
Attends the emperor in his royal court.
 Ant. I know it well.
 Pan. 'T were good, I think, your lordship sent
  him thither:
There shall he practise tilts and tournaments,[b]
Hear sweet discourse, converse with noblemen;
And be in eye of every exercise,
Worthy his youth and nobleness of birth.
 Ant. I like thy counsel; well hast thou ad-
  vis'd:
And, that thou may'st perceive how well I like it,
The execution of it shall make known:
Even with the speediest expedition
I will dispatch him to the emperor's court.
 Pan. To-morrow, may it please you, Don
  Alphonso,
With other gentlemen of good esteem,
Are journeying to salute the emperor,
And to commend their service to his will.
 Ant. Good company; with them shall Proteus
  go:
And,—in good time.[a]—Now will we break with
 him.[b]

Enter PROTEUS.

Pro. Sweet love! sweet lines! sweet life!
Here is her hand, the agent of her heart;
Here is her oath for love, her honour's pawn:
O, that our fathers would applaud our loves,

[a] *In good time.* As Antonio is declaring his intention Proteus appears; the speaker, therefore, breaks off with the expression, "in good time"—apropos.
[b] *Break with him.* Break the matter to him,—a form which repeatedly occurs.

To seal our happiness with their consents!
O heavenly Julia!

Ant. How now? what letter are you reading there?

Pro. May't please your lordship, 't is a word or two
Of commendation sent from Valentine,
Deliver'd by a friend that came from him.

Ant. Lend me the letter; let me see what news.

Pro. There is no news, my lord; but that he writes
How happily he lives, how well-beloved,
And daily graced by the emperor;
Wishing me with him, partner of his fortune.

Ant. And how stand you affected to his wish?

Pro. As one relying on your lordship's will,
And not depending on his friendly wish.

Ant. My will is something sorted with his wish:
Muse not that I thus suddenly proceed;
For what I will, I will, and there an end.
I am resolv'd, that thou shalt spend some time
With Valentinus in the emperor's court;
What maintenance he from his friends receives,
Like exhibition* thou shalt have from me.
To-morrow be in readiness to go:

* *Exhibition.* Stipend, allowance. The word is still used in this sense in our universities.

Excuse it not, for I am peremptory.

Pro. My lord, I cannot be so soon provided;
Please you, deliberate a day or two.

Ant. Look, what thou want'st shall be sent after thee;
No more of stay; to-morrow thou must go.—
Come on, Panthino; you shall be employ'd
To hasten on his expedition.

[*Exeunt* ANT. *and* PAN.

Pro. Thus have I shunn'd the fire, for fear of burning;
And drench'd me in the sea, where I am drown'd:
I fear'd to shew my father Julia's letter,
Lest he should take exceptions to my love;
And with the vantage of mine own excuse
Hath he excepted most against my love.
O, how this spring of love resembleth
The uncertain glory of an April day;
Which now shews all the beauty of the sun,
And by and by a cloud takes all away!

Re-enter PANTHINO.

Pan. Sir Proteus, your father calls for you;
He is in haste; therefore, I pray you go.

Pro. Why, this it is! my heart accords thereto;
And yet a thousand times it answers, no.

[*Exeunt.*

ILLUSTRATIONS OF ACT I.

¹ SCENE.—"*I will be thy Beadsman, Valentine.*"

THE Anglo-Saxon *bead*,—a prayer,—something prayed,—has given the name to the mechanical help which the ritual of the early church associated with the act of praying. To drop a ball down a string at every prayer, whether enjoined by the priest or by voluntary obligation, has been the practice of the Romish church for many centuries. In our language the ball, from its use, came to be called the bead. To "bid the beads," and to "pray," were synonymous. Burnet, in his History of the Reformation, says, "The form of *bidding* prayer was not begun by King Henry, as some have weakly imagined, but was used in the times of popery, as will appear by the form of *bidding the beads* in King Henry the Seventh's time. The way was, first, for the preacher to name and open his text, and then to call on the people to go to their prayers, and to tell them what they were to pray for; after which all the people said their *beads* in a general silence, and the minister kneeled down also and said his." We find the expression "*bedes bydding*" in the Vision of Pierce Plowman, which was written, according to Tyrwhitt, about 1362. In the same remarkable poem we also find *Bedman*—headman, or headsman. A beadsman, in the sense of "I will be thy beadsman," is one who offers up prayers for the welfare of another. In this general sense it was used by Sir Henry Lee to Queen Elizabeth. (See Illustration 10.) "Thy poor daily orator and beadsman" was the common subscription to a petition to any great man or person in authority. We retain the substance, though not the exact form, of this courtly humiliation, even to the present day, when we memorialize the Crown and the Houses of Parliament, and seek to propitiate those authorities by the unmeaning assurance that their "petitioners shall ever pray." But the great men of old did not wholly depend upon the efficacy of their prayers for their welfare, which proceeded from the expectation or gratitude of their suitors. They had regularly appointed *beadsmen*, who were paid to weary Heaven with their supplications. It is to this practice that Shakspere alludes, in the speech of Scroop to Richard II.:—

"Thy very beadsmen learn to bend their bows
Of double-fatal yew against thy state."

Johnson, upon this passage, says, "The king's beadsmen were his chaplains." This assertion is partly borne out by an entry in "The Privy Purse Expenses of King Henry VIII.," published by Sir Harris Nicolas:—"Item, to Sir Torche, the king's bede man at the Rood in Greenewiche, for one yere now ended, xl s." The title "Sir" was in these days more especially applied to priests. (See Merry Wives of Windsor.) But the term "Bedesman" was also, we have little doubt, generally applied to any persons, whether of the clergy or laity, who received endowments for the purpose of offering prayers for the sovereign. Henry VII. established such persons upon a magnificent scale. The Harleian MS. No. 1498, in the British Museum, is an indenture made between Henry VII. and John Islipp, Abbot of St. Peter, Westminster, in which the abbot engages to "provide and sustain within the said monastery, in the almshouses there, therefore made and appointed by the said king, thirteen poor men, one of them being a priest;" and the duty of these thirteen poor men is "to pray during the life of the said king, our sovereign lord, for the good and prosperous state of the same king, our sovereign lord, and for the prospering of this his realm." These men are not in the indenture called *bedesmen*; that instrument providing that they "shall be named and called the *Almesse men* of the said king our sovereign lord." The general designation of those who make prayers for others - bedesmen—is here sunk in a name derived from the particular *almesse* (alms), or endowment. The dress of the twelve almsmen is to be a gown and a hood, "and a scochyn to be made and set upon every of the said gowns, and a red rose crowned and embroidered thereupon." In the following design (the figure of which, a monk at his devotions, is from a drawing by Quelinus, a pupil of Rubens) the costume is taken from an illumination in the indenture now recited, which illumination represents the abbot, the priest, and the almsmen receiving the indenture.

The first almsman bears a string of *beads* upon his hand. The "scochyn" made and set upon the gown reminds us of the "badge" of poor Edie

ILLUSTRATIONS OF ACT I.

Ochiltree, in the Antiquary; and this brings us back to "Beadsmen." This prince of mendicants was, as our readers will remember, a "King's Bedesman"—"an order of paupers to whom the kings of Scotland were in the custom of distributing a certain alms, in conformity with the ordinances of the Catholic church, and who were expected, in return, *to pray for the royal welfare and that of the state.*" The similarity in the practices of the "King's Bedesmen" of Scotland, and the "Almesse men" of Henry VII., is precise. "This order," as Sir Walter Scott tells us in his advertisement to the Antiquary, from which the above description is copied, "is still kept up." The "poor orators and beadsmen" of England live now only in a few musty records, or in the allusions of Spenser and Shakspere; and in the same way the "Blue Gowns" or "King's Bedesmen" of Scotland, who "are now seldom to be seen in the streets of Edinburgh," will be chiefly remembered in the imperishable pages of the Author of Waverley.

¹ SCENE I.—"*Nay, give me not the boots.*"

This expression may refer, as Steevens has suggested, to a country sport in harvest-time, in which any offender against the laws of the reaping-season was laid on a bench and slapped with boots. But Steevens has also concluded—and Douce follows up the opinion,—that the allusion is to the instrument of torture called *the Boots.* That horrid engine, as well as the rack and other monuments of the cruelty of irresponsible power, was used in the *question*, in the endeavour to wring a confession out of the accused by terror or by actual torment. This meaning gives a propriety to the allusion which we have not seen noticed. In the passage before us Valentine is bantering Proteus about his mistress—and Proteus exclaims. "Nay, give me not the boots"—do not *torture me to confess* to those love-delinquencies of which you accuse me. The torture of the boots was used principally in Scotland; and Douce has an extract from a very curious pamphlet containing an account of its infliction in the presence of our James I., before he was called to the English crown, upon one Dr. Fein, a supposed wizard, who was charged with raising the storms which the king encountered on his passage from Denmark. The brutal superstition, which led James to the use of this horrid torture, is less revolting than the calculating tyranny which prescribed its application to the unhappy Whig preachers of a century later, as recorded by Burnet, in the case of Macneil, in 1666. Our readers will here again remember Scott, in his powerful scene of Macbriar before the Privy Council of Scotland, —and will think of the wily Lauderdale and his detestable joke when the tortured man has fainted —"he'll scarce ride to-day, though he has had his boots on." Douce says, "the torture of the boot was known in France, and, in all probability, imported from that country." He then gives a representation of it, copied from Millæus's *Praxis criminis persequendi*, Paris, 1541. The wood-cut which we subjoin is from the same book; but we have restored a portion of the original engraving which Douce has omitted—the judges, or examiners, witnessing the torture, and prepared to record the prisoner's deposition under its endurance.

² SCENE I. "*In the sweetest bud The eating canker dwells.*"

This is a figure which Shakspere has often repeated. In the sonnets we have (Sonnet LXX.),—

"Canker vice the sweetest buds doth love."

In King John—

"Now will canker sorrow eat my bud."

In Hamlet,—

"The canker galls the infants of the spring."

The peculiar canker which our poet, a close observer of Nature, must have noted, is described in Midsummer Night's Dream,—

"Some to kill cankers in the musk-rose buds."

And in 1 Henry VI.,—

"Hath not thy rose a canker."

The instrument by which the canker was produced is described in

"The bud bit with an envious worm"

of Romeo and Juliet; and in

"concealment, like a worm i' the bud,
Fed on her damask cheek."

in Twelfth Night.

Shakspere found the "canker worm" in the Old Testament (Joel i. 4). The Geneva Bible, 1561, has "That which is left of the palmer-worm hath the grasshopper eaten, and the residue of the grasshopper hath the *canker-worm* eaten, and the residue of the *canker-worm* hath the caterpillar eaten." The Arabic version of the passage in Joel, renders what is here, and in our received translation, "the palmer-worm" by *dud*, which seems a general denomination for the larva state of an insect, and which applies especially to the "canker-worm." The original Hebrew, which is rendered palmer-worm, is from a verb meaning to cut or shear; the Greek of the Septuagint, by which the same word is rendered, is derived from the verb meaning, to bend. —(See Pictorial Bible, Joel i.) These two words give a most exact description of the "canker-worm;"—of "the canker in the musk-rose buds;"

of the larvæ which are produced in the leaves of many plants, and which find habitation and food by the destruction of the receptacle of their infant existence. These caterpillars are termed "leaf-rollers," and their economy is amongst the most curious and interesting of the researches of entomology. The general operations of the larvæ, and the particular operations of the "cankers in the musk-rose buds," have been described in a little volume entitled, "Insect Architecture." A small dark brown caterpillar, with a black head and six feet, is the "canker worm" of the rose. It derives its specific name *Locotænia Rosana*, from its habits. The grub, produced from eggs deposited in the previous summer or autumn, makes its appearance with the first opening of the leaves, and it constructs its summer tent while the leaves are in their soft and half-expanded state. It weaves them together so strongly, *bending* them (according to the Greek of the Septuagint) and fastening their discs with the silken cords which it spins—that the growth of the bud in which it forms its canopy is completely stopped. Thus secured from the rain and from external enemies, it begins to destroy the inner partitions of its dwelling: it becomes the *cutting* insect of the Hebrew. In this way,

"the most forward bud
Is eaten by the canker ere it blow."

‘ SCENE I.—" *Not so much as a ducat.*"

The ducat—which derives its name from duke, a ducal coin—is repeatedly mentioned in Shakspere. There were two causes for this. First, many of the incidents of his plays were derived from Italian stories, and were laid in Italian scenes; and his characters, therefore, properly use the name of the coin of their country. Thus, ducat occurs in this play—in the Comedy of Errors—in Much Ado about Nothing—in Romeo and Juliet; and, more than all, in the Merchant of Venice. But Italy was the great resort of English travellers in the time of Shakspere; and ducat being a familiar word to him, we find it also in Hamlet, and in Cymbeline. Venice has, at present, its silver ducat—the ducat of eight livres—worth about 3s. 3d. The following representation of its *old* silver ducat is from a coin in the British Museum :—

The gold ducat of Venice is at present worth about 6s. The following representation of its *old* gold ducat is from a print in the Coin Room in the British Museum.

‘ SCENE I.—" *You have testern'd me.*"

A verb is here made out of the name of a coin—the *tester*—which is mentioned twice in Shakspere: 1, by Falstaff, when he praises his recruit Wart, "There's a tester for thee;" and, 2, by Pistol, " Tester I'll have in pouch." We have also testril, which is the same, in Twelfth Night. The value of a tester, teston, testern, or testril, as it is variously written, was supposed to be determined by a passage in Latimer's sermons (1584):— " They brought him a denari, a piece of their current coin that was worth ten of our usual pence—such another piece as our testerne." But the value of the tester, like that of all our ancient coins, was constantly changing, in consequence of the infamous practice of debasing the currency, which was amongst the expedients of bad governments for wringing money out of the people by cheating as well as violence. The French name. *teston*. was applied to a silver coin of Louis XII., 1513, because it bore the king's head; and the English shilling received the same name at the beginning of the reign of Henry VIII.—probably because it had the same value as the French teston. The following representation of the shilling of Henry VIII. is from a specimen in the British Museum. The testons were called in by proclamations in the second and third years of Edward VI., in consequence of the extensive forgeries of this coin by Sir William Sherrington, for which, by an express act of parliament, he was attainted of treason. They are described in these proclamations as "pieces of xiid., commonly called testons." But the base shillings still continued to circulate, and they were, according to Stow, "called down" to the value of ninepence, afterwards to sixpence, and finally to fourpence halfpenny, in the reign of Edward VI.

ILLUSTRATIONS OF ACT I.

The value seems, at last, to have settled to sixpence. Harrison, in his Description of England, says, "Sixpence, usually named the testone." In Shakspere's time it would appear, from the following passage in Twelfth Night, where Sir Toby and Sir Andrew are bribing the Clown to sing, that its value was sixpence :—

"*Sir. To.* Come on; there is sixpence for you: let's have a song.
Sir. A. There 's a testril of me, too."

In the reign of Anne, its value, according to Locke, who distinguishes between the shilling and the tester, was sixpence; and to this day we sometimes hear the name applied to sixpence.

⁶ SCENE II.—"*Best sing it to the tune of* Light o' love."

This was the name of a dance tune, which, from the frequent mention of it in the old poets, appears to have been very popular. Shakspere refers to it again in Much Ado about Nothing, with more exactness: "Light o' love ;—that goes without a burthen ; do you sing it and I'll dance it." We shall give the music (which Sir John Hawkins recovered from an ancient MS.) in that play.

⁷ SCENE II.—"*Injurious wasps ! to feed on such sweet honey.*"

The economy of bees was known to Shakspere with an exactness which he could not have derived from books. The description in 1 Henry V., "So work the honey bees," is a study for the naturalist as well as the poet. He had doubtless not only observed "the lazy, yawning drone," but the "injurious wasps," that plundered the stores which had been collected by those who

"Make boot upon the summer's velvet buds."

These were the fearless robbers to which the pretty pouting Julia compares her fingers :—

"Injurious wasps ! to feed on such sweet honey,
And kill the bees that yield it with your stings."

The metaphor is as accurate as it is beautiful.

⁸ SCENE III.—"*Some to the wars, &c.*"

We have alluded to these lines, somewhat at length, in the Introductory Notice. It would be out of place here to give a more particular detail of what were the wars, and who the illustrious men that went "to try their fortunes there," or to recapitulate "the islands far away," that were sought for or discovered, or to furnish even a list of "the studious universities" to which the eager scholars of Elizabeth's time resorted. The subject is too large for us to attempt its illustration by any minute details. We may, however, extract a passage from Gifford's "Memoirs of Ben Jonson," prefixed to his excellent edition of that great dramatist, which directly bears upon this passage :—

"The long reign of Elizabeth, though sufficiently agitated to keep the mind alert, was yet a season of comparative stability and peace. The nobility, who had been nursed in domestic turbulence, for which there was now no place, and the more active spirits among the gentry, for whom entertainment could no longer be found in feudal grandeur and hospitality, took advantage of the diversity of employment happily opened, and spread themselves in every direction. They put forth, in the language of Shakspere,

'Some, to the wars, to try their fortunes there ;
Some, to discover islands far away;
Some, to the studious universities ;'

and the effect of these various pursuits was speedily discernible. The feelings narrowed and embittered in household feuds, expanded and purified themselves in distant warfare, and a high sense of honour and generosity, and chivalrous valour, ran with electric speed from bosom to bosom, on the return of the first adventurers in the Flemish campaigns ; while the wonderful reports of discoveries, by the intrepid mariners who opened the route since so successfully pursued, faithfully committed to writing, and acting at once upon the cupidity and curiosity of the times, produced an inconceivable effect in diffusing a thirst for novelties among a people, who, no longer driven in hostile array to destroy one another, and combat for interests in which they took little concern, had leisure for looking around them, and consulting their own amusement."

⁹ SCENE III.—"*In having known no travel, &c.*"

There was a most curious practice with reference to travelling in those days, which is well described in Fynes Moryson's Itinerary. Adventurous persons, of slender fortune, deposited a small sum, upon undertaking a distant or perilous journey, to receive a larger sum if they returned alive. Moryson's brother, he tells us, desired to visit Jerusalem and Constantinople, and he "thought this putting out of money to be an honest means of gaining, at least, the charges of his journey." He, therefore, "put out some few hundred pounds, to be repaid twelve hundred pounds, upon his return from those two cities, and to lose it if he died in the journey." We shall have occasion to refer to this practice, in the Tempest, where Shakspere distinctly notices it:

"Each putter out on five for one will bring us Good warrant of," &c.

We have here mentioned this singular sort of bargain, to shew that those who undertook "travel" in those days were considered as incurring serious dangers.

¹⁰ SCENE III.—"*There shall he practise tilts and tournaments.*"

St. Palaye, in his Memoirs of Chivalry, says, that, in their private castles, the gentlemen *practised* the exercises which would prepare them for the public tournaments. This refers to the period which appears to have terminated some half century before the time of Elizabeth, when real warfare was conducted with express reference to the laws of knighthood; and the tourney, with all its magnificent array,—its minstrels, its heralds, and its damosels in lofty towers,—had its hard blows, its wounds, and sometimes its deaths. There were the "Joustes à outrance," or the "Joustes mortelles et à champ," of Froissart. But the "tournaments" that Shakspere sends Proteus to "practise," were the "Joustes of Peace," the "Joustes à Plaisance," the tournaments of gay pennons and pointless lances. They had all the gorgeousness of the old knightly encounters, but they appear to have been regarded only as courtly pastimes, and not as serious preparations for "a well-foughten field." One or two instances from the annals of these times will at least amuse our readers, if they do not quite satisfy them that these combats were as harmless to the combatants as the fierce encounters between other less noble actors—the heroes of the stage.

On Whitson Monday, 1581, a most magnificent tournament was held in the Tilt-yard at Westminster, in honour of the Dauphin, and other noblemen and gentlemen of France, who had arrived as commissioners to the queen. Holinshed describes the proceedings respecting this "Triumph," at great length. A magnificent gallery was erected for the queen and her court, which was called by the combatants the fortress of perfect beauty; "and not without cause, forasmuch as her highness would be there included." Four gentlemen—the Earl of Arundel, the Lord Windsor, Mr. Philip Sydney, and Mr. Fulke Greville—calling themselves the foster-children of Desire, laid claim to this fortress, and vowed to withstand all who should dare to oppose them. Their challenge being accepted by certain gentlemen of the court, they proceeded (in gorgeous apparel, and attended by squires and attendants richly dressed) forthwith to the tilt, and on the following day to the tourney, where they behaved nobly and bravely, but, at length, submitted to the queen, acknowledging that they ought not to have accompanied Desire by Violence, and concluding a long speech, full of the compliments of the day, by declaring themselves thenceforth slaves to the "Fortress of Perfect Beautie." These "Courtlie triumphes" were arranged and conducted in the most costly manner. The queen's gallery was painted in imitation of stone and covered with ivy and garlands of flowers; cannons were bred with perfumed powder; the dresses of the knights and courtiers were of the richest stuff,

and covered with precious stones; and moving mounts, costly chariots, and many other devices were introduced to give effect to the scene.

In the reign of Elizabeth there were annual exercises of arms, which were first commenced by Sir Henry Lee. This worthy knight made a vow to appear armed in the Tilt-yard at Westminster, on the 27th November (the anniversary of the queen's accession) in every year, until disabled by age, where he offered to tilt with all comers, in honour of Her Majesty's accession. He continued the queen's champion until the thirty-third year of her reign, when, having arrived at the sixtieth year of his age, he resigned in favour of George, Earl of Cumberland, who was invested in the office with much form and solemnity in 1590. It was on the 27th November in that year, that Sir Henry Lee, having performed his devoirs in the lists for the last time, and with much applause, accompanied by the Earl of Cumberland, presented himself before the queen, who was seated in her gallery overlooking the lists, and kneeling on one knee, humbly besought Her Majesty to accept the Earl of Cumberland for her knight, to continue the yearly exercises which he was compelled, from infirmities of age, himself to relinquish. The queen graciously accepting the offer, the old knight presented his armour at Her Majesty's feet, and then assisting in fastening the armour of the earl, he mounted him on his horse. This ceremony being performed, he put upon his own person a side coat of "black velvet pointed under the arm, and covered his head (in lieu of a helmet) with a buttoned cap of the country fashion." Then, whilst music was heard proceeding from a magnificent temple which had been erected for the occasion, he presented to the queen, through the hands of three beautiful maidens, a veil curiously wrought, and richly adorned, and other gifts of great magnificence, and declared that, although his youth and strength had decayed, his duty, faith, and love remained perfect as ever; his hands, instead of wielding the lance, should now be held up in prayer for Her Majesty's welfare; and he trusted she would allow him to be her Beadsman, now that he had ceased to incur knightly perils in her service. But the queen complimented him upon his gallantry, and desired that he would attend the future annual jousts, and direct the knights in their proceedings; for indeed his virtue and valour in arms were declared by all to be deserving of command. In the course of the good old knight's career of "virtue and valour in arms," he was joined by many companions, anxious to distinguish themselves in all courtly and chivalrous exercises. One duke, nineteen earls, twenty-seven barons, four knights of the garter, and above one hundred and fifty other knights and esquires, are stated to have taken part in these annual feats of arms.—(See Walpole's Miscellaneous Antiquities, No. I. pp. 41 to 48, which contains an extract from "Honour, Military and Civil." By Sir W. Segur; Norroy: London, 1602.)

If Shakspere had not looked upon these "Annual Exercises of Arms," when he thought of the tournaments "in the emperor's court," he had probably been admitted to the Tilt-yard at Kenilworth, on some occasion of magnificent display by the proud Leicester.

ACT II.

SCENE I.—Milan. *A Room in the Duke's Palace.*

Enter VALENTINE *and* SPEED.

Speed. Sir, your glove.
Val. Not mine; my gloves are on.
Speed. Why then this may be yours, for this is but one.[a]
Val. Ha! let me see: ay, give it me, it's mine:—
Sweet ornament that decks a thing divine!
Ah Silvia! Silvia!
Speed. Madam Silvia! madam Silvia!
Val. How now, sirrah?
Speed. She is not within hearing, sir.
Val. Why, sir, who bade you call her?
Speed. Your worship, sir; or else I mistook.
Val. Well, you'll still be too forward.
Speed. And yet I was last chidden for being too slow.
Val. Go to, sir; tell me, do you know madam Silvia?
Speed. She that your worship loves?
Val. Why, how know you that I am in love?
Speed. Marry, by these special marks: First, you have learned, like sir Proteus, to wreath your arms like a male-content; to relish a love-song, like a Robin-red-breast; to walk alone, like one that had the pestilence; to sigh, like a school-boy that had lost his A. B. C.; to weep, like a young wench that had buried her grandam; to fast, like one that takes diet; to watch, like one that fears robbing; to speak puling, like a beggar at Hallowmas? You were wont, when you laughed, to crow like a cock; when you walked, to walk like one of the lions;[b] when you fasted, it was presently after dinner; when you looked sadly, it was for want of money; and now you are metamorphosed with a mistress, that, when I look on you, I can hardly think you my master.
Val. Are all these things perceived in me?
Speed. They are all perceived without ye.
Val. Without me? they cannot.
Speed. Without you! nay, that's certain, for

---

[a] The quibble here depends upon the pronunciation of *one*, which was anciently pronounced as if it were written *on*.

[b] *To walk like one of the lions,* is thus commented on by Ritson: "If Shakspere had not been thinking of the lions in the Tower, he would have written 'like a lion.'"— Shakspere was thinking dramatically; and he therefore made Speed use an image with which he might be familiar. The firm, decided step of a lion, furnished an apt illustration of the bold bearing of Speed's master before he was a lover. The comparison was not less just, when made with "one of the lions;"—and the use of that comparison was in keeping with Speed's character, whilst the lofty image, "like a lion," would not have been so. The "clownish servant" might compare his master to a caged lion, without being poetical which Shakspere did not intend him to be.

without you were so simple, none else would: but you are so without these follies, that these follies are within you, and shine through you like the water in an urinal; that not an eye that sees you but is a physician to comment on your malady.

Val. But tell me, dost thou know my lady Silvia?

Speed. She that you gaze on so, as she sits at supper?

Val. Hast thou observed that? even she I mean.

Speed. Why, sir, I know her not.

Val. Dost thou know her by my gazing on her, and yet know'st her not?

Speed. Is she not hard favoured, sir?

Val. Not so fair, boy, as well favoured.

Speed. Sir, I know that well enough.

Val. What dost thou know?

Speed. That she is not so fair, as (of you) well favoured.

Val. I mean, that her beauty is exquisite, but her favour infinite.

Speed. That's because the one is painted, and the other out of all count.

Val. How painted? and how out of count?

Speed. Marry, sir, so painted, to make her fair, that no man counts of her beauty.

Val. How esteemest thou me! I account of her beauty.

Speed. You never saw her since she was deformed.

Val. How long hath she been deformed?

Speed. Ever since you loved her.

Val. I have loved her ever since I saw her; and still I see her beautiful.

Speed. If you love her, you cannot see her.

Val. Why?

Speed. Because love is blind. O, that you had mine eyes; or your own eyes had the lights they were wont to have, when you chid at sir Proteus for going ungartered!

Val. What should I see then?

Speed. Your own present folly, and her passing deformity: for he, being in love, could not see to garter his hose;³ and you, being in love, cannot see to put on your hose.

Val. Belike, boy, then you are in love; for last morning you could not see to wipe my shoes.

Speed. True, sir; I was in love with my bed: I thank you, you swing'd me for my love, which makes me the bolder to chide you for yours.

Val. In conclusion, I stand affected to her.

Speed. I would you were set; so your affection would cease.

Val. Last night she enjoined me to write some lines to one she loves.

Speed. And have you?

Val. I have.

Speed. Are they not lamely writ?

Val. No, boy, but as well as I can do them; Peace, here she comes.

Enter SILVIA.

Speed. O excellent motion!ᵃ O exceeding puppet! now will he interpret to her.ᵇ

Val. Madam and mistress, a thousand good-morrows.

Speed. O, 'give ye good even! here's a million of manners.

Sil. Sir Valentine and servant,⁴ to you two thousand.

Speed. He should give her interest, and she gives it him.

Val. As you enjoin'd me, I have writ your letter,
Unto the secret nameless friend of yours;
Which I was much unwilling to proceed in,
But for my duty to your ladyship.

Sil. I thank you, gentle servant: 't is very clerkly done.

Val. Now trust me, madam, it came hardly off;
For, being ignorant to whom it goes,
I writ at random, very doubtfully.

Sil. Perchance you think too much of so much pains?

Val. No, madam; so it stead you, I will write, Please you command, a thousand times as much: And yet,—

Sil. A pretty period! Well, I guess the sequel; And yet I will not name it:—and yet I care not;—
And yet take this again;—and yet I thank you; Meaning henceforth to trouble you no more.

Speed. And yet you will; and yet another yet. [*Aside.*

Val. What means your ladyship? do you not like it?

Sil. Yes, yes; the lines are very quaintly writ: But since unwillingly, take them again; Nay, take them.

Val. Madam, they are for you.

Sil. Ay, ay, you writ them, sir, at my request; But I will none of them; they are for you: I would have had them writ more movingly.

ᵃ *Motion.* A puppet-show. Silvia is the puppet, and Valentine will interpret for her. The master of the show was, in Shakspere's time, often called interpreter to the puppets.
ᵇ Capell and Cambridge edit. give these speeches of Speed as [*Aside.*

81

Val. Please you, I'll write your ladyship another.
Sil. And when it's writ, for my sake read it over:
And if it please you, so: if not, why so.
Val. If it please me, madam! what then?
Sil. Why, if it please you, take it for your labour.
And so good morrow, servant. [*Exit* SILVIA.
Speed. O jest unseen, inscrutable, invisible,
As a nose on a man's face, or a weathercock on a steeple!
My master sues to her; and she hath taught her suitor,
He being her pupil, to become her tutor.
O excellent device! was there ever heard a better?
That my master, being scribe, to himself should write the letter?
Val. How now, sir? what are you reasoning with yourself?
Speed. Nay, I was rhyming; 't is you that have the reason.
Val. To do what?
Speed. To be a spokesman from madam Silvia.
Val. To whom?
Speed. To yourself: why, she wooes you by a figure.
Val. What figure?
Speed. By a letter, I should say.
Val. Why, she hath not writ to me?
Speed. What need she, when she hath made you write to yourself? Why, do you not perceive the jest?
Val. No, believe me.
Speed. No believing you indeed, sir: But did you perceive her earnest?
Val. She gave me none, except an angry word.
Speed. Why, she hath given you a letter.
Val. That's the letter I writ to her friend.
Speed. And that letter hath she deliver'd, and there an end.
Val. I would, it were no worse.
Speed. I'll warrant you 't is as well.

For often have you writ to her; and she, in modesty,
Or else for want of idle time, could not again reply;
Or fearing else some messenger, that might her mind discover,
Herself hath taught her love himself to write unto her lover.—

All this I speak in print," for in print I found it.—
Why muse you, sir? 't is dinner time.

Val. I have dined.
Speed. Ay, but hearken, sir; though the chameleon Love can feed on the air, I am one that am nourished by my victuals, and would fain have meat. O, be not like your mistress; be moved, be moved." [*Exeunt.*

SCENE II.—Verona. *A Room in Julia's House.*

Enter PROTEUS *and* JULIA.

Pro. Have patience, gentle Julia.
Jul. I must, where is no remedy.
Pro. When possibly I can, I will return.
Jul. If you turn not, you will return the sooner:
Keep this remembrance for thy Julia's sake. [*Giving a ring.*
Pro. Why then we'll make exchange;" here, take you this.
Jul. And seal the bargain with a holy kiss.
Pro. Here is my hand for my true constancy;
And when that hour o'erslips me in the day,
Wherein I sigh not, Julia, for thy sake,
The next ensuing hour some foul mischance
Torment me for my love's forgetfulness;"
My father stays my coming; answer not;
The tide is now; nay, not thy tide of tears;
That tide will stay me longer than I should: [*Exit* JULIA.
Julia, farewell.—What! gone without a word?
Ay, so true love should do: it cannot speak;
For truth hath better deeds than words to grace it.

Enter PANTHINO.

Pan. Sir Proteus, you are staid for.
Pro. Go; I come, I come:—
Alas! this parting strikes poor lovers dumb. [*Exeunt.*

SCENE III.—*The same. A Street.*

Enter LAUNCE, *leading a Dog.*

Laun. Nay, 't will be this hour ere I have done weeping; all the kind of the Launces have this very fault: I have received my proportion, like the prodigious son, and am going with sir Proteus to the Imperial's court. I think Crab my dog be the sourest-natured dog that lives: my mother weeping, my father wailing, my sister crying, our maid a howling, our cat wringing her hands, and all our house in a great perplexity, yet did

---

* *In print* With exactness. Speed is repeating, or affects to be repeating, some lines which he has read.

" *Be moved.* Have compassion on me.

not this cruel-hearted cur shed one tear; he is a stone, a very pebble-stone, and has no more pity in him than a dog: a Jew would have wept to have seen our parting; why, my grandam having no eyes, look you, wept herself blind at my parting. Nay, I'll shew you the manner of it: This shoe is my father;—no, this left shoe[a] is my father;—no, no, this left shoe is my mother;—nay, that cannot be so neither:—yes, it is so, it is so; it hath the worser sole; This shoe, with the hole in it, is my mother, and this my father; A vengeance on't! there 't is: now, sir, this staff is my sister; for, look you, she is as white as a lily, and as small as a wand: this hat is Nan, our maid; I am the dog:—no, the dog is himself, and I am the dog,—O, the dog is me, and I am myself; ay, so, so. Now come I to my father; *Father, your blessing;* now should not the shoe speak a word for weeping; now should I kiss my father; well, he weeps on:—now come I to my mother, (O, that she could speak now!) like a wood[a] woman;—well, I kiss her;—why, there 't is; here's my mother's breath up and down; now come I to my sister; mark the moan she makes: now the dog all this while sheds not a tear, nor speaks a word; but see how I lay the dust with my tears.

Enter PANTHINO.

Pan. Launce, away, away, aboard; thy master is shipped, and thou art to post after with oars. What's the matter? why weep'st thou, man? Away, ass; you'll lose the tide, if you tarry any longer.

Laun. It is no matter if the tied were lost; for it is the unkindest tied[b] that ever man tied.

Pan. What's the unkindest tide?

Laun. Why, he that's tied here; Crab, my dog.

Pan. Tut, man, I mean thou'lt lose the flood: and, in losing the flood, lose thy voyage; and, in losing thy voyage, lose thy master; and, in losing thy master, lose thy service; and, in losing thy service,—Why dost thou stop my mouth?

Laun. For fear thou should'st lose thy tongue.

Pan. Where should I lose my tongue?

Laun. In thy tale.

Pan. In thy tail?

Laun. Lose the tide, and the voyage, and the master, and the service, and the tied![c] Why,

man, if the river were dry, I am able to fill it with my tears; if the wind were down, I could drive the boat with my sighs.

Pan. Come, come away, man; I was sent to call thee.

Laun. Sir, call me what thou darest.

Pan. Wilt thou go?

Laun. Well, I will go.   [*Exeunt.*

SCENE IV.—Milan. *A Room in the* Duke's *Palace.*

Enter VALENTINE, SILVIA, THURIO, *and* SPEED.

Sil. Servant.
Val. Mistress.
Speed. Master, sir Thurio frowns on you.
Val. Ay, boy, it's for love.
Speed. Not of you.
Val. Of my mistress then.
Speed. 'T were good you knocked him.
Sil. Servant, you are sad.
Val. Indeed, madam, I seem so.
Thu. Seem you that you are not?
Val. Haply I do.
Thu. So do counterfeits.
Val. So do you.
Thu. What seem I, that I am not?
Val. Wise.
Thu. What instance of the contrary?
Val. Your folly.
Thu. And how quote[a] you my folly?
Val. I quote[b] it in your jerkin.
Thu. My jerkin is a doublet.
Val. Well, then, I'll double your folly.
Thu. How?
Sil. What, angry, sir Thurio? do you change colour?
Val. Give him leave, madam; he is a kind of cameleon.
Thu. That hath more mind to feed on your blood, than live in your air.
Val. You have said, sir.
Thu. Ay, sir, and done too, for this time.
Val. I know it well, sir; you always end ere you begin.

---

[a] *Wood.* Mad; wild.

[b] This quibble, according to Steevens, is found in Lyly's Endymion, 1591.

[c] We give the punctuation of the original edition. Malone prints the passage thus:—
"Lose the tide, and the voyage, and the master, and the service, and the tide!"

---

[a] *Quote.* To mark.

[b] Quote was pronounced *cote*, from the old French *coter.* Hence the quibble,—I coat it in your jerkin,—your short coat, or jacket.

Sil. A fine volley of words, gentlemen, and quickly shot off.
Val. 'T is indeed, madam; we thank the giver.
Sil. Who is that, servant?
Val. Yourself, sweet lady; for you gave the fire: sir Thurio borrows his wit from your ladyship's looks, and spends what he borrows, kindly in your company.
Thu. Sir, if you spend word for word with me, I shall make your wit bankrupt.
Val. I know it well, sir: you have an exchequer of words, and, I think, no other treasure to give your followers; for it appears by their bare liveries that they live by your bare words.
Sil. No more, gentlemen, no more; here comes my father.

Enter DUKE.

Duke. Now, daughter Silvia, you are hard beset.
Sir Valentine, your father's in good health:
What say you to a letter from your friends
Of much good news?
Val.   My lord, I will be thankful
To any happy messenger from thence.
Duke. Know you Don Antonio, your countryman?
Val. Ay, my good lord, I know the gentleman
To be of worth, and worthy estimation,
And not without desert so well reputed.
Duke. Hath he not a son?
Val. Ay, my good lord; a son, that well deserves
The honour and regard of such a father.
Duke. You know him well?
Val. I know him, as myself[a]; for from our infancy
We have convers'd, and spent our hours together:
And though myself have been an idle truant,
Omitting the sweet benefit of time
To clothe mine age with angel-like perfection,
Yet hath sir Proteus, for that's his name,
Made use and fair advantage of his days;
His years but young, but his experience old;
His head unmellow'd, but his judgment ripe;
And, in a word, (for far behind his worth
Come all the praises that I now bestow,)
He is complete in feature,[b] and in mind,
With all good grace to grace a gentleman.

   [a] *Knew,* in folio; *know,* Dyce.
   [b] *Feature* (form or fashion) was applied to the body as well as the face. Thus, in Gower,—
      "Like to a woman in semblance
      Of feature and of countenance."
And, later, in "All Ovid's Elegies, by C. M." (Christopher Marlowe)
      "I fly her lust, but follow beauty's creature,
      I loath her manners, love her body's feature."

Duke. Beshrew me, sir, but if he make this good,
He is as worthy for an empress' love,
As meet to be an emperor's counsellor.
Well, sir; this gentleman is come to me,
With commendation from great potentates;
And here he means to spend his time a-while:
I think, 't is no unwelcome news to you.
Val. Should I have wish'd a thing, it had been he.
Duke. Welcome him then according to his worth;
Silvia, I speak to you: and you, sir Thurio:—
For Valentine, I need not 'cite him to it:
I 'll send him hither to you presently.
                       [*Exit* DUKE.
Val. This is the gentleman, I told your ladyship,
Had come along with me, but that his mistress
Did hold his eyes lock'd in her crystal looks.
Sil. Belike, that now she hath enfranchis'd them,
Upon some other pawn for fealty.
Val. Nay, sure I think she holds them prisoners still.
Sil. Nay, then he should be blind; and, being blind,
How could he see his way to seek out you?
Val. Why, lady, love hath twenty pair of eyes.
Thu. They say, that love hath not an eye at all—
Val. To see such lovers, Thurio, as yourself;
Upon a homely object love can wink.

Enter PROTEUS.

Sil. Have done, have done; here comes the gentleman.
Val. Welcome, dear Proteus!—Mistress, I beseech you,
Confirm his welcome with some special favour.
Sil. His worth is warrant for his welcome hither,
If this be he you oft have wish'd to hear from.
Val. Mistress, it is: sweet lady, entertain him
To be my fellow-servant to your ladyship.
Sil. Too low a mistress for so high a servant.
Pro. Not so, sweet lady; but too mean a servant
To have a look of such a worthy mistress.
Val. Leave off discourse of disability:—
Sweet lady, entertain him for your servant.
Pro. My duty will I boast of, nothing else.
Sil. And duty never yet did want his meed;
Servant, you are welcome to a worthless mistress.
Pro. I 'll die on him that says so, but yourself.

[ACT II.] TWO GENTLEMEN OF VERONA. [Scene IV

Sil. That you are welcome?
Pro.   No; that you are worthless.

    Enter Servant.

Ser. Madam, my lord your father would speak with you.*
Sil. I wait upon his pleasure.   [*Exit* Servant.
  Come, sir Thurio,
Go with me:—Once more, new servant, welcome:
I 'll leave you to confer of home affairs;
When you have done, we look to hear from you.
  Pro. We 'll both attend upon your ladyship.
      [*Exeunt* SILVIA, THURIO, *and* SPEED.
  Val. Now, tell me, how do all from whence you came?
  Pro. Your friends are well, and have them much commended.
  Val. And how do yours?
  Pro.   I left them all in health.
  Val. How does your lady? and how thrives your love?
  Pro. My tales of love were wont to weary you;
I know you joy not in a love-discourse.
  Val. Ay, Proteus, but that life is alter'd now:
I have done penance for contemning love;
Whose high imperious thoughts have punish'd me
With bitter fasts, with penitential groans,
With nightly tears, and daily heart-sore sighs;
For, in revenge of my contempt of love,
Love hath chas'd sleep from my enthralled eyes,
And made them watchers of mine own heart's sorrow.
O, gentle Proteus, love's a mighty lord;
And hath so humbled me, as, I confess,
There is no woe to his correction,[b]
Nor to his service no such joy on earth!
Now, no discourse, except it be of love;
Now can I break my fast, dine, sup, and sleep,
Upon the very naked name of love.
  Pro. Enough; I read your fortune in your eye:
Was this the idol that you worship so?
  Val. Even she; and is she not a heavenly saint?
  Pro. No; but she is an earthly paragon.
  Val. Call her divine.
  Pro.   I will not flatter her.
  Val. O, flatter me; for love delights in praises.
  Pro. When I was sick, you gave me bitter pills;
And I must minister the like to you.
  Val. Then speak the truth by her; if not divine,
Yet let her be a principality,
Sovereign to all the creatures on the earth.

  Pro. Except my mistress.
  Val.   Sweet, except not any;
Except thou wilt except against my love.
  Pro. Have I not reason to prefer mine own?
  Val. And I will help thee to prefer her too:
She shall be dignified with this high honour,—
To bear my lady's train; lest the base earth
Should from her vesture chance to steal a kiss,
And, of so great a favour growing proud,
Disdain to root the summer-swelling flower,
And make rough winter everlastingly.
  Pro. Why, Valentine, what braggardism is this?
  Val. Pardon me, Proteus: all I can is nothing
To her, whose worth makes other worthies[c] nothing;
She is alone.
  Pro. Then let her alone.
  Val. Not for the world: why, man, she is mine own;
And I as rich in having such a jewel,
As twenty seas, if all their sand were pearl,
The water nectar, and the rocks pure gold.
Forgive me, that I do not dream on thee,
Because thou seest me dote upon my love.
My foolish rival, that her father likes,
Only for his possessions are so huge,
Is gone with her along; and I must after,
For love, thou know'st, is full of jealousy.
  Pro. But she loves you?
  Val.   Ay, and we are betroth'd;
Nay, more, our marriage hour,
With all the cunning manner of our flight,
Determin'd of: how I must climb her window;
The ladder made of cords; and all the means
Plotted, and 'greed on, for my happiness.
Good Proteus, go with me to my chamber,
In these affairs to aid me with thy counsel.
  Pro. Go on before; I shall inquire you forth:
I must unto the road,[b] to disembark
Some necessaries that I needs must use;
And then I 'll presently attend you.
  Val. Will you make haste?
  Pro. I will.—   [*Exit* VAL.
Even as one heat another heat expels,
Or as one nail by strength drives out another,
So the remembrance of my former love
Is by a newer object quite forgotten.
Is it her mien[c] or Valentinus' praise,

---

* This speech is given to Thurio in the folio. Theobald assigned it to a servant. Mr. White says Thurio is right, as in the poorly-appointed stage of Shakspere's time Thurio might act as a messenger.
[b] There is no woe compared to his correction.

[a] Mr. White prints *worth as*, and says *worthies* is a palpable misprint, though hitherto unnoticed.
[b] *Road.* Open harbour.
[c] The folio of 1623 reads, "It is mine, or Valentine's praise." Warburton would read, "It is mine eye, &c." This reading Steevens adopts, making the sentence interrogative, "Is it mine eye?" The present reading is that of Malone, and its correctness is supported by the circumstance that *mien* was, in Shakspere's time, spelt *mine*.

Her true perfection, or my false transgression,
That makes me reasonless, to reason thus?
She's fair; and so is Julia, that I love;—
That I did love, for now my love is thaw'd;
Which, like a waxen image 'gainst a fire,
Bears no impression of the thing it was.
Methinks, my zeal to Valentine is cold;
And that I love him not, as I was wont:
O! but I love his lady too, too much;
And that's the reason I love him so little.
How shall I dote on her with more advice,
That thus without advice begin to love her?
'T is but her picture [a] I have yet beheld,
And that hath dazzled [b] my reason's light;
But when I look on her perfections,
There is no reason but I shall be blind.
If I can check my erring love, I will;
If not, to compass her I'll use my skill. [*Exit.*

SCENE V.—*The same. A Street.*

Enter SPEED *and* LAUNCE.

Speed. Launce! by mine honesty, welcome to Milan.[c]

Laun. Forswear not thyself, sweet youth; for I am not welcome. I reckon this always—that a man is never undone till he be hanged; nor never welcome to a place till some certain shot be paid, and the hostess say, welcome.

Speed. Come on, you mad-cap, I'll to the ale-house with you presently; where, for one shot of five-pence, thou shalt have five thousand welcomes. But, sirrah, how did thy master part with Madam Julia?

Laun. Marry, after they closed in earnest, they parted very fairly in jest.

Speed. But shall she marry him?

Laun. No.

Speed. How then? shall he marry her?

Laun. No, neither.

Speed. What, are they broken?

Laun. No, they are both as whole as a fish.

Speed. Why then, how stands the matter with them?

Laun. Marry, thus; when it stands well with him, it stands well with her.

Speed. What an ass art thou! I understand thee not!

Laun. What a block art thou, that thou can'st not! My staff understands me.

Speed. What thou say'st?

Laun. Ay, and what I do, too: look thee, I'll but lean, and my staff understands me.

Speed. It stands under thee, indeed.

Laun. Why, stand under and understand is all one.

Speed. But tell me true, wil' 't be a match?

Laun. Ask my dog: if he say, ay, it will; if he say, no, it will; if he shake his tail, and say nothing, it will.

Speed. The conclusion is then, that it will.

Laun. Thou shalt never get such a secret from me but by a parable.

Speed. 'T is well that I get it so. But, Launce, how say'st thou, that my master is become a notable lover?

Laun. I never knew him otherwise.

Speed. Than how?

Laun. A notable lubber, as thou reportest him to be.

Speed. Why, thou whoreson ass, thou mistakest me.

Laun. Why, fool, I meant not thee, I meant thy master.

Speed. I tell thee, my master is become a hot lover.

Laun. Why, I tell thee, I care not though he burn himself in love. If thou wilt, go with me to the ale-house; if not, thou art an Hebrew, a Jew, and not worth the name of a Christian.

Speed. Why?

Laun. Because thou hast not so much charity in thee, as to go to the ale[a] with a Christian: Wilt thou go?

Speed. At thy service. [*Exeunt.*

SCENE VI.—*The same. A Room in the Palace.*

Enter PROTEUS.

Pro. To leave my Julia, shall I be forsworn;
To love fair Silvia, shall I be forsworn;
To wrong my friend, I shall be much forsworn;
And even that power, which gave me first my oath,
Provokes me to this threefold perjury
Love bade me swear, and love bids me forswear.
O sweet-suggesting love, if thou hast sinn'd,
Teach me, thy tempted subject, to excuse it.
At first I did adore a twinkling star,
But now I worship a celestial sun.
Unheedful vows may heedfully be broken;
And he wants wit, that wants resolved will

---

[a] *Picture.* Her person, which I have seen, has shewn me her "perfections" only as a picture. Dr. Johnson receives the expression in a literal sense.
[b] *Dazzled* is here used as a trisyllable.
[c] The Cambridge edition retains *Padua* of the original, as showing that Shakspere had written the play before he had finally determined on the locality. For the same reason, *Verona* is retained in Act. III. sc. 1 (note a, p. 43).

[a] *Ale.* A rural festival, oftentimes connected with the holidays of the Church, as a Whitson-ale. Launce calls Speed a Jew because he will not go to the Ale (the Church feast) with a Christian.

To learn his wit to exchange the bad for better.—
Fye, fye, unreverend tongue! to call her bad,
Whose sovereignty so oft thou hast preferr'd
With twenty thousand soul-confirming oaths.
I cannot leave to love, and yet I do;
But there I leave to love, where I should love.
Julia I lose, and Valentine I lose:
If I keep them, I needs must lose myself;
If I lose them, thus find I by their loss,
For Valentine, myself: for Julia, Silvia.
I to myself am dearer than a friend:
For love is still most precious in itself;
And Silvia, witness heaven, that made her fair!
Shews Julia but a swarthy Ethiope.
I will forget that Julia is alive,
Rememb'ring that my love to her is dead;
And Valentine I'll hold an enemy,
Aiming at Silvia as a sweeter friend.
I cannot now prove constant to myself,
Without some treachery used to Valentine:—
This night, he meaneth with a corded ladder
To climb celestial Silvia's chamber-window;
Myself in counsel, his competitor:
Now presently I'll give her father notice
Of their disguising, and pretended* flight;
Who, all enraged, will banish Valentine;
For Thurio, he intends, shall wed his daughter:
But, Valentine being gone, I'll quickly cross,
By some sly trick, blunt Thurio's dull proceeding
Love, lend me wings to make my purpose swift,
As thou hast lent me wit to plot this drift! [*Exit.*

SCENE VII.—Verona. *A Room in Julia's House.*

Enter JULIA *and* LUCETTA.

Jul. Counsel, Lucetta! gentle girl, assist me!
And, even in kind love, I do conjure thee,—
Who art the table* wherein all my thoughts
Are visibly character'd and engrav'd,—
To lesson me; and tell me some good mean,
How, with my honour, I may undertake
A journey to my loving Proteus.
Luc. Alas! the way is wearisome and long.
Jul. A true-devoted pilgrim is not weary
To measure kingdoms with his feeble steps;
Much less shall she that hath love's wings to fly;
And when the flight is made to one so dear,
Of such divine perfection, as sir Proteus.
Luc. Better forbear, till Proteus make return.
Jul. O, know'st thou not, his looks are my soul's food?

* *Pretended,*—intended.

Pity the dearth that I have pined in,
By longing for that food so long a time.
Didst thou but know the inly touch of love,
Thou would'st as soon go kindle fire with snow,
As seek to quench the fire of love with words.
Luc. I do not seek to quench your love's hot fire;
But qualify the fire's extreme rage,
Lest it should burn above the bounds of reason.
Jul. The more thou damm'st it up, the more it burns;
The current, that with gentle murmur glides,
Thou know'st, being stopp'd, impatiently doth rage;
But, when his fair course is not hindered,
He makes sweet music with the enamel'd stones,
Giving a gentle kiss to every sedge
He overtaketh in his pilgrimage;
And so by many winding nooks he strays,
With willing sport, to the wild ocean.
Then let me go, and hinder not my course:
I'll be as patient as a gentle stream,
And make a pastime of each weary step,
Till the last step have brought me to my love;
And there I'll rest, as, after much turmoil,
A blessed soul doth in Elysium.
Luc. But in what habit will you go along?
Jul. Not like a woman; for I would prevent
The loose encounters of lascivious men:
Gentle Lucetta, fit me with such weeds
As may beseem some well-reputed page.
Luc. Why then your ladyship must cut your hair.
Jul. No, girl; I'll knit it up in silken strings,
With twenty odd-conceited true-love knots:
To be fantastic, may become a youth
Of greater time than I shall show to be.
Luc. What fashion, madam, shall I make your breeches?
Jul. That fits as well, as—"tell me, good my lord,
"What compass will you wear your farthingale?"
Why, even that fashion thou best lik'st, Lucetta.
Luc. You must needs have them with a cod-piece, madam.
Jul. Out, out, Lucetta! that will be ill-favour'd.
Luc. A round hose, madam, now's not worth a pin,
Unless you have a cod-piece to stick pins on.
Jul. Lucetta, as thou lov'st me, let me have
What thou think'st meet, and is most mannerly:
But tell me, wench, how will the world repute me,
For undertaking so unstaid a journey?
I fear me, it will make me scandaliz'd.

Luc. If you think so, then stay at home, and go not.

Jul. Nay, that I will not.

Luc. Then never dream on infamy, but go.
If Proteus like your journey, when you come,
No matter who 's displeased, when you are gone:
I fear me, he will scarce be pleas'd withal.

Jul. That is the least, Lucetta, of my fear:
A thousand oaths, an ocean of his tears,
And instances of infinite* of love,
Warrant me welcome to my Proteus.

Luc. All these are servants to deceitful men.

Jul. Base men, that use them to so base effect!
But truer stars did govern Proteus' birth!

* *Infinite,*—infinity. The same form of expression occurs in Chaucer:—"although the life of it be stretched with infinite of time."—The reading we give is that of the first folio. The common reading is that of the second folio:—"Instances as infinite."

His words are bonds, his oaths are oracles;
His love sincere, his thoughts immaculate;
His tears, pure messengers sent from his heart;
His heart as far from fraud as heaven from earth.

Luc. Pray heaven, he prove so, when you come to him!

Jul. Now, as thou lov'st me, do him not that wrong,
To bear a hard opinion of his truth:
Only deserve my love, by loving him;
And presently go with me to my chamber,
To take a note of what I stand in need of,
To furnish me upon my longing journey.
All that is mine I leave at thy dispose,
My goods, my lands, my reputation;
Only, in lieu thereof, dispatch me hence:
Come, answer not, but to it presently;
I am impatient of my tarriance. [*Exeunt.*

ILLUSTRATIONS OF ACT II.

¹ SCENE I.—"*Sir, your glove.*"

GLOVES finely perfumed were brought from Italy as presents in the sixteenth century. "A pair of sweet gloves" is mentioned in an inventory of apparel at Hampton Court, temp. Henry VIII.

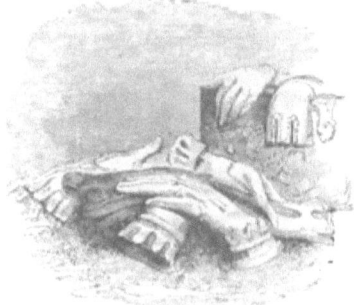

² SCENE I.—"*Beggar at Hallowmas.*"

If we were to look only at the severe statutes against mendicancy, we might suppose that, at the period when Shakspere thus described what he must have commonly seen, there were no beggars in the land but the licensed beggars, which these statutes permitted. Unlicensed beggars were, by the statute of 1572, to be punished, in the first instance, by grievous whipping, and burning through the gristle of the right ear; and for second and third offences they were to suffer death as felons. It is clear that these penal laws were almost wholly inoperative; and Harrison, in his Description of Britain, prefixed to Holinshed,

shows the lamentable extent of vagrancy amongst the "thriftless poor." In our notes upon King Lear, where Edgar describes himself as "Poor Tom, who is whipped from tything to tything, and stock'd, punish'd, and imprison'd," this subject is noticed more at length. Of the "valiant beggar"—the compound of beggar and thief,—Shakspere has given a perfect picture in his "Autolycus," which also furnishes an interesting annotation. In the mean time we give a curious representation of the Beggarman and Beggarwoman, from a manuscript of the Roman de la Rose, in the Harleian Collection (No. 4425). The date of the MS. is somewhat earlier than this play, and these beggars are French; but the costume of rags is not a subject for very nice distinctions either of time or place.

³ SCENE I.—"*He, being in love, could not see to garter his hose.*"

We shall have frequent occasions of mentioning the costly garters of the sixteenth century, and the various fashion of wearing them. Shakspere is here speaking of those of his own time, but at the period to which we have confined the costume of this play, garters of great magnificence appeared round the large slashed hose, both above and below the knee. To go ungartered was the common trick of a fantastic lover, who thereby implied he was too much occupied by his passion to pay attention to his dress.

⁴ SCENE I.—"*Sir Valentine and servant.*"

Sir J. Hawkins says, "Here Silvia calls her lover servant, and again her gentle servant. This was the common language of ladies to their lovers, at the time when Shakspere wrote." Steevens gives several examples of this. Henry James Pye, in his "Comments on the Commentators," mentions that, "in the Noble Gentlemen of Beaumont and Fletcher, the lady's gallant has no other name in the dramatis personæ than servant," and that "mistress and servant are always used for lovers in Dryden's plays." It is clear to us, however, that Shakspere here uses the words in a much more general sense than that which expresses the relations between two lovers. At the very moment that Valentine calls Silvia mistress, he says that he has written for her a letter,—"some lines to one she loves,"—unto a "secret nameless friend;" and what is still stronger evidence that the word "servant" had not the full meaning of lover, but meant a much more general admirer, Valentine introducing Proteus to Silvia, says,

"Sweet lady, entertain him
To be my fellow-servant to your ladyship,"

and Silvia, consenting, says to Proteus,

"Servant, you are welcome to a worthless mistress."

ILLUSTRATIONS OF ACT II.

Now, when Silvia says this, which, according to the meaning which has been attached to the words servant and mistress, would be a speech of endearment, she had accepted Valentine really as her betrothed lover, and she had been told by Valentine that Proteus

"Had come along with me, but that his mistress
Did hold his eyes lock'd in her crystal looks."

It appears, therefore, that we must receive these words in a very vague sense, and regard them as titles of courtesy, derived, perhaps, from the chivalric times, when many a harness'd knight and sportive troubadour described the lady whom they had gazed upon in the tilt-yard as their "mistress," and the same lady looked upon each of the gallant train as a "servant" dedicated to the defence of her honour, or the praise of her beauty.

⁵ SCENE II.—"*Why then we'll make exchange.*"

The priest in Twelfth Night (Act. V. Sc. I.), describes the ceremonial of bethrothing, for which the Catholic church had a ritual:

"A contract of eternal bond of love,
Confirm'd by mutual joinder of your hands,
Attested by the holy close of lips,
Strengthen'd by interchangement of your rings."

This contract was made, in private, by Proteus and Julia; and it was also made by Valentine and Silvia—"we are betroth'd."

⁶ SCENE III.—"*This left shoe.*"

A passage in King John also shews that each foot was formerly fitted with its shoe, a fashion of unquestionable utility, which was revived many years ago:

"Standing on slippers, which his nimble haste
Had falsely thrust upon contrary feet."

⁷ SCENE IV.—"*My jerkin is a doublet.*"

The jerkin, or jacket, was generally worn over the doublet; but occasionally the doublet was worn alone, and, in many instances, is confounded with the jerkin. Either had sleeves or not, as the wearer fancied; for by the inventories and wardrobe accounts of the time, we find that the sleeves were frequently separate articles of dress, and attached to the doublet, jerkin, coat, or even woman's gown, by laces or ribands, at the pleasure of the wearer. A "doblet jaquet" and hose of blue velvet, cut upon cloth of gold, embroidered, and a "doblet hose and jaquet" of purple velvet, embroidered, and cut upon cloth of gold, and lined with black satin, are entries in an inventory of the wardrobe of Henry VIII.
In 1535, a jerkin of purple velvet, with purple satin sleeves, embroidered all over with Venice gold, was presented to the king by Sir Richard Cromwell; and another jerkin of crimson velvet, with wide sleeves of the same coloured satin, is mentioned in the same inventory.

⁸ SCENE VII.—"*The table wherein all my thoughts Are visibly character'd.*"

The allusion is to the table-book, or tables, which were used, as at present, for noting down something to be remembered. Hamlet says:

"My tables,—meet it is I set it down."

They were made sometimes of ivory, and sometimes of slate. The Archbishop of York, in Henry IV, says:

"And, therefore, will he wipe his tables clean."

The table-book of slate is engraved and described in Gesner's treatise, *De Rerum Fossilium Figuris*, 1565; and it has been copied in Douce's Illustrations.

⁹ SCENE VII.—"*And, even in kind love, I do conjure thee.*"

Malone prints the word conjure with an accent on the first syllable, *cónjure*. In the same way, in the next line but one, he marks the accent on *cháracter'd*. Since the publication of our first edition we have been led, through a consideration of the many false theories which have prevailed as to the general versification of Shakspere, to believe that this system of accenting words differently from their ordinary pronunciation, and constantly varying, is a false one. For example, in the passage before us, Malone prints

"And, e'en in kind love, I do cónjure thee."

The emphasis must here be on *kind* and *con*. But read,

"And, *even* in *kind* love, I do *conjure* thee."

placing the emphasis on *love* and *jure*, and the metre is perfect enough, without such a variation from the common pronunciation. Upon a just metrical system there is no difficulty in such passages. Our opinion is much strengthened by the communication of a friend on this subject; and we therefore omit these arbitrary marks.

¹⁰ SCENE VII.—"*A true devoted pilgrim.*"

The comparison which Julia makes between the ardour of her passion, and the enthusiasm of the pilgrim, is exceedingly beautiful. When travelling was a business of considerable danger and personal suffering, the pilgrim, who was not weary

"To traverse kingdoms with his feeble steps,"

to encounter the perils of a journey to Rome, or Loretto, or Compostella, or Jerusalem, was a person to be looked upon as thoroughly in earnest.

ILLUSTRATIONS OF ACT II.

In the time of Shakspere the pilgrimages to the tomb of St. Thomas à Becket, at Canterbury, which Chaucer has rendered immortal, were discontinued; and few, perhaps, undertook the sea voyage to Jerusalem. But the pilgrimage to the shrine of St. James, or St. Jago, the patron-saint of Spain, at Compostella, was undertaken by all classes of Catholics. The house of our Lady at Loretto was, however, the great object of the devotee's vows; and, at particular seasons, there were not fewer than two hundred thousand pilgrims visiting it at once. The Holy House (the *Santa Casa*) is the house in which the Blessed Virgin is said to have been born, in which she was betrothed to Joseph, and where the annunciation of the Angel was made. It is pretended that it was carried, on the 9th of May, 1291, by supernatural means from Galilee to Ternato, in Dalmatia; and from thence removed, on the 10th of December, 1294, to Italy, where it was deposited in a wood at midnight. The Santa Casa (which now stands within the large church of Loretto) consists of one room, the length of which is 31¾ feet, the breadth 13 feet, and the height 18 feet. On the ceiling is painted the Assumption of the Virgin Mary; and other paintings once adorned the walls of the apartment. On the west side is the window through which the Angel is said to have entered the house; and facing it, in a niche, is the image of the Virgin and Child, which was once enriched by the offerings of princes and devotees. The mantle, or robe, which she had on was covered with innumerable jewels of inestimable value, and she had a triple crown of gold enriched with pearls and diamonds, given her by Louis XIII. of France. The niche in which the figure stands was adorned with seventy-one large Bohemian topazes, and on the right side of the image is an angel of cast gold, profusely enriched with diamonds and other gems. A great part of these treasures was taken by Pope Pius VII., in order to pay to France the sum extorted by the treaty of Tolentino, in 1797. They have been partially replaced since by new contributors, among whom have been Murat, Eugene Beauharnois, and other members of the Bonaparte family. There are a few relics considered more valuable than the richest jewels that have been carried away. Notwithstanding the mean appearance of the walls within the Santa Casa, the outside is encased, and adorned with the finest Carrara marble. This work was begun in 1514, in the pontificate of Leo X., and the House of our Lady was consecrated in 1538. The expense of this casing amounted to 50,000 crowns, and the most celebrated sculptors of the age were employed. Bramante was the architect, and Baccio Bandinelli assisted in the sculptures. The whole was completed in 1579, in the pontificate of Gregory XIII. The munificent expenditure upon the house of our Lady at Loretto, had, probably, contributed greatly to make the pilgrimage the most attractive in Europe, when Shakspere wrote.

¹³ Scene VII.——————— "*Such weeds As may beseem some well-reputed page.*"

"Such weeds" are here represented from a print after Paul Veronese. The original painting is, or was, in the French royal collection.

¹⁴ Scene VII.—"*I'll knit it up in silken strings, With twenty odd-conceited true-love knots.*"

The accompanying heads—one from Boissard, "Habitus variarum Orbis Gentium, 1581;" and the other from a print of the sixteenth century, may be supposed to illustrate the fashion of Shakspere's own time here mentioned.

ACT III.

SCENE I.—Milan. *An Ante-room in the Duke's Palace.*

Enter DUKE, THURIO, *and* PROTEUS.

Duke. Sir Thurio, give us leave, I pray, awhile;
We have some secrets to confer about.——
　　　　　　　　　　　　[*Exit* THURIO.
Now, tell me, Proteus, what's your will with me?
　Pro. My gracious lord, that which I would discover,
The law of friendship bids me to conceal:
But, when I call to mind your gracious favours
Done to me, undeserving as I am,
My duty pricks me on to utter that
Which else no worldly good should draw from me.
Know, worthy prince, sir Valentine, my friend,
This night intends to steal away your daughter;
Myself am one made privy to the plot.
I know you have determin'd to bestow her
On Thurio, whom your gentle daughter hates;
And should she thus be stolen away from you,
It would be much vexation to your age.
Thus, for my duty's sake, I rather chose
To cross my friend in his intended drift,
Than, by concealing it, heap on your head
A pack of sorrows, which would press you down,
Being unprevented, to your timeless grave.
　Duke. Proteus, I thank thee for thine honest care;
Which to requite, command me while I live.
This love of theirs myself have often seen,
Haply, when they have judged me fast asleep;
And oftentimes have purpos'd to forbid
Sir Valentine her company, and my court:
But, fearing lest my jealous aim[a] might err,
And so, unworthily, disgrace the man,
(A rashness that I ever yet have shunn'd,)
I gave him gentle looks; thereby to find
That which thyself hast now disclos'd to me.
And, that thou may'st perceive my fear of this,
Knowing that tender youth is soon suggested,[b]
I nightly lodge her in an upper tower,
The key whereof myself have ever kept;
And thence she cannot be convey'd away.
　Pro. Know, noble lord, they have devis'd a mean
How he her chamber-window will ascend,
And with a corded ladder fetch her down;
For which the youthful lover now is gone,
And this way comes he with it presently;
Where, if it please you, you may intercept him.
But, good my lord, do it so cunningly,
That my discovery be not aim'd at;[c]

---

[a] *Aim.* Steevens explains this noun as meaning *guess.* Professor Craik says, "Aim, in old French, *esme, esme* and *estme,* is the same word as *esteem,* and should, therefore, signify properly a judgment or conjecture of the mind." *Julius Cæsar,*'57.

[b] *Suggested*—tempted.

[c] *Aimed at.* Here the word is again stated, both by Steevens and Johnson, to mean, *to guess.* The common interpretation of aim,—to point at, to level at,—will, however, give the meaning of the passage quite as well. At first sight it might appear that the word *aim,* which, literally or metaphorically, is ordinarily taken to mean the act of looking towards a definite object with a precise intention, cannot include the random determination of the mind which we imply by the word *guess.* But we must go a little further. The etymology of both words is somewhat doubtful.

ACT III.] TWO GENTLEMEN OF VERONA. [SCENE I.

For love of you, not hate unto my friend,
Hath made me publisher of this pretence.[b]
  Duke. Upon mine honour, he shall never know
That I had any light from thee of this.
  Pro. Adieu, my lord; sir Valentine is coming.
                            [*Exit.*

Enter VALENTINE.

  Duke. Sir Valentine, whither away so fast?
  Val. Please it your grace, there is a messenger
That stays to bear my letters to my friends,
And I am going to deliver them.
  Duke. Be they of much import?
  Val. The tenor of them doth but signify
My health, and happy being at your court.
  Duke. Nay, then no matter; stay with me a while;
I am to break with thee of some affairs,
That touch me near, wherein thou must be secret.
'Tis not unknown to thee, that I have sought
To match my friend, sir Thurio, to my daughter.
  Val. I know it well, my lord; and, sure, the match
Were rich and honourable; besides, the gentleman
Is full of virtue, bounty, worth, and qualities
Beseeming such a wife as your fair daughter:
Cannot your grace win her to fancy him?
  Duke. No, trust me; she is peevish, sullen, froward,
Proud, disobedient, stubborn, lacking duty;
Neither regarding that she is my child,
Nor fearing me as if I were her father:
And, may I say to thee, this pride of hers,
Upon advice, hath drawn my love from her;
And, where[b] I thought the remnant of mine age

Aim is supposed to be derived from *æstimare*, to weigh attentively; *quæs*, from the Anglo-Saxon *wis-an*, *wis*, to think (See Richardson's Dictionary). Here the separate meanings of the two words almost slide into one and the same. It is certain that in the original and literal use of the word *aim*, in archery, was meant the act of the mind in considering the various circumstances connected with the flight of the arrow, rather than the mere operation of the sense in pointing at the mark. When Locksley, in *Ivanhoe*, tells his adversary, "You have not allowed for the wind, Hubert, or that would have been a better shot," he furnishes Hubert with a new element of calculation for his next aim. There is a passage of Bishop Jewell: "He that seethe no marks must shoote by aym." This certainly does not mean *must shoot at random*—although it may mean *must shoot by guess*,—must shoot by calculation. To give aim, in archery, was the business of one who stood within view of the butts, to call out how near the arrows fell to the mark,—as "Wide on the bow-hand;—wide on the shaft-hand;—short;—gone." To give aim was, therefore, to give the knowledge of a fact, by which the intention, the aim, of the archer might be better regulated in future. In the fifth Act (4th scene) of this comedy, the passage
    "Behold her, that gave aim to all thy oathes,"
has reference to the aim-giver of the butts.
  [a] *Pretence*—design.
  [b] *Where*—whereas.

Should have been cherish'd by her child-like duty,
I now am full resolv'd to take a wife,
And turn her out to who will take her in.
Then let her beauty be her wedding-dower;
For me and my possessions she esteems not.
  Val. What would your grace have me to do in this?
  Duke. There is a lady, sir, in Milan, here,[a]
Whom I affect; but she is nice, and coy,
And nought esteems my aged eloquence:
Now, therefore, would I have thee to my tutor,
(For long agone I have forgot to court:
Besides, the fashion of the time is chang'd;)
How, and which way, I may bestow myself,
To be regarded in her sun-bright eye.
  Val. Win her with gifts, if she respect not words;
Dumb jewels often, in their silent kind,
More than quick words, do move a woman's mind.
  Duke. But she did scorn a present that I sent her.
  Val. A woman sometimes scorns what best contents her:
Send her another; never give her o'er;
For scorn at first makes after-love the more.
If she do frown, 'tis not in hate of you,
But rather to beget more love in you:
If she do chide, 'tis not to have you gone;
For why, the fools are mad, if left alone.
Take no repulse, whatever she doth say;
For, *get you gone*, she doth not mean, *away*;
Flatter, and praise, commend, extol their graces;
Though ne'er so black, say they have angels' faces.
That man that hath a tongue, I say, is no man,
If with his tongue he cannot win a woman.
  Duke. But, she I mean is promis'd by her friends
Unto a youthful gentleman of worth;
And kept severely from resort of men,
That no man hath access by day to her.
  Val. Why then I would resort to her by night.
  Duke. Ay, but the doors be lock'd, and keys kept safe,
That no man hath recourse to her by night.
  Val. What lets,[b] but one may enter at her window?
  Duke. Her chamber is aloft, far from the ground;
And built so shelving, that one cannot climb it
Without apparent hazard of his life.
  Val. Why then, a ladder, quaintly made of cords,

  [a] Mr. Dyce prefers Mr. Collier's correction—
      "There is a lady in Milano here."
Mr. Halliwell reads, "of Verona."
  [b] *Lets*—hinders.

[Act III.]   TWO GENTLEMEN OF VERONA.   [Scene I.

To cast up with a pair of anchoring hooks,
Would serve to scale another Hero's tower,
So bold Leander would adventure it.
  Duke. Now, as thou art a gentleman of blood,
Advise me where I may have such a ladder.
  Val. When would you use it? pray, sir, tell me that.
  Duke. This very night; for love is like a child,
That longs for every thing that he can come by.
  Val. By seven o'clock I'll get you such a ladder.
  Duke. But, hark thee; I will go to her alone;
How shall I best convey the ladder thither?
  Val. It will be light, my lord, that you may bear it
Under a cloak, that is of any length.
  Duke. A cloak as long as thine will serve the turn!
  Val. Ay, my good lord.
  Duke. Then let me see thy cloak:
I'll get me one of such another length.
  Val. Why, any cloak will serve the turn, my lord.
  Duke. How shall I fashion me to wear a cloak?—
I pray thee, let me feel thy cloak upon me.—
What letter is this same? What's here?—*To Silvia?*
And here an engine fit for my proceeding!
I'll be so bold to break the seal for once. [*Reads.*

> My thoughts do harbour with my Silvia nightly;
> And slaves they are to me, that send them flying:
> O, could their master come and go as lightly,
> Himself would lodge, where senseless they are lying.
> My herald thoughts in thy pure bosom rest them;
> While I, their king, that thither them importune,
> Do curse the grace that with such grace hath bless'd them.
> Because myself do want my servants' fortune:
> I curse myself, for they are sent by me,
> That they should harbour where their lord should be.

What's here?

> Silvia, this night I will enfranchise thee.

'T is so; and here's the ladder for the purpose.
Why Phaëton, (for thou art Merops' son,)
Wilt thou aspire to guide the heavenly car,
And with thy daring folly burn the world?
Wilt thou reach stars, because they shine on thee?
Go, base intruder! over-weening slave!
Bestow thy fawning smiles on equal mates;
And think my patience, more than thy desert,
Is privilege for thy departure hence:
Thank me for this, more than for all the favours,
Which, all too much, I have bestow'd on thee.
But if thou linger in my territories,
Longer than swiftest expedition

Will give thee time to leave our royal court,
By heaven, my wrath shall far exceed the love
I ever bore my daughter, or thyself.
Be gone, I will not hear thy vain excuse,
But, as thou lov'st thy life, make speed from hence.   [*Exit* Duke.
  Val. And why not death, rather than living torment?
To die, is to be banish'd from myself;
And Silvia is myself: banish'd from her,
Is self from self: a deadly banishment!
What light is light, if Silvia be not seen?
What joy is joy, if Silvia be not by?
Unless it be to think that she is by,
And feed upon the shadow of perfection.
Except I be by Silvia in the night,
There is no music in the nightingale;
Unless I look on Silvia in the day,
There is no day for me to look upon:
She is my essence; and I leave to be,
If I be not by her fair influence
Foster'd, illumin'd, cherish'd, kept alive.
I fly not death, to fly his deadly doom
Tarry I here, I but attend on death;
But, fly I hence, I fly away from life.

Enter Proteus *and* Launce.

  Pro. Run, boy, run, run, and seek him out.
  Laun. So-ho! so-ho!
  Pro. What seest thou?
  Laun. Him we go to find: there's not a hair on 's head, but 't is a Valentine.
  Pro. Valentine?
  Val. No.
  Pro. Who then? his spirit?
  Val. Neither.
  Pro. What then?
  Val. Nothing.
  Laun. Can nothing speak? Master, shall I strike?
  Pro. Who would'st thou strike?
  Laun. Nothing.
  Pro. Villain, forbear.
  Laun. Why, sir, I'll strike nothing: I pray you,—
  Pro. Sirrah, I say, forbear: Friend Valentine, a word.
  Val. My ears are stopp'd, and cannot hear good news,
So much of bad already hath possess'd them.
  Pro. Then in dumb silence will I bury mine,
For they are harsh, untuneable, and bad.
  Val. Is Silvia dead?
  Pro. No, Valentine.
  Val. No Valentine, indeed, for sacred Silvia!—

Hath she forsworn me?

Pro. No, Valentine.

Val. No Valentine, if Silvia have forsworn me!—
What is your news?

Laun. Sir, there's a proclamation that you are vanish'd.

Pro. That thou art banish'd. O, that's the news;
From hence, from Silvia, and from me thy friend.

Val. O, I have fed upon this woe already,
And now excess of it will make me surfeit.
Doth Silvia know that I am banished?

Pro. Ay, ay; and she hath offer'd to the doom,
(Which, unrevers'd, stands in effectual force,)
A sea of melting pearl, which some call tears:
Those at her father's churlish feet she tender'd;
With them, upon her knees, her humble self;
Wringing her hands, whose whiteness so became them,
As if but now they waxed pale for woe:
But neither bended knees, pure hands held up,
Sad sighs, deep groans, nor silver-shedding tears,
Could penetrate her uncompassionate sire;
But Valentine, if he be ta'en, must die.
Besides, her intercession chaf'd him so,
When she for thy repeal was suppliant,
That to close prison he commanded her,
With many bitter threats of 'biding there.

Val. No more; unless the next word that thou speak'st
Have some malignant power upon my life:
If so, I pray thee, breathe it in mine ear,
As ending anthem of my endless dolour.

Pro. Cease to lament for that thou can'st not help,
And study help for that which thou lament'st.
Time is the nurse and breeder of all good.
Here if thou stay, thou canst not see thy love;
Besides, thy staying will abridge thy life.
Hope is a lover's staff; walk hence with that,
And manage it against despairing thoughts.
Thy letters may be here, though thou art hence:
Which, being writ to me, shall be deliver'd
Even in the milk-white bosom of thy love.[1]
The time now serves not to expostulate;
Come, I'll convey thee through the city gate;
And, ere I part with thee, confer at large
Of all that may concern thy love-affairs:
As thou lov'st Silvia, though not for thyself,
Regard thy danger, and along with me.

Val. I pray thee, Launce, an if thou seest my boy,
Bid him make haste, and meet me at the north-gate.

Pro. Go, sirrah, find him out. Come, Valentine.

Val. O my dear Silvia, hapless Valentine!
[*Exeunt* VALENTINE *and* PROTEUS.

Laun. I am but a fool, look you; and yet I have the wit to think my master is a kind of a knave: but that's all one, if he be but one knave. He lives not now that knows me to be in love: yet I am in love; but a team of horse shall not pluck that from me; nor who 't is I love, and yet 't is a woman: but what woman, I will not tell myself; and yet 't is a milkmaid; yet 't is not a maid, for she hath had gossips: yet 't is a maid, for she is her master's maid, and serves for wages. She hath more qualities than a water-spaniel,—which is much in a bare-christian. Here is the cate-log [*Pulling out a paper*] of her conditions. Imprimis, *She can fetch and carry.* Why, a horse can do no more: nay, a horse cannot fetch, but only carry; therefore is she better than a jade. Item, *She can milk;* look you, a sweet virtue in a maid with clean hands.

Enter SPEED.

Speed. How now, signior Launce? what news with your mastership?

Laun. With my master's ship? why it is at sea.

Speed. Well, your old vice still; mistake the word: What news then in your paper?

Laun. The blackest news that ever thou heard'st.

Speed. Why, man, how black?

Laun. Why, as black as ink.

Speed. Let me read them.

Laun. Fye on thee, jolt-head; thou canst not read.

Speed. Thou liest, I can.

Laun. I will try thee: tell me this: Who begot thee?

Speed. Marry, the son of my grandfather.

Laun. O illiterate loiterer! it was the son of thy grandmother: this proves, that thou canst not read.

Speed. Come, fool, come: try me in thy paper.

Laun. There; and St. Nicholas be thy speed![2]

Speed. Imprimis, *She can milk.*

Laun. Ay, that she can.

Speed. Item, *She brews good ale.*

Laun. And thereof comes the proverb,—Blessing of your heart, you brew good ale.

Speed. Item, *She can sew.*

Laun. That's as much as to say, can she so?

Speed. Item, *She can knit.*

Laun. What need a man care for a stock with a wench, when she can knit him a stock.[a]

Speed. Item, *She can wash and scour.*

Laun. A special virtue; for then she need not be washed and scoured.

Speed. She can spin.

Laun. Then I may set the world on wheels, when she can spin for her living.

Speed. Item, *She hath many nameless virtues.*

Laun. That's as much as to say, bastard virtues; that, indeed, know not their fathers, and therefore have no names.

Speed. Here follow her vices.

Laun. Close at the heels of her virtues.

Speed. Item, *She is not to be kissed fasting, in respect of her breath.*

Laun. Well, that fault may be mended with a breakfast: Read on.

Speed. Item, *She hath a sweet mouth.*

Laun. That makes amends for her sour breath.

Speed. Item, *She doth talk in her sleep.*

Laun. It's no matter for that, so she sleep not in her talk.

Speed. Item, *She is slow in words.*

Laun. O villain, that set this down among her vices! To be slow in words is a woman's only virtue: I pray thee, out with 't; and place it for her chief virtue.

Speed. Item, *She is proud.*

Laun. Out with that too; it was Eve's legacy, and cannot be ta'en from her.

Speed. Item, *She hath no teeth.*

Laun. I care not for that neither, because I love crusts.

Speed. Item, *She is curst.*

Laun. Well; the best is, she hath no teeth to bite.

Speed. She will often praise her liquor.

Laun. If her liquor be good, she shall: if she will not, I will; for good things should be praised.

Speed. Item, *She is too liberal.*

Laun. Of her tongue she cannot; for that's writ down she is slow of: of her purse she shall not; for that I'll keep shut: now of another thing she may; and that cannot I help. Well, proceed.

Speed. Item, *She hath more hair than wit,*[b] *and more faults than hairs, and more wealth than faults.*

Laun. Stop there; I'll have her: she was mine, and not mine, twice or thrice in that last article: Rehearse that once more.

[a] *Stock.*—Stocking.
[b] An old English proverb.

Speed. Item, *She hath more hair than wit,—*

Laun. More hair than wit,—it may be; I'll prove it; The cover of the salt hides the salt,[c] and therefore it is more than the salt; the hair that covers the wit, is more than the wit; for the greater hides the less. What's next?

Speed.—And more faults than hairs,—

Laun. That's monstrous: O, that that were out!

Speed.—And more wealth than faults.

Laun. Why, that word makes the faults gracious: Well, I'll have her: And if it be a match, as nothing is impossible,—

Speed. What then?

Laun. Why, then will I tell thee,—that thy master stays for thee at the north gate.

Speed. For me?

Laun. For thee? ay: who art thou? he hath staid for a better man than thee.

Speed. And must I go to him?

Laun. Thou must run to him, for thou hast staid so long, that going will scarce serve the turn.

Speed. Why didst not tell me sooner? 'pox of your love-letters! [*Exit.*

Laun. Now will he be swinged for reading my letter: An unmannerly slave, that will thrust himself into secrets!—I'll after, to rejoice in the boy's correction. [*Exit.*

SCENE II.—*Milan. A Room in the* Duke's *Palace.*

Enter DUKE *and* THURIO; PROTEUS *behind.*

Duke. Sir Thurio, fear not but that she will love you,
Now Valentine is banish'd from her sight.

Thu. Since his exile she hath despis'd me most,
Forsworn my company, and rail'd at me,
That I am desperate of obtaining her.

Duke. This weak impress of love is as a figure
Trenched in ice; which with an hour's heat
Dissolves to water, and doth lose his form.
A little time will melt her frozen thoughts,
And worthless Valentine shall be forgot.—
How now, sir Proteus? Is your countryman,
According to our proclamation, gone?

Pro. Gone, my good lord.

Duke. My daughter takes his going grievously.

Pro. A little time, my lord, will kill that grief.

Duke. So I believe; but Thurio thinks not so.—
Proteus, the good conceit I hold of thee,
(For thou hast shown some sign of good desert,)
Makes me the better to confer with thee.

Pro. Longer than I prove loyal to your grace,
Let me not live to look upon your grace.
  Duke. Thou know'st, how willingly I would effect
The match between sir Thurio and my daughter.
  Pro. I do, my lord.
  Duke. And also, I think, thou art not ignorant
How she opposes her against my will.
  Pro. She did, my lord, when Valentine was here.
  Duke. Ay, and perversely she persevers so.
What might we do, to make the girl forget
The love of Valentine, and love sir Thurio?
  Pro. The best way is, to slander Valentine
With falsehood, cowardice, and poor descent;
Three things that women highly hold in hate.
  Duke. Ay, but she'll think, that it is spoke in hate.
  Pro. Ay, if his enemy deliver it:
Therefore it must, with circumstance, be spoken
By one whom she esteemeth as his friend.
  Duke. Then you must undertake to slander him.
  Pro. And that, my lord, I shall be loth to do:
'T is an ill office for a gentleman;
Especially, against his very* friend.
  Duke. Where your good word cannot advantage him,
Your slander never can endamage him;
Therefore the office is indifferent,
Being entreated to it by your friend.
  Pro. You have prevail'd, my lord: if I can do it,
By aught that I can speak in his dispraise,
She shall not long continue love to him.
But say, this weed her love from Valentine,
It follows not that she will love sir Thurio.
  Thu. Therefore, as you unwind her love from him,
Lest it should ravel, and be good to none,
You must provide to bottom it on me;[b]
Which must be done, by praising me as much
As you in worth dispraise sir Valentine.
  Duke. And, Proteus, we dare trust you in this kind;
Because we know, on Valentine's report,

You are already love's firm votary,
And cannot soon revolt and change your mind.
Upon this warrant shall you have access,
Where you with Silvia may confer at large;
For she is lumpish, heavy, melancholy,
And, for your friend's sake, will be glad of you;
Where you may temper her, by your persuasion,
To hate young Valentine, and love my friend.
  Pro. As much as I can do, I will effect:—
But you, sir Thurio, are not sharp enough;
You must lay lime, to tangle her desires,
By wailful sonnets, whose composed rhymes
Should be full fraught with serviceable vows.
  Duke. Ay, much is the force of heaven-bred poesy.
  Pro. Say, that upon the altar of her beauty
You sacrifice your tears, your sighs, your heart.
Write till your ink be dry; and with your tears
Moist it again; and frame some feeling line,
That may discover such integrity:
For Orpheus' lute was strung with poet's sinews;
Whose golden touch could soften steel and stones,
Make tigers tame, and huge leviathans
Forsake unsounded deeps to dance on sands.
After your dire lamenting elegies,
Visit by night your lady's chamber-window,
With some sweet consort:[a] to their instruments
Tune a deploring dump;[b] the night's dead silence
Will well become such sweet-complaining grievance.
This, or else nothing, will inherit[c] her.
  Duke. This discipline shews thou hast been in love.
  Thu. And thy advice this night I'll put in practice.
Therefore, sweet Proteus, my direction-giver,
Let us into the city presently
To sort[d] some gentlemen well skill'd in music
I have a sonnet that will serve the turn,
To give the onset to thy good advice.
  Duke. About it, gentlemen.
  Pro. We'll wait upon your grace, till after supper;
And afterward determine our proceedings.
  Duke. Even now about it; I will pardon you.
  [*Exeunt.*

---

a Very. True; real (verus).
b This image, derived from the labours of the sempstress, had found its way into English poetry, before the time of Shakspere:—
  "A *bottom* for your silk, it seems,
  My letters are become,
  Which oft with winding off and on,
  Are wasted whole and some."
      Grange's Garden, 1557.

a The modern concert is the same as the old consort—a band or company.
b Dump. A mournful elegy. Dump, or dumps, for sorrow, was not originally a burlesque term:—
  "My sinews dull, in dumps I stand."—SURREY.
c Inherit. To obtain possession.
d Sort. To choose.

ILLUSTRATIONS OF ACT III.

¹ Scene I.—*"Even in the milk-white bosom of thy love."*

The lady of the sixteenth century had a small pocket in the front of her stays, in which she carried her letters, and other matters which she valued. In the verses which Valentine has addressed to Silvia, he says,

"My herald thoughts in thy pure bosom rest them."

In Hamlet we have the same allusion: "These to her excellent white bosom." A passage in Lord Surrey's Sonnets conveys the same idea, which occurs also in Chaucer's Merchant's Tale:—

"This purse hath she in his bosom hid."

² Scene I.—*"Saint Nicholas be thy speed."*

When Speed is about to read Launce's paper, Launce, who has previously said, "Thou can'st not read," invokes Saint Nicholas to assist him. Saint Nicholas was the patron-saint of scholars. There is a story in Douce how the saint attained this distinction, by discovering that a wicked host had murdered three scholars on their way to school, and by his prayers restored their souls to their bodies. This legend is told in the Life of Saint Nicholas, composed in French verse by *Maitre Wace*, chaplain to Henry II., and which remains in manuscript. By the statutes of St. Paul's School, the scholars are required to attend divine service at the cathedral on the anniversary of this saint. The parish clerks of London were incorporated into a guild, with Saint Nicholas for their patron. These worthy persons were, probably, at the period of their incorporation, more worthy of the name of *clerks* (scholars) than we have been wont in modern times to consider. But why are thieves called Saint Nicholas' clerks in Henry IV.? Warburton says, by a quibble between Nicholas and old Nick. This we doubt. Scholars appear, from the ancient statutes against vagrancy, to have been great travellers about the country. These statutes generally recognise the right of poor scholars to beg; but they were also liable to the penalties of the gaol and the stocks, unless they could produce letters testimonial from the chancellor of their respective universities. It is not unlikely that in the journeys of these hundreds of poor scholars they should have occasionally "taken a purse" as well as begged "an almcasse," and that some of "Saint Nicholas's clerks" should have become as celebrated for the same accomplishments which distinguished Bardolph and Peto at Gadshill, as for the learned poverty which entitled them to travel with a chancellor's licence.

³ Scene I.—*"The cover of the salt hides the salt.*

The large salt-cellar of the dinner-table was a massive piece of plate, with a cover equally substantial. There was only one salt-cellar on the board, which was placed near the top of the table; and the distinction of those who sat above and below the salt was universally recognised. The following representation of a salt-cellar, *a*, with its cover, *b*, presented to Queen Elizabeth, is from "Nicholl's Progresses."

ACT IV.

SCENE I.—*A Forest, near* Mantua.

Enter certain Outlaws.

1 *Out.* Fellows, stand fast; I see a passenger.
2 *Out.* If there be ten, shrink not, but down with 'em.

Enter VALENTINE *and* SPEED.

3 *Out.* Stand, sir, and throw us that you have about you;
If not, we'll make you sit, and rifle you.
Speed. Sir, we are undone! these are the villains
That all the travellers do fear so much.
Val. My friends,—
1 *Out.* That's not so, sir; we are your enemies.
2 *Out.* Peace; we'll hear him.
3 *Out.* Ay, by my beard, will we; for he's a proper man.
Val. Then know, that I have little wealth to lose;
A man I am cross'd with adversity:
My riches are these poor habiliments,
Of which if you should here disfurnish me,
You take the sum and substance that I have.
2 *Out.* Whither travel you?
Val. To Verona.
1 *Out.* Whence came you?
Val. From Milan.
3 *Out.* Have you long sojourn'd there?
Val. Some sixteen months; and longer might have staid,
If crooked fortune had not thwarted me.
1 *Out.* What, were you banish'd thence?
Val. I was.
2 *Out.* For what offence?
Val. For that which now torments me to rehearse:
I kill'd a man, whose death I much repent;
But yet I slew him manfully in fight,
Without false vantage, or base treachery.
1 *Out.* Why, ne'er repent it, if it were done so:
But were you banish'd for so small a fault?
Val. I was, and held me glad of such a doom.
1 *Out.* Have you the tongues?
Val. My youthful travel therein made me happy;
Or else I often had been miserable.
3 *Out.* By the bare scalp of Robin Hood's fat friar,[1]
This fellow were a king for our wild faction.
1 *Out.* We'll have him; sirs, a word.

Speed. Master, be one of them;
It is an honourable kind of thievery.
  Val. Peace, villain!
  2 Out. Tell us this: Have you anything to
    take to?
  Val. Nothing, but my fortune.
  3 Out. Know then, that some of us are gentle-
    men,
Such as the fury of ungovern'd youth
Thrust from the company of awful[a] men :
Myself was from Verona banished,
For practising to steal away a lady,
An heir, and near allied unto the duke.
  2 Out. And I from Mantua, for a gentleman,
Whom, in my mood, I stabb'd unto the heart.
  1 Out. And I, for such like petty crimes as
    these.
But to the purpose,—for we cite our faults,
That they may hold excus'd our lawless lives,
And, partly, seeing you are beautified
With goodly shape; and by your own report
A linguist; and a man of such perfection,
As we do in our quality much want;—
  2 Out. Indeed, because you are a banish'd
    man,
Therefore, above the rest, we parley to you:
Are you content to be our general?
To make a virtue of necessity,
And live, as we do, in this wilderness?
  3 Out. What say'st thou? wilt thou be of our
    consort?
Say, ay, and be the captain of us all :
We'll do thee homage, and be rul'd by thee,
Love thee as our commander, and our king.
  1 Out. But if thou scorn our courtesy, thou
    diest.
  2 Out. Thou shalt not live to brag what we
    have offer'd.
  Val. I take your offer, and will live with you;
Provided that you do no outrages
On silly women, or poor passengers.
  3 Out. No, we detest such vile base practices.
Come, go with us, we'll bring thee to our crews,
And shew thee all the treasure we have got:
Which, with ourselves, all rest at thy dispose.
                              [*Exeunt.*

SCENE II.—Milan. *Court of the Palace.*

Enter PROTEUS.

Pro. Already have I been false to Valentine,
And now I must be as unjust to Thurio.

Under the colour of commending him,
I have access my own love to prefer;
But Silvia is too fair, too true, too holy,
To be corrupted with my worthless gifts.
When I protest true loyalty to her,
She twits me with my falsehood to my friend :
When to her beauty I commend my vows,
She bids me think, how I have been forsworn
In breaking faith with Julia whom I lov'd :
And, notwithstanding all her sudden quips,
The least whereof would quell a lover's hope,
Yet, spaniel-like, the more she spurns my love,
The more it grows, and fawneth on her still.
But here comes Thurio: now must we to her
      window,
And give some evening music to her ear.

Enter THURIO *and Musicians.*

  Thu. How now, sir Proteus? are you crept
    before us?
  Pro. Ay, gentle Thurio; for, you know, that
    love
Will creep in service where it cannot go.
  Thu. Ay, but, I hope, sir, that you love not
    here.
  Pro. Sir, but I do; or else I would be hence.
  Thu. Who? Silvia?
  Pro. Ay, Silvia,—for your sake.
  Thu. I thank you for your own. Now, gen-
    tlemen,
Let's tune, and to it lustily awhile.

Enter Host, *at a distance; and* JULIA *in boy's clothes.*

  Host. Now, my young guest! methinks you're
allycholly; I pray you, why is it?
  Jul. Marry, mine host, because I cannot be
merry.
  Host. Come, we'll have you merry: I'll bring
you where you shall hear music, and see the
gentleman that you ask'd for.
  Jul. But shall I hear him speak?
  Host. Ay, that you shall.
  Jul. That will be music.   [*Music plays.*
  Host. Hark! hark!
  Jul. Is he among these?
  Host. Ay: but peace, let's hear 'em.

SONG.

Who is Silvia? what is she,
  That all our swains commend her?
Holy, fair, and wise is she,
  The heaven such grace did lend her,
That she might admired be.

---

[a] *Awful.* Steevens and others think we should here read *lawful.* But Shakspere, in other places, uses this word in the sense of lawful:—
  "We come within our awful banks again."

Is she kind, as she is fair
  For beauty lives with kindness:
Love doth to her eyes repair,
  To help him of his blindness;
And, being help'd, inhabits there.

Then to Silvia let us sing,
  That Silvia is excelling;
She excels each mortal thing,
  Upon the dull earth dwelling:
To her let us garlands bring.

Host. How now? are you sadder than you were before?

How do you, man; the music likes[a] you not.

Jul. You mistake; the musician likes me not.

Host. Why, my pretty youth?

Jul. He plays false, father.

Host. How? out of tune on the strings?

Jul. Not so; but yet so false that he grieves my very heart-strings.

Host. You have a quick ear.

Jul. Ay, I would I were deaf! it makes me have a slow heart.

Host. I perceive, you delight not in music.

Jul. Not a whit, when it jars so.

Host. Hark, what fine change is in the music!

Jul. Ay; that change is the spite.

Host. You would have them always play but one thing.

Jul. I would always have one play but one thing.
But, host, doth this sir Proteus, that we talk on, Often resort unto this gentlewoman?

Host. I tell you what Launce, his man, told me, he loved her out of all nick.[b]

Jul. Where is Launce?

Host. Gone to seek his dog; which, to-morrow, by his master's command, he must carry for a present to his lady.

Jul. Peace! stand aside! the company parts.

Pro. Sir Thurio, fear not you! I will so plead, That you shalt say, my cunning drift excels.

Thu. Where meet we?

Pro. At saint Gregory's well.

Thu. Farewell. [*Exeunt* THURIO *and Musicians.*

SILVIA *appears above, at her window.*

Pro. Madam, good even to your ladyship.

Sil. I thank you for your music, gentlemen: Who is that, that spake?

Pro. One, lady, if you know his pure heart's truth,
You'd quickly learn to know him by his voice.

Sil. Sir Proteus, as I take it.

Pro. Sir Proteus, gentle lady, and your servant

Sil. What is your will?

Pro. That I may compass[a] yours.

Sil. You have your wish; my will is even this,—
That presently you hie you home to bed.
Thou subtle, perjur'd, false, disloyal man!
Think'st thou, I am so shallow, so conceitless,
To be seduced by thy flattery,
That hast deceiv'd so many with thy vows?
Return, return, and make thy love amends.
For me,—by this pale queen of night I swear,
I am so far from granting thy request,
That I despise thee for thy wrongful suit;
And by and by intend to chide myself,
Even for this time I spend in talking to thee.

Pro. I grant, sweet love, that I did love a lady;
But she is dead.

Jul. 'T were false, if I should speak it;
For I am sure she is not buried. [*Aside.*

Sil. Say that she be; yet Valentine, thy friend,
Survives; to whom, thyself art witness,
I am betroth'd: And art thou not asham'd
To wrong him with thy importunacy?

Pro. I likewise hear that Valentine is dead.

Sil. And so suppose am I; for in his grave
Assure thyself my love is buried.

Pro. Sweet lady, let me rake it from the earth

Sil. Go to thy lady's grave, and call her's thence;
Or, at the least, in her's sepulchre thine.

Jul. He heard not that. [*Aside.*

Pro. Madam, if your heart be so obdurate,
Vouchsafe me yet your picture for my love,

---

[a] *Likes*—pleases.

[b] *Nick.* Beyond all reckoning. The nick was the notch upon the tally stick, by which accounts were kept. An Innkeeper in a play before Shakspere's time—"A Woman never Vexed," says—

——"I have carried
The tallies at my girdle seven years together,
For I did ever love to deal honestly in the nick."

These primitive day-books and ledgers were equally adapted to an alehouse score and a nation's revenue; for, as our readers know, they continued to be used in the English Exchequer till within the last thirty years.

[a] *Compass.* Johnson says that in this passage "the word *will* is ambiguous. He wishes to gain her will; she tells him, if he wants her will he has it." Douce considers that Johnson has mistaken the meaning of the word *compass*, which does not here mean to gain, but to perform. It appears to us that a double ambiguity is here intended. Silvia says "What is your will"—what is your *wish*,—for although Shakspere has accurately distinguished between the two words, as in this play (Act I. Sc. III.),

"My will is something seal'd with his wish,"

he yet often uses them synonymously. Proteus' reply is to the question, is—"That I may compass your's"—*that I may have* your *will within my power*—encompassed—surrounded. Julia, in her answer, receives the word *compass* in its meaning of to *perform*; and distinguishes between *wish* and *will.* "You *have* your wish;"—you may compass—you may perform *my will*—"my will is even this," &c. This latter meaning of *compass* is frequent in Shakspere, as, "You judge it impossible to compass wonders," (1 Hen. VI.) "That were hard to compass." (Tw. Night.) The meaning in which Proteus appears to us to *use* the term, is indicated in the Merry Wives.—"May be the knave bragged of that he could not compass"—of that which was beyond his power.

The picture that is hanging in your chamber;
To that I'll speak, to that I'll sigh and weep:
For, since the substance of your perfect self
Is else devoted, I am but a shadow;
And to your shadow will I make true love.

Jul. If 't were a substance, you would, sure, deceive it,
And make it but a shadow, as I am. [*Aside.*

Sil. I am very loth to be your idol, sir;
But, since your falsehood shall become you well
To worship shadows, and adore false shapes,
Send to me in the morning, and I'll send it:
And so, good rest.

Pro. As wretches have o'er-night,
That wait for execution in the morn.

[*Exeunt* PROTEUS; *and* SILVIA, *from above.*

Jul. Host, will you go?
Host. By my halidom,ᵃ I was fast asleep.
Jul. Pray you, where lies Sir Proteus?
Host. Marry, at my house: Trust me, I think, 't is almost day.
Jul. Not so; but it hath been the longest night That e'er I watched, and the most heaviest.

[*Exeunt.*

SCENE III.—*The same.*

Enter EGLAMOUR.

Egl. This is the hour that madam Silvia
Entreated me to call, and know her mind;
There's some great matter she'd employ me in.—
Madam, madam!

SILVIA *appears above, at her window.*

Sil. Who calls?
Egl. Your servant, and your friend;
One that attends your ladyship's command.
Sil. Sir Eglamour, a thousand times good-morrow.
Egl. As many, worthy lady, to yourself.
According to your ladyship's impose,ᵇ
I am thus early come, to know what service
It is your pleasure to command me in.
Sil. O Eglamour, thou art a gentleman,
(Think not I flatter, for I swear I do not,)
Valiant, wise, remorseful, well accomplish'd.
Thou art not ignorant what dear good will
I bear unto the banish'd Valentine;
Nor how my father would enforce me marry
Vain Thurio, whom my very soul abhorr'd.ᶜ
Thyself hast loved; and I have heard thee say,
No grief did ever come so near thy heart,

As when thy lady and thy true love died,
Upon whose grave thou vow'dst pure chastity.
Sir Eglamour, I would to Valentine,
To Mantua, where, I hear, he makes abode;
And, for the ways are dangerous to pass,
I do desire thy worthy company,
Upon whose faith and honour I repose.
Urge not my father's anger, Eglamour,
But think upon my grief, a lady's grief;
And on the justice of my flying hence,
To keep me from a most unholy match.
Which Heaven and fortune still reward with plagues.
I do desire thee, even from a heart
As full of sorrows as the sea of sands,
To bear me company, and go with me:
If not, to hide what I have said to thee,
That I may venture to depart alone.

Egl. Madam, I pity much your grievances;
Which since I know they virtuously are plac'd,
I give consent to go along with you;
Recking as little what betideth me
As much I wish all good befortune you.
When will you go?
Sil. This evening coming.
Egl. Where shall I meet you?
Sil. At friar Patrick's cell,
Where I intend holy confession.
Egl. I will not fail your ladyship:
Good-morrow, gentle lady.
Sil. Good-morrow, kind sir Eglamour.

[*Exeunt.*

SCENE IV.—*The same.*

Enter LAUNCE, *with his dog.*

When a man's servant shall play the cur with him, look you, it goes hard: one that I brought up of a puppy; one that I saved from drowning, when three or four of his blind brothers and sisters went to it! I have taught him—even as one would say precisely, Thus I would teach a dog. I was sent to deliver him, as a present to mistress Silvia, from my master; and I came no sooner into the dining-chamber, but he steps me to her trencher,ᶜ and steals her capon's leg. O, 't is a foul thing when a cur cannot keepᵉ himself in all companies! I would have, as one should say, one that takes upon him to be a dog indeed, to be, as it were, a dog at all things. If I had not had more wit than he, to take a fault upon me that he did, I think verily he had been hanged for 't; sure as I live he had suffer'd for 't: you shall judge. He thrusts me himself into the company of three or four gentlemen-like dogs,

---

ᵃ *Halidom*—Holiness; *hali* and *dom*,—as in kingdom. Holidame—holy virgin—was a corruption of the term.
ᵇ *Impose*—command.—The word, as a noun, does not occur again in Shakspere.
ᶜ Mr. Dyce has "my very soul abhors," remarking that Hanmer had made the obvious correction.

ᵉ *Keep*—restrain.

under the duke's table: he had not been there (bless the mark) a pissing while, but all the chamber smelt him. *Out with the dog*, says one; *What cur is that?* says another; *Whip him out*, says the third; *Hang him up*, says the duke. I, having been acquainted with the smell before, knew it was Crab; and goes me to the fellow that whips the dogs: *Friend*, quoth I, *you mean to whip the dog? Ay, marry, do I*, quoth he. *You do him the more wrong*, quoth I; *'t was I did the thing you wot of*. He makes me no more ado, but whips me out of the chamber. How many masters would do this for their servant? Nay, I'll be sworn, I have sat in the stocks[b] for puddings he hath stolen, otherwise he had been executed: I have stood on the pillory[c] for geese he hath killed, otherwise he had suffer'd for 't; thou think'st not of this now!—Nay, I remember the trick you served me, when I took my leave of madam Silvia; did not I bid thee still mark me, and do as I do? When didst thou see me heave up my leg, and make water against a gentlewoman's farthingale? didst thou ever see me do such a trick?

Enter PROTEUS *and* JULIA.

Pro. Sebastian is thy name? I like thee well, And will employ thee in some service presently.
Jul. In what you please.—I'll do what I can.
Pro. I hope thou wilt.—How now, you whoreson peasant? [*To* LAUNCE.
Where have you been these two days loitering?
Laun. Marry, sir, I carried mistress Silvia the dog you bade me.
Pro. And what says she to my little jewel?
Laun. Marry, she says, your dog was a cur; and tells you, currish thanks is good enough for such a present.
Pro. But she received my dog?
Laun. No, indeed, did she not: here have I brought him back again.
Pro. What, didst thou offer her this from me?
Laun. Ay, sir; the other squirrel was stolen from me by the hangman's boys in the market-place: and then I offered her mine own; who is a dog as big as ten of yours, and therefore the gift the greater.
Pro. Go, get thee hence, and find my dog again,
Or ne'er return again into my sight.
Away, I say: Stay'st thou to vex me here?
A slave, that still an end turns me to shame.
[*Exit* LAUNCE.
Sebastian, I have entertained thee,
Partly, that I have need of such a youth,
That can with some discretion do my business,

For 't is no trusting to you foolish lowt;
But, chiefly, for thy face and thy behaviour;
Which (if my augury deceive me not)
Witness good bringing up, fortune, and truth:
Therefore know thee, for this I entertain thee.
Go presently, and take this ring with thee,
Deliver it to madam Silvia:
She lov'd me well,[a] deliver'd it to me.
Jul. It seems you lov'd her not to leave[b] her token:
She's dead, belike.
Pro. Not so; I think she lives.
Jul. Alas!
Pro. Why dost thou cry, alas!
Jul. I cannot choose but pity her.
Pro. Wherefore should'st thou pity her?
Jul. Because, methinks, that she lov'd you as well
As you do love your lady Silvia:
She dreams on him that has forgot her love;
You dote on her that cares not for your love.
'T is pity, love should be so contrary;
And thinking on it makes me cry, alas!
Pro. Well, give her that ring, and therewithal
This letter;—that's her chamber.—Tell my lady,
I claim the promise for her heavenly picture.
Your message done, hie home unto my chamber,
Where thou shalt find me sad and solitary.
[*Exit* PROTEUS.
Jul. How many women would do such a message?
Alas, poor Proteus! thou hast entertain'd
A fox, to be the shepherd of thy lambs.
Alas, poor fool! why do I pity him
That with his very heart despiseth me?
Because he loves her, he despiseth me;
Because I love him, I must pity him.
This ring I gave him, when he parted from me,
To bind him to remember my good will:
And now am I (unhappy messenger)
To plead for that, which I would not obtain;
To carry that which I would have refus'd;
To praise his faith, which I would have dispraised.
I am my master's true confirmed love;
But cannot be true servant to my master,
Unless I prove false traitor to myself.
Yet I will woo for him; but yet so coldly,
As, Heaven it knows, I would not have him speed.

Enter SILVIA, *attended*.

Gentlewoman, good day! I pray you, be my mean
To bring me where to speak with madam Silvia

---
[a] She lov'd me well, *who* deliver'd it to me.
[b] To *leave*—to part with.

Sil. What would you with her, if that I be she?
Jul. If you be she, I do entreat your patience
To hear me speak the message I am sent on.
Sil. From whom?
Jul. From my master, sir Proteus, madam.
Sil. O!—he sends you for a picture?
Jul. Ay, madam.
Sil. Ursula, bring my picture there.
                    [*Picture brought.*
Go, give your master this: tell him from me,
One Julia, that his changing thoughts forget,
Would better fit his chamber, than this shadow.
Jul. Madam, please you peruse this letter.——
Pardon me, madam; I have unadvis'd
Deliver'd you a paper that I should not:
This is the letter to your ladyship.
Sil. I pray thee, let me look on that again.
Jul. It may not be; good madam, pardon me.
Sil. There, hold.
I will not look upon your master's lines:
I know they are stuff'd with protestations,
And full of new-found oaths; which he will
    break,
As easily as I do tear his paper.
Jul. Madam, he sends your ladyship this ring.
Sil. The more shame for him that he sends it
    me;
For, I have heard him say a thousand times,
His Julia gave it him at his departure:
Though his false finger have profan'd the ring,
Mine shall not do his Julia so much wrong.
Jul. She thanks you.
Sil. What say'st thou?
Jul. I thank you, madam, that you tender her:
Poor gentlewoman! my master wrongs her
    much.
Sil. Dost thou know her?
Jul. Almost as well as I do know myself:
To think upon her woes I do protest
That I have wept an hundred several times.
Sil. Belike, she thinks that Proteus hath forsook her.
Jul. I think she doth, and that 's her cause of
    sorrow.
Sil. Is she not passing fair?
Jul. She hath been fairer, madam, than she is:
When she did think my master lov'd her well,
She, in my judgment, was as fair as you;
But since she did neglect her looking-glass,
And threw her sun expelling mask away,[7]
The air hath starv'd the roses in her cheeks,
And pinch'd the lily-tincture of her face,
That now she is become as black as I.[a]

[a] In this passage *pinch'd* means painted, and not as Johnson has it, pinch'd with cold. *Black* signifies dark,

Sil. How tall was she?
Jul. About my stature: for, at Pentecost,
When all our pageants of delight were play'd,
Our youth got me to play the woman's part,
And I was trimm'd in madam Julia's gown;
Which serv'd me as fit, by all men's judgment,
As if the garment had been made for me:
Therefore, I know she is about my height.
And, at that time, I made her weep a-good,
For I did play a lamentable part;
Madam, 't was Ariadne, passioning
For Theseus' perjury, and unjust flight;
Which I so lively acted with my tears,
That my poor mistress, moved therewithal,
Wept bitterly; and, would I might be dead,
If I in thought felt not her very sorrow!
Sil. She is beholden to thee, gentle youth!—
Alas, poor lady! desolate and left!—
I weep myself to think upon thy words.
Here, youth, there is my purse; I give thee this
For thy sweet mistress' sake, because thou lov'st
    her.
Farewell.   [*Exit* Silvia.
Jul. And she shall thank you for't, if e'er you
    know her.
A virtuous gentlewoman, mild, and beautiful.
I hope my master's suit will be but cold,
Since she respects my mistress' love so much.
Alas, how love can trifle with itself!
Here is her picture: Let me see; I think,
If I had such a tire, this face of mine
Were full as lovely as is this of hers:
And yet the painter flatter'd her a little,
Unless I flatter with myself too much.
Her hair is auburn, mine is perfect yellow:[a]
If that be all the difference in his love,
I 'll get me such a colour'd periwig.[a]
Her eyes are grey as glass;[b] and so are mine.
Ay, but her forehead 's low, and mine 's as high.
What should it be, that he respects in her,
But I can make respective[c] in myself,

tanned. In the next act Thurio says "my face is black," as opposed to "fair." It is curious that *black, bleak, blight,* are words having a strong affinity; and that, therefore, "the air," which "starv'd the roses," and "pinch'd the lily tincture," so as to make "black," is the same as the withering and *blighting* agency, the *bleak* wind, which covers vegetation with a sterile *blackness*. (See Richardson's Dictionary.)
[a] Capell says the colour of the hair marks this play as of the period of Elizabeth. The auburn, or yellow, of the queen's hair made that colour beautiful.
[b] The glass of Shakspere's time was not of the colourless quality which now constitutes the perfection of glass, but of a light blue tint; hence "as grey as glass." "Eyen as gray as glasse," in the old romances, expresses the pale cerulean hue of those eyes which usually accompany a fair complexion—a complexion belonging to the "auburn" and "yellow" hair of Julia and Silvia.
[c] Steevens interprets *respective* as respectful, respectable; but the true meaning of the word, and the context, shew that Julia says, "What he respects in her, has equal *relation to myself.*"

If this fond love were not a blinded god?
Come, shadow, come, and take this shadow up,
For 't is thy rival. O thou senseless form,
Thou shalt be worshipp'd, kiss'd, lov'd, and ador'd;
And, were there sense in his idolatry,
My substance should be statue* in thy stead.

* The words *statue* and *picture* were often used without distinction. In Massinger's City Madam, Sir John Frugal desires that his daughters

I 'll use thee kindly for thy mistress' sake,
That used me so; or else, by Jove I vow,
I should have scratch'd out your unseeing eyes,
To make my master out of love with thee. [*Exit.*

" may take leave
Of their late suitors' statues."

Luke replies:—" There they hang." Stow, speaking of Queen Elizabeth's funeral, mentions " her statue or picture lying upon the coffin;" and in one of the inventories of Henry the Eighth's furniture, *pictures of earth*—that is, busts of *terra cotta*—are recited.

RECENT NEW READINGS.

Sc. I. p. 50.—" Come, go with us, we'll bring thee to our crews."
" Come, go with us, we'll bring thee to our *cave*."—*Collier.*
Mr. Collier says, in defence of his reading, that the " crews," so to call them, were on the stage, while the " cave " was the place where the treasure was deposited. Crews, however, are companions, and it was not necessary that all the outlaws should be on the stage, leaving the treasure unguarded. Mr. Dyce adopts the correction of *cave*. Mr. Singer has *caves*. Mr. Grant White, in his edition of " The Works of William Shakespeare," published at Boston, U.S., in 1859, adheres to *crews*.

Sc. IV. p. 53.—" The other squirrel was stolen from me by the hangman's boys."
" By the *hangman-boy*."—*Collier.*
The *hangman-boy*, says Mr. Collier, is a rascally boy, a gallows boy. There is no occasion for the change, for the " hangman's boys" are boys dedicated to the hangman. Mr. Dyce and Mr. G. White print " hangman boys."

ILLUSTRATIONS OF ACT IV.

¹ SCENE I.—" *Robin Hood's fat friar.*"

THE jolly Friar Tuck, of the old Robin Hood ballads—the almost equally famous Friar Tuck, of Ivanhoe—is the personage whom the outlaws here invoke. It is unnecessary for us to enter upon the legends

" Of Tuck, the merry friar, which many a sermon made,
 In praise of Robin Hood, his outlaws, and his trade,"

as old Drayton has it. It may be sufficient to give a representation of his " bare scalp." The following illustration is copied, with a little improvement in the drawing, from the Friar in Mr. Tollett's painted window, representing the celebration of May-day. The entire window is given in the Illustrations of All's Well that Ends Well, with a detailed account of the several figures. We may mention here, that the figures, which represent Morris dancers, are very spirited. One of the chief is supposed to be Maid Marian, the Queen of May; and as Marian was the mistress of Robin Hood, who was anciently styled King of May, it has been conjectured that the Friar is Robin's jovial chaplain. At any rate, the figure is not unworthy of Friar Tuck.

Shakspere has two other allusions to Robin Hood. The old duke, in As You Like It, " is already in the forest of Arden, and a many merry men with him, and there they live, like the old Robin Hood of England." Master Silence, that ' merry heart," that " man of mettle," sings, " in the sweet of the night," of

" Robin Hood, Scarlet, and John."

The honourable conditions of Robin's lawless rule over his followers, were evidently in our poet's mind when he makes Valentine say

" I take your offer, and will live with you,
 Provided that you do no outrages
 On silly women, and poor passengers."

² SCENE II.—" *At Saint Gregory's well.*"

This is, as far as we know, the only instance in which holy wells are mentioned by Shakspere. We have already mentioned (see Introductory Notice) that the popular belief in the virtues of these sainted wells, must have been familiar to him. Saint Gregory's well, the place where Proteus and Thurio were to meet, might have been found in some description of Italian and other cities which Shakspere had read; for these wells were often contained within splendid buildings, raised by some devotee to protect the sacred fount from which, he believed, he had derived inestimable advantage. Such was the well of Saint Winifred at Holywell, in Flintshire. This remarkable fountain throws up eighty-four hogsheads every minute, which volume of water forms a considerable stream. The well is enclosed within a beautiful Gothic temple, erected by the mother of Henry VII. The following engraving represents this rich and elegant building.

³ SCENE III.—' *Upon whose grave thou vow'dst pure chastity.*"

Sir Eglamour was selected by Silvia as the companion of her flight, not only as "a gentleman," but as one whose affections were buried in the "grave" of his "lady," and "true love." Steevens says, that it was common for widows and widowers to make solemn vows of chastity, of which the church took account. It is immaterial (for the matter has been controverted) whether Sir Eglamour was a widower, or had made this vow upon the death of one to whom he was betrothed.

⁴ SCENE IV.—"*He steps me to her trencher.*"

That the daughter of a Duke of Milan should eat her capon from a trencher, may appear somewhat strange. It may be noted, however, that the fifth Earl of Northumberland, in 1512, was ordinarily served on wooden trenchers, and that plates of pewter, mean as we may now think them, were reserved in his family for great holidays. The Northumberland Household Book, edited by Bishop Percy, furnishes several entries which establish this. In the privy-purse expenses of Henry VIII. there are also entries regarding trenchers; as, for example, in 1530,—" Item, paied to the s'geant of the pantrye for certen trenchors for the king, xxiijs iiijd."

⁵ SCENE IV.—"*I have sat in the stocks.*"

Launce speaks familiarly of an object that was the terror of vagabonds in every English village,—the "Ancient Castle" of Hudibras,—the

"Dungeon scarce three inches wide;
With roof so low, that under it
They never stand, but lie or sit;
And yet so foul, that whoso is in,
Is to the middle-leg in prison."

Civilization has banished the stocks, with many other relics of a barbarous age. The following representation, which is taken from Fox's Acts and Monuments, and there professes to depict "the straight handling of close prisoners in Lollard's tower," may contribute to preserve the remembrance of this renowned "Fabrick."

⁶ SCENE IV.—"*I have stood on the pillory.*"

The pillory is also abolished in all ordinary cases, and perhaps public opinion will prevent it being ever again used. Our ancestors were ingenious in the varieties of form in which they constructed their pillories. Douce has engraved no less than six specimens of these instruments of punishment. The pillory that was in use amongst us not a quarter of a century ago, appears to have differed very slightly from that of the time of Henry VIII. The following engraved illustration, which represents the infliction of the punishment upon Robert Ockam, in that reign, is copied, like the preceding illustration, from Fox's Martyrs.

⁷ SCENE IV.—"*Sun-expelling mask.*"

Stubbs, in his Anatomie of Abuses, published in 1595, thus describes the masks of the ladies of Elizabeth's time : "When they use to ride abroad they have masks and visors made of velvet, wherewith they cover all their faces, having holes made in them against their eyes, whereout they look."

⁸ SCENE IV.————"*At Pentecost, When all our pageants of delight were play'd.*"

We shall include the general subject of pageants in an illustration of the line in Act V.

"Triumphs, mirth, and rare solemnity."

⁹ SCENE IV.—"*A colour'd periwig.*"

No word has puzzled etymologists more than periwig. It has been referred to a Hebrew, Greek, Latin, and northern origin, and, perhaps, with equal want of success. It is the same word as *perwick*, *periwicke*, and *peruke*. Whiter, in his very curious Etymological Dictionary, thinks it is a compound of two words, or, rather, combinations of sounds, common to many languages. "The wig belonging to the head," he says, "means the *raised up, soft covering*. In the *perruque*, or *perri-wig*, the PRQ, or PR, means, I believe, the *enclosure*, as in *park*." When we smile at Julia's expression, "a colour'd periwig," we must recollect that, in Shakspere's time, the word had not a ludicrous meaning. False hair was worn by ladies long before wigs were adopted by men. In a beautiful passage in the Merchant of Venice, Shakspere more particularly notices this female fashion :

"So are those crisped, snaky, golden locks,
Which make such wanton gambols with the wind,
Upon supposed fairness, often known
To be the dowry of a second head,
The scull that bred them in the sepulchre"

ACT V.

SCENE I.—*The same. An Abbey.*

Enter EGLAMOUR.

Egl. The sun begins to gild the western sky:
And now, it is about the very hour
That Silvia, at friar Patrick's cell, should meet
me.
She will not fail; for lovers break not hours,
Unless it be to come before their time;
So much they spur their expedition.

Enter SILVIA.

See where she comes: Lady, a happy evening!
Sil. Amen, amen! go on, good Eglamour,
Out at the postern by the abbey-wall;
I fear I am attended by some spies.
Egl. Fear not: the forest is not three leagues
off:
If we recover that, we are sure enough. [*Exeunt.*

SCENE II.—*The same. A Room in the* Duke's *Palace.*

Enter THURIO, PROTEUS, *and* JULIA.

Thu. Sir Proteus, what says Silvia to my suit?
Pro. O, sir, I find her milder than she was;
And yet she takes exceptions at your person.
Thu. What, that my leg is too long?
Pro. No; that it is too little.*
Thu. I'll wear a boot, to make it somewhat rounder.
Pro. But love will not be spurr'd to what it loaths.
Thu. What says she to my face?
Pro. She says, it is a fair one.
Thu. Nay, then the wanton lies; my face is black.

* *That it is too little.* "Little" does not sound like as epithet of Shakspere's. Might not he have written "lithe"? Lithe, lithy, lither, are often used in the sense of weak.

Pro. But pearls are fair; and the old saying is, Black men are pearls in beauteous ladies' eyes.
Jul. 'T is true, such pearls as put out ladies' eyes;
For I had rather wink than look on them. [*Aside.*
Thu. How likes she my discourse?
Pro. Ill, when you talk of war.
Thu. But well, when I discourse of love and peace?
Jul. But better, indeed, when you hold your peace. [*Aside.*
Thu. What says she to my valour?
Pro. O, sir, she makes no doubt of that.
Jul. She needs not, when she knows it cowardice. [*Aside.*
Thu. What says she to my birth?
Pro. That you are well deriv'd.
Jul. True; from a gentleman to a fool. [*Aside.*
Thu. Considers she my possessions?
Pro. O, ay; and pities them.
Thu. Wherefore?
Jul. That such an ass should owe them. [*Aside.*
Pro. That they are out by lease.*
Jul. Here comes the duke.

Enter DUKE.

Duke. How now, sir Proteus? how now, Thurio?
Which of you saw sir Eglamour of late?
Thu. Not I.
Pro. Nor I.
Duke. Saw you my daughter?
Pro. Neither.
Duke. Why, then, she 's fled unto that peasant Valentine;
And Eglamour is in her company.
'T is true; for friar Lawrence met them both,
As he in penance wander'd through the forest:
Him he knew well, and guess'd that it was she;
But, being mask'd, he was not sure of it:
Besides, she did intend confession
At Patrick's cell this even; and there she was not:
These likelihoods confirm her flight from hence.
Therefore, I pray you, stand not to discourse,
But mount you presently; and meet with me
Upon the rising of the mountain-foot
That leads towards Mantua, whither they are fled.
Dispatch, sweet gentlemen, and follow me. [*Exit.*
Thu. Why this it is to be a peevish girl,
That flies her fortune when it follows her:

---

* By his possessions, Thurio means his lands; but Proteus, who is bantering him, alludes to his mental endowments, which he says "are out by lease"—are not in his own keeping.

I 'll after; more to be reveng'd on Eglamour,
Then for the love of reckless Silvia. [*Exit*
Pro. And I will follow, more for Silvia's love,
Than hate of Eglamour that goes with her. [*Exit.*
Jul. And I will follow, more to cross that love,
Than hate for Silvia, that is gone for love. [*Exit*

SCENE III.—*Frontiers of Mantua. The Forest.*

Enter SILVIA, *and* Out-laws.

1 Out. Come, come;
Be patient, we must bring you to our captain.
Sil. A thousand more mischances than this one
Have learn'd me how to brook this patiently.
2 Out. Come, bring her away.
1 Out. Where is the gentleman that was with her?
3 Out. Being nimble-footed, he hath out-run us,
But Moyses and Valerius follow him.
Go thou with her to the west end of the wood,
There is our captain: we 'll follow him that 's fled.
The thicket is beset, he cannot 'scape.
1 Out. Come, I must bring you to our captain's cave;
Fear not; he bears an honourable mind,
And will not use a woman lawlessly.
Sil. O Valentine, this I endure for thee.
[*Exeunt.*

SCENE IV.—*Another part of the Forest.*

Enter VALENTINE.

Val. How use doth breed a habit in a man!
This shadowy desert, unfrequented woods,
I better brook than flourishing peopled towns:
Here can I sit alone, unseen of any,
And to the nightingale's complaining notes
Tune my distresses, and record* my woes.
O thou that dost inhabit in my breast,
Leave not the mansion so long tenantless;
Lest, growing ruinous, the building fall,
And leave no memory of what it was!
Repair me with thy presence, Silvia;
Thou gentle nymph, cherish thy forlorn swain
What halloing, and what stir, is this to-day?
These are my mates, that make their wills their law,
Have some unhappy passenger in chase:

---

* *Record*, to sing: thus:—
"Fair Philomel, night-music of the spring,
Sweetly *records* her tuneful harmony."
Drayton's *Eclogues,* 1563.
Douce says that the word was formed from the *recorder*, a sort of flute with which birds were taught to sing.

59

They love me well; yet I have much to do,
To keep them from uncivil outrages.
Withdraw thee, Valentine; who's this comes
    here?   [*Steps aside.*

Enter PROTEUS, SILVIA, *and* JULIA.

Pro. Madam, this service I have done for you,
(Though you respect not aught your servant
    doth,)
To hazard life, and rescue you from him
That would have forc'd your honour and your
    love.
Vouchsafe me, for my meed, but one fair look;
A smaller boon than this I cannot beg,
And less than this, I am sure, you cannot give.
  Val. How like a dream is this I see and hear!
Love, lend me patience to forbear a while.
                                [*Aside.*
  Sil. O miserable, unhappy that I am!
  Pro. Unhappy were you, madam, ere I came;
But, by my coming, I have made you happy.
  Sil. By thy approach thou mak'st me most
    unhappy.
  Jul. And me, when he approacheth to your
    presence.   [*Aside.*
  Sil. Had I been seized by a hungry lion,
I would have been a breakfast to the beast,
Rather than have false Proteus rescue me.
O, Heaven be judge, how I love Valentine,
Whose life's as tender to me as my soul;
And full as much, (for more there cannot be,)
I do detest false perjur'd Proteus:
Therefore be gone, solicit me no more.
  Pro. What dangerous action, stood it next to
    death,
Would I not undergo for one calm look?
O, 't is the curse in love, and still approv'd,*
When women cannot love, where they're belov'd.
  Sil. When Proteus cannot love where he's
    belov'd.
Read over Julia's heart, thy first best love,
For whose dear sake thou didst then read thy
    faith
Into a thousand oaths; and all those oaths
Descended into perjury, to love me.
Thou hast no faith left now, unless thou hadst
    two,
And that's far worse than none; better have
    none
Than plural faith, which is too much by one:
Thou counterfeit to thy true friend!
  Pro.   In love,
Who respects friend?

* *Approv'd*—proved, experienced.

  Sil.   All men but Proteus.
  Pro. Nay, if the gentle spirit of moving words
Can no way change you to a milder form,
I'll woo you like a soldier, at arms' end;
And love you 'gainst the nature of love, force you.
  Sil. O heaven!
  Pro.   I'll force thee yield to my desire.
  Val. Ruffian, let go that rude uncivil touch;
Thou friend of an ill fashion!
  Pro.   Valentine!
  Val. Thou common friend, that's without faith
    or love;
(For such is a friend now;) treacherous man!
Thou hast beguil'd my hopes; nought but mine
    eye
Could have persuaded me: Now I dare not say
I have one friend alive; thou wouldst disprove me.
Who should be trusted when one's own right
    hand
Is perjur'd to the bosom? Proteus,
I am sorry I must never trust thee more,
But count the world a stranger for thy sake.
The private wound is deepest: O time most ac-
    curs'd!
'Mongst all foes, that a friend should be the
    worst.
  Pro. My shame, and guilt, confounds me.—
Forgive me, Valentine: if hearty sorrow
Be a sufficient ransom for offence,
I render it here; I do as truly suffer
As e'er I did commit.
  Val.   Then I am paid;
And once again I do receive thee honest:—
Who by repentance is not satisfied
Is nor of heaven, nor earth; for these are pleas'd;
By penitence the Eternal's wrath's appeas'd:—
And, that my love may appear plain and free,
All that was mine in Silvia, I give thee."

ᵃ This passage has much perplexed the commentators. Pope thinks it very odd that Valentine should give up his mistress at once, without any reason alleged; and, consequently, the two lines spoken by Valentine, after his forgiveness of Proteus,—

"And, that my love may appear plain and free,
   All that was mine, in Silvia, I give thee."

are considered to be interpolated or transposed. Sir W. Blackstone thinks they should be spoken by Thurio. In our first edition we suggested, without altering the text, that the two lines might be spoken by Silvia. A correspondent, however, had the kindness to supply us with an explanation, which, we think, is very preferable, removing, as it appears to do much of the difficulty; although, after all, it might be intended that Valentine, in a fit of romance, should give up his mistress. Our correspondent writes as follows:—"It appears to me that the lines belong properly to Valentine, as given in all the editions, and not to Silvia, as suggested by you. The error of all the previous commentators, and, as I think, the one into which you have fallen, is in understanding the word 'all' to be used by Shakspere, in the above passage, in the sense of 'everything,' or as applying to 'love' in the previous line; whereas it refers to 'wrath' in the line which immediately precedes the above couplet. The

Jul. O me, unhappy! [*Faints.*
Pro. Look to the boy.
Val. Why, boy! why, wag! how now? what's the matter? Look up; speak.
Jul. O good sir, my master charged me to deliver a ring to madam Silvia; which, out of my neglect, was never done.
Pro. Where is that ring, boy?
Jul. Here 't is: this is it. [*Gives a ring.*
Pro. How! let me see: why this is the ring I gave to Julia.
Jul. O, cry your mercy, sir, I have mistook; This is the ring you sent to Silvia.
[*Shews another ring.*
Pro. But, how cam'st thou by this ring? at my depart, I gave this unto Julia.
Jul. And Julia herself did give it me; And Julia herself hath brought it hither.
Pro. How! Julia!
Jul. Behold her that gave aim to all thy oaths,ᵇ And entertain'd them deeply in her heart:
How oft hast thou with perjury cleft the root?ᵇ
O Proteus, let this habit make thee blush!
Be thou asham'd, that I have took upon me
Such an immodest raiment; if shame live
In a disguise of love:
It is the lesser blot, modesty finds,
Women to change their shapes, than men their minds.
Pro. Than men their minds! 't is true; O heaven! were man
But constant, he were perfect: that one error

way in which I would read these three lines is as follows:—
'By penitence the Eternal's wrath 't appeas'd;
And that my love (i.e. for Proteus) may appear plain and free,
All (i.e. the wrath) that was mine in (i.e. on account of) Silvia, I give thee (i.e. give thee up—forego).'
In other words, Valentine, having pardoned Proteus for his treachery to himself, in order to convince him how sincere was his reconciliation (justifying, however, to himself what he was about to do, by the consideration that even

' By penitence the Eternal's wrath's appeas'd '),
also forgives him the insult he had offered to Silvia. The use above suggested of the preposition "in" appears to me to be highly poetical. It distinguishes between Valentine's wrath on his own account for Proteus's treachery to himself, and that of Silvia for the indignity offered her by Proteus, which latter Valentine adopts and makes his own and so calls his wrath in Silvia. The use of the word 'was' also supports this reading. Valentine wishes to express that his wrath was past: had he been speaking of his 'love,' he would have said 'is.'"
Mr. G. White, in his edition of the Plays, calls it "a singular passage," but says that comment belongs rather to the philosopher than the critic, as it appears to be uncorrupted. He calls attention to similar overstrained generosity in Valentine, in Act II. Sc. IV. where he twice earnestly entreats Silvia to accept Proteus as her "lover," on equal terms with him as his "fellow-servant to her."
ᵃ See Note to Act III. Sc. I.
ᵇ "Cleft the root" is an allusion to clearing the pin, in archery, continuing the metaphor from "give aim." To cleave the pin was to break the nail which attached the mark to the butts.

Fills him with faults; makes him run through all sins:
Inconstancy falls off, ere it begins:
What is in Silvia's face, but I may spy
More fresh in Julia's with a constant eye?
Val. Come, come, a hand from either:
Let me be blest to make this happy close;
'T were pity two such friends should be long foes.
Pro. Bear witness, Heaven, I have my wish for ever.
Jul. And I mine.
Enter Outlaws, *with* DUKE *and* THURIO.
Out. A prize, a prize, a prize!
Val. Forbear, forbear, I say; it is my lord the duke.
Your grace is welcome to a man disgrac'd, Banished Valentine.
Duke.   Sir Valentine!
Thu. Yonder is Silvia; and Silvia's mine.
Val. Thurio, give back, or else embrace thy death;
Come not within the measure of my wrath:
Do not name Silvia thine; if once again,
Milan shall not behold thee.ᵃ Here she stands,
Take but possession of her with a touch;—
I dare thee but to breathe upon my love.
Thu. Sir Valentine, I care not for her, I;
I hold him but a fool, that will endanger
His body for a girl that loves him not:
I claim her not, and therefore she is thine.
Duke. The more degenerate and base art thou,
To make such means for her as thou hast done,
And leave her on such slight conditions.—
Now, by the honour of my ancestry,
I do applaud thy spirit, Valentine,
And think thee worthy of an empress' love.
Know then, I here forget all former griefs,
Cancel all grudge, repeal thee home again.—
Plead a new state in thy unrivall'd merit,
To which I thus subscribe,—Sir Valentine,
Thou art a gentleman, and well deriv'd;
Take thou thy Silvia, for thou hast deserv'd her.
Val. I thank your grace; the gift hath made me happy.
I now beseech you, for your daughter's sake,
To grant one boon that I shall ask of you.
Duke. I grant it for thine own, whate'er it be.
Val. These banish'd men, that I have kept withal,
Are men endued with worthy qualities;
Forgive them what they have committed here,

ᵃ The reading of the original edition is "Verona shal' not hold thee." Mr. Collier gives
"Milano shall not hold thee;"
of which Mr. Dyce approves. See remark of the Cambridge editors, Act. II. Sc. V.

And let them be recalled from their exile:
They are reformed, civil, full of good,
And fit for great employment, worthy lord.
    Duke. Thou hast prevail'd; I pardon them,
        and thee;
Dispose of them, as thou know'st their deserts.
Come, let us go; we will include all jars
With triumphs, mirth, and rare solemnity.[1]
    Val. And, as we walk along, I dare be bold
With our discourse to make you[2] grace to
        smile:
What think you of this page, my lord?

    Duke. I think the boy hath grace in him; he
        blushes.
    Val. I warrant you, my lord; more grace than
        boy.
    Duke. What mean you by that saying?
    Val. Please you, I'll tell you as we pass along
That you will wonder what hath fortuned.—
Come Proteus; 't is your penance, but to hear
The story of your loves discovered:
That done, our day of marriage shall be yours;
One feast, one house, one mutual happiness.
                                            [*Exeunt.*

ILLUSTRATIONS OF ACT V.

¹ SCENE IV.—"*Triumphs, mirth, and rare solemnity.*"

MALONE, in a note on this passage, says, "*Triumphs*, in this and many other passages of Shakspere, signify masques and revels." This assertion appears to us to have been hastily made. We have referred to all the passages of Shakspere in which the plural noun "triumphs" is used; and it appears to us to have a signification perfectly distinct from that of masques and revels. And first of Julius Cæsar, Antony says:—

"O, mighty Cæsar! Dost thou lie so low?
Are all thy conquests, glories, triumphs, spoils,
Shrunk to this little measure?"

In Titus Andronicus, Tamora, addressing her conqueror, exclaims,

"We are brought to Rome
To beautify thy triumphs."

In these two quotations we have the original meaning of triumphs—namely, the solemn processions of a conqueror with his captives and spoils of victory. The triumphs of modern times were gorgeous shows, in imitation of those pomps of antiquity. When Columbus, returning from his first voyage, presented to the sovereigns of Castile and Arragon the productions of the countries which he had discovered, the solemn procession on that memorable occasion was a real *Triumph*. But when Edward IV., in Shakspere (Henry VI., Part iii.), exclaims, after his final conquest,

"And now what rests, but that we spend the time
With stately triumphs, mirthful comic shows,
Such as befit the pleasures of the court,"

he refers to those ceremonials which the genius of chivalry had adopted from the mightier pomps of antiquity, imitating something of their splendour, but laying aside their stern demonstrations of outward exultation over their vanquished foes. There were no human captives in massive chains —no lions and elephants led along to the amphitheatre, for the gratification of a turbulent populace. Edward exclaims of his prisoner Margaret—

"Away with her, and waft her hence to France."

The dread of Cleopatra was that of exposure in the Triumph:—

"Shall they hoist me up,
And shew me to the shouting varletry
Of censuring Rome?"

Here, then, was the difference of the Roman and the feudal manners. The triumphs of the middle ages were shows of peace, decorated with the pomp of arms: but altogether mere scenic representations, deriving their name from the more solemn triumphs of antiquity. But they were not masques, as Malone has stated. The Duke of York, in Richard II., asks,

"What news from Oxford? hold these justs and triumphs?"

and for these "justs and triumphs" Aumerle has prepared his "gay apparel." There is one more passage which appears to us conclusive as to the use of the word Triumphs. The passage is in Pericles: Simonides asks,

"Are the knights ready to begin the triumph?"

And when answered that they are, he says—

"Return then, we are ready; and our daughter,
In honour of whose birth these triumphs are,
Sits here, like beauty's child."

The triumph, then, meant the "joustes of peace" which we have noticed in a previous illustration; and the great tournament there mentioned, when Elizabeth sat in her "fortress of perfect beauty," was expressly called a triumph. In the triumph was, of course, included the processions and other "stately" shows that accompanied the sports of the tilt-yard.

In this view of the word triumph we have given an engraved illustration at the foot of the last Act, which represents a procession at Milan of the nobles, and knights, and prelates of Italy, who attended "the emperor in his royal court." The various figures are grouped from particular scenes in the very curious book of Hogheuburg (which we have mentioned in the Introductory Notice), representing the triumphs upon the occasion of the visit of Charles V., to Bologna.

The Duke of Milan, in this play, desires to "include all jars," not only with "triumphs," but with "mirth and rare solemnity." The "mirth" and the "solemnity" would include the "pageant" —the favourite show of the days of Elizabeth. The "masque" (in its highest signification) was a more refined and elaborate device than the pageant; and, therefore, we shall confine the remainder of this illustration to some few general observations on the subject of "pageants."

We may infer, from the expression of Julia in the fourth Act,

"At Pentecost,
When all our pageants of delight were play'd,"

that the pageant was a religious ceremonial, connected with the festivals of the church. And so it originally was. The "pageants" performed at Coventry were, for the most part, "dramatic mysteries;" and the city, according to Dugdale,

ILLUSTRATIONS OF ACT V.

was famous, before the suppression of the monasteries, for the pageants that were played there on Corpus Christi day. "These pageants," says the fine old topographer, "were acted with mighty state and reverence by the fryers of this house, and contained the story of the New Testament, which was composed into old English rhyme. The theatres for the several scenes were very large and high, and being placed upon wheels, were drawn to all the eminent places of the city, for the better advantage of the spectators." It appears, from Mr. Sharp's Dissertation on the Coventry Pageants, that the trading companies were accustomed to perform these plays; and it will be remembered that when Elizabeth was entertained by Leicester at Kenilworth, the "old Coventry play of Hock Tuesday" formed a principal feature of the amusements. The play of Hock Tuesday commemorates the great victory over the Danes, A.D. 1002, and it was exhibited before the queen by Captain Cox and many others from Coventry. The Whitsun plays at Chester, called the Chester Pageants, or Chester Mysteries, were also performed by the trading companies of that ancient city. Archdeacon Rogers, who died in 1569, has left an account of the Whitsun plays, which he saw in Chester, which shews that the pageant-vehicles there, like those of Coventry, were scaffolds upon wheels. Mr. Collier, in his valuable History of the Stage, mentions a fact, given by Hall the historian, that in 1511, at the revels at Whitehall, Henry VIII. and his lords "entered the hall in a pageant on wheels."

It is clear from the passage in which Julia describes her own part in the "pageants of delight,"—

"Ariadne passioning
For Theseus' perjury and unjust flight,"—

that the pageant had begun to assume something of the classical character of the masque. But it had certainly not become the gorgeous entertainment which Jonson has so glowingly described, as "of power to surprise with delight, and steal away the spectators from themselves." The pageant in which Julia acted at Pentecost was probably such as Shakspere had seen in the streets of Coventry, or in some stately baronial hall of his rich county. The "pageant on wheels" in which Henry and his lords entered his hall of revels was evidently the same sort of machine as that described by Dugdale, and which is here copied, with a slight adaptation, from a representation in Sharp's Dissertation.

SUPPLEMENTARY NOTICE.

"ASSUREDLY that criticism of Shakspere will alone be genial which is reverential. The Englishman who, without reverence, a proud and affectionate reverence, can utter the name of William Shakspere, stands disqualified for the office of critic. He wants one at least of the very senses, the language of which he is to employ; and will discourse at best but as a blind man, while the whole harmonious creation of light and shade, with all its subtle interchange of deepening and dissolving colours, rises in silence to the silent *fiat* of the uprising Apollo." * Thus a "reverential" criticism will not only be most genial,—it will be most intelligible. Heminge and Condell, in their Preface to the first collected edition of Shakspere, truly say,—" Read him again and again; and if then you do not like him, surely you are in some manifest danger not to understand him." To love Shakspere best is best to understand him. And yet, from the days of Rymer, who described Othello as a "bloody farce, without salt or savour," we have had a "wilderness" of *critics*, each one endeavouring, "merely by his *ipse dixit*, to treat as contemptible what he has not intellect enough to comprehend, or soul to feel, without assigning any reason, or referring his opinion to any demonstrative principle."† In offering an analysis of the various critical opinions upon each play, we must, of necessity, present our readers with many remarks which are not "reverential." But we trust, also, to be able to shew, in most cases by authorities which *do* refer to some "demonstrative principle," that those who have uttered the name of Shakspere "without reverence," as too many of the commentators have done, are "but stammering interpreters of the general and almost idolatrous admiration of his countrymen."‡

Without any reference to the period of the poet's life in which the Two Gentlemen of Verona was written, Theobald tells us, "This is one of Shakspere's worst plays." Hanmer thinks Shakspere "only enlivened it with some speeches and lines thrown in here and there." Upton determines "that if any proof can be drawn from manner and style, this play must be sent packing, and seek for its parent elsewhere." Johnson, though singularly favourable in his opinion of this play, says of it. "there is a strange mixture of knowledge and ignorance, of care and negligence." Mrs. Lenox (who, in the best slip-slop manner, does not hesitate to pass judgment upon many of the greatest works of Shakspere), says, "'t is generally allowed that the plot, conduct, manners, and incidents of this play are extremely deficient." On the other hand, Pope gives the style of this comedy the high praise of being "natural and unaffected;" although he complains that the familiar parts are "composed of the lowest and most trifling conceits, to be accounted for only by the gross taste of the age he lived in." Johnson says, "when I read this play, I cannot but think that I find, both in the serious and ludicrous scenes, the language and sentiments of Shakspere. It is not, indeed, one of his most powerful effusions; it has neither many diversities

---

* Coleridge, Literary Remains, vol. ii. p. 63.   † Id. p. 11.
‡ Schlegel's Lectures on Dramatic Literature, Black's Translation, vol. ii. p. 164.

SUPPLEMENTARY NOTICE

of character, nor striking delineations of life. But it abounds in γνῶμαι (sententious observations) beyond most of his plays; and few have more lines or passages which, singly considered, are eminently beautiful." Coleridge, the best of critics on Shakspere, has no remark on this play beyond calling it "a sketch." Hazlitt, in a more elaborate criticism, follows out the same idea: "This is little more than the first outlines of a comedy loosely sketched in. It is the story of a novel dramatised with very little labour or pretension; yet there are passages of high poetical spirit, and of inimitable quaintness of humour, which are undoubtedly Shakspere's, and there is throughout the conduct of the fable a careless grace and felicity which marks it for his." We scarcely think that Coleridge and Hazlitt are correct in considering this play "a sketch," if it be taken as a whole In the fifth Act, unquestionably, the outlines "are loosely sketched in." The unusual shortness of that Act would indicate that it is, in some degree, hurried and unfinished. If the text be correct which makes Valentine offer to give up Silvia to Proteus, there cannot be a doubt that the poet intended to have worked out this idea, and to have exhibited a struggle of self-denial, and a sacrifice to friendship, which very young persons are inclined to consider possible. Friendship has its romance as well as love. In the other parts of the comedy there is certainly extremely little that can be called sketchy. They appear to us to be very carefully finished. There may be a deficiency of power, but not of elaboration. A French writer who has analysed all Shakspere's plays (M. Paul Duport), considers that this play possesses a powerful charm, which he attributes to the brilliant and poetical colouring of its style. He thinks, and justly, that a number of graceful comparisons, and of vivid and picturesque images, here take the place of the bold and natural conceptions (the "vital and organic" style, as Coleridge expresses it) which are the general characteristic of his genius. In these elegant generalizations, M. Duport properly recognises the vagueness and indecision of the youthful poet.* The remarks of A. W. Schlegel on this comedy are, as usual, acute and philosophical:—"The Two Gentlemen of Verona paints the irresolution of love, and its infidelity towards friendship, in a pleasant, but, in some degree, superficial manner; we might almost say with the levity of mind which a passion suddenly entertained, and as suddenly given up, pre-supposes. The faithless lover is at last forgiven without much difficulty by his first mistress, on account of his ambiguous repentance. For the more serious part, the premeditated flight of the daughter of a prince, the captivity of her father along with herself by a band of robbers, of which one of the two gentlemen, the faithful and banished friend, has been compulsively elected captain; for all this a peaceful solution is soon found. It is as if the course of the world was obliged to accommodate itself to a transient youthful caprice, called love." † An English writer, who has well studied Shakspere, and has published a volume of very praiseworthy research,‡ distinguished for correct taste and good feeling (although some of its theories may be reasonably doubted), considers this comedy Shakspere's first dramatic production, and imagines that it might have been written at Stratford, and have formed his chief recommendation to the Blackfriars company. He adds,—"This play appears to me enriched with all the freshness of youth; with strong indications of his future matured poetical power and dramatic effect. It is the day-spring of genius, full of promise, beauty, and quietude, before the sun has arisen to its splendour. I can likewise discern in it his peculiar gradual development of character, his minute touches, each tending to complete a portrait; and if these are not executed by the master hand, as shewn in his later plays, they are by the same apprentice-hand, each touch of strength sufficient to harmonize with the whole." Johnson says of this play, "I am inclined to believe that it was not very successful." It is difficult to judge of the accuracy of this belief. The "quietude," the "minute touches," may not have been exactly suited to an audience who had as yet been unaccustomed to the delicate lights and shadows of the Elizabethan drama. Shakspere, in some degree, stood in the same relation to his predecessors, as Raphael did to the earlier painters. The gentle gradations, the accurate distances, the harmony and repose, had to be superadded to the hard outlines, the strong colouring, and the disproportionate parts of the elder artists, in the one case as in the other. But our dramatist, who unquestionably always looked to what the stage demanded from him, however he may have looked beyond the mere wants of his present audience, put enough of attractive matter into the Two Gentlemen

---

* Essais Littéraires sur Shakspere, tome ii. p. 337. Paris, 1828.
† Lectures on Dramatic Art and Literature, Black's translation, vol. ii. p. 156.
‡ Shakspere's Autobiographical Poems, &c. By Charles Armitage Brown. 1838.

TWO GENTLEMEN OF VERONA.

of Verona, to command its popularity. No "clown" that had appeared on the stage before his time could at all approach to Launce in real humour. But the clowns that the celebrated Tarleton represented had mere words of buffoonery put in their mouths; and it is not to be wondered at that Shakspere retained some of their ribaldry. It would be some time before he would be strong enough to assert the rights of his own genius, as he unquestionably did in his later plays. He must, as a young writer, have been sometimes forced into a sacrifice to the popular requirements.

Mr. Boaden, as it is stated by Malone, is of opinion that the Two Gentlemen of Verona contains the germ of other plays which Shakspere afterwards wrote.* The expression, "germ of other plays," is somewhat undefined. There are in this play the germ of several incidents and situations which occur in the poet's maturer works—the germ of some other of his most admired characters—the germ of one or two of his most beautiful descriptions. When Julia is deputed by Proteus to bear a letter to Silvia, urging the love which he ought to have kept sacred for herself, we are reminded of Viola, in Twelfth Night, being sent to plead the duke's passion for Olivia,—although the other circumstances are widely different; when we see Julia wearing her boy's disguise, with a modest archness and spirit, our thoughts involuntary turn not only to Viola, but to Rosalind, and to Imogen, three of the most exquisite of Shakspere's exquisite creations of female characters;—when Valentine, in the forest of Mantua, exclaims,

"How use doth breed a habit in a man!
This shadowy desert, unfrequented woods,
I better brook than flourishing peopled towns,"

we hear the first faint notes of the same delicious train of thought, though greatly modified by the different circumstances of the speaker, that we find in the banished Duke of the Forest of Ardennes:—

"Now my co-mates, and brothers in exile,
Hath not old custom made this life more sweet
Than that of painted pomp?"

When Valentine exclaims,

"And why not death, rather than living torment?"

we recollect the grand passage in Macbeth, where the same thought is exalted, and rendered terrible, by the peculiar circumstances of the speaker's guilt;—

"Better be with the dead,
Whom we, to gain our place, have sent to peace,
Than on the torture of the mind to lie
In restless ecstasy."

There are, generally speaking, resemblances throughout the works of Shakspere, which none but his genius could have preserved from being imitations. But, taking the particular instance before us, when, with matured powers, he came to deal with somewhat similar incidents and characters in other plays, and to repeat the leading idea of a particular sentiment, we can, without difficulty, perceive how vast a difference had been produced by a few years of reflection and experience; —how he had made to himself an entirely new school of art, whose practice was as superior to his own conceptions as embodied in his first works, as it was beyond the mastery of his contemporaries, or of any who have succeeded him. It was for this reason that Pope called the style of the Two Gentlemen of Verona "simple and unaffected." It was opposed to Shakspere's later style, which is teeming with allusion upon allusion, dropped out of the exceeding riches of his glorious imagination. With the exception of the few obsolete words, and the unfamiliar application of words still in use, this comedy has, to our minds, a very modern air. The thoughts are natural and obvious, the images familiar and general. The most celebrated passages have a character of grace rather than of beauty; the elegance of a youthful poet aiming to be correct, instead of the splendour of the perfect artist, subjecting every crude and apparently unmanageable thought to the wonderful alchemy of his all-penetrating genius. Look, in this comedy, at the images, for example, which are derived from external nature, and compare them with the same class of images in the later plays. We might select several illustrations, but one will suffice:—

"As the most favour'd bud
Is eaten by the canker ere it blow;

* Malone's Shakspere, by Boswell, vol. ii. p. 32.

SUPPLEMENTARY NOTICE.

> "Even so by love the young and tender wit
> Is turn'd to folly; blasting in the bud,
> Losing his verdure even in the prime."

Here the image is feeble, because it is generalized. But compare it with the same image in Romeo and Juliet:—

> "But he, his own affection's counsellor,
> Is to himself—I will not say how true,
> But to himself so secret and so close,
> So far from sounding and discovering,
> As is the bud bit with an envious worm,
> Ere he can spread his sweet leaves to the air,
> Or dedicate his beauty to the sun."

Johnson, as we have already seen, considered this comedy to be wanting in "diversity of character." The action, it must be observed, is mainly sustained by Proteus and Valentine, and by Julia and Silvia; and the conduct of the plot is relieved by the familiar scenes in which Speed and Launce appear. The other actors are very subordinate, and we scarcely demand any great diversity of character amongst them; but it seems to us, with regard to Proteus and Valentine, Julia and Silvia, Speed and Launce, that the characters are exhibited, as it were, in pairs, upon a principle of very defined though delicate contrast. We will endeavour to point out these somewhat nice distinctions.

Coleridge says, in 'The Friend,' "It is Shakspere's peculiar excellence, that throughout the whole of his splendid picture gallery (the reader will excuse the acknowledged inadequacy of this metaphor), we find individuality everywhere,—mere portrait nowhere. In all his various characters we still feel ourselves communing with the same nature, which is everywhere present as the vegetable sap in the branches, sprays, leaves, buds, blossoms, and fruits, their shapes, tastes, and odours. Speaking of the effect, that is, his works themselves, we may define the excellence of their method as consisting in that just proportion, that union and interpenetration of the universal and the particular, which must ever pervade all works of decided genius and true science." Nothing can be more just and more happy than this definition of the distinctive quality of Shakspere's works,—a quality which puts them so immeasurably above all other works,—"the union and interpenetration of the universal and the particular." It constitutes the peculiar charm of his matured style,—it furnishes the key to the surpassing excellence of his representations, whether of facts which are cognizable by the understanding or by the senses, in which a single word individualizes the "particular" object described or alluded to, and, without separating it from the "universal," to which it belongs, gives it all the value of a vivid colour in a picture, perfectly distinct, but also completely harmonious. The skill which he attained in this wonderful mastery over the whole world of materials for poetical construction, was the result of continual experiment. In his characters, especially, we see the gradual growth of this extraordinary power, as clearly as we perceive the differences between his early and his matured forms of expression. But it is evident to us, that, in his very earliest delineations of character, he had conceived the principle which was to be developed in "his splendid picture gallery." In the comedy before us, Valentine and Proteus are the "two gentlemen,"—Julia and Silvia the two ladies "beloved,"—Speed and Launce the two "clownish" servants. And yet how different is the one from the other of the same class. The German critic, Gervinus, has honoured us by treating "the two gentlemen," the "two ladies beloved," and the two "clownish servants," on the same principle of contrast. Proteus, who is first represented to us as a lover, is evidently a very cold and calculating one. He is "a votary to fond desire;" but he *complains* of his mistress that she has metamorphosed him:—

> "Made me neglect my studies,—lose my time."

He ventures, however, to write to Julia; and when he has her answer, "her oath for love, her honour's pawn," he immediately takes the most prudent view of their position:—

> "O that our fathers would applaud our loves."

But he has not decision enough to demand this approbation:—

> "I fear'd to shew my father Julia's letter,
> Lest he should take exceptions to my love."

He parts with his mistress in a very formal and well-behaved style;—they exchange rings, but Julia has first offered "this remembrance" for her sake;—he makes a common-place vow of constancy, whilst Julia rushes away in tears;—he quits Verona for Milan, and has a new love at first sight the instant he sees Silvia. The mode in which he sets about betraying his friend, and wooing his new mistress, is eminently characteristic of the calculating selfishness of his nature:—

"If I can check my erring love, I will;
If not, to compass her I'll use my skill."

He is of that very numerous class of men who would always be virtuous, if virtue would accomplish their object as well as vice;—who prefer truth to lying, when lying is unnecessary;—and who have a law of justice in their own minds, which if they can observe they "will;" but "if not,"—if they find themselves poor erring mortals, which they infallibly do,—they think

"Their stars are more in fault than they."

This Proteus is a very contemptible fellow, who finally exhibits himself as a ruffian and a coward, and is punished by the heaviest infliction that the generous Valentine could bestow—his forgiveness. Generous, indeed, and most confiding, is our Valentine—a perfect contrast to Proteus. In the first scene he laughs at the passion of Proteus, as if he knew that it was alien to his nature; but when he has become enamoured himself, with what enthusiasm he proclaims his devotion:—

"Why, man, she is mine own!
And I as rich in having such a jewel
As twenty seas, if all their sand were pearl."

In this passionate admiration we have the germ of Romeo, and so also in the scene where Valentine is banished:—

"And why not death, rather than living torment?"

But here is only a sketch of the strength of a deep and all-absorbing passion. The whole speech of Valentine upon his banishment is forcible and elegant; but compare him with Romeo in the same condition:—

"Heaven is here
Where Juliet lives; and every cat, and dog,
And little mouse, every unworthy thing,
Live here in heaven, and may look on her,
But Romeo may not."

We are not wandering from our purpose of contrasting Proteus and Valentine, by shewing that the character of Valentine is compounded of some of the elements that we find in Romeo; for the strong impulses of both these lovers are as much opposed as it is possible to the subtle devices of Proteus. The confiding Valentine goes to his banishment with the cold comfort that Proteus gives him:—

"Hope is a lover's staff; walk hence with that."

He is compelled to join the outlaws, but he makes conditions with them that exhibit the goodness of his nature; and we hear no more of him till the catastrophe, when his traitorous friend is forgiven with the same confiding generosity that has governed all his intercourse with him. We have little doubt of the corruption, or, at any rate, of the unfinished nature, of the passage in which he is made to give up Silvia to his false friend,—for that would be entirely inconsistent with the ardent character of his love, and an act of injustice towards Julia, which he could not commit. But it is perfectly natural and probable that he should receive Proteus again into his confidence, upon his declaration of "hearty sorrow," and that he should do so upon principle:—

"Who by repentance is not satisfied,
Is nor of heaven, nor earth."

It is, to our minds, quite delightful to find in this, which we consider amongst the earliest of Shakspere's plays, that exhibition of the real Christian spirit of charity which, more or less, pervades all his writings; but which, more than any other quality, has made some persons, who deem their own morality as of a higher and purer order, cry out against them, as giving encouragement to evil doers. We shall have occasion hereafter to speak of the noble lessons which Shakspere teaches *dramatically* (and not according to the childish devices of those who would make the dramatist write a "moral" at the end of five acts, upon the approved plan of a Fable in a spelling-book), and we therefore pass over, for the present, those profound critics who say "he has no moral purpose in view."* But there are some who are not quite so pedantically wise as to affirm "he paid no attention to that retributive justice which, when human affairs are rightly understood, pervades them

* Lardner's Cyclopædia, Literary and Scientific Men, vol. ii. p. 128.

SUPPLEMENTARY NOTICE

all;"* but who yet think that Proteus ought to have been at least banished, or sent to the galleys for a few years with the outlaws;—that Angelo, in Measure for Measure, should have been hanged;—that Leontes, in the Winter's Tale, was not sufficiently punished for his cruel jealousy by sixteen years of sorrow and repentance;—that Iachimo, in Cymbeline, is not treated with poetical justice when Posthumus says,—

> "Kneel not to me:
> The power that I have on you is to spare you;"—

and that Prospero is a very weak magician not to apply his power to a better purpose than only to give his wicked brother and his followers a little passing punishment;—weak indeed, when he has them in his hands, to exclaim,—

> "Though with their high wrongs I am struck to the quick,
> Yet with my nobler reason 'gainst my fury
> Do I take part: the rarer action is
> In virtue than in vengeance: they being penitent,
> The sole drift of my purpose doth extend
> Not a frown further: go release them, Ariel."

Not so thought Shakspere. He, that never represented crime as virtue, had the largest pity for the criminal. "He has never varnished over wild and blood-thirsty passions with a pleasing exterior—never clothed crime and want of principle with a false shew of greatness of soul;"† but, on the other hand, he has never made the criminal a monster, and led us to flatter ourselves that he is not a man. It is as a man, subject to the same infirmities as all are who are born of woman, that he represents Proteus, and Iachimo, and other of the lesser criminals, as receiving pardon upon repentance. It is not so much that they are deserving of pardon, but that it would be inconsistent with the characters of the pardoners that they should exercise their power with severity. Shakspere lived in an age when the vindictive passions were too frequently let loose by men of all sects and opinions,—and much too frequently in the name of that religion which came to teach peace and good will. Is it to be objected to him, then, that wherever he could he asserted the supremacy of charity and mercy;—that he taught men the "quality" of that blessed principle which

> "Droppeth as the gentle dew from heaven;"—

that he proclaimed—no doubt to the annoyance of all self-worshippers—that "the web of our life is of a mingled yarn, good and ill together;"—and that he asked of those who would be hard upon the wretched, "Use every man after his desert, and who shall 'scape whipping?" We may be permitted to believe that this large toleration had its influence in an age of racks and gibbets; and we know not how much of this charitable spirit may have come to the aid of the more authoritative and holier teaching of the same principle,—forgotten even by the teachers, but gradually finding its way into the heart of the multitude,—till human punishments at length were compelled to be subservient to other influences than those of the angry passions, and the laws could only dare to ask for justice, but not for vengeance.

The generous, confiding, courageous, and forgiving spirit of Valentine, are well appreciated by the Duke—"Thou art a gentleman." In this praise is included all the virtues which Shakspere desired to represent in the character of Valentine;—the absence of which virtues he has also indicated in the selfish Proteus. The Duke adds, "and well derived." "Thou art a gentleman" in "thy spirit"—a gentleman in "thy unrivalled merit;" and thou hast the honours of ancestry—the further advantage of honourable progenitors. This line, in one of Shakspere's earliest plays, is a key to some of his personal feelings. He was himself a true gentleman, though the child of humble parents. His exquisite delineations of the female character establish the surpassing refinement and purity of his mind in relation to women;—and thus, if there were no other evidence of the son of the wool-stapler of Stratford being a "gentleman," this one prime feature of the character would be his most pre-eminently. Well then might he, looking to himself, assert the principle that rank and ancestry are additions to the character of the gentleman, but not indispensable component parts. "Thou art a gentleman, and well derived."

We have dwelt so long upon the contrasts in the characters of the "two gentlemen," Proteus and Valentine, that we may appear to have forgotten our purpose of also tracing the distinctive peculiarities of the two ladies "beloved." Julia, in the sweetest feminine tenderness, is entirely

---

* Lardner's Cyclopædia. Literary and Scientific Men, vol. iii. p. 122.
† A. W. Schlegel, Black, vol. ii. p. 137.

TWO GENTLEMEN OF VERONA.

worthy of the poet of Juliet and Imogen. Amidst her deep and sustaining love she has all the playfulness that belongs to the true woman. When she receives the letter of Proteus, the struggle between her affected indifference, and her real disposition to cherish a deep affection, is exceedingly pretty. Then comes, and very quickly, the development of the change which real love works,—the plighting her troth with Proteus,—the sorrow for his absence,—the flight to him,—the grief for his perjury,—the forgiveness. How full of heart and gentleness is all her conduct, after she has discovered the inconstancy of Proteus! How beautiful an absence is there of all upbraiding either of her faithless lover, or of his new mistress. Of the one she says,

"Because I love him, I must pity him;"

the other she describes, without a touch of envy, as

"A virtuous gentlewoman, mild, and beautiful."

Silvia is a character of much less intensity of feeling. She plays with her accepted lover as with a toy given to her for her amusement; she delights in a contest of words between him and his rival Thurio; she avows she is betrothed to Valentine, when she reproves Proteus for his perfidy, but she allows Proteus to send for her picture, which is, at least, not the act of one who strongly felt and resented his treachery to his friend. When she resolves to escape from her prison, she does not go forth to danger and difficulty with the spirit of Julia,—"a true devoted pilgrim,"—but she places herself under the protection of Eglamour—("a very perfect gentle knight," as Chaucer would have called him),

"For the ways are dangerous to pass."

She goes to her banished lover, but she flies from her father—

"To keep me from a most unholy match."

When she encounters Proteus in the forest, she, indeed, spiritedly avows her love for Valentine, and her hatred for himself; nor is there, in any of the slight distinctions which we have pointed out, any real inferiority in her character to that of Julia. She is only more under the influence of circumstances. Julia, by her decision, subdues the circumstances of her situation to her own will.

Turn we now to Speed and Launce, the two "clownish" servants of Valentine and Proteus.

In a note introducing the first scene between Speed and Proteus, Pope says, "This whole scene, like many others in these plays (some of which I believe, were written by Shakspere, and others interpolated by the players), is composed of the lowest and most trifling conceits, to be accounted for only by the gross ,taste of the age he lived in; *populo ut placerent*. I wish I had authority to leave them out." There are passages in Shakspere which an editor would desire to leave out, if he consulted only the standard of taste in his own age; just as there are passages in Pope which we now consider filthy and corrupting, which the wits and fine ladies of the Court of Anne only regarded as playful and piquant. The scenes, however, in which Speed and Launce are prominent, with the exception of a few obscure allusions, which will not be discovered unless a commentator points them out, and of one piece of plain speaking in Launce, which is refinement itself when compared with the classical works of the Dean of St. Patrick's,—these scenes offer a remarkable instance of the reform which Shakspere was enabled to effect in the conduct of the English stage, and which, without doubt, banished a great deal of what had been offensive to good manners, as well as good taste. "The clown" or "fool" of the earlier English drama was introduced into every piece. He came on between the acts, and sometimes interrupted even the scenes by his buffoonery. Occasionally the author set down a few words for him to speak; but out of these he had to spin a monologue of doggerel verses created by his "extemporal wit." The "Jeasts" of Richard Tarleton, the most celebrated of these clowns, were published in 1611; and fortunate it must have been for the morals of our ancestors that Shakspere constructed dialogue for his "Clowns," and insisted on their adhering to it: "Let those that play your clowns speak no more than is set down for them." The "Clown" was the successor of the "Vice" of the old Moralities; and he was the representative of the domestic "Jester" that flourished before and during the age of Shakspere. We shall have frequent occasion to return to this subject. The "clownish" servant was something intermediate between the privileged "fool" of the old drama, and the pert lacquey of the later comedy. But he originally stood in the place of the genuine "Clown;" and his "conceits" are to be regarded partly as a reflection of the manners of the most refined, whose wit, in a great degree, consisted in a play upon words, and partly as a law of the established drama, which even Shakspere could not dispense with, if he had desired so to do. But his instinctive knowledge of the value of

SUPPLEMENTARY NOTICE.

his dramatic materials led him to retain the "Clowns" amongst other inheritances of the old stage; and who that has seen the use he has made of the "*allowed* fool" in Twelfth Night, and As You Like It, and All's Well that Ends Well, and especially in Lear,—of the country clown in Love's Labour's Lost and The Merchant of Venice,—and of the "clownish" or witty servant in the Two Gentlemen of Verona, will regret that he did not cast away what Pope has called "low" and "trifling," determining to retain a machinery equally adapted to the relief of the tragic and the heightening of the comic, and entirely in keeping with what we now call the romantic drama,—an edifice of which Shakspere found the scaffolding raised and the stone quarried, but which it was reserved for him alone to build up upon a plan in which the most apparently incongruous parts were subjected to the laws of fitness and proportion, and wherein even the grotesque (like the grinning heads in our fine Gothic cathedrals) was in harmony with the beautiful and the sublime.

Speed and Launce are both punsters; but Speed is by far the more inveterate one. He begins with a pun—my master "is shipp'd already, and I have play'd the sheep (ship) in losing him." The same play upon words which the ship originates runs through the scene; and we are by no means sure that if Shakspere made Verona a sea-port in ignorance (which we very much doubt),—if, like his own Hotspur, he had "forgot the map,"—whether he would, at any time, have converted Valentine into a land traveller, and have lost his pun upon a better knowledge. Of these apparent violations of propriety we have already spoken in the Introductory Notice. In the scene before us, Speed establishes his character for a "quick wit;" Launce, on the contrary, very soon earns the reputation of "a mad cap" and "an ass." And yet Launce can pun as perseveringly as Speed. But he can do something more. He can throw in the most natural touches of humour amongst his quibbles; and, indeed, he altogether forgets his quibbles when he is indulging his own peculiar vein. That vein is unquestionably drollery,—as Hazlitt has well described it,—the richest farcical drollery. His descriptions of his leave-taking, while "the dog all this while sheds not a tear," and of the dog's misbehaviour when he thrust "himself into the company of three or four gentleman-like dogs," are perfectly irresistible. We must leave thee, Launce; but we leave thee with less regret, for thou hast worthy successors. Thou wert among the first fruits, we think, of the creations of the greatest comic genius that the world has seen, and thou wilt endure for ever, with Bottom, and Malvolio, and Parolles, and Dogberry. Thou wert conceived, perhaps, under that humble roof at Stratford, to gaze upon which all nations have since sent forth their pilgrims! Or, perhaps, when the young poet was, for the first time, left alone in the solitude of London, he looked back upon that shelter of his boyhood, and shadowed out his own parting in thine, Launce!

INTRODUCTORY NOTICE.

STATE OF THE TEXT, AND CHRONOLOGY, OF LOVE'S LABOUR'S LOST.*

This play was one of the fifteen published in Shakspere's lifetime. The first edition appeared in 1598, under the following title: "A pleasant conceited comedie, called Loues Labors Lost. As it was presented before her Highnes this last Christmas. Newly corrected and augmented by W. Shakespere." No subsequent edition appeared in a separate form till 1631. In the first collected edition of Shakspere's plays, the folio of 1623, the text can scarcely be said to differ, except by accident, from the original quarto. The editors of the first folio without doubt took the quarto as their copy. The manifold errors of the press in the Latin words of the first edition have not been corrected in the second. We have still *Dictinima* for *Dictynna*, and *bome* for *bone*. Steevens, in a note to Henry V., observes, "It is very certain that authors, in the time of Shakspere did not correct the press for themselves. I hardly ever saw, in one of the old plays, a sentence of either Latin, Italian, or French without the most ridiculous blunders." This neglect on the part of dramatic authors may be accounted for by the fact that the press was not their medium of publication; but it is remarkable that such errors should have been perpetuated through four of the collected editions of Shakspere's works, and not have been corrected till the time of Rowe and Theobald.

We have seen, from the title of the first edition of Love's Labour's Lost, that when it was presented before Queen Elizabeth, at the Christmas of 1597, it had been "newly corrected and augmented." As no edition of the comedy, before it was corrected and augmented, is known to exist (though, as in the case of the unique Hamlet of 1603, one may some day be discovered), we have no proof that the few allusions to temporary circumstances, which are supposed in some degree to fix the date of the play, may not apply to the augmented copy only. Thus, when Moth refers to "the dancing horse" who was to teach Armado how to reckon what "deuce-ace amounts to," the fact that Banks's horse (See Illustrations to Act I. Scene II.) first appeared in London in 1589 does not prove that the original play might not have been written before 1589. This date gives it an earlier appearance than Malone would assign to it, who first settled it as 1591, and afterwards as 1594. A supposed allusion to "The Metamorphosis of Ajax," by Sir John Harrington, printed in 1596, is equally unimportant with reference to the original composition of the play. The "finished representation of colloquial excellence" † in the beginning of the fifth act, is supposed to be an imitation of a passage in Sidney's "Arcadia," first printed in 1590. The passage might have been introduced in the augmented copy; to say nothing of the fact that the "Arcadia" was known in manuscript before it was printed. Lastly, the mask in the fifth act, where the King and his lords appear in Russian habits, and the allusions to Muscovites which this mask produces, are supposed by Warburton to have been suggested by the public concern for the settlement of a treaty of commerce with Russia, in 1591. But the learned commentator overlooks a passage in Hall's Chronicle, which shows that a mask of Muscovites was a court recreation in the time of Henry VIII.‡

In the *extrinsic* evidence, therefore, which this comedy supplies, there is nothing whatever to

---

* *Love's Labour's Lost.* The title of this play stands as follows in the folio of 1623: "*Loues Labour's Lost.*" The modes in which the genitive case and the contraction of *is* after a substantive, are printed in the titles of other plays in this edition, and in the earlier copies, leads us to believe that the author intended to call his play "Love's Labour is Lost." The apostrophe is not given as the mark of the genitive case in those instances—"*The Winters Tale*,"—"*A Midsummer Nights Dream*,"—(so printed.) But when the verb *is* forms a part of the title, the apostrophe is introduced, as in "*All's well that ends well*." We do not think ourselves justified, therefore, in printing either "Love's Labour Lost," or "Love's Labours Lost,"—as some have recommended.

† Johnson.   ‡ See Illustrations to Act V.

INTRODUCTORY NOTICE.

disprove the theory which we entertain, that, before it had been "corrected and augmented." Love's Labour 's Lost was one of the plays produced by Shakspere about 1589, when, being only twenty-five years of age, he was a joint-proprietor in the Blackfriars Theatre. The *intrinsic* evidence appears to us entirely to support this opinion; and as this evidence involves several curious particulars of literary history, we have to request the reader's indulgence whilst we examine it somewhat in detail.

Coleridge, who always speaks of this comedy as a "*juvenile drama*"—"a young author's first work"—says, "The characters in this play are either impersonated out of Shakspere's own multiformity by imaginative self-position, *or out of such as a country-town and a schoolboy's observation might supply*."* For this production, Shakspere, it is presumed, found neither characters nor plot in any previous romance or drama. "I have not hitherto discovered," says Steevens, "any novel on which this comedy appears to have been founded; and yet the story of it has most of the features of an ancient romance." Steevens might have more correctly said that the story has most of the features which would be derived from an acquaintance with the ancient romances. The action of the comedy, and the higher actors, are the creations of one who was imbued with the romantic spirit of the middle ages—who was conversant "with their Courts of Love, and all that lighter drapery of chivalry, which engaged even mighty kings with a sort of serio-comic interest, and may well be supposed to have occupied more completely the smaller princes."† Our poet himself, in this play, alludes to the Spanish romances of chivalry:

> "This child of fancy that Armado hight,
> For interim to our studies, shall relate
> In high-born words the worth of many a knight
> From tawny Spain, lost in the world's debate."

With these materials, and out of his own "imaginative self-position," might Shakspere have readily produced the King and Princess, the lords and ladies, of this comedy;—and he might have caught the tone of the Court of Elizabeth,—the wit, the play upon words, the forced attempts to say and do clever things,—without any actual contact with the society which was accessible to him after his fame conferred distinction even upon the highest and most accomplished patron. The more ludicrous characters of the drama were unquestionably within the range of "a schoolboy's observation."

And first, of Don Armado, whom Scott calls "the Euphuist."‡ The historical events which are interwoven with the plot of Scott's "Monastery" must have happened about 1562 or 1563, before the authority of the unhappy Queen of Scots was openly trodden under foot by Murray and her rebellious lords; and she had at least the personal liberty, if not the free will, of a supreme ruler. Our great novelist is, as is well known, not very exact in the matter of dates; and in the present instance his licence is somewhat extravagant. Explaining the source of the affectations of his Euphuist, Sir Piercie Shafton, he says—"it was about this period that the only rare poet of his time, the witty, comical, facetiously-quick, and quickly-facetious John Lyly—he that sate at Apollo's table, and to whom Phœbus gave a wreath of his own bays without snatching§—he, in short, who wrote that singularly coxcomical work, called *Euphues and his England*,—was in the very zenith of his absurdity and reputation. The quaint, forced, and unnatural style which he introduced by his 'Anatomy of Wit' had a fashion as rapid as it was momentary—all the Court ladies were his scholars, and to *parler Euphuisme* was as necessary a qualification to a courtly gallant, as those of understanding how to use his rapier, or to dance a measure."‖ This statement is somewhat calculated to mislead the student of our literary history, as to the period of the commencement, and of the duration, of Lyly's influence upon the structure of "polite conversation." "Euphues,—the Anatomy of Wit," was first published in 1580; and "Euphues and his England" in 1581—some eighteen or twenty years after the time when Sir Piercie Shafton (the English Catholic who surrendered himself to the champions of John Knox and the Reformation) explained to Mary of Avenel the merits of the Anatomy of Wit—"that all-to-be-unparalleled volume—that quintessence of human wit—that treasury of quaint invention—that exquisitely-pleasant-to-read, and inevitably-necessary-to-be-remembered manual of all that is worthy to be known."¶ Nor was the fashion of Euphuism as momentary as Scott represents it to have been. The prevalence of this "spurious and unnatural mode of conversation"** is alluded to in Jonson's "Every Man out of his

---

* Literary Remains. vol. ii., p. 102. † Coleridge. Literary Remains, vol. ii., p. 104.
‡ Introduction to the Monastery. § Extract from Blount, the editor of six of Lyly's plays, in 1632.
‖ Monastery, chap. xiv. ¶ Monastery, chap. xiv. ** Gifford's Ben Jonson, vol. ii., p. 230.

LOVE'S LABOUR'S LOST.

Humour," first acted in 1599;—and it forms one of the chief objects of the satire of rare Ben's "Cynthia's Revels," first acted in 1600. But the most important question with reference to Shakspere's employment of the affected phraseology which he puts into the mouth of Armado is, whether this "quaint, forced, and unnatural style" was an imitation of that said to be *introduced* by Lyly; if, indeed, Lyly did more than reduce to a system those innovations of language which had obtained a currency amongst us for some time previous to the appearance of his books. Blount, it is true, says—" our nation are in his debt for a new English which he taught them. Euphues and his England began first that language." It is somewhat difficult precisely to define what "that language" is; but the language of Armado is not very different from that of Andrew Borde, the physician, who, according to Hearne, "gave rise to the name of Merry Andrew, the fool of the mountebank stage." His "Breviary of Health," first printed in 1547, begins thus: " Egregious doctours and maysters of the eximious and arcane science of physicke, of your urbanitie exasperate not your selve."* Nor is Armado's language far removed from the example of "dark words and inkhorn terms" exhibited by Wilson, in his "Arte of Rhetorike" first printed in 1553, where he gives a letter thus devised by a Lincolnshire man for a void benefice :—" Ponderyng, expendyng, and revolutyng with myself, your ingent affabilitie, and ingenious capacitie for mundane affaires, I cannot but celebrate and extoll your magnificall dexteritie above all other. For how could you have adapted suche illustrate prerogative, and dominicall superioritie, if the fecunditie of your ingenie had not been so fertile and wonderfull pregnaunt."† In truth, Armado the braggart, and Holofernes the pedant, both talk in this vein; though the schoolmaster may lean more to the hard words of Lexiphanism, and the fantastic traveller to the quips and cranks of Euphuism. Our belief is, that, although Shakspere might have been familiar with Lyly's Euphues when he wrote Love's Labour's Lost, he did not, in Armado, point at the fashion of the Court "to parley Euphuism."‡ The courtiers in this comedy, be it observed, speak, when they are wearing an artificial character, something approaching to this language, but not the identical language. They, indeed, "trust to speeches penn'd"—they "woo in rhyme"—they employ

"Taffata phrases, silken terms precise
Three-pil'd hyperboles :"—

they exhibit a "constant striving after logical precision, and subtle opposition of thoughts, together with the making the most of every conception or image, by expressing it under the least expected property belonging to it."§ But of no one of them can it be said, "He speaks not like a man of God's making." Ben Jonson, on the contrary, when, in "Cynthia's Revels," he satirized "the special Fountain of Manners, the Court," expressly makes the courtiers talk the very jargon of Euphuism; as for example: "You know I call madam Philautia, my Honour; and she calls me, her Ambition. Now, when I meet her in the presence anon, I will come to her, and say, Sweet Honour, I have hitherto contented my sense with the lilies of your hand, but now I will taste the roses of your lips; and, withal kiss her: to which she cannot but blushing answer, Nay, now you are too ambitious. And then do I reply, I cannot be too ambitious of Honour, sweet lady." But Armado,—

" A refined traveller of Spain;
A man in all the world's new fashion planted,
That hath a mint of phrases in his brain,"—

is the only man of "fire-new words." The pedant even laughs at him as a "fanatical phantasm." But such a man Shakspere might have seen in his own country-town: where, unquestionably, the schoolmaster and the curate might also have flourished. If he had found them in books, Wilson's "Rhetorike" might as well have supplied the notion of Armado and Holofernes, as Lyly's "Euphues" of the one, or Florio's "First Fruits" of the other.

Warburton, in his usual "discourse peremptory," tells us, " by Holofernes is designed a particular character, a pedant and schoolmaster of our author's time, one John Florio, a teacher of the Italian tongue in London, who has given us a small Dictionary of that language, under the title of 'A World of Words.'" What Warburton asserted Farmer upheld. Florio, says Farmer, had given the first affront, by saying, "the plays that they play in England are neither right comedies nor right tragedies ; but representations of histories without any decorum." Florio says this in his "Second Fruites," published in 1591. Now, if Shakspere felt himself aggrieved at this statement,

---

* Quoted in Warton's History of English Poetry, vol. iii., p. 335, 1824.   † Ibid., vol. iv., p. 166.
‡ Blount.   § Coleridge's Literary Remains, vol. ii., p. 104.

INTRODUCTORY NOTICE.

which was true enough of the English drama before his time, he was betrayed by his desire for revenge into very unusual inconsistencies. For, in truth, the making of a teacher of Italian the prototype of a country schoolmaster, who, whilst he lards his phrases with words of Latin, as if he were construing with his class, holds to the good old English pronunciation, and abhors "such rackers of orthography, as to speak, dout, fine, when he should say, doubt," &c., is such an absurdity as Shakspere, who understood his art, would never have yielded to through any instigation of caprice or passion. The probability is, that when Shakspere drew Holofernes, whose name he found in Rabelais,* he felt himself under considerable obligations to John Florio for having given the world "his 'First Fruites;' which yeelde familiar speech, merie proverbes, wittie sentences, and golden sayings." This book was printed in 1578. But, according to Warburton, Florio, in 1598, in the preface to a new edition of his "World of Words," is furious upon Shakspere in the following passage: "There is another sort of leering curs, that rather snarle than bite, whereof I could instance in one, who, lighting on a good sonnet of a gentleman's, a friend of mine, that loved better to be a poet than to be counted so, called the author a Rymer. Let Aristophanes and his comedians make plaies, and scowre their mouths on Socrates, those very mouths they make to vilifie shall be the means to amplifie his virtue." Warburton maintains that the sonnet was Florio's own, and that it was parodied in the "extemporal epitaph on the death of the deer," beginning

"The praiseful princess pierc'd and prick'd a pretty pleasing pricket."

This is very ingenious argument, but somewhat bold; and it appears to us that Thomas Wilson was just as likely to have suggested the alliteration as John Florio. In the "Arte of Rhetorike" which we have already quoted, we find this sentence: "Some use over-muche repetition of one letter, as pitifall povertie prayeth for a penie, but puffed presumpcion passeth not a point." Indeed, there are many existing proofs of the excessive prevalence of alliteration in the end of the sixteenth century. Bishop Andrews is notorious for it. Florio seems to have been somewhat of a braggart, for he always signs his name "Resolute John Florio." But, according to the testimony of Sir William Cornwallis, he was far above the character of a fantastical pedant. Speaking of his translation of Montaigne (the book which has now acquired such interest by bearing Shakspere's undoubted autograph), Sir William Cornwallis says, "divers of his (Montaigne's) pieces I have seen translated; they that understand both languages say very well done; and I am able to say (if you will take the word of ignorance), translated into a style admitting as few idle words as our language will endure."† Holofernes, the pedant, who had "lived long on the alms-basket of words"—who had "been at a great feast of languages and stolen the scraps," was not the man to deserve the praise of writing "a style admitting as few idle words as our language will endure."

As far then as we have been able to trace, the original comedy of Love's Labour's Lost might have been produced by Shakspere without any personal knowledge of the court language of Euphuism,—without any acquaintance with John Florio,—and with a design only to ridicule those extravagancies which were opposed to the maxim of Roger Ascham, the most unpedantic of schoolmasters, "to speake as the common people do, to thinke as wise men do."‡ The further intrinsic evidence that this comedy was a very early production is most satisfactory. Coleridge has a very acute remark—(which in our minds is worth all that has been written about the learning of Shakspere)—as to his early literary habits. "It is not unimportant to notice how strong a presumption the diction and allusions of this play afford, that, though Shakspere's acquirements in the dead languages might not be such as we suppose in a learned education, his habits had, nevertheless, been scholastic, and those of a student. For a young author's first work almost always bespeaks his recent pursuits, and his first observations of life are either drawn from the immediate employments of his youth, and from the characters and images most deeply impressed on his mind in the situations in which those employments had placed him;—or else they are fixed on such objects and occurrences in the world as are easily connected with, and seem to bear upon, his studies and the hitherto exclusive subjects of his meditations."§ The frequent rhymes,—the alternate verses,—the familiar metre which has been called doggerel (but which Anstey and Moore have made classical by wit, and by fun even more agreeable than wit), lines such as

"His face's own margent did quote such amazes,
That all eyes saw his eyes enchanted with gazes,"—

* "De faict, l'en lay enseigna ung grand docteur sophiste, nommé maistre Thubal Holoferne." Gargantua, livre i., chap. xiv. † Essays, 1600. ‡ Toxophilus. Literary Remains, vol. ii., p. 106.

the sonnets full of quaint conceits, or running off into the most playful anacreontics,—the skilful management of the pedantry, with a knowledge far beyond the pedantry,—and the happy employment of the ancient mythology,—all justify Coleridge's belief that the materials of this comedy were drawn from the immediate employments of Shakspere's youth. Still the play, when augmented and corrected, might have received many touches derived from the power which he had acquired by experience. If it were not presumptuous to attempt to put our finger upon such passages, we would say that Biron's eloquent speech at the end of the fourth act, beginning

"Have at you then, affection's men at arms,"—

and Rosaline's amended speech at the end of the play,

"Oft have I heard of you, my lord Biron,"—

must be amongst the more important of these augmentations.

PERIOD OF THE ACTION, AND MANNERS.

There is no historical foundation for any portion of the action of this comedy. There was no Ferdinand King of Navarre. We have no evidence of a difference between France and Navarre as to possessions in Aquitain. We may place, therefore, the period of the action as the period of Elizabeth, for the manners are those of Shakspere's own time. The more remarkable of the customs which are alluded to will be pointed out in our illustrations.

COSTUME.

Cesare Vecellio, at the end of his third book (edit. 1598), presents us with the general costume of Navarre at this period. The women appear to have worn a sort of clog or patten, something like the Venetian chioppine; and we are told in the text that some dressed in imitation of the French, some in the style of the Spaniards, while others blended the fashions of both those nations. The well-known costume of Henri Quatre and Philip II. may furnish authority for the dress of the king and nobles of Navarre, and of the lords attending on the Princess of France, who may herself be attired after the fashion of Marguerite de Valois, the sister of Henry III. of France, and first wife of his successor the King of Navarre. (Vide Montfaucon, Monarchie Française.) We subjoin the Spanish gentleman, and the French lady, of 1589, from Vecellio. For the costume of the Muscovites in the mask (Act V.), see Illustrations.

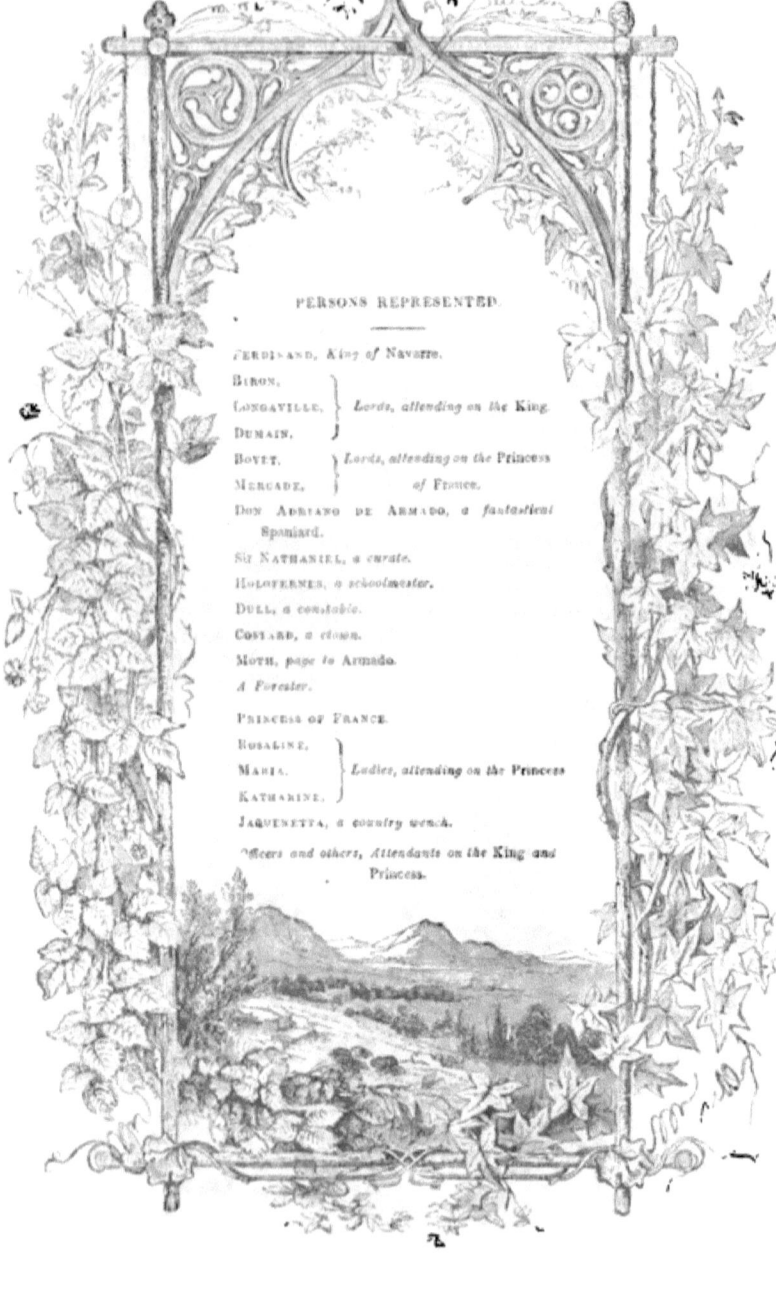

PERSONS REPRESENTED.

FERDINAND, King of Navarre.
BIRON,
LONGAVILLE, } Lords, attending on the King.
DUMAIN,
BOYET, } Lords, attending on the Princess
MERCADE, } of France.
DON ADRIANO DE ARMADO, a fantastical Spaniard.
SIR NATHANIEL, a curate.
HOLOFERNES, a schoolmaster.
DULL, a constable.
COSTARD, a clown.
MOTH, page to Armado.
A Forester.

PRINCESS OF FRANCE.
ROSALINE,
MARIA, } Ladies, attending on the Princess
KATHARINE,
JAQUENETTA, a country wench.

Officers and others, Attendants on the King and Princess.

ACT I.

SCENE I.—Navarre. *A Park, with a Palace in it.*

Enter the KING, BIRON,[a] LONGAVILLE, *and* DUMAIN.

King. Let fame, that all hunt after in their lives,
Live register'd upon our brazen tombs,
And then grace us in the disgrace of death;
When, spite of cormorant devouring time,
The endeavour of this present breath may buy
That honour, which shall bate his scythe's keen edge,
And make us heirs of all eternity.
Therefore, brave conquerors!—for so you are,
That war against your own affections,
And the huge army of the world's desires,—
Our late edict shall strongly stand in force:
Navarre shall be the wonder of the world;
Our court shall be a little Academe,
Still and contemplative in living art.
You three, Biron, Dumain, and Longaville,
Have sworn for three years' term to live with me,
My fellow-scholars, and to keep those statutes,
That are recorded in this schedule here:
Your oaths are past, and now subscribe your names;

That his own hand may strike his honour down,
That violates the smallest branch herein:
If you are armed to do, as sworn to do,
Subscribe to your deep oath, and keep it too.[*]

Long. I am resolv'd: 't is but a three years fast:
The mind shall banquet, though the body pine:
Fat paunches have lean pates; and dainty bits
Make rich the ribs, but bankerout the wits.

Dum. My loving lord, Dumain is mortified.
The grosser manner of these world's baser slaves:
To love, to wealth, to pomp, I pine and die;
With all these living in philosophy.

Biron. I can but say their protestation over,
So much, dear liege, I have already sworn,
That is, To live and study here three years.
But there are other strict observances;
As, not to see a woman in that term;
Which, I hope well, is not enrolled there:
And, one day in a week to touch no food,
And but one meal on every day beside;

---

[a] *Biron.* In all the old copies this name is spelt *Berowne.* In Act. IV. Sc. III. we have a line in which *Biron* rhymes to *moon.* We may, therefore, suppose the pronunciation to have been *Beroon.*

[*] The first folio, and the quartos, read *oaths,* and still retain it. Mr. Dyce says that, in Shakspere's writings, and in those of his contemporaries, there are instances of *it* applied to a preceding plural word. The second folio *lives* "*oaths,* and keep *them* too." The line, as we give it, is a modern alteration, which, Mr. Dyce says, was made without regard to the line a little before,—
"Your oaths are pass'd, and now subscribe your names,"
&c. Addressing the three who had sworn, *your oaths* is correct. But it is not incorrect to call upon them to subscribe their names to the *one* oath which each had taken.

The which, I hope, is not enrolled there:
And then to sleep but three hours in the
  night,
And not be seen to wink of all the day;
(When I was wont to think no harm all night,
And make a dark night too of half the day;)
Which, I hope well, is not enrolled there:
O, these are barren tasks, too hard to keep;
Not to see ladies,—study,—fast,—not sleep.
  King. Your oath is pass'd to pass away from
    these.
  Biron. Let me say no, my liege, an if you
    please;
I only swore, to study with your grace,
And stay here in your court for three years'
    space.
  Long. You swore to that, Biron, and to the
    rest.
  Biron. By yea and nay, sir, then I swore in
    jest.
What is the end of study? let me know.
  King. Why, that to know, which else we
    should not know.
  Biron. Things hid and barr'd, you mean, from
    common sense?
  King. Ay, that is study's godlike recompense.
  Biron. Come on then, I will swear to study so,
To know the thing I am forbid to know:
As thus,—To study where I well may dine,
When I to feast expressly am forbid;*
Or, study where to meet some mistress fine,
When mistresses from common sense are hid:
Or, having sworn too hard-a-keeping oath,
Study to break it, and not break my troth.
If study's gain be thus, and this be so,
Study knows that, which yet it doth not know:
Swear me to this, and I will ne'er say, no.
  King. These be the stops that hinder study
    quite,
And train our intellects to vain delight.
  Biron. Why, all delights are vain; and that
    most vain,
Which, with pain purchas'd, doth inherit pain:
As, painfully to pore upon a book,
  To seek the light of truth; while truth the
    while
Doth falsely blind the eyesight of his look:
  Light, seeking light, doth light of light be-
    guile:
So, ere you find where light in darkness lies,
Your light grows dark by losing of your eyes.

Study me how to please the eye indeed,
  By fixing it upon a fairer eye;
Who dazzling so, that eye shall be his heed,
  And give him light that it was blinded by.
Study is like the heaven's glorious sun,
  That will not be deep-search'd with saucy
    looks;
Small have continual plodders ever won,
  Save base authority from others' books.
These earthly godfathers of heaven's lights,
  That give a name to every fixed star,
Have no more profit of their shining nights,
  Than those that walk, and wot not what they
    are.
Too much to know is, to know nought but fame;
And every godfather can give a name.
  King. How well he's read, to reason against
    reading!
  Dum. Proceeded well, to stop all good pro-
    ceeding!
  Long. He weeds the corn, and still lets grow
    the weeding.
  Biron. The spring is near, when green geese
    are a breeding.
  Dum. How follows that?
  Biron.   Fit in his place and time.
  Dum. In reason nothing.
  Biron.   Something then in rhyme.
  King. Biron is like an envious sneaping frost,
    That bites the first-born infants of the
    spring.
  Biron. Well say I am; why should proud
    summer boast,
Before the birds have any cause to sing?
Why should I join in an ª abortive birth?
At Christmas I no more desire a rose,
Than wish a snow in May's new-fangled shows;
But like of each thing that in season grows.
So you, to study now it is too late,
Climb o'er the house to unlock the little gate,ᵇ
  King. Well, sit you out; go home, Biron;
    adieu!
  Biron. No, my good lord; I have sworn to
    stay with you:
And, though I have for barbarism spoke more,
  Than for that angel knowledge you can say,
Yet, confident I'll keep what I have swore,
  And bide the penance of each three years' day,ᶜ
Give me the paper, let me read the same;
And to the strictest decrees I'll write my name.

ª *Forbid.* The old copies read "to *fast* expressly am forbid." Theobald first supplied *feast.* The converse of the oath is *fast;* and unless we suppose that Biron was *forbid* in two senses—fir-t, in its usual meaning, and then in its ancient mode of making *bid* more emphatical, *for-bid,*—we must adopt the change.

ᵇ For *any Pope gave us an.* Mr. Dyce says *any was* caught from the preceding line.
ᵇ So the quarto of 1598. The folio has,
  "That were to climb o'er the house t' unlock the gate."
ᶜ It is usual to close the sentence at "three years' day;" but the construction requires the rejection of such a pause.

82

King. How well this yielding rescues thee
  from shame!
Biron. [*Reads.*]
Item, That no woman shall come within a mile of my
court—
Hath this been proclaim'd?
Long. Four days ago.
Biron. Let's see the penalty. [*Reads.*]
—On pain of losing her tongue.—
Who devis'd this penalty?
Long. Marry, that did I.
Biron. Sweet lord, and why?
Long. To fright them hence with that dread
  penalty.
Biron. A dangerous law against gentility.ᵃ
[*Reads.*]
Item, If any man be seen to talk with a woman within
the term of three years, he shall endure such public shame
as the rest of the court shall possibly devise.—
This article, my liege, yourself must break;
For, well you know, here comes in embassy
The French king's daughter, with yourself to
  speak,—
A maid of grace, and complete majesty,—
About surrender-up of Aquitain
To her decrepit, sick, and bed-rid father:
Therefore this article is made in vain,
Or vainly comes the admired princess hither.
King. What say you, lords? why, this was
  quite forgot.
Biron. So study evermore is overshot.
While it doth study to have what it would,
It doth forget to do the thing it should:
And when it hath the thing it hunteth most,
'T is won, as towns with fire; so won, so lost.
King. We must, of force, dispense with this
  decree;
She must lieᵇ here on mere necessity
Biron. Necessity will make us all forsworn
  Three thousand times within this three
    years' space:
For every man with his affects is born;
  Not by might master'd, but by special grace.
If I break faith, this word shall speakᶜ for me,
I am forsworn on mere necessity.—
So to the laws at large I write my name:
                                [*Subscribes.*
  And he that breaks them in the least de-
    gree,

Stands in attainder of eternal shame:
Suggestionsᵃ are to others, as to me;
But, I believe, although I seem so loth;
I am the last that will last keep his oath.
But is there no quick recreation granted?
King. Ay, that there is; our court, you know,
  is haunted
With a refined traveller of Spain;
A man in all the world's new fashion planted,
  That hath a mint of phrases in his brain:
One whom the music of his own vain tongue
  Doth ravish, like enchanting harmony;
A man of complements,ᵇ whom right and wrong
  Have chose as umpire of their mutiny:
This child of fancy, that Armado hight,
  For interim to our studies, shall relate,
In high-born words, the worth of many a knight
  From tawny Spain, lost in the world's debate.ᵈ
How you delight, my lords, I know not, I;
But, I protest, I love to hear him lie,
And I will use him for my minstrelsy.
Biron. Armado is a most illustrious wight,
A man of fire-newᶜ words, fashion's own knight.
Long. Costard, the swain, and he, shall be our
  sport;
And, so to study, three years is but short.

Enter DULL, *with a letter, and* COSTARD.

Dull. Which is the duke's own person?
Biron. This, fellow; What wouldst?
Dull. I myself reprehend his own person, for
I am his g ace's tharborough: but I would see
his own person in flesh and blood.
Biron. This is he.
Dull. Signior Arme—Arme—commends you.
There's villainy abroad; this letter will tell you
more.
Cost. Sir, the contempts thereof are as touch-
ing me.
King. A letter from the magnificent Armado.
Biron. How low soever the matter, I hope in
God for high words.
Long. A high hope for a low heaven:ᵈ God
grant us patience!
Biron. To hear? or forbear hearing?

ᵃ *Suggestions*—temptations.
ᵇ *Complements*—a man versed in ceremonial distinctions—in punctilios—a man who brings *forms* to decide the mutiny between right and wrong. *Compliment* and *complement* were originally written without distinction, and though the first may be taken to mean *ceremonies* and the second *accomplishments*, both the one and the other have the same origin—they each make *that perfect which was wanting*. In this passage we have the meaning of *ceremonies*; but in Act III., where Moth says "these are complements," we have the meaning of accomplishments.
ᶜ *Fire-new* and *bran-new*,—that is brand-new,—new off the irons,—have each the same origin.
ᵈ See Illustration, Act I.
ᵉ Capell proposed to read "*laughing*;" which some editors adopt.

ᵃ In the early editions this line is given to Longaville. It seems more properly to belong to Biron, and we therefore receive Theobald's correction, especially as Biron is reading the paper, and the early copies do not mark this when they give the line of comment upon the previous item to Longaville.
ᵇ To *lie*—to reside. We have the sense in Wotton's punning definition of an ambassador—"an honest man sent to lie abroad for the good of his country."
ᶜ The folio reads *break*.

LOVE'S LABOUR'S LOST.

Long. To hear meekly, sir, and to laugh moderately; or to forbear both.

Biron. Well, sir, be it as the style shall give us cause to climb in the merriness.

Cost. The matter is to me, sir, as concerning Jaquenetta. The manner of it is, I was taken with the manner.[a]

Biron. In what manner?

Cost. In manner and form following, sir; all those three: I was seen with her in the manor-house, sitting with her upon the form, and taken following her into the park; which, put together, is in manner and form following. Now, sir, for the manner,—it is the manner of a man to speak to a woman: for the form,—in some form.

Biron. For the following, sir?

Cost. As it shall follow in my correction; And God defend the right!

King. Will you hear this letter with attention?

Biron. As we would hear an oracle.

Cost. Such is the simplicity of man to hearken after the flesh.

King. [*Reads.*]

"Great deputy, the welkin's vicegerent, and sole dominator of Navarre, my soul's earth's God, and body's fostering patron,—"

Cost. Not a word of Costard yet.

King.
"So it is,—"

Cost. It may be so: but if he say it is so, he is, in telling true, but so.[b]

King. Peace!

Cost. —be to me, and every man that dares not fight!

King. No words!

Cost. —of other men's secrets, I beseech you.

King.
"So it is, besieged with sable-coloured melancholy, I did commend the black-oppressing humour to the most wholesome physic of thy health-giving air; and, as I am a gentleman, betook myself to walk. The time when? About the sixth hour; when beasts most graze, birds best peck, and men sit down to that nourishment which is called supper. So much for the time when: Now for the ground which; which, I mean, I walked upon: it is yclept thy park. Then for the place where; where, I mean, I did encounter that obscene and most preposterous event, that draweth from my snow-white pen the ebon-coloured ink, which here thou viewest, beholdest, surveyest, or seest: But to the place where,—It standeth north-north-east and by east from the west corner of thy curious-knotted garden,[b] There did I see that low-spirited swain, that base minnow of thy mirth,

Cost. Me?

King.
—"that unletter'd small-knowing soul,"

---
[a] *Manner.* Costard here talks law-French. A thief was taken *with the mainour* when he was taken with the thing stolen—*hand-habend,* having in the hand.
[b] *So-so* in modern editions. *So* in early copies.

Cost. Me?

King.
—"that shallow vassal,"

Cost. Still me?

King.
—"which as I remember, hight Costard,"

Cost. O me!

King.
—"sorted, and consorted, contrary to thy established proclaimed edict and continent canon, with—with,—O with—but with this I passion to say wherewith,

Cost. With a wench.

King.
—"with a child of our grandmother Eve, a female; or, for thy more sweet understanding, a woman. Him I (as my ever esteemed duty pricks me on) have sent to thee, to receive the meed of punishment, by thy sweet grace's officer, Antony Dull; a man of good repute, carriage, bearing, and estimation.

Dull. Me, an't shall please you; I am Antony Dull.

King.
"For Jaquenetta, (so is the weaker vessel called, which I apprehended with the aforesaid swain,) I keep her as a vessel of thy law's fury; and shall, at the least of thy sweet notice, bring her to trial. Thine, in all compliments of devoted and heart-burning heat of duty,

DON ADRIANO DE ARMADO."

Biron. This is not so well as I looked for, but the best that ever I heard.

King. Ay, the best for the worst. But, sirrah, what say you to this?

Cost. Sir, I confess the wench.

King. Did you hear the proclamation?

Cost. I do confess much of the hearing it, but little of the marking of it.

King. It was proclaimed a year's imprisonment, to be taken with a wench.

Cost. I was taken with none, sir; I was taken with a damosel.

King. Well, it was proclaimed damosel.

Cost. This was no damosel, neither, sir; she was a virgin.

King. It is so varied too; for it was proclaimed virgin.

Cost. If it were, I deny her virginity; I was taken with a maid.

King. This maid will not serve your turn, sir.

Cost. This maid will serve my turn, sir.

King. Sir, I will pronounce your sentence; You shall fast a week with bran and water.

Cost. I had rather pray a month with mutton and porridge.

King. And Don Armado shall be your keeper.—
My lord Biron, see him deliver'd o'er.—

And go we, lords, to put in practice, that
Which each to other hath so strongly sworn.—
[*Exeunt* KING, LONGAVILLE, *and* DUMAIN.
Biron. I 'll lay my head to any good man's hat,
These oaths and laws will prove an idle
scorn.—
Sirrah, come on.
Cost. I suffer for the truth, sir: for true it is,
I was taken with Jaquenetta, and Jaquenetta is
a true girl; and therefore, Welcome the sour
cup of prosperity! Affliction may one day smile
again, and until then, Sit down, Sorrow! *
[*Exeunt*.

SCENE II.—*Another part of the same.*
Armado's House.

Enter ARMADO *and* MOTH.

Arm. Boy, what sign is it, when a man of great spirit grows melancholy?
Moth. A great sign, sir, that he will look sad.
*Arm.*b Why, sadness is one and the self-same thing, dear imp.
Moth. No, no; O lord, sir, no.
Arm. How canst thou part sadness and melancholy, my tender juvenal?
Moth. By a familiar demonstration of the working, my tough senior.
Arm. Why tough senior? why tough senior?
Moth. Why tender juvenal? why tender juvenal?
Arm. I spoke it, tender juvenal, as a congruent epitheton, appertaining to thy young days, which we may nominate tender.
Moth. And I, tough senior, as an appertinent title to your old time, which we may name tough.
Arm. Pretty, and apt.
Moth. How mean you, sir; I pretty, and my saying apt? or I apt, and my saying pretty?
Arm. Thou pretty, because little.
Moth. Little pretty, because little: Wherefore apt?
Arm. And therefore apt, because quick.
Moth. Speak you this in my praise, master?
Arm. In thy condign praise.
Moth. I will praise an eel with the same praise.
Arm. What? that an eel is ingenious?
Moth. That an eel is quick.
Arm. I do say, thou art quick in answers: Thou heatest my blood.

* This is the reading of the first folio, and is adopted by Mr. White, instead of the usual reading of "till then, Sit thee down, Sorrow."
b In the early copies, Armado is called *Braggart* through the scene, after his first words.

Moth. I am answered, sir.
Arm. I love not to be crossed.
Moth. He speaks the mere contrary, crosses * love not him. [*Aside*.
Arm. I have promised to study three years with the duke.
Moth. You may do it in an hour, sir.
Arm. Impossible.
Moth. How many is one thrice told?
Arm. I am ill at reckoning; it fits the spirit of a tapster.
Moth. You are a gentleman, and a gamester, sir.
Arm. I confess both; they are both the varnish of a complete man.
Moth. Then, I am sure, you know how much the gross sum of deuce-ace amounts to.
Arm. It doth amount to one more than two.
Moth. Which the base vulgar call, three.
Arm. True.
Moth. Why, sir, is this such a piece of study? Now here is three studied, ere you 'll thrice wink: and how easy it is to put years to the word three, and study three years in two words, the dancing horse will tell you.4
Arm. A most fine figure!
Moth. To prove you a cipher. [*Aside*.
Arm. I will hereupon confess, I am in love: and, as it is base for a soldier to love, so am I in love with a base wench. If drawing my sword against the humour of affection would deliver me from the reprobate thought of it, I would take Desire prisoner, and ransom him to any French courtier for a new devised courtesy. I think scorn to sigh; methinks, I should outswear Cupid. Comfort me, boy: What great men have been in love?
Moth. Hercules, master.
Arm. Most sweet Hercules!—More authority, dear boy, name more; and, sweet my child, let them be men of good repute and carriage.
Moth. Sampson, master; he was a man of good carriage, great carriage; for he carried the town-gates on his back, like a porter: and he was in love.
Arm. O well-knit Sampson! strong-jointed Sampson! I do excel thee in my rapier, as much as thou didst me in carrying gates. I am in love too,—Who was Sampson's love, my dear Moth?
Moth. A woman, master.

* *Crosses.* A cross is a coin. Moth thinks his master has the poverty as well as pride of a Spaniard.

[Act I.]   LOVE'S LABOUR'S LOST.   [Scene II.]

Arm. Of what complexion?
Moth. Of all the four, or the three, or the two; or one of the four.
Arm. Tell me precisely of what complexion?
Moth. Of the sea water green, sir.
Arm. Is that one of the four complexions?
Moth. As I have read, sir; and the best of them too.
Arm. Green, indeed, is the colour of lovers; but to have a love of that colour, methinks, Sampson had small reason for it. He, surely, affected her for her wit.
Moth. It was so, sir; for she had a green wit.
Arm. My love is most immaculate white and red.
Moth. Most maculate* thoughts, master, are masked under such colours.
Arm. Define, define, well-educated infant.
Moth. My father's wit, and my mother's tongue, assist me.
Arm. Sweet invocation of a child; most pretty, and pathetical!
Moth. If she be made of white and red,
    Her faults will ne'er be known;
For blushing cheeks by faults are bred,
    And fears by pale-white shown:
Then, if she fear, or be to blame,
    By this you shall not know;
For still her cheeks possess the same,
    Which native she doth owe.ᵇ
A dangerous rhyme, master, against the reason of white and red.
Arm. Is there not a ballad, boy, of the King and the Beggar?
Moth. The world was very guilty of such a ballad some three ages since: but, I think, now 't is not to be found; or, if it were, it would neither serve for the writing, nor the tune.
Arm. I will have that subject newly writ o'er, that I may example my digression by some mighty precedent. Boy, I do love that country girl, that I took in the park with the rational hind Costard; she deserves well.
Moth. To be whipped; and yet a better love than my master.   [*Aside.*
Arm. Sing, boy; my spirit grows heavy in love.
Moth. And that 's great marvel, loving a light wench.

    " O vouchsafe
With that thy rare green eye, which never yet
Beheld things maculate."

ᵇ *Owe*—possess.
86

Arm. I say, sing.
Moth. Forbear till this company be past.

Enter DULL, COSTARD, *and* JAQUENETTA.

Dull. Sir, the duke's pleasure is that you keep Costard safe: and you must let him take no delight, nor no penance; but a' must fast three days a-week. For this damsel, I must keep her at the park; she is allowed for the day-woman.ᵃ Fare you well.
Arm. I do betray myself with blushing.—Maid.
Jaq. Man.
Arm. I will visit thee at the lodge.
Jaq. That 's hereby.ᵇ
Arm. I know where it is situate.
Jaq. Lord, how wise you are!
Arm. I will tell thee wonders.
Jaq. With that face?ᶜ
Arm. I love thee.
Jaq. So I heard you say.
Arm. And so farewell.
Jaq. Fair weather after you!
Dull. Come, Jaquenetta, away.
    [*Exeunt* DULL *and* JAQUENETTA.
Arm. Villain, thou shalt fast for thy offences ere thou be pardoned.
Cost. Well, sir, I hope, when I do it, I shall do it on a full stomach.
Arm. Thou shalt be heavily punished.
Cost. I am more bound to you, than your fellows, for they are but lightly rewarded.
Arm. Take away this villain; shut him up.
Moth. Come, you transgressing slave; away.
Cost. Let me not be pent up, sir; I will fast, being loose.
Moth. No, sir; that were fast and loose: thou shalt to prison.
Cost. Well, if ever I do see the merry days of desolation that I have seen, some shall see—
Moth. What shall some see?
Cost. Nay nothing, master Moth, but what

---

* *Day-women* most probably means dairy-woman. In parts of Scotland the term *dey* has been appropriated to dairy-maids; but in England, *deyes* were, perhaps, the lowest class of husbandry servants, generally. In a statute of Richard II., regulating wages, we have "a switcherd, a female labourer, and deye," put down at six shillings yearly. Chaucer describes the diet of his "poore widow" as that of a dry (Nonnes Preestes Tale):—

    " Milk and brown bread, in which she fond no lack,
    Seinde bacon, and sometime an ey or tweye;
    For she was, as it were, a maner dry."

ᵇ *Hereby*—a provincial expression for *as it may happen.* Armado takes it as *hard by.*
ᶜ *With that face?* The folio has "With what face!" The phrase of the quarto, "with *that* face," was a vulgar idiomatic expression in the time of Fielding, who says he took it "verbatim, from very polite conversation."

they look upon. It is not for prisoners to be too silent in their words; and, therefore, I will say nothing: I thank God, I have as little patience as another man; and, therefore, I can be quiet. [*Exeunt* MOTH *and* COSTARD.

Arm. I do affect^a the very ground, which is base, where her shoe, which is baser, guided by her foot, which is basest, doth tread. I shall be forsworn, (which is a great argument of falsehood,) if I love: And how can that be true love, which is falsely attempted? Love is a familiar; love is a devil; there is no evil angel but love. Yet Sampson was so tempted; and he had an excellent strength: yet was Solomon so seduced; and he had a very good wit. Cupid's buttshaft is too hard for Hercules' club, and there-

^a *To affect* is to incline towards, and thence, metaphorically, to love.

fore too much odds for a Spaniard's rapier. The first and second cause^a will not serve my turn; the passado he respects not, the duello he regards not: his disgrace is to be called boy; but his glory is to subdue men. Adieu, valour! rust rapier! be still drum! for your manager is in love; yea, he loveth. Assist me some extemporal god of rhyme, for, I am sure, I shall turn sonnet.^b Devise wit; write pen; for I am for whole volumes in folio. [*Exit.*

^a *First and second cause.* See Illustrations to Romeo and Juliet, Act II., Scene IV., page 43.
^b *Sonnet.* All the old copies have *sonnet*. Hanmer "emended" it into *sonneteer* which is the received reading. To "turn sonneteer" is not in keeping with Armado's style —as "adieu valour—rust rapier;"—and afterwards, "devise wit—write pen." He says, in the same phraseology, he will "turn sonnet;" As at the present day we say, "he can *turn a tune*." Ben Jonson, it will be remembered, speaks of Shakspere's "well-torned and true-filed lines."

ILLUSTRATIONS OF ACT I.

[1] Scene I.—"*A high hope for a low heaven.*"

This is the reading of the early copies; but it was changed by Theobald to *having*. In our first edition we yielded to the universal adoption of the change; but we have become satisfied that *heaven* is the true word, and we restore it accordingly. Mr. Whiter, in his 'Specimen of a Commentary,' has noticed this passage in connexion with his theory of association. The *heaven* here mentioned is the *heaven* of the ancient stage—the covering or internal roof—according to Mr Whiter. (See Henry VI. Part I., Illustrations of Act I.) The "high words" expected in Armado's letter were associated with a "low heaven," as the ranting heroes of the early tragedy mouthed their lofty language beneath a very humble roof. Without adopting Mr. Whiter's theory in its full extent, we may receive the term "*low* heaven," as we receive the term "*highest* heaven" in Henry V., or the "*third* heaven" of some of the old comedies. Biron has somewhat profanely said, "I hope in God for high words;" and Longaville reproves him by saying "your hope is expressed in strong terms for a very paltry gratification—'A high hope for a low heaven.'"

[2] Scene I.—"*In high-born words, the worth of many a knight*
From tawny Spain, lost in the world's debate."

In the variorum editions of Shakspere there is a long dissertation by Warburton, to show that the romances of chivalry were of Spanish origin; and an equally long refutation of this opinion by Tyrwhitt. Tyrwhitt is, undoubtedly, more correct than Warburton; for, although the romances of chivalry took root in Spain, very few were of Spanish growth. Shakspere could have known nothing of these romances through the sources by which they have become familiar to England,—for 'Don Quixote' was not published till 1605; but 'Amadis of Gaul' (asserted by Sismondi to be of Portuguese origin) was translated in 1592; and 'Palmerin of England'—which Southey maintains to be Portuguese—was translated in 1580. It is probable that many of the Spanish romances of the sixteenth century were wholly or partially known in England when Shakspere wrote Love's Labour's Lost; and formed, at least, a subject of conversation amongst the courtiers and men of letters. He, therefore, makes it one of the qualities of Armado to recount "in high-born words" the exploits of the knights of "tawny Spain"—exploits which once received their due meed of admiration, but which "the world's debate,"—the contentions of wars and political changes,—have obscured. The extravagances of these romances, as told by Armado, are pointed at by the king—"I love to hear him lie."

[3] Scene I.—"*Curious knotted garden.*"

We have given, at the end of Act I., a representation of "a curious knotted garden," which will inform our readers better than any description. The beds, or plots, disposed in mathematical symmetry, were the knots. The gardener, in Richard II., comparing England to a neglected garden, says,

" Her fruit-trees all unprun'd, her hedges ruin'd,
Her knots disorder'd."

Milton has exhibited the characteristics of this formal symmetry by a beautiful contrast:—

' Flowers, worthy Paradise, which not nice art
In beds and curious knots, but nature boon
Pour'd forth."

[4] Scene II.—"*The dancing horse will tell you.*"

Our ancestors were fond of learned quadrupeds. "Holden's camel" was distinguished for "ingenious study," as mentioned by John Taylor, the water-poet; there was a superlatively wise elephant, noticed by Donne and Jonson;—but the "dancing horse"—"Banks's horse"—has been celebrated by Shakspere, and Jonson, and Donne, and Hall, and Taylor, and Sir Kenelm Digby, and Sir Walter Raleigh. The name of this wonderful horse was Morocco. Banks first showed his horse in London in 1589; where, in addition to his usual accomplishments of telling the number of pence in a silver coin, and the number of points in throws of the dice, he filled the town with wonder by going to the top of St. Paul's. The fame of Banks's horse led his master to visit the Continent, but he was unfortunate in this step. At Orleans the horse and the master were brought under suspicion of magic; and, to the utter disgrace of papal ignorance and intolerance, poor Banks and his "fine cut" were at last put to death at Rome as Jonson quaintly says,

" Being, beyond the sea, burned for one witch."

ACT II.

SCENE I.—*Another part of the Park. A Pavilion and Tents at a distance.*

Enter the PRINCESS OF FRANCE, ROSALINE, MARIA, KATHARINE, BOYET, Lords, *and other* Attendants.

Boyet. Now, madam, summon up your dearest [a] spirits;
Consider who the king your father sends;
To whom he sends; and what's his embassy:
Yourself, held precious in the world's esteem,
To parley with the sole inheritor
Of all perfections that a man may owe,
Matchless Navarre: the plea of no less weight
Than Aquitain; a dowry for a queen.
Be now as prodigal of all dear grace,
As nature was in making graces dear,
When she did starve the general world beside,
And prodigally gave them all to you.
Prin. Good lord Boyet, my beauty, though but mean,
Needs not the painted flourish of your praise;
Beauty is bought by judgment of the eye,
Not utter'd [b] by base sale of chapmen's [c] tongues:
I am less proud to hear you tell my worth,
Than you much willing to be counted wise
In spending your wit in the praise of mine.
But now to task the tasker,—Good Boyet,
You are not ignorant, all-telling fame
Doth noise abroad, Navarre hath made a vow,
Till painful study shall outwear three years,
No woman may approach his silent court:
Therefore to us seemeth it a needful course,
Before we enter his forbidden gates,
To know his pleasure; and in that behalf,
Bold of your worthiness, we single you
As our best-moving fair solicitor.
Tell him, the daughter of the king of France,
On serious business, craving quick despatch,
Importunes personal conference with his grace.
Haste, signify so much; while we attend,
Like humble-visag'd suitors, his high will.
Boyet. Proud of employment, willingly I go.
[*Exit.*
Prin. All pride is willing pride, and yours is so.
Who are the votaries, my loving lords,
That are vow-fellows with this virtuous duke?

---
a *Dearest*—best.
b To *utter* is to put forth—as we say, "to utter base coin.
c *Chapman* was formerly a seller—a *chapman*, from *ch ap*, a market; and it is still used in this sense legally, as when we say, "dealer and chapman." But it was also used indifferently for seller and buyer: the bargainer on either side was a *chapman, chapman,* or *copeman*.

1 *Lord.* Longaville is one.
Prin.　　　　　　　　　Know you the man?
Mar. I know him, madam; at a marriage feast,
Between lord Perigort and the beauteous heir
Of Jaques Falconbridge solemnized,
In Normandy saw I this Longaville:
A man of sovereign parts he is esteem'd;
Well fitted in the arts, glorious in arms:
Nothing becomes him ill, that he would well.
The only soil of his fair virtue's gloss,
(If virtue's gloss will stain with any soil,)
Is a sharp wit match'd with too blunt a will;
Whose edge hath power to cut, whose will still wills
It should none spare that come within his power.
Prin. Some merry mocking lord, belike; is 't so?
Mar. They say so most, that most his humours know.
Prin. Such short-liv'd wits do wither as they grow.
Who are the rest?
Kath. The young Dumain, a well-accomplish'd youth,
Of all that virtue love for virtue lov'd;
Most power to do most harm, least knowing ill;
For he hath wit to make an ill shape good,
And shape to win grace though he had no wit.
I saw him at the duke Alençon's once;
And much too little of that good I saw,
Is my report,* to his great worthiness.
Ros. Another of these students at that time
Was there with him: If I have heard a truth,
Biron they call him; but a merrier man,
Within the limit of becoming mirth,
I never spent an hour's talk withal:
His eye begets occasion for his wit;
For every object that the one doth catch,
The other turns to a mirth-moving jest;
Which his fair tongue (conceit's expositor)
Delivers in such apt and gracious words,
That aged ears play truant at his tales,
And younger hearings are quite ravished;
So sweet and voluble is his discourse.
Prin. God bless my ladies! are they all in love;
That every one her own hath garnished
With such bedecking ornaments of praise?
Mar. Here comes Boyet.

Re-enter BOYET.

Prin.　　　Now, what admittance, lord?
Boyet. Navarre had notice of your fair approach;

---
* Too little compared to, or in proportion to, his great worthiness.

And he, and his competitors in oath,
Were all address'd to meet you, gentle lady,
Before I came. Marry, thus much I have learnt,
He rather means to lodge you in the field,
(Like one that comes here to besiege his court,)
Than seek a dispensation for his oath,
To let you enter his unpeopled house.
Here comes Navarre.　　[*The Ladies mask.*

Enter KING, LONGAVILLE, DUMAIN, BIRON, *and Attendants.*

King. Fair princess, welcome to the court of Navarre.
Prin. Fair, I give you back again; and, welcome I have not yet: the roof of this court is too high to be yours; and welcome to the wild fields too base to be mine.
King. You shall be welcome, madam, to my court.
Prin. I will be welcome then; conduct me thither.
King. Hear me, dear lady, I have sworn an oath.
Prin. Our lady help my lord! he'll be forsworn.
King. Not for the world, fair madam, by my will.
Prin. Why, will shall break it; will, and nothing else.
King. Your ladyship is ignorant what it is.
Prin. Were my lord so, his ignorance were wise,
Where now his knowledge must prove ignorance.
I hear, your grace hath sworn-out house-keeping:
'T is deadly sin to keep that oath, my lord,
And sin to break it:
But pardon me, I am too sudden bold;
To teach a teacher ill-beseemeth me.
Vouchsafe to read the purpose of my coming,
And suddenly resolve me in my suit.
　　　　　　　　　　　　　[*Gives a paper.*
King. Madam, I will, if suddenly I may.
Prin. You will the sooner, that I were away;
For you'll prove perjur'd, if you make me stay.
Biron. Did not I dance with you in Brabant once?
Ros. Did not I dance with you in Brabant once?
Biron. I know you did.
Ros.　　　　　How needless was it then
To ask the question!
Biron.　　　You must not be so quick.
Ros. 'T is long* of you that spur me with such questions.

---
* *Long of you*—along of you—through you.

Biron. Your wit's too hot, it speeds too fast,
  't will tire.
Ros. Not till it leave the rider in the mire.
Biron. What time o' day?
Ros. The hour that fools should ask.
Biron. Now fair befall your mask! ᵃ
Ros. Fair fall the face it covers!
Biron. And send you many lovers!
Ros. Amen, so you be none.
Biron. Nay, then will I be gone.
King. Madam, your father here doth intimate
The payment of a hundred thousand crowns;
Being but the one half of an entire sum,
Disbursed by my father in his wars.
But say, that he, or we, (as neither have,)
Receiv'd that sum; yet there remains unpaid
A hundred thousand more; in surety of the
  which,
One part of Aquitain is bound to us,
Although not valued to the money's worth.
If then the king your father will restore
But that one half which is unsatisfied,
We will give up our right in Aquitain,
And hold fair friendship with his majesty.
But that, it seems, he little purposeth,
For here he doth demand to have repaid
An hundred thousand crowns; and not demands,
On payment of a hundred thousand crowns,
To have his title live in Aquitain; ᵇ
Which we much rather had depart withal,
And have the money by our father lent,
Than Aquitain so gelded as it is.
Dear princess, were not his requests so far
From reason's yielding, your fair self should
  make
A yielding, 'gainst some reason, in my breast,
And go well satisfied to France again.
  Prin. You do the king my father too much
    wrong,
And wrong the reputation of your name,
In so unseeming to confess receipt
Of that which hath so faithfully been paid.
  King. I do protest, I never heard of it;
And, if you prove it, I 'll repay it back,
Or yield up Aquitain.
  Prin.   We arrest your word:—
Boyet, you can produce acquittances,
For such a sum, from special officers
Of Charles his father.

ᵃ The ladies were masked, and, perhaps, were dressed alike. Biron, subsequently, after an exchange of wit with Rosaline, inquires who Katharine is; and Dumain, in the same manner, asks Boyet as to Rosaline.

ᵇ He requires the re-payment of a hundred thousand crowns,—but does not propose to pay us the other hundred thousand crowns, by which payment he would redeem the mortgage.

  King.   Satisfy me so.
  Boyet. So please your grace, the packet is
    not come,
Where that and other specialties are bound;
To-morrow you shall have a sight of them.
  King. It shall suffice me: at which interview,
All liberal reason I will yield unto.
Meantime, receive such welcome at my hand
As honour, without breach of honour, may
Make tender of to thy true worthiness:
You may not come, fair princess, in my gates;
But here without you shall be so receiv'd,
As you shall deem yourself lodg'd in my
  heart,
Though so denied fair harbour in my house.
Your own good thoughts excuse me, and farewell:
To-morrow we shall visit you again.
  Prin. Sweet health and fair desires consort
    your grace!
  King. Thy own wish wish I thee in every
    place!   [*Exeunt* KING *and his train.*
  Biron. Lady, I will commend you to my own
    heart.
  Ros. 'Pray you, do my commendations; I
    would be glad to see it.
  Biron. I would, you heard it groan.
  Ros. Is the fool sick?
  Biron. Sick at the heart.
  Ros. Alack, let it blood.
  Biron. Would that do it good?
  Ros. My physic says, I.
  Biron. Will you prick 't with your eye?
  Ros. No *poynt*,ᵃ with my knife.
  Biron. Now, God save thy life!
  Ros. And yours from long living!
  Biron. I cannot stay thanksgiving [*Retiring.*
  Dum. Sir, I pray you a word: What lady is
    that same?
  Boyet. The heir of Alençon, Rosaline her
    name.
  Dum. A gallant lady! Monsieur, fare you
    well.   [*Exit.*
  Long. I beseech you a word; What is she in
    the white?
  Boyet. A woman sometimes, if you saw her in
    the light.
  Long. Perchance, light in the light: I desire
    her name.
  Boyet. She hath but one for herself; to desire
    that, were a shame.
  Long. Pray you, sir, whose daughter?

ᵃ *No poynt*—the double negative, as it is commonly called, of the French—*non point.*

Boyet. Her mother's, I have heard.
Long. God's blessing on your beard !
Boyet. Good sir, be not offended :
She is an heir of Falconbridge.
Long. Nay, my choler is ended.
She is a most sweet lady.
Boyet. Not unlike, sir; that may be.
[*Exit* LONG.
Biron. What's her name, in the cap?
Boyet. Katharine, by good hap.
Biron. Is she wedded, or no?
Boyet. To her will, sir, or so.
Biron. You are welcome, sir ; adieu !
Boyet. Farewell to me, sir, and welcome to
you. [*Exit* BIRON.—*Ladies unmask.*
Mar. That last is Biron, the merry mad-cap
lord ;
Not a word with him but a jest.
Boyet. And every jest but a word.
Prin. It was well done of you to take him at
his word.
Boyet. I was as willing to grapple, as he was
to board.
Mar. Two hot sheeps, marry !
Boyet. And wherefore not ships ?
No sheep, sweet lamb, unless we feed on your
lips.
Mar. You sheep, and I pasture ; Shall that
finish the jest ?
Boyet. So you grant pasture for me.
[*Offering to kiss her.*
Mar. Not so, gentle beast ;
My lips are no common, though several they be.ᵃ
Boyet. Belonging to whom ?
Mar. To my fortunes and me.
Prin. Good wits will be jangling : but, gentles, agree :

ᵃ *Common—several.* Shakspere here uses his favourite law-phrases,—which practice has given rise to the belief that he was bred in an attorney's office. But there is here, apparently, some confusion in the use,—occasioned by the word *though.* A "*common,*" as we all know, is unapportioned land ;—a "*several,*" land that is private property. Shakspere uses the word according to this sense in the Sonnets :—
"Why should my heart think that a *several* plot,
Which my heart knows the world's wide common place ?"
But Dr. James has attempted to show that *several*, or *severell*, in Warwickshire, meant the common *field* :—common to a few proprietors, but not common to all. In this way, the word "though" is not contradictory. Maria's lips are "no common, though several"—
"Belonging to whom ?
To my fortunes and me."—
I and my fortunes are the co-proprietors of the common field,—but we will not "grant pasture" to others. Provincial usages are important in the illustration of Shakspere.

This civil war of wits were much better us'd
On Navarre and his book-men ; for here 't is
abus'd.
Boyet. If my observation, (which very seldom
lies,)
By the heart's still rhetoric, disclosed with eyes,
Deceive me not now, Navarre is infected.
Prin. With what ?
Boyet. With that which we lovers entitle,
affected.
Prin. Your reason.
Boyet. Why, all his behaviours did make
their retire
To the court of his eye, peeping thorough desire:
His heart, like an agate, with your print impressed,
Proud with his form, in his eye pride expressed :
His tongue, all impatient to speak and not see,
Did stumble with haste in his eyesight to be ;
All senses to that sense did make their repair,
To feel onlyᵃ looking on fairest of fair :
Methought all his senses were lock'd in his eye,
As jewels in crystal for some prince to buy ;
Who, tend'ring their own worth, from whence
they were glass'd,
Did point out to buy them, along as you pass'd,
His face's own margent did quote such amazes,
That all eyes saw his eyes enchanted with gazes :
I'll give you Aquitain, and all that is his,
An you give him for my sake but one loving
kiss.
Prin. Come, to our pavilion : Boyet is dispos'd—
Boyet. But to speak that in words, which his
eye hath disclos'd :
I only have made a mouth of his eye,
By adding a tongue which I know will not lie.
Ros. Thou art an old love-monger, and speak'st
skilfully.
Mar. He is Cupid's grandfather, and learns
news of him.
Ros. Then was Venus like her mother ; for
her father is but grim.
Boyet. Do you hear, my mad wenches ?
Mar. No.
Boyet. What, then, do you see ?
Ros. Ay, our way to be gone.
Boyet. You are too hard for me.
[*Exeunt.*

ᵃ *To feel only.* Thus the ancient copies. Jackson suggests "*To feed on by.*"

ACT III.

SCENE I.—*Another part of the Park.*

Enter ARMADO *and* MOTH.

Arm. Warble, child; make passionate my sense of hearing.
Moth. Concolinel¹——   [*Singing.*
Arm. Sweet air! Go, tenderness of years! take this key, give enlargement to the swain, bring him festinately hither; I must employ him in a letter to my love.
Moth. Master, will you win your love with a French brawl?²
Arm. How meanest thou? brawling in French?
Moth. No, my complete master: but to jig off a tune at the tongue's end, canary³ to it with your feet, humour it with turning up your eyelids; sigh a note, and sing a note; sometime through the throat, as if you swallowed love with singing love; sometime through the nose, as if you snuffed up love by smelling love; with your hat, penthouse-like, o'er the shop of your eyes; ⁴ with your arms crossed on your thin-belly* doublet, like a rabbit on a spit; or your hands in your pocket, like a man after the old painting; and keep not too long in one tune, but a snip

and away: These are complements,ᵃ these are humours; these betray nice wenches, that would be betrayed without these; and make them men of note, (do you note, men?) that most are affected to these.
Arm. How hast thou purchased this experience?
Moth. By my penny of observation.
Arm. But O,—but O—
Moth. —the hobby-horse is forgot.ᵃ
Arm. Callest thou my love, hobby-horse?
Moth. No, master; the hobby-horse is but a colt, and your love, perhaps, a hackney. But have you forgot your love?
Arm. Almost I had.
Moth. Negligent student! learn her by heart.
Arm. By heart, and in heart, boy.
Moth. And out of heart, master: all those three I will prove.
Arm. What wilt thou prove?
Moth. A man, if I live; and this, by, in, and without, upon the instant: By heart you love her, because your heart cannot come by her: in heart you love her, because your heart is in love with her: and out of heart you love her, being out of heart that you cannot enjoy her.

* The folio has *thin-belly*, as a compound word. The quarto, *thin belly's*.

ᵃ See Note to Act I., Scene I.

Arm. I am all these three.

Moth. And three times as much more, and yet nothing at all.

Arm. Fetch hither the swain; he must carry me a letter.

Moth. A message well sympathised; a horse to be ambassador for an ass!

Arm. Ha, ha! what sayest thou?

Moth. Marry, sir, you must send the ass upon the horse, for he is very slow-gaited: But I go.

Arm. The way is but short; away.

Moth. As swift as lead, sir.

Arm. Thy meaning, pretty ingenious? Is not lead a metal heavy, dull, and slow?

Moth. Minimè, honest master; or rather, master, no.

Arm. I say, lead is slow.

Moth. You are too swift, sir, to say so. Is that lead slow which is fired from a gun?

Arm. Sweet smoke of rhetoric! He reputes me a cannon; and the bullet, that's he:—

I shoot thee at the swain.

Moth. Thump then, and I flee.
[*Exit.*

Arm. A most acute juvenal; voluble and free of grace!

By thy favour, sweet welkin, I must sigh in thy face:

Most rude melancholy, valour gives thee place.

My herald is returned.

Re-enter MOTH *and* COSTARD.

Moth. A wonder, master; here's a Costard broken in a shin.ᵃ

Arm. Some enigma, some riddle: come,—thy l'envoy;—begin.

Cost. No egma, no riddle, no l'envoy; no salve in them all,ᵇ sir: O, sir, plantain, a plain plantain; no l'envoy, no l'envoy, no salve, sir, but a plantain!ᶜ

Arm. By virtue, thou enforcest laughter; thy silly thought, my spleen; the heaving of my lungs provokes me to ridiculous smiling: O, pardon me, my stars! Doth the inconsiderate take salve for l'envoy, and the word l'envoy for a salve?

Moth. Do the wise think them other? is not l'envoy a salve?ᵃ

Arm. No, page: it is an epilogue or discourse, to make plain
Some obscure precedence that hath tofore been said.
I will example it:
The fox, the ape, and the humble-bee,
Were still at odds, being but three.

There's the moral: Now the l'envoy.

Moth. I will add the l'envoy; say the moral again.

Arm. The fox, the ape, and the humble-bee,
Were still at odds, being but three.

Moth. Until the goose came out of door,
And stay'd the odds by adding four.

Now will I begin your moral, and do you follow with my l'envoy.

The fox, the ape, and the humble-bee,
Were still at odds, being but three:

Arm. Until the goose came out of door,
Staying the odds by adding four.ᵇ

Moth. A good l'envoy, ending in the goose;
Would you desire more?

Cost. The boy hath sold him a bargain,ᶜ a goose, that's flat:—

Sir, your pennyworth is good, an your goose be fat.—

To sell a bargain well, is as cunning as fast and loose:

Let me see a fat l'envoy; ay, that's a fat goose.

Arm. Come hither, come hither: How did this argument begin?

Moth. By saying that a Costard was broken in a shin.

Then call'd you for the l'envoy.

Cost. True, and I for a plantain: Thus came your argument in;

Then the boy's fat l'envoy, the goose that you bought,

And he ended the market.

Arm. But tell me; how was there a Costard broken in a shin?

Moth. I will tell you sensibly.

Cost. Thou hast no feeling of it, Moth; I will speak that l'envoy.

ᵃ *Costard broken in a shin.*—Costard is the head.

ᵇ *No salve in them all.* The common reading is "no salve in the mail," which is that of the old copies. We adopt Tyrwhitt's suggestion.

ᶜ When Moth quibbles about Costard and his shin, Armado supposes there is a riddle—and he calls for the l'envoy—the address of the old French poem, which conveyed their moral or explanation. Costard says, he wants no such thing—there is no salve in them all: he wants a plantain for his wound.

ᵃ But the arch page makes a joke out of Costard's blunder, and asks is not l'envoy a salve? He has read of the *Salve!* of the Romans, and has a pun for the eye ready. Dr. Farmer believes that Shakspere had here forgot his small Latin, and thought that the words had the same pronunciation. Poor Shakspere! What a dull dog he must have been at this Latin, according to the no-learning critics.

ᵇ So the quarto of 1598. But the folio makes Armado merely give the moral, and Moth the l'envoy, without these repetitions. The sport which so delights Costard is lost by the omission. (See Illustration.)

ACT III.]   LOVE'S LABOUR'S LOST.   [SCENE I.

I, Costard, running out, that was safely within, fell over the threshold, and broke my shin.
Arm. We will talk no more of this matter.
Cost. Till there be more matter in the shin.
Arm. Marry, Costard, I will enfranchise thee.
Cost. O, marry me to one Frances;—I smell some l'envoy, some goose in this.
Arm. By my sweet soul, I mean, setting thee at liberty, enfreedoming thy person; thou wert immured, restrained, captivated, bound.
Cost. True, true; and now you will be my purgation, and let me loose:
Arm. I give thee thy liberty, set thee from durance; and, in lieu thereof, impose on thee nothing but this: Bear this significant to the country maid Jaquenetta: there is remuneration; [*giving him money*] for the best ward of mine honour is rewarding my dependents. Moth, follow. [*Exit.*
Moth. Like the sequel, I.—Signor Costard, adieu.
Cost. My sweet ounce of man's flesh! my incony* Jew! [*Exit* MOTH.
Now will I look to his remuneration. Remuneration! O, that's the Latin word for three farthings: three farthings—remuneration.—What's the price of this inkle? a penny.—No, I'll give you a remuneration: why, it carries it.—Remuneration!—why, it is a fairer name than French crown. I will never buy and sell out of this word.

Enter BIRON.

Biron. O, my good knave Costard! exceedingly well met.
Cost. Pray you, sir, how much carnation ribbon may a man buy for a remuneration?
Biron. What is a remuneration?
Cost. Marry, sir, halfpenny farthing.
Biron. O, why then, three-farthings-worth of silk.
Cost. I thank your worship: God be with you!
Biron. O, stay, slave; I must employ thee: As thou wilt win my favour, good my knave, Do one thing for me that I shall entreat.
Cost. When would you have it done, sir?
Biron. O, this afternoon.
Cost. Well, I will do it, sir: Fare you well.
Biron. O, thou knowest not what it is.
Cost. I shall know, sir, when I have done it.

Biron. Why, villain, thou must know first.
Cost. I will come to your worship to-morrow morning.
Biron. It must be done this afternoon. Hark slave, it is but this;—
The princess comes to hunt here in the park,
And in her train there is a gentle lady;
When tongues speak sweetly, then they name her name,
And Rosaline they call her: ask for her;
And to her white hand see thou do commend
This seal'd-up counsel. There's thy guerdon, go.ᵃ   [*Gives him money.*
Cost. Gardon,—O sweet gardon! better than remuneration; eleven-pence farthing better Most sweet gardon!—I will do it, sir, in print.—Gardon—remuneration.   [*Exit.*
Biron. O!—And I, forsooth, in love! I, that have been love's whip;
A very beadle to a humorous sigh;
A critic; nay, a night-watch constable;
A domineering pedant o'er the boy,
Than whom no mortal so magnificent!
This wimpled,ᵇ whining, purblind, wayward boy;
This senior-junior, giant-dwarf, Dan Cupid;
Regent of love-rhymes, lord of folded arms,
The anointed sovereign of sighs and groans,
Liege of all loiterers and malcontents,
Dread prince of plackets, king of codpieces,
Sole imperator, and great general
Of trotting paritors,⁷ O my little heart!—
And I to be a corporal of his field,⁸
And wear his colours like a tumbler's hoop!⁹
What? I love! I sue! I seek a wife!
A woman, that is like a German clock,¹⁰
Still a repairing; ever out of frame;
And never going aright, being a watch,
But being watch'd that it may still go right?
Nay, to be perjur'd, which is worst of all;
And, among three, to love the worst of all;
A whitely wanton with a velvet brow,
With two pitch balls stuck in her face for eyes;
Ay, and, by heaven, one that will do the deed,
Though Argus were her eunuch and her guard!

ᵃ We deviate, for once, from a resolution not to dwell upon the commendation, or dispraise, of our labours by other editors, for the purpose of expressing our grateful sense of this note by Mr. White:—
"In the original Biron is represented as giving this French name for remuneration correctly, and the clown as mispronouncing it,—a trifling but characteristic distinction, neglected by all editors hitherto, except Mr. Knight—even by the careful Capell. It would not be worthy of particular mention, except to remind the reader that there are many hundreds of like restorations of the original text (aside from those of more importance), which are silently made for the first time in this edition."

ᵇ *Wimpled*—veiled.

---

* *Incony Jew.*—Incony is thought to be the same as the Scotch *canny*—which is our *knowing—cunning. Jew* is, perhaps, Costard's superlative notion of a clever fellow.

95

[Act III.]   LOVE'S LABOUR'S LOST.   [Scene I.

And I to sigh for her! to watch for her!
To pray for her? Go to; it is a plague
That Cupid will impose for my neglect
Of his almighty dreadful little might.

Well, I will love, write, sigh, pray, sue, and
  groan;
Some men must love my lady, and some Joan.
                                                [Exit.

RECENT NEW READINGS.

Sc. 1. p. 93.—"By my *penny* of observation."
  "By my *pain* of observation."—*Collier*.
Pain is explained as "*the pains* he [Moth] had taken in observing the characters of men and women." The connexion between "purchased" and "penny" need hardly be shown. Certainly the Corrector had taken *no pains* in observing Moth's character when he made this bald attempt to turn wit into common-place.
Sc. 1. p. 93.—"*Sirrah*, Costard, I will enfranchise thee."

"Sirrah, Costard, *marry*, I will enfranchise thee."—*Collier*.
  The word *marry* is certainly required; and we have taken the liberty not to follow Mr. Collier by its insertion after Costard, but to substitute it for the "*Sirrah*" of the original.
Sc. 1. p. 93.—"A *whitely* wanton with a velvet brow."
  "A *witty* wanton with a velvet brow."—*Collier*.
  We agree with Mr. Dyce that *whitely* (in the old editions *whitly*) "is a questionable reading, Rosaline being, as we learn from several places of the play, dark-complexioned."

ILLUSTRATIONS OF ACT III.

¹ SCENE I.—"*Concolinel.*"

THIS was doubtless the burthen of some tender air, that would "make passionate the sense of hearing." Steevens has shown that, when songs were introduced in the old comedies, the author was, in many cases, content to leave the selection of the song to the player or to the musician, indicating the place of its introduction by a stage direction.

² SCENE I.—"*A French brawl.*"

The Elizabethan gallants must have required very serious exercises in the academy of dancing, to win their loves. The very names of the dances are enough to astound those for whom the mysteries of the quadrille are sufficiently difficult: "Coratitoes, lavoltos, jigs, measures, pavins, brawls, galliards, canaries." (Brome's 'City Wit.') The name of the brawl is derived from the French *branle*, a shaking or swinging motion; and with this dance, which was performed by persons uniting hands in a circle, balls were usually opened. The opening was calculated to put the parties considerably at their ease, if the *branle* be correctly described in a little book of dialogues printed at Antwerp, 1579: "Un des gentilhommes et une des dames, estans les premiers en la danse, laissent les autres (qui cependant continuent la danse), et, se mettans dedans la dicte compagnie, vont baisans par ordre toutes les personnes qui y sont : à sçavoir, le gentilhomme les dames, et la dame les gentilshommes. Puis, ayant achevé leurs baisemens, au lieu qu'ils estoyent les premiers en la danse, se mettent les derniers. E. ceste façon de faire se continue par le gentilhomme et la dame qui sont les plus prochains, jusques à ce qu'on vienne aux derniers." We are obliged to Douce for this information; but we have often looked upon the fine old seat of the Hatton family at Stoke, the scene of Gray's "long story," and marvelled at its

"Rich windows that exclude the light,
And passages that lead to nothing,"

without being aware that the "grave Lord Keeper" had such arduous duties to perform :—

"Full oft within the spacious walls,
  When he had fifty winters o'er him,
My grave Lord-Keeper led the brawls;
  The seal and maces danc'd before him.
His bushy beard, and shoe-strings green,
  His high-crown'd hat, and satin doublet,
Mov'd the stout heart of England's queen,
  Though Pope and Spaniard could not trouble it."

ILLUSTRATIONS OF ACT III.

With regard to the musical character of the *brawl* or *branle* (anciently *bransle*), it is described by De Castilbon as a gay, round dance, the air is short, and *en rondeau*, i.e. ending at each repetition with the first part. Mersenne (*Harmonie Universelle*, 1636) enumerates and describes several kinds of *branle* and gives examples, in notes, of each. In the *Orchesographie* of Thoinot Arbeau (1588) is the annexed specimen of this dance:—

³ SCENE I.—"*Canary to it.*"

Canary, or *canaries*, an old lively dance. Sir John Hawkins is quite mistaken in supposing this to be of English invention; it most probably originated in Spain, though, from the name, many have attributed its origin to the Canary Islands, instead of concluding, what is most likely, that it was there imported from the civilized mother-country. Thoinot Arbeau and Mersenne both give the tune, but in different forms. That of the latter is thus noted:—

Purcell, in his opera, *Dioclesian*, (1691,) introduces a *canaries*, wh ch, as well as the above from Mersenne, seems modelled after that published by Arbeau. Purcell's is set for four bowed instruments, accompanied, most probably, by hautboys; and as the work in which it appears is very rare, and the tune but little if at all known, we here insert an adaptation of it, which retains all the notes in the original·

⁴ SCENE I.—"*With your hat, penthouse-like.*"

In the extremely clever engraved title-page to Burton's "Anatomy of Melancholy," the inamorato, who wears " his hat pent-house like o'er the shop of his eyes," is represented as an example of love melancholy. We have given the figure at the end of Act III., as an impersonation of Moth's description: which may also refer to Biron's ner vocation.

LOVE'S LABOUR'S LOST.

'SCENE I.—"*The hobby-horse is forgot.*"

The hobby-horses which people ride in the present day are generally very quiet animals, which give little offence to public opinion. But the hobby-horse to which Shakspere here alludes, and to which he has alluded also in Hamlet, was an animal considered by the Puritans so dangerous that they exerted all their power to banish him from the May-games. The people, however, clung to him with wonderful pertinacity; and it is most probably for this reason that, when an individual cherishes a small piece of folly which he is unwilling to give up, it is called his hobby-horse. The hobby-horse was turned out of the May-games with Friar Tuck and Maid Marian, as savouring something of popery; and some wag wrote his epitaph as described by Hamlet,—

"For, O, for, O, the hobby-horse is forgot."

The hobby-horse of the May-games required a person of considerable skill to manage him, although his body was only of wicker-work, and his head and neck of pasteboard. Sogliardo, in Ben Jonson's 'Every Man out of his Humour,' describes how he danced in him :—

"*Sogliardo.*—Nay, look you, sir, there's ne'er a gentleman in the country has the like humours for the hobby-horse as I have; I have the method for the threading of the needle and all, the——

Carlo.—How, the method!

Sog.—Ay, the leigerity for that, and the whighhie, and the daggers in the nose, and the travels of the egg from finger to finger, and all the humours incident to the quality. The horse hangs at home in my parlour. I'll keep it for a monument as long as I live, sure."

Strutt, in his antiquarian romance of 'Queen-hoo Hall,' has described at length the gambols of the hobby-horse and the dragon and Friar Tuck, which, perhaps, may be as well understood from the following engraving.

'SCENE I.—"*The boy hath sold him a bargain.*"

This comedy is running over with allusions to country sports—one of the many proofs that in its original shape it may be assigned to the author's greenest years. The sport which so delights Costard about the fox, the ape, and the humble-bee, has been explained by Capell, whose lumbering and obscure comments upon Shakspere have been pillaged and sneered at by the other commentators. In this instance they take no notice of him. It seems, according to Capell, that "selling a bargain" consisted in drawing a person in by some stratagem to proclaim himself fool by his own lips; and thus, when Moth makes his master repeat the l'envoy ending in the goose, he proclaims himself a goose, according to the rustic wit, which Costard calls "selling a bargain well." "Fast and loose," to which he alludes, was another holiday sport; and the goose that ended the market alludes to the proverb "three women and a goose make a market."

ILLUSTRATIONS OF ACT III.

⁷ SCENE I.—"*Of trotting paritors.*"

The paritor, apparitor, is the officer of the Ecclesiastical Court who carries out citations—often, in old times, against offenders who were prompted by the

"Liege of all loiterers."

⁸ SCENE I.—"*And I to be a corporal of his field.*"

A corporal of the field was an officer in some degree resembling our *aide-de-camp*, according to a passage in Lord Strafford's Letters. But, according to Styward's 'Pathway of Martial Discipline,'

1581, of four corporals of the field, two had charge of the shot, and two of the pikes and bills.

⁹ SCENE I.—"*And wear his colours like a tumbler's hoop.*"

The tumbler was a great itinerant performer in the days of Shakspere, as he is still. His hoop, which was a necessary accompaniment of his feats, was adorned with ribands. Strutt, in his 'Sports,' has given us some representations of the antics which these ancient promoters of mirth exhibited; and they differ very slightly from those which still delight the multitude at country fairs.

SCENE I.—"*Like a German clock.*"

The Germans were the great clock-makers of the sixteenth century. The clock at Hampton Court, which, according to the inscription, was set up in 1540, is said to be the first ever made in England. Sir Samuel Meyrick possessed a table-clock of German manufacture, the representations of costume on which show it to be of the time of Elizabeth. It has a double set of hours, namely, from one to twenty-four, which was probably peculiar to the clocks of this period, as we may gather from Othello :—

"He'll watch the horologe a double set."

It is most probable that the German clock,

"Still a repairing; ever out of frame;
And never going aright,"

was of the common kind which we now call Dutch clocks.

ACT IV.

SCENE I.—*Another part of the Park.*

Enter the PRINCESS, ROSALINE, MARIA, KA-
THARINE, BOYET, *Lords, Attendants, and a*
Forester.

Prin. Was that the king, that spurr'd his
  horse so hard
Against the steep uprising of the hill?
  Boyet. I know not; but, I think, it was not
    be.
  Prin. Whoe'er he was, he show'd a mount-
    ing mind.
Well, lords, to-day we shall have our despatch;
On Saturday we will return to France.—
Then, forester, my friend, where is the bush,
That we must stand and play the murderer in?¹
  For. Here by, upon the edge of yonder cop-
    pice;
A stand, where you may make the fairest shoot.
  Prin. I thank my beauty, I am fair that
    shoot,
And thereupon thou speak'st, the fairest shoot.
  For. Pardon me, madam, for I meant not so.
  Prin. What, what! first praise me, and then
    again say, no?
O short-liv'd pride! Not fair? alack for woe!
  For. Yes, madam, fair.
  Prin.   Nay, never paint me now;
Where fair is not, praise cannot mend the brow.

Here, good my glass,ᵃ take this for telling true;
        [*Giving him money.*
Fair payment for foul words is more than due.
  For. Nothing but fair is that which you in-
    herit.
  Prin. See, see, my beauty will be sav'd by
    merit.
O heresy in fair, fit for these days!
A giving hand, though foul, shall have fair
    praise.—
But come, the bow:—Now mercy goes to kill,
And shooting well is then accounted ill.
Thus will I save my credit in the shoot:
Not wounding, pity would not let me do't;
If wounding, then it was to show my skill,
That more for praise, than purpose, meant to kill.
And, out of question, so it is sometimes;
Glory grows guilty of detested crimes;
When, for fame's sake, for praise, an outward
    part,
We bend to that the working of the heart:
As I, for praise alone, now seek to spill
The poor deer's blood, that my heart means no
    ill.
  Boyet. Do not curstᵇ wives hold that self-
    sovereigntyᶜ

ᵃ *Good my glass.* The Forester is the metaphorical glass of the Princess.
ᵇ *Curst*—shrewish.
ᶜ *Self-sovereignty*—used in the same way as self-sufficiency.—not a sovereignty over themselves, but *in themselves*.

101

Only for praise' sake, when they strive to be
Lords o'er their lords?
 Prin. Only for praise: and praise we may
 afford
To any lady that subdues a lord.

Enter COSTARD.

Boyet. Here comes a member of the com-
 monwealth.
 Cost. God dig-you-den[a] all! Pray you, which
is the head lady?
 Prin. Thou shalt know her, fellow, by the
'est that have no heads.
 Cost. Which is the greatest lady, the highest?
 Prin. The thickest, and the tallest.
 Cost. The thickest, and the tallest! it is so;
 truth is truth.
An your waist, mistress, were as slender as my
 wit,
One of these maids' girdles for your waist should
 be fit.
Are not you the chief woman? you are the
 thickest here.
 Prin. What's your will, sir? what's your will?
 Cost. I have a letter from monsieur Biron to
 one lady Rosaline.
 Prin. O, thy letter, thy letter; he's a good
 friend of mine:
Stand aside, good bearer.—Boyet, you can carve;
Break up this capon.
 Boyet. I am bound to serve.—
This letter is mistook, it importeth none here;
It is writ to Jaquenetta.
 Prin. We will read it, I swear:
Break the neck of the wax, and every one give
 ear.
 Boyet. [*Reads.*]

 * By heaven, that thou art fair is most infallible; true,
that thou art beauteous; truth itself, that thou art lovely:
More fairer than fair, beautiful than beauteous, truer than
truth itself, have commiseration on thy heroical vassal!
The magnanimous and most illustrate king Cophetua set
eye upon the pernicious and indubitate beggar Zenelophon;
and he it was that might rightly say, *veni, vidi, vici;* which
to annotanize[b] in the vulgar, (O base and obscure vulgar!)
videlicet, he came, saw, and overcame; he came, one; saw,
two; overcame, three. Who came? the king; Why did he
come? to see; Why did he see? to overcome: To whom
came he? to the beggar; What saw he? the beggar; Who
overcame he? the beggar: The conclusion is victory; On
whose side? the king's; the captive is enrich'd; On whose
side? the beggar's: The catastrophe is a nuptial: On whose
side? the king's?—no, on both in one, or one in both. I
am the king; for so stands the comparison: thou the beggar; for so witnesseth thy lowliness. Shall I command thy
love? I may: Shall I enforce thy love? I could: Shall I

 [a] *Dig-you-den.* The popular corruption of *give you good
den.*
 [b] In the folio and quarto, *annothanize.* Mr. Dyce advo-
cates the modern *anatomise.*

entreat thy love? I will: What shalt thou exchange for
rags? robes; For titles, titles; For thyself, me. Thus, ex-
pecting thy reply, I profane my lips on thy foot, my eyes on
thy picture, and my heart on thy every part.
 Thine, in the dearest design of industry,
 DON ADRIANO DE ARMADO.'

Thus dost thou hear the Nemean lion roar
 'Gainst thee, thou lamb, that standest as his
 prey;
Submissive fall his princely feet before,
 And he from forage will incline to play:
But if thou strive, poor soul, what art thou then?
Food for his rage, repasture for his den.
 Prin. What plume of feathers is he that in-
 dited this letter?
What vane? what weather-cock? did you ever
 hear better?
 Boyet. I am much deceived, but I remember
 the style.
 Prin. Else your memory is bad, going o'er it
 erewhile.
 Boyet. This Armado is a Spaniard, that keeps
 here in court;
A phantasm, a Monarcho,[2] and one that makes
 sport
To the prince, and his book-mates.
 Prin. Thou, fellow, a word:
Who gave thee this letter?
 Cost. I told you; my lord.
 Prin. To whom shouldst thou give it?
 Cost. From my lord to my lady.
 Prin. From which lord, to which lady?
 Cost. From my lord Biron, a good master of
 mine;
To a lady of France, that he call'd Rosaline.
 Prin. Thou hast mistaken his letter. Come,
 lords, away.
Here, sweet, put up this; 't will be thine another
 day.   [*Exit* PRINCESS *and train.*
 Boyet. Who is the suitor? who is the suitor?*
 Ros. Shall I teach you to know?
 Boyet. Ay, my continent of beauty.
 Ros. Why, she that bears the bow.
Finely put off!
 Boyet. My lady goes to kill horns; but, if
 thou marry,
Hang me by the neck, if horns that year mis-
 carry.
Finely put on!
 Ros. Well then, I am the shooter.
 Boyet. And who is your deer?

 * *Suitor.* The old copies read "who is the *shooter?*"
But Boyet asks, "who is the suitor?"—and Rosaline gives
him a quibbling answer—"she that bears the bow." We
see, then, that *suitor* and *shooter* were pronounced alike in
Shakspere's day; and that the Scotch and Irish pronunciation of this word, which we laugh at now, is nearer the
old English than our own pronunciation.

Ros. If we choose by the horns, yourself come not near.
Finely put on, indeed!—
Mar. You still wrangle with her, Boyet, and she strikes at the brow.
Boyet. But she herself is hit lower: Have I hit her now?
Ros. Shall I come upon thee with an old saying, that was a man when king Pepin of France was a little boy, as touching the hit it?
Boyet. So I may answer thee with one as old, that was a woman when queen Guinever of Britain was a little wench, as touching the hit it.
Ros. [*Singing.*]
   Thou canst not hit it, hit it, hit it,
   Thou canst not hit it, my good man.
Boyet.
   An I cannot, cannot, cannot,
   An I cannot, another can.
             [*Exeunt* Ros. *and* Kath.
Cost. By my troth, most pleasant! how both did fit it!
Mar. A mark marvellous well shot; for they both did hit it.
Boyet. A mark! O, mark but that mark; A mark says my lady!
Let the mark have a prick in 't to mete at, if it may be.
Mar. Wide o' the bow hand! I' faith, your hand is out.
Cost. Indeed, a' must shoot nearer, or he 'll ne'er hit the clout.
Boyet. An if my hand be out, then, belike your hand is in.
Cost. Then will she get the upshot by cleaving the pin.
Mar. Come, come, you talk greasily, your lips grow foul.
Cost. She 's too hard for you at pricks, sir; challenge her to bowl.
Boyet. I fear too much rubbing; Good night, my good owl.
            [*Exeunt* Boyet *and* Maria.
Cost. By my soul, a swain! a most simple clown!
Lord, lord! how the ladies and I have put him down!
O' my troth, most sweet jests! most incony vulgar wit!
When it comes so smoothly off, so obscenely, as it were, so fit.
Armado o' the one side,—O, a most dainty man!
To see him walk before a lady, and to bear her fan!
To see him kiss his hand! and how most sweetly a' will swear!
And his page o' t' other side, that handful of wit!
Ah, heavens, it is a most pathetical nit!
Sola, sola!   *Shouting within.*
           [*Exit* Costard, *running*.

SCENE II.—*The same.*

Enter Holofernes,[a] *Sir* Nathaniel, *and* Dull.

Nath. Very reverent sport, truly; and done in the testimony of a good conscience.
Hol. The deer was, as you know, *sanguis*,—in blood;[b] ripe as a pomewater,[c] who now hangeth like a jewel in the ear of *cœlo*,—the sky, the welkin, the heaven; and anon falleth like a crab, on the face of *terra*,—the soil, the land, the earth.
Nath. Truly, master Holofernes, the epithets are sweetly varied, like a scholar at the least: But, sir, I assure ye, it was a buck of the first head.
Hol. Sir Nathaniel, *haud credo*.
Dull. 'T was not a *haud credo*; t' was a pricket[d]
Hol. Most barbarous intimation! yet a kind of insinuation, as it were *in via*, in way, of explication; *facere*, as it were, replication, or, rather, *ostentare*, to show, as it were, his inclination, after his undressed, unpolished, uneducated, unpruned, untrained, or rather unlettered, or, ratherest, unconfirmed fashion,—to insert again my *haud credo* for a deer.
Dull. I said, the deer was not a *haud credo*; 't was a pricket.
Hol. Twice sod simplicity, *bis coctus*!—O thou monster ignorance, how deformed dost thou look!
Nath. Sir, he hath never fed of the dainties that are bred in a book; he hath not eat paper, as it were; he hath not drunk ink: his intellect is not replenished; he is only an animal, only sensible in the duller parts;
And such barren plants are set before us, that we thankful should be
(Which we of taste and feeling are) for those parts that do fructify in us more than he.

---

[a] In the old editions Holofernes is distinguished as "The Pedant."
[b] All the old copies have this reading. Steevens would read " in *sanguis*—blood."
[c] *Pomewater*—a species of apple
[d] *Pricket* Dull contradicts Sir Nathaniel as to the age of the buck. The parson asserts that it was "a buck of the first head"—the constable says it was "a pricket." The buck acquires a new name every year as he approaches to maturity. The first year he is a fawn; the second, a pricket;—the third, a sorrell;—the fourth, a soare;—the fifth, a buck of the first head;—the sixth, a complete buck.

For as it would ill become me to be vain, indiscreet, or a fool,
So, were there a patch set on learning, to see him in a school :
But *omne bene*, say I; being of an old father's mind,
Many can brook the weather, that love not the wind.

Dull. You two are bookmen : Can you tell me by your wit,
What was a month old at Cain's birth, that's not five weeks old as yet?

Hol. Dictynna, good man Dull; Dictynna, good man Dull.

Dull. What is Dictynna?

Nath. A title to Phœbe, to Luna, to the moon.

Hol. The moon was a month old, when Adam was no more ;
And raught[a] not to five weeks, when he came to five-score.
The allusion holds in the exchange.

Dull. 'T is true indeed; the collusion holds in the exchange.

Hol. God comfort thy capacity! I say, the allusion holds in the exchange.

Dull. And I say the pollution holds in the exchange; for the moon is never but a month old : and I say beside, that 't was a pricket that the princess killed.

Hol. Sir Nathaniel, will you hear an extemporal epitaph on the death of the deer? and, to humour the ignorant, I have called the deer the princess killed, a pricket.

Nath. *Perge*, good master Holofernes, *perge*; so it shall please you to abrogate scurrility.

Hol. I will something affect the letter ;[b] for it argues facility.

The praiseful princess pierc'd and prick'd a pretty pleasing pricket ;
Some say a sore ; but not a sore, till now made sore with shooting.
The dogs did yell ; put l to sore, then sorel jumps from thicket ;
Or pricket, sore, or else sorel ; the people fall a hooting.
If sore be sore, then L to sore makes fifty sores ;[c] O sore L !
Of one sore I an hundred make, by adding but one more L.

Nath. A rare talent !

Dull. If a talent be a claw,[d] look how he claws him with a talent.

Hol. This is a gift that I have, simple, simple ; a foolish extravagant spirit, full of forms, figures, shapes, objects, ideas, apprehensions, motions, revolutions : these are begot in the ventricle of memory, nourished in the womb of *pia mater*, and delivered upon the mellowing of occasion : But the gift is good in those in whom it is acute, and I am thankful for it.

Nath. Sir, I praise the Lord for you; and so may my parishioners ; for their sons are well tutored by you, and their daughters profit very greatly under you : you are a good member of the commonwealth.

Hol. Mehercle, if their sons be ingenious, they shall want no instruction : if their daughters be capable, I will put it to them : But, *vir sapit qui pauca loquitur*. A soul feminine saluteth us.

Enter JAQUENETTA *and* COSTARD.

Jaq. God give you good morrow, master person.[a]

Hol. Master person, *quasi* pers-on. And if one should be pierced, which is the one ?

Cost. Marry, master schoolmaster, he that is likest to a hogshead.

Hol. Of piercing a hogshead ! a good lustre of conceit in a turf of earth; fire enough for a flint, pearl enough for a swine : 't is pretty ; it is well.

Jaq. Good master parson, be so good as read me this letter; it was given me by Costard, and sent me from Don Armado; I beseech you, read it.

Hol. Fauste. precor gelidâ quando pecus omne sub umbrâ
Ruminat,—and so forth. Ah, good old Mantuan ![b]
I may speak of thee as the traveller doth of Venice :
—— *Vinegia, Vinegia,*
Chi non te vede, ei non te pregia.[c]
Old Mantuan! old Mantuan! Who understandeth thee not, loves thee not.—*Ut, re, sol, la, mi, fa.*[d]—Under pardon, sir, what are the

---

[a] *Master person.* The derivation of *parson* was, perhaps, commonly understood in Shakspere's time, and *parson* and *person* were used indifferently. Blackstone has explained the word : " A parson, *persona ecclesiœ*, is one that hath full possession of all the rights of a parochial church. He is called *parson, persona*, because by his *person*, the church, which is an invisible body, is represented."—*Commentaries*, b. i.

[b] The good old Mantuan was Joh. Baptist Mantuanus, a Carmelite, whose Eclogues were translated into English by George Turberville, in 1567. His first Eclogue commences with *Fauste, precor gelidâ*; and Farnaby, in his preface to Martial, says that pedants thought more highly of the *Fauste, precor gelidâ*, than of the *Arma virumque cano*. Here, again, the unlearned Shakspere hits the mark when he meddles with learned masters.

[c] A proverbial expression applied to Venice, which we find thus in Ho—ll's Letters :—
" Venetia, Venetia, chi non te vede, non te pregia,
Ma chi t'ha troppo veduto le dispregia."

[d] The pedant is in his altitudes. He has quoted Latin and Italian ; and in his self-satisfaction he *sol-fas*, to recreate himself and to show his musical skill.

---

[a] *Raught*—reached.
[b] *Affect the letter*—affect alliteration.
[c] The pedant brings in the Roman numeral L, as the sign of fifty.
[d] Talon was formerly written *talent*.

contents? Or, rather, as Horace says in his— What, my soul, verses?

Nath. Ay, sir, and very learned.

Hol. Let me hear a staff, a stanza, a verse; *Lege, domine.*

Nath.

If love make me forsworn, how shall I swear to love?
Ah, never faith could hold, if not to beauty vowed!
Though to myself forsworn, to thee I'll faithful prove:
Those thoughts to me were oaks, to thee like osiers bowed.*
Study his bias leaves, and makes his book thine eyes,
Where all those pleasures live, that art would comprehend:
If knowledge be the mark, to know thee shall suffice;
Well learned is that tongue, that well can thee commend;
All ignorant that soul, that sees thee without wonder;
(Which is to me some praise, that I thy parts admire;)
Thy eye Jove's lightning bears, thy voice his dreadful thunder,
Which, not to anger bent, is music, and sweet fire.
Celestial as thou art, oh pardon, love, this wrong,
That sings heaven's praise with such an earthly tongue!

Hol. You find not the apostrophes, and so miss the accent: let me supervise the canzonet. Here are only numbers ratified; but, for the elegancy, facility, and golden cadence of poesy, *caret.* Ovidius Naso was the man: and why, indeed, Naso; but for smelling out the odoriferous flowers of fancy, the jerks of invention? *Imitari,* is nothing: so doth the hound his master, the ape his keeper, the tired horse his rider. But damosella virgin, was this directed to you?

Jaq. Ay, sir, from one Monsieur Biron, one of the strange queen's lords.

Hol. I will overglance the superscript. "To the snow-white hand of the most beauteous lady Rosaline." I will look again on the intellect of the letter, for the nomination of the party writing to the person written unto: "Your ladyship's in all desired employment, BIRON." Sir Nathaniel, this Biron is one of the votaries with the king; and here he hath framed a letter to a sequent of the stranger queen's, which, accidentally, or by the way of progression, hath miscarried.—Trip and go, my sweet; deliver this paper into the royal hand of the king; it may concern much: Stay not thy compliment; I forgive thy duty; adieu.

Jaq. Good Costard, go with me.—Sir, God save your life!

Cost. Have with thee, my girl.

[*Exeunt* COST. *and* JAQ.

Nath. Sir, you have done this in the fear of

* "You find not the apostrophes," says Holofernes. We judge it, therefore, right to print vowed and bowed, instead of vow'd and bow'd.

God, very religiously; and, as a certain father saith——

Hol. Sir, tell not me of the father, I do fear colourable colours. But, to return to the verses: Did they please you, Sir Nathaniel?

Nath. Marvellous well for the pen.

Hol. I do dine to-day at the father's of a certain pupil of mine; where if, before repast, it shall please you to gratify the table with a grace, I will, on my privilege I have with the parents of the aforesaid child or pupil, undertake your *ben venuto;* where I will prove those verses to be very unlearned, neither savouring of poetry, wit, nor invention: I beseech your society.

Nath. And thank you too: for society (saith the text) is the happiness of life.

Hol. And, certes, the text most infallibly concludes it.—Sir, [*to* DULL] I do invite you too; you shall not say me, nay: *pauca verba.* Away; the gentles are at their game, and we will to our recreation. [*Exeunt.*

SCENE III.—*Another part of the same.*

Enter BIRON, *with a paper.*

Biron. The king he is hunting the deer; I am coursing myself: they have pitched a toil; I am toiling in a pitch; pitch that defiles; defile! a foul word. Well, Sit thee down, sorrow! for so they say the fool said, and so say I, and I the fool. Well proved, wit! By the Lord, this love is as mad as Ajax: it kills sheep; it kills me, I a sheep: Well proved again on my side! I will not love: If I do, hang me; i' faith, I will not. O, but her eye,—by this light, but for her eye, I would not love her; yes, for her two eyes. Well, I do nothing in the world but lie, and lie in my throat. By heaven, I do love: and it hath taught me to rhyme, and to be melancholy; and here is part of my rhyme, and here my melancholy. Well, she hath one o' my sonnets already: the clown bore it, the fool sent it, and the lady hath it: sweet clown, sweeter fool, sweetest lady! By the world, I would not care a pin if the other three were in: Here comes one with a paper; God give him grace to groan. [*Gets up into a tree.*

Enter the KING, *with a paper.*

King. Ah me!

Biron. [*Aside.*] Shot, by heaven!—Proceed, sweet Cupid; thou hast thump'd him with thy bird-bolt under the left pap:—I' faith secrets.—

King. [*Reads.*]

So sweet a kiss the golden sun gives not
To those fresh morning drops upon the rose,
As thy eye-beams, when their fresh rays have smote
The night of dew that on my cheeks down flows;
Nor shines the silver moon one half so bright
Through the transparent bosom of the deep,
As doth thy face through tears of mine give light
Thou shin'st in every tear that I do weep,
No drop but as a coach doth carry thee,
So ridest thou triumphing in my woe:
Do but behold the tears that swell in me,
And they thy glory through my grief will show:
But do not love thyself; then thou wilt keep
My tears for glasses, and still make me weep.
O queen of queens, how far dost thou excel!
No thought can think, nor tongue of mortal tell.—

How shall she know my griefs? I'll drop the paper;
Sweet leaves shade folly. Who is he comes here? [*Steps aside.*

Enter LONGAVILLE, *with a paper.*

What, Longaville! and reading! listen, ear.
Biron. Now, in thy likeness, one more fool, appear! [*Aside.*
Long. Ah me! I am forsworn.
Biron. Why, he comes in like a perjure, wearing papers.[b] [*Aside.*
King. In love, I hope; Sweet fellowship in shame! [*Aside.*
Biron. One drunkard loves another of the name. [*Aside.*
Long. Am I the first that have been perjur'd so?
Biron. [*Aside.*] I could put thee in comfort; not by two, that I know:
Thou mak'st the triumviry, the corner cap of society,
The shape of Love's Tyburn that hangs up simplicity.
Long. I fear, these stubborn lines lack power to move:
O sweet Maria, empress of my love
These numbers will I tear and write in prose.
Biron. [*Aside.*] O, rhymes are guards[c] on wanton Cupid's hose:
Disfigure not his slop.[d]
Long. This same shall go. — [*He reads the sonnet.*

Did not the heavenly rhetoric of thine eye
('Gainst whom the world cannot hold argument)
Persuade my heart to this false perjury!
'ows for thee broke deserve not punishment.

[a] Smot – the old preterite of *smote*.
[b] The *perjure*—the perjurer—when exposed on the pillory – wore "papers of perjury."
[c] *Guards*—the hems or boundaries of a garment—generally ornamented.
[d] The original has *shop*. Theobald introduced *slop*: *hose*, as a part of dress, is a *slop*.

106

A woman I forswore; but, I will prove,
Thou being a goddess, I forswore not thee:
My vow was earthly, thou a heavenly love;
Thy grace being gain'd, cures all disgrace in me.
Vows are but breath, and breath a vapour is:
Then thou, fair sun, which on my earth dost shine,
Exhal'st this vapour vow; in thee it is:
If broken then, it is no fault of mine,
If by me broke. What fool is not so wise,
To lose an oath to win a paradise?

Biron. [*Aside.*] This is the liver vein, which makes flesh a deity;
A green goose, a goddess: pure, pure idolatry.
God amend us, God amend! we are much out o' the way.

Enter DUMAIN, *with a paper.*

Long. By whom shall I send this?—Company I stay. [*Stepping aside.*
Biron. [*Aside.*] All hid, all hid, an old infant play:
Like a demi-god here sit I in the sky,
And wretched fools' secrets heedfully o'er-eye.
More sacks to the mill![1] O heavens, I have my wish;
Dumain transform'd: four woodcocks in a dish!
Dum. O most divine Kate!
Biron. O most profane coxcomb [*Aside.*
Dum. By heaven, the wonder of a mortal eye!
Biron. By earth she is not, corporal:[a] there you lie. [*Aside.*
Dum. Her amber hairs for foul have amber coted.[b]
Biron. An amber-colour'd raven was well noted. [*Aside.*
Dum. As upright as the cedar.
Biron. Stoop, I say;
Her shoulder is with child. [*Aside.*
Dum. As fair as day.
Biron. Ay, as some days; but then no sun must shine. [*Aside.*
Dum. O that I had my wish!
Long. And I had mine!
[*Aside.*
King. And I mine too, good lord! [*Aside.*
Biron. Amen, so I had mine: Is not that a good word? [*Aside.*
Dum. I would forget her; but a fever she Reigns in my blood, and will remember'd be.

[a] *She is not, corporal.* The received reading is, "She is but corporal." Ours is the ancient reading; and Douce repudiates the modern change. Biron calls Dumain, corporal, as he had formerly named himself (Act III.) "corporal of his field,"—of Cupid's field.
[b] *Coted*—quoted.

Biron. A fever in your blood! why, then
    incision
Would let her out in saucers; Sweet misprision!
                                     [*Aside.*
Dum. Once more I'll read the ode that I have
    writ.
Biron. Once more I'll mark how love can
    vary wit.   [*Aside.*
Dum.
> On a day, (alack the day!)
> Love, whose month is ever May,
> Spied a blossom, passing fair,
> Playing in the wanton air.
> Through the velvet leaves the wind,
> All unseen, 'gan passage find;
> That the lover, sick to death,
> Wish'd himself the heaven's breath.
> Air, quoth he, thy cheeks may blow;
> Air, would I might triumph so!
> But, alack, my hand is sworn
> Ne'er to pluck thee from thy thorn:
> Vow, alack, for youth unmeet,
> Youth so apt to pluck a sweet
> Do not call it sin in me,
> That I am forsworn for thee:
> Thou for whom Jove would swear
> Juno but an Ethiop were;
> And deny himself for Jove,
> Turning mortal for thy love.[3]

This will I send; and something else more plain,
That shall express my true love's fasting pain.
O, would the King, Biron, and Longaville,
Were lovers too! Ill, to example ill,
Would from my forehead wipe a perjur'd note;
For none offend, where all alike do dote.
    Long. Dumain, [*advancing*] thy love is far
        from charity,
That in love's grief desir'st society:
You may look pale, but I should blush, I know,
To be o'erheard, and taken napping so.
    King. Come, sir, [*advancing*] you blush · as
        his your case is such;
You chide at him, offending twice as much:
You do not love Maria; Longaville
Did never sonnet for her sake compile;
Nor never lay his wreathed arms athwart
His loving bosom, to keep down his heart.
I have been closely shrouded in this bush,
And mark'd you both, and for you both did
    blush.
I heard your guilty rhymes, observ'd your
    fashion;
Saw sighs reek from you, noted well your
    passion;
Ah me! says one; O Jove! the other cries;
One, her hairs were gold, crystal the other's
    eyes:

---

[a] Pope introduced ev'n—other editors even—neither of which is the reading of the originals, or required by the rhythm.

You would for paradise break faith and troth;
                                     [*To* Long.
And Jove, for your love, would infringe an oath.
                                    [*To* Dumain.
What will Biron say, when that he shall hear
Faith infringed, which such zeal did swear?
How will he scorn! how will he spend his wit!
How will he triumph, leap, and laugh at it!
For all the wealth that ever I did see,
I would not have him know so much by me.
    Biron. Now step I forth to whip hypocrisy.—
Ah, good my liege, I pray thee, pardon me:
                            [*Descends from the tree.*
Good heart, what grace hast thou, thus to reprove
These worms for loving, that art most in love?
Your eyes do make no coaches; in your tears,
There is no certain princess that appears;
You'll not be perjur'd, 'tis a hateful thing;
Tush, none but minstrels like of sonneting.
But are you not ashamed? nay, are you not,
All three of you, to be thus much o'ershot?
You found his mote; the king your mote[a] did
    see;
But I a beam do find in each of three.
O, what a scene of foolery have I seen,
Of sighs, of groans, of sorrow, and of teen!
O me, with what strict patience have I sat,
To see a king transformed to a gnat!
To see great Hercules whipping a gig,
And profound Solomon tuning a jig,
And Nestor play at push-pin with the boys,
And critic Timon laugh at idle toys!
Where lies thy grief, O tell me, good Dumain?
And, gentle Longaville, where lies thy pain?
And where my liege's? all about the breast :—
A caudle, ho!
    King.   Too bitter is thy jest.
Are we betray'd thus to thy over-view?
    Biron. Not you to me, but I betray'd by
        you:[b]
I, that am honest; I, that hold it sin
To break the vow I am engaged in;
I am betray'd, by keeping company
With men like men,[c] of strange inconstancy.
When shall you see me write a thing in rhyme?
Or groan for Joan? or spend a minute's time
In pruning me? When shall you hear that I
Will praise a hand, a foot, a face, an eye,
A gait, a state, a brow, a breast, a waist,
A leg, a limb?—

---

[a] *Mote.* The quarto and folio have each the synonymous word moth.
[b] The original has —
    "Not you by me, but I betray'd to you."
Monck Mason suggested the transposition.
[c] *Men like men.* So the old copies. The epithet *strange* was introduced in the second folio. Sidney Walker communicated to Mr. Dyce, who adopted it, the reading—
    "With men like you, men of inconstancy."

King. Soft; whither away so fast?
A true man, or a thief, that gallops so?
  Biron. I post from love; good lover, let me go.

  Enter JAQUENETTA *and* COSTARD.

  Jaq. God bless the king!
  King. What present hast thou there?
  Cost. Some certain treason.
  King. What makes treason here?
  Cost. Nay, it makes nothing, sir.
  King. If it mar nothing neither,
The treason, and you, go in peace away together.
  Jaq. I beseech your grace, let this letter be
    read;
Our parson misdoubts it; it was treason, he
    said.
  King. Biron, read it over.
        [*Giving him the letter.*
Where hadst thou it?
  Jaq. Of Costard.
  King. Where hadst thou it?
  Cost. Of Dun Adramadio, Dun Adramadio.
  King. How now! what is in you? why dost
    thou tear it?
  Biron. A toy, my liege, a toy; your grace
    needs not fear it.
  Long. It did move him to passion, and there-
    fore let's hear it.
  Dum. It is Biron's writing, and here is his
    name.   [*Picks up the pieces.*
  Biron. Ah, you whoreson loggerhead, [*to*
    COSTARD] you were born to do me
    shame.—
Guilty, my lord, guilty; I confess, I confess.
  King. What?
  Biron. That you three fools lack'd me fool to
    make up the mess;
He, he, and you; and you, my liege, and I,
Are pick-purses in love, and we deserve to die.
O, dismiss this audience, and I shall tell you
    more.
  Dum. Now the number is even.
  Biron.   True, true; we are four:—
Will these turtles be gone?
  King.   Hence, sirs; away.
  Cost. Walk aside the true folk, and let the trai-
    tor stay.   [*Exeunt* COST. *and* JAQ.
  Biron. Sweet lords, sweet lovers, O let us
    embrace!
As true we are, as flesh and blood can be:
The sea will ebb and flow, heaven show his
    face;
Young blood doth not obey an old decree:
We cannot cross the cause why we are born;
Therefore, of all hands must we be forsworn.

  King. What, did these rent lines show some
    love of thine?
  Biron. Did they, quoth you? Who sees the
    heavenly Rosaline,
That, like a rude and savage man of Inde,
  At the first opening of the gorgeous east,
Bows not his vassal head: and, strucken blind,
  Kisses the base ground with obedient breast?
What peremptory eagle-sighted eye
  Dares look upon the heaven of her brow,
That is not blinded by her majesty?
  King. What zeal, what fury hath inspir'd thee
    now?
My love, her mistress, is a gracious moon;
  She, an attending star, scarce seen a light.
  Biron. My eyes are then no eyes, nor I
    Biron:
O, but for my love, day would turn to night!
Of all complexions, the cull'd sovereignty
  Do meet, as at a fair, in her fair cheek;
Where several worthies make one dignity;
  Where nothing wants, that want itself doth
    seek.
Lend me the flourish of all gentle tongues,—
  Fie, painted rhetoric! O, she needs it not
To things of sale a seller's praise belongs;
  She passes praise: then praise too short
    doth blot.
A wither'd hermit, five-score winters worn,
  Might shake off fifty, looking in her eye:
Beauty doth varnish age, as if new-born,
  And gives the crutch the cradle's infancy.
O, 't is the sun that maketh all things shine!
  King. By heaven, thy love is black as ebony!
  Biron. Is ebony like her? O wood divine!
A wife of such wood were felicity.
O, who can give an oath? where is a book?
  That I may swear, beauty doth beauty lack:
If that she learn not of her eye to look:
  No face is fair, that is not full so black.
  King. O paradox! Black is the badge of hell,
  The hue of dungeons, and the school of
    night!
And beauty's crest becomes the heavens well.
  Biron. Devils soonest tempt, resembling spirits
    of light.
O, if in black my lady's brows be deck'd,
  It mourns, that painting, and usurping hair,
Should ravish doters with a false aspect;
  And therefore is she born to make black
    fair.
Her favour turns the fashion of the days;
  For native blood is counted painting now;
And therefore red, that would avoid dispraise,
  Paints itself black to imitate her brow.

Dum. To look like her, are chimney-sweepers
   black.
Long. And, since her time, are colliers counted
   bright.
King. And Ethiops of their sweet complexion
   crack.
Dum. Dark needs no candles now, for dark
   is light.
Biron. Your mistresses dare never come in
   rain,
   For fear their colours should be wash'd away.
King. 'T were good, yours did; for, sir, to tell
   you plain,
   I'll find a fairer face not wash'd to-day.
Biron. I'll prove her fair, or talk till dooms-
   day here.
King. No devil will fright thee then so much
   as she.
Dum. I never knew man hold vile stuff so dear.
Long. Look, here's thy love: my foot and her
   face see.   [*Showing his shoe.*
Biron. O, if the streets were paved with thine
   eyes,
   Her feet were much too dainty for such
   tread!
Dum. O vile! then as she goes, what upward
   lies
   The street should see as she walk'd over head.
King. But what of this? Are we not all in love?
Biron. O, nothing so sure; and thereby all
   forsworn.
King. Then leave this chat; and, good Biron,
   now prove
   Our loving lawful, and our faith not torn.
Dum. Ay, marry, there;—some flattery for
   this evil.
Long. O, some authority how to proceed;
   Some tricks, some quillets,[a] how to cheat the
   devil.
Dum. Some salve for perjury.
Biron.   O, 't is more than need!—
Have at you then, affection's men at arms;
Consider, what you first did swear unto;—
To fast,—to study,—and to see no woman;—
Flat treason 'gainst the kingly state of youth.
Say, can you fast? your stomachs are too young;
And abstinence engenders maladies.
And where that you have vow'd to study, lords,
In that each of you hath forsworn his book:
Can you still dream, and pore, and thereon
   look?
For when would you, my lord, or you, or you,
Have found the ground of study's excellence,
Without the beauty of a woman's face?
From women's eyes this doctrine I derive:
They are the ground, the books, the academes,
From whence doth spring the true Promethean
   fire.
Why, universal plodding prisons up
The nimble spirits in the arteries;
As motion, and long-during action, tires
The sinewy vigour of the traveller.
Now, for not looking on a woman's face,
You have in that forsworn the use of eyes;
And study too, the causer of your vow:
For where is any author in the world,
Teaches such beauty as a woman's eye?
Learning is but an adjunct to ourself,
And where we are, our learning likewise is.
Then, when ourselves we see in ladies' eyes,
With ourselves,—
Do we not likewise see our learning there?
O, we have made a vow to study, lords;
And in that vow we have forsworn our books:
For when would you, my liege, or you, or you,[b]
In leaden contemplation, have found out
Such fiery numbers, as the prompting eyes
Of beauty's tutors have enrich'd you with?
Other slow arts entirely keep the brain;
And therefore finding barren practisers,
Scarce show a harvest of their heavy toil:
But love, first learned in a lady's eyes,
Lives not alone immured in the brain;[b]
But with the motion of all elements,
Courses as swift as thought in every power;
And gives to every power a double power,
Above their functions and their offices.
It adds a precious seeing to the eye;
A lover's eyes will gaze an eagle blind;
A lover's ear will hear the lowest sound,
When the suspicious head of theft is stopp'd;
Love's feeling is more soft, and sensible,
Than are the tender horns of cockled snails;
Love's tongue proves dainty Bacchus gross in
   taste:
For valour, is not love a Hercules,
Still climbing trees in the Hesperides?
Subtle as sphinx; as sweet, and musical,
As bright Apollo's lute, strung with his hair;
And, when love speaks, the voice of all the gods
Makes heaven drowsy with the harmony.[b]
Never durst poet touch a pen to write,
Until his ink were temper'd with love's sighs.

---

[a] *Quillet* and *quodlibet* each signify a fallacious subtilty—what you please—an argument without foundation. Milton says "let not human *quillets* keep back divine authority."

[b] This fine passage has been mightily obscured by the commentators. The meaning appears to us so clear amidst the blaze of poetical beauty, that an explanation is scarcely wanted:—When love speaks, the responsive harmony of the voice of all the gods makes heaven drowsy.

O, then his lines would ravish savage ears,
And plant in tyrants mild humility.
From women's eyes this doctrine I derive:
They sparkle still the right Promethean fire;
They are the books, the arts, the academes,
That show, contain, and nourish all the world;
Else, none at all in aught proves excellent;
Then fools you were these women to forswear;
Or, keeping what is sworn, you will prove fools
For wisdom's sake, a word that all men love;
Or for love's sake, a word that loves all men;
Or for men's sake, the authors of these women;
Or women's sake, by whom we men are men;
Let us once lose our oaths, to find ourselves,
Or else we lose ourselves to keep our oaths:
It is religion to be thus forsworn:
For charity itself fulfils the law;
And who can sever love from charity?
    King. Saint Cupid, then! and soldiers, to the
        field!
    Biron. Advance your standards, and upon
        them lords;
Pell-mell, down with them! but be first advis'd,
In conflict that you get the sun of them.

Long. Now to plain-dealing; lay these gloves
        by;
Shall we resolve to woo these girls of France?
    King. And win them too: therefore let us
        devise
Some entertainment for them in their tents.
    Biron. First, from the park let us conduct
        them thither;
Then, homeward, every man attach the hand
Of his fair mistress: in the afternoon
We will with some strange pastime solace them,
Such as the shortness of the time can shape;
For revels, dances, masks, and merry hours,
Fore-run fair Love, strewing her way with
        flowers.
    King. Away, away! no time shall be omitted.
That will be time, and may by us be fitted.
    Biron. Allons! Allons!—Sow'd cockle reap'd
        no corn;
    And justice always whirls in equal mea-
        sure:
Light wenches may prove plagues to men for-
        sworn;
If so, our copper buys no better treasure.
                                    [*Exeunt.*

RECENT NEW READINGS.

Sc. I. p. 101.—" O heresy in *fair*, fit for these days!"
" O heresy in *faith*, fit for these days!"—*Collier.*
The context shows that *fair* is the right word: it is used for beauty, as it often was. (See Comedy of Errors.)
Sc. I. p. 103.—" Lousing babies in her eyes, his passion to declare."—*Collier.*
This is a new line, inserted after—
" To see him kiss his hand! and how most sweetly a' will swear!"
Is the new line Shakspere's or the Corrector's? In Fletcher's 'Loyal Subject,' first printed in 1647, we have the very words:—
    " Look babies in your eyes, my pretty sweet one."
Massinger, too, has the same words in 'The Renegade,' and Herrick repeats the image. The Corrector had not far to seek for a new rhyming line. We cannot suppose he lived after Moore, who popularised the image.

Sc. III p. 108.—" The hue of dungeons, and the *school* of night."
This is the reading of the original, and is adopted by Tieck in his translation, as giving the notion of something dark, wearisome, and comfortless. Theobald corrected it to *scowl*, and also suggested *stole*. Mr. Collier's Corrector gives *shade*, which Mr. White has adopted; and Mr. Dyce suggests *soil*.
Sc. III. p. 109.—" Teaches such *beauty* as a woman's eye."
" Teaches such *learning* as a woman's eye."—*Collier.*
The name æsthetics is modern; but Shakspere might, out of his own self-consciousness, have known that the philosophy of beauty was a science. Mr. Staunton would prefer *study*, if changed at all; Mr. White gives *learning*, and says *beauty* is an easy misprint.

ILLUSTRATIONS OF ACT IV.

¹ SCENE I.—   "*Where is the bush,
That we must stand and play the murderer in?*"

ROYAL and noble ladies, in the days of Elizabeth, delighted in the somewhat unrefined sport of shooting deer with a cross-bow. In the "alleys green" of Windsor or of Greenwich Parks, the queen would take her stand on an elevated platform, and, as the pricket or the buck was driven past her, would aim the death-shaft, amidst the acclamations of her admiring courtiers. The ladies, it appears, were skilful enough at this sylvan butchering. Sir Francis Leake writes to the Earl of Shrewsbury, " Your lordship has sent me a very great and fat stag, the welcomer being stricken by your right honourable lady's hand." The practice was as old as the romances of the middle ages; but in those days the ladies were sometimes not so expert as the Countess of Shrewsbury; for, in the history of Prince Arthur, a fair huntress wounds Sir Launcelot of the Lake, instead of the stag at which she aims.

² SCENE I.—"*A Monarcho.*"

This allusion is to a mad Italian, commonly called the *monarch*, whose epitaph, or description, was written by Churchyard, in 1580. His notion was, that he was sovereign of the world; and one of his conceits, recorded by Scot in his "Discovery of Witchcraft," 1584, was, that all the ships that came into the port of London belonged to him.

³ SCENE III.—"*On a day,*" &c.

This exquisite canzonet was published in the miscellany called "The Passionate Pilgrim," and it also appears in "England's Helicon," 1614. The line,

"Thou for whom Jove would swear,"

reads thus, in all the old copies; but some modern editors have tampered with the rhythm, by giving us

"Thou for whom even Jove would swear."

In the same way, the fine pause after the third syllable of

"There to meet with Macbeth,"

has been sought to be destroyed by thrusting in another syllable.

This ode, as Shakspere terms it, was set to music upwards of seventy years ago, by Jackson, *of Exeter*, for three men's voices, and a more beautiful, finished, and masterly composition, of the kind, the English school of music cannot produce:—for that we have a school, and one of which we need not be ashamed, will soon cease to be denied. The composer calls this *An Elegy*. This name is not quite consistent with our notion of the word Elegy ;—but amongst the Greeks and Romans it did not necessarily mean a mournful poem—it was merely verses to be sung Jackson uses the word in somewhat too scholarly a manner. He was a man of letters, possessing a very superior understanding, and not a mere musician. Indeed, it is but fair to add, that really original and great composers have generally been men of strong minds; the exceptions are only enough in number to prove the rule.

⁴ SCENE III.—"*That, like a rude and savage man of Inde.*"

Shakspere might have found an account of the Ghebers, or fire-worshipers of the East, in some of the travellers whose works had preceded Hakluyt's collection. Nothing can be finer or more accurate than this description. The Ghebers, as the elegant poet of "Lalla Rookh" tells us, were not blind idolaters; they worshipped the Creator in the most splendid of his works :—

"Yes,—I am of that impious race,
Those Slaves of Fire who, morn and even,
Hail their Creator's dwelling-place
Among the living lights of heaven!"

⁵ SCENE III.—"*For when would you, my liege, or you, or you.*"

It will be observed that this line is almost a repetition of a previous one,

"For when would you, my lord, or you, or you;"

and in the same manner throughout this speech the most emphatic parts of the reasoning are repeated with variations. Upon this, conjecture goes to work; and it is pronounced that the lines are unnecessarily repeated. Some of the commentators understood little of rhythm, and they were not very accurate judges of rhetoric. One of the greatest evidences of skill in an orator is the enforcement of an idea by repetition, without repeating the precise form of its original announcement. The speech of Ulysses in the third act of Troilus and Cressida,

"Time hath, my lord, a wallet on his back,"

is a wonderful example of this art.

ACT V.

SCENE I.—*Another part of the same.*

Enter HOLOFERNES, *Sir* NATHANIEL, *and* DULL.

Hol. Satis quod sufficit.

Nath. I praise God for you, sir; your reasons at dinner have been sharp and sententious; pleasant without scurrility, witty without affection,[a] audacious without impudency, learned without opinion, and strange without heresy. I did converse this *quondam* day with a companion of the king's, who is intituled, nominated, or called, Don Adriano de Armado.

Hol. Novi hominem tanquam te: His humour is lofty, his discourse peremptory, his tongue filed,[b] his eye ambitious, his gait majestical, and his general behaviour vain, ridiculous, and thrasonical.[c] He is too picked, too spruce, too affected, too odd, as it were, too peregrinate, as I may call it.

Nath. A most singular and choice epithet.

[*Takes out his table-book.*

Hol. He draweth out the thread of his verbosity finer than the staple of his argument. I abhor such fanatical fantasms, such insociable and point-devise[*] companions; such rackers of orthography, as to speak, dout, fine, when he should say, doubt; det, when he should pronounce debt;—d, e, b, t; not d, e, t:—he clepeth a calf, cauf; half, hauf; neighbour, *vocatur*, nebour; neigh, abbreviated, ne: This is abhominable, (which he would call abominable,) it insinuateth me of insanie; *Ne intelligis domine?* to make frantic, lunatic.

Nath. Laus Deo bone intelligo.

Hol. Bone?——*bone*, for *bene: Priscian* a little scratch'd; 't will serve.

Enter ARMADO, MOTH, *and* COSTARD.

Nath. Videsne quis venit?
Hol. Video et gaudeo.
Arm. Chirra! [*To* MOTH.
Hol. Quare Chirra, not sirrah?

---

[*] *Point-devise*—nice to excess, and, sometimes, adverbially, for exactly, with the utmost nicety. Gifford thinks this must have been a mathematical phrase. Other examples of its use are found in Shakspere—and in Holinshed, Drayton, and Ben Jonson. The phrase, Douce says, "has been supplied from the labours of the needle. *Poinct*, in the French language, denotes a stitch; *devisé*, anything invented, disposed, or arranged. *Point-devisé* was therefore a particular sort of patterned lace worked with the needle; and the term *point-lace* is still familiar to every female." It is incorrect to write *point-de-vice*, as is usually done.

[a] *Affection*—affectation.
[b] *Filed*—polished.
[c] *Thrasonical*—from Thraso, the boasting soldier of Terence.

[Act V.] LOVE'S LABOUR'S LOST. [Scene I.]

Arm. Men of peace, well encounter'd.
Hol. Most military sir, salutation.
Moth. They have been at a great feast of languages, and stolen the scraps.
　　　　　　　　　　　　[*To* Costard *aside.*
Cost. O, they have lived long on the almsbasket of words! I marvel, thy master hath not eaten thee for a word; for thou art not so long by the head as *honorificabilitudinitatibus*:[1] thou art easier swallowed than a flap-dragon.
Moth. Peace; the peal begins.
Arm. Monsieur, [*to* Hol.] are you not letter'd?
Moth. Yes, yes; he teaches boys the hornbook:—
What is a, b, spelt backward with a horn on his head?
Hol. Ba, *pueritia*, with a horn added.
Moth. Ba, most silly sheep, with a horn:—You hear his learning.
Hol. Quis, quis, thou consonant?
Moth. The third of the five vowels, if you repeat them; or the fifth, if I.[2]
Hol. I will repeat them, a, e, i.—
Moth. The sheep: the other two concludes it; o, u.
Arm. Now, by the salt wave of the Mediterraneum, a sweet touch, a quick venew of wit;[3] snip, snap, quick and home; it rejoiceth my intellect: true wit.
Moth. Offer'd by a child to an old man; which is wit-old.
Hol. What is the figure? what is the figure?
Moth. Horns.
Hol. Thou disputest like an infant: go, whip thy gig.
Moth. Lend me your horn to make one, and I will whip about your infamy *circum circa*; A gig of a cuckold's horn!
Cost. An I had but one penny in the world, thou shouldst have it to buy gingerbread: hold, there is the very remuneration I had of thy master, thou halfpenny purse of wit, thou pigeon-egg of discretion. O, an the heavens were so pleased that thou wert but my bastard! what a joyful father wouldst thou make me! Go to; thou hast it *ad dunghill*, at the fingers' ends, as they say.
Hol. O, I smell false Latin; dunghill for *unguem*.
Arm. Arts-man, *præambula*; we will be singled from the barbarous. Do you not educate youth at the charge-house on the top of the mountain?
Hol. Or, *mons*, the hill.

Arm. At your sweet pleasure, for the mountain.
Hol. I do, sans question.
Arm. Sir, it is the king's most sweet pleasure and affection, to congratulate the princess at her pavilion, in the posteriors of this day; which the rude multitude call the afternoon.
Hol. The posterior of the day, most generous sir, is liable, congruent, and measurable for the afternoon: the word is well cull'd, chose; sweet and apt, I do assure you, sir, I do assure.
Arm. Sir, the king is a noble gentleman; and my familiar, I do assure you, very good friend:—For what is inward between us, let it pass:—I do beseech thee, remember thy courtesy:[a]—I beseech thee, apparel thy head:—And among other importunate and most serious designs,—and of great import indeed, too;—but let that pass:—for I must tell thee, it will please his grace (by the world) sometime to lean upon my poor shoulder; and with his royal finger, thus, dally with my excrement, with my mustachio: but, sweet heart, let that pass. By the world, I recount no fable; some certain special honours it pleaseth his greatness to impart to Armado, a soldier, a man of travel, that hath seen the world: but let that pass.—The very all of all is, —but, sweet heart, I do implore secrecy,—that the king would have me present the princess, sweet chuck, with some delightful ostentation, or show, or pageant, or antic, or fire-work. Now, understanding that the curate and your sweet self are good at such eruptions, and sudden breaking out of mirth, as it were, I have acquainted you withal, to the end to crave your assistance.
Hol. Sir, you shall present before her the nine worthies.—Sir Nathaniel, as concerning some entertainment of time, some show in the posterior of this day, to be rendered by our assistance,—the king's command, and this most gallant, illustrate, and learned gentleman,—before the princess; I say, none so fit as to present the nine worthies.
Nath. Where will you find men worthy enough to present them?
Hol. Joshua, yourself; myself, or this gallant gentleman, Judas Maccabæus; this swain, be-

---

[a] *Remember thy courtesy.* Theobald is of opinion that the passage should read—remember *not* thy courtesy,—that is, do not take thy hat off. Jackson thinks it should be, remember *my* courtesy. It appears to us that the text is right; and that its construction is—for what is confidential between us, let it pass—notice it not—I do beseech thee, remember thy courtesy—remember thy obligation to silence as a gentleman. Holofernes then bows; upon which Armado says, I beseech thee, apparel thy head; and then goes on with his confidential communications, which he finishes by saying—Sweet heart, I do implore secrecy.

cause of his great limb or joint, shall pass Pompey the Great; the page, Hercules.

Arm. Pardon, sir, error: he is not quantity enough for that worthy's thumb: he is not so big as the end of his club.

Hol. Shall I have audience? he shall present Hercules in minority: his *enter* and *exit* shall be strangling a snake; and I will have an apology for that purpose.

Moth. An excellent device! so, if any of the audience hiss, you may cry: Well done, Hercules! now thou crushest the snake! that is the way to make an offence gracious; though few have the grace to do it.

Arm. For the rest of the worthies?—

Hol. I will play three myself.

Moth. Thrice-worthy gentleman!

Arm. Shall I tell you a thing?

Hol. We attend

Arm. We will have, if this fadge* not, an antic.

I beseech you, follow.

Hol. Via, goodman Dull! thou hast spoken no word all this while.

Dull. Nor understood none neither, sir.

Hol. Allons! we will employ thee

Dull. I'll make one in a dance, or so; or I will play on the tabor to the worthies, and let them dance the hay.

Hol. Most dull, honest Dull, to our sport, away. [*Exeunt.*

SCENE II.—*Another part of the same. Before the Princess's Pavilion.*

Enter the PRINCESS, KATHARINE, ROSALINE, *and* MARIA.

Prin. Sweet hearts, we shall be rich ere we depart,
If fairings come thus plentifully in:
A lady wall'd about with diamonds!
Look you, what I have from the loving king.

Ros. Madam, came nothing else along with that?

Prin. Nothing, but this? yes, as much love in rhyme,
As would be cramm'd up in a sheet of paper,
Writ on both sides of the leaf, margent and all;
That he was fain to seal on Cupid's name.

Ros. That was the way to make his godhead wax;*
For he hath been five thousand years a boy.

Kath. Ay, and a shrewd unhappy gallows too.

Ros. You'll ne'er be friends with him; he kill'd your sister.

Kath. He made her melancholy, sad, and heavy;
And so she died: had she been light, like you,
Of such a merry, nimble, stirring spirit,
She might have been a grandam ere she died:
And so may you; for a light heart lives long.

Ros. What's your dark meaning, mouse, of this light word?

Kath. A light condition in a beauty dark.

Ros. We need more light to find your meaning out.

Kath. You'll mar the light, by taking it in snuff;
Therefore, I'll darkly end the argument.

Ros. Look, what you do; you do it still i' the dark.

Kath. So do not you; for you are a light wench.

Ros. Indeed, I weigh not you; and therefore light.

Kath. You weigh me not,—O, that's you care not for me.

Ros. Great reason; for, Past cure is still past care.

Prin. Well bandied both; a set of wit[b] well play'd.
But Rosaline, you have a favour too:
Who sent it? and what is it?

Ros. I would, you knew:
An if my face were but as fair as yours,
My favour were as great; be witness this.
Nay, I have verses too, I thank Biron:
The numbers true; and, were the numb'ring too,
I were the fairest goddess on the ground:
I am compar'd to twenty thousand fairs.
O, he hath drawn my picture in his letter!

Prin. Anything like?

Ros. Much, in the letters; nothing in the praise.

Prin. Beauteous as ink; a good conclusion.

Kath. Fair as a text B in a copy-book.

Ros. 'Ware pencils! Ho! let me not die your debtor,
My red dominical, my golden letter:
O that your face were not so full of O's![c]

---

a Fadge. This word is from the Anglo-Saxon *fegan*—to join together, and hence to fit, to agree. Somner gives this derivation, and explains that things will not *fadge* when they cannot be brought together, so as to serve to that end whereto they are designed. In Warner's "Albion's England," we have this passage, which is quoted in Mr. Richardson's valuable Dictionary:—
 "It hath beene when as hearte loue
  Did trente and tie the knot,
  Though now, if gold but lack in graines,
  The wedding fadgeth not."

b Set of wit.—Set is a term used at tennis.
c Rosaline twits Katharine that her face is marked with the small pox; *not so* is omitted in the folio.

Kath. A pox of that jest! and I beshrew all shrows!
Prin. But, Katharine, what was sent to you from fair Dumain?
Kath. Madam, this glove.
Prin. Did he not send you twain?
Kath. Yes, madam; and moreover,
Some thousand verses of a faithful lover;
A huge translation of hypocrisy,
Vilely compil'd, profound simplicity.
Mar. This, and these pearls, to me sent Longaville;
The letter is too long by half a mile.
Prin. I think no less: Dost thou not wish in heart,
The chain were longer, and the letter short?
Mar. Ay, or I would these hands might never part.
Prin. We are wise girls, to mock our lovers so.
Ros. They are worse fools to purchase mocking so.
That same Biron I'll torture ere I go.
O, that I knew he were but in by the week!
How I would make him fawn, and beg, and seek;
And wait the season, and observe the times,
And spend his prodigal wits in bootless rhymes,
And shape his service wholly to my behests;[a]
And make him proud to make me proud that jests!
So portent-like would I o'ersway his state,
That he should be my fool, and I his fate.
Prin. None are so surely caught, when they are catch'd,
As wit turn'd fool: folly, in wisdom hatch'd,
Hath wisdom's warrant, and the help of school;
And wit's own grace to grace a learned fool.
Ros. The blood of youth burns not with such excess,
As gravity's revolt to wantonness.[b]
Mar. Folly in fools bears not so strong a note,
As foolery in the wise, when wit doth dote;
Since all the power thereof it doth apply,
To prove, by wit, worth in simplicity

Enter BOYET.

Prin. Here comes Boyet, and mirth is in his face.
Boyet. O, I am stabb'd with laughter! Where's her grace?
Prin. Thy news, Boyet?

Boyet. Prepare, madam, prepare!—
Arm, wenches, arm! encounters mounted are
Against your peace: Love doth approach disguis'd,
Armed in arguments; you'll be surpris'd:
Muster your wits; stand in your own defence;
Or hide your heads like cowards, and fly hence.
Prin. Saint Dennis to Saint Cupid! What are they,
That charge their breath against us? say, scout, say.
Boyet. Under the cool shade of a sycamore,
I thought to close mine eyes some half an hour;
When, lo! to interrupt my purpos'd rest,
Toward that shade I might behold address'd
The king and his companions: warily
I stole into a neighbour thicket by,
And overheard what you shall overhear;
That, by and by, disguis'd they will be here.
Their herald is a pretty knavish page,
That well by heart hath conn'd his embassage
Action, and accent, did they teach him there;
"Thus must thou speak, and thus thy body bear:"
And ever and anon they made a doubt,
Presence majestical would put him out;
"For," quoth the king, "an angel shalt thou see,
Yet fear not thou, but speak audaciously."
The boy replied, "An angel is not evil;
I should have fear'd her, had she been a devil."
With that all laugh'd, and clapp'd him on the shoulder,
Making the bold wag by their praises bolder.
One rubb'd his elbow, thus; and fleer'd, and swore,
A better speech was never spoke before:
Another with his finger and his thumb,
Cried, "Via! we will do't, come what will come:"
The third he caper'd and cried, "All goes well;"
The fourth turn'd on the toe, and down he fell.
With that, they all did tumble on the ground,
With such a zealous laughter, so profound,
That in this spleen ridiculous appears,
To check their folly, passion's solemn tears.
Prin. But what, but what, come they to visit us?
Boyet. They do, they do; and are apparel'd thus,—
Like Muscovites, or Russians,' as I guess.[a]
Their purpose is, to parle, to court, and dance:
And every one his love-feat will advance
Unto his several mistress; which they'll know
By favours several, which they did bestow.

[a] See Introductory Notice, p. 76.

Prin. And will they so? the gallants shall be
 task'd:—
For, ladies, we will every one be mask'd;
And not a man of them shall have the grace,
Despite of suit, to see a lady's face.
Hold, Rosaline, this favour thou shalt wear,
And then the king will court thee for his dear;
Hold, take thou this, my sweet, and give me
 thine;
So shall Biron take me for Rosaline.—
And change your favours too; so shall your
 loves
Woo contrary, deceiv'd by these removes.
  Ros. Come on then; wear the favours most
   in sight.
  Kath. But, in this changing, what is your
   intent?
  Prin. The effect of my intent is, to cross
   theirs:
They do it but in mocking merriment;
And mock for mock is only my intent.
Their several counsels they unbosom shall
To loves mistook; and so be mock'd withal,
Upon the next occasion that we meet,
With visages display'd, to talk and greet.
  Ros. But shall we dance, if they desire us to't?
  Prin. No; to the death we will not move a
   foot:
Nor to their penn'd speech render we no grace:
But, while 't is spoke, each turn away her face.
  Boyet. Why, that contempt will kill the
   speaker's heart,
And quite divorce his memory from his part.
  Prin. Therefore I do it; and, I make no
   doubt,
The rest will ne'er come in, if he be out.
There's no such sport as sport by sport o'er-
 thrown;
To make theirs ours, and ours none but our
 own:
So shall we stay, mocking intended game;
And they, well mock'd, depart away with shame.
   [*Trumpets sound within.*
  Boyet. The trumpet sounds; be mask'd, the
   maskers come. [*The ladies mask.*

Enter the KING, BIRON, LONGAVILLE, *and* DU-
MAIN, *in Russian habits and masked;* MOTH,
Musicians *and* Attendants.

  Moth. "All hail the richest beauties on the
   earth!"
  Boyet. Beauties no richer than rich taffata.
  Moth. "A holy parcel of the fairest dames,"
   [*The ladies turn their backs to him.*

"That ever turn'd their"—backs—"to mortal
 views!"
  Biron. "Their eyes," villain, "their eyes!"
  Moth. "That ever turn'd their eyes to mortal
   views! Out"—
  Boyet. True; *out*, indeed.
  Moth. "Out of your favours, heavenly spirits,
   vouchsafe
Not to behold "—
  Biron. "Once to behold," rogue.
  Moth. "Once to behold with your sun-beamed
   eyes,"——" with your sun-beamed eyes "—
  Boyet. They will not answer to that epithet,
You were best call it, daughter-beamed eyes.
  Moth. They do not mark me, and that brings
   me out.
  Biron. Is this your perfectness? begone, you
   rogue.
  Ros. What would these strangers? know
   their minds, Boyet:
If they do speak our language, 't is our will
That some plain man recount their purposes:
Know what they would.
  Boyet. What would you with the princess?
  Biron. Nothing but peace, and gentle visitation.
  Ros. What would they, say they?
  Boyet. Nothing but peace, and gentle visitation.
  Ros. Why, that they have; and bid them
   so be gone.
  Boyet. She says, you have it, and you may
   be gone.
  King. Say to her, we have measur'd many
   miles,
To tread a measure with her on the grass.
  Boyet. They say that they have measur'd
   many a mile.
To tread a measure* with you on this grass.
  Ros. It is not so: ask them how many inches
Is in one mile: if they have measur'd many,
The measure then of one is easily told.
  Boyet. If, to come hither you have measur'd
   miles,
And many miles, the princess bids you tell,
How many inches do fill up one mile.
  Biron. Tell her, we measure them by weary
   steps.
  Boyet. She hears herself.
  Ros.   How many weary steps,
Of many weary miles you have o'ergone,
Are number'd in the travel of one mile?
  Biron. We number nothing that we spend for
   you;

---

* *Tread a measure.* The measure was a grave courtly
dance, of which the steps were slow and measured, like
those of a modern minuet. (See Illustrations to Romeo and
Juliet, Act I.)

Act V.] LOVE'S LABOUR'S LOST. [Scene II.

Our duty is so rich, so infinite,
That we may do it still without accompt.
Vouchsafe to show the sunshine of your face,
That we, like savages, may worship it.
 Ros. My face is but a moon, and clouded too.
 King. Blessed are clouds, to do as such clouds do!
Vouchsafe, bright moon, and these thy stars, to shine
(Those clouds remov'd) upon our watery eyne.
 Ros. O vain petitioner! beg a greater matter;
Thou now request'st but moonshine in the water.
 King. Then, in our measure, vouchsafe but one change:
Thou bidd'st me beg; this begging is not strange.
 Ros. Play, music, then: nay, you must do it soon. [*Music plays.*
Not yet;—no dance:—thus change I like the moon.
 King. Will you not dance? How come you thus estrang'd?
 Ros. You took the moon at full; but now she's chang'd.
 King. Yet still she is the moon, and I the man.
The music plays; vouchsafe some motion to it.
 Ros. Our ears vouchsafe it.
 King.   But your legs should do it.
 Ros. Since you are strangers, and come here by chance,
We'll not be nice: take hands;—we will not dance.
 King. Why take we hands then?
 Ros.   Only to part friends:—
Court'sy, sweet hearts; and so the measure ends.
 King. More measure of this measure; be not nice.
 Ros. We can afford no more at such a price.
 King. Prize you yourselves; What buys your company?
 Ros.   Your absence only.
 King.   That can never be.
 Ros. Then cannot we be bought: and so adieu;
Twice to your visor, and half once to you!
 King. If you deny to dance, let's hold more chat.
 Ros. In private then.
 King.   I am best pleas'd with that.
       [*They converse apart.*
 Biron. White-handed mistress, one sweet word with thee.
 Prin. Honey, and milk, and sugar; there is three.

 Biron. Nay then, two treys, (an if you grow so nice,)
Metheglin, wort, and malmsey;—Well run, dice!
There's half a dozen sweets.
 Prin.   Seventh sweet, adieu.
Since you can cog,[*] I'll play no more with you.
 Biron. One word in secret.
 Prin.   Let it not be sweet.
 Biron. Thou griev'st my gall.
 Prin.   Gall? bitter.
 Biron.   Therefore meet.
       [*They converse apart.*
 Dum. Will you vouchsafe with me to change a word?
 Mar. Name it.
 Dum.   Fair lady,—
 Mar.   Say you so? Fair lord,—
Take that for your fair lady.
 Dum.   Please it you,
As much in private, and I'll bid adieu.
       [*They converse apart.*
 Kath. What, was your visor made without a tongue?
 Long. I know the reason, lady, why you ask.
 Kath. O, for your reason! quickly, sir; I long.
 Long. You have a double tongue within your mask,
And would afford my speechless visor half.
 Kath. Veal, quoth the Dutchman;—Is not veal a calf?
 Long. A calf, fair lady?
 Kath.   No, a fair lord calf.
 Long. Let's part the word.
 Kath.   No, I'll not be your half:
Take all, and wean it; it may prove an ox.
 Long. Look, how you butt yourself in these sharp mocks!
Will you give horns, chaste lady? do not so.
 Kath. Then die a calf, before your horns do grow.
 Long. One word in private with you, ere I die.
 Kath. Bleat softly then, the butcher hears you cry.   [*They converse apart.*
 Boyet. The tongues of mocking wenches are as keen
As is the razor's edge invisible,
Cutting a smaller hair than may be seen;
Above the sense of sense: so sensible

---
[*] Biron says, "Well run, dice!" The Princess says he can *cog*.—To cog the dice is to load them,—and thence generally, to defraud.

117

Seemeth their conference; their conceits have wings,
Fleeter than arrows, bullets, wind, thought, swifter things.
Ros. Not one word more, my maids; break off, break off.
Biron. By heaven, all dry-beaten with pure scoff!
King. Farewell, mad wenches; you have simple wits.
[*Exeunt* KING, Lords, MOTH, *Music, and Attendants.*
Prin. Twenty adieus, my frozen Muscovits.—
Are these the breed of wits so wonder'd at?
Boyet. Tapers they are, with your sweet breaths puff'd out.
Ros. Well-liking wits[a] they have; gross, gross; fat, fat.
Prin. O poverty in wit, kingly-poor flout!
Will they not, think you, hang themselves to-night?
Or ever, but in visors, show their faces?
This pert Biron was out of countenance quite.
Ros. O! they were all in lamentable cases!
The king was weeping-ripe for a good word.
Prin. Biron did swear himself out of all suit.
Mar. Dumain was at my service, and his sword:
No point,[b] quoth I; my servant straight was mute.
Kath. Lord Longaville said, I came o'er his heart;
And trow you, what he call'd me?
Prin. Qualm, perhaps.
Kath. Yes, in good faith.
Prin. Go, sickness as thou art!
Ros. Well, better wits have worn plain statute-caps.[b]
But will you hear? the king is my love sworn.
Prin. And quick Biron hath plighted faith to me.
Kath. And Longaville was for my service born.
Mar. Dumain is mine as sure as bark on tree.
Boyet. Madam, and pretty mistresses, give ear:
Immediately they will again be here
In their own shapes; for it can never be,
They will digest this harsh indignity.
Prin. Will they return?
Boyet. They will, they will, God knows,
And leap for joy, though they are lame with blows:

Therefore, change favours; and, when they repair,
Blow like sweet roses in this summer air.
Prin. How blow? how blow? speak to be understood.
Boyet. Fair ladies, mask'd, are roses in their bud;
Dismask'd, their damask sweet commixture shown,
Are angels vailing clouds,[a] or roses blown.
Prin. Avaunt, perplexity! What shall we do,
If they return in their own shapes to woo?
Ros. Good madam, if by me you'll be advis'd
Let's mock them still, as well known, as disguis'd:
Let us complain to them what fools were here,
Disguis'd like Muscovites, in shapeless gear;
And wonder what they were; and to what end
Their shallow shows, and prologue vilely penn'd,
And their rough carriage so ridiculous,
Should be presented at our tent to us.
Boyet. Ladies, withdraw: the gallants are at hand.
Prin. Whip to our tents, as roes run over land.
[*Exeunt* PRINCESS, ROS., KATH., *and* MARIA.

Enter the KING, BIRON, LONGAVILLE, *and* DUMAIN, *in their proper habits.*

King. Fair sir, God save you! Where is the princess?
Boyet. Gone to her tent: Please it your majesty,
Command me any service to her thither?
King. That she vouchsafe me audience for one word.
Boyet. I will; and so will she, I know, my lord. [*Exit.*
Biron. This fellow pecks up wit, as pigeons peas,[b]
And utters it again when Jove doth please:
He is wit's peddler; and retails his wares
At wakes, and wassails, meetings, markets, fairs;
And we that sell by gross, the Lord doth know,
Have not the grace to grace it with such show.
This gallant pins the wenches on his sleeve;
Had he been Adam, he had tempted Eve:
He can carve too, and lisp: Why, this is he,
That kiss'd away his hand in courtesy;
This is the ape of form, monsieur the nice,
That, when he plays at tables, chides the dice

---

[a] *Well-liking* is used in the same sense in which the young of the wild goats in Job are said to be in *good-liking.*

[b] See note on Act II. Scene I.

[a] To vail—to avale—to cause to fall down; the clouds open as the angels descend.

[b] *Pecks.* So the quarto; the folio *picks.* We adopt the reading which more distinctly expresses the action of a bird with its beak.

[Act V.] LOVE'S LABOUR'S LOST. [Scene II.

In honourable terms; nay, he can sing
A mean* most meanly; and, in ushering,
Mend him who can: the ladies call him, sweet;
The stairs, as he treads on them, kiss his feet:
This is the flower that smiles on every one,
To show his teeth as white as whales'[b] bone:
And consciences, that will not die in debt,
Pay him the due of honey-tongued Boyet.
  King. A blister on his sweet tongue, with my heart,
That put Armado's page out of his part!

Enter the PRINCESS, *ushered by* BOYET; ROSALINE, MARIA, KATHARINE, *and* Attendants.

  Biron. See where it comes!—Behaviour, what wert thou,
Till this man show'd thee? and what art thou now?
  King. All hail, sweet madam, and fair time of day!
  Prin. Fair, in all hail, is foul, as I conceive.
  King. Construe my speeches better, if you may.
  Prin. Then wish me better, I will give you leave.
  King. We came to visit you; and purpose now
To lead you to our court: vouchsafe it then.
  Prin. This field shall hold me: and so hold your vow:
Nor God, nor I, delights in perjur'd men.
  King. Rebuke me not for that which you provoke;
The virtue of your eye must break my oath.
  Prin. You nickname virtue: vice you should have spoke;
For virtue's office never breaks men's troth.
Now, by my maiden honour, yet as pure
As the unsullied lily, I protest,
A world of torments though I should endure,
I would not yield to be your house's guest:
So much I hate a breaking-cause to be
Of heavenly oaths, vow'd with integrity.
  King. O, you have liv'd in desolation here,
Unseen, unvisited, much to our shame.
  Prin. Not so, my lord, it is not so, I swear;
We have had pastimes here, and pleasant game;
A mess of Russians left us but of late.

---

  a A mean most meanly. The mean, in vocal music, is an intermediate part; a part—whether tenor, or second soprano, or contra-tenor—between the two extremes of highest and lowest.
  b Whales' bone. The tooth of the walrus. The word *whales'* is here a dissyllable.

  King. How, madam? Russians?
  Prin. Ay, in truth, my lord;
Trim gallants, full of courtship, and of state.
  Ros. Madam, speak true:—It is not so, my lord;
My lady (to the manner of the days),
In courtesy, gives undeserving praise.
We four, indeed, confronted were with four
In Russian habit; here they staid an hour,
And talk'd apace; and in that hour, my lord,
They did not bless us with one happy word.
I dare not call them fools; but this I think,
When they are thirsty, fools would fain have drink.
  Biron. This jest is dry to me. Gentle sweet,
Your wit makes wise things foolish; when we greet
With eyes best seeing heaven's fiery eye,
By light we lose light: Your capacity
Is of that nature, that to your huge store
Wise things seem foolish, and rich things but poor.
  Ros. This proves you wise and rich, for in my eye,—
  Biron. I am a fool, and full of poverty.
  Ros. But that you take what doth to you belong,
It were a fault to snatch words from my tongue.
  Biron. O, I am yours, and all that I possess.
  Ros. All the fool mine?
  Biron. I cannot give you less.
  Ros. Which of the visors was it that you wore?
  Biron. Where? when? what visor? why demand you this?
  Ros. There, then, that visor; that superfluous case,
That hid the worse, and show'd the better face.
  King. We are descried: they'll mock us now downright.
  Dum. Let us confess, and turn it to a jest.
  Prin. Amaz'd, my lord? Why looks your highness sad?
  Ros. Help, hold his brows! he'll swoon! Why look you pale?—
Sea-sick, I think, coming from Muscovy.
  Biron. Thus pour the stars down plagues for perjury.
Can any face of brass hold longer out?—
Here stand I, lady; dart thy skill at me;
Bruise me with scorn, confound me with a flout;
Thrust thy sharp wit quite through my ignorance;
Cut me to pieces with thy keen conceit;
And I will wish thee never more to dance,
Nor never more in Russian habit wait.

O! never will I trust to speeches penn'd,
　　Nor to the motion of a schoolboy's tongue;
Nor never come in visor to my friend;
　　Nor woo in rhyme, like a blind harper's
　　　song:
Taffata phrases, silken terms precise,
Three-pil'd hyperboles, spruce affectation,[*]
Figures pedantical; these summer-flies
　　Have blown me full of maggot ostentation:
I do forswear them: and I here protest,
　　By this white glove, (how white the hand,
　　　God knows!)
Henceforth my wooing mind shall be express'd
　　In russet yeas, and honest kersey noes:
And, to begin, wench,—so God help me, la!—
My love to thee is sound, sans crack or flaw.
　　Ros. Sans sans, I pray you.
　　Biron.　　　　　　　Yet I have a trick
Of the old rage:—bear with me, I am sick;
I 'll leave it by degrees. Soft, let us see:—
Write, "Lord have mercy on us,"[b] on those
　　three;
They are infected, in their hearts it lies;
They have the plague, and caught it of your eyes:
These lords are visited; you are not free,
For the Lord's tokens on you do I see.
　　Prin. No, they are free, that gave these tokens
　　　to us.
　　Biron. Our states are forfeit, seek not to
　　　undo us.
　　Ros. It is not so. For how can this be true,
That you stand forfeit, being those that sue?
　　Biron. Peace; for I will not have to do with
　　　you.
　　Ros. Nor shall not, if I do as I intend.
　　Biron. Speak for yourselves, my wit is at an end.
　　King. Teach us, sweet madam, for our rude
　　　transgression
Some fair excuse.
　　Prin.　　　　　　The fairest is confession.
Were you not here, but even now, disguis'd?
　　King. Madam, I was.
　　Prin.　　　　　　And were you well advis'd?
　　King. I was, fair madam.
　　Prin.　　　　　　When you then were here,
What did you whisper in your lady's ear?

　　King. That more than all the world I did
　　　respect her.
　　Prin. When she shall challenge this, you will
　　　reject her.
　　King. Upon mine honour, no.
　　Prin.　　　　　　Peace, peace, forbear;
Your oath once broke, you force not to forswear.
　　King. Despise me, when I break this oath of
　　　mine.
　　Prin. I will: and therefore keep it:—Rosa-
　　　line,
What did the Russian whisper in your ear?
　　Ros. Madam, he swore that he did hold me
　　　dear
As precious eyesight: and did value me
Above this world: adding thereto, moreover,
That he would wed me, or else die my lover.
　　Prin. God give thee joy of him! the noble
　　　lord
Most honourably doth uphold his word.
　　King. What mean you, madam? by my life,
　　　my troth,
I never swore this lady such an oath.
　　Ros. By heaven you did; and to confirm it
　　　plain,
You gave me this: but take it, sir, again.
　　King. My faith, and this, the princess I did
　　　give;
I knew her by this jewel on her sleeve.
　　Prin. Pardon me, sir, this jewel did she
　　　wear;
And lord Biron, I thank him, is my dear:—
What; will you have me, or your pearl again?
　　Biron. Neither of either; I remit both twain.
I see the trick on 't;—Here was a consent,
(Knowing aforehand of our merriment,)
To dash it like a Christmas comedy:
Some carry-tale, some please-man, some slight
　　zany,
Some mumble-news, some trencher-knight, some
　　Dick,—
That smiles his cheek in years,[a] and knows the
　　trick
To make my lady laugh, when she 's dispos'd,—
Told our intents before: which once disclos'd,
The ladies did change favours; and then we,
Following the signs, woo'd but the sign of she.
Now, to our perjury to add more terror,
We are again forsworn: in will, and error.

---

[*] *Affection* is the old reading; modern editors read a*ffecti-
ation*; but affection is used in the same sense in the beginning of this Act. On the other hand, we have *affectation*
in the Merry Wives of Windsor;—Malone, who prefers
affection, has not stated the necessity of anglicising *hyperboles*, reading it hy-per-boles, if we retain *affection*. Without
affectation the line has imperfect rhythm, and there is no
rhyme to *ostentation*.
  [b] *Lord have mercy on us*. The fearful inscription on
houses visited with the plague.
120

[a] *In years.* Malone reads *in jeers*. We have in Twelfth
Night, "He doth smile his cheek into more lines than are
in the new map." The character which Biron gives of
Boyet is not that of a jeerer; he is a carry-tale—a please-
man. The *in years* is supposed by Warburton to mean into
wrinkles. Tieck ingeniously gives an explanation of the
supposed wrinkles. Boyet is neither young nor old, but
he has smiled so continually, that his cheek, which in
respect of years would have been smooth, has become
wrinkled through too much smiling.

Much upon this it is :—Aud might not you
[*To* BOYET.
Forestal our sport, to make us thus untrue?
Do not you know my lady's foot by the squire,[a]
And laugh upon the apple of her eye?
And stand between her back, sir, and the fire,
Holding a trencher, jesting merrily?
You put our page out: Go, you are allow'd;[b]
Die when you will, a smock shall be your shroud
You leer upon me, do you? there's an eye,
Wounds like a leaden sword.
    Boyet.   Full merrily
Hath this brave manage, this career, been run.
    Biron. Lo, he is tilting straight! Peace; I
have done.

           Enter COSTARD.

Welcome, pure wit! thou partest a fair fray.
    Cost. O Lord, sir, they would know,
Whether the three worthies shall come in, or no.
    Biron. What, are there but three?
    Cost.   No, sir; but it is vara fine,
For every one pursents three.
    Biron.   And three times thrice is nine.
    Cost. Not so, sir; under correction, sir; I
hope, it is not so:
You cannot beg us,[c] sir, I can assure you, sir;
        we know what we know:
I hope, sir, three times thrice, sir,—
    Biron.   Is not nine.
    Cost. Under correction, sir, we know whereuntil it doth amount.
    Biron. By Jove, I always took three threes
        for nine.
    Cost. O Lord, sir, it were pity you should get
your living by reckoning, sir.
    Biron. How much is it?
    Cost. O Lord, sir, the parties themselves, the
actors, sir, will show whereuntil it doth amount:
for mine own part, I am, as they say, but to
parfect one man, in one poor man; Pompion
the great, sir.
    Biron. Art thou one of the worthies?
    Cost. It pleased them to think me worthy of
Pompion the great: for mine own part, I know
not the degree of the worthy; but I am to
stand for him.
    Biron. Go, bid them prepare.
    Cost. We will turn it finely off, sir; we will
        take some care.   [*Exit* COSTARD.
    King. Biron, they will shame us, let them not
        approach.

    Biron. We are shame-proof, my lord: and
't is some policy
To have one show worse than the king's and his
        company.
    King. I say, they shall not come.
    Prin. Nay, my good lord, let me o'er-rule
        you now:
That sport best pleases that doth least know how:
Where zeal strives to content, and the contents
Die in the zeal of that which it presents;
Their form confounded makes most form in
        mirth;
When great things labouring perish in their birth.
    Biron. A right description of our sport, my
lord.

           Enter ARMADO.

    Arm. Anointed, I implore so much expense
of thy royal sweet breath, as will utter a brace
of words.
    [ARMADO *converses with the* KING, *and delivers him a paper.*
    Prin. Doth this man serve God?
    Biron. Why ask you?
    Prin. He speaks not like a man of God's
making.
    Arm. That's all one, my fair, sweet, honey
monarch: for, I protest, the schoolmaster is
exceedingly fantastical; too, too vain; too, too
vain; But we will put it, as they say, to *fortuna
della guerra.* I wish you the peace of mind,
most royal couplement!   [*Exit* ARMADO.
    King. Here is like to be a good presence of
worthies: He presents Hector of Troy; the
swain, Pompey the great; the parish curate,
Alexander; Armado's page, Hercules; the
pedant, Judas Machabæus.
And if these four worthies in their first show
        thrive,
These four will change habits, and present the
other five.
    Biron. There is five in the first show.
    King. You are deceiv'd, 't is not so.
    Biron. The pedant, the braggart, the hedgepriest, the fool, and the boy:—
Abate a throw at novum;[a] and the whole world
        again
Cannot prick out five such, take each one in his
        vein.
    King. The ship is under sail, and here she
        comes amain.
    [*Seats brought for the* KING, PRINCESS, *&c.*

---

[a] *The squire—esquierre,* a rule, or square.
[b] *Allow'd.* You are an allow'd fool. As in Twelfth Night—
    "There is no slander in an allow'd fool."

[a] *Abate a throw. Novum,* or *quinquenove,* was a game at dice, of which nine and five were the principal throws. Biron therefore says, Abate a throw—that is, leave out the nine,— and the world cannot prick out five such.

Pageant of the Nine Worthies.

Enter COSTARD, *armed, for* Pompey.

Cost. "I Pompey am,"—
Boyet.   You lie, you are not he.
Cost. "I Pompey am,"—
Boyet.   With libbard's [a] head on knee.
Biron. Well said, old mocker; I must needs be friends with thee.
Cost. "I Pompey am, Pompey surnam'd the big,"—
Dum. The great.
Cost. It is great, sir;—"Pompey surnam'd the great;
That oft in field, with targe and shield, did make my foe to sweat:
And travelling along this coast, I here am come by chance;
And lay my arms before the legs of this sweet lass of France."
If your ladyship would say, "Thanks, Pompey," I had done.
Prin. Great thanks, great Pompey.
Cost. 'T is not so much worth; but, I hope, I was perfect: I made a little fault in "great".
Biron. My hat to a halfpenny, Pompey proves the best worthy.

Enter NATHANIEL, *armed, for* Alexander.

Nath. "When in the world I liv'd, I was the world's commander;
By east, west, north, and south, I spread my conquering might:
My 'scutcheon plain declares that I am Alisander."
Boyet. Your nose says, no, you are not; for it stands too right.
Biron. Your nose smells, no, in this, most tender-smelling knight.
Prin. The conqueror is dismay'd: Proceed, good Alexander.
Nath. "When in the world I liv'd, I was the world's commander;"—
Boyet. Most true, 't is right; you were so, Alisander.
Biron. Pompey the great,—
Cost.   Your servant, and Costard.
Biron. Take away the conqueror, take away Alisander.

Cost. O, sir, [*to* NATH.] you have overthrown Alisander the conqueror! You will be scraped out of the painted cloth for this: your lion, that holds his poll-ax sitting on a close stool, will be given to A-jax: he will be the ninth worthy. A conqueror, and afeard to speak! run away for shame, Alisander. [NATH. *retires.*] There, an't shall please you; a foolish mild man; an honest man, look you, and soon dash'd! He is a marvellous good neighbour, in sooth; and a very good bowler: [b] but, for Alisander, alas, you see how 't is;—a little o'erparted: [a]—But there are worthies a coming will speak their mind in some other sort.

Prin. Stand aside, good Pompey.

Enter HOLOFERNES *for* Judas, *and* MOTH *for* Hercules.

Hol. "Great Hercules is presented by this imp,
    Whose club kill'd Cerberus, that three-headed *canus*;
And, when he was a babe, a child, a shrimp,
    Thus did he strangle serpents in his *manus*:
Quoniam, he seemeth in minority;
Ergo, I come with this apology."—
Keep some state in thy *exit*, and vanish.
                        [MOTH *retires.*

Hol. "Judas, I am,"—
Dum. A Judas!
Hol. Not Iscariot, sir,—
"Judas, I am, yclepcd Machabæus."
Dum. Judas Machabæus clipt, is plain Judas.
Biron. A kissing traitor:—How art thou prov'd Judas?
Hol. "Judas, I am,"—
Dum. The more shame for you, Judas.
Hol. What mean you, sir?
Boyet. To make Judas hang himself.
Hol. Begin, sir; you are my elder.
Biron. Well follow'd: Judas was hang'd on an elder.[b]
Hol. I will not be put out of countenance.
Biron. Because thou hast no face.
Hol. What is this?
Boyet. A cittern-head.[c]
Dum. The head of a bodkin.
Biron. A death's face in a ring.
Long. The face of an old Roman coin, scarce seen.
Boyet. The pummel of Cæsar's faulchion.
Dum. The carv'd-bone face on a flask.[d]

---

[a] *O'erparted*—overparted, not quite equal to his part.
[b] The common tradition was that Judas hanged himself on an elder-tree. Thus, in Ben Jonson's "Every Man out of his Humour," "He shall be your Judas, and you shall be his elder-tree to hang on."
[c] *A cittern-head.* It appears from several passages in the old dramas, that the head of a cittern, gittern, or guitar, was terminated with a face.
[d] *Flask.* A soldier's powder horn which was often elaborately carved.

---

[a] *Libbard*—leopard.

Biron. St. George's half-cheek in a brooch.
Dum. Ay, and in a brooch of lead.
Biron. Ay, and worn in the cap of a toothdrawer.
And now, forward; for we have put thee in countenance.
Hol. You have put me out of countenance.
Biron. False: we have given thee faces.
Hol. But you have out-fac'd them all.
Biron. An thou wert a lion, we would do so.
Boyet. Therefore, as he is an ass, let him go.
And so adieu, sweet Jude! nay, why dost thou stay?
Dum. For the latter end of his name.
Biron. For the ass to the Jude; give it him:
—Jud-as, away.
Hol. This is not generous; not gentle; not humble.
Boyet. A light for monsieur Judas: it grows dark, he may stumble.
Prin. Alas, poor Machabæus, how hath he been baited!

Enter ARMADO, *armed, for* Hector.

Biron. Hide thy head, Achilles; here comes Hector in arms.
Dum. Though my mocks come home by me, I will now be merry.
King. Hector was but a Trojan in respect of this.
Boyet. But is this Hector?
Dum. I think Hector was not so clean-timbered.
Long. His leg is too big for Hector.
Dum. More calf, certain.
Boyet. No; he is best indued in the small.
Biron. This cannot be Hector.
Dum. He's a god or a painter; for he makes faces.
Arm. "The armipotent Mars, of lances the almighty,
Gave Hector a gift,"—
Dum. A gilt nutmeg.
Biron. A lemon.
Long. Stuck with cloves.
Dum. No, cloven.
Arm. Peace!
"The armipotent Mars, of lances the almighty,
  Gave Hector a gift, the heir of Ilion:
A man so breath'd, that certain he would fight, yea,
  From morn till night, out of his pavilion.
I am that flower,"—
Dum. That mint.
Long. That columbine.
Arm. Sweet lord Longaville, rein thy tongue.

Long. I must rather give it the rein, for it runs against Hector.
Dum. Ay, and Hector's a greyhound.
Arm. The sweet war-man is dead and rotten; sweet chucks, beat not the bones of the buried: when he breath'd, he was a man—But I will forward with my device: Sweet royalty, [*to the* PRINCESS] bestow on me the sense of hearing.
  [BIRON *whispers* COSTARD.
Prin. Speak, brave Hector; we are much delighted.
Arm. I do adore thy sweet grace's slipper.
Boyet. Loves her by the foot.
Dum. He may not by the yard.
Arm. "This Hector far surmounted Hannibal,"—
Cost. The party is gone, fellow Hector, she is gone; she is two months on her way.
Arm. What meanest thou?
Cost. Faith, unless you play the honest Trojan, the poor wench is cast away: she's quick; the child brags in her belly already; 't is yours.
Arm. Dost thou infamonize me among potentates? thou shalt die.
Cost. Then shall Hector be whipped, for Jaquenetta that is quick by him; and hanged, for Pompey that is dead by him.
Dum. Most rare Pompey!
Boyet. Renowned Pompey!
Biron. Greater than great, great, great, great Pompey! Pompey, the huge!
Dum. Hector trembles.
Biron. Pompey is moved:—More Ates, more Ates; stir them on! stir them on!
Dum. Hector will challenge him.
Biron. Ay, if he have no more man's blood in 's belly than will sup a flea.
Arm. By the north pole, I do challenge thee.
Cost. I will not fight with a pole, like a northern man;* I'll slash; I'll do it by the sword:—I pray you, let me borrow my arms again.
Dum. Room for the incensed worthies.
Cost. I'll do it in my shirt.
Dum. Most resolute Pompey!
Moth. Master, let me take you a button-hole lower. Do you not see, Pompey is uncasing for the combat? What mean you? you will lose your reputation.
Arm. Gentlemen, and soldiers, pardon me; I will not combat in my shirt.
Dum. You may not deny it; Pompey hath made the challenge.
Arm. Sweet bloods, I both may and will.
Biron. What reason have you for 't?

Arm. The naked truth of it is, I have no shirt; I go woolward for penance.[a]

Boyet. True, and it was enjoin'd him in Rome for want of linen: since when, I'll be sworn, he wore none but a dishclout of Jaquenetta's; and that 'a wears next his heart, for a favour.

Enter MERCADE.

Mer. God save you, madam!
Prin. Welcome, Mercade;
But that thou interrupt'st our merriment.
Mer. I am sorry, madam; for the news I bring
Is heavy in my tongue. The king, your father—
Prin. Dead, for my life.
Mer. Even so; my tale is told.
Biron. Worthies, away; the scene begins to cloud.
Arm. For mine own part, I breathe free breath: I have seen the day of wrong through the little hole of discretion, and I will right myself like a soldier. [*Exeunt Worthies.*
King. How fares your majesty?
Prin. Boyet, prepare; I will away to-night.
King. Madam, not so; I do beseech you, stay.
Prin. Prepare, I say.—I thank you, gracious lords,
For all your fair endeavours; and entreat,
Out of a new-sad soul, that you vouchsafe
In your rich wisdom, to excuse, or hide,
The liberal opposition of our spirits:
If over-boldly we have borne ourselves
In the converse of breath, your gentleness
Was guilty of it.—Farewell, worthy lord!
A heavy heart bears not a nimble[b] tongue:
Excuse me so, coming so short of thanks
For my great suit so easily obtain'd.
King. The extreme part of time extremely form[c]
All causes to the purpose of his speed;
And often, at his very loose, decides
That which long process could not arbitrate:
And though the mourning brow of progeny
Forbid the smiling courtesy of love,
The holy suit which fain it would convince;
Yet, since love's argument was first on foot,
Let not the cloud of sorrow justle it
From what it purpos'd; since, to wail friends lost,
Is not by much so wholesome, profitable,
As to rejoice at friends but newly found.

---
[a] *Woolward*, wanting the shirt, so as to leave the woollen cloth of the outer coat next the skin.
[b] *Humble* in old editions. Theobald reads *nimble*, which is now generally accepted.
[c] This is Mr. Dyce's reading: old copies have *parts*.

Prin. I understand you not; my griefs are double.
Biron. Honest plain words best pierce the ear of grief;—
And by these badges understand the king.
For your fair sakes have we neglected time;
Play'd foul play with our oaths. Your beauty, ladies,
Hath much deform'd us, fashioning our humours
Even to the opposed end of our intents:
And what in us hath seem'd ridiculous,—
As love is full of unbefitting strains;
All wanton as a child, skipping, and vain;
Form'd by the eye, and, therefore, like the eye
Full of stray[a] shapes, of habits, and of forms,
Varying in subjects as the eye doth roll
To every varied object in his glance:
Which party-coated presence of loose love
Put on by us, if, in your heavenly eyes,
Have misbecom'd our oaths and gravities,
Those heavenly eyes, that look into these faults,
Suggested us to make: Therefore, ladies,
Our love being yours, the error that love makes
Is likewise yours: we to ourselves prove false,
By being once false for ever to be true
To those that make us both,—fair ladies, you:
And even that falsehood, in itself a sin,
Thus purifies itself, and turns to grace.
Prin. We have receiv'd your letters, full of love;
Your favours, the embassadors of love;
And, in our maiden council, rated them
At courtship, pleasant jest, and courtesy,
As bombast,[b] and as lining to the time:
But more devout than this, in our respects,
Have we not been; and therefore met your loves
In their own fashion, like a merriment.
Dum. Our letters, madam, show'd much more than jest.
Long. So did our looks.
Ros.   We did not quote them so.
King. Now, at the latest minute of the hour,
Grant us your loves.
Prin.   A time, methinks, too short
To make a world-without-end bargain in:
No, no, my lord, your grace is perjur'd much,
Full of dear guiltiness; and, therefore this,—
If for my love (as there is no such cause)
You will do aught, this shall you do for me:
Your oath I will not trust; but go with speed
To some forlorn and naked hermitage,

---
[a] *Full of stray shapes.* The old copies read *straying*; the modern *strange.* Coleridge suggested *stray.*
[b] *Bombast*, from *bombagia*, cotton-wool used as stuffing.

Remote from all the pleasures of the world;
There stay, until the twelve celestial signs
Have brought about their annual reckoning:
If this austere insociable life
Change not your offer made in heat of blood;
If frosts, and fasts, hard lodging, and thin weeds,
Nip not the gaudy blossoms of your love,
But that it bear this trial, and last love;
Then, at the expiration of the year,
Come challenge, challenge me by these deserts,
And, by this virgin palm, now kissing thine,
I will be thine; and, till that instant, shut
My woeful self up in a mourning house;
Raining the tears of lamentation
For the remembrance of my father's death.
If this thou do deny, let our hands part;
Neither intitled in the other's heart.

King. If this, or more than this, I would deny,
To flatter up these powers of mine with rest,
The sudden hand of death close up mine eye!
Hence ever then my heart is in thy breast.

Biron. And what to me, my love? and what to me?*

Dum. But what to me, my love? but what to me?

Kath. A wife!—A beard, fair health, and honesty;
With three-fold love I wish you all these three.

Dum. O, shall I say, I thank you, gentle wife?

Kath. Not so, my lord;—a twelvemonth and a day
I'll mark no words that smooth-fac'd wooers say:
Come when the king doth to my lady come,
Then, if I have much love, I'll give you some.

Dum. I'll serve thee true and faithfully till then.

Kath. Yet swear not, lest you be forsworn again.

Long. What says Maria?

Mar. At the twelvemonth's end,
I'll change my black gown for a faithful friend.

Long. I'll stay with patience; but the time is long.

---

* The following lines here occur in all the old editions:—
"*Ros.* You must be purged too, your sins are rank;
You are attaint with faults and perjury;
Therefore, if you my favour mean to get,
A twelvemonth shall you spend, and never rest,
But seek the weary beds of people sick."
There can be no doubt, we think, that Rosaline's speech should be omitted, and Biron left without an answer to his question. This is Coleridge's suggestion. Rosaline's answer being so beautifully expanded in her subsequent speech, we have little doubt that these five lines did occur in the original play, and were not struck out of the copy when it was "augmented and amended." The theory stands upon a different ground from Biron's oratorical repetitions, in the fourth Act. Coleridge differs from Warburton as to the propriety of omitting Biron's question. He says:—"It is quite in Biron's character; and Rosaline not answering it immediately, Dumain takes up the question."

Mar. The liker you; few taller are so young.

Biron. Studies my lady? mistress, look on me,
Behold the window of my heart, mine eye,
What humble suit attends thy answer there;
Impose some service on me for thy love.

Ros. Oft have I heard of you, my lord Biron,
Before I saw you: and the world's large tongue
Proclaims you for a man replete with mocks;
Full of comparisons and wounding flouts;
Which you on all estates will execute,
That lie within the mercy of your wit:
To weed this wormwood from your fruitful brain,
And, therewithal, to win me, if you please,
(Without the which I am not to be won,)
You shall this twelvemonth term from day to day
Visit the speechless sick, and still converse
With groaning wretches; and your task shall be,
With all the fierce endeavour of your wit,
To enforce the pained impotent to smile.

Biron. To move wild laughter in the throat of death?
It cannot be; it is impossible:
Mirth cannot move a soul in agony.

Ros. Why, that's the way to choke a gibing spirit,
Whose influence is begot of that loose grace
Which shallow laughing hearers give to fools
A jest's prosperity lies in the ear
Of him that hears it, never in the tongue
Of him that makes it: then, if sickly ears,
Deaf'd with the clamours of their own dear groans,
Will hear your idle scorns, continue them,*
And I will have you, and that fault withal;
But, if they will not, throw away that spirit,
And I shall find you empty of that fault,
Right joyful of your reformation.

Biron. A twelvemonth? well, befal what will befal,
I'll jest a twelvemonth in an hospital.

Prin. Ay, sweet my lord; and so I take my leave. [*To the* KING.

King. No, madam, we will bring you on your way.

Biron. Our wooing doth not end like an old play;
Jack hath not Jill: these ladies' courtesy
Might well have made our sport a comedy.

King. Come, sir, it wants a twelvemonth and a day,
And then 't will end.

Biron. That's too long for a play.

---

* *Them*—Mr. Dyce's correction of *then*.

[Act V.]   LOVE'S LABOUR'S LOST.   [Scene II.

Enter ARMADO.

Arm. Sweet majesty, vouchsafe me,—
Prin. Was not that Hector?
Dum. The worthy knight of Troy.
Arm. I will kiss thy royal finger, and take leave: I am a votary; I have vowed to Jaquenetta to hold the plough for her sweet love three years. But, most esteemed greatness, will you hear the dialogue that the two learned men have compiled, in praise of the owl and the cuckoo? it should have followed in the end of our show.
King. Call them forth quickly, we will do so.
Arm. Holla! approach.

Enter HOLOFERNES, NATHANIEL, MOTH, COSTARD, *and others.*

This side is Hiems, winter; This Ver, the spring; the one maintained by the owl, the other by the cuckoo. Ver, begin.

SONG.

1.

Spring   When daisies pied, and violets blue,
   And lady-smocks all silver-white,
   And cuckoo-buds of yellow hue,
   Do paint the meadows with delight,
The cuckoo then, on every tree,
Mocks married men, for thus sings he,
   Cuckoo;
Cuckoo, cuckoo,—O word of fear,
Unpleasing to a married ear!

II.

When shepherds pipe on oaten straws,
   And merry larks are ploughmen's clocks,
When turtles tread, and rooks, and daws,
   And maidens bleach their summer smocks,
The cuckoo then, on every tree,
Mocks married men, for thus sings he,
   Cuckoo;
Cuckoo, cuckoo,—O word of fear,
Unpleasing to a married ear!

III.

Winter   When icicles hang by the wall,
   And Dick the shepherd blows his nail,
And Tom bears logs into the hall,
   And milk comes frozen home in pail,
When blood is nipp'd, and ways be foul,
Then nightly sings the staring owl,
   To-who;
To-whit, tu-who, a merry note,
While greasy Joan doth keel the pot.

IV.

When all aloud the wind doth blow,
   And coughing drowns the parson's saw,
And birds sit brooding in the snow,
   And Marian's nose looks red and raw,
When roasted crabs hiss in the bowl,
Then nightly sings the staring owl,
   To-who;
To-whit, to-who, a merry note,
While greasy Joan doth keel the pot.

Arm. The words of Mercury are harsh after the songs of Apollo. You, that way; we, this way.   [*Exeunt.*

ILLUSTRATIONS OF ACT V.

¹ Scene I.—"*Honorificabilitudinitatibus.*"

Taylor, the water-poet, has given us a syllable more of this delight of schoolboys—*honorificiubilitudinitatibus*. But he has not equalled Rabelais, who has thus furnished the title of a book that might puzzle Paternoster Row :—*Antipericatametaparbengedamphicribrationes.*

² Scene I.—"*The fifth, if I.*"

The pedant asks who is the silly sheep—quis, quis? "The third of the five vowels if you repeat them," says Moth; and the pedant does repeat them—a, e, I; the other two clinches it, says Moth, o, u (O you). This may appear a poor conundrum, and a low conceit, as Theobald has it, but the satire is in opposing the pedantry of the boy to the pedantry of the man, and making the pedant have the worst of it in what he calls "a quick venew of wit."

³ Scene I.—"*Venew of wit.*"

Steevens and Malone fiercely contradict each other as to the meaning of the word *renew*. "The cut-and-thrust notes on this occasion exhibit a complete match between the two great Shaksperian masters of defence," says Douce. This industrious commentator gives us five pages to determine the controversy; the argument of which amounts to this, that *renew* and *bout* equally denote a *hit* in fencing.

⁴ Scene II.— "*And are apparell'd thus,— Like Muscovites, or Russians.*"

For the Russian or Muscovite habits assumed by the king and nobles of Navarre, we are indebted to Vecellio. At page 303 of the edition of 1598, we find a noble Muscovite whose attire sufficiently corresponds with that described by Hall in his account of a Russian masque at Westminster, in the reign of Henry VIII., quoted by Ritson in illustration of this play.

"In the first year of King Henry VIII.," says the chronicler, "at a banquet made for the foreign ambassadors in the Parliament-chamber at Westminster, came the Lord Henry Earl of Wiltshire, and the Lord Fitzwalter, in two long gowns of yellow satin traversed with white satin, and in every bend* of white was a bend of crimson satin, after the fashion of Russia or Russland, with furred hats of grey on their heads, either of them having an hatchet in their hands, and boots with pikes turned up." The boots in Vecellio's print have no "pikes turned up," but we perceive the "long gown" of figured satin or damask, and the "furred hat." At page 283 of the same work we are presented also with the habit of the Grand Duke of Muscovy, a rich and imposing costume which might be worn by his majesty of Navarre himself.

* By *bend* is meant a broad diagonal stripe. It is an heraldic term, and constantly used in the description of dresses by writers of the middle ages.

⁵ Scene II.—"*Better wits have worn plain statute-caps.*"

By an act of parliament of 1571, it was provided that all above the age of six years, except the nobility and other persons of degree, should, on sabbath-days and holidays, wear caps of wool, manufactured in England. This was one of the laws for the encouragement of trade, which so occupied the legislatorial wisdom of our ancestors, and which the people, as constantly as they were enacted, evaded, or openly violated. This very law was repealed in 1597. Those to whom the law applied, and wore the statute-caps, wore citisens, and artificers, and labourers; and thus, as the nobility continued to wear their bonnets and feathers, Rosaline says, "*better wits have worn plain statute caps.*"

⁶ SCENE II.—"*You cannot beg us.*"
Costard means to say we are not idiots. One of the most abominable corruptions of the feudal system of government was for the sovereign, who was the legal guardian of idiots, to grant the wardship of such an unhappy person to some favourite, granting with the idiot the right of using his property. Ritson, and Douce more correctly, give a curious anecdote illustrative of this custom, and of its abuse.—
"The Lord North begg'd old Bladwell for a foole (though he could never prove him so), and having him in his custodie as a lunaticke, he carried him to a gentleman's house, one day, that was his neighbour. The L. North and the gentleman retir'd awhile to private discourse, and left Bladwell in the dining-roome, which was hung with a faire hanging; Bladwell walking up and downe, and viewing the imagerie, spyed a foole at last in the hanging, and without delay drawes his knife, flyes at the foole, cutts him cleane out, and layes him on the floore; my Lord and the gentleman coming in againe, and finding the tapestrie thus defac'd, he ask'd Bladwell what he meant by such a rude uncivill act; he answered, Sir, be content, I have rather done you a courtesie than a wrong, for, if ever my L. N. had seene the foole there he would have begg'd him, and so you might have lost your whole suite." (Harl. MS. 6395.)

⁷ SCENE II.—"*Pageant of the nine worthies.*"
The genuine worthies of the old pageant were Joshua, David, Judas Maccabeus, Hector, Alexander, Julius Cæsar, Arthur, Charlemagne, and Godfrey of Bulloigne. Sometimes Guy of Warwick was substituted for Godfrey of Bulloigne. These redoubted personages, according to a manuscript in the British Museum (Harl. 2057), were clad in complete armour, with crowns of gold on their heads, every one having his esquire to bear before him his shield and pennon at arms. According to this manuscript, these "Lords" were dressed as three Hebrews, three Infidels, and three Christians. Shakspere overthrew the just proportion of age and country, for he gives us four infidels, Hector, Pompey, Alexander, and Hercules, out of the five of the schoolmaster's pageant. In the MS. of the Harleian Collection, which is a Chester pageant, with illuminations, the *Four Seasons* conclude the representation of the Nine Worthies. Shakspere must have seen such an exhibition, and have thence derived the songs of *Ver* and *Hiems*.

LOVE'S LABOUR'S LOST.

⁸ SCENE II.—" *A very good bowler.*"

The preceding engraving of the bowls of the sixteenth century is designed from Strutt's 'Sports and Pastimes.' The sport, according to Strutt, appears to have prevailed in the fourteenth century, for he has given us figures of three persons engaged in bowling, from a manuscript of that date.

⁹ SCENE II.—" *I will not fight with a pole, like a northern man.*"

The old quarter-staff play of England was most practised in the north. Strutt, in his 'Sports,' and Ritson, in his 'Robin Hood Poems,' have given us representations of these loving contests, from which the following engraving has been designed.

¹⁰ SCENE II.—" *When daisies pied.*"

The first two stanzas of this song are set to music by Dr. Arne, with all that justness of conception and simple elegance of which he was so great a master, and which are conspicuous in nearly all of his compositions that are in union with Shakspere's words. The song having been "married" to music, it would not be well to disturb the received reading. Yet the deviations from all the original copies must be noted. There is a transposition in the first four lines, to meet the alternate rhymes in the subsequent verses. In the original we find :—

" When daisies pied, and violets blue,
And cuckoo-buds of yellow hue,
And lady-smocks all silver-white,
Do paint the meadows with delight."

In the third and fourth verses,

" *To-who*"

is a modern introduction to correspond with "Cuckoo;" but "*To-who*" alone is not the song of the owl—it is "*Tu-whit, to-who.*" The original lines stand thus :—

" Then nightly sings the staring owl,
Tu-whit, to-who,
A merry note."

Did not the original music vary with the varying form of the metre ?

SUPPLEMENTARY NOTICE.

CHARLES LAMB was wont to call Love's Labour's Lost the Comedy of Leisure. 'T is certain that in the commonwealth of King Ferdinand of Navarre we have,

"all men idle, all;
And women too."

The courtiers, in their pursuit of "that angel knowledge," waste their time in subtle contentions, how that angel is to be won;—the ladies from France spread their pavilions in the sunny park, and there keep up their round of jokes with their "wit's peddler," Boyet, "the nice;"—Armado listens to his page while he warbles "Concolinel;"—Jaquenetta, though she is "allowed for the day," seems to have no dairy to look after;—Costard acts as if he were neither ploughman nor swineherd, and born for no other work than to laugh for ever at Moth, and, in the excess of his love for that "pathetical nit," to exclaim, "An I had but one penny in the world, thou shouldst have it to buy gingerbread;"—the schoolmaster appears to be without scholars, the curate without a cure, the constable without watch and ward. There is, indeed, one parenthesis of real business connected with the progress of the action—the difference between France and Navarre, in the matter of Aquitain. But the settlement of this business is deferred till "to-morrow"—the "packet of specialities" is not come; and whether Aquitain goes back to France, or the hundred thousand crowns return to Navarre, we never learn. This matter, then, being postponed till a more fitting season, the whole set abandon themselves to what Dr. Johnson calls "strenuous idleness." The king and his courtiers forswear their studies, and every man becomes a lover and a sonneteer;—the refined traveller of Spain resigns himself to his passion for the dairy-maid; the schoolmaster and the curate talk learnedly after dinner; and, at last, the king, the nobles, the priest, the pedant, the braggart, the page, and the clown, join in one dance of mummery, in which they all laugh, and are laughed at. But still all this idleness is too energetic to warrant us in calling this the Comedy of Leisure. Let us try again. Is it not the Comedy of Affectations?

Molière, in his 'Précieuses Ridicules,' has admirably hit off one affectation that had found its way into the private life of his own times. The ladies aspired to be wooed after the fashion of the Grand Cyrus. Madelon will be called Polixène, and Cathos Aminte. They dismiss their plain

LOVE'S LABOUR'S LOST.

honest lovers, because marriage ought to be at the end of the romance, and not at the beginning. They dote upon Mascarille (the disguised lacquey) when he assures them "Les gens de qualité savent tout sans avoir jamais rien appris." They are in ecstasies at everything. Madelon is "furieusement pour les portraits;"—Cathos loves "terriblement les énigmes." Even Mascarille's ribbon is "furieusement bien choisi;"—his gloves "sentent terriblement bons;"—and his feathers are "effroyablement belles." But in the 'Précieuses Ridicules,' Molière, as we have said, dealt with one affectation;—in Love's Labour's Lost Shakspere presents us almost every variety of affectation that is founded upon a misdirection of intellectual activity. We have here many of the forms in which cleverness is exhibited as opposed to wisdom, and false refinement as opposed to simplicity. The affected characters, even the most fantastical, are not fools; but, at the same time, the natural characters, who, in this play, are chiefly the women, have their intellectual foibles. All the modes of affectation are developed in one continued stream of fun and drollery;—every one is laughing at the folly of the other, and the laugh grows louder and louder as the more natural characters, one by one, trip up the heels of the more affected. The most affected at last join in the laugh with the most natural; and the whole comes down to "plain kersey yea and nay,"—from the syntax of Holofernes, and the "fire-new words" of Armado, to "greasy Joan," and "roasted crabs."—Let us hastily review the comedy under this aspect.

The affectation of the King and his courtiers begins at the very beginning of the play. The mistake upon which they set out, in their desire to make their Court "a little academe," is not an uncommon one. It is the attempt to separate the contemplative from the active life; to forego duties for abstractions; to sacrifice innocent pleasures for plans of mortification, difficult to be executed, and useless if carried through. Many a young student has been haunted by the same dream; and he only required to be living in an age when vows bound mankind to objects of pursuit that now present but the ludicrous side, to have had his dreams converted into very silly realities. The resistance of Biron to the vow of his fellows is singularly able,—his reasoning is deep and true and ought to have turned them aside from their folly:—

> "Study is like the heaven's glorious sun,
> That will not be deep-search'd with saucy looks;
> Small have continual plodders ever won,
> Save base authority from others' books."

But the vow is ratified, and its abjuration will only be the result of its practical inconvenience. The "French king's daughter," the "admired princess," is coming to confer with the King and his Court, who have resolved to talk with no woman for three years:—

> "So study evermore is overshot."

But the "child of fancy" appears—the "fantastic"—the "magnificent"—the "man of great spirit who grows melancholy"—he who "is ill at reckoning because it fitteth the spirit of a tapster"—he who confesses to be a "gentleman and a gamester," because "both are the varnish of a complete man." How capitally does Moth, his page, hit him off, when he intimates that only "the base vulgar" call dence-ace three! And yet this indolent piece of refinement is

> "A man in all the world's new fashions planted,
> That hath a mint of phrases in his brain."

and he himself has no mean idea of his abilities—he is "for whole volumes in folio." Moth, who continually draws him out to laugh at him, is an embryo wag, whose common sense is constantly opposed to his master's affectations; and Costard is another cunning bit of nature, though cast in a coarser mould, whose heart runs over with joy at the tricks of his little friend, this "nit of mischief."

The Princess and her train arrive at Navarre. We have already learnt to like the King and his lords, and have seen their fine natures shining through the affectations by which they are clouded. We scarcely require, therefore, to hear their eulogies delivered from the mouths of the Princess's ladies, who have appreciated their real worth. Biron, however, has all along been our favourite; and we feel that, in some degree, he deserves the character which Rosaline gives him :—

SUPPLEMENTARY NOTICE.

> ———— "A merrier man,
> Within the limit of becoming mirth
> I never spent an hour's talk withal:
> His eye begets occasion for his wit;
> For every object that the one doth catch,
> The other turns to a mirth-moving jest;
> Which his fair tongue (conceit's expositor)
> Delivers in such apt and gracious words,
> That aged ears play truant at his tales,
> And younger hearings are quite ravished;
> So sweet and voluble is his discourse.'

But, with all this disposition to think highly of the nobles of the self-denying Court, the "mad wenches" of France are determined to use their "civil war of wits," on "Navarre and his book-men," for their absurd vows; and well do they keep their determination. Boyet is a capital courtier, always ready for a gibe at the ladies, and always ready to bear their gibes. Costard thinks he is "a most simple clown;" but Biron more accurately describes him at length:—

> ———— "Why, this is he,
> That kiss'd away his hand in courtesy:
> This is the ape of form, monsieur the nice,
> That, when he plays at tables chides the dice
> In honourable terms; nay, he can sing
> A mean most meanly: and, in ushering,
> Mend him who can: the ladies call him, sweet;
> The stairs, as he treads on them, kiss his feet."

We are very much tempted to think that, in his character of Boyet, Shakspere had in view that most amusing coxcomb Master Robert Laneham, whose letter from Kenilworth, in which he gives the following account of himself, was printed in 1575:—"Always among the gentlewomen with my good will, and when I see company according, then I can be as lively too. Sometimes I foot it with dancing; now with my gittern and else with my cittern; then at the virginals; ye know nothing comes amiss to me; then carol I up a song withal, that by and by they come flocking about me like bees to honey, and ever they cry, ' Another, good Laneham, another.' "

Before the end of Navarre's first interview with the Princess, Boyet has discovered that he is "infected." At the end of the next Act we learn from Biron himself that he is in the same condition. Away then goes the vow with the King and Biron. In the fourth Act we find that the infection has spread to all the lords; but the love of the King and his courtiers is thoroughly characteristic. It may be sincere enough, but it is still love fantastical.—It hath taught Biron "to rhyme and to be melancholy." The King drops his paper of poesy; Longaville reads his sonnet, which makes "flesh a deity;" and Dumain, in his most beautiful anacreontic,—as sweet a piece of music as Shakspere ever penned,—shows " how love can vary wit." The scene in which each lover is detected by the other, and all laughed at by Biron, till he is detected himself, is thoroughly dramatic; and there is perhaps nothing finer in the whole range of the Shaksperian comedy than the passage where Biron casts aside his disguises, and rises to the height of poetry and eloquence. The burst when the "rent lines" discover "some love" of Biron is incomparably fine:—

> ———— " Who sees the heavenly Rosaline,
> That, like a rude and savage man of Inde,
> At the first opening of the gorgeous east,
> Bows not his vassal head; and, strucken blind,
> Kisses the base ground with obedient breast?'

The famous speech of Biron, which follows, is perhaps unmatched as a display of poetical rhetoric, except by the speeches of Ulysses to Achilles in the third Act of Troilus and Cressida. Coleridge has admirably described this speech of Biron. "It is logic clothed in rhetoric;—but observe how Shakspere, in his two-fold being of poet and philosopher, avails himself of it to convey profound truths in the most lively images,—the whole remaining faithful to the character supposed to utter the lines, and the expressions themselves constituting a further development of that character."* The rhetoric of Biron produces its effect. "Now to plain dealing," says Longaville; but Biron, the

* Literary Remains, vol. ii., p. 106.

LOVES LABOUR'S LOST.

merry man whose love is still half fun, is for more circuitous modes than laying their hearts at the feet of their mistresses. He is of opinion that

> "Revels, dances, masks, and merry hours,
> Fore-run fair Love,"

and he therefore recommends "some strange pastime" to solace the dames. But "the gallants will be task'd."

King and Princess, lords and ladies, must make way for the great pedants. The *form* of affectation is now entirely changed. It is not the cleverness of rising superior to all other men by despising the "affects" to which every man is born;—it is not the cleverness of labouring at the most magnificent phrases to express the most common ideas;—but it is the cleverness of two persons using conventional terms, which they have picked up from a common source, and which they believe sealed to the mass of mankind, instead of employing the ordinary colloquial phrases by which ideas are rendered intelligible. This is pedantry—and Shakspere shows his excellent judgment in bringing a brace of pedants upon the scene. In O'Keefe's 'Agreeable Surprise,' and in Colman's 'Heir at Law,' we have a single pedant,—the one talking Latin to a milk-maid, and the other to a tallow-chandler. This is farce. But the pedantry of Holofernes and the curate is comedy. They each address the other in their freemasonry of learning. They each flatter the other. But for the rest of the world they look down upon them. "Sir," saith the curate, excusing the "twice-sod simplicity" of Goodman Dull, "he hath never fed of the dainties that are bred in a book; he hath not eat paper, as it were; he hath not drunk ink: his intellect is not replenished." But Goodman Dull has his intellect stimulated by this abuse. He has heard the riddles of the "ink-horn" men, and he sports a riddle of his own:—

> "You two are bookmen: Can you tell by your wit,
> What was a month old at Cain's birth, that's not five weeks old as yet?"

The answer of Holofernes is the very quintessence of pedantry. He gives Goodman Dull the hardest name for the moon in the mythology. Goodman Dull is with difficulty quieted. Holofernes then exhibits his poetry; and he "will something affect the letter, for it argues facility." He produces, as all pedants attempt to produce, not what is good when executed, but what is difficult of execution. Satisfied with his own performances—'the gift is good in those in whom it is acute, and I am thankful for it'—he is profuse in his contempt for other men's productions. He undertakes to prove Biron's canzonet "to be very unlearned, neither savouring of poetry, wit, nor invention." The portrait is two hundred years old, and yet how many of the present day might sit for it! Holofernes, however, is not meant by Shakspere for a blockhead. He is made of better stuff than the ordinary run of those who "educate youth at the charge-house." Shakspere has taken care that we should see flashes of good sense amidst his folly. To say nothing of the curate's commendations of his "reasons at dinner," we have his own description of Armado, to show how clearly he could discover the ludicrous side of others. The pedant can see the ridiculous in pedantry of another stamp. But the poet also takes care that the ridiculous side of "the two learned men" shall still be prominent. Moth and Costard are again brought upon the scene to laugh at those who "have been at a great feast of languages, and have stolen the scraps." Costard himself is growing affected. He has picked up the fashion of being clever, and he has himself stolen *honorificabilitudinitatibus* out of "the alms-basket of words." But business proceeds:— Holofernes will present before the Princess the nine worthies, and he will play three himself. The soul of the schoolmaster is in this magnificent device; and he looks down with most self-satisfied pity on honest Dull, who has spoken no word, and understood none.

The ladies have received verses and jewels from their lovers; but they trust not to the verses — they think them "bootless rhymes," the effusions of "prodigal wits:"—

> "Folly in fools bears not so strong a note,
> As foolery in the wise."

When Boyet discloses to the Princess the scheme of the mask of Muscovites she is more confirmed in her determination to laugh at the laughers:—

> "They do it but in mocking merriment,
> And mock for mock is only my intent."

SUPPLEMENTARY NOTICE.

The affectation of "speeches penn'd" is overthrown in a moment by the shrewdness of the women, who encounter the fustian harangue with prosaic action. Moth comes in crammed with others' affectations:—

> "All hail, the richest beauties on the earth!
> A holy parcel of the fairest dames"—

The ladies turn their backs on him—

> "That ever turn'd their—backs—to mortal views?"

Biron in vain gives him the cue—"their eyes, villain, their eyes!"—"the pigeon-egg of discretion" has ceased to be discreet—he is out, and the speech is ended. The maskers will try for themselves. They each take a masked lady apart, and each finds a wrong mistress, who has no sympathy with him. The keen breath of "mocking wenches" has puffed out all their fine conceits:—

> "Well, better wits have worn plain statute-caps."

The sharp medicine has had its effect. The King and his lords return without their disguises; and, being doomed to hear the echo of the laugh at their folly, they come down from their stilts to the level ground of common sense:—from "taffata phrases" and "figures pedantical" to

> "Russet yeas, and honest kersey noes."

But the worthies are coming; we have not yet done with the affectations and the mocking merriment. Biron maliciously desires "to have one show worse than the king's and his company." Those who have been laughed at now take to laughing at others. Costard, who is the most natural of the worthies, comes off with the fewest hurts. He has performed Pompey marvellously well, and he is not a little vain of his performance—"I hope I was perfect." When the learned curate breaks down as Alexander, the apology of Costard for his overthrow is inimitable: "There, an't shall please you; a foolish mild man; an honest man, look you, and soon dash'd! He is a marvellous good neighbour in sooth, and a very good bowler; but, for Alisander, alas! you see how 't is; a little o'erparted." Holofernes comes off worse than the curate—"Alas, poor Machabœus how hath he been baited!" We feel, in spite of our inclination to laugh at the pedant, that his remonstrance is just—"This is not generous, not gentle, not humble." We know that to be generous, to be gentle, to be humble, are the especial virtues of the great; and Shakspere makes us see that the schoolmaster is right. Lastly, comes Armado. His discomfiture is still more signal. The malicious trick that Biron suggests to Costard shows that Rosaline's original praise of him was not altogether deserved—that his merriment was not always

> "Within the limit of becoming mirth."

The affectations of Biron are cast aside, but he has a natural fault to correct, worse than any affectation; and beautifully does Rosaline hold up to him the glass which shows him how

> "to choke a gibing spirit,
> Whose influence is begot of that loose grace
> Which shallow laughing hearers give to fools."

The affectations are blown into thin air. The King and his courtiers have to turn from speculation to action—from fruitless vows to deeds of charity and piety. Armado is about to apply to what is useful: "I have vowed to Jaquenetta to hold the plough for her sweet love three years." The voices of the pedants are heard no more in scraps of Latin.—They are no longer "singled from the barbarous."—But, on the contrary, "the dialogue that the two learned men have compiled, in praise of the owl and the cuckoo," is full of the most familiar images, expressed in the most homely language. Shakspere, unquestionably, to our minds, brought in this most characteristic song—(a song that he might have written and sung in the chimney-corner of his father's own kitchen, long before he dreamt of having a play acted before Queen Elizabeth)—to mark, by an emphatic close, the triumph of simplicity over false refinement.

[Part of Windsor Castle, built in the time of Elizabeth.]

INTRODUCTORY NOTICE.

STATE OF THE TEXT, AND CHRONOLOGY, OF THE MERRY WIVES OF WINDSOR.

The first edition of this play was published in 1602, under the following title: 'A most pleasaunt and excellent conceited Comedy of Sir John Falstaffe, and the Merry Wives of Windsor. Entermixed with sundrie variable and pleasing humors of Sir Hugh the Welch Knight, Justice Shallow, and his wise Cousin M. Slender. With the swaggering vaine of Ancient Pistoll and Corporall Nym. By William Shakespeare. As it hath bene divers times acted by the Right Honourable my Lord Chamberlaines Servants; Both before her Majestie and else where. London: Printed by T. C. for Arthur Johnson,' &c. &c. 1602. The same copy was reprinted in 1619. The comedy as it now stands first appeared in the folio of 1623; and the play in that edition contains very nearly twice the number of lines that the quarto contains. The succession of scenes is the same in both copies, except in one instance; but the speeches of the several characters are greatly elaborated in the amended copy, and several of the characters not only heightened, but new distinctive features given to them. For example, the *Slender* of the present comedy—one of the most perfect of the minor characters of Shakspere—is a very inferior conception in the first copy. Our Slender has been worked up out of the first rough sketch, with touches at once delicate and powerful. Again, the *Justice Shallow* of the quarto is an amusing person—but he is not the present Shallow; we have not even the repetitions which identify him with the Shallow of Henry IV. We point out these matters here, for the purpose of shewing that, although the quarto of 1602 was most probably piratically published when the play had been re-modelled, and was reprinted without alteration in 1619 (the amended copy then remaining unpublished), the copy of that first edition must not be considered as an imperfect transcript of the complete play. The differences between the two copies are produced by the alterations of the author working upon his first sketch. The extent of these changes and elaborations can only be satisfactorily perceived by comparing the two copies, scene by scene. We have given a few examples in our foot-notes; and we here subjoin the scene at Herne's Oak, which has no doubt been completely re-written:—

INTRODUCTORY NOTICE.

QUARTO OF 1602.

Qui. You fairies that do haunt these shady groves
Look round about the wood if you can spy
A mortal that doth haunt our sacred round:
If such a one you can espy, give him his due,
And leave not till you pinch him black and blue.
Give them their charge, Puck, ere they part away.
 Sir Hugh. Come hither, Peane, go to the country houses,
And when you find a slut that lies asleep,
And all her dishes foul, and room unswept,
With your long nails pinch her till she cry,
And swear to mend her sluttish housewifery.
 Fai. I warrant you, I will perform your will.
 Hu. Where's Pead? Go and see where brokers sleep,
And fox-eyed serjeants, with their mace,
Go lay the proctors in the street,
And pinch the lousy serjeant's face:
Spare none of these when th' are a bed,
But such whose nose looks blue and red.
 Qui. Away, begone, his mind fulfil,
And look that none of you stand still.
Some do that thing, some do this,
All do something, none amiss.
 Sir Hugh. I smell a man of middle earth.
 Fal. God bless me from that Welch fairy.
 Quic. Look every one about this round,
And if that any here be found,
For his presumption in this place,
Spare neither leg, arm, head, nor face.
 Sir Hugh. See I have spied one by good luck,
His body man, his head a buck.
 Fal. God send me good fortune now, and I care not.
 Quick. Go strait, and do as I command,
And take a taper in your hand,
And set it to his fingers' ends,
And if you see it him offends,
And that he starteth at the flame,
Then he is mortal, know his name
If with an F it doth begin,
Why then be sure he's full of sin.
About it then, and know the truth,
Of this same metamorphosed youth.
 Sir Hugh. Give me the tapers, I will try
And if that he love venery.

FOLIO OF 1623.

Quick. Fairies, black, grey, green, and white
You moonshine-revellers, and shades of night,
You orphan-heirs of fixed destiny,
Attend your office and your quality.
Crier Hobgoblin, make the fairy oyes.
 Pist. Elves, list your names; silence, you airy toys.
Cricket, to Windsor chimneys shalt thou leap:
Where fires thou find'st unrak'd, and hearths unswept,
There pinch the maids as blue as bilberry:
Our radiant queen hates sluts and sluttery.
 Fal. They are fairies; he that speaks to them shall die.
I'll wink and couch: no man their works must eye.
 [*Lies down upon his face.*
 Eva. Where's Pede?—Go you, and where you find a maid,
That, ere she sleep, has thrice her prayers said,
Raise up the organs of her fantasy,
Sleep she as sound as careless infancy;
But those as sleep and think not on their sins,
Pinch them, arms, legs, backs, shoulders, sides, and shins.
 Quick. About, about;
Search Windsor castle, elves, within and out:
Strew good luck, ouphes, on every sacred room;
That it may stand till the perpetual doom,
In state as wholesome, as in state 'tis fit;
Worthy the owner, and the owner it.
The several chairs of order look you scour
With juice of balm, and every precious flower:
Each fair instalment, coat, and several crest,
With loyal blazon, evermore be blest!
And nightly, meadow-fairies, look you sing,
Like to the Garter's compass, in a ring:
The expressure that it bears green let it be.
More fertile-fresh than all the field to see;
And, *Hony soit qui mal y pense*, write
In emerald tufts, flowers purple, blue, and white:
Like sapphire, pearl, and rich embroidery,
Buckled below fair knight-hood's bending knee:
Fairies use flowers for their charactery.
Away; disperse: But, till 'tis one o'clock,
Our dance of custom, round about the oak
Of Herne the Hunter let us not forget.
 Eva. Pray you, lock hand in hand; yourselves in order set.
And twenty glow-worms shall our lanterns be,
To guide our measure round about the tree.
But, stay: I smell a man of middle earth.
 Fal. Heavens defend me from that Welch fairy!
Lest he transform me to a piece of cheese!
 Pist. Vild worm, thou wast o'erlooked even in thy birth.
 Quick. With trial-fire touch me his finger end:
If he be chaste, the flame will back descend
And turn him to no pain; but if he start,
It is the flesh of a corrupted heart.
 Pist. A trial, come.
 Eva. Come, will this wood take fire?
 [*They burn him with their tapers.*
 Fal. Oh, oh, oh!
 Quick. Corrupt, corrupt, and tainted in desire!
About him, fairies; sing a scornful rhyme;
And, as you trip, still pinch him to your time.

The quarto copy of the Merry Wives of Windsor being so completely different from the amended play, affords little assistance in the settlement of the text. Indeed, following the folio of 1623, there are very few real difficulties. Modern editors appear to us to have gone beyond their proper line of duty in "rescuing" lines from the quarto which the author had manifestly superseded by other passages. We have, for the most part, rejected these restorations, as they are called, but have given the passages in our foot-notes.

But, if the quarto is not to be taken as a guide in the formation of a text, it appears to us,

MERRY WIVES OF WINDSOR.

viewed in connexion with some circumstances which we shall venture to point out as heretofore in some degree unregarded, to be a highly interesting literary curiosity.

Malone, contrary to his opinion with regard to the quarto edition of Henry V., says of the quarto of the Merry Wives of Windsor, "The old edition in 1602, like that of Romeo and Juliet, is apparently a rough draught, and not a mutilated or imperfect copy." His view, therefore, of the period when this play was written, applies to the "rough draught." Malone's opinion of the date of this sketch is thus stated in his 'Chronological Order:'—

"The following line in the earliest edition of this comedy,

'Sail like my pinnace to those golden shores,'

shews that it was written after Sir Walter Raleigh's return from Guiana in 1596.

"The first sketch of the Merry Wives of Windsor was printed in 1602. It was entered in the books of the Stationers' Company on the 18th of January, 1601-2, and was therefore probably written in 1601, after the two parts of King Henry IV., being, it is said, composed at the desire of Queen Elizabeth, in order to exhibit Falstaff in love, when all the pleasantry which he could afford in any other situation was exhausted. But it may not be thought so clear that it was written after King Henry V. Nym and Bardolph are both hanged in King Henry V., yet appear in The Merry Wives of Windsor. Falstaff is disgraced in the Second Part of King Henry IV., and dies in King Henry V.; but, in the Merry Wives of Windsor, he talks as if he were yet in favour at court: 'If it should come to the ear of the court how I have been transformed,' &c : and Mr. Page discountenances Fenton's addresses to his daughter because he 'kept company with the wild prince and with Pointz.' These circumstances seem to favour the supposition that this play was written between the First and Second Parts of King Henry IV. But that it was not written then, may be collected from the tradition above mentioned. The truth, I believe, is, that though it ought to be read (as Dr. Johnson has observed) between the Second Part of King Henry IV. and King Henry V., it was written after King Henry V., and after Shakspere had killed Falstaff. In obedience to the royal commands, having revived him, he found it necessary at the same time to revive all those persons with whom he was wont to be exhibited, Nym, Pistol, Bardolph, and the Page: and disposed of them as he found it convenient, without a strict regard to their situations, or catastrophes in former plays."

The opinion that this comedy was written after the two parts of Henry IV. is not quite in consonance with the tradition that Queen Elizabeth desired to see Falstaff in love; for Shakspere might have given this turn to the character in Henry V., after the announcement in the Epilogue to the second Part of Henry IV.—"our humble author will continue the story, with Sir John in it." Malone's theory, therefore, that it was produced after Henry V., is in accordance with the tradition as received by him with such an implicit belief. George Chalmers, however, in his 'Supplemental Apology,' laughs at the tradition, and at Malone's theory. He believes that the three historical plays and the comedy were successively written in 1596, and in 1597, but that Henry V. was produced the last. He says " In it (Henry V.) Falstaff does not come out upon the stage, but dies of a sweat, after performing less than the attentive auditors were led to expect: and in it, ancient Pistol appears as the husband of Mistress Quickly; who also dies, during the ancient's absence in the wars of France. Yet do the commentators bring the knight to life, and revive and unmarry the dame, by assigning the year 1601 as the epoch of the Merry Wives of Windsor. Queen Elizabeth is said by the critics to have commanded these miracles to be worked in 1601,—a time when she was in no proper mood for such fooleries. The tradition on which is founded the story of Elizabeth's command to exhibit the facetious knight in love, I think too improbable for belief." Chalmers goes on to argue that after Falstaff's disgrace at the end of the second Part of Henry IV. (which is followed in Henry V. by the assertion that " the King has killed his heart") he was not in a fit condition for " a speedy appearance amongst the Merry Wives of Windsor;" and further, that if it be true, as the first Act of the second Part evinces, that Sir John, soon after doing good service at Shrewsbury, was sent off, with some charge, to Lord John of Lancaster at York, he could not consistently saunter to Windsor, after his rencounter with the Chief Justice." Looking at these contradictions, Chalmers places "the true epoch of this comedy in 1596;" and affirms "*that its proper place is before the first Part of Henry IV.*" We had been strongly impressed with the same opinion before we had seen the passage in Chalmers, which is not given under his view of the

INTRODUCTORY NOTICE

chronology of 'The Merry Wives of Windsor.' But we are quite aware that the theory is at first sight open to objection: though it is clearly not so objectionable as Malone's assertion that Shakspere revived his dead Falstaff, Quickly, Nym, and Bardolph; and it perhaps gets rid of the difficulties which belong to Dr. Johnson's opinion that "the present play ought to be read between Henry IV. and Henry V." The question, altogether, appears to us very interesting as a piece of literary history; and we therefore request the indulgence of our readers whilst we examine it somewhat in detail.

And first, of the *tradition* upon which Malone builds. Dennis, in an epistle prefixed to 'the Comical Gallant,' an alteration of this play which he published in 1702, says,—"This Comedy was written at her (Queen Elizabeth's) command, and by her direction, and she was so eager to see it acted that she commanded it to be finished in fourteen days; and was afterwards, as tradition tells us, very well pleased at the representation." The tradition, however, soon became more circumstantial; for Rowe and Pope and Theobald each inform us that Elizabeth was so well pleased with *the Falstaff of the two Parts of Henry IV.*, that she commanded a play to be written by Shakspere in which he should shew the Knight in Love. Malone considers that the tradition, as given by Dennis, came to him from Dryden, who received it from Davenant. The more circumstantial tradition was furnished by Gildon, who published it in his 'Remarks on Shakspeare's Plays,' in 1710. The tradition, as stated by Dennis, is not inconsistent with the belief that the Merry Wives of Windsor (of course we speak of the Sketch) was produced *before* the two Parts of Henry IV. The more circumstantial tradition is completely reconcilable only with Malone's theory, that Shakspere, *continuing* the comic characters of the Historical Plays in the Merry Wives of Windsor, ventured upon the daring experiment of reviving the dead.

Malone, according to his theory, believes that the Sketch of the Merry Wives of Windsor, "finished in fourteen days," was written in 1601; Chalmers that it was written in 1596. We are inclined to think that the period of the production of the original Sketch might have been even earlier than 1596.

Raleigh returned from his expedition to Guiana in 1596, having sailed in 1595. In the present text of the Merry Wives (Act I., Sc. III.) Falstaff says, "Here's another letter to her: she bears the purse too; she is *a region in Guiana*, all gold and bounty. I will be cheater to them both, and they shall be exchequers to me: they shall be my East and West Indies." In the original Sketch the passage stands thus: "Here is another letter to her; she bears the purse too. They shall be exchequers to me and I'll be cheaters to them both. They shall be my East and West Indies." In the amended text we have, subsequently,

"Sail like my pinnace to those golden shores."

which line is found in the quarto, *the* being in the place of *those*. This line *alone* is taken by Malone to shew that the Comedy, in its first unfinished state, "was written after Sir Walter Raleigh's return from Guiana in 1596." Surely this is not precise enough. *Golden shores* were spoken of metaphorically before Raleigh's voyage; but the *region in Guiana* is a very different indication. To our minds it shews that the Sketch was written *before* Raleigh's return;—the finished play after Guiana was known and talked of.

'The Fairy Queen' of Spenser was published in 1596. "The whole plot," says Chalmers, "which was laid by Mrs. Page, to be executed at the hour of fairy revel, around Herne's Oak, by urchins, ouphes, and fairies, green and white, was plainly an allusion to the *Fairy Queen* of 1596, which for some time after its publication was the universal talk." A *general* mention of fairies and fairy revels might naturally occur without any allusion to Spenser; and thus in the original Sketch we have only such a general mention. But in the amended copy of the folio *the Fairy Queen* is presented to the audience three times as a familiar name. If these passages may be taken to allude to 'The Fairy Queen' of Spenser, we have another proof (as far as such proof can go) that the original Sketch, in which they do *not* occur, was written before 1596.

Again, in Falstaff's address to the Merry Wives at Herne's Oak, we have—"Let the sky rain potatoes, . . . and snow eringoes." The words *potatoes* and *eringoes* are in Lodge's 'Devils Incarnate,' 1596;—but they are *not* found in the original sketch of this Comedy.

Whatever may be the date of the original Sketch, there can be no doubt, we think, that the play, as we have received it from the folio of 1623, was enlarged and revived after the production

MERRY WIVES OF WINDSOR.

of Henry IV. Some would assign this revival to the time of James I. The passages which indicate this, according to Malone and Chalmers, are those in which Falstaff says "You'll complain of me to the *King*,"—the word being *Council* in the quarto: "these *Knights* will hack;"—(See Act II. Scene 1) Mrs. Quickly's allusion to *Coaches* (See Illustration); the poetical description of the insignia of the Garter; and the mention of the "*Cotsall*" games. But as not one of these passages is found in the original quarto, the question of the date of the sketch remains untouched by them. The *exact* date is of very little importance, because we do not know the *exact* dates of the two Parts of Henry IV. But, before we leave this branch of the subject we may briefly notice a matter which is in itself curious, and hitherto unnoticed.

In the original Sketch we have the following passage:—

> "*Doctor.* Where be my host de gartir!
> *Host.* O, here sir, in perplexity.
> *Doctor.* I cannot tell vat he dad,
> But be-gar I will tell you von ting.
> Dere be a *Germane* duke come to de court
> Has cosened all the hosts of Brainford
> And Reading."

In the folio the passage stands thus:

> "*Caius.* Vere is mine *Host de Jarterre?*
> *Host.* Here, master doctor, in perplexity and doubtful dilemma.
> *Caius.* I cannot tell vat is dat: but it is tell a me, dat you make grand preparation for a duke *de Jarmany*; by my trot, dere is no duke dat de court is know to come."

In the original Sketch we have the story of the "cozenage" of my Host of the Garter, by some Germans, who pretended to be of the retinue of a German Duke. Now, if we knew that a real German Duke had visited Windsor—(a rare occurrence in the days of Elizabeth) we should have the date of the comedy pretty exactly fixed. The circumstance would be one of those local and temporary allusions which Shakspere seized upon to arrest the attention of his audience. In 1592, a German Duke did visit Windsor. We had access, through the kindness of Mr. T. Rodd, to a narrative printed in the old German language, of the journey to England of the Duke of Würtemberg, in 1592, which narrative, drawn up by his Secretary, contains a daily journal of his proceedings. He was accompanied by a considerable retinue, and travelled under the name of "the Count Mombeliard."

The title of this work may be translated as follows:—

'A short and true description of the bathing journey* which his Serene Highness the Right Honourable Prince and Lord Frederick, Duke of Würtemburg, and Teck, Count of Mümpelgart, Lord (Baron) of Heidenheim, Knight of the two ancient royal orders of St. Michael, in France, and of the Garter, in England, &c., &c., lately performed, in the year 1592, from Mümpelgart, into the celebrated kingdom of England, afterwards returning through the Netherlands, until his arrival again at Mümpelgart. Noted down from day to day in the briefest manner, by your Princely Grace's gracious command, by your fellow-traveller and Private Secretary. Printed at Tübingen, by Erhardo Cellio, in 1602.'

This curious volume contains a sort of passport from Lord Howard, addressed to all Justices of Peace, Mayors, and Bailiffs, which we give without correction of the orthography:—

"Theras this nobleman, Counte Mombeliard, is to passe ouer Contrye in England, in to the lowe Countryes, Thise schal be to wil and command you in heer Majts. name for such, and is heer pleasure to see him fournissed with post horses in his trauail to the sea side, and there to soecke up such schippinge as schalbe fit for his transportations, *he pay nothing for the same*, for wich tis schalbe your sufficient warrante soo see that your faile noth thereof at your perilles. From Bifleete, the 2 of September, 1592. Your friend, C. HOWARD."

The "German duke" visited Windsor; was shewn "the splendidly beautiful and royal castle;"

---

* The Author, in an address to the reader, explains that this title, though it may appear strange, as only one bathing-place is visited, has been adopted, because as in the "usual bathing-journeys it is common to assemble together, as well all sorts of strange persons out of foreign places and nations, as known friends and sick people, even so in the description of this bathing-journey will be found all sorts of curious things, and strange (marvellous) histories."

INTRODUCTORY NOTICE.

hunted in the "parks full of fallow-deer and other game;" heard the music of an organ, and of other instruments, with the voices of little boys, as well as a sermon an hour long, in a church covered with lead; and, after staying two days, departed for Hampton Court.* His grace and his suite must have caused a sensation at Windsor. Probably mine Host of the Garter had really made "grand preparation for a Duke de Jarmany;"—at any rate he would believe Bardolph's story,— "the Germans desire to have three of your horses." Was there any dispute about the ultimate payment for the Duke's horses, for which he was "to pay nothing?" Was my host out of his reckoning when he said, "they shall have my horses, but I'll make them pay?" We have little doubt that the passages which relate to the German Duke (all of which with slight alteration, are in the original sketch,) have reference to the Duke of Würtemburg's visit to Windsor in 1592,—a matter to be forgotten in 1601, when Malone says the sketch was written; and somewhat stale in 1596, which Chalmers assigns as its date.

We now proceed to the more interesting point—was the Merry Wives of Windsor produced, either *after* the first Part of Henry IV., *after* the second Part, *after* Henry V., or *before* all of these Historical Plays? Let us first, state the difficulties which inseparably belong to the circumstances under which the similar characters of the Historical Plays and the Comedy are found, if the Comedy is to be received as a *continuation* of the Historical Plays.

The Falstaff of the two Parts of Henry IV., who dies in Henry V., but who, according to Malone, comes alive again in the Merry Wives, is found at Windsor living lavishly at the Garter Inn, sitting "at ten pounds a week,"—with Bardolph and Nym and Pistol and the Page, his "followers." At what point of his previous life is Falstaff in this flourishing condition? At Windsor he is represented as having committed an outrage upon one Justice Shallow. Could this outrage have been perpetrated after the borrowing of the "thousand pound," which was unpaid at the time of Henry the Fifth's coronation; or did it take place before Falstaff and Shallow renewed their youthful acquaintance under the auspices of Justice Silence? Johnson says "this play should be read between King Henry IV. and King Henry V." that is, after Falstaff's renewed intercourse with Shallow, the borrowing of the thousand pounds, and the failure of his schemes at the coronation. Another writer says "it ought rather to be read between the first and the second Part of King Henry IV.,"—that is, before Falstaff had met Shallow at his seat in Gloucestershire, at which meeting Shallow recollects nothing that had taken place at Windsor, and had clean forgotten the outrages of Falstaff upon his keeper, his dogs, and his deer. But Falstaff had been surrounded by much more important circumstances than had belonged to his acquaintance with Master Shallow. He had been the intimate of a Prince — he had held high charge in the royal army. We learn indeed that he is a "soldier" when he addresses Mrs. Ford; but he entirely abstains from any of those allusions to his royal friend which might have been supposed to be acceptable to a Merry Wife of Windsor. In the folio copy of the amended play, we have, positively, not one allusion to his connexion with the Court. In the quarto there is one solitary passage, which would apply to any Court—to that of Elizabeth, as well as to that of Henry V.—"Well, if the flue wits of the Court hear this, they'll so whip me with their keen jests that they'll melt me out like tallow." In the same quarto, when Falstaff hears the noise of hunters at Herne's Oak, he exclaims, "I'll lay my life the mad Prince of Wales is stealing his father's deer." This points apparently at the Prince of Henry IV.; but we think it had reference to the Prince of the 'Famous Victories,'—a character with whom Shakspere's audience was familiar. The passage is left out in the amended play; but we find another passage which certainly is meant for a link, however slight, between the Merry Wives and Henry IV.: Page objects to Fenton that "he kept company with the wild Prince and with Poins." The corresponding passage in the quarto is "the gentlemen is wild—he knows too much."

What does Shallow do at Windsor—he who inquired "how a good yoke of bullocks at Stamford fair?"—Robert Shallow, of Glostershire, "a poor esquire of this county, and one of the king's justices of the peace?" It is true that we are told by Slender that he was "in the county of Gloster, justice of peace and *coram*," — but this information is first given us in the amended edition. In the sketch, *Master* Shallow (we do not find even his name of Robert) is indeed a "cavalero justice," according to our Host of the Garter, but his commission may be in Berkshire for aught that the poet tells us to the contrary. Slender, indeed is, "as good as is any in Glostershire, under the degree of

---

* We have given the description of the Parks in the Local Illustration of Act II.

MERRY WIVES OF WINDSOR.

a squire," and he is Shallow's cousin;—but of Shallow "the local habitation" is undefined enough to make us believe that he might have been a son, or indeed a father (for he says, "I am fourscore,") of the real Justice Shallow. Again:—In Henry IV., Part I., we have a *Hostess* without a name,—the "good pint-pot" who is exhorted by Falstaff "love thy *husband*;"—in Henry IV., Part II., we have Hostess *Quickly*,—"a poor *widow*," according to the Chief Justice, to whom Falstaff owes himself and his money too;—In Henry V., this good Hostess is "*the quondam Quickly*," who has married Pistol, and who, if the received opinion be correct, died before her husband returned from the wars of Henry V. Where shall we place the *Mistress Quickly*, than whom "never a woman in Windsor knows more of Anne's mind,"—and who defies all angels "but in the way of honesty?"—She has evidently had no previous passages with Sir John Falstaff;—she is "a foolish carrion" only,—Dr. Caius's nurse, or his dry nurse, or his cook, or his laundry;—she has not heard Falstaff declaim, "as like one of these harlotry players as I ever see;"—she has not sate with him by a sea-coal fire, when goodwife Keech, the butcher's wife, came in and called her "gossip Quickly;"—she did not see him "fumble with the sheets, and play with flowers, and smile upon his fingers' ends," when "there was but one way." Falstaff and Quickly are strangers. She is to him either "goodwife" or "good maid,"—and at any rate only "fair woman." Surely, we cannot place Mistress Quickly of the Merry Wives after Henry V., when she was dead; or after the second Part of Henry IV., when she was a "poor widow;" or before the second Part, when she had a husband and children. She must stand alone in the Merry Wives,—an undefined predecessor of the famous Quickly of the Boar's Head.

But Pistol and Bardolph—are they not the same "irregular humorists" (as they are called in the original list of characters to the second Part of Henry IV.,) acting with Falstaff under the same circumstances? We think not. The Pistol of the Merry Wives is not the "ancient" Pistol of the second Part of Henry IV. and of Henry V., nor is Bardolph the "corporal" Bardolph of the second Part of Henry IV., nor the "lieutenant" Bardolph of Henry V. In the title-page, indeed, of the sketch, published as we believe without authority as a substitute for the more complete play, we have "the swaggering vaine (vein) of *ancient* Pistoll and *corporal* Nym." Corporal Nym is no companion of Falstaff in the Historical Plays, for he first makes his appearance in the Henry V. Neither Pistol, nor Bardolph, nor Nym, appear in the Merry Wives to be soldiers serving under Falstaff. They are his "cogging companions" of the first sketch; they are his "coney-catching rascals" of the amended play;—in both they are his "followers" whom he can turn away, discard, cashier; but Falstaff is not their "captain."

It certainly does appear to us that these anomalous positions in which the characters common to the Merry Wives of Windsor and the Henry IV. and Henry V. are placed, furnish a very strong presumption that the Comedy was *not a continuation* of the Histories. That the Merry Wives of Windsor was a continuation of Henry V. appears to us impossible. Malone does not think it very clear that the Merry Wives of Windsor "was written after King Henry V. Nym and Bardolph are both *hanged* in King Henry V., yet appear in the Merry Wives of Windsor. Falstaff is disgraced in the second part of King Henry IV., and *dies* in King Henry V.; but in the Merry Wives of Windsor he talks as if he were yet in favour at court." Assuredly these are very natural objections to the theory that the Comedy was written after Henry V.; but Malone disposes of the difficulty by the summary process of *revival*. Did ever any the most bungling writer of imagination proceed upon such a principle as is here imputed to the most skilful of dramatists?—Would any audience ever endure such a violence to their habitual modes of thought? Would the readers of the Spectator have tolerated the revival of Sir Roger de Coverley in the Guardian? Could the mother of the Mary of Avenel of the Monastery be found alive in the Abbot, except through the agency of the White Lady? The conception is much too monstrous.

Every person who has written on the *character* of Falstaff admits the inferiority of the *butt* of the Merry Wives of Windsor to the *wit* of the Boar's Head. It is remarkable that in Morgann's very elaborate Essay on the Character of Falstaff not one of his characteristics is derived from the Comedy. It has been regretted, by more than one critic, that Shakspere should have carried on the disgrace of Falstaff in the conclusion of Henry IV., to the further humiliation of the scenes at Datchet Mead and Herne's Oak; and, what is worse, that Shakspere should in the Comedy have exaggerated the vices of Falstaff, and brought him down from his intellectual eminence. Shakspere found somewhat similar incidents to the adventures of Falstaff with Mrs. Ford in a 'Story of

INTRODUCTORY NOTICE.

the two Lovers of Pisa,' published in Tarleton's 'Newes out of Purgatorie,' 1590. In that story an intrigue is carried on, with no innocent intentions on the part of the lady, with a young man who makes the old husband his confidant, as Falstaff makes Brook, and whose escapes in chests and up chimneys may have suggested the higher comedy of the buck-basket and the wise woman of Brentford. The story is given at length in Malone's edition of our poet. But Shakspere desired to show a butt and a dupe—not a successful gallant; a husband jealous without cause—not an unhappy old man plotting against his betrayers. He gave the whole affair a ludicrous turn. He made the lover old and fat and avaricious;—betrayed by his own greediness and vanity into the most humiliating scrapes, so that his complete degradation was the natural denouement of the whole adventure, and the progress of his shame the proper source of merriment. Could the adroit and witty Falstaff of Henry IV. have been selected by Shakspere for such an exhibition? In truth the Falstaff of the Merry Wives, *especially as we have him in the first sketch*, is not at all adroit, and not very witty. Read the very first scene in which Falstaff appears in this comedy. To Shallow's reproaches he opposes no weapon but impudence, and that not of the sublime kind which so astounds us in the Henry IV. Read further the scene in which he discloses his views upon the Merry Wives to Pistol and Nym. Here Pistol is the wit:—

"*Fal.* My honest lads, I will tell you what I am about.
Pist. Two yards and more.
Fal. No quips now, Pistol."

Again, in the same scene:—

"*Fal.* Sometimes the beam of her view gilded my foot, sometimes my portly belly.
Pist. Then did the sun on dunghill shine."

There can be no doubt, however, that when the comedy was re-modelled, which certainly was done after the production of Henry IV., the character of Falstaff was much heightened. But still the poet kept him far behind the Falstaff of Henry IV. Falstaff's descriptions, first to Bardolph and then to Brook, of his buck-basket adventure, are amongst the best things in the comedy, and they are very slightly altered from the original sketch. But compare them with any of the racy passages of the Falstaff of the Boar's Head, and after the comparison we feel ourselves in the presence of a being of far lower powers of intellect than the Falstaff "unimitated, unimitable." Is this acknowledged inferiority of the Falstaff of the Merry Wives most easily reconciled with the theory that he was produced before or after the Falstaff of the Henry IV.? That Elizabeth might have suggested the Merry Wives, originally, upon some traditionary tale of Windsor—that it might have been acted in the gallery which she built at Windsor, and which still bears her name— we can understand; but we cannot reconcile the belief that Shakspere produced the Falstaff of the Merry Wives after the Falstaff of Henry IV. with our unbounded confidence in the habitual power of such a poet. To him Falstaff was a thing of reality. He had drawn a man altogether different from other men, but altogether in nature. Could *he* much lower the character of that man? Another and a feebler dramatist might have given us the Falstaff of the Merry Wives as an imitation of the Falstaff of Henry IV.; but Shakspere *must* have abided by the one Falstaff that he had made after such a wondrous fashion of truth and originality.

And then Justice Shallow—never-to-be-forgotten Justice Shallow!—The Shallow who will bring Falstaff "before the Council" is not the Shallow who with him "heard the chimes at midnight." The Shallow of the Sketch of the Merry Wives has not even Shallow's trick of repetition. In the amended Play this characteristic may be recognised; but in the sketch there is not a trace of it. For example, in the first Scene of the finished play we find Shallow talking somewhat like the great Shallow, especially about the fallow greyhound; in the sketch this passage is altogether wanting. In the Sketch he says to Page, "Though he be a knight he shall not think to carry it so away. Master Page, I will not be wrong'd." In the finished play we have, "He hath wrong'd me indeed he hath, at a word he hath: believe me, Robert Shallow, esquire, saith he is wrong'd." And Bardolph too! Could it be predicated that the Bardolph of a comedy which was produced after the Henry IV. would want those "meteors and exhalations" which characterise the Bardolph who was a standing joke to Falstaff and the Prince? Would his zeal cease to "burn in his nose?" Absolutely, in the first Sketch, there is not the slightest allusion to that face which ever "blushed extempore." One mention, indeed, there is in the complete play of the "red face," and one supposed allusion of "Scarlet and John." The commentators have wished to show that Bardolph

MERRY WIVES OF WINDSOR.

in both copies is called "a tinder-box" on account of his nose; but this is not very clear. And then Pistol is not the magnificent bully of the second Part of Henry IV., and of Henry V. He has "affectations," as Sir Hugh mentions, and speaks "in Latin," as Slender has it;—but he is here literally "a tame cheater," but not without considerable cleverness. "Why then the world's mine oyster" is essentially higher than the obscure bombast of the real Pistol. Of Mistress Quickly we have already spoken as to the circumstances in which she is placed; and these circumstances are so essentially different that we can scarcely recognise any marked similarity of character in the original Sketch.

Having, then, seen the great and insuperable difficulties which belong to the theory that the Merry Wives of Windsor was written *after* the Histories, let us consider what difficulties, both of situation and character, present themselves under the other theory, that the Comedy was produced *before* the Histories.

First, is it irreconcilable with the tradition referring to Queen Elizabeth? It is not so, if we adopt the tradition as related by Dennis—this Comedy was written by Queen Elizabeth's command, and finished in fourteen days. This statement of the matter is plain and simple; because it is disembarrassed of those explanations and inferences which never belong to any popular tradition, but are superadded by ingenious persons who have a theory to establish. We can perfectly understand how the Merry Wives of Windsor, as we have it in the first Sketch, might have been produced by Shakspere in a fortnight;—and how such a slight and lively piece, containing many local allusions, and perhaps some delineations of real characters, might have furnished the greatest solace to Elizabeth some seven or eight years before the end of the sixteenth century, after mornings busily employed in talking politics with Leicester, or in translating Boetius in her own private chamber. The manners throughout, and without any disguise, are those of Elizabeth's own time. Leave out the line in the amended play of "the mad Prince and Poins,"—and the line in the Sketch about "the wild Prince killing his father's deer"—and the whole play (taken apart from the Histories) might with much greater propriety be acted with the costume of the age of Elizabeth. It is for this reason, most probably, that we find so little of pure poetry either in the Sketch or the finished performance. As Shakspere placed his characters in his own country, with the manners of his own days, he made them speak like ordinary human beings, shewing

> "—— deeds, and language, such as men do use,
> And persons such as Comedy would choose,
> When she would shew an image of the times,
> And sport with human follies, not with crimes."*

We may believe, therefore, the tradition (without adopting the circumstances which make it difficult of belief) and accept the theory that the Merry Wives of Windsor was written before the Henry IV.

Secondly, is the theory that the Comedy was produced *before* the Histories, irreconcilable with the *contradictory circumstances* which render the other theory so difficult of admission. Assuming that the Comedy was written before the Histories, it can be read without any violence to our indelible recollections of the situations of the characters in the Henry IV. and Henry V. It must be read with a conviction that if there be any connexion of the action at all, it is a very slight one—and that this action precedes the Henry IV. by some indefinite period. Then, the Falstaff who in the quiet shades of Windsor did begin to perceive he was "made an ass" had not acquired the experience of the city, for before he knew Hal he "knew nothing;"—then the fair maid Quickly, who afterwards contrived to have a husband and be a poor widow without changing her name, knew no higher sphere than the charge of Dr. Caius's laundry and kitchen;— then Pistol was not an ancient, certainly had not married the quondam Quickly, had not made the dangerous experiment of jesting with Fluellen, and occasionally talked like a reasonable being;— then Shallow had some unexplained business which took him from Glostershire to Windsor, travelled without his man Davy, had not lent a thousand pounds to Sir John Falstaff, and was not quite so silly and so delightful as when he had drunk "too much sack at supper" toasting "all the cavaleroes about London;"—then, lastly, Bardolph was not "Master Corporate Bardolph," and certainly Nym and he had not been hanged.

Thirdly, does the theory of the production of the Merry Wives of Windsor *before* Henry IV.

---

* Ben Jonson. Prologue to 'Every Man in his Humour.'

INTRODUCTORY NOTICE.

and Henry V., furnish a proper solution of the remarkable inferiority in the Comedy of several of the characters which are common to both? If we accept the opinion that the Falstaff, the Shallow, the Quickly, the Pistol, Bardolph, and Nym, of the Merry Wives, were all originally conceived by the poet before the characters with similar names in the Henry IV. and Henry V.; and that after they had been in some degree adopted in the Historical Plays, Shakspere remodelled the Merry Wives, and heightened the resemblances of character which the resemblances of name implied,— the inferiority in several of these characters, especially in the Sketch, will be accounted for, without assuming, with Johnson, that "the poet approached as near as he could to the work enjoined him; yet having perhaps in the former play completed his own idea, seems not to have been able to give Falstaff all his former powers of entertainment." Johnson's opinion proceeds upon the very just assumption that *continuations* are, for the most part, inferior to original conceptions. But the Merry Wives could not have been proposed as a continuation of the Henry IV. and the Henry V., even if it had been written after those plays. If it were written after the Histories the author certainly mystified all the new circumstances as compared with those which had preceded them, for the purpose of destroying the idea of continuation. This appears to us too violent an assumption. But no other can be maintained. To attribute such interminable contradictions to negligence, is to assume that Shakspere was not only the greatest of poets, but of blunderers.

And now we must hazard a conjecture. The reader will remember that in the Introductory Notice to Henry IV. we gave a brief account of the evidence by which it has been attempted to shew that the Falstaff of the *first* Part of Henry IV. was originally called *Oldcastle*. If that were the case, and the balance of evidence is in favour of that opinion, the whole matter seems to us clearer. Let it be remembered that Falstaff and Bardolph are the only characters that are common to the *first* Part of Henry IV. and the Merry Wives of Windsor; for in the original copy of Henry IV. Part I. the person who stands amongst the modern list of characters as Quickly is invariably called *the Hostess*. If the Falstaff, then, of Henry IV. were originally Oldcastle, we have only Bardolph left in common to the two dramas. Was Bardolph originally called so in Henry IV. Part I.? When Poins proposes to the Prince to go to Gadshill he says, in the original copy, "I have a jest to execute that I cannot manage alone,—Falstaff, Harvey, Rossil and Gadshill shall rob these men," &c. We now read "Falstaff, Bardolph, Peto, and Gadshill," &c. It has been conjectured that Harvey and Rossil were the names of actors; but as *Oldcastle* remains where we now read Falstaff in one place of the original copy, might not in the same way Bardolph have been originally *Harvey* or *Rossil*? This point, however, is not material. If Shakspere were compelled, by a strong expression of public opinion, to remove the name of *Oldcastle* from the first Part of Henry IV., the name of *Falstaff* was ready to his hand as a substitute. He had drawn a *knight, fat and unscrupulous*, as he had represented *Oldcastle*, but far his inferior in wit, humour, inexhaustible merriment, presence of mind, and intellectual activity. The transition was not inconsistent from the Falstaff of the Merry Wives to the Falstaff of Henry IV. The character, when Shakspere remodelled the first sketch of the comedy, required some elevation;—but it still might stand at a long distance, without offence to an audience who knew that the inferior creation was first produced. With Falstaff Shakspere might have transferred Bardolph to the first Part of Henry IV., but materially altered. The base Hungarian wight who would "the spigot wield," had, as a tapster, his nose a "fiery kitchen" to roast malt-worms; and he was fit to save him "a thousand marks in links and torches." When, further, Falstaff had completely superseded Oldcastle in the first Part of Henry IV., Shakspere might have adopted Pistol and Shallow and Quickly in the second Part,—but greatly changed;—and lastly, have introduced Nym to the Henry V. unchanged. All this being accomplished, he would naturally have remodelled the first sketch of the Merry Wives,—making the relations between the characters of the comedy and of the histories closer, but still of purpose keeping the situations sufficiently distinct. He thus for ever connected the Merry Wives with the Historical Plays. The Falstaff of the comedy must now belong to the age of Henry IV.; but to be understood he must, we venture to think, be regarded as the embryo Falstaff.

We request that it may be borne in mind that the entire argument which we have thus advanced is founded upon a conviction that the original Sketch, as published in the quarto of 1602, is an authentic production of our poet. Had no such Sketch existed, we must have reconciled the difficulties of believing the Merry Wives of Windsor to have been produced *after* Henry IV. and Henry V., as we

MERRY WIVES OF WINDSOR.

best might have done. Then we must have acknowledged that the characters of Falstaff and Shallow and Quickly were the same in the Comedy and the Henry IV., though represented *under different circumstances*. Then we must have believed that the contradictory situations were to be explained by the determination of Shakspere boldly to disregard the circumstances which resulted from his compliance with the commands of Elizabeth—" to shew Falstaff in love." But that sketch being preserved to us, it is much easier, we think, to believe that it was produced before the Histories; and that the characters were subsequently heightened, and more strikingly delineated, to assimilate them to the characters of the Histories. After all, we have endeavoured, whilst we have expressed our own belief, fairly to present both sides of the question. The point, we think, is of interest to the lovers of Shakspere; for inferring that the comedy is a continuation of the history, the inferiority of the Falstaff of the Merry Wives to the Falstaff of Henry IV., implies a considerable abatement of the poet's skill. On the other hand, the conviction that the sketch of the comedy preceded the history—that it was an early play—and that it was subsequently remodelled—is consistent with the belief in the progression of that extraordinary intellect which acquired greater vigour the more its powers were exercised.

COSTUME.

The costume of this Comedy is, of course, the same with that of the two parts of Henry IV., and, therefore, for its general description we must refer our readers to the notice affixed to Part I. of that play. Chaucer, however, who wrote his Canterbury Tales towards the close of the previous reign, gives us a few hints for the habit of some of the principal characters in the Merry Wives. Dr. Caius, for instance, should be clothed, like the Doctor of Physic, "in sanguine and in perse," (i. e. in purple and light blue) the gown being "lined with tafata and sendal." In " the Testament of Cresseyde" Chaucer speaks of a Physician in "a scarlet gown," and "furred well, as such a one ought to be;" but scarlet and purple were terms used indifferently one for the other, and the phrase "scarlet *red*" was generally used to designate that colour which we now call scarlet.

The Franklin or Country gentleman—the Master Page, or Master Ford of this play—is merely said to have worn an anelace or knife, and a white silk gipciere or purse hanging at his girdle.

The young 'Squire may furnish us with the dress of Master Fenton. He is described as wearing a short gown, with sleeves long and wide, and embroidered "as it were a mead, all full of fresh flowers white and red." Falstaff, when dressed as Herne the Hunter, should be attired like his Yeoman, in a coat and hood of green, with a horn slung in a green baldrick.

The Wife of Bath is said to have worn, on a Sunday, or holyday, kerchiefs on her head of the finest manufacture, but in such a quantity as to weigh nearly a pound.—When abroad, she wore "a hat as broad as is a buckler or a targe." Her stockings were of fine scarlet red, and her shoes "full moist and new." The high-crowned hats and point lace aprons, in which the Merry Wives of Windsor have been usually depicted, are of the seventeenth, instead of the fifteenth century.

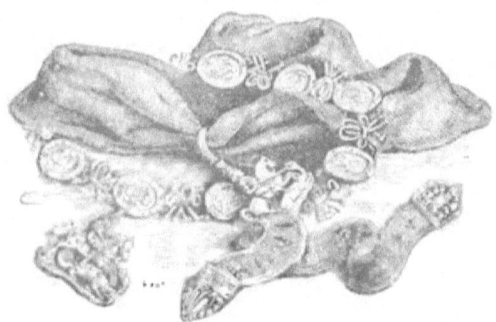

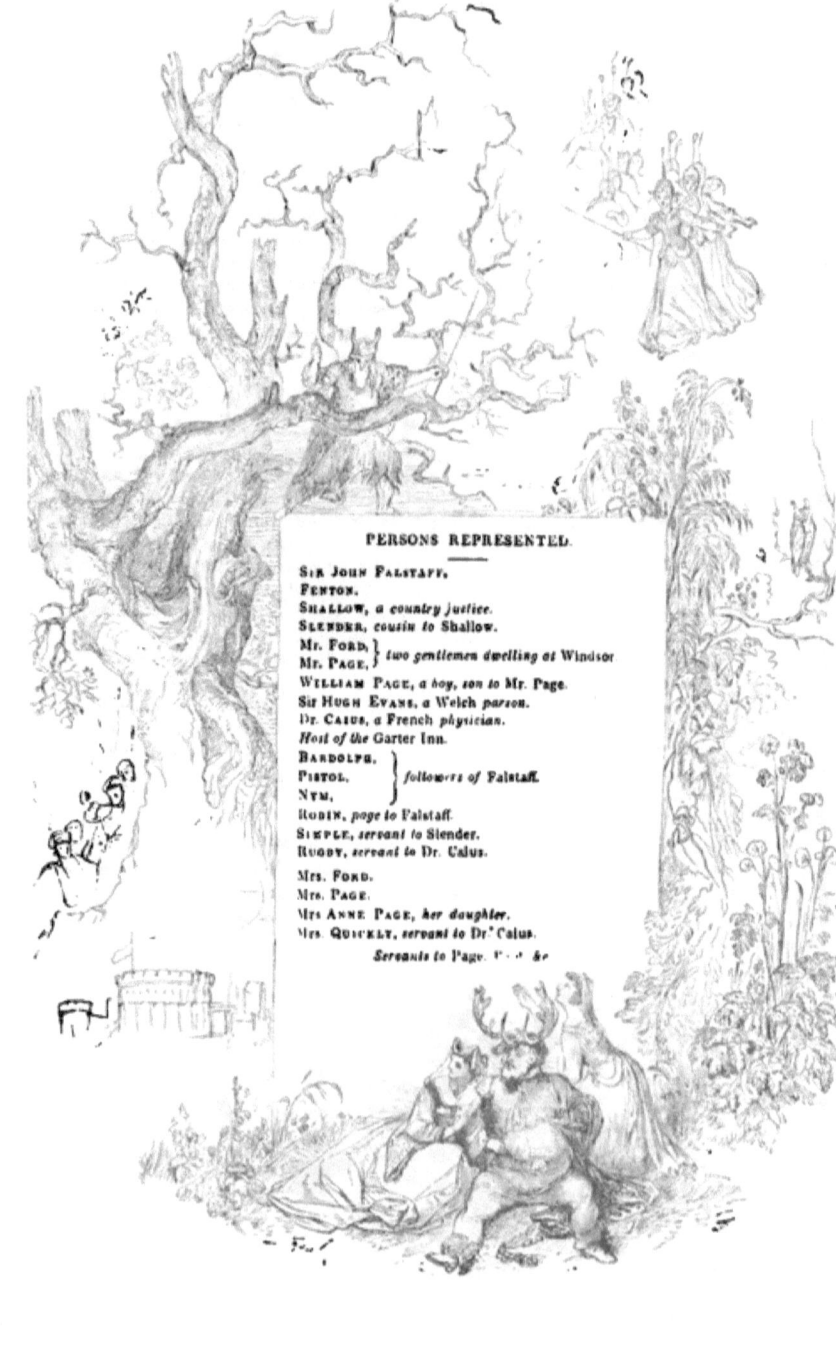

PERSONS REPRESENTED.

SIR JOHN FALSTAFF.
FENTON.
SHALLOW, *a country justice.*
SLENDER, *cousin to* Shallow.
MR. FORD, } *two gentlemen dwelling at* Windsor
MR. PAGE,
WILLIAM PAGE, *a boy, son to* Mr. Page.
SIR HUGH EVANS, *a Welch parson.*
Dr. CAIUS, *a French physician.*
Host of the Garter Inn.
BARDOLPH.
PISTOL. } *followers of Falstaff.*
NYM.
ROBIN, *page to* Falstaff.
SIMPLE, *servant to* Slender.
RUGBY, *servant to* Dr. Caius.

Mrs. FORD.
Mrs. PAGE.
Mrs ANNE PAGE, *her daughter.*
Mrs QUICKLY, *servant to* Dr Caius.

Servants to Page, *&c.*

[" I pray you, sir, walk in."]

ACT I.

SCENE I.—Windsor. *Garden Front of* Page's *House.*

Enter Justice SHALLOW, SLENDER, *and Sir* HUGH EVANS.

Shal. Sir Hugh,[1] persuade me not; I will make a Star-chamber[a] matter of it: if he were twenty sir John Falstaffs, he shall not abuse Robert Shallow, esquire.

Slen. In the county of Gloster, justice of peace, and *coram.*

Shal. Ay, cousin Slender, and *Cust-alorum.*[b]

Slen. Ay, and *ratolorum* too; and a gentleman born, master parson; who writes himself *armigero;* in any bill, warrant, quittance, or obligation, *armigero.*[a]

Shal. Ay, that I do; and have done[b] any time these three hundred years.

Slen. All his successors, gone before him, have don't; and all his ancestors, that come after him, may: they may give the dozen white luces in their coat.

Shal. It is an old coat.

Eva. The dozen white louses do become an old coat well; it agrees well, passant: it is a familiar beast to man, and signifies love.

Shal. The luce is the fresh fish; the salt fish is an old coat.[2]

Slen. I may quarter, coz?

Shal. You may, by marrying.

---

[a] So in Ben Jonson, (Magnetic Lady, Act III. Sc. IV.):
"There is a Court above, of the Star-chamber,
To punish routs and riots."

[b] *Cust alorum* is meant for an abridgment of *Custos Rotulorum.* Slender, not understanding the abbroviation, adds, "and *rotolorum* too."

---

[a] The Justice signed his attestations, "Jurat' coram me, Roberto Shallow, *armigero.*"

[b] *Have done—we have done—*"his successors, gone before him," as Slender explains it.

Eva. It is marring, indeed, if he quarter it.
Shal. Not a whit.
Eva. Yes, py'r-lady; if he has a quarter of your coat there is but three skirts for yourself, in my simple conjectures: but that is all one: If sir John Falstaff have committed disparagements unto you, I am of the church, and will be glad to do my benevolence, to make atonements and compromises between you.
Shal. The Council shall hear it; it is a riot.
Eva. It is not meet the Council hear a riot; there is no fear of Got in a riot: the Council, look you, shall desire to hear the fear of Got, and not to hear a riot; take your vizaments* in that.
Shal. Ha! o' my life, if I were young again the sword should end it.
Eva. It is petter that friends is the sword, and end it: and there is also another device in my prain, which, peradventure, prings goot discretions with it: There is Anne Page, which is daughter to master George Page, which is pretty virginity.
Slen. Mistress Anne Page? She has brown hair, and speaks small like a woman.
Eva. It is that fery person for all the 'orld, as just as you will desire; and seven hundred pounds of monies, and gold, and silver, is her grandsire upon his death's-bed, (Got deliver to a joyful resurrection!) give, when she is able to overtake seventeen years old: it were a goot motion if we leave our pribbles and prabbles, and desire a marriage between master Abraham and mistress Anne Page.
Shal. Did her grandsire leave her seven hundred pound?
Eva. Ay, and her father is make her a petter penny.
Shal. I know the young gentlewoman; she has good gifts.
Eva. Seven hundred pounds, and possibilities, is goot gifts.
Shal. Well, let us see honest master Page: Is Falstaff there?
Eva. Shall I tell you a lie? I do despise a liar as I do despise one that is false; or as I despise one that is not true. The knight, sir John, is there; and, I beseech you, be ruled by your well-willers. I will peat the door [*knocks*] for master Page. What, hoa! Got pless your house here!

Enter PAGE.

Page. Who's there?

Eva. Here is Got's plessing, and your friend, and justice Shallow: and here young master Slender; that, peradventures, shall tell you another tale, if matters grow to your likings.
Page. I am glad to see your worships well: I thank you for my venison, master Shallow.
Shal. Master Page, I am glad to see you; Much good do it your good heart! I wished your venison better; it was ill killed:—How doth good mistress Page?—and I thank* you always with my heart, la; with my heart.
Page. Sir, I thank you.
Shal. Sir, I thank you; by yea and no, I do.
Page. I am glad to see you, good master Slender.
Slen. How does your fallow greyhound, sir? I heard say he was out-run on Cotsall.[3]
Page. It could not be judg'd, sir.
Slen. You'll not confess, you'll not confess.
Shal. That he will not;—'tis your fault, 'tis your fault:—'Tis a good dog.
Page. A cur, sir.
Shal. Sir, he's a good dog, and a fair dog; Can there be more said? he is good, and fair. Is sir John Falstaff here?
Page. Sir, he is within; and I would I could do a good office between you.
Eva. It is spoke as a Christians ought to speak.
Shal. He hath wrong'd me, master Page.
Page. Sir, he doth in some sort confess it.
Shal. If it be confess'd it is not redress'd; is not that so, master Page? He hath wrong'd me; indeed he hath;—at a word he hath;—believe me; Robert Shallow, esquire, saith he is wrong'd.
Page. Here comes sir John.

Enter Sir JOHN FALSTAFF, BARDOLPH, NYM, *and* PISTOL.

Fal. Now, master Shallow; you'll complain of me to the king?
Shal. Knight, you have beaten my men, killed my deer, and broke open my lodge.
Fal. But not kiss'd your keeper's daughter.
Shal. Tut, a pin! this shall be answer'd.
Fal. I will answer it straight;—I have done all this:—That is now answer'd.
Shal. The Council shall know this.
Fal. 'Twere better for you if it were known in counsel;[b] you'll be laughed at.

---

^a *I thank you.* So the folio. The early quartos, "I love you."
^b *Counsel.* Steevens adopts the spelling of the first quarto—*Counsell* and *counsell.* The folio, in both cases, has *counsell.* In the distinction which Steevens has suggested, Falstaff makes a small jest—quibbling between the *Council* of the Star-chamber and *counsel* in the sense of a man's private advisers. Probably Steevens is right.

---

^a *Vizaments*—advisements.

Eva. Pauca verba, sir John, goot worts.

Fal. Good worts! good cabbage.ᵃ—Slender, I broke your head; what matter have you against me?

Slen. Marry, sir, I have matter in my head against you; and against your coney-catchingᵇ rascals, Bardolph, Nym, and Pistol. [They carried me to the tavern and made me drunk, and afterwards picked my pocket.ᶜ]

Bard. You Banbury cheese!ᵈ

Slen. Ay, it is no matter.

Pist. How now, Mephostophilus?ᵉ

Slen. Ay, it is no matter.

Nym. Slice, I say! *pauca, pauca*; slice! that's my humour.

Slen. Where's Simple, my man?—can you tell, cousin?

Eva. Peace: I pray you! Now let us understand: There is three umpires in this matter, as I understand: that is—master Page, *fidelicet*, master Page; and there is myself, *fidelicet*, myself; and the three party is, lastly and finally, mine host of the Garter.

Page. We three, to hear it and end it between them.

Eva. Fery goot: I will make a prief of it in my note-book; and we will afterwards 'ork upon the cause, with as great discreetly as we can.

Fal. Pistol,—

Pist. He hears with ears.

Eva. The tevil and his tam! what phrase is this, *He hears with ear*? Why, it is affectations.

Fal. Pistol, did you pick master Slender's purse?

Slen. Ay, by these gloves, did he, (or I would I might never come in mine own great chamber again else,) of seven groats in mill-sixpences,ᶠ and two Edward shovel-boards, that cost me two shilling and two pence a-piece of Yead Miller, by these gloves.

Fal. Is this true, Pistol?

Eva. No; it is false, if it is a pick-purse.

Pist. Ha, thou mountain-foreigner!—Sir John and master mine,

I combat challenge of this latten bilbo:ᶠ
Word of denial in thy labrasᵍ here;

Word of denial: froth and scum, thou liest!

Slen. By these gloves, then 'twas he.

Nym. Be advis'd, sir, and pass good humours; I will say, *marry trap*, with you, if you run the nuthook's humourᵃ on me: that is the very note of it.

Slen. By this hat, then, he in the red face had it: for though I cannot remember what I did when you made me drunk, yet I am not altogether an ass.

Fal. What say you, Scarlet and John?

Bard. Why, sir, for my part, I say, the gentleman had drunk himself out of his five sentences.

Eva. It is his five senses: fie, what the ignorance is!

Bard. And being fap,ᵇ sir, was, as they say, cashier'd: and so conclusions passed the careers.ᶜ

Slen. Ay, you spake in Latin then too: but 'tis no matter: I'll ne'er be drunk whilst I live again, but in honest, civil, godly company, for this trick: if I be drunk, I'll be drunk with those that have the fear of God, and not with drunken knaves.

Eva. So Got 'udge me, that is a virtuous mind.

Fal. You hear all these matters denied, gentlemen; you hear it.

Enter Mistress ANNE PAGE *with wine; Mistress* FORD *and Mistress* PAGE *following.*

Page. Nay, daughter, carry the wine in; we'll drink within. [*Exit* ANNE PAGE.

Slen. O heaven! this is mistress Anne Page.

Page. How now, mistress Ford?

Fal. Mistress Ford, by my troth, you are very well met: by your leave, good mistress.
[*kissing her.*

Page. Wife, bid these gentlemen welcome: Come, we have a hot venison pasty to dinner; come, gentlemen, I hope we shall drink down all unkindness.
[*Exeunt all but* SHAL. SLENDER, *and* EVANS.

Slen. I had rather than forty shillings, I had my book of Songs and Sonnetsᵃ here:—

Enter SIMPLE.

How now, Simple! Where have you been? I must wait on myself, must I? You have not the Book of Riddles about you, have you?

ᵃ *Worts* was the generic name of cabbages;—we have still *cole-wort.*
ᵇ *Coney-catcher* was synonymous with *sharper.*
ᶜ The passage between brackets is not in the folio.
ᵈ In "Jack Drum's Entertainment" (1601) we have, "you are like a Banbury cheese—nothing but paring."
ᵉ *Mephostophilus* is an evil spirit in the old story of "Sir John Faustus;"—but a very inferior demon to the extraordinary creation of Goethe.
ᶠ *Bilbo* is a sword;—a *latten bilbo*—a sword made of a thin latten plate—expresses Pistol's opinion of Slender's weakness.
ᵍ *Labras*, lips;—" word of denial in thy *labras*," is equivalent to "the lie in thy teeth."

ᵃ The *nuthook* was used by the thief to hook portable commodities out of a window,—and thus Nym, in his queer fashion means, "If you say I'm a thief."
ᵇ *Fap*, a cant word for *drunk.*
ᶜ *Careers.* In the *manège* to run a *career* was to gallop a horse violently backwards and forwards.

Sim. Book of Riddles? why, did you not lend it to Alice Shortcake upon Allhallowmas last, a fortnight afore Michaelmas?*

Shal. Come, coz; come, coz; we stay for you. A word with you, coz: marry, this, coz; There is, as 'twere, a tender, a kind of tender, made afar off by sir Hugh here:—Do you understand me?

Slen. Ay, sir, you shall find me reasonable; if it be so, I shall do that that is reason.

Shal. Nay, but understand me.

Slen. So I do, sir.

Eva. Give ear to his motions, master Slender: I will description the matter to you, if you be capacity of it.

Slen. Nay, I will do as my cousin Shallow says: I pray you, pardon me; he's a justice of peace in his country, simple though I stand here.

Eva. But that is not the question; the question is concerning your marriage.

Shal. Ay, there's the point, sir.

Eva. Marry, is it; the very point of it; to mistress Anne Page.

Slen. Why, if it be so I will marry her upon any reasonable demands.

Eva. But can you affection the 'oman? Let us command to know that of your mouth or of your lips; for divers philosophers hold that the lips is parcel of the mouth:—Therefore, precisely, can you carry your good will to the maid?

Shal. Cousin Abraham Slender, can you love her?

Slen. I hope, sir,—I will do as it shall become one that would do reason.

Eva. Nay, Got's lords and his ladies, you must speak possitable, if you can carry her your desires towards her.

Shal. That you must: Will you, upon good dowry, marry her?

Slen. I will do a greater thing than that, upon your request, cousin, in any reason.

Shal. Nay, conceive me, conceive me, sweet coz; what I do is to pleasure you, coz: Can you love the maid?

Slen. I will marry her, sir, at your request; but if there be no great love in the beginning, yet heaven may decrease it upon better acquaintance, when we are married and have more occasion to know one another: I hope, upon familiarity will grow more contempt;[b] but if you say, *marry her,* I will marry her, that I am freely dissolved, and dissolutely.

Eva. It is a fery discretion answer; save, the faul' is in the 'ort dissolutely: the 'ort is, according to our meaning, resolutely;—his meaning is good.

Shal. Ay, I think my cousin meant well.

Slen. Ay, or else I would I might be hanged, la.

Re-enter ANNE PAGE.

Shal. Here comes fair mistress Anne:—Would I were young for your sake, mistress Anne!

Anne. The dinner is on the table; my father desires your worship's company.

Shal. I will wait on him, fair mistress Anne.

Eva. Od's plessed will! I will not be absence at the grace.

[*Exeunt* SHALLOW *and Sir* H. EVANS

Anne. Will't please your worship to come in, sir?

Slen. No, I thank you, forsooth, heartily; I am very well.

Anne. The dinner attends you, sir.

Slen. I am not a-hungry, I thank you, forsooth. Go, sirrah, for all you are my man, go, wait upon my cousin Shallow: [*Exit* SIMPLE.] A justice of peace sometime may be beholden to his friend for a man:—I keep but three men and a boy yet, till my mother be dead: But what though? yet I live like a poor gentleman born.

Anne. I may not go in without your worship they will not sit till you come.

Slen. I'faith, I'll eat nothing; I thank you as much as though I did.

Anne. I pray you, sir, walk in.

Slen. I had rather walk here, I thank you; I bruised my shin the other day with playing at sword and dagger with a master of fence,* three veneys for a dish of stewed prunes; and, by my troth, I cannot abide the smell of hot meat since. Why do your dogs bark so? be there bears i' the town.

Anne. I think there are, sir; I heard them talked of.

Slen. I love the sport well; but I shall as soon quarrel at it, as any man in England:—You are afraid if you see the bear loose, are you not?

Anne. Ay, indeed, sir.

Slen. That's meat and drink to me now: I have seen Sackerson[7] loose twenty times; and have taken him by the chain: but, I warrant you, the women have so cried and shriek'd at it,

---

* Theobald proposed *Martlemas.*
b *Contempt.* The folio reads *content*—the word which Slender meant to use. But the poor soul was thinking of his copy-book adage,—" too much familiarity breeds contempt."

ANN PAGE AND SLENDER.

Slender. "I had rather walk here, I thank you."
  Merry Wives of Windsor. Act I., sc. I.

that it pass'd:ᵃ—but women, indeed, cannot abide 'em; they are very ill favoured rough things.

Re-enter PAGE.

Page. Come, gentle master Slender, come; we stay for you.

Slen. I'll eat nothing, I thank you, sir.

Page. By cock and pye, you shall not choose, sir: come, come.

Slen. Nay, pray you, lead the way.

Page. Come on, sir.

Slen. Mistress Anne, yourself shall go first.

Anne. Not I, sir; pray you, keep on.

Slen. Truly, I will not go first; truly, la: I will not do you that wrong.

Anne. I pray you, sir.

Slen. I'll rather be unmannerly than troublesome; you do yourself wrong, indeed, la.

[*Exeunt.*

SCENE II.—*The same.*

Enter Sir HUGH EVANS *and* SIMPLE.

Eva. Go your ways, and ask ofᵇ Doctor Caius' house,—which is the way: and there dwells one mistress Quickly, which is in the manner of his nurse, or his dry nurse, or his cook, or his laundry,ᶜ his washer, and his wringer.

Sim. Well, sir.

Eva. Nay, it is petter yet:—give her this letter; for it is a 'oman that altogether's acquaintance with mistress Anne Page: and the letter is, to desire and require her to solicit your master's desires to mistress Anne Page: I pray you, begone; I will make an end of my dinner; there's pippins and cheese to come. [*Exeunt.*

SCENE III.—*A Room in the* Garter Inn.

Enter FALSTAFF, HOST, BARDOLPH, NYM, PISTOL, *and* ROBIN.

Fal. Mine host of the Garter.—

Host. What says my bully-rook?ᵈ Speak scholarly and wisely.

Fal. Truly, mine host, I must turn away some of my followers.

Host. Discard, bully Hercules; cashier: let them wag; trot, trot.

Fal. I sit at ten pounds a week.

Host. Thou'rt an emperor, Cæsar, Keisar, and Pheezar. I will entertain Bardolph; he shall draw, he shall tap: said I well, bully Hector?

Fal. Do so, good mine host.

Host. I have spoke; let him follow: Let me see thee froth and lime:ᵃ I am at a word; follow. [*Exit* HOST.

Fal. Bardolph, follow him: a tapster is a good trade; an old cloak makes a new jerkin; a withered servingman a fresh tapster: Go; adieu.

Bard. It is a life that I have desired; I will thrive. [*Exit* BARD.

Pist. O base Hungarianᵇ wight! wilt thou the spigot wield?

Nym. He was gotten in drink: Is not the humour conceited? [His mind is not heroic, and there's the humour of it.ᵉ]

Fal. I am glad I am so acquit of this tinder-box; his thefts were too open; his filching was like an unskilful singer,—he kept not time.

Nym. The good humour is to steal at a minute's rest.ᵈ

Pist. Convey, the wise it call: Steal! foh; a fico for the phrase.

Fal. Well, sirs, I am almost out at heels.

Pist. Why then let kibes ensue.

Fal. There is no remedy; I must coney-catch; I must shift.

Pist. Young ravens must have food.

Fal. Which of you know Ford of this town?

Pist. I ken the wight; he is of substance good.

Fal. My honest lads, I will tell you what I am about.

ᵃ *It pass'd*—it *surpass'd*; or, it *pass'd expression*—a common mode of referring to something **extraordinary.** Thus in Act IV. Scene 11, "this passes."

ᵇ *Of Dr. Caius' house*—ask *for* **Dr. Caius' house**—ask which is the **way.**

ᶜ *Laundry.* Sir Hugh means to say *launder*, or *laundress.*

ᵈ Douce says that *bully-rock* is not derived from the *rook* of chess—but that it means a hectoring, cheating sharper. We scarcely think that the Host would have applied such offensive terms to Falstaff, who sat "at ten pounds a week." Rowe has *bully-rock*, which Mr. Whit) adopts, showing, by quotations from Sedley and others, that a *bully-rock* was a brave dashing fellow.

ᵃ *Froth, and lime*, in the folio. The reading of the quarto is "*froth and lime*," which is interpreted to *froth* the beer and *lime* the **sack.** Steevens says the beer was frothed by putting **soap in the tankard**, and the sack made sparkling by lime **in the glass.** He does not give **us** his authority for these retail mysteries of the drawer's craft. Mr. Staunton prints, "**let me see** thee froth and lime;" assuming *Froth* and *Lime* **to be an** old cant term for a tapster.

ᵇ *Hungarian.* So the folio. The quarto, which **has** supplied the ordinary reading, gives **us** *Gongarian.* The editors have retained 'Gongarian' because they find a similar epithet in one of the old bombast plays. *Hungarian* means a gipsy—and is equivalent to the *Bohemian* of Quentin Durward. In this play the Host calls Simple a 'Bohemian Tartar.' Bishop Hall in his Satires has a punning couplet,—

"So sharp and meagre that who should **them** see
Would swear they lately came from Hungary,"—

and therefore Malone says that "**a** Hungarian signified **a** nungry, starved fellow."

ᶜ The passage in brackets **was inserted by** Theobald, **from** the quarto.

ᵈ See *Recent New Readings*, p. 155.

Pist. Two yards, and more.

Fal. No quips now, Pistol: Indeed I am in the waist two yards about; but I am now about no waste; I am about thrift. Briefly, I do mean to make love to Ford's wife; I spy entertainment in her; she discourses, she carves,[a] she gives the leer of invitation: I can construe the action of her familiar style; and the hardest voice of her behaviour, to be English'd rightly, is, I am sir John Falstaff's.

Pist. He hath studied her will, and translated her will,[b] out of honesty into English.

Nym. The anchor is deep: Will that humour pass?

Fal. Now, the report goes, she has all the rule of her husband's purse; he hath a legion of angels.[c]

Pist. As many devils entertain; and, 'To her boy,' say I.

Nym. The humour rises; it is good: humour me the angels.

Fal. I have writ me here a letter to her: and here another to Page's wife; who even now gave me good eyes too; examin'd my parts with most judicious œiliads; sometimes the beam of her view gilded my foot, sometimes my portly belly.

Pist. Then did the sun on dunghill shine.

Nym. I thank thee for that humour.

Fal. O, she did so course o'er my exteriors with such a greedy intention, that the appetite of her eye did seem to scorch me up like a burning glass! Here's another letter to her: she bears the purse too; she is a region in Guiana, all gold and bounty. I will be cheater to them both, and they shall be exchequers to me; they shall be my East and West Indies, and I will trade to them both. Go, bear thou this letter to mistress Page; and thou this to mistress Ford: we will thrive, lads, we will thrive.

Pist. Shall I sir Pandarus of Troy become, And by my side wear steel? then, Lucifer take all!

Nym. I will run no base humour: here, take the humour letter; I will keep the 'haviour of reputation.

Fal. Hold, sirrah, [*to* Rob.] bear you these letters tightly;
Sail like my pinnace[b] to these golden shores.—
Rogues, hence, avaunt! vanish like hail-stones, go;
Trudge, plod away i' the hoof; seek shelter, pack!
Falstaff will learn the humour of the age,[c]
French thrift, you rogues; myself, and skirted page. [*Exeunt* FALSTAFF *and* ROBIN.

Pist. Let vultures gripe thy guts! for gourd and fullam holds,
And high and low beguile the rich and poor;[d]
Tester I'll have in pouch, when thou shalt lack,
Base Phrygian Turk!

Nym. I have operations,[e] which be humours of revenge.

Pist. Wilt thou revenge?

Nym. By welkin, and her stars!

Pist. With wit, or steel?

Nym. With both the humours, I;
I will discuss the humour of this love to Ford.[f]

Pist. And I to Page shall eke unfold,
How Falstaff, varlet vile,
His dove will prove, his gold will hold,
And his soft couch defile.

Nym. My humour shall not cool: I will incense Ford to deal with poison; I will possess him with yellowness, for the revolt of mien[g] is dangerous: that is my true humour.

Pist. Thou art the Mars of malcontents: I second thee; troop on. [*Exeunt.*

SCENE IV.—*A room in Dr.* Caius's *House.*

Enter Mrs. QUICKLY, SIMPLE, *and* RUGBY.

Quick. What, John Rugby!—I pray thee,

---

[a] *Tightly*—briskly, cleverly.
[b] *Pinnace*—a small vessel attached to, or in company with, a larger.
[c] The folio has *honour*; the quarto, *humour*.
[d] *Gourd*, *fullam*, *high and low*, were cant terms for false dice. Pistol will have his tester in pouch, by cheating at play.
[e] The quarto reads, "I have operations *in my head*."
[f] The editors have altered "Ford" to "Page," and "Page" to "Ford," because "the very reverse of this happens." Steevens says, "Shakspere is frequently guilty of these little forgetfulnesses." And yet the quarto gives us the reading which the editors adopt. But had Shakspere, who was not quite so forgetful as they represent, no reason for making the change? Nym suggests the scheme of betraying Falstaff, and it was natural that Ford being first mention'd by Sir John, and Ford's wife being most the subject of conversation, Nym should first propose to "discuss the humour of this love" to Ford. How the worthies arranged their plans afterwards has little to do with the matter; and it is to be observed that they are together when the disclosure takes place to both husbands.
[g] *Mien*. This is *mine* in the folio; but *mien* was thus spelt. By "the revolt of mien" Nym may intend the change of complexion—the yellowness of jealousy. Or he may intend by "the revolt of *mine*," *my* revolt. The matter is not worth discussing.

go to the casement, and see if you can see my master, master Doctor Caius, coming: if he do, i'faith, and find any body in the house, here will be an old abusing of God's patience and the king's English.

Rug. I'll go watch.   [*Exit* RUGBY.

Quick. Go; and we'll have a posset for't soon at night, in faith, at the latter end of a sea-coal fire. An honest, willing, kind fellow, as ever servant shall come in house withal; and, I warrant you, no tell-tale, nor no breed-bate:[a] his worst fault is that he is given to prayer; he is something peevish that way; but nobody but has his fault;—but let that pass. Peter Simple you say your name is?

Sim. Ay, for fault of a better.

Quick. And master Slender's your master?

Sim. Ay, forsooth.

Quick. Does he not wear a great round beard, like a glover's paring knife?

Sim. No, forsooth: he hath but a little wee face, with a little yellow beard; a cane-coloured beard.[b]

Quick. A softly-sprighted man, is he not?

Sim. Ay, forsooth: but he is as tall a man of his hands as any is between this and his head; he hath fought with a warrener.

Quick. How say you?—O, I should remember him: Does he not hold up his head, as it were? and strut in his gait?

Sim. Yes, indeed, does he.

Quick. Well, heaven send Anne Page no worse fortune! Tell master parson Evans I will do what I can for your master: Anne is a good girl, and I wish—

Re-enter RUGBY.

Rug. Out, alas! here comes my master.

Quick. We shall all be shent:[c] Run in here, good young man; go into this closet. [*Shuts* SIMPLE *in the closet.*] He will not stay long.—What, John Rugby! John, what John, I say! Go, John, go inquire for thy master; I doubt he be not well, that he comes not home:—*and down, down, adown-a,* &c.   [*Sings.*

---
[a] *Bate* is *strife.* It is "debate."
[b] The ordinary reading is "a *Cain*-coloured beard." Cain and Judas, according to Theobald, were represented in the old tapestries with yellow beards. But surely the representation was not so general as to become the popular designation of a colour; whereas the colour of cane is intelligible to all. The quarto confirms this:—
" *Quick.* He has as it were a *whay*-coloured beard.
 Sim. Indeed my master's beard is *kane*-coloured."
The spelling of the folio is, however, "*Caine*-coloured."
[c] *Shent,* roughly handled.

Enter Doctor CAIUS.

Caius. Vat is you sing? I do not like dese toys; Pray you, go and vetch me in my closet *un boitier verd;* a box, a green-a box; Do intend vat I speak? a green-a box.

Quick. Ay, forsooth, I'll fetch it you. I am glad he went not in himself: if he had found the young man, he would have been horn-mad.
   [*Aside.*

Caius. Fe, fe, fe, fe! ma foi, il fait fort chaud. Je m'en vais à la Cour,—la grande affaire.

Quick. Is it this, sir?

Caius. Ouy; mette le au mon pocket; *Depêche* quickly:—Vere is dat knave Rugby?

Quick. What, John Rugby! John!

Rug. Here, sir.

Caius. You are John Rugby, and you are Jack Rugby: Come, take-a your rapier, and come after my heel to de court.

Rug. 'Tis ready, sir, here in the porch.

Caius. By my trot, I tarry too long;—Od's me! *Qu'ay j'oublié?* dere is some simples in my closet dat I vill not for the varld I shall leave behind.

Quick. Ah me! he'll find the young man there, and be mad!

Caius. O diable, diable! vat is in my closet?—Villainy! *larron!* [*Pulling* SIMPLE *out.*] Rugby, my rapier.

Quick. Good master, be content.

Caius. Verefore shall I be content-a?

Quick. The young man is an honest man.

Caius. Vat shall de honest man do in my closet? dere is no honest man dat shall come in my closet.

Quick. I beseech you, be not so flegmatick: hear the truth of it: He came of an errand to me from parson Hugh.

Caius. Vell.

Sim. Ay, forsooth, to desire her to—

Quick. Peace, I pray you.

Caius. Peace-a your tongue:—Speak-a your tale.

Sim. To desire this honest gentlewoman, your maid, to speak a good word to Mrs. Anne Page for my master, in the way of marriage.

Quick. This is all, indeed, la; but I'll ne'er put my finger in the fire, and need not.

Caius. Sir Hugh send-a you?—Rugby, *baillez* me some paper: Tarry you a little-a while.
   [*Writes.*

Quick. I am glad he is so quiet: if he had been thoroughly moved you should have heard him so loud and so melancholy.—But notwithstanding, man, I'll do your master what good I can: and the very yea and the no is, the French doctor, my master,— I may call him my master, look you, for I keep his house; and I wash, wring, brew, bake, scour, dress meat and drink, make the beds, and do all myself:—

Sim. 'Tis a great charge to come under one body's hand.

Quick. Are you avis'd o'that? you shall find it a great charge: and to be up early and down late;—but notwithstanding, (to tell you in your ear; I would have no words of it;) my master himself is in love with mistress Anne Page: but notwithstanding that, I know Anne's mind,— that's neither here nor there.

Caius. You jack'nape; give-a dis letter to sir Hugh; by gar, it is a challenge: I will cut his troat in de park; and I vill teach a scurvy jack-a-nape priest to meddle or make:—you may be gone; it is not good you tarry here:—by gar, I vil cut all his two stones; by gar, he shall not have a stone to trow at his dog. [*Exit* SIMPLE.

Quick. Alas, he speaks but for his friend.

Caius. It is no matter-a for dat:—do not you tell-a me dat I shall have Anne Page for myself? —by gar, I will kill de Jack Priest; and I have appointed mine host of *de Jarterre* to measure our weapon:—by gar, I vill myself have Anne Page.

Quick. Sir, the maid loves you, and all shall be well: we must give folks leave to prate: What, the good-jer!

Caius. Rugby, come to de court vid me:—By gar, if I have not Anne Page, I shall turn your head out of my door:—Follow my heels, Rugby.
[*Exeunt* CAIUS *and* RUGBY.

Quick. You shall have An fools-head of your own. No, I know Anne's mind for that: never a woman in Windsor knows more of Anne's mind than I do; nor can do more than I do with her, I thank heaven.

Fent. [*Within.*] Who's within there? ho!

Quick. Who's there, I trow? Come near the house, I pray you.

Enter FENTON.

Fent. How now, good woman; how dost thou?

Quick. The better that it pleases your good worship to ask.

Fent. What news? how does pretty mistress Anne?

Quick. In truth, sir, and she is pretty, and honest, and gentle; and one that is your friend, I can tell you that by the way; I praise heaven for it.

Fent. Shall I do any good, think'st thou? Shall I not lose my suit?

Quick. Troth, sir, all is in his hands above: but notwithstanding, master Fenton, I'll be sworn on a book, she loves you:—Have not your worship a wart above your eye?

Fent. Yes, marry, have I; what of that?

Quick. Well, thereby hangs a tale;—good faith, it is such another Nan;—but, I detest, an honest maid as ever broke bread;—We had an hour's talk of that wart:—I shall never laugh but in that maid's company! But, indeed, she is given too much to allicholly and musing: But for you—Well, go to.

Fent. Well, I shall see her to-day; Hold, there's money for thee; let me have thy voice in my behalf: if thou seest her before me, commend me.

Quick. Will I? i'faith, that we will; and I will tell your worship more of the wart, the next time we have confidence; and of other wooers.

Fent. Well, farewell; I am in great haste now. [*Exit.*

Quick. Farewell to your worship.—Truly, an honest gentleman; but Anne loves him not; for I know Anne's mind as well as another does:— Out upon't! what have I forgot? [*Exit.*

RECENT NEW READINGS.

Sc. III. p. 155.—" Steal at a *minute's* rest."
"Steal at a *minim's* rest."—*Singer.*
The same correction had been proposed by Mr. Langton. But to rest, to set up a rest, was a phrase of card-playing, equivalent to standing upon the game. The player was allowed time to make up his mind. Bardolph's thefts were too open; he did not deliberate. Nym would pause. We believe the original reading, which we give, is right. If Nym only paused while he could count two—the time of a minim, he would be as rash as Bardolph. Mr. Collier's 'Corrector' anticipated (? adopted) Langton and Singer.

Sc. III. p. 156.—" She is a region in Guiana, all gold and *homily.*"
" She is a region in Guiana, all gold and *beauty.*"—*Collier.*
In favour of the correction, Mr. Collier says, " Guiana was famous for its beauty as well as for its gold, and thus the parallel between it and Mrs. Page is more exact." But Falstaff nowhere speaks of Mrs. Page as a beauty. He writes to her, " you are not young." She herself says, " Have I 'scaped love-letters in the holiday time of my beauty, and am I now a subject for them?" Falstaff thinks *only* of her money, and her bounty is parting with it. " She bears the purse too."

[Master of fence.]

ILLUSTRATIONS OF ACT I.

¹ SCENE I.—"*Sir Hugh, persuade me not.*"

WE find several instances in Shakspere of a priest being called *Sir*: as, *Sir Hugh* in this comedy; *Sir Oliver* in As You Like It; *Sir Topas* in Twelfth Night; and *Sir Nathaniel* in Love's Labour's Lost.—In a curious treatise quoted by Todd, entitled 'A Decacordon of Ten Quodlibetical Questions concerning Religion and State, &c., newly imprinted, 1602,' we have the following magniloquent explanation of the matter:—

"By the laws armorial, civil, and of arms, a *Priest* in his place in civil conversation is always before any Esquire, as being a *Knight's fellow* by his holy orders: and the third of the three *Sirs*, which only were in request of old (no baron, viscount, earl, nor marquis being then in use) to wit. *Sir* King, *Sir* Knight, and *Sir* Priest; this word *Dominus*, in Latin, being a noun substantive common to them all. as *Dominus* meus Rex, *Dominus* meus Joab, *Dominus Sacerdos*: and afterwards, when honours began to take their subordination one under another, and titles of princely dignity to be hereditary to succeeding posterity (which happened upon the fall of the Roman empire) then *Dominus* was in Latin applied to all noble and generous hearts, even from the king to the meanest *Priest*, or temporal person of gentle blood, coat-armour perfect, and ancestry. But *Sir* in English was restrained to these four; *Sir* Knight, *Sir* Priest, *Sir* Graduate, and in common speech *Sir* Esquire: so as always since distinction of titles were, *Sir* Priest was ever the second."

Fuller, in his Church History, gives us a more homely version of the title. After saying that anciently there were in England more Sirs than Knights, he adds, "Such priests as have the addition of Sir before their Christian name were men not graduated in the university, being in orders, but not in degrees, whilst others entitled masters had commenced in the arts." In a note in Smith's Antiquities of Westminster, Mr. John Sidney Hawkins gives us the following explanation of the passage in Fuller:—

"It was, probably, only a translation of the Latin *dominus*, which in strictness means, when applied to persons under the degree of knighthood, nothing more than master, or, as it is now written, Mr. In the university persons would rank according to their academical degrees only, and there was, consequently, no danger of confusion between baronets and knights and those of the clergy, but to preserve the distinction which Fuller points out, it seems to have been thought necessary to translate *dominus*, in this case, by the appellative Sir; for had *magister* been used instead of *dominus*, or had *dominus* been rendered master, non-graduates, to whom it had been applied, would have been mistaken for *magistri artium*, masters of arts."

² SCENE I.—"*The luce is the fresh fish; the salt fish is an old coat.*"

This speech is an heraldic puzzle. It is pretty clear that "the dozen white luces" apply to the arms of the Lucy family. In Ferne's Blazon of

ILLUSTRATIONS OF ACT I.

Gentry, 1586, we have, "signs of the coat should something agree with the name. It is the coat of Geffray Lord Lucy. He did bear gules, three *lucies* bariant [hauriant] argent." The luce is *a pike*,—"the fresh fish;" not the "familiar beast to man." So far is clear; but why "the salt fish is an old coat" is not so intelligible.

Since our first edition we have received an ingenious explanation from a correspondent, "A Lover of Heraldry."

"The arms of the Lucies (now quartered by the Duke of Northumberland), are gules, three lucies hauriant, argent. The fish is called hauriant in heraldry when it is drawn erect, or in the act of springing up to draw in the air. Now Shallow is not a very exact herald, and does not apply the special term *hauriant* to the luce, but the term *saltant* or *saliant*, which expresses the same thing, but is only used of beasts, like lions, &c. The first part of the sentence is merely in answer to what Sir Hugh has just said, explaining what the luce is. 'The luce is the fresh fish,' *i.e.* the large fresh-water fish, the pike. Then he goes on in conclusion, but without any opposition of the latter part of his sentence to the first,—'The salt fish (*i.e.* the fish or luce *saltant*) is an old coat.' Without taking it as a strict and formed adjective, in Shallow's mouth the *salt luceis* may mean the *saltant lucies*."

³ SCENE I.—"*I heard say he was out-run on Cotsall.*"

The Cotswold Hills in Gloucestershire, like many other places, were anciently famous for rural sports. In the Second Part of Henry IV., Shallow mentions "Will Squele, a Cotswold man," as one of his four swinge bucklers. But Cotswold subsequently became famous for "the yearly celebration of Mr. Robert Dover's Olympick Games."

⁴ SCENE I.—"*Seven groats in mill sixpences.*"

How Slender could be robbed of two shillings and fourpence in sixpences would require his own ingenuity to explain. The mill sixpences coined in 1561 and 1562 were the first milled money used in this kingdom. We subjoin a representation from a beautiful specimen in the British Museum.

⁵ SCENE I.—"*I had rather than forty shillings, I had my book of songs and sonnets here.*"

The exquisite bit of nature of poor Slender wanting his book of Songs and Sonnets, and his book of Riddles, to help him out in his talk with Anne Page, is not found in the original Sketch.

⁶ SCENE I.—"*Master of fence.*"

Steevens informs us that "master of defence, on this occasion, does not simply mean a professor of the art of fencing, but a person who had taken his master's degree in it;" and he adds, that in this art there were three degrees, a master, a provost, and a scholar. We doubt whether Slender, "on this occasion," meant very precisely to indicate the quality of the professor with whom he played at sword and dagger.

⁷ SCENE I.—"*Sackerson loose.*"

The inquiry of Slender "be there bears i' the town?" furnishes a proof of the universality of the practice of bear-baiting. In the time of Henry VIII. the bear gardens on Bank-side were open on Sundays; and the price of admission was a halfpenny. That it was a barbarous custom we can have no doubt. Master Laneham, in his letters from Kenilworth, tells us that when the bear was loose from the dogs, it was a matter of goodly relief to him to shake his ears twice or thrice. Sackerson was a celebrated bear exhibited in Paris Garden in Southwark. In a collection of epigrams by Sir John Davies we have the lines:—

"Publius, a student of the common law,
To Paris-garden doth himself withdraw;—
Leaving old Ployden, Dyer, and Brooke alone,
To see old Harry Hunkes and Sacarson."

The following representation of "Sackerson loose" has been composed by Mr. Buss upon the authority of a description in Strutt's 'Sports and Pastimes.' If Slender had "taken him by the chain," Sackerson

MERRY WIVES OF WINDSOR.

and Slender must have been equals in simplicity. Slender's triumph of manhood over the women, who "so cried and shrieked at it," is exquisite. The passage is wonderfully improved from the corresponding one in the original sketch :—

"*Slen.* What, have you bears in your town, mistress Anne, your dogs bark so.
Anne. I cannot tell master Slender, I think there be.
Slen. Ha, how say you? I warrant you're afraid of a bear 'at loose, are you not?
Anne. Yes, trust me.
Slen. Now that's meat and drink to me. I'll run to a bear, and take her by the muzzle, you never saw the like. But indeed I cannot blame you, for they are marvellous rough things.
Anne. Will you go in to dinner, master Slender? The meat stays for you.
Slen. No faith, not I, I thank you I cannot abide the smell of hot meat, ne'er since I broke my shin. I'll tell you how it came, by my troth. A fencer and I played three venies for a dish of stewed prunes, and I with my ward defending my head, he hit my shin; yes, faith."

[Sackerson horse.]

LOCAL ILLUSTRATION.

In the original editions of this comedy we have no descriptions of the scenes, such as, 'Street in Windsor,' 'Windsor Park,' 'Field near Frogmore.' These necessary explanations were added by Rowe; but we may collect from the text that Shakspere had a perfect knowledge of the localities of Windsor. Having the advantage of the same local experience, we shall attempt to follow the poet in these passages; and, without going into any minute descriptions, endeavour to shew what was the Windsor of our ancestors, and such as it presented itself to Shakspere's observation.

Although we have reason to believe that the action of this play might originally have belonged to the time of Elizabeth, yet the connexion of some of the characters as they now stand with characters of the historical plays of Henry IV., must place the period of the action about two centuries before Shakspere's own age. We have felt it necessary, therefore, in the arrangement of the illustrations, to give some notion of the Windsor of the time of Henry IV.; and the very tasteful designs which have been made by Mr. Creswick have especial reference to this object. At that period the town of Windsor no doubt consisted of scattered houses, surrounded with trees and gardens, approaching the castle, but not encroaching upon the ancient fortifications. The line of the walls and circular towers on the west and south sides next the town, was then unobstructed; and the moat or ditch by which the castle was then surrounded on all sides was open. In the time of Henry IV., Windsor, although in many respects splendid as a palace, must externally have presented the character of a very strong fortress. Its terraces, which were commenced by Elizabeth, and finished by Charles II., did not conceal the stern grandeur of the walls standing boldly upon the rock of chalk. The windows of the towers were little more than loopholes; and the only appearance of natural ornament was probably the clustering ivy in which the rook and starling had long built unmolested. The site of the present splendid chapel of St. George was occupied by a meaner edifice, which Edward IV

ILLUSTRATIONS OF ACT I.

pulled down, substituting that exquisite gem which is now amongst our best preserved ecclesiastical monuments. The buildings which were added by Henry VII., and by Elizabeth, at the western end of the north front of the Upper Ward, were of a more ornamental character than the older parts of the castle, indicating the establishment of an order of things in which the monarch and the people could dwell more in security.

We shall here very briefly describe the Illustrations which have reference to the castle and town of Windsor.

The architectural Illustration at the head of the Introductory Notice exhibits the gallery which was built by Elizabeth in 1583. Sir Jeffrey Wyatville has preserved this building almost unaltered. The few changes which he has introduced in the lower part have had the effect of giving it a character of unity. Our view exhibits it as it stood before the late improvements.

We have imagined Page's house as standing in the High Street, a little to the north of the present Town Hall, but on the opposite side. The description of the first scene of Act I , as we received it from Rowe, is, 'Windsor—before Page's house;' but as Anne Page enters with wine, it would seem more proper that the characters should assemble in the garden front than in the street, and Mr. Creswick's design has therefore been made upon this principle. The street front of Page's house is exhibited at the head of Act II. A market cross is shewn in this design. That of Windsor was erected in 1380, but demolished during the civil wars of Charles I. The very ancient church (see Act IV. Scene VI.) which stood on the east side of the street, and which is represented in our sketch, was pulled down about 1814. The houses, it must be observed, of this design, as well as of the other street scenes, are imaginary; for Windsor, as compared with other places of antiquity, is most singularly deficient in relics of our old domestic architecture. there being very few houses in the town more than a century old, and of those few which may date from the beginning of the seventeenth century, the external character has been changed during our own recollection The design at the head of Act III. has its locality in the ancient Peascod Street; from the lower part of which the round tower, or keep, is a very conspicuous and picturesque object. We, of course, present this remarkable building as it was seen before the recent improvements. The locality of Ford's house, at the head of Act IV., is fixed in Thames Street. What we imagined a quarter of a century ago, has been accomplished. The mean houses which stood on the west and north-west sides of the street have been removed, and the fine old tower at the north-western angle has been cleared to its base.

["Here's the twin brother of thy letter."]

ACT II.

SCENE I.—*Before Page's House.*

Enter Mistress PAGE, *with a Letter.*

Mrs. Page. What! have I 'scaped love-letters in the holy-day time of my beauty, and am I now a subject for them? Let me see: [*Reads.*

> 'Ask me no reason why I love you; for though love use reason for his precisian, he admits him not for his counsellor:^a You are not young, no more am I; go to then, there's sympathy: you are merry, so am I; Ha! ha! then there's more sympathy: you love sack, and so do I; Would you desire better sympathy? Let it suffice thee, mistress Page, (at the least, if the love of a soldier can suffice,) that I love thee. I will not say, pity me, 'tis not a soldier-like phrase; but I say, love me. By me,
>   Thine own true knight,
>   By day or night,
>   Or any kind of light,
>   With all his might,
>   For thee to fight, *John Falstaff.*'^b

What a Herod of Jewry is this!—O wicked,

---

^a Johnson would read *physician* instead of *precisian;* not Farmer, as Mr. Collier says. Farmer only adopted it. Johnson, in his 'Dictionary,' published before his Shakspere, defines *precisian* as "one who limits or restrains," quoting this passage as an authority. The *precisian* of Shakspere's time was the same as the puritan, to whom was commonly ascribed the mere show of sanctity: "I will set my countenance like a precisian."

^b The corresponding letter in the quarto furnishes a striking example of the careful mode in which this play was elaborated from the first Sketch:—

"Mistress Page, I love you. Ask me no reason, because they're impossible to allege. You are fair, and I am fat. You love sack, so do I. As I am sure I have no mind but to love, so I know you have no heart but to grant. A soldier doth not use many words where he knows a letter may serve for a sentence. I love you, and so I leave you
   "Yours, Sir John Falstaff."

wicked world!—one that is well nigh worn to pieces with age, to shew himself a young gallant! What an unweighed behaviour hath this Flemish drunkard¹ picked (with the devil's name) out of my conversation, that he dares in this manner assay me? Why, he hath not been thrice in my company!—What should I say to him?—I was then frugal of my mirth;—heaven forgive me! Why I'll exhibit a bill in the parliament for the putting down of men.^a How shall I be revenged on him? for revenged I will be, as sure as his guts are made of puddings.

Enter Mistress FORD.

Mrs. Ford. Mistress Page! trust me, I was going to your house!

Mrs. Page. And trust me, I was coming to you. You look very ill.

Mrs. Ford. Nay, I'll ne'er believe that; I have to shew to the contrary.

Mrs. Page. 'Faith, but you do, in my mind.

Mrs. Ford. Well, I do, then; yet, I say, I could shew you to the contrary; O, mistress Page, give me some counsel!

Mrs. Page. What's the matter, woman?

Mrs. Ford. O woman, if it were not for one trifling respect, I could come to such honour!

---

^a Theobald would read *fat* men, because the quarto has "I shall trust *fat* men the worse while I live, for his sake." The folio has a corresponding passage to this—"I shall think the worse of *fat* men, as long as I have an eye to make difference of men's liking;"—and the quarto has no parallel to "a bill in parliament."

Mrs. Page. Hang the trifle, woman; take the honour: What is it?—dispense with trifles;—what is it?

Mrs. Ford. If I would but go to hell for an eternal moment, or so, I could be knighted.

Mrs. Page. What? thou liest!—Sir Alice Ford! These knights will hack;[a] and so thou shouldst not alter the article of thy gentry.

Mrs. Ford. We burn day-light:[b]—here, read, read:—perceive how I might be knighted.—I shall think the worse of fat men, as long as I have an eye to make difference of men's liking: And yet he would not swear; praised women's modesty; and gave such orderly and well-behaved reproof to all uncomeliness,—that I would have sworn his disposition would have gone to the truth of his words: but they do no more adhere and keep place together than the hundredth psalm to the tune of *Green sleeves.*[c] What tempest, I trow, threw this whale with so many tuns of oil in his belly, ashore at Windsor? How shall I be revenged on him? I think the best way were to entertain him with hope, till the wicked fire of lust have melted him in his own grease. Did you ever hear the like?

Mrs. Page. Letter for letter; but that the name of Page and Ford differs!—To thy great comfort in this mystery of ill opinions, here's the twin-brother of thy letter: but let thine inherit first; for, I protest, mine never shall. I warrant he hath a thousand of these letters, writ with blank space for different names, (sure more,) and these are of the second edition: He will print them out of doubt; for he cares not what he puts into the press when he would put us two. I had rather be a giantess, and lie under mount Pelion. Well, I will find you twenty lascivious turtles, ere one chaste man.

Mrs. Ford. Why, this is the very same; the very hand, the very words: What doth he think of us?

Mrs. Page. Nay, I know not: It makes me almost ready to wrangle with mine own honesty. I'll entertain myself like one that I am not acquainted withal; for, sure, unless he know some strain[a] in me, that I know not myself, he would never have boarded me in this fury.

Mrs. Ford. Boarding, call you it? I'll be sure to keep him above deck.

Mrs. Page. So will I; if he come under my hatches I'll never to sea again. Let's be reveng'd on him: let's appoint him a meeting; give him a show of comfort in his suit; and lead him on with a fine baited delay, till he hath pawn'd his horses to mine Host of the Garter.

Mrs. Ford. Nay, I will consent to act any villainy against him, that may not sully the chariness of our honesty. O, that my husband saw this letter! it would give eternal food to his jealousy.

Mrs. Page. Why, look, where he comes; and my good man too; he's far from jealousy as I am from giving him cause; and that, I hope, is an unmeasurable distance.

Mrs. Ford. You are the happier woman.

Mrs. Page. Let's consult together against this greasy knight: Come hither. [*They retire.*

Enter FORD, PISTOL, PAGE, *and* NYM.

Ford. Well, I hope it be not so.

Pist. Hope is a curtall[a] dog in some affairs: Sir John affects thy wife.

Ford. Why, sir, my wife is not young.

Pist. He woos both high and low, both rich and poor,

Both young and old, one with another, Ford;

He loves thy galley-mawfry; Ford, perpend.

Ford. Love my wife?

Pist. With liver burning hot: Prevent, or go thou,

Like sir Actæon he, with Ringwood at thy heels:—

O, odious is the name!

Ford. What name, sir?

Pist. The horn, I say: Farewell.

Take heed; have open eye; for thieves do foot by night:

Take heed, ere summer comes, or cuckoo birds do sing.—

Away, sir corporal Nym.—

Believe it, Page; he speaks sense.[b]

[*Exit* PISTOL.

Ford. I will be patient; I will find out this.

Nym. And this is true; [*to* PAGE.] I like not the humour of lying. He hath wronged me in some humours: I should have borne the humoured letter to her; but I have a sword, and it shall bite upon my necessity. He loves your wife; there's the short and the long. My

---

[a] *Will hack.* James I. would make fifty knights before breakfast; and therefore "these knights will hack"—will become common; and for this cause the honour of being "Sir Alice Ford" would not "alter the article of thy gentry" —would not add any lustre to thy gentry. The passage was added in the folio, and it furnishes a proof that the play was enlarged after the accession of James.

[b] *We burn day-light*—we waste our time like those who use "lamps by day." See Romeo and Juliet, Act I. Sc. IV.

[c] *Strain*—turn, humour disposition

[a] *Curtall-dog.* This is not literally a dog without a tail, as it is explained generally; nor is it spelt *curtail.* The "curtal dog" is, like the "curtal friar,"—an expression of contempt. The worthless dog may have a short tail, and the Franciscan friar *might wear a short garment;* and thus they each may be *curtailed.* But the word came to express some general defect, and is here used in that sense.

[b] Pistol confirms what Nym has been saying, aside, to Page.

name is corporal Nym; I speak, and I avouch. 'Tis true:—my name is Nym, and Falstaff loves your wife.—Adieu! I love not the humour of bread and cheese. Adieu. [*Exit* NYM.

Page. The humour of it, quoth 'a! here's a fellow frights humour out of his wits.

Ford. I will seek out Falstaff.

Page. I never heard such a drawling, affecting rogue.

Ford. If I do find it, well.

Page. I will not believe such a Cataian,* though the priest o' the town commended him for a true man.

Ford. 'T was a good sensible fellow: Well.

Page. How now, Meg?

Mrs. Page. Whither go you, George?—Hark you.

Mrs. Ford. How now, sweet Frank? why art thou melancholy?

Ford. I melancholy! I am not melancholy. —Get you home, go.

Mrs. Ford. 'Faith, thou hast some crotchets in thy head now.—Will you go, mistress Page?

Mrs. Page. Have with you.—You'll come to dinner, George? Look, who comes yonder: she shall be our messenger to this paltry knight. [*Aside to Mrs.* FORD.

Enter Mrs. QUICKLY.

Mrs. Ford. Trust me, I thought on her: she'll fit it.

Mrs. Page. You are come to see my daughter Anne?

Quick. Ay, forsooth. And I pray, how does good mistress Anne?

Mrs. Page. Go in with us and see; we have an hour's talk with you.

[*Exeunt Mrs.* PAGE, *Mrs.* FORD, *and Mrs.* QUICKLY.

Page. How now, master Ford?

Ford. You heard what this knave told me; did you not?

Page. Yes. And you heard what the other told me?

Ford. Do you think there is truth in them?

Page. Hang 'em, slaves; I do not think the knight would offer it: but these that accuse him in his intent towards our wives are a yoke of his discarded men: very rogues, now they be out of service.

Ford. Were they his men?

Page. Marry were they.

Ford. I like it never the better for that.— Does he lie at the Garter?

Page. Ay, marry, does he. If he should intend this voyage towards my wife, I would turn her loose to him; and what he gets more of her than sharp words, let it lie on my head.

Ford. I do not misdoubt my wife; but I would be loth to turn them together: A man may be too confident: I would have nothing lie on my head: I cannot be thus satisfied.

Page. Look, where my ranting host of the Garter comes: there is either liquor in his pate, or money in his purse, when he looks so merrily. —How now, mine host?

Enter HOST *and* SHALLOW.

Host. How now, bully-rook! thou'rt a gentleman: cavalero justice, I say.

Shal. I follow, mine host, I follow.—Good even, and twenty, good master Page! Master Page, will you go with us? we have sport in hand.

Host. Tell him, cavalero-justice; tell him, bully-rook.

Shal. Sir, there is a fray to be fought, between sir Hugh the Welch priest, and Caius the French doctor.

Ford. Good mine host o' the Garter, a word with you.

Host. What say'st thou, my bully-rook?

[*They go aside.*

Shal. Will you [*to* PAGE.] go with us to behold it? My merry host hath had the measuring of their weapons; and, I think, hath appointed them contrary places: for, believe me, I hear the parson is no jester. Hark, I will tell you what our sport shall be.

Host. Hast thou no suit against my knight, my guest-cavalier?

Ford. None, I protest: but I'll give you a pottle of burnt sack to give me recourse to him, and tell him my name is Brook:ᵃ only for a jest.

Host. My hand, bully; thou shalt have egress and regress; said I well? and thy name shall be Brook: It is a merry knight. Will you go on, heers?ᵇ

---

* Warburton says, *Cataian* meant a liar, because the old travellers in Cathay, such as Marco Polo and Mandeville, told incredible stories of that country. Steevens says that Cataian meant a sharper, the Chinese being held to be of thievish propensities.

ᵃ The folio throughout gives the assumed name of Ford as *Broome*; the quartos *Brooke*. We must adopt the reading of *Brook*, for we otherwise lose a jest which the folio gives us—"Such Brooks are welcome to me that o'erflow such liquor." For a century after Shakspere, however, the stage-name was Broome. In Johnson's Lives of the Poets (Life of Fenton) we have the following anecdote: "Fenton was one day in the company of Broome, his associate, and Ford, a clergyman. * * * They determined all to see the Merry Wives of Windsor, which was acted that night; and Fenton, as a dramatic poet, took them to the stage-door, where the door-keeper, inquiring who they were, was told that they were three very necessary men Ford, Broome, and Fenton. The name in the play which Pope restored to *Brook* was then *Broome*. See New Readings.

ᵇ *Heers.* The folio reads *an-heires*—the parallel pas-

Shal. Have with you, mine host.
Page. I have heard the Frenchman hath good skill in his rapier.[a]
Shal. Tut, sir, I could have told you more: In these times you stand on distance, your passes, stoccadoes, and I know not what: 'tis the heart, master Page; 'tis here, 'tis here. I have seen the time with my long sword I would have made you four tall fellows skip like rats.
Host. Hero, boys, here, here! shall we wag?
Page. Have with you:—I had rather hear them scold than fight.

[*Exeunt* HOST, SHALLOW, *and* PAGE.

Ford. Though Page be a secure fool, and stands so firmly on his wife's frailty, yet I cannot put off my opinion so easily: She was in his company at Page's house; and, what they made there I know not. Well, I will look further into 't: and I have a disguise to sound Falstaff: If I find her honest, I lose not my labour; if she be otherwise, 'tis labour well bestowed.

[*Exit.*

SCENE II.—*A Room in the* Garter Inn.

Enter FALSTAFF *and* PISTOL.

Fal. I will not lend thee a penny.[a]
Pist. Why, then the world's mine oyster, Which I with sword will open.
Fal. Not a penny. I have been content, sir, you should lay my countenance to pawn: I have grated upon my good friends for three reprieves for you and your coach-fellow, Nym; or else you had looked through the grate, like a gemini of baboons. I am damned in hell, for swearing to gentlemen my friends you were good soldiers and tall fellows: and when mistress Bridget lost the handle of her fan, I took 't upon mine honour thou hadst it not.
Pist. Didst not thou share? hadst thou not fifteen pence?
Fal. Reason, you rogue, reason: Think'st thou I'll endanger my soul *gratis?* At a word, hang no more about me, I am no gibbet for you:

—go.—A short knife and a throng;[a]—to your manor of Pickt-hatch,[b] go.—You'll not bear a letter for me, you rogue!—You stand upon your honour!—Why, thou unconfinable baseness, it is as much as I can do to keep the terms of my honour precise. I, I, I myself sometimes, leaving the fear of heaven on the left hand, and hiding mine honour in my necessity, am fain to shuffle, to edge, and to lurch; and yet you, rogue, will ensconce your rags, your cat-a-mountain looks, your red-lattice phrases,[c] and your bold-beating oaths, under the shelter of your honour! You will not do it, you?
Pist. I do relent. What would thou more of man?

Enter ROBIN.

Rob. Sir, here's a woman would speak with you.
Fal. Let her approach.

Enter Mistress QUICKLY.

Quick. Give your worship good-morrow.
Fal. Good-morrow, good wife.
Quick. Not so, an't please your worship.
Fal. Good maid, then.
Quick. I'll be sworn; as my mother was, the first hour I was born.
Fal. I do believe the swearer: What with me?
Quick. Shall I vouchsafe your worship a word or two?
Fal. Two thousand, fair woman: and I'll vouchsafe thee the hearing.
Quick. There is one mistress Ford, sir;—I pray, come a little nearer this ways:—I myself dwell with master doctor Caius.
Fal. Well, on. Mistress Ford, you say,—
Quick. Your worship says very true: I pray your worship, come a little nearer this ways.
Fal. I warrant thee, nobody hears;—mine own people, mine own people.
Quick. Are they so? Heaven bless them, and make them his servants!
Fal. Well: Mistress Ford;—what of her?
Quick. Why, sir, she's a good creature. Lord, lord! your worship's a wanton: Well, heaven forgive you, and all of us, I pray!
Fal. Mistress Ford;—come, mistress Ford,—
Quick. Marry, this is the short and the long of it; you have brought her into such a canaries, as 'tis wonderful. The best courtier of them all, when the court lay at Windsor, could never have

---

[a] sage in the quarto is, "here boys, shall we wag?" The ordinary reading is, "will you go on, *hearts?*" Malone would read, "will you go and *hear us!*" Boaden proposes, "will you go, *Cavaleiros?*" We think that the Host, who, although he desires to talk with the German gentlemen who "speak English," is fond of using foreign words which he has picked up from his guests, such as cavalero, Francisco, and sciletto, employs the Dutch *Heer*, or the German *Heer*,—Sir,—Master. Both words are pronounced nearly alike. He says, "will you go on, *heers!*" Theobald proposed *mynheers*, which is perhaps right.
[a] The passage in the quarto is thus:—
"*Fal.* I'll not lend thee a penny.
Pist. I will retort the sum in equipage.
Fal. Not a penny."
The editors could not be satisfied to receive the beautiful answer of Pistol, "Why then the world's mine oyster," &c., without retaining the weaker passage, "I will retort the sum in equipage."

[a] *A short knife*, &c. A knife to cut purses, and a mob to find them amongst.
[b] *Pickt-hatch* is mentioned in one of Ben Jonson's Epigrams, in company with "Marsh Lambeth and White Fryers." Each of these was an *Alsatia* in Shakspere's day.
[c] *Red-lattice phrases*—ale-house terms. Thus Falstaff's page in Henry IV says; "he called me, even now, my lord, through a *red lattice*."

brought her to such a canary. Yet there has been knights, and lords, and gentlemen, with their coaches; I warrant you, coach after coach, letter after letter, gift after gift; smelling so sweetly, (all musk) and so rushling, I warrant you, in silk and gold; and in such alligant terms; and in such wine and sugar of the best, and the fairest, that would have won any woman's heart; and, I warrant you, they could never get an eye-wink of her.—I had myself twenty angels given me this morning; but I defy all angels, (in any such sort, as they say,) but in the way of honesty:—and, I warrant you, they could never get her so much as sip on a cup with the proudest of them all: and yet there has been earls, nay, which is more, pensioners; but, I warrant you, all is one with her.

Fal. But what says she to me? be brief, my good she Mercury.

Quick. Marry, she hath received your letter; for the which she thanks you a thousand times: and she gives you to notify, that her husband will be absence from his house between ten and eleven.

Fal. Ten and eleven?

Quick. Ay, forsooth; and then you may come and see the picture, she says, that you wot of; master Ford, her husband, will be from home. Alas! the sweet woman leads an ill life with him; he's a very jealousy man: she leads a very frampold* life with him, good heart.

Fal. Ten and eleven: Woman, commend me to her; I will not fail her.

Quick. Why you say well: But I have another messenger to your worship: Mistress Page hath her hearty commendations to you too;—and let me tell you in your ear, she's as fartuous a civil modest wife, and one (I tell you) that will not miss you morning nor evening prayer, as any is in Windsor, whoe'er be the other: and she bade me tell your worship that her husband is seldom from home; but, she hopes, there will come a time. I never knew a woman so dote upon a man; surely, I think you have charms, la; yes, in truth.

Fal. Not I, I assure thee: setting the attraction of my good parts aside I have no other charms.

Quick. Blessing on your heart for't!

Fal. But, I pray thee, tell me this: has Ford's wife and Page's wife acquainted each other how they love me?

Quick. That were a jest, indeed!—they have not so little grace, I hope:—that were a trick, indeed! But mistress Page would desire you to send her your little page, of all loves: her husband has a marvellous infection to the little page: and, truly, master Page is an honest man Never a wife in Windsor leads a better life than she does; do what she will, say what she will, take all, pay all, go to bed when she list, rise when she list, all is as she will; and, truly, she deserves it: for if there be a kind woman in Windsor, she is one. You must send her your page; no remedy.

Fal. Why, I will.

Quick. Nay, but do so then: and, look you he may come and go between you both; and, in any case, have a nay-word, that you may know one another's mind, and the boy never need to understand any thing; for 'tis not good that children should know any wickedness; old folks, you know, have discretion, as they say, and know the world.

Fal. Fare thee well: commend me to them both; there's my purse; I am yet thy debtor. —Boy, go along with this woman.——This news distracts me!

[*Exeunt* QUICKLY *and* ROBIN.

Pist. This punk is one of Cupid's carriers:— Clap on more sails; pursue, up with your fights; Give fire; she is my prize, or ocean whelm them all!

[*Exit* PISTOL.

Fal. Say'st thou so, old Jack? go thy ways; I'll make more of thy old body than I have done. Will they yet look after thee? Wilt thou, after the expense of so much money, be now a gainer? Good body, I thank thee: Let them say, 'tis grossly done; so it be fairly done no matter.

Enter BARDOLPH.

Bard. Sir John, there's one master Brook below would fain speak with you, and be acquainted with you; and hath sent your worship a morning's draught of sack.

Fal. Brook is his name?

Bard. Ay, sir.

Fal. Call him in; [*Exit* BARDOLPH.] Such Brooks are welcome to me that o'erflow such liquor. Ah! ha! mistress Ford and mistress Page, have I encompassed you? go to; *via!*

Re-enter BARDOLPH, *with* FORD *disguised.*

Ford. Bless you, sir.

---

* *Of all loves.* This pretty antique phrase is now obsolete. We have it in Othello: "the general so likes your music, that he desires you, of all loves, to make no more noise with it."

b *Fights*—Dryden, in his Tragedy of Amboyna, has
 "Up with your *fights*
 And your nettings prepare."
It appears that *fights* were waste-cloths, to conceal the men. *coverts*, says Mr. White, from Cole's English Dict. 1677.

---

* *Frampold*—fretful, uneasy.

Fal. And you, sir: Would you speak with me?

Ford. I make bold to press with so little preparation upon you.

Fal. You're welcome. What's your will? Give us leave, drawer. [*Exit* BARDOLPH.

Ford. Sir, I am a gentleman that have spent much; my name is Brook.

Fal. Good master Brook, I desire more acquaintance of you.

Ford. Good sir John, I sue for yours: not to charge you; for I must let you understand I think myself in better plight for a lender than you are: the which hath something emboldened me to this unseasoned intrusion: for they say, if money go before all ways do lie open.

Fal. Money is a good soldier, sir, and will on.

Ford. Troth, and I have a bag of money here troubles me: if you will help to bear it, sir John, take all, or half, for easing me of the carriage.

Fal. Sir, I know not how I may deserve to be your porter.

Ford. I will tell you, sir, if you will give me the hearing.

Fal. Speak, good master Brook; I shall be glad to be your servant.

Ford. Sir, I hear you are a scholar,—I will be brief with you,—and you have been a man long known to me, though I had never so good means, as desire, to make myself acquainted with you. I shall discover a thing to you, wherein I must very much lay open mine own imperfection: but, good sir John, as you have one eye upon my follies, as you hear them unfolded, turn another into the register of your own; that I may pass with a reproof the easier, sith you yourself know how easy it is to be such an offender.

Fal. Very well, sir; proceed.

Ford. There is a gentlewoman in this town, her husband's name is Ford.

Fal. Well, sir.

Ford. I have long loved her, and I protest to you, bestowed much on her; followed her with a doting observance; engrossed opportunities to meet her; fee'd every slight occasion that could but niggardly give me sight of her; not only bought many presents to give her, but have given largely to many, to know what she would have given: briefly, I have pursued her as love hath pursued me, which hath been on the wing of all occasions. But whatsoever I have merited, either in my mind, or in my means, meed, I am sure, I have received none; unless experience be a jewel; that I have purchased at an infinite rate; and that hath taught me to say this·

Love like a shadow flies, when substance love pursues;
Pursuing that that flies, and flying what pursues.

Fal. Have you received no promise of satisfaction at her hands?

Ford. Never.

Fal. Have you importuned her to such a purpose?

Ford. Never.

Fal. Of what quality was your love then?

Ford. Like a fair house built on another man's ground; so that I have lost my edifice, by mistaking the place where I erected it.

Fal. To what purpose have you unfolded this to me?

Ford. When I have told you that I have told you all. Some say, that, though she appear honest to me, yet, in other places, she enlargeth her mirth so far that there is shrewd construction made of her. Now, sir John, here is the heart of my purpose: You are a gentleman of excellent breeding, admirable discourse, of great admittance, authentic in your place and person, generally allowed for your many war-like, court-like, and learned preparations.

Fal. O, sir!

Ford. Believe it, for you know it:—There is money: spend it, spend it; spend more; spend all I have; only give me so much of your time in exchange of it, as to lay an amiable siege to the honesty of this Ford's wife: use your art of wooing, win her to consent to you; if any man may you may as soon as any.

Fal. Would it apply well to the vehemency of your affection, that I should win what you would enjoy? Methinks, you prescribe to yourself very preposterously.

Ford. O, understand my drift! she dwells so securely on the excellency of her honour, that the folly of my soul dares not present itself; she is too bright to be looked against. Now, could I come to her with any detection in my hand, my desires had instance and argument to commend themselves: I could drive her then from the ward of her purity, her reputation, her marriage vow, and a thousand other her defences, which now are too too strongly embattled against me: What say you to't, sir John?

Fal. Master Brook, I will first make bold with your money; next, give me your hand; and last, as I am a gentleman, you shall, if you will, enjoy Ford's wife.

Ford. O good sir!

Fal. I say you shall.

Ford. Want no money, sir John, you shall want none.

Fal. Want no mistress Ford, master Brook,

you shall want none. I shall be with her, (I may tell you,) by her own appointment; even as you came in to me, her assistant, or go-between, parted from me: I say, I shall be with her between ten and eleven; for at that time the jealous rascally knave, her husband, will be forth. Come you to me at night; you shall know how I speed.

Ford. I am blest in your acquaintance. Do you know Ford, Sir?

Fal. Hang him, poor cuckoldly knave! I know him not:—yet I wrong him to call him poor; they say the jealous wittolly knave hath masses of money; for the which his wife seems to me well-favoured. I will use her as the key of the cuckoldly rogue's coffer; and there's my harvest-home.

Ford. I would you knew Ford, sir; that you might avoid him if you saw him.

Fal. Hang him, mechanical salt-butter rogue! I will stare him out of his wits; I will awe him with my cudgel: it shall hang like a meteor o'er the cuckold's horns: master Brook, thou shalt know I will predominate over the peasant, and thou shalt lie with his wife.—Come to me soon at night:—Ford's a knave, and I will aggravate his stile; thou, master Brook, shalt know him for knave and cuckold:—come to me soon at night. [*Exit.*

Ford. What a damned Epicurean rascal is this!—My heart is ready to crack with impatience.—Who says, this is improvident jealously? My wife hath sent to him, the hour is fixed, the match is made. Would any man have thought this?—See the hell of having a false woman! My bed shall be abused, my coffers ransacked, my reputation gnawn at; and I shall not only receive this villainous wrong, but stand under the adoption of abominable terms, and by him that does me this wrong. Terms! names! —Amaimon sounds well; Lucifer, well; Barbason, well; yet they are devils' additions, the names of fiends! but cuckold! wittol-cuckold! the devil himself hath not such a name. Page is an ass, a secure ass! he will trust his wife, he will not be jealous; I will rather trust a Fleming with my butter, parson Hugh the Welchman with my cheese, an Irishman with my aqua-vitæ bottle, or a thief to walk my ambling gelding, than my wife with herself: then she plots, then she ruminates, then she devises; and what they think in their hearts they may effect they will break their hearts but they will effect. Heaven be praised for my jealousy!—Eleven o'clock the hour.—I will prevent this, detect my wife, be revenged on Falstaff, and laugh at Page. I will

about it; better three hours too soon than a minute too late. Fie, fie, fie! cuckold! cuckold! cuckold! [*Exit.*

SCENE III.—*Field near Windsor.*

Enter CAIUS *and* RUGBY.

Caius. Jack Rugby!

Rug. Sir.

Caius. Vat is de clock, Jack?

Rug. 'Tis past the hour, sir, that sir Hugh promised to meet.

Caius. By gar, he has save his soul, dat he is no come; he has pray his Pible vell, dat he is no come: by gar, Jack Rugby, he is dead already if he be come.

Rug. He is wise, sir; he knew your worship would kill him if he came.

Caius. By gar, de herring is no dead so as I vill kill him. Take your rapier, Jack; I vill tell you how I vill kill him.

Rug. Alas, sir, I cannot fence.

Caius. Villainy, take your rapier.

Rug. Forbear; here's company.

Enter HOST, SHALLOW, SLENDER, *and* PAGE.

Host. 'Bless thee, bully doctor.

Shal. Save you, master doctor Caius.

Page. Now, good master doctor.

Slen. Give you good-morrow, sir.

Caius. Vat be all you, one, two, tree, four, come for?

Host. To see thee fight, to see thee foin, to see thee traverse, to see thee here, to see thee there; to see thee pass thy punto, thy stock, thy reverse, thy distance, thy montánt. Is he dead, my Ethiopian? is he dead, my Francisco? ha, bully! What says my Æsculapius? my Galen? my heart of elder? ha! is he dead, bully Stale? is he dead?

Caius. By gar, he is de coward Jack priest of de vorld; he is not show his face.

Host. Thou art a Castilian,* king Urinal! Hector of Greece, my boy!

Caius. I pray you, bear vitness that me have stay six or seven, two, tree hours for him, and he is no come.

Shal. He is the wiser man, master doctor: he is a curer of souls and you a curer of bodies; if you should fight, you go against the hair of your professions; is it not true, master Page?

Page. Master Shallow, you have yourself been a great fighter, though now a man of peace.

* *Castilian.*—The Host ridicules the Doctor through his ignorance of English. He is a "heart of elder," the elder being filled with soft pith;—he is a Castilian, that name being an opprobrious designation for the Spaniards, whom the English of Elizabeth's time hated as much as their descendants were accustomed to hate the French.

Shal. Bodykins, master Page, though I now be old, and of the peace, if I see a sword out my finger itches to make one: though we are justices, and doctors, and churchmen, master Page, we have some salt of our youth in us; we are the sons of women, master Page.

Page. 'Tis true, master Shallow.

Shal. It will be found so, master Page. Master doctor Caius, I am come to fetch you home. I am sworn of the peace; you have shewed yourself a wise physician, and sir Hugh hath shewn himself a wise and patient churchman: you must go with me, master doctor.

Host. Pardon, guest justice:—ah, monsieur Mock-water.*

Caius. Mock-vater! vat is dat?

Host. Mock-water, in our English tongue, is valour, bully.

Caius. By gar, then I have as much mock-vater as de Englishman:— Scurvy jack-dog priest! by gar, me vill cut his ears.

Host. He will clapper-claw thee tightly, bully.

Caius. Clapper-de-claw! vat is dat?

Host. That is, he will make thee amends.

Caius. By gar, me do look he shall clapper-de-claw me; for, by gar, me vill have it.

Host. And I will provoke him to't, or let him wag.

Caius. Me tank you for dat.

Host. And moreover, bully,—But first, master guest, and master Page, and eke cavalero Slender, go you through the town to Frogmore.
[*Aside to them.*

Page. Sir Hugh is there, is he?

Host. He is there: see what humour he is in; and I will bring the doctor about by the fields: will it do well?

Shal. We will do it.

Page. Shal. and Slen. Adieu, good master doctor. [*Exeunt* PAGE, SHALLOW, *and* SLENDER.

Caius. By gar, me vill kill de priest; for he speak for a jack-an-ape to Anne Page.

Host. Let him die: sheath thy impatience; throw cold water on thy choler: go about the fields with me through Frogmore; I will bring thee where mistress Anne Page is, at a farm-house, a feasting: and thou shalt woo her: Cry'd game?* said I well?

Caius. By gar, me tank you for dat: by gar, I love you; and I shall procure-a you de good guest, de earl, de knight, de lords, de gentlemen, my patients.

Host. For the which I will be thy adversary toward Anne Page; said I well?

Caius. By gar, t'is good; vell said.

Host. Let us wag then.

Caius. Come at my heels, Jack Rugby.
[*Exeunt.*

* *Cry'd game.* So the folio. Warburton proposed to read *cry'd aim,* and much learning has been expended in support of this reading. Those who retain the original *cry'd game* suppose that the Host addresses Dr. Caius by this as a name, in the same way that he calls him "heart of elder." Mr. Dyce has "Cried I aim I." Mr. White retains "cried game," believing it to be a colloquial phrase of which the meaning can only be guessed at. Mr. Collier's corrected copy has "Curds and cream."

* *Mock-water.* So the original; it was changed by Farmer to *muck water.* Lord Chadworth suggests that as the lustre of a diamond is called its *water,* mock-water may mean a *counterfeit* valour. Surely this is very daring. *Mock-water,* or *muck-water,* was some allusion to the profession of Caius.

("At a farm-house, a feasting.")

ILLUSTRATIONS OF ACT II.

¹ SCENE I.—"*This Flemish drunkard.*"

THE English of the days of Elizabeth accused the people of the Low Countries with having taught them to drink to excess. The "men of war" who had campaigned in Flanders, according to Sir John Smythe, in his 'Discourses,' 1590, introduced this vice amongst us; "whereof it is come to pass that now-a-days there are very few feasts where our said men of war are present, but that they do invite and procure all the company, of what calling soever they be, to carousing and quaffing; and, because they will not be denied their challenges, they, with many new conges, ceremonies, and reverences, drink to the health and prosperity of princes; to the health of counsellors, and unto the health of their greatest friends both at home and abroad: in which exercise they never cease till they be dead drunk, or, as the Flemings say, Doot dronken." He adds: "and this aforesaid detestable vice hath within these six or seven years taken wonderful root amongst our English nation, that in times past was wont to be of all nations of Christendom one of the soberest."

² SCENE I. (also ACT V. SC. V.)—"*Green sleeves.*"

This appears to have been a very popular song in Shakspere's time, and, judging from an allusion to it in Fletcher's Tragi-Comedy, 'The Loyal Subject,' as well as from a pamphlet entered at Stationers' Hall, in February, 1580, under the title of 'A representation against *Green Sleeves,* by W Elderton,' was thought gross, even in an age when what was in gay society called polite conversation was rarely free from indelicacy, and the drama teemed with jokes and expressions that now would not be tolerated in the servants' hall. The original words of *Green Sleeves* have not descended to us, but the tune was too good to be condemned to that oblivion which has been the fate of the verses to which it was first set; hence many adapted their poetical effusions to it, and among those extant, is "a new courtly sonnet of the Lady Greensleeves," reprinted in *Ellis's Specimens of the Early English Poets,* from an extremely scarce miscellany, called '**A Handful of Pleasant Delites***, &c.,* by Clement Robinson, and others, 12mo, 1584. This sonnet contains some curious particulars respecting female dress and manners, during the sixteenth century. At the time too when it was the fashion, in England and in France, to set sacred words to popular tunes, this air, among others, was selected for the purpose, as we learn from the books of the Stationers' Company, wherein appears, in September, 1580, the following entry—"*Greensleeves,* moralized to the Scriptures."

Greensleeves is to be found in all the editions of *The Dancing-master* that have come under our notice. In the seventeenth (1721) which is the best, it takes the title of "Greensleeves and yellow lace." It was introduced by Gay, or his friend Dr. Pepusch, in 'The Beggars' Opera,' set to the song, "Since laws were made for every degree," and is still well known, in quarters where ancient customs are yet kept up in all their rude simplicity, as "Christmas comes but once a year." Sir J. Hawkins, in the Appendix to his History of Music, gives the first strain only; why he omitted the latter half is not stated.* In all the copies of the air it appears in the now obsolete measure of six crotchets. In *The Dancing Master* it is set in the key of A minor; in *The Beggars' Opera,* in G minor. We here give it in a measure universally understood, and have added such a base as seems to us to be in keeping with a vocal melody between two and three hundred years old.

* In 'A collection of national English airs,' edited by W. Chappell, (a very interesting work, shewing great research) this tune is inserted in the key of E minor, with a moving base by Dr. Crotch.

ILLUSTRATIONS OF ACT II.

¹ SCENE I.—"*I have heard the Frenchman hath good skill in his rapier.*"

Shallow ridicules the formalities that belong to the use of the rapier, which those of the old school thought a cowardly weapon. The introduction of the rapier into England was ascribed to one Rowland York, who is thus spoken of in Carleton's 'Thankful Remembrance of God's Mercy,' 1625: "He was a Londoner, famous among the cutters of his time, for bringing in a new kind of fight,—to run the point of the rapier into a man's body. This manner of fight he brought first into England, with great admiration of his audaciousness; when in England, before that time, the use was, with little bucklers, and with broad swords, to strike, and not to thrust; and it was accounted unmanly to strike under the girdle." This passage from Carleton appears to be an inaccurate statement from Darcie's 'Annals of Elizabeth,' wherein it is said that Rowland York was the first that brought into England "that wicked and pernicious fashion to fight in the fields, in duels, with a rapier called a tucke, only for the thrust," &c. Douce distinguishes between the *rapier* generally, and the *tucke for the thrust*. It appears, however, from other authorities, that the rapier was in use in the time of Henry VIII.; and Douce holds that " it is impossible to decide that this weapon, which, with its name, we received from the French, might not have been known as early as the reign of Henry IV., or even of Richard II."

² SCENE II.—"*I will not lend thee a penny.*"

This passage requires no comment; but some of our readers may be pleased with the representation of the silver penny of Elizabeth.

³ SCENE II.—"*Coach after coach.*"

"Coaches," says Malone, "as appears from Howe's continuation of Stow's Chronicle, did not come into general use till the year 1605." Chalmers, on the contrary, has shewn us, from the 'Journals of Parliament,' that a bill was introduced during the session of 1601 to restrain the *excessive use* of coaches. We subjoin from a print by Hoefnagel, dated 1582, a very interesting illustration representing one of Elizabeth's visits to Nonsuch, by which we shall perceive that the form of state-coaches, whether for sovereigns or lord mayors, has not materially altered.

⁴ SCENE II.—"*Nay, which is more, pensioners.*"

Pensioners might have been put higher than earls by Mistress Quickly, on account of their splendid dress. Shakspere alludes to this in " A Midsummer Night's Dream: "

"The cowslips tall her pensioners be,
In their gold coats spots you see."

But the pensioners of Elizabeth were also men of large fortune. Tyrwhitt illustrates the passage before us, from Gervase Holles's Life of the First Earl of Clare: "I have heard the Earl of Clare say, that when he was pensioner to the queen, he did not know a worse man of the whole band than himself; and that all the world knew he had then an inheritance of £4,000 a year."

⁷ SCENE II.—"*Hath sent your worship a morning's draught of sack.*"

Presents of wine were often sent from one guest in a tavern to another,—sometimes by way of a friendly memorial, and sometimes as an introduction to acquaintance. "Ben Jonson was at a tavern, and in comes Bishop Corbet (but not so then) into the next room. Ben Jonson calls for a quart of raw wine, and gives it to the tapster

MERRY WIVES OF WINDSOR.

'Sirrah, says he, 'carry this to the gentleman in the next chamber, and tell him, I sacrifice my service to him.' The fellow did, and in those words. 'Friend,' says Dr. Corbet, 'I thank him for his love : but pr'ythee tell him from me that he is mistaken ; for sacrifices are always burnt.'"
—*Merry Passages and Jeasts*, Harl. MSS. 6395.

[Nonsuch House.]

LOCAL ILLUSTRATION.

It is not very easy to define the spot where, according to the mischievous arrangement of mine Host of the Garter, Dr. Caius waited for Sir Hugh Evans. Sir Hugh. we know, waited for Dr. Caius near Frogmore ; for the host tells Shallow, and Page, and Slender, "Go you through the town to Frogmore ;" and he takes the doctor to meet Sir Hugh " about the fields through Frogmore." The stage-direction for this third scene of the second Act is " Windsor Park." But had Caius waited in Windsor Park he would have been near Frogmore, and it would not have been necessary to go through the town, or through the fields. We should be inclined, therefore, to place the locality of the third scene in the meadows near the Thames on the west side of Windsor, and we have altered the stage direction accordingly. Frogmore was probably a small village in Shakspere's time; and at any rate it had its farm-house, where Anne Page was "a feasting." "Old Windsor way" was farther than Frogmore from Windsor, so that Simple had little chance of finding Caius in that direction. The park,—the little park as it is now called,—undoubtedly came close to the castle ditch on the south-east. Some of the oaks not a quarter of a mile from the castle, and which appear to have formed part of an avenue, are of great antiquity. Of the supposed locality of Herne's Oak in this park we shall speak in the fifth Act. The forest, perhaps, stretched up irregularly towards the castle, unenclosed, with meadows and common fields interposing. The connexion between the forest and the castle by the Long Walk was made in the Reign of Anne, the town receiving a grant for the property then enclosed. The description of Windsor nearest to the period of this comedy, is that of Lord Surrey's Poem, 1546, a stanza of which will be found in Henry IV. Part II. Our readers will not be displeased to have it presented to them entire :—

So cruel prison how could betide, alas !
 As proud Windsor ! where I in lust and joy,
 With a king's son, my childish years did pass,
 In greater feast than Priam's sons of Troy.
Where each sweet place returns a taste full sour.
 The large green courts, where we were wont to hove,*
 With eyes cast up unto the Maiden's Tower,
 And easy sighs, such as folk draw in love.
The stately seats, the ladies bright of hue,
 The dances short, long tales of great delight;
 With words, and looks, that tigers could but rue,
 Where each of us did plead the other's right.
The palme-play,† where, despoiled ‡ for the game,

* Linger, or hover.   † Tennis-court.   ‡ Stript.

ILLUSTRATIONS OF ACT II.

With dazed eyes oft we by gleams of love,
Have miss'd the ball, and got sight of our dame,
To bait her eyes, which kept the lends above.
The gravel'd ground, with sleeves tied on the helm,
On foaming horse with swords and friendly hearts;
With chere, as though one should another whelm,
Where we have fought, and chased oft with darts.
With silver drops the meads yet spread for ruth;
In active games of nimbleness and strength,
Where we did strain, trained with swarms of youth,
Our tender limbs, that yet shot up in length.
The secret groves, which oft we made resound
Of pleasant plaint, and of our ladies' praise;
Recording soft what grace each one had found,
What hope of speed, what dread of long delays.
The wild forest, the clothed holts with green;
With reins availed, and swiftly-breathed horse,
With cry of hounds, and merry blasts between,
Where we did chase the fearful hart of force.

The Journal of the Secretary of the Duke of Wartemberg, described in the Introductory Notice, contains the following curious description of the Parks of Windsor, in 1592:—

"Her Majesty appointed a respectable elderly English nobleman to attend upon your Princely Grace, and required and ordered the same not only to shew to your Princely Grace the splendidly beautiful and royal castle of Windsor, but also to make the residence pleasant and merry with shooting and hunting the numerous herds of game ; for it is well known that the aforesaid place, Windsor, has upwards of sixty parks adjoining each other, full of fallow-deer and other game, of all sorts of colours, which may be driven from one park (all being enclosed with hedges) to another, and thus one can enjoy a splendid and royal sport.

"The hunters (deer or park keepers) who live in separate but excellent houses, as had been appointed, made excellent sport for your Princely Grace. In the first Park your Princely Grace shot a fallow deer through the thigh, and it was soon after captured by the dogs. In the next you hunted a stag for a long time over a broad and pleasant plain, with a pack of remarkably good hounds ; your Princely Grace first shot it with an English crossbow, and the hounds at length outwearied and captured it.

"In the third you loosed a stag, but somewhat too quickly, for he was caught too soon, and almost before he came right out upon the plain.

"These three deer were sent to Windsor, and were presented to your Princely Grace: one of these was done justice to in the apartments of Monsieur de Beauvois, the French ambassador."

["Nay, keep your way, little gallant."]

ACT III.

SCENE I.—*A Field near* Frogmore.

Enter Sir Hugh Evans *and* Simple.

Eva. I pray you now, good master Slender's serving-man, and friend Simple by your name, which way have you looked for master Caius, that calls himself Doctor of Physic?

Sim. Marry, sir, the pittie-ward,* the park-ward, every way; old Windsor way, and every way but the town way.

Eva. I most fehemently desire you, you will also look that way.

Sim. I will, sir.

Eva. Pless my soul! how full of cholers I am, and trempling of mind!—I shall be glad if he have deceived me:—how melancholies I am.! I will knog his urinals about his knave's costard, when I have good opportunities for the 'ork— pless my soul! [*Sings.*

> To shallow rivers, to whose falls
> Melodious birds sing madrigals ;
> There will we make our peds of roses.
> And a thousand fragrant posies.
> To shallow—

'Mercy on me! I have a great dispositions to cry.

> Melodious birds sing madrigals ;
> When as I sat in Pabylon,—
> And a thousand vagram posies.
> To shallow—

---

* *Pittie-ward.* Steevens changed this to *city-ward*, which he exp'sins "*towards London;*"—as if Windsor were as near the city as Whitechapel. *Pittie-ward* is undoubtedly right, and is of the same import as *petty-ward*. A part of Windsor Castle is still called the *lower ward*, and in the same way another part might have been known as the *park-ward*.

Sim. Yonder he is coming, this way, Sir Hugh.

Eva. He's welcome:

> To shallow rivers, to whose falls !—

Heaven prosper the right!—What weapons is he?

Sim. No weapons, sir: There comes my master, master Shallow, and another gentleman from Frogmore, over the stile, this way.

Eva. Pray you, give me my gown; or else keep it in your arms.

Enter Page, Shallow, *and* Slender.

Shal. How now, master parson? Good-morrow, good sir Hugh. Keep a gamester from the dice, and a good student from his book, and it is wonderful.

Slen. Ah, sweet Anne Page!

Page. Save you, good sir Hugh!

Eva. Pless you from his mercy sake, all of you!

Shal. What! the sword and the word! do you study them both, master parson?

Page. And youthful still, in your doublet and hose, this raw rheumatic day?

Eva. There is reasons and causes for it.

Page. We are come to you to do a good office, master parson.

Eva. Fery well: What is it?

Page. Yonder is a most reverend gentleman, who belike, having received wrong by some person, is at most odds with his own gravity and patience, that ever you saw.

175

Shal. I have lived fourscore years and upward; I never heard a man of his place, gravity, and learning, so wide of his own respect.

Eva. What is he?

Page. I think you know him; master doctor Caius, the renowned French Physician.

Eva. Got's will, and his passion of my heart! I had as lief you would tell me of a mess of porridge.

Page. Why?

Eva. He has no more knowledge in Hibocrates and Galen,—and he is a knave besides; a cowardly knave, as you would desires to be acquainted withal.

Page. I warrant you, he's the man should fight with him.

Slen. O, sweet Anne Page!

Shal. It appears so, by his weapons:—Keep them asunder;—here comes doctor Caius.

Enter HOST, CAIUS, *and* RUGBY.

Page. Nay, good master parson, keep in your weapon.

Shal. So do you, good master doctor.

Host. Disarm them, and let them question; let them keep their limbs whole, and hack our English.

Caius. I pray you let-a me speak a word vit your ear; Vereforc vill you not meet a-me?

Eva. Pray you, use your patience: in good time.

Caius. By gar, you are de coward, de Jack dog, John ape.

Eva. Pray you, let us not be laughing-stogs to other men's humours; I desire you in friendship, and I will one way or other make you amends:—I will knog your urinal about your knave's cogscomb [for missing your meetings and appointments.]*

Caius. Diable!—Jack Rugby,—mine *Host de Jarterre,* have I not stay for him, to kill him? have I not, at de place I did appoint.

Eva. As I am a christians soul, now, look you, this is the place appointed; I'll be judgment by mine host of the Garter.

Host. Peace, I say, Guallia and Gaul; French and Welch; soul-curer and body-curer.

Caius. Ay, dat is very good! excellent!

Host. Peace, I say; hear mine host of the Garter. Am I politic? am I subtle? am I a Machiavel? Shall I lose my doctor? no; he gives me the potions, and the motions. Shall I lose my parson? my priest? my sir Hugh? no: he gives me the proverbs and the no-verbs.—[Give me thy hand, terrestrial; so:]—Give me thy hand, celestial; so.——Boys of art, I have deceived you both; I have directed you to wrong places; your hearts are mighty, your skins are whole, and let burnt sack be the issue,—Come, lay their swords to pawn:—Follow me, lads of peace; follow, follow, follow.

Shal. Trust me, a mad host:—Follow, gentlemen, follow.

Slen. O, sweet Anne Page!

[*Exeunt* SHALLOW, SLENDER, PAGE, *and* HOST.

Caius. Ha! do I perceive dat? have you make-a de sot of us? ha, ha!

Eva. This is well; he has made us his vlouting-stog.—I desire you that we may be friends; and let us knog our prains together, to be revenge ou this same scall,[b] scurvy, cogging companion, the host of the Garter.

Caius. By gar, vit all my heart; he promise to bring me vere is Anne Page; by gar, he deceive me too.

Eva. Well, I will smite his noddles:—Pray you, follow. [*Exeunt.*

SCENE II.—*The Street in* Windsor.

Enter MISTRESS PAGE *and* ROBIN.

Mrs. Page. Nay, keep your way, little gallant; you were wont to be a follower, but now you are a leader: Whether had you rather lead mine eyes, or eye your master's heels?

Rob. I had rather, forsooth, go before you like a man, than follow him like a dwarf.

Mrs. Page. O you are a flattering boy; now, I see, you'll be a courtier.

Enter FORD.

Ford. Well met, mistress Page: Whither go you?

Mrs. Page. Truly, sir, to see your wife; Is she at home?

Ford. Ay; and as idle as she may hang together, for want of company. I think if your husbands were dead, you two would marry.

Mrs. Page. Be sure of that,—two other husbands.

Ford. Where had you this pretty weathercock?

Mrs. Page. I cannot tell what the dickens

---

* The passage in brackets is not in the folio, but is found in the quarto. The address of the Host to the Doctor as terrestrial, and to the Parson as celestial, is too humorous to be lost.

b *Scall*—scald.—Thus Fluellen, "scald knave."

his name is my husband had him of: What do you call your knight's name, sirrah?

Rob. Sir John Falstaff.

Ford. Sir John Falstaff!

Mrs. Page. He, he; I can never hit on's name.—There is such a league between my good man and he!—Is your wife at home, indeed?

Ford. Indeed, she is.

Mrs. Page. By your leave, sir:—I am sick, till I see her. [*Exeunt Mrs.* PAGE *and* ROBIN.

Ford. Has Page any brains? hath he any eyes? bath he any thinking? Sure, they sleep; he hath no use of them. Why, this boy will carry a letter twenty miles, as easy as a cannon will shoot point-blank twelve score. He pieces out his wife's inclination; he gives her folly motion and advantage: and now she's going to my wife, and Falstaff's boy with her. A man may hear this shower sing in the wind!—and Falstaff's boy with her!—Good plots!—they are laid; and our revolted wives share damnation together. Well; I will take him, then torture my wife, pluck the borrowed veil of modesty from the so seeming mistress Page, divulge Page himself for a secure and wilful Actæon; and to these violent proceedings all my neighbours shall cry aim.* [*Clock strikes.*] The clock gives me my cue, and my assurance bids me search; There I shall find Falstaff: I shall be rather praised for this than mocked; for it is as positive as the earth is firm that Falstaff is there: I will go.

Enter PAGE, SHALLOW, SLENDER, HOST, *Sir* HUGH EVANS, CAIUS, *and* RUGBY.

Shal. Page, &c. Well met, master Ford.

Ford. Trust me, a good knot: I have good cheer at home; and, I pray you all go with me.

Shall. I must excuse myself, master Ford.

Slen. And so must I, sir; we have appointed to dine with mistress Anne, and I would not break with her for more money than I'll speak of.

Shall. We have lingered about a match between Anne Page and my cousin Slender, and this day we shall have our answer.

Slen. I hope I have your good will, father Page.

Page. You have, master Slender; I stand wholly for you:—but my wife, master doctor, is for you altogether.

* Cry aim. See Note to Two Gentlemen of Verona, Act III., Sc. I.

COMEDIES.—VOL. I.   N

Caius. Ay, by gar; and de maid is love a-me; my nursh a Quickly tell me so mush.

Host. What say you to young master Fenton? he capers, he dances, he has eyes of youth, he writes verses, he speaks holiday, he smells April and May; he will carry't, he will carry't; 'tis in his buttons;* he will carry't.

Page. Not by my consent, I promise you. The gentleman is of no having: he kept company with the wild Prince and Poins; he is of too high a region, he knows too much. No, he shall not knit a knot in his fortunes with the finger of my substance: if he take her, let him take her simply; the wealth I have waits on my consent, and my consent goes not that way.

Ford. I beseech you, heartily, some of you go home with me to dinner: besides your cheer, you shall have sport; I will show you a monster. —Master doctor, you shall go;—so shall you, master Page;—and you, sir Hugh.

Shall. Well, fare you well:—we shall have the freer wooing at master Page's.

[*Exeunt* SHALLOW *and* SLENDER.

Caius. Go home, John Rugby; I come anon.
[*Exit* RUGBY.

Host. Farewell, my hearts: I will to my honest knight Falstaff, and drink canary with him. [*Exit* HOST.

Ford. [*Aside.*] I think I shall drink in pipe-wine⁵ first with him; I will make him dance. Will you go, gentles?

All. Have with you, to see this monster.
[*Exeunt.*

SCENE III.—*A room in Ford's House.*

Enter Mrs. FORD *and Mrs.* PAGE.

Mrs. Ford. What, John! What, Robert!

Mrs. Page. Quickly, quickly. Is the buck-basket—

Mrs. Ford. I warrant:—What, Robin, I say.

Enter Servants, with a basket.

Mrs. Page. Come, come, come.

Mrs. Ford. Here, set it down.

Mrs. Page. Give your men the charge; we must be brief.

Mrs. Ford. Marry, as I told you before, John, and Robert, be ready here hard by in the brew-house; and when I suddenly call you, come forth, and (without any pause or stagger-

---

a Probably an allusion to the custom of wearing the flower called *Bachelor's buttons*. But a very similar phrase is common in the midland counties:—"It does not lie in your breeches," meaning it is not within your compass. "Tis in his buttons," therefore means, he is the man to do it.
b *Pipe-wine.* Ford will *pipe* while Falstaff *dances.*

177

ing), take this basket on your shoulders: that done, trudge with it in all haste, and carry it among the whitsters[a] in Datchet mead, and there empty it in the muddy ditch, close by the Thames side.

Mrs. Page. You will do it?

Mrs. Ford. I have told them over and over; they lack no direction: Be gone, and come when you are called. [*Exeunt* Servants.

Mrs. Page. Here comes little Robin.

Enter ROBIN.

Mrs. Ford. How now, my eyas-musket?[b] what news with you?

Rob. My master, sir John, is come in at your back-door, mistress Ford; and requests your company.

Mrs. Page. You little Jack-a-lent,[c] have you been true to us?

Rob. Ay, I'll be sworn: My master knows not of your being here; and hath threatened to put me into everlasting liberty if I tell you of it; for, he swears, he'll turn me away.

Mrs. Page. Thou'rt a good boy; this secrecy of thine shall be a tailor to thee, and shall make thee a new doublet and hose. I'll go hide me.

Mrs. Ford. Do so:—Go tell thy master, I am alone. Mistress Page, remember you your cue. [*Exit* ROBIN.

Mrs. Page. I warrant thee; if I do not act it, hiss me. [*Exit Mrs.* PAGE.

Mrs. Ford. Go to then; we'll use this unwholesome humidity, this gross watery pumpion. We'll teach him to know turtles from jays.

Enter FALSTAFF.

Fal. Have I caught thee, my heavenly jewel?[d] Why, now let me die, for I have lived long enough; this is the period of my ambition. O this blessed hour!

Mrs. Ford. O sweet sir John!

Fal. Mistress Ford, I cannot cog, I cannot prate, mistress Ford. Now shall I sin in my wish: I would thy husband were dead. I'll speak it before the best lord, I would make thee my lady.

Mrs. Ford. I your lady, sir John! alas, I should be a pitiful lady.

Fal. Let the court of France shew me such another. I see how thine eye would emulate the diamond: Thou hast the right arched beauty[a] of the brow, that becomes the ship-tire, the tire-valiant, or any tire of Venetian admittance.

Mrs. Ford. A plain kerchief, sir John: my brows become nothing else; nor that well neither.

Fal. Thou art a tyrant[b] to say so: thou would'st make an absolute courtier; and the firm fixture of thy foot would give an excellent motion to thy gait, in a semi-circled farthingale. I see what thou wert if Fortune thy foe were not; Nature thy friend:[c] Come, thou canst not hide it.

Mrs. Ford. Believe me, there's no such thing in me.

Fal. What made me love thee? let that persuade thee there's something extraordinary in thee. Come, I cannot cog, and say thou art this and that, like a many of these lisping hawthorn buds, that come like women in men's apparel, and smell like Bucklersbury in simple-time:[2] I cannot: but I love thee; none but thee; and thou deservest it.

Mrs. Ford. Do not betray me, sir. I fear you love mistress Page.

Fal. Thou might'st as well say I love to walk by the Counter-gate; which is as hateful to me as the reek of a lime-kiln.

Mrs. Ford. Well, heaven knows how I love you; and you shall one day find it.

Fal. Keep in that mind; I'll deserve it.

Mrs. Ford. Nay, I must tell you, so you do; or else I could not be in that mind.

Rob. [*within.*] Mistress Ford, mistress Ford! here's mistress Page at the door, sweating, and

---

[a] *Whitsters.*—A launder is still called a whitster; but the whitsters of the Thames were probably akin to the blanchisseuses of the Seine, and washed in the same fashion.

[b] *Eyas-musket.* The musket is the small sparrow-hawk; the eyas is a general name for a very young hawk—the first of five several names by which a falcon is called in its first year. Spenser has a pretty image connected with the eyas:

"Youthful gay
Like eyas-hawk up mounts into the skies,
His newly budded pinions to essay."

[c] *Jack-a-lent.* A puppet thrown at in Lent. Thus in Ben Jonson's Tale of a Tub:

"on an Ash Wednesday,
Where thou didst stand six weeks the Jack o' Lent
For boys to hurl three throws a penny at thee."

[d] "Have I caught my heavenly jewel," is the first line of a song in Sidney's Astrophel and Stella. In the quarto the line stands without the *thee* of the present text.

---

[a] *Arched beauty.* Thus the folio; the quarto, which the modern editors follow, has arched bent. Surely a bent arch is a term in which the epithet might be dispensed with.

[b] *Tyrant.* So the folio; the quarto, traitor.

[c] The passage in the folio stands thus: "I see what thou wert if Fortune thy foe, were not Nature thy friend." It is not found in the quarto. Upon Pope's correction the common reading is, "I see what thou wert, if Fortune thy foe were not Nature is thy friend." Boswell proposes to retain the old reading, with its original punctuation, and explains it thus,—"If Fortune *being* thy foe, Nature were not thy friend." But what would Mrs. Ford be, if both Fortune and Nature were leagued against her—if Fortune were her foe and Nature not her friend! "Fortune, my foe," was the beginning of an old ballad. We do not think that a perfect sense can be made of the passage as it stands. Mr. Collier proposes to read it thus:—"Nature *being* thy friend."

blowing, and looking wildly, and would needs speak with you presently.

Fal. She shall not see me: I will ensconce me behind the arras.

Mrs. Ford. Pray you, do so: she's a very tattling woman. [FALSTAFF *hides himself.*

Enter Mistress PAGE *and* ROBIN.

What's the matter? how now?

Mrs. Page. O mistress Ford, what have you done? You're shamed, you're overthrown, you're undone for ever.

Mrs. Ford. What's the matter, good mistress Page?

Mrs. Page. O well-a-day, mistress Ford! having an honest man to your husband, to give him such cause of suspicion!

Mrs. Ford. What cause of suspicion?

Mrs. Page. What cause of suspicion?—Out upon you! how am I mistook in you!

Mrs. Ford. Why, alas! what's the matter?

Mrs. Page. Your husband's coming hither, woman, with all the officers in Windsor, to search for a gentleman that, he says, is here now in the house, by your consent, to take an ill advantage of his absence: You are undone.

Mrs. Ford. 'Tis not so, I hope.*

Mrs. Page. Pray heaven it be not so, that you have such a man here; but 'tis most certain your husband's coming with half Windsor at his heels to search for such a one. I come before to tell you. If you know yourself clear, why I am glad of it: but if you have a friend here, convey, convey him out. Be not amazed; call all your senses to you; defend your reputation, or bid farewell to your good life for ever.

Mrs. Ford. What shall I do?—There is a gentleman, my dear friend; and I fear not mine own shame so much as his peril: I had rather than a thousand pound he were out of the house.

Mrs. Page. For shame, never stand *you had rather,* and *you had rather;* your husband's here at hand; bethink you of some conveyance: in the house you cannot hide him.— O, how have you deceived me!—Look, here is a basket; if he be of any reasonable stature, he may creep in here; and throw foul linen upon him, as if it were going to bucking: Or, it is whiting-time, send him by your two men to Datchet mead.

Mrs. Ford. He's too big to go in there: What shall I do?

Re-enter FALSTAFF.

Fal. Let me see't, let me see't! O let me see't! I'll in, I'll in; follow your friend's counsel;—I'll in.

Mrs. Page. What! Sir John Falstaff! Are these your letters, knight?

Fal. I love thee.* Help me away: let me creep in here; I'll never—
[*He goes into the basket; they cover him with foul linen.*

Mrs. Page. Help to cover your master, boy: Call your men, mistress Ford:—You dissembling knight!

Mrs. Ford. What John, Robert, John! [*Exit* ROBIN. *Re-enter* Servants.] Go take up these clothes here, quickly; where's the cowl-staff?[b] look, how you drumble; carry them to the laundress in Datchet mead; quickly, come.

Enter FORD, PAGE, CAIUS, *and Sir* HUGH EVANS.

Ford. Pray you, come near: if I suspect without cause, why then make sport at me, then let me be your jest; I deserve it.—How now! whither bear you this?

Serv. To the laundress, forsooth.

Mrs. Ford. Why, what have you to do whither they bear it? You were best meddle with buck-washing.

Ford. Buck? I would I could wash myself of the buck! Buck, buck, buck? Ay, buck; I warrant you, buck; and of the season too, it shall appear. [*Exeunt* Servants *with the basket.*] Gentlemen, I have dreamed to-night; I'll tell you my dream. Here, here, here be my keys; ascend my chambers, search, seek, find out: I'll warrant we'll unkennel the fox:—Let me stop this way first:—so, now uncape.

Page. Good master Ford be contented: you wrong yourself too much.

Ford. True, master Page.—Up, gentlemen; you shall see sport anon: follow me, gentlemen.
[*Exit.*

Eva. This is fery fantastical humours and jealousies.

Caius. By gar, 'tis no de fashion of France: it is not jealous in France.

Page. Nay, follow him, gentlemen; see the issue of his search.
[*Exeunt* EVANS, PAGE, *and* CAIUS.

---

* In the modern editions, Mrs. Ford says, before "'Tis not so, I hope,"—"speak louder,"—recovered by Steevens from "the two elder quartos." We have no hesitation in rejecting this restoration. In the second Scene of the fourth Act, where Falstaff again hides himself upon the interruption of Mrs. Page, Mrs. Ford says, "speak louder," which is not found in the two elder quartos. By such restorations as these, the care of the poet to avoid repetitions in the more skilful arrangement of his materials is rendered useless.

* Another restoration from the quarto:—" I love thee and none but thee."
[b] A *cowl-staff* is explained to be a staff used for carrying a basket with two handles.

Act III.] MERRY WIVES OF WINDSOR. [Scene IV.

Mrs. Page. Is there not a double excellency in this?

Mrs. Ford. I know not which pleases me better, that my husband is deceived, or sir John.

Mrs. Page. What a taking was he in, when your husband asked what was in the basket!*

Mrs. Ford. I am half afraid he will have need of washing; so throwing him into the water will do him a benefit.

Mrs. Page. Hang him, dishonest rascal! I would all of the same strain were in the same distress.

Mrs. Ford. I think my husband hath some special suspicion of Falstaff's being here; for I never saw him so gross in his jealousy till now.

Mrs. Page. I will lay a plot to try that: And we will yet have more tricks with Falstaff: his dissolute disease will scarce obey this medicine.

Mrs. Ford. Shall we send that foolish carrion, mistress Quickly, to him, and excuse his throwing into the water; and give him another hope, to betray him to another punishment?

Mrs. Page. We will do it; let him be sent for to-morrow eight o'clock, to have amends.

Re-enter FORD, PAGE, CAIUS, *and Sir* HUGH EVANS.

Ford. I cannot find him: may be the knave bragged of that he could not compass.

Mrs. Page. Heard you that?

Mrs. Ford. You use me well, master Ford, do you?

Ford. Ay, I do so.

Mrs. Ford. Heaven make you better than your thoughts!

Ford. Amen.

Mrs. Page. You do yourself mighty wrong, master Ford.

Ford. Ay, ay; I must bear it.

Eva. If there be any pody in the house, and in the chambers, and in the coffers, and in the presses, heaven forgive my sins at the day of judgment!

Caius. By gar, nor I too; dere is no bodies.

Page. Fie, fie, master Ford! are you not ashamed? What spirit, what devil suggests this imagination? I would not have your distemper in this kind, for the wealth of Windsor Castle.

Ford. 'Tis my fault, master Page: I suffer for it.

Eva. You suffer for a pad conscience: your wife is as honest a 'omans as I will desires amoug five thousand, and five hundred too.

Caius. By gar, I see 'tis an honest woman.

Ford. Well;—I promised you a dinner:—Come, come, walk in the park: I pray you pardon me; I will hereafter make known to you why I have done this.—Come, wife;—come, mistress Page; I pray you pardon me; pray heartily, pardon me.

Page. Let's go in, gentlemen; but, trust me, we'll mock him. I do invite you to-morrow morning to my house to breakfast: after, we'll a birding together; I have a fine hawk for the bush: Shall it be so?

Ford. Any thing.

Eva. If there is one, I shall make two in the company.

Caius. If there be one or two, I shall make a de tird.

Ford. Pray you go, master Page.

Eva. I pray you now, remembrance to-morrow on the lousy knave, mine host.

Caius. Dat is good; by gar, vit all my heart.

Eva. A lousy knave; to have his gibes and his mockeries. [*Exeunt.*

SCENE IV.—*A Room in* Page's *House*.

Enter FENTON *and Mistress* ANNE PAGE.

Fent. I see I cannot get thy father's love; Therefore no more turn me to him, sweet Nan.

Anne. Alas! how then?

Fent. Why, thou must be thyself. He doth object, I am too great of birth; And that, my state being gall'd with my expense, I seek to heal it only by his wealth: Besides these, other bars he lays before me,— My riots past, my wild societies; And tells me, 'tis a thing impossible I should love thee, but as a property.

Anne. May be, he tells you true.

Fent. No, heaven so speed me in my time to come! Albeit, I will confess thy father's wealth Was the first motive that I woo'd thee, Anne: Yet, wooing thee, I found thee of more value Than stamps in gold, or sums in sealed bags; And 'tis the very riches of thyself That now I aim at.

Anne. Gentle master Fenton, Yet seek my father's love; still seek it, sir · If opportunity and humblest suit

---

a *What was in the basket.* The folio has *who;* but we are justified in printing *what* from Falstaff's speech to Brook:—"—*that the jealous knave their master in the door; who asked them once or twice what they had in their basket!*"

* *Scene IV.* In the quartos, this scene, although much shorter than in the folio, follows the fifth scene, where Falstaff relates his Thames adventure. The skill of the dramatist is shewn in the interposition of an episode between the beginning and end of the catastrophe of the buck-basket.

Cannot attain it, why then.—Hark you hither.
            [*They converse apart.*
Enter SHALLOW, SLENDER, *and* Mrs. QUICKLY.

Shal. Break their talk, mistress Quickly; my kinsman shall speak for himself.

Slen. I'll make a shaft or a bolt on't: slid, 'tis but venturing.

Shal. Be not dismay'd.

Slen. No, she shall not dismay me: I care not for that,—but that I am afeard.

Quick. Hark ye; master Slender would speak a word with you.

Anne. I come to him.—This is my father's choice.

O, what a world of vile ill-favour'd faults
Looks handsome in three hundred pounds a-year!   [*Aside.*

Quick. And how does good master Fenton? Pray you, a word with you.

Shal. She's coming; to her, coz. O boy, thou hadst a father!

Slen. I had a father, mistress Anne;—my uncle can tell you good jests of him:—Pray you, uncle, tell mistress Anne the jest, how my father stole two geese out of a pen, good uncle.

Shal. Mistress Anne, my cousin loves you.

Slen. Ay, that I do; as well as I love any woman in Glostershire.

Shal. He will maintain you like a gentlewoman.

Slen. Ay, that I will, come cut and long-tail,[a] under the degree of a 'squire.

Shal. He will make you a hundred and fifty pounds jointure.

Anne. Good master Shallow, let him woo for himself.

Shal. Marry, I thank you for it; I thank you for that good comfort. She calls you, coz: I'll leave you.

Anne. Now, master Slender.

Slen. Now, good mistress Anne.

Anne. What is your will?

Slen. My will? 'od's heartlings, that 's a pretty jest, indeed! I ne'er made my will yet, I thank heaven; I am not such a sickly creature, I give heaven praise.

Anne. I mean, master Slender, what would you with me?

Slen. Truly, for mine own part, I would little or nothing with you: Your father, and my uncle,

have made motions: if it be my luck, so; if not, happy man be his dole! They can tell you how things go better than I can: You may ask your father; here he comes.

Enter PAGE *and Mistress* PAGE.

Page. Now, master Slender:—Love him, daughter Anne.—
Why, how now! what does master Fenton here? You wrong me, sir, thus still to haunt my house: I told you, sir, my daughter is dispos'd of.

Fent. Nay, master Page, be not impatient.

Mrs. Page. Good master Fenton, come not to my child.

Page. She is no match for you.

Fent. Sir, will you hear me?

Page.   No, good master Fenton.
Come, master Shallow; come, son Slender, in :—
Knowing my mind, you wrong me, master Fenton.
            [*Exeunt* PAGE, SHALLOW, *and* SLENDER.

Quick. Speak to mistress Page.

Fent. Good mistress Page, for that I love your daughter
In such a righteous fashion as I do,
Perforce, against all checks, rebukes, and manners,
I must advance the colours of my love,
And not retire: Let me have your good will.

Anne. Good mother, do not marry me to yond' fool.

Mrs. Page. I mean it not; I seek you a better husband.

Quick. That 's my master, master doctor.

Anne. Alas, I had rather be set quick 'i the earth,
And bowl'd to death with turnips.[a]

Mrs. Page. Come, trouble not yourself: Good master Fenton,
I will not be your friend, nor enemy:
My daughter will I question how she loves you,
And as I find her, so am I affected;
'Till then, farewell, sir:—She must needs go in; Her father will be angry.
            [*Exeunt Mrs.* PAGE *and* ANNE.

Fent. Farewell, gentle mistress; farewell, Nan.

Quick This is my doing now.—Nay, said I, will you cast away your child on a fool, and a physician?[b] Look on master Fenton:—this is my doing.

---

[a] *Cut and long-tail.* The commentators give us a world of dissertation to prove, and to disprove, that unlawful dogs had their tails cut by the forest laws; and it seems to be settled that such dogs were only maimed on the fore-foot. *Come cut and long tail* appears to mean, come people of all degrees—*long tail* as opposed to *bob tail*, a member of the worshipful firm of Tag, Rag, & Co.

[a] It is said that this is a proverb in the southern counties. We never heard it. In Ben Jonson's Bartholomew Fair, there is a similar notion: "Would I had been set in the ground, all but the head of me, and had my brains bowl'd at." The refined cruelties of oriental despotism suggested the punishment of burying an offender in this manner. Sir Thomas Roe, in his voyage to the East Indies, tells a story of the Mogul murdering one of his women in this barbarous fashion.

[b] The *fool* was Slender, patronized by Master Page; the *physician*, Dr. Caius, whose suit Mistress Page favoured.

[Act III.] MERRY WIVES OF WINDSOR. [Scene V.

Fent. I thank thee; and I pray thee, once to-night
Give my sweet Nan this ring: There's for thy pains. [*Exit.*
Quick. Now heaven send thee good fortune! A kind heart he hath; a woman would run through fire and water for such a kind heart. But yet, I would my master had mistress Anne; or I would master Slender had her: or, in sooth, I would master Fenton had her: I will do what I can for them all three; for so I have promised, and I'll be as good as my word; but speciously for master Fenton. Well, I must of another errand to sir John Falstaff from my two mistresses. What a beast am I to slack it? [*Exit.*

SCENE V.—*A Room in the* Garter Inn.

Enter FALSTAFF *and* BARDOLPH.

Fal. Bardolph, I say,—
Bard. Here, sir.
Fal. Go fetch me a quart of sack; put a toast in't. [*Exit* BARD.] Have I lived to be carried in a basket, like a barrow of butcher's offal; and to be thrown in the Thames? Well, if I be served such another trick, I'll have my brains ta'en out, and butter'd, and give them to a dog for a new year's gift. The rogues slighted me into the river with as little remorse as they would have drowned a bitch's blind puppies, fifteen i' the litter: and you may know by my size that I have a kind of alacrity in sinking; if the bottom were as deep as hell I should down. I had been drowned but that the shore was shelvy and shallow,—a death that I abhor; for the water swells a man; and what a thing should I have been when I had been swelled! I should have been a mountain of mummy.

Re-enter BARDOLPH *with the wine.*

Bard. Here's mistress Quickly, sir, to speak with you.
Fal. Come let me pour in some sack to the Thames water; for my belly's as cold as if I had swallowed snow-balls for pills to cool the reins. Call her in.
Bard. Come in, woman.

Enter Mrs. QUICKLY.

Quick. By your leave; I cry you mercy: Give your worship good-morrow.
Fal. Take away these chalices: Go, brew me a pottle of sack finely.
Bard. With eggs, sir?
Fal. Simple of itself; I'll no pullet-sperm in my brewage.—[*Exit* BARDOLPH.]—How now?

Quick. Marry, sir, I came to your worship from mistress Ford.
Fal. Mistress Ford! I have had ford enough; I was thrown into the ford: I have my belly full of ford.
Quick. Alas the day! good heart, that was not her fault: she does so take on with her men; they mistook their erection.
Fal. So did I mine, to build upon a foolish woman's promise.
Quick. Well, she laments, sir, for it, that it would yearn your heart to see it. Her husband goes this morning a birding: she desires you once more to come to her between eight and nine. I must carry her word quickly: she'll make you amends, I warrant you.
Fal. Well, I will visit her: Tell her so; and bid her think what a man is: let her consider his frailty, and then judge of my merit.
Quick. I will tell her.
Fal. Do so. Between nine and ten, say'st thou?
Quick. Eight and nine, sir.
Fal. Well, be gone: I will not miss her.
Quick. Peace be with you, sir. [*Exit.*
Fal. I marvel I hear not of master Brook; he sent me word to stay within: I like his money well. O here he comes.

Enter FORD.

Ford. Bless you, sir!
Fal. Now, master Brook? you come to know what hath passed between me and Ford's wife.
Ford. That, indeed, sir John, is my business.
Fal. Master Brook, I will not lie to you: I was at her house the hour she appointed me.
Ford. And sped* you, sir?
Fal. Very ill-favouredly, master Brook.
Ford. How so, sir? Did she change her determination?
Fal. No, master Brook; but the peaking cornuto her husband, master Brook, dwelling in a continual 'larum of jealousy, comes me in the instant of our encounter, after we had embraced, kissed, protested, and, as it were, spoke the prologue of our comedy; and at his heels a rabble of his companions, thither provoked and instigated by his distemper, and forsooth, to search his house for his wife's love.
Ford. What, while you were there?
Fal. While I was there.
Ford. And did he search for you and could not find you?
Fal. You shall hear. As good luck would have

---
* *Sped you.* Malone would read *how sped you?* But *sped you* does not require the addition.

it comes in one mistress Page; gives intelligence of Ford's approach; and, in her invention and Ford's wife's distraction, they conveyed me into a buck-basket.

Ford. A buck-basket?

Fal. Yes, a buck-basket: rammed me in with foul shirts and smocks, socks, foul stockings, greasy napkins; that, master Brook, there was the rankest compound of villainous smell that ever offended nostril.

Ford. And how long lay you there?

Fal. Nay, you shall hear, master Brook, what I have suffered to bring this woman to evil for your good. Being thus crammed in the basket, a couple of Ford's knaves, his hinds, were called forth by their mistress, to carry me in the name of foul clothes to Datchet-lane: they took me on their shoulders; met the jealous knave their master in the door; who asked them once or twice what they had in their basket: I quaked for fear lest the lunatic knave would have searched it; but fate, ordaining he should be a cuckold, held his hand. Well: on went he for a search, and away went I for foul clothes. But mark the sequel, master Brook: I suffered the pangs of three several deaths: first, an intolerable fright, to be detected with a jealous rotten bell-wether: next, to be compassed, like a good bilbo, in the circumference of a peck, hilt to point, heel to head: and then, to be stopped in, like a strong distillation, with stinking clothes that fretted in their own grease: think of that, —a man of my kidney,—think of that; that am as subject to heat, as butter; a man of continual dissolution and thaw; it was a miracle to 'scape suffocation. And in the height of this bath, when I was more than half stewed in grease, like a Dutch dish, to be thrown into the Thames, and cooled, glowing hot, in that surge, like a horseshoe; think of that,—hissing hot,—think of that, master Brook.

Ford. In good sadness, sir, I am sorry that for my sake you have suffered all this. My suit then is desperate; you'll undertake her no more.

Fal. Master Brook, I will be thrown into Etna, as I have been thrown into Thames, ere I will leave her thus. Her husband is this morning gone a birding: I have received from her another embassy of meeting; 'twixt eight and nine is the hour, master Brook.

Ford. 'Tis past eight already, sir.

Fal. Is it? I will then address me to my appointment. Come to me at your convenient leisure, and you shall know how I speed; and the conclusion shall be crowned with your enjoying her: Adieu. You shall have her, master Brook; master Brook, you shall cuckold Ford. [*Exit.*

Ford. Hum! ha! is this a vision? is this a dream? do I sleep? Master Ford, awake; awake, master Ford; there's a hole made in your best coat, master Ford. This 'tis to be married! this 'tis to have linen and buck-baskets!—Well, I will proclaim myself what I am: I will now take the lecher; he is at my house: he cannot 'scape me; 'tis impossible he should; he cannot creep into a halfpenny purse, nor into a pepper-box; but, lest the devil that guides him should aid him, I will search impossible places. Though what I am I cannot avoid, yet to be what I would not shall not make me tame: If I have horns to make me mad, let the proverb go with me, I'll be horn mad. [*Exit.*

ILLUSTRATIONS OF ACT III.

¹ Scene I.—"*To shallow rivers, to whose falls.*"

The exquisite little poem whence this couplet is quoted, has, strange to say, never yet, as a whole, been "married to immortal *notes*;" though the first, second, fourth, and fifth stanzas are set as a four-part glee by Webbe, and, of the kind, a more beautiful composition cannot be named.

Sir John Hawkins says, "The tune to which the former (*i.e.* Marlowe's poem) was sung, I have lately discovered in a MS. as old as Shakspere's time, and it is as follows." He then gives the melody only, as below. To this we have added a simple bass and accompaniment, such as we can imagine the composer himself designed. For the period in which it was written, the air has merit, though the false accentuation, the contempt or ignorance of prosody, in the ninth bar, will be obvious to all.

MERRY WIVES OF WINDSOR

The lines which Sir Hugh Evans hums over are a scrap of a song which we find in that delicious pastoral scene of Isaac Walton, where the anglers meet the milk-maid and her mother, and hear them sing "That smooth song which was made by Kit Marlowe, now at least fifty years ago; .... old fashioned poetry, but choicely good." Sir Hugh Evans in his "trempling of mind" misquotes the lines, introducing a passage from the old version of the 137th Psalm,

"When as I sat in Babylon."

Warburton, who had the good taste to print in his edition of Shakspere this poem, with the 'answer to it,' which was made by Sir Walter Raleigh, in his younger days," according to Walton, assigns that of 'The Passionate Shepherd' to Shakspere himself. It is found in the edition of Shakspere's Sonnets, printed by Jaggard in 1599; but is given to Marlowe in 'England's Helicon,' 1600. We cannot omit this "old fashioned poetry, but choicely good." The verses are variously printed in different collections. Our copy is taken from Percy's Reliques; with the exception of the stanza in brackets.

THE PASSIONATE SHEPHERD TO HIS LOVE.

" Come live with me, and be my love,
And we will all the pleasures prove
That hills and vallies, dale and field,
And all the craggy mountains yield.

There will we sit upon the rocks,
And see the shepherds feed their flocks
By shallow rivers, to whose falls
Melodious birds sing madrigals
There will I make thee beds of roses
With a thousand fragrant posies,
A cap of flowers, and a kirtle
Imbroider'd all with leaves of myrtle;
A gown made of the finest wool,
Which from our pretty lambs we pull;
Slippers lined choicely for the cold ;
With buckles of the purest gold ;
A belt of straw and ivy buds,
With coral clasps, and amber studs:
And if these pleasures may thee move,
Then live with me, and be my love.
[Thy silver dishes for thy meat,
As precious as the gods do eat,
Shall on an ivory table be
Prepar'd each day for thee and me]
The shepherd swains shall dance and sing
For thy delight each May morning :
If these delights thy mind may move,
Then live with me and be my love."

¹ SCENE III.—" *Bucklersbury in simple time.*"

Bucklersbury, in the time of Shakspere, was chiefly inhabited by druggists, who then did the office of the herbalist, and filled the air with the fragrance of rosemary and lavender in "simple time." The materials for the following representation are derived from Aggas's Map of London, 1568.

[Bucklersbury.]

ILLUSTRATIONS OF ACT III.

LOCAL ILLUSTRATION.

When Mistress Ford is plotting the adventure of the buck-basket with Mistress Page, she directs her servants thus: "Take this basket on your shoulders; that done, trudge with it in all haste, and carry it among the whitsters in Datchet Mead, and there empty it in the muddy ditch close by the Thames side." When Falstaff describes his misfortune to Bardolph, he says, "Have I lived to be carried in a basket like a barrow of butcher's offal, and to be thrown into the Thames..... The rogues slighted me into the river..... I had been drowned, but that the shore was shelvy and shallow." Again to Ford he says, "A couple of Ford's knaves, his hinds, were called forth by their mistress to carry me in the name of foul clothes to Datchet Lane." Datchet Mead, although the name is not now in use, was all that flat ground, now enclosed by a wall, lying under the north terrace. The street which leads to it is still called Datchet Lane. The road now passes round the park wall to Datchet by a very circuitous route; but before the enclosure of the mead in the time of William III. the road passed across it. It is probable, therefore, that the shore being "shelvy and shallow," the Thames overflowed the mead in part; so that the whitsters might "bleach their summer smocks" upon the wide plain which the Thames still occasionally inundates. Probably some creek flowed into it, which Mistress Ford denominated a "muddy ditch." The most ancient representation which we can find of this locality, is a print published in the time of Queen Anne, in which the mead is represented as enclosed by its present wall, within which is a triple belt of elms, with two formal avenues at equal distances, and an enormous embanked pond in the centre. The river below Windsor Bridge divides into two streams as at present. The locality of the design at the end of this Act, is placed as near as may be to Datchet Lane. We subjoin a view of the old bridge connecting Windsor and Eton, as given in this very curious print. The vignette which we have given at the end of Act I., as the scene where Mr. Page trained his "fallow greyhound," is the western extremity of Runnemede.

("Out of my door, you witch.")

ACT IV.

SCENE I.—*The Street*.

Enter Mrs. PAGE, *Mrs.* QUICKLY, *and* WILLIAM.

Mrs. Page. Is he at master Ford's already, think'st thou?

Quick. Sure he is by this; or will be presently: but truly he is very courageous mad, about his throwing into the water. Mistress Ford desires you to come suddenly.

Mrs. Page. I'll be with her by-and-by; I'll but bring my young man here to school. Look, where his master comes; 'tis a playing day, I see.

Enter Sir HUGH EVANS.

How now, sir Hugh? no school to-day?

Eva. No; master Slender is let the boys leave to play.

Quick. Blessing of his heart!

Mrs. Page. Sir Hugh, my husband says my son profits nothing in the world at his book. I pray you, ask him some questions in his accidence.

Eva. Come hither, William; hold up your head; come.

Mrs. Page Come on, sirrah: hold up your head; answer your master, be not afraid.

Eva. William, how many numbers is in nouns?

Will. Two.

Quick. Truly, I thought there had been one number more; because they say, od's nouns.

Eva. Peace your tattlings. What is *fair*, William?

Will. Pulcher.

Quick. Poulcats! there are fairer things than poulcats, sure.

Eva. You are a very simplicity 'oman; I pray you, peace. What is *lapis*, William?

Will. A stone.

Eva. And what is a stone, William?

Will. A pebble.

Eva. No, it is *lapis*; I pray you remember in your prain.

Will. Lapis.

Eva. That is a good William. What is he, William, that does lend articles?

Will. Articles are borrowed of the pronoun; and be thus declined, *Singulariter, nominativo, hic, hæc, hoc.*

Eva. Nominativo, hig, hag, hog;—pray you, mark: *genitivo, hujus*: Well, what is your *accusative case?*

Will. Accusativo, hinc.
Eva. I pray you, have your remembrance, child; *Accusativo, hing, hang, hog.*
Quick. Hang hog is Latin for bacon, I warrant you[a]
Eva. Leave your prabbles, 'oman. What is the focative case, William?
Will. O—*vocativo*, O.
Eva. Remember, William, focative is, *caret.*
Quick. And that's a good root.
Eva. 'Oman, forbear.
Mrs. Page. Peace.
Eva. What is your *genitive case plural*, William?
Will. Genitive case?
Eva. Ay.
Will. Genitive,—*horum, harum, horum.*
Quick. 'Vengeance of Jenny's case! fie on her!—never name her, child, if she be a whore.
Eva. For shame, 'oman.
Quick. You do ill to teach the child such words: he teaches him to hick and to hack, which they'll do fast enough of themselves, and to call horum;—fie upon you!
Eva. 'Oman, art thou lunatics? hast thou no understandings for thy cases, and the numbers of the genders? Thou art as foolish christian creatures as I would desires.
Mrs. Page. Prithee, hold thy peace.
Eva. Shew me now, William, some declensions of your pronouns.
Will. Forsooth, I have forgot.
Eva. It is *qui, quæ, quod*; if you forget your *quies*, your *quæs*, and your *quods*, you must be preeches. Go your ways, and play, go.
Mrs. Page. He is a better scholar than I thought he was.
Eva. He is a good sprag[b] memory. Farewell, mistress Page.
Mrs. Page. Adieu, good sir Hugh. [*Exit Sir* HUGH.] Get you home, boy.—Come, we stay too long. [*Exeunt.*

SCENE II.—*A Room in Ford's House.*

Enter FALSTAFF *and Mrs.* FORD.

Fal. Mistress Ford, your sorrow hath eaten up my sufferance: I see you are obsequious in your love, and I profess requital to a hair's breadth; not only, mistress Ford, in the simple office of love, but in all the accoutrement, complement, and ceremony of it. But are you sure of your husband now?
Mrs. Ford. He's a birding, sweet sir John.
Mrs. Page. [*Within.*] What hoa, gossip Ford! what hoa!
Mrs. Ford. Step into the chamber, sir John. [*Exit* FALSTAFF.

Enter Mrs. PAGE.

Mrs. Page. How now, sweetheart? who's at home beside yourself?
Mrs. Ford. Why, none but mine own people.
Mrs. Page. Indeed?
Mrs. Ford. No, certainly;—Speak louder. [*Aside.*
Mrs. Page. Truly, I am so glad you have no body here.
Mrs. Ford. Why?
Mrs. Page. Why, woman, your husband is in his old lunes* again: he so takes on yonder with my husband; so rails against all married mankind; so curses all Eve's daughters, of what complexion soever; and so buffets himself on the forehead, crying *Peer-out, peer-out!* that any madness I ever yet beheld seemed but tameness, civility, and patience, to this his distemper he is in now; I am glad the fat knight is not here.
Mrs. Ford. Why, does he talk of him?
Mrs. Page. Of none but him; and swears he was carried out, the last time he searched for him, in a basket: protests to my husband he is now here; and hath drawn him and the rest of their company from their sport, to make another experiment of his suspicion; but I am glad the knight is not here: now he shall see his own foolery.
Mrs. Ford. How near is he, mistress Page?
Mrs. Page. Hard by; at street end; he will be here anon.
Mrs. Ford. I am undone!—the knight is here.
Mrs. Page. Why then you are utterly ashamed, and he's but a dead man. What a woman are you?—Away with him, away with him; better shame than murder.
Mrs. Ford. Which way should he go? how should I bestow him? Shall I put him into the basket again?

Re-enter FALSTAFF.

Fal. No, I'll come no more i' the basket: May I not go out ere he come?

* *Lunes.* The folio has *lines*; the quarto, "his old vein." Theobald changed *lines* to *lunes*, which is the received reading. Old *lines* may be the same as old *courses*, old humours, old vein.

---

[a] *Hang hog, &c.* This joke is in all probability derived from the traditional anecdote of Sir Nicholas Bacon, which is told by Lord Bacon in his Apophthegms: "Sir Nicholas Bacon being judge of the Northern Circuit, when he came to pass sentence upon the malefactors, was by one of them mightily importuned to save his life. When nothing he had said would avail, he at length desired his mercy on account of kindred. Prithee, said my lord, how came that in? Why if it please you, my lord, your name is *Bacon* and mine is *Hog*, and in all ages Hog and Bacon are so near kindred that they are not to be separated. Ay but, replied the Judge, you and I cannot be of kindred unless you be hanged; for Hog is not Bacon till it be well hang'd."
[b] *Sprag*—quick, lively.

[ACT IV.]   MERRY WIVES OF WINDSOR.   [SCENE II.

Mrs. Page. Alas, three of master Ford's brothers watch the door with pistols, that none shall issue out; otherwise you might slip away ere he came. But what make you here?

Fal. What shall I do?—I'll creep up into the chimney.

Mrs. Ford. There they always use to discharge their birding pieces: Creep into the kiln hole.

Fal. Where is it?

Mrs. Ford. He will seek there, on my word. Neither press, coffer, chest, trunk, well, vault, but he hath an abstract for the remembrance of such places, and goes to them by his note: There is no hiding you in the house.

Fal. I'll go out then.

Mrs. Page. If you go out in your own semblance, you die, sir John. Unless you go out disguised.—

Mrs. Ford. How might we disguise him?

Mrs. Page. Alas the day, I know not. There is no woman's gown big enough for him; otherwise he might put on a hat, a muffler, and a kerchief, and so escape.

Fal. Good hearts devise something: any extremity, rather than a mischief.

Mrs. Ford. My maid's aunt, the fat woman of Brentford, has a gown above.

Mrs. Page. On my word, it will serve him; she is as big as he is: and there's her thrum'd hat, and her muffler too: Run up, sir John.

Mrs. Ford. Go, go, sweet sir John: mistress Page and I will look some linen for your head.

Mrs. Page. Quick, quick; we'll come dress you straight: put on the gown the while.
[*Exit* FALSTAFF.

Mrs. Ford. I would my husband would meet him in this shape: he cannot abide the old woman of Brentford; he swears she's a witch; forbade her my house, and hath threatened to beat her.

Mrs. Page. Heaven guide him to thy husband's cudgel; and the devil guide his cudgel afterwards!

Mrs. Ford. But is my husband coming?

Mrs. Page. Ay, in good sadness, is he; and talks of the basket too, howsoever he hath had intelligence.

Mrs. Ford. We'll try that; for I'll appoint my men to carry the basket again, to meet him at the door with it, as they did last time.

Mrs. Page. Nay, but he'll be here presently: let's go dress him like the witch of Brentford.

Mrs. Ford. I'll first direct my men what they shall do with the basket. Go up, I'll bring linen for him straight. [*Exit.*

Mrs. Page. Hang him, dishonest varlet! we cannot misuse him enough.[a]

We'll leave a proof, by that which we will do,
Wives may be merry and yet honest too:
We do not act that often jest and laugh;
'Tis old but true, Still swine eat all the draff.
[*Exit.*

Re-enter Mrs. FORD, *with two* Servants.

Mrs. Ford. Go, sirs, take the basket again on your shoulders; your master is hard at door; if he bid you set it down, obey him: quickly, despatch. [*Exit.*

1 *Serv.* Come, come, take it up.

2 *Serv.* Pray heaven it be not full of knight again.[b]

1 *Serv.* I hope not; I had as lief bear so much lead.

Enter FORD, PAGE, SHALLOW, CAIUS, *and Sir* HUGH EVANS.

Ford. Ay, but if it prove true, master Page, have you any way then to unfool me again.—Set down the basket, villain:—Somebody call my wife:—Youth in a basket! [c]—O, you panderly rascals! there's a knot, a ging,[d] a pack, a conspiracy against me: Now shall the devil be shamed. What! wife, I say!—Come, come forth. Behold what honest clothes you send forth to bleaching.

Page. Why, this passes! Master Ford, you are not to go loose any longer; you must be pinioned.

Eva. Why, this is lunatics! this is mad as a mad dog!

Shal. Indeed, master Ford, this is not well; indeed.

Enter Mrs. FORD.

Ford. So say I too, sir.—Come, hither, mistress Ford; mistress Ford, the honest woman, the modest wife, the virtuous creature, that hath

---

[a] The folio of 1623 reads "*misuse enough.*" The second folio inserted *him*—"we cannot misuse him enough,"— which is the received reading. Malone says *him* was accidentally omitted.

[b] *Full of knight.* So the folio of 1623. The second folio has "full of *the* knight," which is the received reading. The article destroys the wit. The servant uses *knight* as he would say *lead.*

[c] We print the speech as in the folio,—and, if properly read, it most vividly presents the incoherent and abrupt mode in which a mind overwrought by passion expresses its thoughts. Ford exclaims "Somebody call my wife." He then cries out to the supposed disturber of his peace—"Youth in a basket"—and instantly turns upon the people of his household with reproaches. Malone found "*come out here*" in the old quarto, and foisted it in after "youth in a basket;" whereas "O you panderly rascals" to "what, wife! I say," is parenthetical; and "come, **come** forth" is addressed to the "youth in a basket," and **not** to Mistress Ford.

[d] *Ging*—gang.

189

the jealous fool to her husband:—I suspect without cause. mistress, do I?

Mrs. Ford. Heaven be my witness you do, if you suspect me of any dishonesty.

Ford. Well said, brazen-face; hold it out.— Come forth, sirrah.

[*Pulls the clothes out of the basket.*

Page. This passes!

Mrs. Ford. Are you not ashamed? let the clothes alone.

Ford. I shall find you anon.

Eva. 'Tis unreasonable! Will you take up your wife's clothes? Come away.

Ford. Empty the basket, I say.

Mrs. Ford. Why, man, why,—

Ford. Master Page, as I am a man, there was one conveyed out of my house yesterday in this basket: Why may not he be there again? In my house I am sure he is: my intelligence is true; my jealousy is reasonable: Pluck me out all the linen.

Mrs. Ford. If you find a man there, he shall die a flea's death.

Page. Here's no man.

Shal. By my fidelity, this is not well, master Ford; this wrongs you.

Eva. Master Ford, you must pray, and not follow the imaginations of your own heart: this is jealousies.

Ford. Well, he's not here I seek for.

Page. No, nor no where else, but in your brain.

Ford. Help to search my house this one time: if I find not what I seek, shew no colour for my extremity, let me for ever be your table-sport; let them say of me, As jealous as Ford, that searched a hollow walnut for his wife's leman. Satisfy me once more; once more search with me.

Mrs. Ford. What hoa, mistress Page! come you, and the old woman, down; my husband will come into the chamber.

Ford. Old woman! What old woman's that?

Mrs. Ford. Why, it is my maid's aunt of Brentford.

Ford. A witch, a quean, an old cozening quean! Have I not forbid her my house? She comes of errands, does she? We are simple men; we do not know what's brought to pass under the profession of fortune-telling. She works by charms, by spells, by the figure, and such daubery as this is; beyond our element: we know nothing.—Come down, you witch, you hag you; come down I say.

Mrs. Ford. Nay, good, sweet husband;—good gentlemen, let him not strike the old woman.

Enter FALSTAFF *in women's clothes, led by* Mrs. PAGE.

Mrs. Page. Come, mother Prat, come, give me your hand.

Ford. I'll prat her:——Out of my door, you witch, [*beats him,*] you rag, you baggage, you polecat, you ronyon! out! out! I'll conjure you, I'll fortune-tell you. [*Exit* FALSTAFF.

Mrs. Page. Are you not ashamed? I think you have killed the poor woman.

Mrs. Ford. Nay, he will do it:—'Tis a goodly credit for you.

Ford. Hang her, witch!

Eva. By yea and no, I think, the 'oman is a witch indeed: I like not when a 'oman has a great peard; I spy a great peard under her muffler.

Ford. Will you follow, gentlemen? I beseech you, follow; see but the issue of my jealousy: if I cry out thus upon no trail, never trust me when I open again.

Page. Let's obey his humour a little further: Come, gentlemen.

[*Exeunt* PAGE, FORD, SHALLOW, *and* EVANS.

Mrs. Page. Trust me, he beat him most pitifully.

Mrs. Ford. Nay, by the mass, that he did not; he beat him most unpitifully, methought.

Mrs. Page. I'll have the cudgel hallowed and hung o'er the altar; it hath done meritorious service.

Mrs. Ford. What think you? May we, with the warrant of womanhood, and the witness of a good conscience, pursue him with any further revenge?

Mrs. Page. The spirit of wantonness is, sure, scared out of him; if the devil have him not in fee-simple, with fine and recovery, he will never, I think, in the way of waste, attempt us again.*

Mrs. Ford. Shall we tell our husbands how we have served him?

Mrs. Page. Yes, by all means; if it be but to scrape the figures out of your husband's brains. If they can find in their hearts the poor unvirtuous fat knight shall be any further afflicted, we two will still be the ministers.

Mrs. Ford. I'll warrant they'll have him publicly shamed: and, methinks, there would be

---

* This is one of the many examples of Shakspere's legal knowledge. He certainly knew much more of law than his commentators. Ritson, upon this passage, says, "fee-simple is the largest estate, and fine and recovery the strongest assurance, known to English law." Surely the passage means that the devil had Falstaff as an entire estate, with the power of barring entail—of disposing of him according to his own desire;—as absolute a power as any self-willed person, such as "the devil is said to be, could wish.

no period to the jest,"^a should he not be publicly shamed.

Mrs. Page. Come, to the forge with it then, shape it: I would not have things cool.
[*Exeunt.*

SCENE III.—*A Room in the* Garter Inn.

Enter HOST *and* BARDOLPH.

Bard. Sir, the Germans desire to have three of your horses: the duke himself will be tomorrow at court, and they are going to meet him.

Host. What duke should that be comes so secretly? I hear not of him in the court: Let me speak with the gentlemen; they speak English?

Bard. Ay, sir; I'll call them to you.

Host. They shall have my horses; but I'll make them pay, I'll sauce them: they have had my house a week at command; I have turned away my other guests: they must come off; I'll sauce them: Come.
[*Exeunt.*

SCENE IV.—*A Room in* Ford's *House.*

Enter PAGE, FORD, *Mrs.* PAGE, *Mrs.* FORD, *and* Sir HUGH EVANS.

Eva. 'Tis one of the pest discretions of a 'oman as ever I did look upon.

Page. And did he send you both these letters at an instant?

Mrs. Page. Within a quarter of an hour.

Ford. Pardon me, wife: Henceforth do what thou wilt;
I rather will suspect the sun with cold^b
Than thee with wantonness: now doth thy honour stand,
In him that was of late an heretic,
As firm as faith.

Page. 'Tis well, 'tis well; no more:
Be not as extreme in submission
As in offence;
But let our plot go forward: let our wives
Yet once again, to make us public sport,
Appoint a meeting with this old fat fellow,
Where we may take him, and disgrace him for it.

Ford. There is no better way than that they spoke of.

Page. How! to send him word they'll meet him in the park at midnight, fie, fie; he'll never come.

Eva. You say, he has been thrown in the rivers; and has been grievously peaten, as an old 'oman; methinks, there should be terrors in him that he should not come; methinks, his flesh is punished, he shall have no desires.

Page. So think I too.

Mrs. Ford. Devise but how you'll use him when he comes,
And let us two devise to bring him thither.

Mrs. Page. There is an old tale goes, that Herne the hunter,
Sometime a keeper here in Windsor forest,
Doth all the winter time, at still midnight,
Walk round about an oak, with great ragg'd horns;
And there he blasts the tree, and takes^a the cattle;
And makes milch-kine yield blood, and shakes a chain
In a most hideous and dreadful manner:
You have heard of such a spirit; and well you know,
The superstitious idle-headed eld
Received, and did deliver to our age,
This tale of Herne the hunter for a truth.

Page. Why, yet there want not many that do fear
In deep of night to walk by this Herne's oak:
But what of this?

Mrs. Ford. Marry, this is our device;
That Falstaff at that oak shall meet with us,
[Disguised like Herne, with huge horns on his head.^b]

Page. Well, let it not be doubted but he'll come,
And in this shape: When you have brought him thither,
What shall be done with him? what is your plot?

Mrs. Page. That likewise have we thought upon, and thus:

---

^a *Takes*—seizes with disease. As in Lear,
"Strike her young bones,
Ye *taking* airs."

^b This line is not in the folio; but it is certainly wanting. The passage in the quarto in which this line occurs is a remarkable example of the care with which the first sketch has been improved.

"Hear my device.
Oft have you heard since *Horne* the hunter died,
That women to affright their little children
Says that he walks in shape of a great stag.
Now, for that Falstaffe hath been so deceived
As that he dares not venture to the house.
We'll send him word to meet us in the field,
Disguised like Horne, with huge horns on his head.
The hour shall be just between twelve and one,
And at that time we will meet him both:
Then would I have you present there at hand,
With little boys disguised and drest like fairies,
For to affright fat Palstaffe in the woods."

---

^a *No period to the jest*—we should have to keep on the jest in other forms, unless his public shame concluded it. There would be no end to the jest.

^b *Cold.* The folio reads *gold.* Rowe changed the word to *cold*, which is perhaps the true reading. To suspect the sun with *gold* may mean to suspect the sun of being corrupted with gold; yet with *cold* (*of* cold) is more properly in apposition with *wantonness* (*of* wantonness).

Nan Page my daughter, and my little son,
And three or four more of their growth, we'll dress
Like urchins, ouphes,[a] and fairies, green and white,
With rounds of waxen tapers on their heads,
And rattles in their hands; upon a sudden,
As Falstaff, she, and I, are newly met,
Let them from forth a saw-pit rush at once
With some diffused[b] song; upon their sight,
We two in great amazedness will fly:
Then let them all encircle him about,
And fairy-like, to-pinch[c] the unclean knight;
And ask him, why, that hour of fairy revel,
In their so sacred paths he dares to tread,
In shape profane.
  Mrs. Ford.   And till he tell the truth,
Let the supposed fairies pinch him sound,
And burn him with their tapers.
  Mrs. Page.   The truth being known,
We'll all present ourselves; dis-horn the spirit,
And mock him home to Windsor.
  Ford.   The children must
Be practised well to this, or they'll ne'er do 't.
  Eva. I will teach the children their behaviours;
and I will be like a jack-an-apes also, to burn
the knight with my taber.
  Ford. That will be excellent. I'll go buy them vizards.
  Mrs. Page. My Nan shall be the queen of all the fairies,
Finely attired in a robe of white.
  Page. That silk will I go buy!—and in that time
Shall master Slender steal my Nan away, [*Aside.*
And marry her at Eton.—Go, send to Falstaff straight.
  Ford. Nay, I'll to him again, in name of Brook;
He'll tell me all his purpose: Sure, he'll come.
  Mrs. Page. Fear not you that: Go, get us properties,
And tricking for our fairies.
  Eva. Let us about it: It is admirable pleasures, and fery honest knaveries.
                [*Exeunt* Page, Ford, *and* Evans.
  Mrs. Page. Go, mistress Ford,
Send quickly to Sir John, to know his mind.
                            [*Exit Mrs.* Ford.
I'll to the doctor; he hath my good will,

[a] *Ouphes*—goblins.
[b] *Diffused*—wild.
[c] *To pin.* A *to* as a prefix to a verb is frequent in Spenser: as
    "With locks all loose, and raiment all to-tore."
We find it in Milton's Comus:
    "Were all to-ruffled and sometimes impair'd."

And none but he, to marry with Nan Page.
That Slender, though well landed, is an idiot;
And he my husband best of all affects:
The doctor is well money'd, and his friends
Potent at court; he, none but he, shall have her,
Though twenty thousand worthier come to crave her.   [*Exeunt.*

SCENE V.—*A Room in the* Garter Inn.

Enter Host *and* Simple.

  Host. What would'st thou have, boor? what, thick-skin? speak, breathe, discuss; brief, short, quick, snap.
  Sim. Marry, sir, I come to speak with sir John Falstaff from master Slender.
  Host. There's his chamber, his house, his castle, his standing-bed, and truckle-bed;[a] 'tis painted about with the story of the prodigal, fresh and new: Go, knock and call; he'll speak like an Anthropophaginian unto thee. Knock, I say.
  Sim. There's an old woman, a fat woman, gone up into his chamber: I'll be so bold as stay, sir, till she come down; I come to speak with her, indeed.
  Host. Ha! a fat woman! the knight may be robbed: I'll call.—Bully knight! Bully sir John! speak from thy lungs military: Art thou there? it is thine host, thine Ephesian, calls.
  Fal. [*above.*] How now, mine host?
  Host. Here's a Bohemian-Tartar tarries the coming down of thy fat woman. Let her descend, bully, let her descend; my chambers are honourable: Fye! privacy? fye!

Enter Falstaff.

  Fal. There was, mine host, an old fat woman even now with me; but she 's gone.
  Sim. Pray you, sir, was 't not the wise woman of Brentford?[a]
  Fal. Ay, marry, was it, muscle-shell: What would you with her?
  Sim. My master, sir, my master Slender, sent to her, seeing her go thorough the streets, to know, sir, whether one Nym, sir, that beguiled him of a chain, had the chain, or no.
  Fal. I spake with the old woman about it.
  Sim. And what says she, I pray, sir?
  Fal. Marry, she says, that the very same man that beguiled master Slender of his chain cozened him of it.
  Sim. I would I could have spoken with the

[a] *Wise-woman.* Scott, in his Discovery of Witchcraft says—"At this day it is indifferent to say in the English tongue, She is a *witch*, or she is a *wise-woman*."

woman herself: I had other things to have spoken with her too, from him.

Fal. What are they? let us know.

Host. Ay, come; quick.

Sim. I may not conceal them, sir.

Host. Conceal them, or thou diest.

Sim. Why, sir, they were nothing but about mistress Ann Page; to know if it were my master's fortune to have her, or no.

Fal. 'Tis, 'tis his fortune.

Sim. What, sir?

Fal. To have her,—or no: Go; say, the woman told me so.

Sim. May I be bold to say so, sir?

Fal. Ay, sir Tike; who more bold?

Sim. I thank your worship: I shall make my master glad with these tidings. [*Exit* SIMPLE.

Host. Thou art clerkly, thou art clerkly, sir John: Was there a wise woman with thee?

Fal. Ay, that there was, mine host; one that hath taught me more wit than ever I learned before in my life; and I paid nothing for it neither, but was paid for my learning.

Enter BARDOLPH.

Bard. Out, alas, sir! cozenage! meer cozenage.

Host. Where be my horses? speak well of them, varletto.

Bard. Run away with the cozeners: for so soon as I came beyond Eton, they threw me off, from behind one of them, in a slough of mire; and set spurs and away, like three German devils, three Doctor Faustuses.

Host. They are gone but to meet the duke, villain: do not say they be fled; Germans are honest men.

Enter Sir HUGH EVANS.

Eva. Where is mine host?

Host. What is the matter, sir?

Eva. Have a care of your entertainments: there is a friend of mine come to town, tells me there is three cousin germans, that has cozened all the hosts of Readings, of Maidenhead, of Colebrook, of horses and money. I tell you for good-will, look you: you are wise, and full of gibes and vlouting-stogs; and 'tis not convenient you should be cozened: Fare you well. [*Exit.*

Enter Dr. CAIUS.

Caius. Vere is mine *Host de Jarterre?*

Host. Here, master doctor, in perplexity, and doubtful dilemma.

Caius. I cannot tell vat is dat: But it is tell-a me, dat you make grand preparation for a duke de *Jarmany:* by my trot, dere is no duke dat de court is know to come: I tell you for good vill; adieu. [*Exit.*

Host. Hue and cry, villain, go:—assist me, knight; I am undone: fly, run, hue and cry, villain! I am undone!

[*Exeunt* HOST *and* BARDOLPH.

Fal. I would all the world might be cozened; for I have been cozened and beaten too. If it should come to the ear of the court, how I have been transformed, and how my transformation hath been washed and cudgelled, they would melt me out of my fat, drop by drop, and liquor fisherman's boots with me. I warrant, they would whip me with their fine wits, till I were as crest-fallen as a dried pear. I never prospered since I foreswore myself at *primero*. Well, if my wind were but long enough to say my prayers, I would repent.—

Enter Mistress QUICKLY.

Now! whence come you?

Quick. From the two parties, forsooth.

Fal. The devil take one party, and his dam the other, and so they shall be both bestowed! I have suffered more for their sakes, more, than the villainous inconstancy of man's disposition is able to bear.

Quick. And have not they suffered? Yes, I warrant; speciously one of them; mistress Ford, good heart, is beaten black and blue, that you cannot see a white spot about her.

Fal. What tell'st thou me of black and blue? I was beaten myself into all the colours of the rainbow; and I was like to be apprehended for the witch of Brentford; but that my admirable dexterity of wit, my counterfeiting the action of an old woman, deliver'd me, the knave constable had set me i' the stocks, i' the common stocks, for a witch.

Quick. Sir, let me speak with you in your chamber: you shall hear how things go; and, I warrant, to your content. Here is a letter will say somewhat. Good hearts, what ado here is to bring you together! Sure, one of you does not serve heaven well that you are so crossed.

Fal. Come up into my chamber. [*Exeunt.*

SCENE VI.—*Another room in the* Garter Inn.

Enter FENTON *and* HOST.

Host. Master Fenton, talk not to me; my mind is heavy, I will give over all.

Fent. Yet hear me speak: Assist me in my purpose,
And, as I am a gentleman, I'll give thee
A hundred pounds in gold, more than your loss.

Host. I will hear you, master Fenton; and I will, at the least, keep your counsel.

Fent. From time to time I have acquainted you
With the dear love I bear to fair Ann Page;
Who, mutually, hath answered my affection
(So far forth as herself might be her chooser,)
Even to my wish: I have a letter from her
Of such contents as you will wonder at;
The mirth whereof so larded with my matter,
That neither, singly, can be manifested,
Without the shew of both,—wherein fat Falstaff*
Hath a great scene: the image of the jest
I'll shew you here at large. Hark, good mine host:
To-night at Herne's oak, just 'twixt twelve and one,
Must my sweet Nan present the fairy queen:
The purpose why, is here; in which disguise,
While other jests are something rank on foot,
Her father hath commanded her to slip
Away with Slender, and with him at Eton
Immediately to marry: she hath consented:
Now, sir,
Her mother, even strong against that match,
And firm for doctor Caius, hath appointed
That he shall likewise shuffle her away,
While other sports are tasking of their minds,
And at the deanery, where a priest attends,
Straight marry her: to this her mother's plot
She, seemingly obedient, likewise hath
Made promise to the doctor.—Now thus it rests:
Her father means she shall be all in white;
And in that habit, when Slender sees his time
To take her by the hand, and bid her go,
She shall go with him: her mother hath intended,
The better to denote her to the doctor,
(For they must all be mask'd and vizarded,)
That, quaint in green, she shall be loose enrob'd
With ribbands pendant, flaring 'bout her head;
And when the doctor spies his vantage ripe,
To pinch her by the hand, and, on that token,
The maid hath given consent to go with him.

Host. Which means she to deceive? father or mother?

Fent. Both, my good host, to go along with me:
And here it rests,—that you'll procure the vicar
To stay for me at church, 'twixt twelve and one,
And, in the lawful name of marrying,
To give our hearts united ceremony.

Host. Well, husband your device; I'll to the vicar:
Bring you the maid, you shall not lack a priest.

Fent. So shall I ever more be bound to thee;
Besides, I'll make a present recompense.
(Exeunt.)

* This line in the folio is
"Without the shew of both; fat Falstaff."
In the quarto, wherein, which appears necessary.

["Sometime a keeper here in Windsor Forest."]

ILLUSTRATIONS OF ACT IV.

¹ Scene II.—"*I spy a great peard under her muffler.*"

THE *muffler* covered a portion of the face—sometimes the lower part, sometimes the upper. It was enacted, says Douce, by a Scottish statute in 1457, that "na woman cum to kirk, nor mercat, with her face *muffaled*, or covered that scho may not be kend." Yet the ladies of Scotland, according to Warton, continued *muzzled* during three reigns. Douce gives us the following figures—the first and third from Josh. Ammon's *Theatrum Mulierum*,—the second, from Speed's Map of England, being the costume of a countrywoman in the time of James I.

² Scene V.—"*His standing bed and truckle bed.*"

The standing bed was for the master, the truckle bed for the servant. (See Illustration to Romeo and Juliet, Act II.)

RECENT NEW READING.

LOCAL ILLUSTRATION.

ETON was probably a village in the time of Henry IV. It is scarcely necessary to say that the present College was founded by Henry VI. The church where Anne Page was "immediately to marry" with Slender, was probably the ancient parish church, which has long since fallen to decay.

In Scene III. Bardolph informs the Host that the Germans desire to have three of his horses; the duke himself will be to-morrow at Court, and they are going to meet him. Mine Host, although he hears not in the Court of the Duke "who comes so secretly," says the Germans shall have his horses. He is indeed in "perplexity and doubtful dilemma" when he is told of the "three cousin germans, that has cozened all the hosts of Reading, of Maidenhead, of Colebrook, of horses and money." In the extracts which we gave of the 'Bathing Journey' of the Duke of Würtemberg, &c. we felt it necessary to confine ourselves to what especially related to Windsor. Mr. Halliwell, in his folio Shakespeare, Vol. II. has given a translation of some portions, which we purposely omitted. We had said with reference to the hosts of Reading, of Maidenhead, of Colebrook, that Shakspere was probably familiar with the road from London to Maidenhead in his journeys to Stratford through Oxford. In the original sketch the Germans Duke has "cozened all the hosts of Braintford and Reading." This would imply such a knowledge of the course of the Duke of Würtemberg—in conjunction with the subsequent passage in the folio—of the cozening of the hosts of Reading, Maidenhead, and Colebrook, as would render it not improbable that Shakspere was acquainted with the curious volume which we first brought into notice. According to this narrative, Elizabeth, on being made officially acquainted with the arrival of his Highness in London, despatched from the residence of the court at Reading, a page of honour to convey him thither, in a coach sent by the Queen. They travelled from London in this coach with post-horses. At noon they dined at Hounsloe; towards night they reached Maidenhaide; and on the next morning arrived about noon at Reading. We need not follow the narration of the interviews of the Queen and the Duke during two days. On the third day, the Queen having left Reading with her court; his Highness, in company with the French ambassador, travelled back towards London, and in the evening arrived at Windsor, which is described as twelve miles from Reading. Here he stayed two days, seeing the castle, as noticed in our Local Illustration to Act II. From this narrative we may judge that the cozenage of our Host of the Garter was practised upon him during the period when the Duke had travelled from London to Reading, and back again to Windsor.

[ETON.]

[Herne's Oak — 'Sixty years since.']

ACT V.

SCENE I.—*A Room in the* Garter Inn.

Enter FALSTAFF *and Mrs.* QUICKLY.

Fal. Prithee, no more prattling:—go. I'll hold: This is the third time; I hope, good luck lies in odd numbers. Away, go; they say there is divinity in odd numbers, either in nativity, chance, or death.—Away.

Quick. I'll provide you a chain: and I'll do what I can to get you a pair of horns.

Fal. Away, I say; time wears: hold up your head, and mince.   [*Exit Mrs.* QUICKLY.

Enter FORD.

How now, master Brook? Master Brook, the matter will be known to-night, or never. Be you in the Park about midnight, at Herne's oak, and you shall see wonders.

Ford. Went you not to her yesterday, sir, as you told me you had appointed?

Fal. I went to her, master Brook, as you see, like a poor old man: but I came from her, master Brook, like a poor old woman. That same knave, Ford her husband, hath the finest mad devil of jealousy in him, master Brook, that ever governed frenzy. I will tell you:—He beat me grievously, in the shape of a woman; for in the shape of man, master Brook. I fear not Goliah with a weaver's beam; because I know also, life is a shuttle. I am in haste; go along with me; I'll tell you all, master Brook. Since I pluck'd geese, play'd truant, and whipp'd top, I knew not what it was to be beaten, till lately. Follow me: I'll tell you strange things of this knave Ford: on whom to-night I will be revenged, and I will deliver his wife into your hand.—Follow: Strange things in hand, master Brook! follow.   [*Exeunt.*

SCENE II.—Windsor Park.

Enter PAGE, SHALLOW, *and* SLENDER.

Page. Come, come; we'll couch i' the castle ditch, till we see the light of our fairies.—Remember, son Slender, my daughter.

Slen. Ay, forsooth; I have spoke with her, and we have a nay-word, how to know one another. I come to her in white, and cry, *mum;* she cries *budget;* and by that we know one another.

Shal. That's good too: but what needs either your *mum,* or her *budget?* the white will decipher her well enough.—It hath struck ten o'clock.

Page. The night is dark; light and spirits will become it well. Heaven prosper our sport! No man means evil but the devil, and we shall know him by his horns. Let's away; follow me.   [*Exeunt.*

SCENE III.—*The Street in* Windsor.

Enter Mrs. PAGE, *Mrs.* FORD, *and Dr.* CAIUS.

Mrs. Page. Master Doctor, my daughter is in green: when you see your time, take her by the hand, away with her to the deanery, and despatch it quickly: Go before into the park; we two must go together.

Caius. I know vat I have to do; Adieu.

Mrs. Page. Fare you well, sir.   [*Exit* CAIUS. My husband will not rejoice so much at the abuse of Falstaff, as he will chafe at the doctor's marrying my daughter: but 'tis no matter; better a little chiding than a great deal of heartbreak.

Mrs. Ford. Where is Nan now, and her troop of fairies? and the Welch devil, Hugh?

Mrs. Page. They are all couched in a pit hard by Herne's oak, with obscured lights; which, at the very instant of Falstaff's and our meeting, they will at once display to the night.

Mrs. Ford. That cannot choose but amaze him.

Mrs. Page. If he be not amazed, he will be mocked; if he be amazed, he will every way be mocked.

Mrs. Ford. We'll betray him finely.

Mrs. Page. Against such lewdsters, and their lechery,
Those that betray them do no treachery.

Mrs. Ford. The hour draws on. To the oak, to the oak!   [*Exeunt.*

SCENE IV.—Windsor Park.

Enter Sir HUGH EVANS, *and Fairies.*

Eva. Trib, trib, fairies; come; and remember your parts: be pold, I pray you; follow me into the pit; and when I give the watch-'ords, do as I pid you; Come, come; trib, trib.   [*Exeunt.*

SCENE V.—*Another part of the Park.*

Enter FALSTAFF, *disguised with a buck's head on.*

Fal. The Windsor bell hath struck twelve; the minute draws on: Now, the hot-blooded gods assist me:—Remember, Jove, thou wast a bull for thy Europa; love set on thy horns. O powerful love! that, in some respects, makes a beast a man; in some other, a man a beast. You were also, Jupiter, a swan, for the love of Leda:—O, omnipotent love! how near the god drew to the complexion of a goose?—A fault done first in the form of a beast;—O Jove, a beastly fault! and then another fault in the semblance of a fowl; think on't, Jove; a foul fault. When gods have hot backs, what shall poor men do? For me, I am here a Windsor stag; and the fattest, I think, i' the forest: Send me a cool rut-time, Jove, or who can blame me to piss my tallow? Who comes here? my doe?

Enter Mrs. FORD *and Mrs.* PAGE.

Mrs. Ford. Sir John? art thou there, my deer? my male deer?

Fal. My doe with the black scut?—Let the sky rain potatoes; let it thunder to the tune of *Green sleeves;* hail kissing-comfits, and snow eringoes;[a] let there come a tempest of provocation, I will shelter me here.   [*Embracing her.*

Mrs. Ford. Mistress Page is come with me, sweetheart.

Fal. Divide me like a bribe-buck, each a haunch: I will keep my sides to myself, my shoulders for the fellow of this walk, and my horns I bequeath your husbands. Am I a woodman?[b] ha! Speak I like Herne the hunter? —Why, now is Cupid a child of conscience; he makes restitution. As I am a true spirit, welcome!   [*Noise within.*

Mrs. Page. Alas! what noise!

Mrs. Ford. Heaven forgive our sins!

Fal. What should this be?

Mrs. Ford. } Away, away.   [*They run off.*
Mrs. Page. }

Fal. I think the devil will not have me damned, lest the oil that is in me should set hell on fire; he would never else cross me thus.

Enter Sir HUGH EVANS *like a satyr; Mrs.* QUICKLY, *and* PISTOL; ANNE PAGE, *as the Fairy Queen, attended by her brother and others, dressed like fairies, with waxen tapers on their heads.*

Quick. Fairies, black, grey, green, and white, You moon-shine revellers, and shades of night,

---

[a] Holinshed tells us that in 1583 was performed "a very stately tragedy named Dido, wherein the queen's banquet (with Æneas' narration of the destruction of Troy,) was lively described in a *marchpaine pattern,*—the tempest wherein it hailed small confects, rained rose-water, and snew an artificial kind of snow."

[b] Do I understand woodman's craft—the hunter's art.

You orphan-heirs of fixed destiny,
Attend your office and your quality.
Crier Hobgoblin, make the fairy oyes.*
  Pist. Elves, list your names; silence, you airy
    toys.
  Cricket, to Windsor chimneys shalt thou leap:
Where fires thou find'st unrak'd, and hearths
    unswept,
There pinch the maids as blue as bilberry:
Our radiant queen hates sluts and sluttery.
  Fal. They are fairies; he that speaks to them
    shall die:
I'll wink and couch: no man their works must
    eye.   [*Lies down upon his face.*
  Eva. Where's Pede?—Go you, and where
    you find a maid,
That, ere she sleep, has thrice her prayers said,
Raise up the organs of her fantasy.[b]
Sleep she as sound as careless infancy;
But those as sleep and think not on their sins,
Pinch them, arms, legs, backs, shoulders, sides,
    and shins

  Anne. About, about;
Search Windsor-castle, elves, within and out:
Strew good luck, ouphes, on every sacred room;
That it may stand till the perpetual doom,
In state as wholesome, as in state 'tis fit;
Worthy the owner, and the owner it.
The several chairs of order look you scour
With juice of balm, and every precious flower:
Each fair instalment, coat, and several crest,
With loyal blazon, evermore be blest!
And nightly, meadow-fairies, look, you sing,
Like to the Garter's compass, in a ring:
The expressure that it bears, green let it be,
More fertile-fresh than all the field to see;
And, *Hony soit qui mal y pense,*[c] write,
In emerald tufts, flowers purple, blue, and white:
Like sapphire, pearl, and rich embroidery,
Buckled below fair knight-hood's bending knee:
Fairies use flowers for their charactery.
Away; disperse: But, till 'tis one o'clock,
Our dance of custom, round about the oak
Of Herne the Hunter, let us not forget.
  Eva. Pray you, lock hand in hand; yourselves
    in order set:
And twenty glow-worms shall our lanterns be,
To guide our measure round about the tree.
But, stay: I smell a man of middle earth.
  Fal. Heavens defend me from that Welch fairy!
Lest he transform me to a piece of cheese!

  Pist. Vild worm, thou wast overlook'd even
    in thy birth.
  Anne. With trial-fire touch me his finger-end.
If he be chaste, the flame will back descend
And turn him to no pain; but if he start,
It is the flesh of a corrupted heart.
  Pist. A trial, come.
  Eva.   Come, will this wood take fire?
    [*They burn him with their tapers.*
  Fal. Oh, oh, oh!
  Anne. Corrupt, corrupt, and tainted in desire!
About him, fairies; sing a scornful rhyme;
And, as you trip, still pinch him to your time.*

SONG.
  Fye on sinful fantasy!
  Fye on lust and luxury!
  Lust is but a bloody fire,
  Kindled with unchaste desire,
  Fed in heart; whose flames aspire,
  As thoughts do blow them, higher and higher
  Pinch him, fairies, mutually;
  Pinch him for his villainy;
  Pinch him, and burn him, and turn him about,
  Till candles, and star-light, and moon-shine be out

During this song, the fairies pinch Falstaff.
Doctor Caius *comes one way, and steals away
a fairy in green;* Slender *another way, and
takes off a fairy in white; and* Fenton *comes,
and steals away Mrs.* Anne Page. *A noise of
hunting is made within. All the fairies run
away.* Falstaff *pulls off his buck's head, and
rises.*

Enter Page, Ford, *Mrs.* Page, *and Mrs.* Ford.
They lay hold on him.

  Page. Nay, do not fly; I think, we have
    watch'd you now:
Will none but Herne the hunter serve your turn?
  Mrs. Page. I pray you, come; hold up the
    jest no higher:
Now, good sir John, how like you Windsor
    wives?
See you these, husband? do not these fair yokes
Become the forest better than the town?
  Ford. Now, sir, who's a cuckold now?—Master
Brook, Falstaff's a knave, a cuckoldly knave;

---

  * The *oyes,* the oyez, of the crier of a proclamation, was clearly a monosyllable, rhyming to *toys.*
  [b] *Elevate* her fancy.
  [c] *Pense* is a dissyllable—a proof that Shakspere knew the distinction between French verse and prose.

  * Theobald here inserts a speech from the quarto; "It is right; judged he is full of lecheries and iniquity." Theobald says "this speech is very much in character for Sir Hugh." He forgets that the real actors of the comedy are here speaking in assumed characters. Pistol has a speech or two; but all traces of Pistol's own character are suppressed. The entire scene is elevated into pure poetry in the amended edition, and none of the coarseness of the original is retained. For example, in the quarto, Sir Hugh says,

    "Where's Pede?
    Go and see where brokers sleep,
    And fox eyed serjeants with their mace;
    Go lay the proctors in the street,
    And pinch the lousy serjeant's face;
    Spare none of these when they're a-bed
    But such whose nose looks blue and red."

ACT V.] MERRY WIVES OF WINDSOR. [SCENE V.

here are his horns, master Brook: And, master Brook, he hath enjoyed nothing of Ford's but his buck-basket, his cudgel, and twenty pounds of money, which must be paid to master Brook; his horses are arrested for it, master Brook.

Mrs. Ford. Sir John, we have had ill luck; we could never meet. I will never take you for my love again, but I will always count you my deer.

Fal. I do begin to perceive that I am made an ass.

Ford. Ay, and an ox too; both the proofs are extant.

Fal. And these are not fairies? I was three or four times in the thought they were not fairies: and yet the guiltiness of my mind, the sudden surprize of my powers, drove the grossness of the foppery into a received belief, in despite of the teeth of all rhyme and reason, that they were fairies. See now, how wit may be made a Jack-a-lent, when 't is upon ill employment.

Eva. Sir John Falstaff, serve Got, and leave your desires, and fairies will not pinse you.

Ford. Well said, fairy Hugh.

Eva. And leave you your jealousies too, I pray you.

Ford. I will never mistrust my wife again, till thou art able to woo her in good English.

Fal. Have I laid my brain in the sun, and dried it, that it wants matter to prevent so gross o'er-reaching as this? Am I ridden with a Welch goat too? Shall I have a coxcomb of frize? 'T is time I were choked with a piece of toasted cheese.

Eva. Seese is not good to give putter; your pelly is all putter.

Fal. Seese and putter! have I lived to stand at the taunts of one that makes fritters of English? This is enough to be the decay of lust and late-walking through the realm.

Mrs. Page. Why, sir John, do you think, though we would have thrust virtue out of our hearts by the head and shoulders, and have given ourselves without scruple to hell, that ever the devil could have made you our delight?

Ford. What, a hodge-pudding? a bag of flax?

Mrs. Page. A puffed man?

Page. Old, cold, withered, and of intolerable entrails?

Ford. And one that is as slanderous as Satan?

Page. And as poor as Job?

Ford. And as wicked as his wife?

Eva. And given to fornications, and to taverns, and sack, and wine, and metheglins, and to drinkings, and swearings, and starings, pribbles and prabbles?

Fal. Well, I am your theme: you have the start of me; I am dejected; I am not able to answer the Welch flannel: ignorance itself is a plummet o'er me; use me as you will.

Ford. Marry, sir, we 'll bring you to Windsor, to one master Brook, that you have cozened of money, to whom you should have been a pander: over and above that you have suffered, I think, to repay that money will be a biting affliction.[a]

Page. Yet be cheerful, knight: thou shalt eat a posset to-night at my house; where I will desire thee to laugh at my wife that now laughs at thee: Tell her master Slender hath married her daughter.

Mrs. Page. Doctors doubt that; if Anne Page be my daughter, she is, by this, doctor Caius' wife. [*Aside.*

Enter SLENDER.

Slen. Whoo, ho! ho! father Page!

Page. Son! how now? how now, son? have you despatched?

Slen. Despatched!—I 'll make the best in Glocestershire know on 't; would I were hanged, la, else.

Page. Of what, son?

Slen. I came yonder at Eton to marry mistress Anne Page, and she's a great lubberly boy. If it had not been i' the church, I would have swinged him, or he should have swinged me. If I did not think it had been Anne Page would I might never stir, and 't is a post-master's boy.

Page. Upon my life then you took the wrong.

Slen. What need you tell me that? I think so, when I took a boy for a girl: If I had been married to him, for all he was in woman's apparel, I would not have had him.

Page. Why, this is your own folly. Did not I tell you how you should know my daughter by her garments?

Slen. I went to her in white,[b] and cry'd *mum*, and she cry'd *budget*, as Anne and I had appointed; and yet it was not Anne, but a post-master's boy.[c]

Mrs. Page. Good George, be not angry: I knew of your purpose; turned my daughter into green; and, indeed, she is now with the doctor at the deanery, and there married.

---

[a] The whole scene being changed, three lines are here often foisted in from the quarto:
" *Mrs. Ford.* Nay, husband, let that go to make amends:
Forgive that sum, and so we 'll all be friends.
Ford. Well, here's my hand; all's forgiven at last."

[b] The folio has *green*, which Pope changed to *white*, also changing, in the next speech, *white* to *green*.

[c] Two other lines are here introduced in the same way:
" *Eva.* Jeshu! Master Slender, cannot you see but many pays?
Page. O, I am vexed at heart: What shall I do?"

200

Enter Caius.

Caius. Vere is mistress Page? By gar, I am cozened; I ha' married *un garçon*, a boy; *un paisan*, by gar, a boy; it is not Anne Page: by gar, I am cozened.

Mrs. Page. Why, did you take her in green?

Caius. Ay, be gar, and 'tis a boy; be gar, I'll raise all Windsor. [*Exit* Caius.

Ford. This is strange: Who hath got the right Anne?

Page. My heart misgives me: Here comes master Fenton.

Enter Fenton *and* Anne Page.

How now, master Fenton?

Anne. Pardon, good father! good, my mother, pardon!

Page. Now, mistress? how chance you went not with master Slender?

Mrs. Page. Why went you not with master doctor, maid?

Fent. You do amaze her: Hear the truth of it.
You would have married her most shamefully,
Where there was no proportion held in love.
The truth is, she and I, long since contracted,
Are now so sure that nothing can dissolve us.
The offence is holy that she hath committed:
And this deceit loses the name of craft,

Of disobedience, or unduteous title;
Since therein she doth evitate and shun
A thousand irreligious cursed hours,
Which forced marriage would have brought upon her.

Ford. Stand not amaz'd: here is no remedy:
In love, the heavens themselves do guide the state;
Money buys lands, and wives are sold by fate.

Fal. I am glad, though you have ta'en a special stand to strike at me, that your arrow hath glanced.

Page. Well, what remedy? Fenton, heaven give thee joy!
What cannot be eschew'd must be embrac'd.

Ful. When night-dogs run all sorts of deer are chas'd.*

Mrs. Page. Well, I will muse no further master Fenton,
Heaven give you many, many merry days!
Good husband, let us every one go home,
And laugh this sport o'er by a country fire;
Sir John and all.

Ford. Let it be so:—Sir John,
To master Brook you yet shall hold your word;
For he, to-night, shall lie with mistress Ford. [*Exeunt.*

* We have also another line restored—rescued, as the editors say—good in itself, but out of place:
"*Era* I will dance and eat plums at your wedding."

RECENT NEW READINGS.

It was suggested to us by Dr. Maginn, for our 'Library Edition,' that these poetical speeches belong to *Anne*, as the Fairy Queen. In all previous modern editions they are all very inappropriately given to *Quickly*. We have traced the origin of this mistake, which is perfectly evident. In the original quarto we have not a word of the arrangement for *Anne* to "present the Fairy Queen." These lines are only found in the folio:—

"To-night, at Herne's oak, just 'twixt twelve and one,
Must my sweet Nan present the fairy queen."

But in the quarto edition, in the stage-direction of this scene, we have, "Enter Sir Hugh like a satyr, and boys dressed like fairies." What the Queen had to say was greatly elaborated in the folio; and there the stage-direction is for the entrance, without any designation of "Anne Page, Fairies, Page, Ford, Quickly," &c. We have no doubt that the poet having determined that Anne should "present the fairy queen," these speeches unquestionably belong to her, and we have made the change accordingly. Mr. Dyce and Mr. Staunton adopt the change; Mr. White, in his edition of the Plays, contends that *Quickly* is right, but he says it has been the "invariable custom since Malone's time," to substitute "*Anne Page* as the *Fairy Queen*" when the characters enter, while the speeches were given to *Quickly*. "The inconsistency was avoided by Mr. Collier at the suggestion of Mr. Harness." He goes on to say that *Qui.* and *Quic* could not have been invariably misprinted for *Qu.*; that the speeches of *Pistol* and *Sir Hugh* are as much inconsistent with the characters as those of *Mrs. Quickly*; that they were all assuming parts, and were lightly masked; and that *Anne Page* did not play the Fairy Queen, for, as she assured her lover, she intended to deceive her father and mother, "and she did so."

(Oak, and Avenue of Elms, Windsor Home Park.)

LOCAL ILLUSTRATION OF ACT V.

THE question whether the Herne's Oak of Shakspere is at present existing, or whether it was cut down some sixty years before, had become, at the time of the publication of our first edition, a subject of much controversy. Mr. Jesse, the author of those very agreeable volumes, 'Gleanings in Natural History,' maintained that the identical tree was still standing. The Quarterly Review, on the contrary, asserted that the tree had been cut down. At Windsor there were many believers in the present Herne's Oak, and many non-believers. We have bestowed some care in the investigation of the question; and we shall endeavour to present to our readers the result of our inquiries in connexion with our own early recollections.*

The memory of the editor carries him back to Windsor as it was forty years ago. The castle was then almost uninhabited. The king and his family lived in an ugly barrack-looking building called the Queen's Lodge, which stood opposite the south front of the castle. The great quadrangle, the terrace, and every part of the Home Park, was a free playground for the boys of Windsor. The path to Datchet passed immediately under the south terrace, direct from west to east, and it abruptly descended into the Lower Park, at a place called Dodd's Hill. From this path several paths diverged in a south-easterly direction towards the dairy at Frogmore; and one of these went close by a little dell, in which long rank grass, and fern, and low thorns grew in profusion. Near this dell stood several venerable oaks. Our earliest recollections associate this place with birds'-nests and mushrooms; but some five or six years later we came to look here for the "oak with great ragg'd horns," to which we had been introduced in the newly discovered world of Shakspere. There was an oak, whose upper branches were much decayed, standing some thirty or forty yards from the deep side of the dell; and there was another oak with fewer branches, whose top was

* We had better keep the dates as they stand in this illustration, as published in 1839, in the first edition of the 'Pictorial Shakspere.'

MERRY WIVES OF WINDSOR.

also bare, standing in the line of the avenue near the park wall. We have heard each of these oaks called Herne's Oak; but the application of the name to the oak in the avenue is certainly more recent. That tree, as we first recollect it, had not its trunk bare. Its dimensions were comparatively small, and it seemed to us to have no pretensions to the honour which it occasionally received. The old people, however, used to say that Herne's Oak was cut down or blown down, and certainly our own impressions were that Herne's Oak was gone. One thing however consoled us. The little dell was assuredly the "pit hard by Herne's Oak" in which Anne Page and her troop of fairies "couched with obscured lights." And so we for ever associated this dell with Shakspere.

Years passed on—Windsor ceased to be familiar to us. When Mr. Jesse, however, published his second series of Gleanings in 1834, we were pleased to find this passage: "The most interesting tree, at Windsor, for there can be little doubt of its identity, is the celebrated Herne's Oak. There is indeed a story prevalent in the neighbourhood respecting its destruction. It was stated to have been felled by command of his late Majesty George III about fifty years ago, under peculiar circumstances. The whole story, the details of which it is unnecessary to enter upon, appeared so improbable, that I have taken some pains to ascertain the inaccuracy of it, and have now every reason to believe that it is perfectly unfounded." But we were not quite satisfied with Mr. Jesse's description of this oak. In his 'Gleanings' he says, "In following the footpath which leads from the Windsor-road to Queen Adelaide's Lodge, in the Little Park, about half way on the right, a dead tree may be seen close to an avenue of elms. This is what is pointed out as Herne's Oak." Now we distinctly recollected that one of the trees, which some persons said was Herne's Oak, was not only close to an avenue of elms but formed part of the avenue; the other oak which pretended to the name was some distance from the avenue. Mr. Jesse goes on to say :—

"The footpath which leads across the park is stated to have passed, in former times, close to Herne's Oak. The path is now at a little distance from it, and was, probably, altered, in order to protect the tree from injury."

Here again was the manifestation of some imperfect local knowledge, which led us to doubt Mr. Jesse's strong assertion of the tree's identity. The footpath, so far from being altered to protect the tree from injury, was actually made, for the first time, some five-and-twenty years ago, when the ancient footpath to Datchet, which crossed the upper part of the park, passing, as we have mentioned, under the south terrace, was diverted by order of the magistrates, in order to give a greater privacy to the castle. The present pathway to Datchet was then first made, and a causeway was carried across the little dell. One of the paths from the castle to the dairy went near this dell, but it was on the more northern side, and not far from the other tree which some persons called Herne's Oak. Indeed, we were by no means sure that Mr. Jesse's description did not apply to this other tree. The expression "*close* to the avenue" might include it. Certainly his engraving was much more like that tree, as we recollect it, than the tree *in* the avenue.

Towards the end of 1838, the following passage in 'The Quarterly Review,' came to destroy the little hope which we had indulged that Mr. Jesse had restored to us Herne's Oak :—

"Among his anecdotes of celebrated English oaks, we were surprised to find Mr. Loudon adopting (at least so we understand him) an apocryphal story about Herne's Oak, given in the lively pages of Mr. Jesse's *Gleanings*. That gentleman, if he had taken any trouble, might have ascertained that the tree in question was cut down one morning, by order of King George III., when in a state of great, but transient, excitement ; the circumstance caused much regret and astonishment at the time."

Mr. Jesse replied to this statement, in a letter addressed to the editor of the 'Times,' dated Nov. 28, 1838. Mr. Jesse says that the story thus given was often repeated by George IV., who, however, always added 'that tree was supposed to have been Herne's Oak, but it was not.' Mr. Jesse adds, that the tree thus cut down, which stood near the castle, was an elm. We may take the liberty of mentioning that George IV. did not *always* add that the tree cut down was *not* Herne's Oak; and this we know from the very best authority—the King's own statement to Mr. Croker, who furnished the information to us. We have a letter in which that gentleman says that the cutting down of Herne's Oak was mentioned by George IV., as one of the results of his father's mental indisposition. Mr. Jesse goes on to say, that soon after the circumstance referred to, three large old oak trees were blown down in a gale of wind in the Little Park ; and one of them, supposed to be Herne's Oak, was cut up and made into boxes and other Shaksperian relics. Mr Jesse, however, conceives that the matter is put beyond doubt by the following statement :—

"To set the matter at rest, however, I will now repeat the substance of some information given to me relative to Herne's Oak, by Mr. Ingalt, the present respectable bailiff and manager of Windsor Home Park. He states that he was appointed to that situation by George III., about forty years ago. On receiving his appointment he was directed to attend upon the King at the Castle, and on arriving there he found His Majesty with 'the old Lord Wiuchilsea.' After a little delay, the King set off to walk in the park, attended by Lord Winchilsea, and Mr Ingalt was desired to follow them Nothing was said to him until the King stopped opposite an oak tree. He then turned to Mr. Ingalt and said, 'I brought you here to point out this tree to you. I commit it to your especial charge, and take care that no damage is ever done to it. I had rather that every tree in the park should be cut down than that this tree should be hurt. *This is Herne's Oak*.' Mr. Ingalt added, that this was the tree still standing near Queen Elizabeth's Walk, and is the same tree which I have mentioned and given a sketch of in my *Gleanings in Natural History*. Sapless and leafless it certainly is, and its rugged bark has all disappeared.

'Its boughs are moss'd with age,
'And high top bald with gray antiquity;'—

ILLUSTRATIONS OF ACT V.

but there it stands, and long may it do so, an object of interest to every admirer of our immortal bard. In this state it has been, probably, long before the recollection of the oldest person living. Its trunk appears, however, sound, like a piece of ship-timber, and it has always been protected by a strong fence round it—a proof of the care which has been taken of the tree, and of the interest which is attached to it."

Mr. Engall (not Ingalt), "the present respectable bailiff and manager of Windsor Home Park," certainly did not reside at Windsor forty years ago. He is not now what may he called an old man; and he was originally about the person of George III. at one of those seasons of affliction which were so distressing to his Majesty's family, and to his subjects. The conversation thus reported by Mr. Jesse, is entirely at variance with much earlier recollections of George III., which we shall presently shew.

We are here relieved from the doubt as to which tree Mr. Jesse originally intended to describe as Herne's Oak, by the following passage of his letter to the 'Times.' "King William III. was a great planter of avenues, and to him we are indebted for those in Hampton Court and Bushy Park, and also those at Windsor. All these have been made in a straight line, with the exception of one in the Home Park, which diverges a little, *so as to take in Herne's Oak as a part of the avenue*—a proof, at least, that Wiliam III. preferred distorting his avenue to cutting down the tree in order to make way for it in a direct line, affording another instance of the care taken of this tree 150 years ago."

With our own recollections of the localities still vivid, we have recently visited the favourite haunts of our boyhood in the Little Park. Our sensations were not pleasurable. The spot is so changed, that we could scarcely recognise it. We lamented twenty-five years ago that the common footpath to Datchet should have been carried through the picturesque dell, near which all tradition agreed that Herne's Oak stood; but we were not prepared to find that, during the alterations of the castle, the most extensive and deepest part of the dell, all on the north of the path, had been filled up and made perfectly level. Our old favourite thorns are now all buried, and the antique roots of the old trees that stood in and about the dell are covered up. Surely the rubbish of the castle might have been conveyed to a less interesting place of deposit. The smaller and shallower part of the dell, that on the south of the path, has been half filled up, and what remains is of a formal and artificial character. Mr. Jesse seems quite unaware of the change that has taken place in the locality, for in his *Gleanings* he says: " I was glad to find a pit hard by, where Nan and her troop of fairies, and the Welsh Devil Evans, might all have couch'd, without being perceived by the 'fat Windsor stag' when he spake like Herne the hunter. The pit above alluded to has recently had a few thorns planted in it; and the circumstance of its being near the oak, with the diversion of the footpath, seem to prove the identity of the tree, in addition to the traditions respecting it." The divergence of the avenue which Mr. Jesse, somewhat enthusiastically, attributes to the respect of William III. for Herne's Oak, must, we fear, be assigned to less poetical motives. The avenue, we understand, formed the original boundary of the Park in that direction. It diverges at least 120 yards before it reaches Mr. Jesse's Herue's Oak ; and there is little doubt that the meadow on the south of the avenue after it diverges, which in our remembrance was a separate enclosure, was formerly a common field. The engraving at the head of this Illustration is a most faithful delineation of the oak which Mr. Jesse calls Herne's. It is now perfectly hare down to the very roots. "In this state," says Mr. Jesse, "it has been, probably, long before the recollection of the oldest person living." He adds, "It has always been protected by a strong fence round it." In our own recollection this tree was unprotected by any fence, and its upper part only was withered and without bark. So far from Herne the hunter having blasted it, it appears to have suffered a premature decay, and it felldown in 1863. This tree was of small girth compared with other trees about it. It was not more than fifteen feet in circumference at the largest part, while there is a magnificent oak at about 200 yards' distance whose girth is nearly thirty feet. The engraving at the end of this notice is a representation of that beautiful tree.

The subject, after the publication of our first edition, was investigated with great acuteness by Dr. Bromet, and his conclusions are given in a very interesting letter in the 'Gentleman's Magazine,' for April, 1841. He collected a variety of testimony from various persons, which went to prove that a tree called Herne's Oak was cut down some sixty years before, and that the tree which now pretends to the honour—"*this* oak"—had acquired the name in very modern times:—"Its present name was not conferred upon it until some time after the demolition of another old tree, formerly possessing that title." This entirely agrees with our own personal recollections of the talk of Windsor about Herne's Oak. But Dr. Bromet justly observes that the "strongest proof" against the claims of Mr. Jesse's oak, is "Collier's map of 1742," which actually points out 'Sir John Falstaff's oak' as being, *not in the present avenue, but outside it, near the edge of the pit.*

The engraving of an oak at the head of Act V. is copied without alteration from a drawing made in the year 1800, by Mr. W. Delamotte, the Professor of Landscape Drawing at Sandhurst, who was a pupil of Benjamin West, under whose care he was placed in 1792. Mr. Delamotte has often heard his master lament that Herne's Oak had been cut down, to the great annoyance, as Mr. West stated, of the King and the royal family. According to Mr. West's account of the circumstance, the King had directed all the trees in the park to be numbered ; and upon the representation of the bailiff, whose name was Robinson, that certain trees encumbered the ground, directions were given to fell those trees, and Herne's Oak was amongst the condemned. Mr. West, who was residing at Windsor at the time, traced this oak to the spot where it was conveyed, and obtained a large piece of one of its knotty arms, which Mr. Delamotte has often seen. Mr. Ralph West, however, the eldest son of the President, who, as a youth, was distinguished for his love of art, and his great skill as a draftsman, made a drawing of this tree before it was felled, and Mr. Delamotte's drawing, which he has kindly granted us permission to engrave, was a copy of this valuable sketch. The locality of the tree, as indicated by the position of the castle in this sketch, perfectly corresponds with the best traditions.

We might here dismiss the subject, had we not been favoured with a communication, in accordance with the views which we have already taken. Mr. Nicholson, the eminent landscape draftsman, has furnished Mr. Crofton Croker, who has taken a kind interest in our work, with the following information:—

About the year 1800, he was on a visit to the Dowager Countess of Kingston, at Old Windsor; and his mornings were chiefly employed in sketching, or rather making studies of the old trees in the Forest. This circumstance one day led the conversation of some visitors to Lady Kingston to Herne's Oak. Mrs. Boufoy and her daughter, Lady Ely, were present; and as they were very much with the royal family, Mr. Nicholson requested Lady Ely to procure for him any information that she could from the King, respecting Herne's Oak, which, considering His Majesty's tenacious memory and familiarity with Windsor, the King could probably give better than any one else.

In a very few days, Lady Ely informed Mr. Nicholson that she had made the inquiry he wished of the King, who told her that "when he (George III.) was a young man, it was represented to him that there were a number of old oaks in the park which had become unsightly objects, and that it would be desirable to take them down; he gave immediate directions that such trees as were of this description should be removed; but he was afterwards sorry that he had given such an order inadvertently, because he found that, among the rest, the remains of Herne's Oak had been destroyed.

There is a third version of the popular belief regarding the removal of Herne's Oak, which differs from the preceding statements, and yet is sufficiently circumstantial. The best information we have gathered on the subject is derived from a letter obligingly communicated to us, written by the son of Mr. John Piper, of Cambridge, formerly a gunmaker at Windsor, and of which the following are extracts. It will be remarked how closely this statement of Mr. Piper agrees with the information derived from Collier's plan:—

"My father states that about sixty-four years since, there was a deep chalk-pit sunk inside the park at Windsor, nearly opposite the Hope Inn (which is now nearly filled up again, and through which the road to Datchet now runs). The chalk was taken in immense quantities from this pit to fill up the ditch which then ran round the castle, it being considered it would render the foundations of the castle and connected buildings more secure, as in many places they were giving way. The removal of the chalk from the pit for this purpose, in some measure undermined a fine oak tree, which stood on the upper side of the pit, nearest the castle. Shortly after a storm came and blew this tree down, and this circumstance created a great sensation at the time, as *that* tree was considered to be the identical Herne's Oak of Shakspere notoriety. My father had in his boyish days very frequently played in the pit and round the tree, and its locality is therefore strongly impressed on his memory, although now between sixty and seventy years since." The letter then concludes thus:—"My father wishes me to add that it must not be inferred that there was no pit existing *previous* to the removal of the chalk for the purpose stated." There was before then such a pit as described in Act V. Scene III. where Mrs. Page says,

"They are all couched in a pit close to Herne's oak."

[Oak, near the site of Herne's Oak.]

[Windsor, 1839.]

SUPPLEMENTARY NOTICE.

RIGHTLY to appreciate this Comedy, it is, we conceive, absolutely necessary to dissociate it from the Historical plays of Henry IV., and Henry V. Whether Shakspere produced the original sketch of the Merry Wives of Windsor before those plays, and remodelled it after their appearance,—or whether he produced both the original sketch, and the finished performance, when his audiences were perfectly familiar with the Falstaff, Shallow, Pistol, Nym, Bardolph, and Mistress Quickly of Henry IV., and Henry V.,—it is perfectly certain that *he* did not intend the Merry Wives as a continuation. It is impossible, however, not to associate the period of the comedy with the period of the histories. For although the characters which are common to all the dramas act in the comedy under very different circumstances, and are, to our minds, not only different in their moods but in some of their distinctive features, they must each be received as identical—*alter et idem*. Still the connexion must be as far as possible removed from our view, that we may avoid comparisons which the author certainly was desirous to avoid, when in remodelling the comedy he introduced no circumstances which could connect it with the histories; and when he not only did not reject what would be called the anachronisms of the first sketch, but in the perfect play heaped on such anachronisms with a profuseness that is not exhibited in any other of his dramas. We must, therefore, not only dissociate the characters of the Merry Wives from the similar characters of the histories; but suffer our minds to slide into the belief that the manners of the times of Henry IV. had sufficient points in common with those of the times of Elizabeth, to justify the poet in taking no great pains to distinguish between them. We must suffer ourselves to be carried away with the nature and fun of this comedy, without encumbering our minds with any precise idea of the social circumstances under which the characters lived. We must not startle, therefore, at the mention of Star-chambers, and Edward shovel-boards, and Sackerson, and Guiana, and rapiers, and Flemish drunkards, and coaches, and pensioners. The characters speak in the language of truth and nature, which belongs to all time; and we must forget that they sometimes use the expressions of a particular time to which they do not in strict propriety belong.

The critics have been singularly laudatory of this comedy. Warton calls it "the most complete specimen of Shakspere's comic powers." Johnson says, "This comedy is remarkable for the variety and number of the personages, who exhibit more characters appropriated and discriminated than perhaps can be found in any other play . . . . . Its general power, that power by which all works of genius shall finally be tried, is such, that perhaps it never yet had reader or spectator who did not think it too soon at the end." We agree with much of this; but we certainly cannot agree with Warton that it is "the most complete specimen of Shakspere's comic powers." We cannot forget As You Like It, and Twelfth Night, and Much Ado about Nothing. We cannot forget those exquisite combinations of the highest wit with the purest poetry, in which the

MERRY WIVES OF WINDSOR.

wit flows from the same everlasting fountain as the poetry,—both revealing all that is most intense and profound and beautiful and graceful in humanity. Of those qualities which put Shakspere above all other men that ever existed, the Merry Wives of Windsor exhibits few traces. Some of the touches, however, which no other hand could give, are to be found in Slender, and we think in Quickly. Slender, little as he has to do, is the character that most frequently floats before our fancy when we think of the Merry Wives of Windsor. Slender and Anne Page are the favourites of our modern school of English painting, which has attempted, and successfully, to carry the truth of the Dutch School into a more refined region of domestic art. We do not wish Anne Page to have been married to Slender, but in their poetical alliance they are inseparable. It is in the remodelled play that we find, for the most part, such Shaksperian passages in the character of Slender as, "If I be drunk, I'll be drunk with those that have the fear of God, and not with drunken knaves,"—which resolve, as Evans says, shews his "virtuous mind." In the remodelled play, too, we find the most peculiar traces of the master-hand in Quickly,—such as, "His worst fault is that he is given to prayer; he is something peevish that way;" and "the boy never need to understand anything, for 'tis not good that children should know any wickedness. Old folks, you know, have discretion, as they say, and know the world;" and again, "Good hearts! what ado there is to bring you together, sure one of you does not serve heaven well that you are so crossed." Johnson objects to this latter passage as profane; but he overlooks the extraordinary depth of the satire Shakspere's profound knowledge of the human heart is as much displayed in these three little sentences as in his Hamlet and his Iago.

The principal action of this comedy—the adventures of Falstaff with the Merry Wives—sweeps on with a rapidity of movement which hurries us forward to the denouement as irresistibly as if the actors were under the influence of that destiny which belongs to the empire of tragedy. No reverses, no disgraces, can save Falstaff from his final humiliation. The net is around him, but he does not see the meshes;—he fancies himself the deceiver, but he is the deceived. He will stare Ford "out of his wits," he will "awe him with his cudgel," yet he lives "to be carried in a basket like a barrow of butcher's offal, and to be thrown into the Thames." But his confidence is undaunted: "I will be thrown into Etna, as I have been into Thames, ere I will leave her;" yet "since I plucked geese, played truant, and whipped top, I knew not what it was to be beaten till lately." Lastly, he will rush upon a third adventure: "This is the third time, I hope good luck lies in odd numbers;" yet his good luck ends in "I do begin to perceive that I am made an ass." The real jealousy of Ford most skilfully helps on the merry devices of his wife; and with equal skill does the poet make him throw away his jealousy, and assist in the last plot against the "unclean knight." The misadventures of Falstaff are most agreeably varied. The disguise of the old woman of Brentford puts him altogether in a different situation to his suffocation in the buck basket; and the fairy machinery of Herne's Oak carries the catastrophe out of the region of comedy into that of romance.

The movement of the principal action is beautifully contrasted with the occasional repose of the other scenes. The Windsor of the time of Elizabeth is presented to us, as the quiet country town, sleeping under the shadow of its neighbour the castle. Amidst its gabled houses, separated by pretty gardens, from which the elm and the chestnut and the lime throw their branches across the unpaved road, we find a goodly company, with little to do but gossip and laugh, and make sport out of each other's cholers and weaknesses. We see Master Page training his "fallow greyhound;" and we go with Master Ford "a-birding." We listen to the "pribbles and prabbles" of Sir Hugh Evans and Justice Shallow, with a quiet satisfaction; for they talk as unartificial men ordinarily talk, without much wisdom, but with good temper and sincerity. We find ourselves in the days of ancient hospitality, when men could make their fellows welcome without ostentatious display, and half a dozen neighbours "could drink down all unkindness" over "a hot venison pasty." The more busy inhabitants of the town have time to tattle, and to laugh, and be laughed at. Mine Host of the Garter is the prince of hosts; he is the very soul of fun and good temper;—he is not solicitous whether Falstaff sit "at ten pounds a week" or at two;—he readily takes "the withered serving man for a fresh tapster;"—his confidence in his own cleverness is delicious:—"am I politic, am I subtle, am I a Machiavel?"—the Germans "shall have my horses, but I'll make them pay I'll sauce them." When he loses his horses, and his "mind is heavy," we rejoice that Fenton will give him "a hundred pound in gold" more than his loss. His contrivances to manage the fray

207

SUPPLEMENTARY NOTICE.

between the furious French doctor, and the honest Welsh parson, are productive of the happiest situations. Caius waiting for his adversary—" de herring is no dead so as I vill kill him "—is capital. But Sir Hugh, with his,—

> "There will we make our peds of roses,
> And a thousand fragrant posies,
> To shallow—

Mercy on me ! I have a great dispositions to cry,"—is inimitable.

With regard to the under-plot of Fenton and Anne Page—the scheme of Page to marry her to Slender—the counter-plot of her mother, "firm for Dr. Caius"—and the management of the lovers to obtain a triumph out of the devices against them—it may be sufficient to point out how skilfully it is interwoven with the Herne's Oak adventure of Falstaff. Though Slender "went to her in white, and cry'd, mum, and she cry'd budget, . . . yet it was not Anne, but a postmaster's boy;"—though Caius did "take her in green," he "ha' married un garçon, a boy; un paisan;"—but Anne and Fenton

> ————————" long since contracted,
> Are now so sure, that nothing can dissolve them."

Over all the misadventures of that night, when "all sorts of deer were chas'd," Shakspere throws his own tolerant spirit of forgiveness and content :—

> "Good husband, let us every one go home,
> And laugh this sport o'er by a country fire;
> Sir John and all."

[Restoration of the Second Temple of Diana, at Ephesus.]

INTRODUCTORY NOTICE.

State of the Text, and Chronology, of the Comedy of Errors.

The Comedy of Errors was first printed in the folio collection of Shakspere's Plays in 1623. There can be no doubt that it was therein printed from the author's manuscript. Appearing for the first time after the death of Shakspere, this copy presents many typographical errors; and in a few passages the text is manifestly corrupt. The difficulties, however, are not very considerable; and the original copy is decidedly better, for the most part, than the modern innovations. Malone, in adhering to this text, was more distinctly opposed to Steevens than in other plays, in which he has, though evidently contrary to his own better opinion, adopted the suggestions of Steevens and others, who introduced what they considered amendments, but which amendments were founded upon an imperfect knowledge of the phraseology and metre of their author. The rejections by Malone of the changes of Steevens are here made with somewhat more of pertinacity, and perhaps of ill-temper, than was common with him.

The Comedy of Errors was clearly one of Shakspere's very early plays. It was probably untouched by its author after its first production. We have here no existing sketch to enable us to trace what he introduced, and what he corrected, in the maturity of his judgment. It was, we imagine, one of the pieces for which he would manifest little solicitude after his genius was fully developed. The play is amongst those mentioned by Meres in 1598. The only allusion in it which can be taken to fix a date, is that which is supposed to refer to the civil contests of France

INTRODUCTORY NOTICE.

upon the accession of Henry IV. We have noticed this passage in our Illustrations of Act III.; but we are by no means sure that the *equivoque* in the description of France, "arm'd and reverted, making war against her heir," is to be received with reference to the war of the League. The spelling of *heire* in the original copy is not conclusive; for the words *heire* and *haire* are confounded in other places of the early copies of Shakspere's dramas. At any rate, the change of *heire* to *haire* in the second folio shows that the supposed allusion to Henry IV. was forgotten in 1632.

We must depend, then, upon the internal evidence of this being a very early play. This evidence consists,

1. In the great prevalence of that measure which was known to our language as early as the time of Chaucer, by the name of "rime dogerel." This peculiarity is found only in three of our author's plays, —in Love's Labour's Lost, in the Taming of the Shrew, and in the Comedy of Errors. But this measure was a distinguishing characteristic of the early English drama. It prevails very much more in this play than in Love's Labour's Lost; for prose is here much more sparingly introduced. The doggrel seems to stand half-way between prose and verse, marking the distinction between the language of a work of art, and that of ordinary life, in the same way that the recitative does in a musical composition. It is to be observed, too, in the Comedy of Errors, that this measure is very carefully regulated by somewhat strict laws:—

"We came into the world like brother and brother,
And now let 's go hand in hand, not one before another."

This concluding passage, which is cast in the same mould as the other similar verses of the play, is much more regular in its structure than the following in Love's Labour's Lost:—

"And such barren plants are set before us, that we thankful should be,
Which we of taste and feeling are, for those parts that do fructify in us more than he."

The latter line almost reminds us of 'Mrs. Harris's Petition,' which, according to Swift, "Humbly sheweth

"That I went to warm myself in Lady Betty's chamber, because I was cold,
And I had in a purse seven pounds, four shillings and sixpence, besides farthings, in money and gold."

The measure in the Comedy of Errors was formed by Shakspere upon his rude predecessors. In some of these it is not only occasionally introduced, but constitutes the great mass of the dialogue. In 'Gammer Gurton's Needle,' for example, a long play of five acts, which has been called the first English comedy, the doggrel measure prevails throughout, as in the concluding lines:—

"But now, my good masters, since we must be gone,
And leave you behind us, here all alone,
Since at our lasting ending, thus merry we be,
For Gammer Gurton's Needle's sake, let us have a plaudytie."

The supposed earlier comedy of 'Ralph Roister Doister' is composed in the same measure. Nor was it in humorous performances alone that this structure of verse (which Shakspere always uses as a vehicle of fun) was introduced. In 'Damon and Pithias,' a serious play, which was probably produced about 1570, the sentence of Dionysius is thus pronounced upon Pithias:—

"Pithias, seeing thou takest me at my word, take Damon to thee;
For two months he is thine; unbind him; I set him free;
Which time once expired, if he appear not the next day by noon,
Without further delay thou shalt lose thy life, and that full soon."

There cannot, we think, be a stronger proof that the Comedy of Errors was an early play of our author, than its agreement, in this particular, with the models which Shakspere found in his almost immediate predecessors.

2. In Love's Labour's Lost, Romeo and Juliet, A Midsummer-Night's Dream, and the Comedy of Errors, alternate rhymes are very frequently introduced. Shakspere obtained the mastery over this species of verse in the Venus and Adonis, "the first heir of his invention," as he himself calls it. He writes it with extraordinary facility—with an ease and power that strikingly contrast with the more laboured elegiac stanzas of modern times. Nothing can be more harmonious, or the har-

COMEDY OF ERRORS.

many more varied, than this measure in Shakspere's hands. Take, for example, the well-known lines in the Venus and Adonis, which, themselves the most perfect music, have been allied to one of the most successful musical compositions of the present day:—

> "Bid me discourse, I will enchant thine ear,
> Or, like a fairy, trip upon the green,
> Or, like a nymph, with long dishevell'd hair,
> Dance on the sands, and yet no footing seen."

Compare these with the following in Love's Labour's Lost:—

> "A wither'd hermit, five-score winters worn,
> Might shake off fifty, looking in her eye:
> Beauty doth varnish age, as if new born,
> And gives the crutch the cradle's infancy."

Or with these, in Romeo and Juliet:—

> "If I profane with my unworthiest hand
> This holy shrine, the gentle sin is this,—
> My lips, two blushing pilgrims, ready stand,
> To smooth that rough touch with a tender kiss."

Or with some of the lines in A Midsummer-Night's Dream, such as,

> "Why should you think that I should woo in scorn?
> Scorn and derision never come in tears:
> Look, when I vow I weep; and vows so born,
> In their nativity all truth appears."

Or, lastly, with the exquisite address of Antipholus of Syracuse to Luciana, in the third act of the Comedy of Errors.

> "Teach me, dear creature, how to think and speak.
> Lay open to my earthy gross conceit,
> Smother'd in errors, feeble, shallow, weak,
> The folded meaning of your words' deceit."

There was clearly a time in Shakspere's poetical life when he delighted in this species of versification; and in many of the instances in which he has employed it in the dramas we have mentioned, the passages have somewhat of a fragmentary appearance, as if they were not originally cast in a dramatic mould, but were amongst those scattered thoughts of the young poet which had shaped themselves into verse, without a purpose beyond that of embodying his feeling of the beautiful and the harmonious. When the time arrived that he had fully dedicated himself to the great work of his life, he rarely ventured upon cultivating these offshoots of his early versification. The doggrel was entirely rejected—the alternate rhymes no longer tempted him by their music to introduce a measure which is scarcely akin with the dramatic spirit—the couplet was adopted more and more sparingly—and he finally adheres to the blank verse which he may almost be said to have created,—in his hands certainly the grandest as well as the sweetest form in which the highest thoughts were ever unfolded to listening humanity.

Supposed Source of the Plot.

The commentators have puzzled themselves, after their usual fashion, with the evidence which this play undoubtedly presents of Shakspere's ability to read Latin, and their dogged resolution to maintain the opinion that in an age of grammar-schools our poet never could have attained that common accomplishment. The speech of Ægeon, in the first scene,

> "A heavier task could not have been impos'd
> Than I to speak my griefs unspeakable,"—

INTRODUCTORY NOTICE.

is, they admit, an imitation of the

"Infandum, Regina, jubes renovare dolorem"

of Virgil.

"Thou art an elm, my husband, I a vine,"

is in Catullus, Ovid, and Horace. The "owls" that "suck our breath" are the "*striges*" of Ovid. The apostrophe of Dromio to the virtues of "beating"—" When I am cold he heats me with beating, when I am warm he cools me with beating; I am waked with it when I sleep; rais'd with it when I sit; driven out of doors with it when I go from home; welcomed home with it when I return;"—is modelled upon Cicero:—"Hæc studia adolescentiam agunt, senectutem oblectant, secundas res ornant, adversis perfugium ac solatium præbent, delectant domi, non impediunt foris, pernoctant nobiscum, peregrinantur, rusticantur." The burning of the conjurer's beard is an incident copied from the twelfth book of Virgil's Æneid, where Corinæus singes "the goodly bush of hair" of Ebusus, in a manner scarcely consistent with the dignity of heroic poetry. Lastly, in the original copy of the Comedy of Errors, the Antipholus of Ephesus is called *Sereptus*—a corruption of the epithet by which one of the twin brothers in Plautus is distinguished—*Menæchmus Surreptus*. There was a translation of this comedy of Plautus, to which we shall presently more fully advert. "If the poet had not dipped into the original Plautus," says Capell, "*Surreptus* had never stood in his copy, the translation having no such *agnomen*, but calling one brother simply *Menæchmus*, the other *Sosicles*." With all these admissions on the part of some of those who proclaimed that Farmer had made a wonderful discovery when he attempted to prove that Shakspere did not know the difference between *clarus* and *carus*—(See Henry V., Act v., Illustration)—they will not swerve from their belief that his mind was so constituted as to be incapable of attaining that species of knowledge which was of the easiest attainment in his own day,—and for the teaching of which a school was expressly endowed at Stratford-upon-Avon. Steevens says, "Shakspere might have taken the general plan of this comedy from a translation of the Menæchmi of Plautus, by W. W., i.e. (according to Wood) William Warner, in 1595." Ritson thinks that Shakspere was under no obligation to this translation; but that the Comedy of Errors "was not originally his, but proceeded from some inferior playwright, who was *capable* of reading the Menæchmi without the help of a translation." Malone entirely disagrees with Ritson's theory that this comedy was founded upon an earlier production; but sets up a theory of his own to get over the difficulty started by Ritson, that not a single name, word, or line, is taken from Warner's translation. A play called 'The Historie of Error' was enacted before Queen Elizabeth, "by the children of Powles," in 1576; and from this piece, says Malone, "it is extremely probable that he was furnished with the fable of the present comedy," as well as the designation of "*surreptus*." Here is, unquestionably, a very early play of Shakspere,—and yet Steevens maintains that it was taken from a translation of Plautus, published in 1595; the play has no resemblance, beyond the general character of the incidents, to this translation,—and therefore Ritson pronounces that it is not entirely Shakspere's work;—and while Malone denies this, he guesses that the Comedy of Errors was founded upon a much older play. And why all this contradictory hypothesis? Simply, because these most learned men are resolved to hold their own heads higher than Shakspere, by maintaining that he could not do what they could—read Plautus in the original. We have not a doubt that the Comedy of Errors was written at least five years before the publication of Warner's translation of the Menæchmi; and, further, that Shakspere in the composition of his own play was perfectly familiar with the Menæchmi of Plautus. In Hamlet he gives, in a word, the characteristics of two ancient dramatists; —his criticism is decisive as to his familiarity with the originals: "Seneca cannot be too *heavy*, nor Plautus too *light*." We shall furnish a few extracts from this translation of 1595; whence it will be seen, incidentally, that the lightness of the free and natural old Roman is wondrously loaded by the prosaic hand of Master William Warner.

The original argument of the Menæchmi, it will be perceived, at once gave Shakspere the epithet *surreptus*, as well as furnished him with some of the characters of his play, much more distinctly than the translation, which we present with it:—

COMEDY OF ERRORS.

[PLAUTUS.]

"Mercator Siculus, cui erant gemini filii;
Ei, surrepto altero, mors obtigit.
Nomen surreptitii illi indit qui domi est
Avus paternus, facit Menæchmum Sosiclem.
Et is germanum, postquam adolevit, quæritat
Circum omnes oras. Post Epidamnum devenit:
Hic fuerat auctus ille surreptitius
Menæchmum civem credunt omnes advenam:
Eumque appellant, meretrix, uxor et socer.
Ii se cognoscunt fratres postremò invicem."

[WARNER.]

"Two twinborn sons, a Sicill merchant had,
Menæchmus one, and Sosicles the other:
The first his father lost a little lad,
The grandsire named the latter like his brother.
This (grown a man) long travel took to seek
His brother, and to Epidamnum came,
Where th' other dwelt enrich'd, and him so like,
That citizens there take him for the same:
Father, wife, neighbours, each mistaking either,
Much pleasant error, ere they meet together."

This argument is almost sufficient to point out the difference between the plots of Plautus and of Shakspere. It stands in the place of the beautiful narrative of Ægeon, in the first scene of the Comedy of Errors. In Plautus we have no broken-hearted father bereft of both his sons: he is dead; and the grandfather changes the name of the one child who remains to him. Shakspere does not stop to tell us how the twin-brothers bear the same name; nor does he explain the matter any more in the case of the Dromios, whose introduction upon the scene is his own creation. In Plautus, the brother, Menæchmus Sosicles, who remained with the grandsire, comes to Epidamnum, in search of his twin-brother who was stolen, and he is accompanied by his servant Messenio; but all the perplexities that are so naturally occasioned by the confusion of the two twin-servants are entirely wanting. The mistakes are carried on by the "meretrix, uxor, et socer," (softened by Warner into "father, wife, neighbours"). We have "Medicus," the prototype of Doctor Pinch; but the mother of the twins is not found in Plautus. We scarcely need say that the Parasite and the Father-in-law have no place in Shakspere's comedy. The scene in the Comedy of Errors is changed from Epidamnum to Ephesus; but we have mention of Epidamnum once or twice in the play.

The Menæchmi opens with the favourite character of the Roman comedy—the Parasite; the scene is at Epidamnum. The Parasite is going to dine with Menæchmus, who comes out from his house, upbraiding his jealous wife. But his wife is not jealous without provocation.

"Hanc modò uxori intus palam surripui; ad scortum fero."

The Antipholus of Shakspere does not propose to dine with one "pretty and wild," and to bestow "the chain" upon his hostess, till he has been provoked by having his own doors shut upon him. Our poet has thus preserved some sympathy for his Antipholus, which the Menæchmus of Plautus forfeits upon his first entrance. Menæchmus and the Parasite go to dine with Erotium (meretrix). Those who talk of Shakspere's anachronisms have never pointed out to us what formidable liberties the translators of Shakspere's time did not scruple to take with their originals. Menæchmus gives very precise directions for his dinner, after the most approved Roman fashion:—

"Jube igitur nobis tribus apud te prandium accurarier,
Atque aliquid scitamentorum de foro obsonarier,
Glandionidem suillam, laridum pernonidum, aut
Sinciput, aut polimenta porcina, aut aliquid ad eum modum."

This passage W. W. thus interprets:—"Let a good dinner be made for us three. Hark ye, some oysters, a mary-bone pie or two, some artichokes, and potato roots; let our other dishes be as you please." In reading this bald attempt to transfuse the Roman luxuries into words accommodated to English ideas, we are forcibly reminded how "rare Ben" dealt with the spirit of antiquity in such matters:—

"The tongues of carps, dormice, and camels' heels
Boil'd in the spirit of sol, and dissolv'd pearl,
Apicius' diet, 'gainst the epilepsy:
And I will eat these broths with spoons of amber
Headed with diamond and carbuncle.
My foot-boy shall eat pheasants, calver'd salmons
Knots, godwits, lampreys: I myself will have
The beards of barbels serv'd, instead of sallads;
Oil'd mushrooms" &c.—*Alchemist*, Act ii., sc. 1.

INTRODUCTORY NOTICE.

The second Act in Plautus opens with the landing of Menæchmus Sosicles and Messenio, at Epidamnum. The following is Warner's translation of the scene:—

"*Men.* Surely, Messenio, I think seafarers never take so comfortable a joy in any thing as, when they have been long tost and turmoiled in the wide seas, they hap at last to ken land.

Mes. I'll be sworn, I should not be gladder to see a whole country of mine own, than I have been at such a sight. But I pray, wherefore are we now come to Epidamnum? must we needs go to see every town that we hear of?

Men. Till I find my brother, all towns are alike to me; I must try in all places.

Mes. Why then, let's even as long as we live seek your brother: six years now have we roamed about thus, Istria, Hispania, Massylia, Illyria, all the upper sea, all high Greece, all haven towns in Italy. I think if we had sought a needle all th's time we must needs have found it, had it been above ground. It cannot be that he is alive; and to seek a dead man thus among the living, what folly is it?

Men. Yea, could I but once find any man that could certainly inform me of his death, I were satisfied; otherwise I can never desist seeking: little knowest thou, Messenio, how near my heart it goes.

Mes. This is washing of a blackamoor. Faith, let's go home, unless ye mean we should write a story of our travail.

Men. Sirrah, no more of these saucy speeches. I perceive I must teach you how to serve me, not to rule me.

Mes. Ay, so, now it appears what it is to be a servant. Well, I must speak my conscience. Do ye hear, sir? Faith I must tell you one thing, when I look into the lean estate of your purse, and consider advisedly of your decaying stock, I hold it very needful to be drawing homeward, lest in looking your brother, we quite lose ourselves. For this assure yourself, this town, Epidamnum, is a place of outrageous expenses, exceeding in all riot and lasciviousness; and (I hear, as full of ribalds, parasites, drunkards, catchpoles, coney-catchers, and sycophants, as it can hold. Then for courtezans, why here's the currentest stamp of them in the world. You must not think here to scape with as light cost as in other places. The very name shows the nature, no man comes hither *sine damno*.

Men. You say very well indeed; give me my purse into mine own keeping, because I will so be the safer, *sine damno*."

Steevens considered that the description of Ephesus in the Comedy of Errors,

"They say, this town is full of cozenage," &c.

was derived from Warner's translation, where "ribalds, parasites, drunkards, catch-poles, coney-catchers, sycophants, and courtezans," are found; the *voluptarii, potatores, sycophantæ, palpatores*, and *meretrices* of Plautus. But surely the "jugglers," "sorcerers," "witches," of Shakspere are not these. With his exquisite judgment, he gave Ephesus more characteristic "liberties of sin." The cook of the courtezan, in Plautus, first mistakes the wandering brother for the prodigate of Epidamnum. Erotium next encounters him, and with her he dines; and, leaving her, takes charge of a cloak which the Menæchmus of Epidamnum had given her. In the Comedy of Errors the stranger brother dines with the wife of him of Ephesus. The Parasite next meets with the wanderer, and being enraged that the dinner is finished in his absence, resolves to disclose the infidelities of Menæchmus to his jealous wife. The "errors" proceed, in the maid of Erotium bringing him a chain which she says he had stolen from his wife: he is to cause it to be made heavier and of a newer fashion. The traveller goes his way with the cloak and the chain. The jealous wife and the Parasite lie in wait for the faithless husband, who the Parasite reports is carrying the cloak to the dyer's; and they fall with their reproaches upon the Menæchmus of Epidamnum, who left the courtezan to attend to his business. A scene of violence ensues; and the bewildered man repairs to Erotium for his dinner. He meets with reproaches only; for he knows nothing of the cloak and the chain. The stranger Menæchmus, who has the cloak and chain, encounters the wife of his brother, and of course he utterly denies any knowledge of her. Her father comes to her assistance, upon her hastily sending for him. He first reproaches his daughter for her suspicions of her husband, and her shrewish temper: Luciana reasons in a somewhat similar way with Adriana, in the Comedy of Errors;—and the Abbess is more earnest in her condemnation of the complaining wife. The scene in Plautus wants all the elevation that we find in Shakspere; and the old man seems to think that the wife has little to grieve for, as long as she has food, clothes, and servants. Menæchmus, the traveller, of course cannot comprehend all this; and the father and daughter agree that he is mad, and send for a doctor. He escapes from the discipline which is preparing for him; and the doctor's assistants lay hold of Menæchmus, the citizen. He is rescued by Messenio, the servant of the traveller, who mistakes him for his master, and begs his freedom. The servant going to his inn meets with his real master; and, while disputing with him, the Menæchmus of Epidamnum joins them. Of course, the *éclaircissement* is the natural consequence of the presence of both upon the same scene. The brothers resolve to leave Epidam-

COMEDY OF ERRORS.

num together; the citizen making proclamation that he will sell all his goods, and adding, with his accustomed loose notions of conjugal duty,

"Venibit uxor quoque etiam, si quis emptor venerit."

Hazlitt has said, "This comedy is taken very much from the Menæchmi of Plautus, and is not an improvement on it." We think he is wrong in both assertions.

PERIOD OF THE ACTION.

We have noticed some of the anachronisms which the translator of Plautus, in Shakspere's time did not hesitate to introduce into his performance. W. W. did not do this ignorantly; for he was a learned person; and, we are told in an address of "The Printer to his Readers," had "divers of this poet's comedies Englished, for the use and delight of his private friends, who in Plautus' own words are not able to understand them." There was, no doubt, a complete agreement as to the principle of such anachronisms in the writers of Shakspere's day. They employed the conventional ideas of their own time instead of those which properly belonged to the date of their story; they translated images as well as words; they were addressing uncritical readers and spectators, and they thought it necessary to make themselves intelligible by speaking of familiar instead of recondite things. Thus W. W. not only gives us mary-bone pies and potatoes, instead of the complicated messes of the Roman sensualist, but he talks of constables and toll-gatherers, Bedlam fools, and claret. In Douce's Essay 'On the Anachronisms and some other Incongruities of Shakspere,' the offences of our poet in the Comedy of Errors are thus summed up:—"In the *ancient* city of Ephesus we have ducats, marks, and guilders, and the *Abbess of a Nunnery*. Mention is also made of several modern European kingdoms, and of America; of Henry the Fourth of France,* of Turkish tapestry, a rapier, and a striking-clock; of Lapland sorcerers, Satan, and even of Adam and Noah. In one place Antipholus calls himself a *Christian*. As we are unacquainted with the immediate source whence this play was derived, it is impossible to ascertain whether Shakspere is responsible for these anachronisms." The ducats, marks, guilders, tapestry, rapier, striking-clock, and Lapland sorcerers, belong precisely to the same class of anachronisms as those we have already exhibited from the pen of the translator of Plautus. Had Shakspere used the names of Grecian or Roman coins, his audience would not have understood him. Such matters have nothing whatever to do with the period of a dramatic action. But we think Douce was somewhat hasty in proclaiming that the *Abbess of a Nunnery*, Satan, Adam and Noah, and Christian, were anachronisms, in connexion with the "ancient city of Ephesus."

Douce, seeing that the Comedy of Errors was suggested by the Menæchmi of Plautus, considers, no doubt, that Shakspere intended to place his action at the same period as the Roman play. It is manifest to us that he intended precisely the contrary. The Menæchmi contains invocations in great number to the ancient divinities;—Jupiter and Apollo are here familiar words. From the first line of the Comedy of Errors to the last we have not the slightest allusion to the classical mythology. Was there not a time, then, even in the *ancient* city of Ephesus, when there might be an Abbess,—men might call themselves Christians,—and Satan, Adam, and Noah might be names of common use? We do not mean to affirm that Shakspere intended to select the Ephesus of Christianity—the great city of churches and councils—for the dwelling-place of Antipholus, any more than we think that Duke Solinus was a real personage—that "Duke Menaphon, his most renowned uncle," ever had any existence—or that even his name could be found in any story more trustworthy than that of Greene's 'Arcadia.' The truth is, that in the same way that *Ardennes* was a sort of *terra incognita* of chivalry, the poets of Shakspere's time had no hesitation in placing the fables of the romantic ages in classical localities, leaving the periods and the names perfectly undefined and unappreciable. Who will undertake to fix a period for the action of Sir Philip Sydney's great romance, when the author has conveyed his reader into the fairy or pastoral land, and informed him what manner of life the inhabitants of that region lead?" We cannot open a page of Sydney's 'Arcadia' without being struck with what we are accustomed to call anachronisms,—and these from a very severe critic, who, in his

---

* *Mention is certainly not made of Henry IV.; there is a supposed allusion to him*

INTRODUCTORY NOTICE

'Defence of Poesy,' denounces with merciless severity all violation of the unities of the drama. One example will suffice:—Histor and Damon sing a "double sestine." The classical spirit that pervades the following lines belongs to the "true Arcadian" age:—

> "O Mercury, foregoer to the evening,
> O heavenly huntress of the savage mountains,
> O lovely star entitled of the morning,
> While that my voice doth fill these woful valleys,
> Vouchsafe your silent ears to plaining music,
> Which oft hath echo tired in secret forests."

But to what period belong the following lines of the "Phaleuciacs," which Zelmene sings, whose voice "strains the canary-birds!"

> "Her cannons be her eyes, mine eyes the walls be,
> Which at first volley gave too open entry,
> Nor rampier did abide; my brain was up-blown,
> Undermined with a speech the piercer of thoughts."

Warton has prettily said, speaking of Spenser, "*exactness* in his poem would have been like the cornice which a painter introduced in the grotto of Calypso." Those who would define everything in poetry are the makers of corniced grottos. As we are not desirous of belonging to this somewhat obsolete fraternity, to which even Warton himself affected to belong when he wrote what is truly an apology for the Fairy Queen, we will leave our readers to decide,—whether Duke Solinus reigned at Ephesus before "the great temple, after having risen with increasing splendour from seven repeated misfortunes, was finally burnt by the Goths in their third naval invasion;"* or whether he presided over the decaying city, somewhat nearer to the period when Justinian "filled Constantinople with its statues, and raised his church of St. Sophia on its columns;"† or, lastly, whether he approached the period of its final desolation, when the "candlestick was removed out of its place," and the Christian Ephesus became the Mohammadan Aiasaluck.

But decide as our readers may,—and if they decide not at all they will not derive less satisfaction from the perusal of this drama,—it becomes necessary for the demands of the modern stage that the scenery and costume should belong to some definite period. Our coadjutor, Mr. Planché, has felt considerable difficulty in this particular; and the short notice which he gives on the subject of costume aims at greater precision than we should consider necessary with reference to the poetical character of this play. This desire for exactness is, to a certain extent, an evil;—and it is an evil which necessarily belongs to what, at first appearance, is a manifest improvement in the modern stage. The exceeding beauty and accuracy of scenery and dress in our days is destructive, in some degree, to the *poetical* truth of Shakspere's dramas. It takes them out of the region of the broad and universal, to impair their freedom and narrow their range by a typographical and chronological minuteness. When the word "Thebes" was exhibited upon a painted board to Shakspere's audience, their thoughts of that city were in subjection to the descriptions of the poet; but if a pencil as magical as that of Stanfield had shown them a Thebes that the child might believe to be a reality, the words to which they listened would have been comparatively uninteresting, in the easier gratification of the senses instead of the intellect. Poetry must always have something of the vague and indistinct in its character. The exact has its own province. Let Science explore the wilds of Africa, and map out for us where there are mighty rivers and verdant plains in the places where the old geographers gave us pictures of lions and elephants to designate undiscovered desolation. But let Poetry still have its undefined countries; let Arcadia remain unsurveyed; let us not be too curious to inquire whether Dromio was an ancient heathen or a Christian, nor whether Bottom the weaver lived precisely at the time when Theseus did battle with the Centaurs.

* Gibbon, chap. x. † Chandler.
‡ See Sydney's Defence of Poesy. "What child is there that, coming to a play, and seeing Thebes written in great letters upon an old door, doth believe that it is Thebes?" This rude device was probably employed in the representation of the *Thebais* of Seneca, translated by Newton, 1581.

COMEDY OF ERRORS.

Costume.

The costume of this Comedy must, we fear, be left conventional. The two masters, as well as the two servants, must of course be presumed to have been attired precisely alike, or the difference of dress would at least have called forth some remark, had it not led to an immediate éclaircissement; and yet that the Syracusan travellers, both master and man, should by mere chance be clothed in garments not only of the same fashion, but of the same colour, as those of their Ephesian brethren, is beyond the bounds of even stage probability. Were the scene laid during the classical era of Greece, as in 'the Menæchmi,' on which our Comedy was founded, the absurdity would not be quite so startling, as the simple tunic of one slave *might* accidentally resemble that of another; and the chlamys and petasus of the upper classes were at least of one general form, and differed but occasionally in colour; but the appearance of an Abbess renders it necessary to consider the events as passing at the time when Ephesus had become famed amongst the Christian cities of Asia Minor, and at least as late as the first establishment of religious communities (*i. e.* in the fourth century).

We can only recommend to the artist the Byzantine Greek paintings and illuminations, or the costume adopted from them for Scriptural designs by the early Italian masters.

[Medal of Ephesus.]

PERSONS REPRESENTED.

SOLINUS, *Duke of* Ephesus.
ÆGEON, *a merchant of* Syracuse.

ANTIPHOLUS *of* Ephesus, } *twin brothers, and sons to*
ANTIPHOLUS *of* Syracuse, } *Ægeon and Æmilia, but unknown to each other.*

DROMIO *of* Ephesus, } *twin brothers, and Attendants on*
DROMIO *of* Syracuse, } *the two* Antipholuses.
BALTHAZAR, *a merchant.*
ANGELO, *a goldsmith.*
A merchant, friend to Antipholus *of* Syracuse.
PINCH, *a schoolmaster, and a conjurer.*

ÆMILIA, *wife to* Ægeon, *an Abbess at* Ephesus.
ADRIANA, *wife to* Antipholus *of* Ephesus.
LUCIANA, *her sister.*
LUCE, *her servant.*
A Courtezan.

Gaoler Officers, and other Attendants.

SCENE.—EPHESUS.

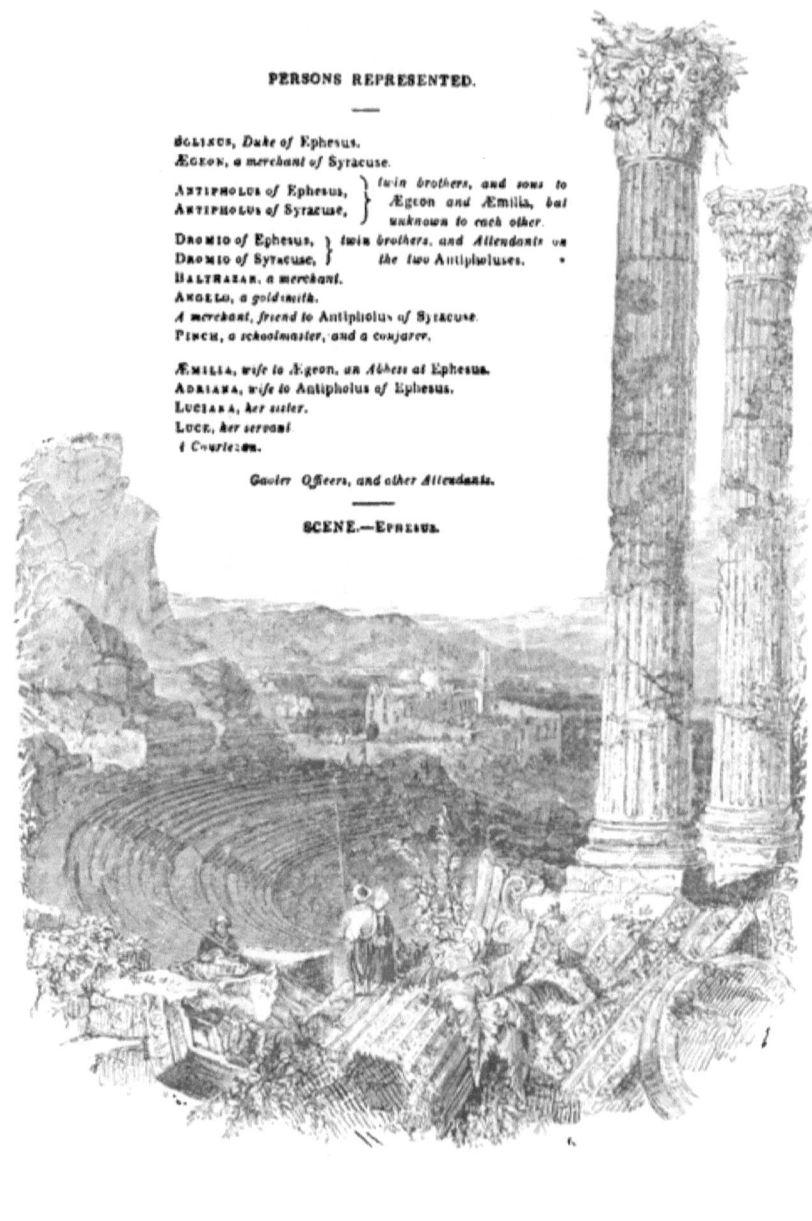

[Ephesus.]

ACT I.

SCENE I.—*A Hall in the* Duke's *Palace.*

Enter DUKE, ÆGEON, Gaoler, Officers, *and other* Attendants.

Æge. Proceed, Solinus, to procure my fall,
And, by the doom of death, end woes and all.
  Duke. Merchant of Syracusa, plead no more;
I am not partial, to infringe our laws;
The enmity and discord, which of late
Sprung from the rancorous outrage of your duke
To merchants, our well-dealing countrymen,—
Who, wanting gilders to redeem their lives,
Have sealed his rigorous statutes with their bloods,—
Excludes all pity from our threat'ning looks.
For, since the mortal and intestine jars
'Twixt thy seditious countrymen and us,
It hath in solemn synods been decreed,
Both by the Syracusans[a] and ourselves,
To admit no traffic to our adverse towns:
Nay, more, If any, born at Ephesus,
Be seen at any Syracusan marts and fairs,
Again, If any Syracusan born,
Come to the bay of Ephesus, he dies,
His goods confiscate to the duke's dispose;
Unless a thousand marks be levied,
To quit the penalty, and to ransom him.
Thy substance, valued at the highest rate,
Cannot amount unto a hundred marks;
Therefore, by law thou art condemn'd to die.
  Æge. Yet this my comfort; when your words are done,
My woes end likewise with the evening sun.
  Duke. Well, Syracusan, say, in brief, the cause
Why thou departedst from thy native home;
And for what cause thou cam'st to Ephesus.
  Æge. A heavier task could not have been impos'd,
Than I to speak my griefs unspeakable:

[a] *Syracusans.*—In the first folio, Syracusians, as we now read, is invariably spelt Syracusians. In Malone's edition (1821), the old spelling is restored, Boswell stating that it has the sanction of Bentley, in his Epistles of Phalaris. We have considered that Syracusians is an error of the early typography; for the Syracusani of the Latin naturally becomes the Syracusans of the English. Mr. Dyce, as well as Mr. Staunton, Mr. Grant White in his American edition, and the Cambridge editors, hold to *Syracusians.*

Yet, that the world may witness that my end
Was wrought by nature,[a] not by vile offence,
I'll utter what my sorrow gives me leave.
In Syracusa was I born; and wed
Unto a woman, happy but for me,
And by me, too, had not our hap been bad.[b]
With her I liv'd in joy; our wealth increas'd,
By prosperous voyages I often made
To Epidamnum, till my factor's death,
And the great care of goods at random left,[c]
Drew me from kind embracements of my spouse:
From whom my absence was not six months old,
Before herself (almost at fainting under
The pleasing punishment that women bear,)
Had made provision for her following me,
And soon, and safe, arrived where I was.
There had she not been long, but she became
A joyful mother of two goodly sons;
And, which was strange, the one so like the other
As could not be distinguish'd but by names.
That very hour, and in the self-same inn,
A poor mean woman was delivered[d]
Of such a burden, male twins, both alike:
Those, for their parents were exceeding poor,
I bought, and brought up to attend my sons.
My wife, not meanly proud of two such boys,
Made daily motions for our home return:
Unwilling I agreed; alas, too soon.
We came aboard:
A league from Epidamnum had we sail'd,
Before the always-wind-obeying deep
Gave any tragic instance of our harm:
But longer did we not retain much hope;
For what obscured light the heavens did grant
Did but convey unto our fearful minds
A doubtful warrant of immediate death;
Which, though myself would gladly have embrac'd,
Yet the incessant weepings of my wife,
Weeping before for what she saw must come,
And piteous plainings of the pretty babes,
That mourn'd for fashion, ignorant what to fear,
Forc'd me to seek delays for them and me.
And this it was,—for other means was none.—
The sailors sought for safety by our boat,
And left the ship, then sinking-ripe, to us:
My wife, most careful for the latter-born,

[a] *By nature*—by the impulses of nature, by natural affection,—as opposed to *vile offence*, the violation of the municipal laws of Ephesus.
[b] The word *too* in this line was supplied in the second folio.
[c] The first folio reads:—
"And he great care of goods at random left."
Malone made the text easy and clear by the substitution of *the*.
[d] The word *poor* in this line was added in the second folio.

Had fasten'd him unto a small spare mast,
Such as sea-faring men provide for storms:
To him one of the other twins was bound,
Whilst I had been like heedful of the other.
The children thus dispos'd, my wife and I,
Fixing our eyes on whom our care was fix'd,
Fasten'd ourselves at either end the mast;
And floating straight, obedient to the stream,
Were carried towards Corinth, as we thought.
At length the sun, gazing upon the earth,
Dispers'd those vapours that offended us;
And, by the benefit of his wish'd light,
The seas wax'd calm, and we discovered
Two ships from far making amain to us,
Of Corinth that, of Epidaurus this:
But ere they came,—O, let me say no more!
Gather the sequel by that went before.
  Duke. Nay, forward, old man, do not break off so;
For we may pity, though not pardon thee.
  Æge. O, had the gods done so, I had not now
Worthily term'd them merciless to us!
For ere the ships could meet by twice five leagues,
We were encounter'd by a mighty rock;
Which being violently borne upon,
Our helpful ship was splitted in the midst,
So that, in this unjust divorce of us,
Fortune had left to both of us alike
What to delight in, what to sorrow for.
Her part, poor soul! seeming as burdened
With lesser weight, but not with lesser woe,
Was carried with more speed before the wind;
And in our sight they three were taken up
By fishermen of Corinth, as we thought.
At length, another ship had seized on us;
And, knowing whom it was their hap to save,
Gave healthful welcome to their shipwreck'd guests;
And would have reft the fishers of their prey,
Had not their bark been very slow of sail,
And therefore homeward did they bend their course.
Thus have you heard me sever'd from my bliss;
That by misfortunes was my life prolong'd,
To tell sad stories of my own mishaps.
  Duke. And, for the sake of them thou sorrowest for,
Do me the favour to dilate at full
What hath befall'n of them, and thee, till now.
  Æge. My youngest boy, and yet my eldest care,
At eighteen years became inquisitive
After his brother; and importun'd me,

That his attendant, (so his case was like,^a
Reft of his brother, but retain'd his name,)
Might bear him company in the quest of him:
Whom whilst I labour'd of a love to see,
I hazarded the loss of whom I lov'd.
Five summers have I spent in farthest Greece,
Roaming clean through the bounds of Asia,
And, coasting homeward, came to Ephesus;
Hopeless to find, yet loath to leave unsought,
Or that, or any place that harbours men.
But here must end the story of my life;
And happy were I in my timely death,
Could all my travels warrant me they live.

Duke. Hapless Ægeon, whom the fates have
    mark'd
To bear the extremity of dire mishap!
Now, trust me, were it not against our laws,
Against my crown, my oath, my dignity,
Which princes, would they, may not disannul,
My soul should sue as advocate for thee.
But, though thou art adjudged to the death,
And passed sentence may not be recall'd
But to our honour's great disparagement,
Yet will I favour thee in what I can:
Therefore, merchant, I'll limit thee this day,
To seek thy help by beneficial help:
Try all the friends thou hast in Ephesus.
Beg thou, or borrow, to make up the sum,
And live; if no, then thou art doom'd to die :—
Gaoler, take him into thy custody.

Gaol. I will, my lord.

Æge. Hopeless, and helpless, doth Ægeon
    wend,
But to procrastinate his lifeless end. [*Exeunt.*

SCENE II.—*A public Place.*

Enter ANTIPHOLUS *and* DROMIO *of* Syracuse,
    and a Merchant.

Mer. Therefore, give out, you are of Epi-
    damnum,
Lest that your goods too soon be confiscate.
This very day, a Syracusan merchant
Is apprehended for arrival here;
And, not being able to buy out his life,
According to the statute of the town,
Dies ere the weary sun set in the west
There is your money that I had to keep.

Ant. S. Go, bear it to the Centaur, where we
    host,
And stay there, Dromio, till I come to thee.
Within this hour it will be dinner-time :
Till that, I'll view the manners of the town,

Peruse the traders, gaze upon the buildings,
And then return, and sleep within mine inn;
For with long travel I am stiff and weary.
Get thee away.

Dro. S. Many a man would take you at your
    word,
And go indeed, having so good a mean.
    [*Exit* DRO. S.

Ant. S. A trusty villain, sir, that very oft,
When I am dull with care and melancholy,
Lightens my humour with his merry jests.
What, will you walk with me about the town,
And then go to my inn and dine with me?

Mer. I am invited, sir, to certain merchants,
Of whom I hope to make much benefit;
I crave your pardon. Soon at five o'clock,^a
Please you, I'll meet with you upon the mart,
And afterward consort you till bed-time ;
My present business calls me from you now.

Ant. S. Farewell till then: I will go lose
    myself,
And wander up and down, to view the city.

Mer. Sir, I commend you to your own content.
    [*Exit* Merchant.

Ant. S. He that commends me to mine own
    content
Commends me to the thing I cannot get.
I to the world am like a drop of water,
That in the ocean seeks another drop;
Who, falling there to find his fellow forth,
Unseen, inquisitive, confounds himself :
So I, to find a mother and a brother,
In quest of them, unhappy, lose myself.

Enter DROMIO *of* Ephesus.

Here comes the almanack of my true date.—
What now? How chance, thou art return'd so
    soon?

Dro. E. Return'd so soon! rather approach'd
    too late :
The capon burns, the pig falls from the spit;
The clock hath strucken twelve upon the bell,
My mistress made it one upon my cheek :
She is so hot, because the meat is cold;
The meat is cold, because you come not home;
You come not home, because you have no
    stomach;
You have no stomach, having broke your fast;
But we, that know what 't is to fast and pray,
Are penitent ^b for your default to-day.

^a *Soon at five o'clock.*—This is ordinarily printed, "Soon, at five o'clock." But Antipholus says—
"Within this hour it will be dinner-time."
The time of dinner was *twelve;* therefore five o'clock would not have been *soon.* We must therefore understand the phrase as *about five o'clock.*

^b *Penitent,*—In the sense of doing penance.

Ant. S. Stop in your wind, sir; tell me this,
    I pray:
Where have you left the money that I gave you?
    Dro. E. O,—sixpence, that I had o' Wednes-
        day last,
To pay the saddler for my mistress' crupper;
The saddler had it, sir; I kept it not.
    Ant. S. I am not in a sportive humour now:
Tell me, and dally not, where is the money?
We being strangers here, how dar'st thou trust
So great a charge from thine own custody?
    Dro. E. I pray you, jest, sir, as you sit at
        dinner:
I from my mistress come to you in post;
If I return, I shall be post indeed;[a]
For she will score your fault upon my pate.
Methinks, your maw, like mine, should be your
    clock,
And strike you home without a messenger.
    Ant. S. Come, Dromio, come, these jests are
        out of season;
Reserve them till a merrier hour than this:
Where is the gold I gave in charge to thee?
    Dro. E. To me, sir? why you gave no gold
        to me.
    Ant. S. Come on, sir knave; have done your
        foolishness,
And tell me how thou hast dispos'd thy charge.
    Dro. E. My charge was but to fetch you fro'
        the mart
Home to your house, the Phœnix, sir, to dinner;
My mistress and her sister stay for you.
    Ant. S. Now, as I am a christian, answer me,
In what safe place you have bestow'd[b] my money;

Or I shall break that merry sconce of yours,
That stands on tricks when I am undispos'd:
Where is the thousand marks thou hadst of me?
    Dro. E. I have some marks of yours upon
        my pate,
Some of my mistress' marks upon my shoulders,
But not a thousand marks between you both.
If I should pay your worship those again,
Perchance, you will not bear them patiently.
    Ant. S. Thy mistress' marks? what mistress,
        slave, hast thou?
    Dro. E. Your worship's wife, my mistress at
        the Phœnix;
She that doth fast till you come home to dinner,
And prays, that you will hie you home to dinner.
    Ant. S. What, wilt thou flout me thus unto
        my face,
Being forbid? There, take you that, sir knave.
    Dro. E. What mean you, sir? for God's sake,
        hold your hands;
Nay, an you will not, sir, I'll take my heels.
    [*Exit* Dro. E.
    Ant. S. Upon my life, by some device or
        other,
The villain is o'er-raught[a] of all my money.
They say, this town is full of cozenage;
As, nimble jugglers that deceive the eye,
Dark-working sorcerers that change the mind,
Soul-killing witches that deform the body,
Disguised cheaters, prating mountebanks,
And many such like liberties of sin:[b]
If it prove so, I will be gone the sooner.
I'll to the Centaur, to go seek this slave;
I greatly fear my money is not safe.   [*Exit.*

---

[a] *I ... indeed.*—The post of a shop was used as the tally-board of a publican is now used, to keep the score
[b] *Bestow'd,*—stowed, deposited.

[a] *O'er-raught,*—over-reached.
[b] *Liberties of sin,*—Some would read *libertines.*

["We were encountered by a mighty rock."]

ILLUSTRATIONS OF ACT I.

Scene I

¹ " *It hath in solemn synods been decreed,
Both by the Syracusans and ourselves,
To admit no traffic to our adverse towns:
Nay more, If any, born at Ephesus,
Be seen at any Syracusian marts and fairs,
Again, If any Syracusian born,
Come to the bay of Ephesus he dies
His goods confiscate to the duke's dispose;
Unless a thousand marks be levied,
To quit the penalty, and to ransom him.*"

The offence which Ægeon had committed, and the penalty which he had incurred, are pointed out with a minuteness, by which the poet doubtless intended to convey his sense of the gross injustice of such enactments. In 'The Taming of the Shrew,' written most probably about the same period as 'The Comedy of Errors,' the jealousies of commercial states, exhibiting themselves in violent decrees and impracticable regulations, are also depicted by the same powerful hand:—

" *Tra.* What countryman, I pray?
Ped.   Of Mantua.
Tra. Of Mantua, sir?—marry, God forbid!
And come to Padua, careless of your life?
Ped. My life, sir! how, I pray! for that goes hard.
Tra. 'T is death for any one in Mantua
To come to Padua; know you not the cause?
Your ships are staid at Venice; and the duke
For private quarrel 'twixt your duke and him,
Hath publish'd and proclaim'd it openly.*"

At the commencement of the reign of Elizabeth, the just principles of foreign commerce were asserted in a very remarkable manner in the preamble to a statute (1 Eliz. c. 13): "Other foreign princes, finding themselves aggrieved with the said several acts"—(statutes prohibiting the export or import of merchandise by English subjects in any but English ships)—"as thinking that the same were made to the hurt and prejudice of their country and navy, have made like penal laws against such as should ship out of their countries in any other vessels than of their several countries and dominions; by reason whereof there hath not only grown great displeasure between the foreign princes and the kings of this realm, but also the merchants have been sore grieved and endamaged." The inevitable consequences of commercial jealousies between rival states—the retaliations that invariably attend these "narrow and malignant politics," as Hume forcibly expresses it—are here clearly set forth. But in five or six years afterwards we had acts "for setting her Majesty's people on work," forbidding the importation of foreign wares ready wrought, "to the intent that her Highness's subjects might be employed in making thereof." These laws were directed against the productions of the Netherlands; and they were immediately followed by counter-proclamations, forbidding the carrying into England of any matter or thing out of which the same wares might be made; and prohibiting the importation in the Low Countries of all English manufactures, under pain of confiscation. Under these laws, the English merchants were driven from town to town—from Antwerp to Embden, from Embden to Hamburgh; their ships seized, their goods confiscated. Retaliation of course followed, with all the complicated injuries of violence begetting violence. The instinctive wisdom of our poet must have seen the folly and wickedness of such proceedings; and we believe that these passages are intended to mark his sense of them. The same brute force, which would confiscate the goods and burn the ships of the merchant, would put the merchant himself to death, under another state of society. He has stigmatised the principle of commercial jealousy by carrying out its consequences under an unconstrained despotism.

[Remains of Gate at Ephesus.]

ACT II.

SCENE I.—*A public Place.*

Enter ADRIANA *and* LUCIANA.

Adr. Neither my husband, nor the slave return'd,
That in such haste I sent to seek his master!
Sure, Luciana, it is two o'clock.
　Luc. Perhaps, some merchant hath invited him,
And from the mart he's somewhere gone to dinner.
Good sister, let us dine, and never fret:
A man is master of his liberty:
Time is their master; and, when they see time,
They'll go, or come: If so, be patient, sister.
　Adr. Why should their liberty than ours be more?
　Luc. Because their business still lies out o' door.
　Adr. Look, when I serve him so, he takes it ill.[a]
　Luc. O, know, he is the bridle of your will.
　Ad.. There's none but asses will be bridled so.
　Luc. Why, headstrong liberty is lash'd with woe.[b]
There's nothing situate under heaven's eye
But hath his bound, in earth, in sea, in sky:
The beasts, the fishes, and the winged fowls,
Are their males' subjects, and at their controls:
Men, more divine, the masters of all these,
Lords of the wide world, and wild watery seas,
Indued with intellectual sense and souls,
Of more pre-eminence than fish and fowls,
Are masters to their females, and their lords:
Then let your will attend on their accords.
　Adr. This servitude makes you to keep unwed.
　Luc. Not this, but troubles of the marriage-bed.
　Adr. But were you wedded you would bear some sway.

[a] *Ill.* This is the reading of the second folio, which is necessary for the rhyme. The original has *thus.*
[b] *Lash'd with woe.*—A *lace,* a *leash,* a *latch,* a *lash,* is each a form of expressing what binds or fastens; and thus "headstrong liberty," and "woe," are bound together,—are inseparable.

Luc. Ere I learn love, I'll practise to obey.
Adr. How if your husband start some other where?ᵃ
Luc. Till he come home again, I would forbear.
Adr. Patience, unmov'd, no marvel though she pause;
They can be meek that have no other cause.
A wretched soul, bruis'd with adversity,
We bid be quiet when we hear it cry;
But were we burden'd with like weight of pain,
As much, or more, we should ourselves complain:
So thou, that hast no unkind mate to grieve thee,
With urging helpless patience would relieve me:
But, if thou live to see like right bereft,
This fool-begg'd patience ᵇ in thee will be left.
Luc. Well, I will marry one day, but to try;—
Here comes your man, now is your husband nigh.

Enter DROMIO *of* Ephesus.

Adr. Say, is your tardy master now at hand?
Dro. E. Nay, he is at two hands with me, and that my two ears can witness.
Adr. Say, did'st thou speak with him? know'st thou his mind?
Dro. E. Ay, ay, he told his mind upon mine ear. Beshrew his hand, I scarce could understand it.
Luc. Spake he so doubtfully thou couldst not feel his meaning?
Dro. E. Nay, he struck so plainly I could too well feel his blows; and withal so doubtfully that I could scarce understand them.ᶜ
Adr. But say, I prithee, is he coming home? It seems he hath great care to please his wife.
Dro. E. Why, mistress, sure my master is horn-mad.
Adr. Horn-mad, thou villain?
Dro. E. I mean not cuckold mad; but, sure, he's stark mad:
When I desir'd him to come home to dinner, He asked me for a thousand marks in gold:

'"'T is dinner-time,' quoth I; 'My gold,' quoth he;
'Your meat doth burn,' quoth I; 'My gold,' quoth he;
'Will you come home?' quoth I; 'My gold,' quoth he:
'Where is the thousand marks I gave thee, villain?'
'The pig,' quoth I, 'is burn'd;' 'My gold,' quoth he:
'My mistress, sir,' quoth I; 'Hang up thy mistress;
I know not thy mistress; out on thy mistress!'
Luc. Quoth who?
Dro. E. Quoth my master:
'I know,' quoth he, 'no house, no wife, no mistress;'
So that my errand, due unto my tongue,
I thank him, I bare home upon my shoulders;
For, in conclusion, he did beat me there.
Adr. Go back again, thou slave, and fetch him home.
Dro. E. Go back again, and be new beaten home?
For God's sake send some other messenger.
Adr. Back, slave, or I will break thy pate across.
Dro. E. And he will bless that cross with other beating:
Between you I shall have a holy head.
Adr. Hence, prating peasant; fetch thy master home.
Dro. E. Am I so round with you, as you with me,
That like a football you do spurn me thus?ᵃ
You spurn me hence, and he will spurn me hither:
If I last in this service you must case me in leather. [*Exit.*
Luc. Fye, how impatience loureth in your face!
Adr. His company must do his minions grace,
Whilst I at home starve for a merry look.
Hath homely age the alluring beauty took
From my poor cheek? then he hath wasted it:
Are my discourses dull? barren my wit?
If voluble and sharp discourse be marr'd,
Unkindness blunts it, more than marble hard.
Do their gay vestments his affections bait?
That's not my fault, he's master of my state:
What ruins are in me that can be found
By him not ruin'd? then is he the ground

ᵃ **Johnson** would read, "start some other *here.*" But *where* has here the power of a noun, and is used, as in Henry VIII., "the king hath sent me *otherwhere.*" We have lost this mode of using *where* in composition; but we retain *otherwise*, in a different *guise;* we understand *otherwhile,* at a different time; and we can therefore have no difficulty with *otherwhere,* in a different *place.*

ᵇ The allusion is to the practice of "begging a fool" for the guardianship of his fortune. (See Love's Labour's Lost, Illustrations of Act V.) This abominable prerogative of the Crown seems to have been continued as late as the time of Congreve. In the 'Way of the World,' on Witwould's inquiring what he should do with the fool, his brother, Petulant, replies, "Beg him for his estate, that I may beg you afterwards, and so have but one trouble with you both."

ᶜ *Understand them,*—stand under them. We have the same quibble in the Two Gentlemen of Verona—"My staff understands me." Milton does not disdain to make Belial, "in gamesome mood," use a similar playupon words. (See Paradise Lost, book vi. v. 625.)

ᵃ To be *round* with any one is to be plain-spoken; as in Hamlet: "Let her be *round* with him." Dromio uses the word in a double sense, when he alludes to the foot-ball.

Of my defeatures:* My decayed fair
A sunny look of his would soon repair;
But, too unruly deer, he breaks the pale,
And feeds from home: poor I am but his stale.[b]
  Luc. Self-harming jealousy!—fye, beat it hence.
  Adr. Unfeeling fools can with such wrongs dispense.
I know his eye doth homage otherwhere;
Or else, what lets it but he would be here?
Sister, you know he promis'd me a chain;—
Would that alone alone he would detain,[c]
So he would keep fair quarter with his bed!
I see, the jewel best enamelled
Will lose his beauty; and though gold 'bides still,
That others touch, yet often touching will[d]
Wear gold; and so no man that hath a name,
But falsehood and corruption doth it shame.[e]
Since that my beauty cannot please his eye,
I'll weep what's left away, and weeping die.
  Luc. How many fond fools serve mad jealousy! [*Exeunt.*

SCENE II.—*The same.*

Enter ANTIPHOLUS *of Syracuse.*

  Ant. S. The gold I gave to Dromio is laid up
Safe at the Centaur; and the heedful slave
Is wander'd forth, in care to seek me out.
By computation, and mine host's report,
I could not speak with Dromio, since at first
I sent him from the mart: See, here he comes.

Enter DROMIO *of Syracuse.*

How now, sir? is your merry humour alter'd?
As you love strokes, so jest with me again.
You know no Centaur? you receiv'd no gold?

---

[a] *Defeatures.* Adriana asserts that her *defeatures*, her decayed fair—*fair* being used as a noun for beauty, and *defeatures* for the change in her features for the worse—have been caused by her husband's neglect. In Othello we have "*defeat* thy favours," meaning disguise thy countenance.

[b] *Stale* is stalking-horse; thus, in Ben Jonson's Catiline—
  "dull, stupid Lentulus,
  My *stale*, with whom I stalk."

[c] In the first folio we have
  "Would that alone a love he would detain."
The obvious error, says Malone, was corrected in the second folio. Mr. Dyce has pointed out that the repetition of *alone* has a precedent in Lucrece:—
  "But I alone, alone must sit and pine."
This emphasises the sentiment, but here the second *alone* perplexes the sense.

[d] *That others touch.* The Cambridge editors ingeniously suggest "*the jester's touch.*"

[e] This passage has been altered by Pope, Warburton, and Steevens, from the original; and it is so impossible to gain tolerable reading without changing the text, that we leave it as it is commonly received. In the first folio the reading is—
  "I see the jewel best enamelled
  Will lose his beauty; *yet* the gold bides still
  That others touch; *and* often touching will
  Where gold; and no man, that hath a name,
  By falsehood and corruption doth it shame."

Your mistress sent to have me home to dinner?
My house was at the Phœnix? Wast thou mad,
That thus so madly thou didst answer me?
  Dro. S. What answer, sir? when spake I such a word?
  Ant. S. Even now, even here, not half an hour since.
  Dro. S. I did not see you since you sent me hence,
Home to the Centaur, with the gold you gave me.
  Ant. S. Villain, thou didst deny the gold's receipt,
And told'st me of a mistress, and a dinner;
For which, I hope, thou felt'st I was displeas'd.
  Dro. S. I am glad to see you in this merry vein:
What means this jest? I pray you, master, tell me.
  Ant. S. Yea, dost thou jeer, and flout me in the teeth?
Think'st thou I jest? Hold, take thou that, and that. [*Beating him.*
  Dro. S. Hold, sir, for God's sake: now your jest is earnest:
Upon what bargain do you give it me?
  Ant. S. Because that I familiarly sometimes
Do use you for my fool, and chat with you,
Your sauciness will jest upon my love,
And make a common of my serious hours.[a]
When the sun shines let foolish gnats make sport,
But creep in crannies when he hides his beams.
If you will jest with me know my aspect,
And fashion your demeanour to my looks,
Or I will beat this method in your sconce.
  Dro. S. Sconce, call you it? so you would leave battering, I had rather have it a head: an you use these blows long, I must get a sconce for my head, and insconce it[b] too; or else I shall seek my wit in my shoulders. But, I pray sir, why am I beaten?
  Ant. S. Dost thou not know?
  Dro. S. Nothing, sir; but that I am beaten.
  Ant. S. Shall I tell you why?
  Dro. S. Ay, sir, and wherefore; for, they say, every why hath a wherefore.
  Ant. S. Why, first,—for flouting me; and then, wherefore,—
For urging it the second time to me.
  Dro. S Was there ever any man thus beaten out of season?

---

[a] The "serious hours" of Antipholus are his *private hours*. The "sauciness" of Dromio intrudes upon those hours, and deprives his master of his exclusive possession of them,—makes them "*a common*" property.

[b] *Insconce it*—defend it—fortify it.

When, in the why, and the wherefore, is neither
  rhyme nor reason?—
Well, sir, I thank you.

Ant. S. Thank me, sir? for what?

Dro. S. Marry, sir, for this something that you gave me for nothing.

Ant. S. I'll make you amends next, to give you nothing for something. But, say, sir, is it dinner-time?

Dro. S. No, sir; I think the meat wants that I have.

Ant. S. In good time, sir, what's that?

Dro. S. Basting.

Ant. S. Well, sir, then 't will be dry.

Dro. S. If it be, sir, I pray you eat none of it.

Ant. S. Your reason?

Dro. S. Lest it make you choleric, and purchase me another dry basting.

Ant. S. Well, sir, learn to jest in good time. There's a time for all things.

Dro. S. I durst have denied that, before you were so choleric.

Ant. S. By what rule, sir?

Dro. S. Marry, sir, by a rule as plain as the plain bald pate of father Time himself.

Ant. S. Let's hear it.

Dro. S. There's no time for a man to recover his hair, that grows bald by nature.

Ant. S. May he not do it by fine and recovery?[a]

Dro. S. Yes, to pay a fine for a periwig,[b] and recover the lost hair of another man.

Ant. S. Why is Time such a niggard of hair, being, as it is, so plentiful an excrement?

Dro. S. Because it is a blessing that he bestows on beasts: and what he hath scanted men in hair, he hath given them in wit.

Ant. S. Why, but there's many a man hath more hair than wit.

Dro. S. Not a man of those but he hath the wit to lose his hair.

Ant. S. Why, thou didst conclude hairy men plain dealers without wit.

Dro. S. The plainer dealer, the sooner lost: Yet he loseth it in a kind of jollity.

Ant. S. For what reason?

Dro. S. For two; and sound ones too.

Ant. S. Nay, not sound, I pray you.

Dro. S. Sure ones then.

Ant. S. Nay, not sure, in a thing falsing.[a]

Dro. S. Certain ones then.

Ant. S. Name them.

Dro. S. The one, to save the money that he spends in tiring;[b] the other, that at dinner they should not drop in his porridge.

Ant. S. You would all this time have proved there is no time for all things.

Dro. S. Marry, and did, sir; namely, in no time to recover hair lost by nature.

Ant. S. But your reason was not substantial, why there is no time to recover.

Dro. S. Thus I mend it: Time himself is bald, and therefore, to the world's end, will have bald followers.

Ant. S. I knew 't would be a bald conclusion: But soft! who wafts us yonder?

Enter ADRIANA *and* LUCIANA.

Adr. Ay, ay, Antipholus, look strange, and frown;
Some other mistress hath thy sweet aspects:
I am not Adriana, nor thy wife.
The time was once, when thou unurg'd would'st vow
That never words were music to thine ear,
That never object pleasing in thine eye,
That never touch well-welcome to thy hand,
That never meat sweet savour'd in thy taste,
Unless I spake, or look'd, or touch'd, or carv'd to thee.
How comes it now, my husband, oh, how comes it,
That thou art then estranged from thyself?
Thyself I call it, being strange to me,
That, undividable, incorporate,
Am better than thy dear self's better part.
Ah, do not tear away thyself from me;
For know, my love, as easy may'st thou fall[c]
A drop of water in the breaking gulph,
And take unmingled thence that drop again,
Without addition or diminishing,
As take from me thyself, and not me too.
How dearly would it touch thee to the quick
Should'st thou but hear I were licentious?

---

[a] *Falsing*—the participle of the obsolete verb *to false.* Shakspere uses this verb once, viz. in Cymbeline, Act II., Scene III:—
  "'T is gold
  Which buys admittance: oft it doth; yea, and makes
  Diana's rangers *false* themselves."
In Chaucer (Rom. of the Rose), we have—
  "They *falsen* ladies traitorously."
The verb is commonly used by Spenser,—as
  "Thou *falsed* hast thy faith with perjury."

[b] *Tiring*—attiring. In the folio we have *trying*, an obvious typographical error, corrected by Pope. Mr. Collier, Mr. Dyce, and Mr. White, suggest *trimming*.

[c] *Fall* is here used as a verb active

---

[a] [In this, as in all Shakspere's early plays, and in his Poems, we have the professional jokes of the attorney's office in great abundance
[b] *Periwig*. This, the word in the folio, is ordinarily printed *peruke*

And that this body, consecrate to thee,
By ruffian lust should be contaminate?
Would'st thou not spit at me, and spurn at me,
And hurl the name of husband in my face,
And tear the stain'd skin of[a] my harlot brow,
And from my false hand cut the wedding ring,
And break it with a deep-divorcing vow?
I know thou canst; and therefore see thou do it.
I am possess'd with an adulterate blot;
My blood is mingled with the grime of lust:[b]
For, if we two be one, and thou play false,
I do digest the poison of thy flesh,
Being strumpeted by thy contagion.
Keep then fair league and truce with thy true bed;
I live dis-stain'd,[c] thou, undishonoured.

  Ant. S. Plead you to me, fair dame? I know you not:
In Ephesus I am but two hours old,
As strange unto your town, as to your talk;
Who, every word by all my wit being scann'd,
Want wit in all one word to understand.

  Luc. Fye, brother! how the world is chang'd with you:
When were you wont to use my sister thus?
She sent for you by Dromio home to dinner.

  Ant. S. By Dromio?

  Dro. S. By me?

  Adr. By thee; and this thou didst return from him,—
That he did buffet thee, and, in his blows
Denied my house for his, me for his wife.

  Ant. S. Did you converse, sir, with this gentlewoman?
What is the course and drift of your compact?

  Dro. S. I, sir? I never saw her till this time.

  Ant. S. Villain, thou liest; for even her very words
Didst thou deliver to me on the mart.

  Dro. S. I never spake with her in all my life.

  Ant. S. How can she thus then call us by our names,
Unless it be by inspiration?

  Adr. How ill agrees it with your gravity,
To counterfeit thus grossly with your slave,
Abetting him to thwart me in my mood?
Be it my wrong, you are from me exempt,[d]
But wrong not that wrong with a more contempt.

Come, I will fasten on this sleeve of thine:
Thou art an elm, my husband, I, a vine;[a]
Whose weakness, married to thy stronger state,
Makes me with thy strength to communicate:
If aught possess thee from me, it is dross,
Usurping ivy, briar, or idle[b] moss;
Who, all for want of pruning, with intrusion
Infect thy sap, and live on thy confusion.

  Ant. S. To me she speaks; she moves me for her theme:
What, was I married to her in my dream?
Or sleep I now, and think I hear all this?
What error drives our eyes and ears amiss?
Until I know this sure, uncertainly[c]
I'll entertain the offer'd[d] fallacy.

  Luc. Dromio, go bid the servants spread for dinner.

  Dro. S. O, for my beads! I cross me for a sinner.
This is the fairy land;[e]—O, spite of spites!
We talk with goblins, owls,[e] and elvish sprites;
If we obey them not, this will ensue,
They'll suck our breath, or pinch us black and blue.

  Luc. Why, prat'st thou to thyself, and answer'st not?
Dromio, thou drone, thou snail, thou slug, thou sot!

  Dro. S. I am transformed, master, am not I?

  Ant. S. I think thou art, in mind, and so am I.

  Dro. S. Nay, master, both in mind, and in my shape.

  Ant. S. Thou hast thine own form.

  Dro. S. No, I am an ape.

  Luc. If thou art chang'd to aught, 't is to an ass.

  Dro. S. 'T is true; she rides me, and I long for grass.

---

[a] When Milton uses this classical image, in Paradise Lost,
"They led the vine
To wed the elm; she, spous'd, about him twines
Her marriageable arms,"
the annotators of our great epic poet naturally give us the parallel passages in Catullus, in Ovid, in Virgil, in Horace. Shakspere unquestionably had the image from the same sources. It appears to us that this line of Shakspere is neither a translation nor an imitation of any of the well-known classical passages; but a transfusion of the spirit of the ancient poets by one who was familiar with them.

[b] *Idle*—useless, fruitless,—as in "deserts *idle*." An *addle* egg is an *idle* egg. Shakspere plays upon the words in Troilus and Cressida: "If you love an *addle* egg as well as you love an *idle* head, you would eat chickens i' the shell."

[c] *Sure, uncertainty.*—We adopt the reading of the Cambridge Editors.

[d] *Offer'd*—In the first folio, *freed*.

[e] *Owls*—Theobald changed *owls* to *ouphes*, upon the plea that owls could not suck breath and pinch. Warburton maintains that the owl here is the *stria* of the ancients—the destroyer of the cradled infant—
"Nocte volant, puerosque petunt nutricis egentes,
Et vitiant cunis corpora rapta suis."
Ovid, Fasti, lib. vi.

[f] *Elvish* is wanting in the first folio, but is found in the second, misprinted "elves."

---

[a] *Of*—so the folio; Steevens unnecessarily substituted *off*.
[b] *Grime*—suggested by Warburton instead of *crime* in the folio.
[c] *Dis-stained* in the folio.
[d] *Exempt.* Johnson says the word here means *separated*. But surely Adriana intends to say that she must bear the wrong; that Antipholus, being her husband, is released, acquitted, *exempt*, from any consequences of this wrong.

'T is so, I am an ass; else it could never be,
But I should know her as well as she knows
    me.
  Adr. Come, come, no longer will I be a
    fool,
To put the finger in the eye and weep,
Whilst man, and master, laugh my woes to
    scorn.
Come, sir, to dinner; Dromio, keep the gate:—
Husband, I 'll dine above with you to-day,
And shrive you of a thousand idle pranks:
Sirrah, if any ask you for your master,
Say, he dines forth, and let no creature enter.
Come, sister:—Dromio, play the porter well.
  Ant. S. Am I in earth, in heaven, or in hell?
Sleeping, or waking? mad, or well advis'd?
Known unto these, and to myself disguis'd!
I 'll say as they say, and persever so,
And in this mist at all adventures go.
  Dro. S. Master, shall I be porter at the gate?
  Adr. Ay; and let none enter, lest I break
    your pate.
  Luc. Come, come, Antipholus, we dine too
    late.   [*Exeunt.*

[Remains of Aqueduct at Ephesus.]

ILLUSTRATIONS OF ACT II.

[1] SCENE II.—"*This is the fairy land.*"

In the first act we have the following description of the unlawful arts of Ephesus:—

> "They say this town is full of cozenage;
> As, nimble jugglers that deceive the eye,
> Dark-working sorcerers that change the mind,
> Soul-killing witches that deform the body,
> Disguised cheaters, prating mountebanks,
> And many such like liberties of sin."

't was observed by Capell that "the character given of Ephesus in this place is the very same that it had with the ancients, which may pass for some note of the poet's learning." It was scarcely necessary, however, for Shakspere to search for this ancient character of Ephesus in more recondite sources than the most interesting narrative of St. Paul's visit to the city, given in the 19th chapter of the Acts of the Apostles. In the 13th verse we find mention of "certain of the vagabond Jews *exorcists;*" and in the 19th verse we are told that "many of them also which used *curious arts* brought their books together, and burned them before all men." The ancient proverbial term, *Ephesian Letters*, was used to express every kind of charm or spell.

[Syracuse.]

ACT III.

SCENE I.—*The same.*

Enter ANTIPHOLUS *of* Ephesus, DROMIO *of* Ephesus, ANGELO, *and* BALTHAZAR.

Ant. E. Good signior Angelo, you must excuse us all:
My wife is shrewish, when I keep not hours:
Say, that I linger'd with you at your shop,
To see the making of her carcanet,*
And that to-morrow you will bring it home.
But here's a villain, that would face me down
He met me on the mart; and that I beat him,
And charg'd him with a thousand marks in gold;
And that I did deny my wife and house:—
Thou drunkard, thou, what didst thou mean by this?

---

* *Carcanet*—a chain, or necklace. In Harrington's Orlando Furioso we have—
   "About his neck a *carknet* rich he ware."

Dro. E. Say what you will, sir, but I know what I know:
That you beat me at the mart, I have your hand to show:
If the skin were parchment, and the blows you gave were ink,
Your own handwriting would tell you what I think.
Ant. E. I think thou art an ass.
Dro. E.   Marry, so it doth appear
By the wrongs I suffer and the blows I bear.
I should kick, being kick'd; and, being at that pass,
You would keep from my heels, and beware of an ass.
Ant. E. You are sad, signior Balthazar:
'Pray God, our cheer
May answer my good will, and your good welcome here.

Bal. I hold your dainties cheap, sir, and your welcome dear.
Ant. E. O, signior Balthazar, either at flesh or fish,
A table full of welcome makes scarce one dainty dish.
Bal. Good meat, sir, is common; that every churl affords.
Ant. E. And welcome more common; for that's nothing but words.
Bal Small cheer, and great welcome, makes a merry feast.
Ant. E. Ay, to a niggardly host, and more sparing guest,
But though my cates be mean, take them in good part;
Better cheer may you have, but not with better heart.
But, soft; my door is lock'd. Go bid them let us in.
Dro. E. Maud, Bridget, Marian, Cicely, Gillian, Jen'!
Dro. S. [*Within.*] Mome,* malt-horse, capon, coxcomb, idiot, patch![b]
Either get thee from the door, or sit down at the hatch:
Dost thou conjure for wenches, that thou call'st for such store,
When one is one too many? Go, get thee from the door.
Dro. E. What patch is made our porter? my master stays in the street.
Dro. S. Let him walk from whence he came, lest he catch cold on's feet.
Ant. E. Who talks within there? ho! open the door.
Dro. S. Right, sir, I'll tell you when, an you'll tell me wherefore.
Ant. E. Wherefore? for my dinner; I have not din'd to-day.
Dro. S. Nor to-day here you must not; come again when you may.
Ant. E. What art thou, that keep'st me out from the house I owe?
Dro. S. The porter for this time, sir, and my name is Dromio.
Dro. E. O villain, thou hast stolen both mine office and my name;
The one ne'er got me credit, the other mickle blame.

If thou had'st been Dromio to-day in my place,
Thou wouldst have chang'd thy face for a name, or thy name for an ass.
Luce. [*Within.*] What a coil is there! Dromio, who are those at the gate?
Dro. E. Let my master in, Luce.
Luce.   Faith no; he comes too late;
And so tell your master.
Dro. E.   O Lord, I must laugh;—
Have at you with a proverb.—Shall I set in my staff?
Luce. Have at you with another: that's,— When? can you tell?
Dro. S. If thy name be called Luce, Luce, thou hast answer'd him well.
Ant. E. Do you hear, you minion? you'll let us in, I hope?
Luce. I thought to have ask'd you.
Dro. S.   And you said, no.
Dro. E. So, come, help; well struck; there was blow for blow.
Ant. E. Thou baggage, let me in.
Luce.   Can you tell for whose sake.
Dro. E. Master, knock the door hard.
Luce.   Let him knock till it ake.
Ant. E. You'll cry for this, minion, if I beat the door down.
Luce. What needs all that, and a pair of stocks in the town?
Adr. [*Within.*] Who is that at the door, that keeps all this noise?
Dro. S. By my troth your town is troubled with unruly boys.
Ant. E. Are you there, wife? you might have come before.
Adr. Your wife, sir knave! go, get you from the door.
Dro. E. If you went in pain, master, this knave would go sore.
Ang. Here is neither cheer, sir, nor welcome; we would fain have either.
Bal. In debating which was best, we shall part with neither.[a]
Dro. E. They stand at the door, master; bid them welcome hither.
Ant. E. There is something in the wind, that we cannot get in.
Dro. E. You would say so, master, if your garments were thin.
Your cake here is warm within; you stand here in the cold:
It would make a man mad as a buck to be so bought and sold.

a Part with—depart with.

a Mome. It is difficult to attach a precise meaning to mome. Some say it is one who plays in a mummery, a buffoon. The derivation is French, and a modern French Dictionary explains it as a young thief, and says it is applied to the *gamins* of Paris.
b Patch is a pretender, a deceitful fellow, one who is patched up. *Patch*, as applied to a fool, has only a secondary meaning. Shakspere uses *patchery* in the sense of roguery: "Here is such patchery, such juggling, and such knavery."—(Troilus and Cressida.)

Ant. E. Go, fetch me something, I'll break ope the gate.

Dro. S. Break any breaking here, and I'll break your knave's pate.

Dro. E. A man may break a word with you, sir; and words are but wind.

Ay, and break it in your face, so he break it not behind.

Dro. S. It seems, thou wantest breaking; Out upon thee, hind!

Dro. E. Here's too much, out upon thee! I pray thee, let me in.

Dro. S. Ay. when fowls have no feathers, and fish have no fin.

Ant. E. Well, I'll break in; Go, borrow me a crow.

Dro. E. A crow without feather; master, mean you so?

For a fish without a fin, there's a fowl without a feather:

If a crow help us in, sirrah, we'll pluck a crow together.

Ant. E. Go, get thee gone, fetch me an iron crow.

Bal. Have patience, sir, O let it not be so.
Herein you war against your reputation,
And draw within the compass of suspect
The unviolated honour of your wife.
Once this,ᵃ—Your long experience of her wisdom,
Her sober virtue, years, and modesty,
Plead on her part some cause to you unknown;
And doubt not, sir, but she will well excuse
Why at this time the doors are made against you.ᵇ
Be rul'd by me; depart in patience,
And let us to the Tiger all to dinner:
And, about evening, come yourself alone,
To know the reason of this strange restraint.
If by strong hand you offer to break in,
Now in the stirring passage of the day,
A vulgar comment will be made of it;
And that supposed by the common rout
Against your yet ungalled estimation,
That may with foul intrusion enter in,
And dwell upon your grave when you are dead:
For slander lives upon succession;
For ever housed, where it gets possession.

Ant. E. You have prevail'd. I will depart in quiet,
And, in despite of mirth, mean to be merry.
I know a wench of excellent discourse;
Pretty and witty; wild, and, yet too, gentle;—
There will we dine: this woman that I mean,
My wife (but, I protest, without desert,)

ᵃ *Once this*—once for all.
ᵇ To make the door is still a provincial expression.

Hath oftentimes upbraided me withal;
To her will we to dinner. Get you home,
And fetch the chain; by this, I know, 't is made:
Bring it, I pray you, to the Porpentine;*
For there's the house; that chain will I bestow
(Be it for nothing but to spite my wife,)
Upon mine hostess there: good sir, make haste:
Since mine own doors refuse to entertain me,
I'll knock elsewhere, to see if they'll disdain me.

Ang. I'll meet you at that place, some hour hence.

Ant. E. Do so. This jest shall cost me some expence. [*Exeunt.*

SCENE II.—*The same.*

Enter LUCIANA *and* ANTIPHOLUS *of Syracuse.*

Luc. And may it be that you have quite forgot
A husband's office? shall, Antipholus,
Even in the spring of love, thy love-springs rot?
Shall love, in building, grow so ruinous?ᵇ
If you did wed my sister for her wealth,
Then, for her wealth's sake, use her with more kindness:
Or, if you like elsewhere, do it by stealth;
Muffle your false love with some show of blindness:
Let not my sister read it in your eye;
Be not thy tongue thy own shame's orator;
Look sweet, speak fair, become disloyalty;
Apparel vice like virtue's harbinger:
Bear a fair presence, though your heart be tainted;
Teach sin the carriage of a holy saint;
Be secret-false: What need she be acquainted?
What simple thief brags of his own attaint?
'T is double wrong to truant with your bed,
And let her read it in thy looks at board:
Shame hath a bastard fame, well managed;
Ill deeds are doubled with an evil word.
Alas, poor women! make us but believe,
Being compact of credit,ᶜ that you love us;
Though others have the arm, show us the sleeve
We in your motion turn, and you may move us.

* *Porpentine.* This word, which has the same meaning as Porcupine, is invariably used throughout the early editions of Shakspere. It was no doubt the familiar word in Shakspere's time, and ought not to be changed.

ᵇ *Ruinate,* instead of *ruinous,* is the reading of the folio. To make a rhyme to *ruinate,* Theobald inserted the word *hate,* in the second line—" Shall, Antipholus, *hate,*"—shall hate not thy love-springs? The correction of *ruinate* to *ruinous,* suggested by Steevens, though not adopted by him, is much more satisfactory. It is to be observed that Antipholus is the prevailing orthography of the folio, though in some places we have Antipholis. *Love-springs* are the early shoots of love, as in the Venus and Adonis—
"This canker that eats up love's tender *spring.*"

ᶜ *Compact of credit*—credulous.

Then, gentle brother, get you in again;
  Comfort my sister, cheer her, call her wife:
'T is holy sport, to be a little vain,[a]
  When the sweet breath of flattery conquers
    strife.
Ant. S. Sweet mistress, (what your name is else,
    I know not,
  Nor by what wonder you do hit of mine,)
Less, in your knowledge, and your grace, you
    show not,
  Than our earth's wonder; more than earth
    divine.
Teach me, dear creature, how to think and speak;
  Lay open to my earthy gross conceit,
Smother'd in errors, feeble, shallow, weak,
  The folded meaning of your words' deceit.
Against my soul's pure truth why labour you,
  To make it wander in an unknown field?
Are you a god? would you create me new?
  Transform me then, and to your power I'll
    yield.
But if that I am I, then well I know,
  Your weeping sister is no wife of mine,
Nor to her bed no homage do I owe;
  Far more, far more, to you do I decline.
O, train me not, sweet mermaid, with thy note,
  To drown me in thy sister flood of tears;
Sing, siren, for thyself, and I will dote:
  Spread o'er the silver waves thy golden hairs,
And, as a bed,[b] I'll take thee and there lie;
  And, in that glorious supposition, think
He gains by death, that hath such means to die:—
Let love,[c] being light, be drowned if she sink!
Luc. What, are you mad, that you do reason
    so?
Ant. S. Not mad, but mated;[d] how, I do not
    know.
Luc. It is a fault that springeth from your eye.
Ant. S. For gazing on your beams, fair sun,
    being by.
Luc. Gaze where you should, and that will
    clear your sight.
Ant. S. As good to wink, sweet love, as look
    on night.
Luc. Why call you me love? call my sister so.
Ant. S. Thy sister's sister.

---

[a] *Vain*—Johnson interprets this *light of tongue.*
[b] *Bed*—the first folio reads *bud.* The second folio, *bed.* "The golden hairs" which are "spread o'er the silver waves" will form the bed of the lover. Mr. Dyce would read—
  "And as a *bride* I'll take thee."
[c] *Love* is here used as the queen of love. In the Venus and Adonis, Venus, speaking of herself, says—
  "Love is a spirit, all compact with fire,
  Not gross to sink, but light, and will aspire."
[d] *To mate—to amate—*is to make senseless,—to stupify or in a dream. *Maton* (A. S.) is to dream.

Luc. That's my sister.
Ant. S. No;
It is thyself, mine own self's better part;
Mine eye's clear eye, my dear heart's dearer
    heart;
My food, my fortune, and my sweet hope's aim,
My sole earth's heaven, and my heaven's claim.
Luc. All this my sister is, or else should be.
Ant. S. Call thyself sister, sweet, for I aim thee
Thee will I love, and with thee lead my life;
Thou hast no husband yet, nor I no wife:
Give me thy hand.
Luc.   O, soft, sir, hold you still;
I'll fetch my sister, to get her good will.
  [*Exit* Luc.

Enter from the house of ANTIPHOLUS *of* Ephesus
  DROMIO *of* Syracuse.

Ant. S. Why, how now, Dromio? where
    run'st thou so fast?
Dro. S. Do you know me, sir? am I Dromio?
    am I your man? am I myself?
Ant. S. Thou art Dromio, thou art my man,
    thou art thyself.
Dro. S. I am an ass, I am a woman's man,
    and besides myself.
Ant. S. What woman's man? and how be-
    sides thyself?
Dro. S. Marry, sir, besides myself, I am due
    to a woman; one that claims me, one that haunts
    me, one that will have me.
Ant. S. What claim lays she to thee?
Dro. S. Marry, sir, such claim as you would
    lay to your horse; and she would have me as a
    beast: not that, I being a beast, she would have
    me; but that she, being a very beastly creature,
    lays claim to me.
Ant. S. What is she?
Dro. S. A very reverent body; ay, such a one
    as a man may not speak of, without he say, sir
    reverence:[a] I have but lean luck in the match,
    and yet is she a wondrous fat marriage.
Ant. S. How dost thou mean a fat mar-
    riage?
Dro. S. Marry, sir, she's the kitchen-wench,
    and all grease; and I know not what use to put
    her to, but to make a lamp of her, and run from
    her by her own light. I warrant, her rags, and
    the tallow in them, will burn a Poland winter:
    if she lives till doomsday, she'll burn a week
    longer than the whole world.
Ant. S. What complexion is she of?
Dro. S. Swart, like my shoe, but her face no-

---

[a] See Illustrations to Romeo and Juliet, Act I. When anything offensive was spoken of, this form of apology was used.

thing like so clean kept. For why? she sweats;
a man may go over shoes in the grime of it.
 Ant. S. That's a fault that water will mend.
 Dro. S. No, sir, 't is in grain; Noah's flood could not do it.
 Ant. S. What's her name?
 Dro. S. Nell, sir;—but her name and three quarters, that is an ell and three quarters, will not measure her from hip to hip.
 Ant. S. Then she bears some breadth?
 Dro. S. No longer from head to foot, than from hip to hip; she is spherical, like a globe. I could find out countries in her.[1]
 Ant. S. In what part of her body stands Ireland?
 Dro. S. Marry, sir, in her buttocks. I found it out by the bogs.
 Ant. S. Where Scotland?[2]
 Dro. S. I found it by the barrenness; hard, in the palm of the hand.
 Ant. S. Where France?
 Dro. S. In her forehead; armed and reverted, making war against her hair.[3]
 Ant. S. Where England?
 Dro. S. I looked for the chalky cliffs, but I could find no whiteness in them: but I guess, it stood in her chin, by the salt rheum that ran between France and it.
 Ant. S. Where Spain?
 Dro. S. Faith, I saw it not; but I felt it, hot in her breath.
 Ant. S. Where America, the Indies?[4]
 Dro. S. O, sir, upon her nose, all o'er embellished with rubies, carbuncles, sapphires, declining their rich aspect to the hot breath of Spain; who sent whole armadas of carracks to be ballast at her nose.
 Ant. S. Where stood Belgia, the Netherlands?
 Dro. S. O, sir, I did not look so low. To conclude, this drudge, or diviner, laid claim to me; called me Dromio; swore, I was assured[a] to her; told me what privy marks I had about me, as the mark of my shoulder, the mole in my neck, the great wart on my left arm, that I, amazed, ran from her as a witch:
And, I think, if my breast had not been made of faith, and my heart of steel,
She had transform'd me to a curtail-dog, and made me turn i' the wheel.[b]

 Ant. S. Go, hie thee presently, post to the road;
And if the wind blow any way from shore,
I will not harbour in this town to-night.
If any bark put forth, come to the mart,
Where I will walk, till thou return to me.
If every one knows us, and we know none,
'T is time, I think, to trudge, pack, and be gone.
 Dro. S. As from a bear a man would run for life,
So fly I from her that would be my wife.
 [Exit

 Ant. S. There's none but witches do inhabit here;
And therefore 't is high time that I were hence.
She, that doth call me husband, even my soul
Doth for a wife abhor: but her fair sister,
Possess'd with such a gentle sovereign grace,
Of such enchanting presence and discourse,
Hath almost made me traitor to myself.
But, lest myself be guilty to[*] self-wrong,
I'll stop mine ears against the mermaid's song.

 Enter ANGELO

 Ang. Master Antipholus?
 Ant. S. Ay, that's my name.
 Ang. I know it well, sir. Lo, here is the chain;
I thought to have ta'en you at the Porpentine:
The chain unfinish'd made me stay thus long.
 Ant. S. What is your will that I should do with this?
 Ang. What please yourself, sir; I have made it for you.
 Ant. S. Made it for me, sir! I bespoke it not.
 Ang. Not once, nor twice, but twenty times you have:
Go home with it, and please your wife withal;
And soon at supper-time I'll visit you,
And then receive my money for the chain.
 Ant. S. I pray you, sir, receive the money now,
For fear you ne'er see chain, nor money more.
 Ang. You are a merry man, sir; fare you well. [Exit
 Ant. S. What I should think of this, I cannot tell:

---

[a] *Assured*—affianced.
[b] We have printed these two lines as verse. The doggrel, like some of Swift's similar attempts, contains a superabundance of syllables; but we have little doubt that Dromio's description of the kitchen-maid was intended to conclude emphatically with rhyme.

[*] *Guilty to*—not *of*,—was the phraseology of Shakspere's time.

But this I think, there's no man is so vain
That would refuse so fair an offer'd chain.
I see, a man here needs not live by shifts,
When in the streets he meets such golden gifts.

I'll to the mart, and there for Dromio stay;
If any ship put out then straight away.

[*Exit.*

Sing, Siren.

ILLUSTRATIONS OF ACT III.

¹ SCENE II.—"*I could find out countries in her.*"

SHAKSPERE most probably had the idea from Rabelais, in the passage where Friar John maps out the head and chin of Panurge (L. 3. c. 28.) "Ta barbe par les distinctions du gris, du blanc, du tanné, et du noir, me semble une mappe-monde. Regarde ici. Voilà Asie. Ici sont Tigris et Euphrates. Voilà Afrique. Ici est la montaigne de la Lune. Vois-tu les palus du Nil? Deçà est Europe. Vois-tu Thelême? Ce touppet ici tout blanc, sont les monts Hyperborées."

² SCENE II.—"*Where Scotland?*"

In the 'Merchant of Venice,' where Portia describes her suitors to Nerissa, we have an allusion,—sarcastic although playful,—to the ancient contests of Scotland with England, and of the support which France generally rendered to the weaker side:

Ner. "What think you of the Scottish lord, his neighbour?

Por. That he hath a neighbourly charity in him; for he borrowed a box of the ear of the Englishman, and swore he would pay him again, when he was able: I think the Frenchman became his surety, and sealed under for another."

The word *Scottish* is found in the original quarto of this play, but in the folio of 1623 it is changed to *other*. Malone considers that the 'Merchant of Venice' being performed in the time of James, the allusion to Scotland was suppressed by the Master of the Revels; but that the more offensive allusion to the "barrenness" of Scotland, in the passage before us being retained in the original folio edition, is a proof that the 'Comedy of Errors' was not revived after the accession of the Scottish monarch to the English throne.

³ SCENE II.—"*Making war against her hair.*"

It seems to be pretty generally agreed that this passage is an allusion to the war of the League. In the first folio we have the spelling *heire*, although in the second folio it was changed to *haire*. Upon the assassination of Henry III., in August, 1589, the great contest commenced between his *heir*, Henry of Navarre, and the Leaguers, who opposed his succession. In 1591 Elizabeth sent an armed force to the assistance of Henry. If the supposition that this allusion was meant by Shakspere be correct, the date of the play is pretty exactly determined; for the war of the League was in effect concluded by Henry's renunciation of the Protestant faith in 1593.

⁴ SCENE II.—"*Where America, the Indies?*"

This is certainly one of the boldest anachronisms in Shakspere; for, although the period of the action of the 'Comedy of Errors' may include a range of four or five centuries, it must certainly be placed before the occupation of the city by the Mohammedans, and therefore some centuries before the discovery of America.

[Remains of the Gymnasium, Ephesus.]

ACT IV.

SCENE I.—*The same.*

Enter a Merchant, ANGELO, *and an* Officer.

Mer. You know, since Pentecost the sum is
 due,
And since I have not much importun'd you,
Nor now I had not, but that I am bound
To Persia, and want gilders for my voyage:
Therefore make present satisfaction,
Or I'll attach you by this officer.
 Ang. Even just the sum that I do owe to you,
Is growing to me* by Antipholus:
And, in the instant that I met with you,
He had of me a chain; at five o'clock,
I shall receive the money for the same:
Pleaseth you walk with me down to his house,
I will discharge my bond, and thank you too.

Enter ANTIPHOLUS *of* Ephesus, *and* DROMIO *of*
 Ephesus.

 Off. That labour may you save; see where he
 comes.
 Ant. E. While I go to the goldsmith's house,
 go thou
And buy a rope's end; that will I bestow
Among my wife and her confederates,
For locking me out of my doors by day.
But soft, I see the goldsmith:—get thee gone;
Buy thou a rope, and bring it home to me.

———
 * *Growing to me—accruing to me.*
240

Dro. E. I buy a thousand pound a year! I
 buy a rope! [*Exit* DROMIO.
 Ant. E. A man is well holp up that trusts to
 you.
I promised your presence, and the chain;
But neither chain, nor goldsmith, came to me:
Belike, you thought our love would last too long,
If it were chain'd together; and therefore came
 not.
 Ang. Saving your merry humour, here's the
 note
How much your chain weighs to the utmost carat;
The fineness of the gold, and chargeful fashion;
Which doth amount to three odd ducats more
Than I stand debted to this gentleman:
I pray you, see him presently discharg'd,
For he is bound to sea, and stays but for it.
 Ant. E. I am not furnish'd with the present
 money;
Besides I have some business in the town:
Good signior, take the stranger to my house,
And with you take the chain, and bid my wife
Disburse the sum on the receipt thereof;
Perchance, I will be there* as soon as you.
 Ang. Then you will bring the chain to her
 yourself?
 Ant. E. No; bear it with you, lest I come
 not time enough.

———
 * *I will,* instead of *I shall,* is a Scotticism, says Douce
(an Englishman); it is an Irishism, says Reed (a Scotsman); and an ancient Anglicism, says Malone (an Irishman).

Ang. Well, sir, I will: Have you the chain about you?

Ant. E. An if I have not, sir, I hope you have;
Or else you may return without your money.

Ang. Nay, come, I pray you, sir, give me the chain;
Both wind and tide stays for this gentleman,
And I, to blame, have held him here too long.

Ant. E. Good lord, you use this dalliance to excuse
Your breach of promise to the Porpentine:
I should have chid you for not bringing it,
But, like a shrew, you first begin to brawl.

Mer. The hour steals on; I pray you, sir, despatch.

Ang. You hear, how he importunes me; the chain—

Ant. E. Why, give it to my wife, and fetch your money.

Ang. Come, come, you know I gave it you even now;
Either send the chain, or send me by some token.

Ant. E. Fye! now you run this humour out of breath:
Come, where 's the chain? I pray you, let me see it.

Mer. My business cannot brook this dalliance:
Good sir, say, whe'r you 'll answer me, or no;
If not, I 'll leave him to the officer.

Ant. E. I answer you! What should I answer you?

Ang. The money, that you owe me for the chain.

Ant. E. I owe you none, till I receive the chain.

Ang. You know, I gave it you half an hour since.

Ant. E. You gave me none; you wrong me much to say so.

Ang. You wrong me more, sir, in denying it:
Consider, how it stands upon my credit.

Mer. Well, officer, arrest him at my suit.

Off. I do; and charge you in the duke 's name, to obey me.

Ang. This touches me in reputation:—
Either consent to pay this sum for me,
Or I attach you by this officer.

Ant. E. Consent to pay thee that I never had!
Arrest me, foolish fellow, if thou dar'st.

Ang. Here is thy fee; arrest him, officer.
I would not spare my brother in this case,
If he should scorn me so apparently.

Off. I do arrest you, sir; you hear the suit.

Ant. E. I do obey thee, till I give thee bail:
But, sirrah, you shall buy this sport as dear
As all the metal in your shop will answer.

Ang. Sir, sir, I shall have law in Ephesus,
To your notorious shame, I doubt it not.

Enter DROMIO *of* Syracuse.

Dro. S. Master, there is a bark of Epidamnum,
That stays but till her owner comes aboard,
And then, sir, she bears away: our fraughtage, sir,
I have convey'd aboard; and I have bought
The oil, the balsamum, and aqua-vitæ.
The ship is in her trim; the merry wind
Blows fair from land: they stay for nought at all,
But for their owner, master, and yourself.

Ant. E. How now! a madman? Why thou peevish[a] sheep,
What ship of Epidamnum stays for me?

Dro. S. A ship you sent me to, to hire waftage.

Ant. E. Thou drunken slave, I sent thee for a rope;
And told thee to what purpose, and what end.

Dro. S. You sent me, sir, for a rope's-end as soon:
You sent me to the bay, sir, for a bark.

Ant. E. I will debate this matter at more leisure,
And teach your ears to list me with more heed.
To Adriana, villain, hie thee straight:
Give her this key, and tell her, in the desk
That 's cover'd o'er with Turkish tapestry,
There is a purse of ducats; let her send it;
Tell her, I am arrested in the street,
And that shall bail me: hie thee, slave; be gone.
On, officer, to prison till it come.

[*Exeunt* Merchant, ANGELO, Officer, *and* ANT. E.

Dro. S. To Adriana! that is where we din'd,
Where Dowsabel did claim me for her husband:
She is too big, I hope, for me to compass.
Thither I must, although against my will,
For servants must their masters' minds fulfil.

[*Exit*

SCENE II.—*The same.*

Enter ADRIANA *and* LUCIANA.

Adr. Ah, Luciana, did he tempt thee so?
Might'st thou perceive austerely in his eye
That he did plead in earnest, yea, or no?
Look'd he or red, or pale; or sad or merrily?

---

[a] *Peevish—silly. Sheep* and *ship* were pronounced alike
Thus Speed's jest in the Two Gentlemen of Verona—
"Twenty to one then he is shipp'd already,
And I have play'd the sheep in losing him."

What observation mad'st thou in this case,
Of his heart's meteors tilting in his face?
   Luc. First, he denied you had in him no
      right.[a]
   Adr. He meant, he did me none; the more
      my spite.
   Luc. Then swore he, that he was a stranger
      here.
   Adr. And true he swore, though yet forsworn
      he were.
   Luc. Then pleaded I for you.
   Adr.   And what said he?
   Luc. That love I begg'd for you, he begg'd
      of me.
   Adr. With what persuasion did he tempt thy
      love?
   Luc. With words that in an honest suit might
      move.
First, he did praise my beauty: then, my speech.
   Adr. Did'st speak him fair?
   Luc.   Have patience, I beseech.
   Adr. I cannot, nor I will not, hold me still;
My tongue, though not my heart, shall have his
     will.
He is deformed, crooked, old, and sere,
Ill-fac'd, worse-bodied, shapeless every where;
Vicious, ungentle, foolish, blunt, unkind;
Stigmatical[b] in making, worse in mind.
   Luc. Who would be jealous then of such a
      one?
No evil lost is wail'd when it is gone.
   Adr. Ah! but I think him better than I say,
     And yet would herein others' eyes were
      worse:
Far from her nest the lapwing cries, away;[1]
     My heart prays for him, though my tongue
      do curse.

      Enter DROMIO *of Syracuse.*

   Dro. S. Here, go: the desk, the purse; sweet
      now, make haste.
   Luc. How hast thou lost thy breath?
   Dro. S.   By running fast.
   Adr. Where is thy master, Dromio? is he
      well?
   Dro. S. No, he's in Tartar limbo, worse than
      hell.
A devil in an everlasting garment hath him,
One whose hard heart is button'd up with
     steel;
A fiend, a fairy, pitiless and rough;
A wolf, nay, worse,—a fellow all in buff;[c]

A back-friend, a shoulder-clapper, one that coun-
     termands
The passages of alleys, creeks, and narrow
     lands;
A hound that runs counter, and yet draws dry
     foot well;[2]
One that, before the judgment, carries poor souls
     to hell.[d]
   Adr. Why, man, what is the matter?
   Dro. S. I do not know the matter; he is
      'rested on the case.
   Adr. What, is he arrested? tell me, at whose
      suit.
   Dro. S. I know not at whose suit he is ar-
      rested, well;
But is in a suit of buff, which 'rested him,
     that can I tell:
Will you send him, mistress, redemption, the
     money in his desk?
   Adr. Go fetch it, sister.—This I wonder at,
                        [*Exit* LUCIANA.
That he, unknown to me, should be in debt:—
Tell me, was he arrested on a band?[e]
   Dro. S. Not on a band, but on a stronger
     thing;
A chain, a chain: do you not hear it ring?
   Adr. What, the chain?
   Dro. S. No, no, the bell: 't is time that I were
      gone.
It was two ere I left him, and now the clock
     strikes one.
   Adr. The hours come back! that did I never
      hear.
   Dro. S. O yes. If any hour meet a sergeant,
      a' turns back for very fear.
   Adr. As if time were in debt! how fondly
      dost thou reason!
   Dro. S. Time is a very bankrout, and owes
     more than he's worth, to season.
Nay, he's a thief too: Have you not heard men
     say,
That time comes stealing on by night and day?
If he be in debt, and theft, and a sergeant in the
     way,
Hath he not reason to turn back an hour in a
     day?

      Enter LUCIANA.

   Adr. Go, Dromio; there's the money, bear it
     straight;
     And bring thy master home immediately.
Come, sister; I am press'd down with conceit;
Conceit, my comfort, and my injury.
                             [*Exeunt.*

---

[a] The modern construction would be, "He denied you
had in him a right;" but this was Shakspere's phraseology,
and that of his time.
[b] *Stigmatical*—branded in form—with a mark upon him.

[c] *Band—bond.*
[d] *He* is Malone's correction of the original *I.* Mr. Dyce
adopts that of Rowe, "If a be."

SCENE III.—*The same.*

Enter ANTIPHOLUS *of* Syracuse.

Ant. S. There's not a man I meet but doth salute me
As if I were their well-acquainted friend;
And every one doth call me by my name.
Some tender money to me, some invite me;
Some other give me thanks for kindnesses;
Some offer me commodities to buy:
Even now a tailor call'd me in his shop,
And show'd me silks that he had bought for me,
And, therewithal, took measure of my body.
Sure, these are but imaginary wiles,
And Lapland sorcerers inhabit here.

Enter DROMIO *of* Syracuse.

Dro. S. Master, here's the gold you sent me for: What, have you got [rid of^a] the picture of Old Adam new apparelled?
Ant. S. What gold is this? What Adam dost thou mean?
Dro. S. Not that Adam that kept the paradise, but that Adam that keeps the prison: he that goes in the calf's-skin that was killed for the prodigal; he that came behind you, sir, like an evil angel, and bid you forsake your liberty.
Ant. S. I understand thee not.
Dro. S. No? why, 't is a plain case: he that went like a base-viol, in a case of leather; the man, sir, that, when gentlemen are tired, gives them a fob,^b and 'rests them; he, sir, that takes pity on decayed men, and gives them suits of durance; he that sets up his rest to do more exploits with his mace, than a morris-pike.
Ant. S. What! thou mean'st an officer?
Dro. S. Ay, sir, the sergeant of the band; he, that brings any man to answer it that breaks his band; one that thinks a man always going to bed, and says, 'God give you good rest!'
Ant. S. Well, sir, there rest in your foolery. Is there any ship puts forth to-night? may we be gone?
Dro. S. Why, sir, I brought you word an hour since, that the bark Expedition put forth to-night; and then were you hindered by the sergeant, to tarry for the hoy Delay: Here are the angels that you sent for, to deliver you.
Ant. S. The fellow is distract, and so am I;
And here we wander in illusions;
Some blessed power deliver us from hence!

Enter a Courtezan.

Cour. Well met, well met, master Antipholus. I see, sir, you have found the goldsmith now: Is that the chain you promis'd me to-day?
Ant. S. Satan, avoid! I charge thee tempt me not!
Dro. S. Master, is this mistress Satan?
Ant. S. It is the devil.
Dro. S. Nay, she is worse, she is the devil's dam; and here she comes in the habit of a light wench; and thereof comes, that the wenches say, 'God damn me,' that's as much as to say, 'God make me a light wench.' It is written, they appear to men like angels of light: light is an effect of fire, and fire will burn; ergo, light wenches will burn. Come not near her.
Cour. Your man and you are marvellous merry, sir.
Will you go with me? We'll mend our dinner here.
Dro. S. Master, if you do, expect spoon-meat, so bespeak a long spoon.
Ant. S. Why, Dromio?
Dro. S. Marry, he must have a long spoon that must eat with the devil.
Ant. S. Avoid thee,^a fiend! what tell'st thou me of supping?
Thou art, as you are all, a sorceress:
I conjure thee to leave me, and be gone.
Cour. Give me the ring of mine you had at dinner,
Or, for my diamond, the chain you promis'd;
And I'll begone, sir, and not trouble you.
Dro. S. Some devils ask but the paring of one's nail,
A rush, a hair, a drop of blood, a pin,
A nut, a cherry-stone; but she, more covetous,
Would have a chain.
Master, be wise; an' if you give it her,
The devil will shake her chain, and fright us with it.
Cour. I pray you, sir, my ring, or else the chain;
I hope you do not mean to cheat me so.
Ant. S. Avaunt, thou witch! Come, Dromio, let us go.
Dro. S. Fly pride, says the peacock: Mistress, that you know.
[*Exeunt* ANT. S. *and* DRO. S.
Cour. Now, out of doubt, Antipholus is mad,
Else would he never so demean himself:
A ring he hath of mine worth forty ducats,
And for the same he promis'd me a chain;
Both one, and other, he denies me now.
The reason that I gather he is mad,

^a Theobald inserted *rid of*; and they appear necessary,—for the " follow all in buff" was not with the Antipholus of Syracuse.
^b *Fob* in the original. Mr. Halliwell suggests *sop.*

^a *Avoid thee*—then in first folio; the fourth folio, *thou*; Mr. Dyce, *thee;* Mr. White, *thou.*

(Besides this present instance of his rage,)
Is a mad tale he told to-day at dinner,
Of his own doors being shut against his entrance.
Belike, his wife, acquainted with his fits,
On purpose shut the doors against his way.
My way is now, to hie home to his house,
And tell his wife, that, being lunatic,
He rush'd into my house, and took perforce
My ring away: This course I fittest choose;
For forty ducats is too much to lose. [*Exit.*

SCENE IV.—*The same.*

Enter ANTIPHOLUS *of* Ephesus, *and an* Officer.

Ant. E. Fear me not, man, I will not break away:
I 'll give thee, ere I leave thee, so much money
To warrant thee, as I am 'rested for.
My wife is in a wayward mood to-day;
And will not lightly trust the messenger:
That I should be attach'd in Ephesus,*
I tell you, 't will sound harshly in her ears.—

Enter DROMIO *of* Ephesus, *with a rope's end.*

Here comes my man; I think he brings the money.
How now, sir? have you that I sent you for?
Dro. E. Here's that, I warrant you, will pay them all.
Ant. E. But where's the money?
Dro. E. Why, sir, I gave the money for the rope.
Ant. E. Five hundred ducats, villain, for a rope?
Dro. E. I 'll serve you, sir, five hundred at the rate.
Ant. E. To what end did I bid thee hie thee home?
Dro. E. To a rope's end, sir: and to that end am I return'd.
Ant. E. And to that end, sir, I will welcome you. [*Beating him.*
Off. Good sir, be patient.
Dro. E. Nay, 't is for me to be patient; I am in adversity.
Off. Good now, hold thy tongue.
Dro. E. Nay, rather persuade him to hold his hands.
Ant. E. Thou whoreson, senseless villain!

* This is ordinarily printed—
"And will not lightly trust the messenger,
That I should be attach'd in Ephesus."
As we print the passage, his wife will not lightly, easily, trust the messenger with the money; for it will sound harshly in her ears that her husband should be attached in Ephesus.

Dro. E. I would I were senseless, sir, that I might not feel your blows.
Ant. E. Thou art sensible in nothing but blows, and so is an ass.
Dro. E. I am an ass, indeed; you may prove it by my long ears. I have served him from the hour of my nativity to this instant, and have nothing at his hands for my service, but blows; when I am cold, he heats me with beating: when I am warm, he cools me with beating: I am waked with it, when I sleep; raised with it, when I sit; driven out of doors with it, when I go from home; welcomed home with it, when I return: nay, I bear it on my shoulders, as a beggar wont her brat: and, I think, when he hath lamed me, I shall beg with it from door to door.

Enter ADRIANA, LUCIANA, *and the* Courtezan, *with* PINCH, *and others.*

Ant. E. Come, go along; my wife is coming yonder.
Dro. E. Mistress, *respice finem*, respect your end; or rather to prophesy, like the parrot, 'Beware the rope's end.'
Ant. E. Wilt thou still talk? [*Beats him.*
Cour. How say you now? is not your husband mad?
Adr. His incivility confirms no less.
Good doctor Pinch, you are a conjurer;
Establish him in his true sense again,
And I will please you what you will demand.
Luc. Alas, how fiery and how sharp he looks!
Cour. Mark, how he trembles in his extasy!
Pinch. Give me your hand, and let me feel your pulse.
Ant. E. There is my hand, and let it feel your ear.
Pinch. I charge thee, Satan, hous'd within this man,
To yield possession to my holy prayers,
And to thy state of darkness hie thee straight;
I conjure thee by all the saints in heaven.
Ant. E. Peace, doting wizard, peace; I am not mad.
Adr. O, that thou wert not, poor distressed soul!
Ant. E. You minion, you, are these your customers?
Did this companion with the saffron face
Revel and feast it at my house to-day,
Whilst upon me the guilty doors were shut,
And I denied to enter in my house?
Adr. O husband, God doth know, you din'd at home,
Where 'would you had remain'd until this time,
Free from these slanders, and this open shame!

Ant. E. Din'd at home! Thou villain, what say'st thou?

Dro. E. Sir, sooth to say, you did not dine at home.

Ant. E. Were not my doors lock'd up, and I shut out?

Dro. E. Perdy, your doors were lock'd and you shut out.

Ant. E. And did not she herself revile me there?

Dro. E. Sans fable, she herself revil'd you there.

Ant. E. Did not her kitchen-maid rail, taunt, and scorn me?

Dro. E. Certes, she did; the kitchen-vestal scorn'd you.

Ant. E. And did not I in rage depart from thence?

Dro. E. In verity, you did;—my bones bear witness,

That since have felt the vigour of his rage.

Adr. Is 't good to sooth him in these contraries?

Pinch. It is no shame; the fellow finds his vein,

And, yielding to him, humours well his frenzy.

Ant. E. Thou hast suborn'd the goldsmith to arrest me.

Adr. Alas! I sent you money to redeem you, By Dromio here, who came in haste for it.

Dro. E. Money by me? heart and good-will you might,

But, surely, master, not a rag of money.

Ant. E. Went'st not thou to her for a purse of ducats?

Adr. He came to me, and I deliver'd it.

Luc. And I am witness with her, that she did.

Dro. E. God and the rope-maker, hear me witness,

That I was sent for nothing but a rope!

Pinch. Mistress, both man and master is possess'd;

I know it by their pale and deadly looks:

They must be bound, and laid in some dark room.

Ant. E. Say, wherefore didst thou lock me forth to-day?

And why dost thou deny the bag of gold?

Adr. I did not, gentle husband, lock thee forth.

Dro. E. And, gentle master, I receiv'd no gold;

But I confess, sir, that we were lock'd out.

Adr. Dissembling villain, thou speak'st false in both.

Ant. E. Dissembling harlot, thou art false in all;

And art confederate with a damned pack,

To make a loathsome abject scorn of me:

But with these nails I'll pluck out these false eyes,

That would behold in me this shameful sport.

[PINCH *and his* Assistants *bind* ANT. E. *and* DRO. E.

Adr. O, bind him, bind him, let him not come near me.

Pinch. More company; the fiend is strong within him.

Luc. Ah me, poor man! how pale and wan he looks!

Ant. E. What, will you murder me? Thou gaoler, thou,

I am thy prisoner: wilt thou suffer them To make a rescue?

Off. Masters, let him go:

He is my prisoner, and you shall not have him.

Pinch. Go, bind this man, for he is frantic too.

Adr. What wilt thou do, thou peevish officer?

Hast thou delight to see a wretched man

Do outrage and displeasure to himself?

Off. He is my prisoner; if I let him go,

The debt he owes will he requir'd of me.

Adr. I will discharge thee, ere I go from thee:

Bear me forthwith unto his creditor,

And, knowing how the debt grows, I will pay it.

Good master doctor, see him safe convey'd

Home to my house. O most unhappy day!

Ant. E. O most unhappy strumpet!

Dro. E. Master, I am here enter'd in bond for you.

Ant. E. Out on thee, villain! wherefore dost thou mad me?

Dro. E. Will you be bound for nothing? be mad, good master; cry, the devil.—

Luc. God help, poor souls, how idly do they talk!

Adr. Go bear him hence.—Sister, go you with me.—

[*Exeunt* PINCH *and* Assistants, *with* ANT. E. *and* DRO. E.

Say now, whose suit is he arrested at?

Off. One Angelo, a goldsmith. Do you know him?

Adr. I know the man: What is the sum he owes?

Off. Two hundred ducats.

Adr. Say, how grows it due?

Off. Due for a chain your husband had of him.

Adr. He did bespeak a chain for me, but had it not.

Cour. When as your husband, all in rage, to-day,
Came to my house, and took away my ring,
(The ring I saw upon his finger now,)
Straight after, did I meet him with a chain.

Adr. It may be so, but I did never see it:—
Come, gaoler, bring me where the goldsmith is;
I long to know the truth hereof at large.

Enter ANTIPHOLUS *of* Syracuse, *with his rapier drawn, and* DROMIO *of* Syracuse.

Luc. God, for thy mercy! they are loose again.
Adr. And come with naked swords; let's call more help,
To have them bound again.
Off.   Away, they'll kill us.
            [*Exeunt* Officer, ADR. *and* LUC.

Ant. S. I see, these witches are afraid of swords.

Dro. S. She, that would be your wife, now ran from you.

Ant. S. Come to the Centaur; fetch our stuff from thence;
I long that we were safe and sound aboard.

Dro. S. Faith, stay here this night, they will surely do us no harm; you saw they speak us fair, give us gold: methinks, they are such a gentle nation, that but for the mountain of mad flesh that claims marriage of me, I could find in my heart to stay here still, and turn witch.

Ant. S. I will not stay to-night for all the town;
Therefore away, to get our stuff* aboard.
                                    [*Exeunt.*

* *Stuff*—baggage. "The king's stuff" is often mentioned in the orders issued for royal progresses.

RECENT NEW READING.

Sc. II. p. 212.—" A devil in an everlasting garment hath him.
One whose hard heart is button'd up with steel."
" A devil in an everlasting garment hath him, *fell*;
One whose hard heart is button'd up with steel.
Who has no touch of mercy, cannot feel."—*Collier.*

The additions are considered by Mr. Collier as valuable things that had been lost. We consider them as sentimental stuff, very much out of character—added in a more recent period than that of Shakspere, to make couplets.

['Far from her nest, the lapwing cries.']

ILLUSTRATIONS OF ACT IV.

¹ SCENE II.—"*Far from her nest, the lapwing cries, away.*"

This image was a favourite one with the Elizabethan writers. In Lily's Campaspe, 1584, we have, "You resemble the lapwing, who crieth most where her nest is not." Greene and Nash also have the same allusion, which Shakspere repeats in Measure for Measure :—

"With maids to seem the lapwing, and to jest,
Tongue far from heart."

² SCENE II.—"*A fellow all in buff.*"

The prince asks Falstaff, "Is not a buff jerkin a most sweet robe of durance?" The buff jerkin, according to Dromio's definition, is "an everlasting garment," worn by "a shoulder-clapper." The commentators have thrown away much research upon these passages. Steevens maintains that *everlasting* and *durance* were technical names for very strong and durable cloth; but there can be no doubt, we think, that the occupation of the bailiff being somewhat dangerous, in times when men were ready to resist the execution of the law with the sword and rapier, he was clothed with the ox-skin, the buff, which in warfare subsequently took the place of the heavier coat of mail. It is by no means clear, from the passage before us, that the bailiff did not even wear a sort of armour :—

"One whose hard heart is button'd up with steel."

³ SCENE II.—"*A hound that runs counter, and yet draws dry-foot well.*"

The hound that runs counter runs upon a false course; but the hound that draws dry-foot well, follows the game by the scent of the foot, as the blood-hound is said to do. The bailiff's dog-like attributes were not inconsistent; for he was a serjeant of the *counter prison*, and followed his game as Brainworm describes in 'Every Man in his Humour:' "Well, the truth is, my old master intends to follow my young master, dry-foot, over Moor-fields to London this morning."

⁴ SCENE II.—"*One that, before the judgment, carries poor souls to hell.*"

The arrest "before judgment" is that upon *mesne-process*, and Shakspere is here employing his legal knowledge. It appears that Hell was the name of a place of confinement under the Exchequer Chamber for the debtors of the Crown. It is described by that name in the Journals of the House of Commons on the occasion of the coronation of William and Mary.

⁵ SCENE IV.—"*Here's that, I warrant you, will pay them all.*"

Dr. Gray has the following note on this passage: "If the honest countryman in the Isle of Axholm in Lincolnshire, where they grow little else but hemp, had been acquainted with Shakspere's Works, I should have imagined that he borrowed his jest from hence. At the beginning of the rebellion in 1641, a party of the parliament soldiers, seeing a man sowing somewhat, asked him what it was he was sowing, for they hoped to reap his crop. 'I am sowing of hemp, gentlemen,' (says he,) 'and I hope I have enough for you all.'"

(Remains of the Amphitheatre at Ephesus.)

ACT V.

SCENE I.—*The same.*

Enter Merchant *and* ANGELO.

Ang. I am sorry, sir, that I have hinder'd you;
But, I protest, he had the chain of me,
Though most dishonestly he doth deny it.
　Mer. How is the man esteem'd here in the city?
　Ang. Of very reverent reputation, sir,
Of credit infinite, highly belov'd,
Second to none that lives here in the city;
His word might bear my wealth at any time.
　Mer. Speak softly: yonder, as I think, he walks.

Enter ANTIPHOLUS *and* DROMIO *of* Syracuse.

Ang. 'T is so; and that self chain about his neck,
Which he forswore, most monstrously, to have.
Good sir, draw near to me, I'll speak to him.
Signior Antipholus, I wonder much
That you would put me to this shame and trouble;
And not without some scandal to yourself,
With circumstance and oaths, so to deny
This chain, which now you wear so openly:
Beside the charge, the shame, imprisonment,
You have done wrong to this my honest friend;
Who, but for staying on our controversy,

Had hoisted sail, and put to sea to-day:
This chain you had of me, can you deny it?
　Ant. S. I think I had; I never did deny it.
　Mer. Yes, that you did, sir; and forswore it too.
　Ant. S. Who heard me to deny it, or forswear it?
　Mer. These ears of mine, thou knowest, did hear thee:
Fye on thee, wretch! 't is pity, that thou liv'st
To walk where any honest men resort.
　Ant. S. Thou art a villain to impeach me thus:
I'll prove mine honour and mine honesty
Against thee presently, if thou dar'st stand.
　Mer. I dare, and do defy thee for a villain.
　　　　　　　　　　　　　　　　　[They draw

Enter ADRIANA, LUCIANA, Courtezan, *and others.*

Adr. Hold, hurt him not, for God's sake; he is mad;
Some get within him,[a] take his sword away:
Bind Dromio too, and bear them to my house.
　Dro. S. Run, master, run; for God's sake, take a house.[b]
This is some priory.—In, or we are spoil'd.
　　　　[Exeunt ANT. S. *and* DRO. S. *to the Priory.*

[a] *Get within him.* Close with him.
[b] *Take a house.* Take to a house; take the shelter of a house.

Enter the Abbess.

Abb. Be quiet, people. Wherefore throug you hither?

Adr. To fetch my poor distracted husband hence:
Let us come in, that we may bind him fast,
And bear him home for his recovery.

Ang. I knew he was not in his perfect wits.

Mer. I am sorry now that I did draw on him.

Abb. How long hath this possession held the man?

Adr. This week he hath been heavy, sour, sad,
And much different from the man he was;
But, till this afternoon, his passion
Ne'er brake into extremity of rage.

Abb. Hath he not lost much wealth by wrack of sea?
Buried some dear friend? Hath not else his eye
Stray'd his affection in unlawful love?
A sin, prevailing much in youthful men,
Who give their eyes the liberty of gazing.
Which of these sorrows is he subject to?

Adr. To none of these, except it be the last;
Namely, some love, that drew him oft from home.

Abb. You should for that have reprehended him.

Adr. Why, so I did.

Abb. Ay, but not rough enough.

Adr. As roughly as my modesty would let me.

Abb. Haply, in private.

Adr. And in assemblies too.

Abb. Ay, but not enough.

Adr. It was the copy of our conference:
In bed, he slept not for my urging it;
At board, he fed not for my urging it;
Alone, it was the subject of my theme;
In company, I often glanced it;
Still did I tell him it was vile and bad.

Abb. And therefore came it that the man was mad:
The venom clamours of a jealous woman
Poison more deadly than a mad dog's tooth.
It seems, his sleeps were hinder'd by thy railing:
And thereof comes it, that his head is light.
Thou say'st, his meat was sauc'd with thy upbraidings:
Unquiet meals make ill digestions,
Thereof the raging fire of fever bred;
And what's a fever but a fit of madness
Thou say'st, his sports were hinder'd by thy brawls:
Sweet recreation barr'd, what doth ensue
But moody and dull melancholy,

Kinsman to grim and comfortless despair,[a]
And, at her heels, a huge infectious troop
Of pale distemperatures, and foes to life?
In food, in sport, and life-preserving rest
To be disturb'd, would mad or man, or beast:
The consequence is then, thy jealous fits
Have scar'd thy husband from the use of wits.

Luc. She never reprehended him but mildly,
When he demean'd himself rough, rude and wildly.
Why bear you these rebukes, and answer not?

Adr. She did betray me to my own reproof.—
Good people, enter, and lay hold on him.

Abb. No, not a creature enters in my house.

Adr. Then, let your servants bring my husband forth.

Abb. Neither; he took this place for sanctuary,
And it shall privilege him from your hands,
Till I have brought him to his wits again,
Or lose my labour in assaying it.

Adr. I will attend my husband, be his nurse,
Diet his sickness, for it is my office,
And will have no attorney but myself;
And therefore let me have him home with me.

Abb. Be patient: for I will not let him stir,
Till I have used the approved means I have,
With wholesome syrups, drugs, and holy prayers
To make of him a formal man again:
It is a branch and parcel of mine oath,
A charitable duty of my order;
Therefore depart, and leave him here with me.

Adr. I will not hence, and leave my husband here;
And ill it doth beseem your holiness,
To separate the husband and the wife.

Abb. Be quiet, and depart, thou shalt not have him. [*Exit* Abbess.

Luc. Complain unto the duke of this indignity.

Adr. Come, go; I will fall prostrate at his feet,
And never rise until my tears and prayers
Have won his grace to come in person hither,
And take perforce my husband from the abbess.

Mer. By this, I think, the dial points at five:
Anon, I'm sure, the duke himself in person
Comes this way to the melancholy vale,—
The place of death[b] and sorry execution,
Behind the ditches of the abbey here.

Ang. Upon what cause?

---

[a] Capell took an amusing method of correcting the supposed confusion in the sex of melancholy, reading thus:—
"But moody and dull melancholy, *kinsWoman* to grim and comfortless despair."
This is as good as "I studied at the *U-Niversity* of Gottingen."

[b] *Place of death*—the original, *depth*.

Mer. To see a reverend Syracusan merchant,
Who put unluckily into this bay
Against the laws and statutes of this town,
Beheaded publicly for his offence.
    Aug. See, where they come; we will behold
        his death.
    Luc. Kneel to the duke, before he pass the
        abbey.

Enter DUKE, *attended;* ÆGEON, *bare-headed;
with the* Headsman *and other* Officers.

    Duke. Yet once again proclaim it publicly,
If any friend will pay the sum for him,
He shall not die, so much we tender him.
    Adr. Justice, most sacred duke,. against the
        abbess!
    Duke. She is a virtuous and a reverend lady;
It cannot be that she hath done thee wrong.
    Adr. May it please your grace, Antipholus,
        my husband,—
Whom I made lord of me and all I had,
At your important letters,—this ill day
A most outrageous fit of madness took him;
That desperately he hurried through the street,
(With him his bondman, all as mad as he,)
Doing displeasure to the citizens .
By rushing in their houses, bearing thence
Rings, jewels, any thing his rage did like.
Once did I get him bound, and sent him home,
Whilst to take order for the wrongs I went,
That here and there his fury had committed.
Anon, I wot not by what strong escape,[a]
He broke from those that had the guard of him;
And, with his mad attendant and himself,
Each one with ireful passion, with drawn swords,
Met us again, and, madly bent on us,
Chased us away; till, raising of more aid,
We came again to bind them: then they fled
Into this abbey, whither we pursued them;
And here the abbess shuts the gates on us,
And will not suffer us to fetch him out,
Nor send him forth, that we may bear him hence.
Therefore, most gracious duke, with thy command,
Let him be brought forth, and borne hence for
    help.
    Duke. Long since, thy husband serv'd me in
        my wars;
And I to thee engag'd a prince's word,
When thou didst make him master of thy bed,
To do him all the grace and good I could.
Go, some of you, knock at the abbey-gate,
And bid the lady abbess come to me;
I will determine this, before I stir.

[a] *Strong escape.* Escape effected by strength.

Enter a Servant.
    Serv. O mistress, mistress, shift and save
        yourself!
My master and his man are both broke loose,
Beaten the maids a-row,[a] and bound the doctor,
Whose beard they have singed off with brands
    of fire;
And ever as it blazed, they threw on him
Great pails of puddled mire to quench the hair:
My master preaches patience to him, and the
    while
His man with scissors nicks him like a fool:[b]
And, sure, unless you send some present help,
Between them they will kill the conjurer.
    Adr. Peace, fool, thy master and his man are
        here;
And that is false thou dost report to us.
    Serv. Mistress, upon my life, I tell you true;
I have not breath'd almost since I did see it.
He cries for you, and vows, if he can take you,
To scotch your face,[c] and to disfigure you:
                                [*Cry within.*
Hark, hark, I hear him, mistress; fly, be gone.
    Duke. Come, stand by me, fear nothing:
Guard with halberds.
    Adr. Ah me, it is my husband! Witness you
That he is borne about invisible:
Even now we hous'd him in the abbey here;
And now he's there, past thought of human
    reason.

Enter ANTIPHOLUS *and* DROMIO *of* Ephesus.

    Ant. E. Justice, most gracious duke, oh, grant
        me justice!
Even for the service that long since I did thee,
When I bestrid thee in the wars, and took
Deep scars to save thy life; even for the blood
That then I lost for thee, now grant me justice!
    Æge. Unless the fear of death doth make me
        dote,
I see my son Antipholus and Dromio.
    Ant. E. Justice, sweet prince, against that
        woman there.
She whom thou gav'st to me to be my wife;
That hath abused and dishonoured me,
Even in the strength and height of injury!
Beyond imagination is the wrong
That she this day hath shameless thrown on
    me.
    Duke. Discover how, and thou shalt find me
        just.

[a] *A-row*—on row. One after the other.
[b] It was the custom to shave, or crop, the heads of idiots. "Crop, the conjurer," was probably a nickname for the unhappy natural.
[c] *Scotch.* The folio *scorch.* Warburton made the correction, of which Steevens disapproved.

[Act V.] COMEDY OF ERRORS. [Scene I.

Ant. E. This day, great duke, she shut the
   doors upon me,
While she with harlots*·feasted in my house.
   Duke. A grievous fault: Say, woman, didst
      thou so?
   Adr. No, my good lord;—myself, he, and my
      sister,
To-day did dine together: So befal my soul
As this is false he burdens me withal!
   Luc. Ne'er may I look on day, nor sleep on
      night,
But she tells to your highness simple truth!
   Ang. O perjur'd woman! they are both for-
      sworn.
In this the madman justly chargeth them.
   Ant. E. My liege, I am advised what I say;
Neither disturbed with the effect of wine,
Nor heady-rash, provok'd with raging ire,
Albeit my wrongs might make one wiser mad.
This woman lock'd me out this day from dinner:
That goldsmith there, were he not pack'd with her,
Could witness it, for he was with me then;
Who parted with me to go fetch a chain,
Promising to bring it to the Porpentine,
Where Balthazar and I did dine together.
Our dinner done, and he not coming thither,
I went to seek him: In the street I met him;
And in his company that gentleman.
There did this perjur'd goldsmith swear me down,
That I this day of him receiv'd the chain,
Which, God he knows, I saw not: for the which,
He did arrest me with an officer.
I did obey; and sent my peasant home
For certain ducats: he with none return'd.
Then fairly I bespoke the officer,
To go in person with me to my house.
By the way we met
My wife, her sister, and a rabble more
Of vile confederates; along with them
They brought one Pinch, a hungry lean-faced
   villain,
A mere anatomy, a mountebank,
A thread-bare juggler, and a fortune-teller;
A needy, hollow-ey'd, sharp-looking wretch,
A living dead man: this pernicious slave,
Forsooth, took on him as a conjurer,
And gazing in mine eyes, feeling my pulse,
And with no face, as 't were, outfacing me,
Cries out, I was possess'd: then altogether
They fell upon me, bound me, bore me thence;
And in a dark and dankish vault at home

* A *harlot* was, originally, a *hireling*. Thus in Chaucer's
'Sompnoure's Tale':—
   "A sturdy *harlot* went hem ay behind,
      That was his hostes man."

There left me and my man, both bound together;
Till gnawing with my teeth my bonds in sunder,
I gain'd my freedom, and immediately
Ran hither to your grace; whom I beseech
To give me ample satisfaction
For these deep shames, and great indignities.
   Ang. My lord, in truth, thus far I witness with
      him,
That he dined not at home, but was lock'd out.
   Duke. But had he such a chain of thee, or no?
   Ang. He had, my lord: and when he ran in
      here,
These people saw the chain about his neck.
   Mer. Besides, I will be sworn, these ears of
      mine
Heard you confess you had the chain of him,
After you first forswore it on the mart,
And, thereupon, I drew my sword on you;
And then you fled into this abbey here,
From whence, I think, you are come by miracle.
   Ant. E. I never came within these abbey walls,
Nor ever didst thou draw thy sword on me;
I never saw the chain, so help me heaven!
And this is false you burden me withal.
   Duke. Why, what an intricate impeach is this!
I think you all have drunk of Circe's cup.
If here you hous'd him, here he would have
   been:
If he were mad, he would not plead so coldly.
You say he dined at home; the goldsmith here
Denies that saying:—Sirrah, what say you?
   Dro. E. Sir, he dined with her there, at the
      Porpentine.
   Cour. He did; and from my finger snatch'd
      that ring.
   Ant. E. 'T is true, my liege, this ring I had of
      her.
   Duke. Saw'st thou him enter at the abbey
      here?
   Cour. As sure, my liege, as I do see your
      grace.
   Duke. Why, this is strange:—Go call the
      abbess hither;
I think, you are all mated, or stark mad.
      [*Exit an* Attendant.
   Ægе. Most mighty duke, vouchsafe me speak
      a word;
Haply, I see a friend will save my life,
And pay the sum that may deliver me.
   Duke. Speak freely, Syracusan, what thou
      wilt.
   Ægе. Is not your name, sir, call'd Antipholus?
And is not that your bondman Dromio?
   Dro. E. Within this hour I was his bondman,
      sir,

ACT V.]　　　　　　COMEDY OF ERRORS.　　　　　　[SCENE I

But he, I thank him, gnaw'd in two my cords:
Now am I Dromio, and his man, unbound.
　Æge. I am sure you both of you remember me.
　Dro. E. Ourselves we do remember, sir, by
　　　　you;
For lately we were bound, as you are now.
You are not Pinch's patient, are you, sir?
　Æge. Why look you strange on me? you
　　know me well.
　Ant. E. I never saw you in my life, till now.
　Æge. Oh! grief hath chang'd me, since you
　　saw me last;
And careful hours, with Time's deformed hand,
Have written strange defeatures in my face:
But tell me yet, dost thou not know my voice?
　Ant. E. Neither.
　Æge.　　　　Dromio, nor thou?
　Dro. E. No, trust me, sir, nor I.
　Æge.　　　　　　I am sure thou dost.
　Dro. E. Ay, sir? but I am sure I do not; and
whatsoever a man denies you are now bound to
believe him.
　Æge. Not know my voice! O, time's extre-
　　mity!
Hast thou so crack'd and splitted my poor tongue,
In seven short years, that here my only son
Knows not my feeble key of untun'd cares?
Though now this grained face of mine be hid
In sap-consuming winter's drizzled snow,
And all the conduits of my blood froze up,
Yet hath my night of life some memory,
My wasting lamps some fading glimmer left,
My dull deaf ears a little use to hear:
All these old witnesses (I cannot err,)
Tell me, thou art my son Antipholus.
　Ant. E. I never saw my father in my life.
　Æge. But seven years since, in Syracusa, boy,
Thou know'st we parted: but, perhaps, my son,
Thou sham'st to acknowledge me in misery.
　Ant. E. The duke, and all that know me in
　　the city,
Can witness with me that it is not so;
I ne'er saw Syracusa in my life.
　Duke. I tell thee, Syracusan, twenty years
Have I been patron to Antipholus,
During which time he ne'er saw Syracusa:
I see, thy age and dangers make thee dote.

Enter the Abbess, *with* ANTIPHOLUS *of* Syracuse,
　　and DROMIO *of* Syracuse.

　Abb. Most mighty Duke, behold a man much
　　wrong'd.　　[*All gather to see him.*
　Adr. I see two husbands, or mine eyes de-
　　ceive me.
　Duke. One of these men is genius to the other;

And so of these: Which is the natural man,
And which the spirit? Who deciphers them?
　Dro. S. I, sir, am Dromio; command him
　　away.
　Dro. E. I, sir, am Dromio; pray, let me stay.
　Ant. S. Ægeon, art thou not? or else his
　　ghost?
　Dro. S. O, my old master, who hath bound
　　him here?
　Abb. Whoever bound him, I will loose his
　　bonds,
And gain a husband by his liberty:
Speak, old Ægeon, if thou be'st the man
That had'st a wife once call'd Æmilia,
That bore thee at a burden two fair sons:
O, if thou be'st the same Ægeon, speak,
And speak unto the same Æmilia!
　Æge. If I dream not, thou art Æmilia:
If thou art she, tell me, where is that son
That floated with thee on the fatal raft?
　Abb. By men of Epidamnum, he, and I,
And the twin Dromio, all were taken up:
But, by and by, rude fishermen of Corinth
By force took Dromio and my son from them,
And me they left with those of Epidamnum:
What then became of them I cannot tell;
I, to this fortune that you see me in.
　Duke. Why, here begins his morning story
　　right.
These two Antipholuses, these two so like,
And these two Dromios, one in semblance,—
Besides her urging of her wrack at sea,—
These are the parents to these children,
Which accidentally are met together.
Antipholus, thou cam'st from Corinth first?
　Ant. S. No, sir, not I; I came from Syracuse.
　Duke. Stay, stand apart; I know not which is
　　which.
　Ant. E. I came from Corinth, my most gra-
　　cious lord.
　Dro. E. And I with him.
　Ant. E. Brought to this town by that most
　　famous warrior
Duke Menaphon, your most renowned uncle.
　Adr. Which of you two did dine with me to-day?
　Ant. S. I, gentle mistress.
　Adr.　　　And are not you my husband?
　Ant. E. No, I say nay to that.
　Ant. S. And so do I, yet she did call me so,
And this fair gentlewoman, her sister here,
Did call me brother:—What I told you then,
I hope I shall have leisure to make good;
If this be not a dream I see and hear.
　Ang. That is the chain, sir, which you had of
　　me

Ant. S. I think it be, sir; I deny it not.
Ant. E. And you, sir, for this chain arrested me.
Ang. I think I did, sir; I deny it not.
Adr. I sent you money, sir, to be your bail,
By Dromio; but I think he brought it not.
Dro. E. No, none by me.
Ant. S. This purse of ducats I receiv'd from you,
And Dromio my man did bring them me:
I see, we still did meet each other's man,
And I was ta'en for him, and he for me,
And thereupon these Errors are arose.
Ant. E. These ducats pawn I for my father here.
Duke. It shall not need; thy father hath his life.
Cour. Sir, I must have that diamond from you.
Ant. E. There, take it; and much thanks for my good cheer.
Abb. Renowned duke, vouchsafe to take the pains
To go with us into the abbey here,
And hear at large discoursed all our fortunes:
And all that are assembled in this place,
That by this sympathized one day's error
Have suffer'd wrong, go, keep us company,
And we shall make full satisfaction.
Twenty-five years have I but gone in travail
Of you, my sons; and, till this present hour,
My heavy burden ne'er delivered:[a]
The duke, my husband, and my children both,

[a] The passage in the original stands thus:—
 "*Thirty-three* years have I but gone in travail
 Of you, my sons, *nor* till this present hour
 My heavy burthen *are* delivered."

Theobald altered the number to *twenty-five.* The alterations of *and* for *nor,* and *ne'er* for *are,* we adopt from Mr. Dyce. Mr. White has "burthen *here* delivered," which, he says, removes the necessity of altering *nor* to *and.*

And you the calendars of their nativity,
Go to a gossip's feast, and joy with me;
After so long grief, such festivity![a]
Duke. With all my heart I'll gossip at this feast.
[*Exeunt* DUKE, Abbess, ÆGEON, Courtezan, Merchant, ANGELO, *and* Attendants.
Dro. S. Master, shall I fetch your stuff from shipboard?
Ant. E. Dromio, what stuff of mine hast thou embark'd?
Dro. S. Your goods, that lay at host, sir, in the Centaur.
Ant. S. He speaks to me; I am your master, Dromio:
Come, go with us; we'll look to that anon:
Embrace thy brother there, rejoice with him.
[*Exeunt* ANT. S. *and* E., ADR. *and* LUC.
Dro. S. There is a fat friend at your master's house,
That kitchen'd me for you to-day at dinner;
She now shall be my sister, not my wife.
Dro. E. Methinks you are my glass, and not my brother:
I see, by you, I am a sweet-faced youth.
Will you walk in to see their gossiping?
Dro. S. Not I, sir; you are my elder.
Dro. E. That's a question: how shall we try it?
Dro. S. We will draw cuts for the senior: till then, lead thou first.
Dro. E. Nay, then thus:
We came into the world like brother and brother:
And now let's go hand in hand, not one before another. [*Exeunt.*

[a] *Festivity.* Johnson suggested this word instead of *nativity* in the original.

ILLUSTRATION OF THE ENGRAVINGS.

The period of the action in this comedy being so necessarily undefined, we have preferred to select our Pictorial Illustrations from the most authentic representations of the existing remains of ancient Ephesus, and from views of the present state of that celebrated city, of Corinth, and of Syracuse. It may be convenient here to furnish a brief explanation of these Illustrations.

The Temple of Diana is thus described by Pococke:—

"The Temple of Diana is situated towards the south-west corner of the plain, having a lake on the west side, now become a morass, extending westward to the Cayster. This building and the courts about it were encompassed every way with a strong wall, that to the west of the lake and to the north was likewise the wall of the city; there is a double wall to the south. Within these walls were four courts: that is, one on every side of the temple, and on each side of the court to the west there was a large open portico, or colonnade, extending to the lake, on which arches of bricks were turned for a covering. The front of the temple was to the east. The temple was built on arches, to which there is a descent. I went a great way in, till I was stopped either by earth thrown down, or by the water. They consist of several narrow arches, one within another. It is probable they extended to the porticos on each side of the western court, and served for foundations to those pillars. This being a morassy ground, made the expense of such a foundation so necessary; on which, it is said, as much was bestowed as on the fabric above ground. It is probable, also, that the shores [sewers] of the city passed this way into the lake. I saw a great number of pipes made of earthenware in these passages; but it may be questioned whether they were to convey the filth of the city under these passages, or the water from the lake to the basin which was to the east of the temple, or to any other part of the city. In the front of the temple there seems to have been a grand portico. Before this part there lay three pieces of red granite pillars, each being about fifteen feet long, and one of grey broken into two pieces; they were all three feet and a half in diameter. There are four pillars of the former sort in the mosque of St. John, at the village of Aiasalouck. I saw also a fine entablature; and on one of the columns in the mosque there is a most beautiful composite capital, which, without doubt, belonged to it. There are great remains of the pillars of the temple, which were built of large hewn stone, and probably cased with marble; but, from what I saw of one part, I had reason to conclude that arches of brick were turned on them, and that the whole temple, as well as these pillars, was incrusted with rich marbles. On the stonework of the middle grand apartment there are a great number of small holes, as if designed in order to fix the marble casing. It is probable that the statue of the great goddess Diana of the Ephesians was either in the grand middle compartment or opposite to it."

The engraving of the Temple restored is principally founded upon the descriptions of Pococke, who has given an imaginary ground-plan.

The 'Antiquities of Ionia,' published by the Dilettanti Society, and the 'Voyage Pittoresque de la Grèce,' of M. Choiseul Gouffier, have furnished the authorities for the other engravings of Ephesian remains.

Of the modern population of Ephesus the following striking description was furnished by Chandler sixty years ago. The place is now far more desolate and wretched:—

"The Ephesians are now a few Greek peasants, living in extreme wretchedness, dependence, and insensibility; the representatives of an illustrious people, and inhabiting the wreck of their greatness; some, the substructions of the glorious edifices which they raised; some, beneath the vaults of the Stadium, once the crowded scene of their diversions; and some, by the abrupt precipices in the sepulchres which received their ashes. We employed a couple of them to pile stones, to serve instead of a ladder at the arch of the Stadium, and to clear a pedestal of the portico by the theatre from rubbish. We had occasion for another to dig at the Corinthian temple; and, sending to the Stadium, the whole tribe, ten or twelve, followed; one

ILLUSTRATION OF THE ENGRAVINGS.

playing all the time on a rude lyre, and at times striking the sounding-board with the fingers of his left hand in concert with the strings. One of them had on a pair of sandals of goat-skin, laced with thongs, and not uncommon. After gratifying their curiosity, they returned back as they came, with their musician in front. Such are the present citizens of Ephesus, and such is the condition to which that renowned city has been gradually reduced. It was a ruinous place when the Emperor Justinian filled Constantinople with its statues, and raised the church of St. Sophia on its columns. Since then it has been almost quite exhausted. A herd of goats was driven to it for shelter from the sun at noon; and a noisy flight of crows from its marble quarries seemed to insult its silence. We heard the partridge call in the area of the theatre and of the Stadium. The glorious pomp of its heathen worship is no longer remembered; and Christianity, which was here nursed by apostles, and fostered by general councils, until it increased to fulness of stature, barely lingers on in an existence hardly visible."

[Thalia.]

SUPPLEMENTARY NOTICE

COLERIDGE has furnished the philosophy of all just criticism upon the Comedy of Errors in a note, which we shall copy entire from his Literary Remains:—

"The myriad-minded man, our, and all men's, Shakspere, has in this piece presented us with a legitimate farce in exactest consonance with the philosophical principles and character of farce, as distinguished from comedy and from entertainments. A proper farce is mainly distinguished from comedy by the license allowed, and even required, in the fable, in order to produce strange and laughable situations. The story need not be probable, it is enough that it is possible. A comedy would scarcely allow even the two Antipholuses; because, although there have been instances of almost indistinguishable likeness in two persons, yet these are mere individual accidents, *casus ludentis naturæ*, and the *rerum* will not excuse the *inverisimile*. But farce dares add the two Dromios, and is justified in so doing by the laws of its end and constitution. In a word, farces commence in a postulate, which must be granted."

This postulate granted, it is impossible to imagine any dramatic action to be managed with more skill than that of the Comedy of Errors. Hazlitt has pronounced a censure upon the play which is in reality a commendation :—"The curiosity excited is certainly very considerable, though not of the most pleasing kind. We are teased as with a riddle, which, notwithstanding, we try to solve." To excite the curiosity, by presenting a riddle which we should try to solve, was precisely what Plautus and Shakspere intended to do. Our poet has made the riddle more complex by the introduction of the two Dromios, and has therefore increased the excitement of our curiosity. But whether this excitement be pleasing or annoying, and whether the riddle amuse or tease us, entirely depends upon the degree of attention which the reader or spectator of the farce is disposed to bestow upon it. Hazlitt adds, "In reading the play, from the sameness of the names of the two Antipholuses and the two Dromios, as well from their being constantly taken for each other by those who see them, it is difficult, without a painful effort of attention, to keep the characters distinct in the mind. And again, on the stage, either the complete similarity of their persons and dress must produce the same perplexity whenever they first enter, or the identity of appearance, which the story supposes, will be destroyed. We still, however, having a clue to the

SUPPLEMENTARY NOTICE.

difficulty, can tell which is which, merely from the contradictions which arise, as soon as the different parties begin to speak; and we are indemnified for the perplexity and blunders into which we are thrown, by seeing others thrown into greater and almost inextricable ones." Hazlitt has here, almost undesignedly, pointed out the source of the pleasure which, with an "effort of attention,"—not a "painful effort," we think,—a reader or spectator of the Comedy of Errors is sure to receive from this drama. We have "a clue to the difficulty;"—we know more than the actors in the drama;—we may be a little perplexed, but the deep perplexity of the characters is a constantly-increasing triumph to us. We have never seen the play; but one who has thus describes the effect:—" Until I saw it on the stage, (not mangled into an opera,) I had not imagined the extent of the mistakes, the drollery of them, their unabated continuance, till, at the end of the fourth act, they reached their climax with the assistance of Dr. Pinch, when the audience in their laughter rolled about like waves.*" Mr. Brown adds, with great truth, " To the strange contrast of grave astonishment among the actors, with their laughable situations in the eyes of the spectators, who are let into the secret, is to be ascribed the irresistible effect." The spectators, the readers, have the clue, are let into the secret, by the story of the first Scene. Nothing can be more beautifully managed, or is altogether more Shaksperian, than the narrative of Ægeon; and that narrative is so clear and so impressive, that the reader never forgets it amidst all the errors and perplexities which follow. The Duke who, like the reader or spectator, has heard the narrative, instantly sees the real state of things when the *dénouement* is approaching:—

" Why, here begins his morning story right."

The reader or spectator has seen it all along,—certainty by an effort of attention, for without the effort the characters would be confounded like the vain shadows of a morning dream;—and, having seen it, it is impossible, we think, that the constant readiness of the reader or spectator to solve the riddle should be other than pleasurable. It appears to us that every one of an *audience* of the Comedy of Errors, who keeps his eyes open, will, after he has become a little familiar with the persons of the two Antipholuses and the two Dromios, find out some clue by which he can detect a difference between each, even without "the practical contradictions which arise, as soon as the different parties begin to speak." Schlegel says, "In such pieces we must always pre-suppose, to give an appearance of truth to the senses at least, that the parts by which the misunderstandings are occasioned are played with masks; and this the poet, no doubt, observed.". Whether masks, properly so called, were used in Shakspere's time in the representation of this play, we have some doubt. But, unquestionably, each pair of persons selected to play the twins must be of the same height,—with such general resemblances of the features as may be made to appear identical by the colour and false hair of the tiring-room,—and be dressed with apparently perfect similarity. But let every care be observed to make the deception perfect, and yet the observing spectator will detect a difference between each; some peculiarity of the voice, some "trick o' the eye," some dissimilarity in gait, some minute variation in dress. We once knew two adult twin-brothers who might have played the Dromios without the least aids from the arts of the theatre. They were each stout, their stature was the same, each had a sort of shuffle in his walk, the voice of each was rough and unmusical, and they each dressed without any manifest peculiarity. One of them had long been a resident in the country town where we lived within a few doors of him, and saw him daily; the other came from a distant county to stay with our neighbour. Great was the perplexity. It was perfectly impossible to distinguish between them, at first, when they were apart; and we well remember walking some distance with the stranger, mistaking him for his brother, and not discovering the mistake (which he humoured) till we saw his total ignorance of the locality. But after seeing this *Dromio erraticus* a few times the perplexity was at an end. There was a difference which was palpable, though not exactly to be defined. If the features were alike, their expression was somewhat varied; if their figures were the same, the one was somewhat more erect than the other; if their voices were similar, the one had a different mode of accentuation from the other; if they each wore a blue coat with brass buttons, the one was decidedly more slovenly than the other in his general appearance. If we had known them at all intimately, we probably should have ceased to think that the outward points of identity were even greater than the points of difference. We should have, moreover, learned the difference of their characters. It appears to us, then, that as this farce of real life was very soon at an end, when we had become a little

* Shakespeare's Autobiographical Poems &c. By Charles Armitage Brown.

COMEDY OF ERRORS.

familiar with the peculiarities in the persons of these twin-brothers—so the spectator of the Comedy of Errors will very soon detect the differences of the Dromios and Antipholuses; and that, while his curiosity is kept alive by the effort of attention which is necessary for this detection, the riddle will not only not tease him, but its perpetual solution will afford him the utmost satisfaction.

But has not Shakspere himself furnished a clue to the understanding of the Errors, by his marvellous skill in the delineation of character? Some one has said that if our poet's dramas were printed without the names of the persons represented being attached to the individual speeches, we should know who is speaking by his wonderful discrimination in assigning to every character appropriate modes of thought and expression. It appears to us that this is unquestionably the case with the characters of each of the twin-brothers in the Comedy of Errors.

The Dromio of Syracuse is described by his master as

> "A trusty villain, sir; that very oft,
> When I am dull with care and melancholy,
> Lightens my humour with his merry jests."

But the wandering Antipholus herein describes himself: he is a prey to "care and melancholy." He has a holy purpose to execute, which he has for years pursued without success:—

> "He that commends me to mine own content
> Commends me to the thing I cannot get.
> I to the world am like a drop of water
> That in the ocean seeks another drop."

Sedate, gentle, loving, the Antipholus of Syracuse is one of Shakspere's amiable creations. He beats his slave according to the custom of slave-beating; but he laughs with him and is kind to him almost at the same moment. He is an enthusiast, for he falls in love with Luciana in the midst of his perplexities, and his lips utter some of the most exquisite poetry:—

> "O, train me not, sweet mermaid, with thy note,
> To drown me in thy sister's flood of tears;
> Sing, syren, for thyself, and I will dote:
> Spread o'er the silver waves thy golden hairs."

But he is accustomed to habits of self-command, and he resolves to tear himself away even from the syren:—

> "But, lest myself be guilty to self-wrong,
> I'll stop mine ears against the mermaid's song."

As his perplexities increase, he ceases to be angry with his slave:—

> "The fellow is distract and so am I;
> And here we wander in illusions:
> Some blessed power deliver us from hence."

Unlike the Menæchmus Sosicles of Plautus, he refuses to dine with the courtezan. He is firm yet courageous when assaulted by the Merchant. When the Errors are clearing up, he modestly adverts to his love for Luciana; and we feel that he will be happy.

Antipholus of Ephesus is decidedly inferior to his brother, in the quality of his intellect and the tone of his morals. He is scarcely justified in calling his wife "shrewish." Her fault is a too sensitive affection for him. Her feelings are most beautifully described in that address to her supposed husband:—

> "Come, I will fasten on this sleeve of thine;
> Thou art an elm, my husband, I a vine;
> Whose weakness, married to thy stronger state,
> Makes me with thy strength to communicate:
> If aught possess thee from me, it is dross,
> Usurping ivy, briar, or idle moss."

The classical image of the elm and the vine would have been sufficient to express the feelings of a fond and confiding woman; the exquisite addition of the

> "Usurping ivy, briar, or idle moss,"

conveys the prevailing uneasiness of a loving and doubting wife. Antipholus of Ephesus has somewhat hard measure dealt to him throughout the progress of the Errors;—but he deserves it. His doors are shut against him, it is true;—in his impatience he would force his way into his house, against the remonstrances of the good Balthazar:

> "Your long experience of her wisdom,
> Her sober virtue, years, and modesty,
> Plead on her part some cause to you unknown."

He departs, but not "in patience;"—he is content to dine from home, but not at "the Tiger." His resolve—

> "That chain will I bestow
> (Be it for nothing but to spite my wife)
> Upon mine hostess,"—

would not have been made by his brother, in a similar situation. He has spited his wife; he has dined with the courtezan. But he is not satisfied:

> "Go thou
> And buy a rope's end; that will I bestow
> Among my wife and her confederates."

We pity him not when he is arrested, nor when he receives the "rope's end" instead of his "ducats." His furious passion with his wife, and the foul names he bestows on her, are quite in character; and when he has

> "Beaten the maids a-row, and bound the doctor,"

we cannot have a suspicion that the doctor was practising on the right patient. In a word, we cannot doubt that, although the Antipholus of Ephesus may be a brave soldier, who took "deep scars" to save his prince's life,—and that he really has a right to consider himself much injured,—he is strikingly opposed to the Antipholus of Syracuse; that he is neither sedate, nor gentle, nor truly-loving;—that he has no habits of self-command;—that his temperament is sensual;—and that, although the riddle of his perplexity is solved, he will still find causes of unhappiness, and entertain

> "a huge infectious troop
> Of pale distemperatures."

The characters of the two Dromios are not so distinctly marked in their points of difference, at the first aspect. They each have their "merry jests;" they each bear a beating with wonderful good temper; they each cling faithfully to their master's interests. But there is certainly a marked difference in the quality of their mirth. The Dromio of Ephesus is precise and antithetical, striving to utter his jests with infinite gravity and discretion, and approaching a pun with a sly solemnity that is prodigiously diverting:—

> "The capon burns, the pig falls from the spit;
> The clock hath strucken twelve upon the bell;
> My mistress made it one upon my cheek:
> She is so hot, because the meat is cold."

Again:—

> "I have some marks of yours upon my pate,
> Some of my mistress' marks upon my shoulders,
> But not a thousand marks between you both."

He is a formal humourist, and, we have no doubt, spoke with a drawling and monotonous accent, fit for his part in such a dialogue as this:—

> "*Ant. E.* Were not my doors lock'd up, and I shut out?
> *Dro. E.* Perdy, your doors were lock'd, and you shut out.
> *Ant. E.* And did not she herself revile me there?
> *Dro. E.* Sans fable, she herself revil'd you there.
> *Ant. E.* Did not her kitchen-maid rail, taunt, and scorn me?
> *Dro. E.* Certes, she did; the kitchen-vestal scorn'd you."

On the contrary, the "merry jests" of Dromio of Syracuse all come from the outpouring of his gladsome heart. He is a creature of prodigious animal spirits, running over with fun and queer similitudes. He makes not the slightest attempt at arranging a joke, but utters what comes uppermost with irrepressible volubility. He is an untutored wit; and we have no doubt gave his tongue as active exercise by hurried pronunciation and variable emphasis, as could alone make his long descriptions endurable by his sensitive master. Look at the dialogue in the second Scene of Act II., where

COMEDY OF ERRORS.

Antipholus, after having repressed his jests, is drawn into a tilting-match of words with him, in which the merry slave has clearly the victory. Look, again, at his description of the "kitchen-wench,"—coarse, indeed, in parts, but altogether irresistibly droll. The twin-brother was quite incapable of such a flood of fun. Again, what a prodigality of wit is displayed in his description of the bailiff! His epithets are inexhaustible. Each of the Dromios is admirable in his way; but we think that he of Syracuse is as superior to the twin-slave of Ephesus as our old friend Launce is to Speed, in the Two Gentlemen of Verona. These distinctions between the Antipholuses and Dromios have not, as far as we know, been before pointed out;—but they certainly do exist, and appear to us to be defined by the great master of character with singular force as well as delicacy. Of course the characters of the twins could not be violently contrasted, for that would have destroyed the illusion. They must still

"Go hand in hand, not one before another."

[Noble Huntsmen.]

INTRODUCTORY NOTICE.

State of the Text, and Chronology, of the Taming of the Shrew.

The Taming of the Shrew was first printed in the folio collection of Shakspere's Plays in 1623. But it is to be observed that, although this play had not been previously published, in the entry of the books of the Stationers' Company of the claim of the publishers of this first collected edition to "Mr. William Shakespeare's Comedies, Histories, and Tragedies, so many of the said copies *as are not formerly entered to other men,*" the Taming of the Shrew is not recited in the list. In the books of the Stationers' Company we have the following entry, May 2, 1594:—'Peter Shorte. A pleasant conceyted hystorie called the Tayminge of a Shrowe.' In the same year 'A pleasant conceited Historie called the Taming of a Shrew,' was printed by Peter Short for Cuthbert Burbie. We shall have occasion to speak fully of this play, which unquestionably preceded Shakspere's 'Taming of the Shrew.' On the 22nd January, 1606, we find an entry to 'Mr. Ling, of 'Taminge of a Shrew.' In 1607, Nicholas Ling published a new edition of the play which was printed for 'Cuthbert Burbie' in 1594. On the 19th November, 1607, John Smythick (or Smethwick) entered Hamlet, Romeo and Juliet, Love's Labour's Lost, and 'The Taminge of a Shrew.' Smethwick had become, by assignment, the proprietor of Hamlet, Romeo and Juliet, and Love's Labour's Lost, which had previously been published by others; and he ultimately became a proprietor of the first folio. The entry of 1607 might possibly have secured his copyright in Shakspere's 'Taming of the Shrew,' to which it might have referred, as he enters three others of Shakspere's plays on the same day. But Ling, who *did* publish the old 'Taming of a Shrew,' also enters with it Love's Labour's Lost, and Romeo and Juliet, in 1606. The entry of John Smethwick, although not varying from the entry of the preceding year by Ling, of the title of the 'Taming of

INTRODUCTORY NOTICE.

a Shrew,' might, as we say, have referred to Shakspere's comedy; but it might also have referred to a transfer of the earlier comedy from Ling.

Malone originally assigned the Taming of the Shrew to as late a period as 1606. He was led to this determination by the entry at Stationers' Hall, by Smethwick, in 1607; by the fact that Meres does not mention this play as Shakspere's in his list of 1598; and that the line

"This is the way to kill a wife with kindness,"

may be taken to allude to the play of Thomas Heywood (of which the second edition appeared in 1607,) of 'A Woman Killed with Kindness.' Malone subsequently assigned this comedy to 1596. Mr. Collier says, 'Although it is not enumerated by Meres, in 1598, among the plays Shakespeare had then written, and although in Act IV. Sc. I. it contains an allusion to Heywood's 'Woman Killed with Kindness,'* which was not produced until after 1600, Malone finally fixed upon 1596 as the date when the Taming of the Shrew was produced. His earlier conjecture of 1606 *seems much more probable;* and his only reason for changing his mind was that the versification resembled the 'old comedies antecedent to the time' of Shakespeare, and in this notion he was certainly well-founded." † Malone's statement, with regard to the internal evidence of the date of this comedy, is somewhat fuller than Mr. Collier's quotation:—"I had supposed the piece now under consideration to have been written in the year 1606. On a more attentive perusal of it, and more experience in our author's style and manner, I am persuaded that it was one of his *very early productions*, and near, in point of time, to the Comedy of Errors, Love's Labour's Lost, and the Two Gentlemen of Verona. In the old comedies, antecedent to the time of our author's writing for the stage, (if indeed they deserve that name,) a kind of doggrel measure is often found, which, as I have already observed, Shakspeare adopted in some of those pieces which were undoubtedly among his early compositions: I mean his Errors, and Love's Labour's Lost. This kind of metre, being found also in the play before us, adds support to the supposition that it was one of his early productions." Mr. Collier, however, doubts whether the Taming of the Shrew can be treated altogether as one of Shakspere's performances:—"I am satisfied," he says, "that *more than one hand* (perhaps at distant dates) was concerned in it, and that Shakespeare had little to do with any of the scenes in which Katharine and Petruchio are not engaged." Farmer had previously expressed the same opinion, declaring the Induction to be in our poet's best manner, and a great part of the play in his worst, or even below it. To this Steevens replies:—"I know not to whom I could impute this comedy, if Shakspeare was not its author. I think his hand is visible in almost every scene, though perhaps not so evidently as in those which pass between Katharine and Petruchio." Mr. Collier judges that "the underplot much resembles the dramatic style of William Haughton, author of an extant comedy, called 'Englishmen for my Money,' which was produced prior to 1598."

It will be necessary for us, in the first instance, to take a connected view of the obligations of the writer of the 'Taming of *the* Shrew' to the older play which we have already mentioned; and this examination will dispose of that section of our Introductory Notice which we usually give under the head of 'Supposed Sources of the Plot.'

'The Taming of a Shrew,' first appeared in 1594, under the following title : ' A pleasant conceited Historie called the taming of a Shrew. As it was sundry times acted by the Right honourable the Earle of Pembrooke his servants. Printed at London by Peter Short, and are to be sold by Cuthbert Burbie, at his shop at the Royal Exchange, 1594.'‡ The Comedy opens with an Induction, the characters of which are a Lord, Slie, a Tapster, Page, Players, and Huntsmen. The incidents are precisely the same as those of the play which we call Shakspere's. We have inserted, in the Illustration of the Induction, a specimen of the dialogue of this other play. There is this difference in the management of the character of Sly in the anonymous comedy, that, during the whole of the performance of the 'Taming of *a* Shrew,' he occasionally makes his remarks; and is finally carried back to the alehouse door in a state of sleep. In Shakspere we lose this most diverting personage before the end of the first Act. After our poet had fairly launched him in the Induction, and given a tone to his subsequent demeanour during the play, the performer of the character was perhaps

---

* We really doubt whether the line to which Mr. Collier refers can be called an allusion to the title of Heywood's play. It is only the repetition of a common expression, from which expression, we believe, Heywood's play took its title.
† History of Dramatic Poetry, p. 78.
‡ We copy this title from Mr. Collier's History of Dramatic Poetry. This edition was unknown to the commentators. That of 1606, which Steevens reprinted, has no material variations from this very rare copy.

264

TAMING OF THE SHREW.

allowed to continue the dialogue extemporally. We doubt, by the way, whether this would have been permitted after Shakspere had prescribed that the clowns should "speak no more than what is set down for them."

The scene of the old 'Taming of a Shrew' is laid at Athens; that of Shakspere's at Padua. The Athens of the one and the Padua of the other are resorts of learning; the old play opening thus:—

> "Welcome to Athens, my beloved friend,
> To Plato's school, and Aristotle's walks."

Alfonso, a merchant of Athens, (the Baptista of Shakspere,) has three daughters, Kate, Emelia, and Phylema. Aurelius, son of the duke of Cestus, (Sestos,) is enamoured of one, Polidor of another, and Feraudo (the Petrucio of Shakspere) of Kate, the Shrew. The merchant hath sworn, before he will allow his two younger daughters to be addressed by suitors, that

> "His eldest daughter first shall be espous'd."

The wooing of the Kate of the old play by Ferando is exactly in the same spirit as the wooing by Petrucio; so is the marriage; so the lenten entertainment of the bride in Ferando's country-house; so the scene with the Tailor and Haberdasher; so the prostrate obedience of the tamed Shrew. The under-plot, however, is essentially different. The lovers of the younger sisters do not woo them in assumed characters; though a merchant is brought to personate the Duke of Cestus. The real duke arrives, as Vincentio arrives in our play, to discover the imposture; and his indignation occupies much of the latter part of the action, with sufficient tediousness. All parties are ultimately happy and pleased; and the comedy ends with the wager, as in Shakspere, about the obedience of the several wives, the Shrew pronouncing a homily upon the virtue and beauty of submission, which sounds much more hypocritical even than that of the Kate of our poet. We request our readers to turn to the specimens we have given, in the Illustrations to each Act, of the passages which are distinctly parallel to those of Shakspere. There cannot be a doubt that the anonymous author and Shakspere sometimes used the same images and forms of expression,— occasionally whole lines; the incidents of those scenes in which the process of taming the shrew is carried forward, are invariably the same. The audience would equally enjoy the surprise and self-satisfaction of the drunken man when he became a lord; equally relish the rough wooing of the master of "the taming school;" rejoice at the dignity of the more worthy gender when the poor woman was denied "beef and mustard;" and ho'd their sides with convulsive laughter, when the tailor was driven off with his gown and the haberdasher with his cap. Shakspere took these incidents as he found them; perhaps, for the purposes of the stage, he could not have improved them.

This undoubted resemblance involves some necessity for conjecture, with very little guide from evidence. The first and most obvious hypothesis is that 'The Taming of a Shrew' was an older play than Shakspere's, and that he borrowed from that comedy. The question then arises, who was its author?

In our Pictorial Edition of this play, published in October, 1839, we expressed an opinion that Robert Greene might have been the author of 'The Taming of a Shrew,' and that the charge supposed to be made by Greene against Shakspere in his 'Groat's-worth of Wit,' published after his death in 1592, of being "an upstart crow, beautified with our feathers," had reference to a plagiarism from some play more unequivocally belonging to Greene than the plays upon which it was held that 'Henry VI.' was founded. The whole of this question afterwards underwent a much fuller examination by us in our 'Essay on the Three Parts of Henry VI.' &c. in which our views were greatly modified with reference to the precise nature of Greene's complaint. But we may here, without anticipating that fuller discussion, refer only to the point of Greene's probable authorship of 'The Taming of a Shrew.'

The dramatic works of Greene, which have been collected as his, are only six in number; and one was written in connexion with Lodge. The 'Orlando Furioso' is known to have been his, by having been mentioned by a contemporary writer. This play, in its form of publication, appears to us to bear a striking resemblance to the 'Taming of a Shrew.' The title of the first edition is as follows: 'The Historie of Orlando Furioso, one of the twelve Pieres of France. As it was plaid before the Queenes Maiestie. London. Printed by John Danter for Cuthbert Burble, and are to be sold at his Shop nere the Royal Exchange. 1594.' Compare this with the title of the 'Taming of a Shrew.' Each is 'a Historie;' each is without an author's name; each is pub lished by Cuthbert Burbie; each is published in the same year, 1594. Might not the recent death of Greene,—the reputation which he left behind him,—the unhappy circumstances attending his death, for he perished in extreme poverty,—and the remarkable controversy between Nash and Harvey, in 1592, "principally touching Robert Greene,"—have led the bookseller to procure and publish copies of these plays, if they were both written by him? It is impossible, we think, not to be struck with the striking resemblance of these anonymous performances, in the structure of the verse, the extravagant employment of mythological allusions, the laboured finery intermixed with feebleness, and the occasional outpouring of a rich and gorgeous fancy. In the comic parts, too, it appears to us that there is an equal similarity in the two plays—a mixture of the vapid and the coarse, which looks like the attempt of an educated man to lower himself to an uninformed audience. It is very difficult to establish these opinions without being tedious; but we may compare a detached passage or two:—

ORLANDO FURIOSO.

"*Orl.* Is not my love like those purple-colour'd swans,
That gallop by the coach of Cynthia?
Org. Yes, marry is she, my lord.
Orl. Is not her face silver'd like that milk-white shape,
When Jove came dancing down to Semele?
Org. It is, my lord.
Orl. Then go thy ways, and climb up to the clouds,
And tell Apollo, that Orlando sits
Making of verses for Angelica.
And if he do deny to send me down
The shirt which Delanira sent to Hercules,
To make me brave upon my wedding-day,
Tell him, I'll pass the Alps, and up to Meroe,
(I know he knows that watery lakish hill,)
And pull the harp out of the minstrel's hands,
And pawn it unto lovely Proserpine,
That she may fetch the fair Angelica."

TAMING OF A SHREW.

"*Fer.* Tush, Kate, these words add greater love in me,
And make me think thee fairer than before:
Sweet Kate, thou lovelier than Diana's purple robe,
Whiter than are the snowy Apennines,
Or icy hair that grows on Boreas' chin.
Father, I swear by Ibis' golden beak,
More fair and radiant is my bonny Kate,
Than silver Xanthus when he doth embrace
The ruddy Simois at Ida's feet;
And care not thou, sweet Kate, how I be clad;
Thou shalt have garments wrought of Median silk,
Enchas'd with precious jewels fetch'd from far
By Italian merchants, that with Russian stems
Plough up huge furrows in the terrene main."

Take a passage, also, of the prose, or comic, parts of the two plays, each evidently intended for the clowns:—

"*Tom.* Sirrah Ralph, an thou 'lt go with me, I 'll let thee see the bravest madman that ever thou sawest.
Ralph. Sirrah Tom, I believe it was he that was at our town o' Sunday; I 'll tell thee what he did, sirrah. He came to our house when all our folks were gone to church, and there was nobody at home but I, and I was turning of the spit, and he comes in and bade me fetch him some drink. Now, I went and fetched him some; and ere I came again, by my troth, he ran away with the roast meat, spit and all, and so we had nothing but porridge to dinner.
Tom. By my troth, that was brave; but, sirrah, he did so course the boys last Sunday; and if ye call him madman, he'll run after you, and tickle your ribs so with flap of leather that he hath, as it passeth."

"*San.* Boy, oh disgrace to my person! Zounds, boy, of your face, you have many boys with such pickadenaunts, I am sure. Zounds, would you not have a bloody nose for this?
Boy. Come, come, I did but jest; where is that same piece of pie that I gave thee to keep?
San. The pie? Ay, you have more mind of your belly than to go see what your master does.
Boy. Tush, 't is no matter, man; I prithee give it me, I am very hungry I promise thee.
San. Why you may take it, and the devil burst you with it! one cannot save a bit after supper, but you are always ready to munch it up.
Boy. Why, come, man, we shall have good cheer anon at the bride-house, for your master's gone to church to be married already, as there 's such cheer as passeth.
San. O brave! I would I' had eat no meat this week, for I have never a corner left in my belly."

'The Historie of Alphonsus, King of Aragon,'—one of the plays published with Greene's name, after his death,—furnished a passage or two which may be compared with the old 'Taming of a Shrew:'—

ALPHONSUS KING OF ARAGON.

Thou shalt ere long be monarch of the world.
All christen'd kings, with all your pagan dogs,
Shall bend their knees unto Iphigena.
The Indian soil shall be thine at command,
Where every step thou settest on the ground
Shall be received on the golden mines.
Rich Pactolus, that river of account,
Which doth descend from top of Tivole mount
Shall be thine own, and all the world beside."

TAMING OF A SHREW.

—"When I cross'd the bubbling Canibey,
And sailed along the crystal Hellespont,
I fill'd my coffers of the wealthy mines;
Where I did cause millions of labouring Moors
To undermine the caverns of the earth,
To seek for strange and new-found precious stones,
And dive into the sea to gather pearl,
As fair as Juno offer'd Priam's son;
And you shall take your liberal choice of all."

TAMING OF THE SHREW.

" Go, pack thou hence unto the Stygian lake,
And make report unto thy traitorous sire,
How well thou hast enjoy'd the diadem,
Which he by treason set upon thy head;
And if he ask thee who did send thee down,
Alphonsus say, who now must wear thy crown.
  *   *   *   *   *
What, is he gone? the devil break his neck!
The fiends of hell torment his traitorous corpse!
Is this the quittance of Belinus' grace,
Which he did show unto that thankless wretch,
That runagate, that rakehell, yea, that thief?"

" I swear by fair Cynthia's burning rays,
By Merops' head, and by seven-mouthed Nile,
Had I but known ere thou hadst wedded her,
Were in thy breast the world's immortal soul,
This angry sword should rip thy hateful chest,
And hew thee smaller than the Libyan sands.
  *   *   *   *   *
That damned villain that hath deluded me,
Whom I did send for guide unto my son.
Oh that my furious force could cleave the earth,
That I might muster bands of hellish fiends,
To rack his heart and tear his impious soul!"

Malone has conjectured that Greene or Peele wrote this play; but he has also assigned it to Kyd adopting Farmer's opinion. Upon the latter supposition, Mr. Collier observes that "there certainly is not anything like sufficient resemblance in point of style to warrant the belief." Greene possessed the readiest pen of all his contemporaries, and undoubtedly produced many more plays than the six which have come down to us as his.

So far did we express our original opinion that Greene was the author of 'The Taming of a Shrew.' But that opinion underwent some considerable change, from the just respect which we entertained for the critical sagacity and the diligence with which a correspondent in the United States attempted to show that Marlowe was the author of that play. We were of opinion that our correspondent had clearly made out that Marlowe has as good a title to the work as Greene—perhaps a better. Be it one or the other, they each belonged to the same school of poetry; Shakspere created a new school. But there are passages and incidents in 'The Taming of a Shrew' which are unlike Marlowe; such as the scenes with Sly; these are unlike Greene also: they are fused more readily into Shakspere's own materials, because they are natural. We now propose a second theory, altogether different from our previous notion, from that of our correspondent, and from that of any other writer. Was there not an older play than 'The Taming of a Shrew,' which furnished the main plot, some of the characters, and a small part of the dialogue, both to the author of 'The Taming of a Shrew,' and the author of 'The Taming of the Shrew?' This play we may believe, without any violation of fact or probability, to have been used as rude material for both authors to work upon. There was competition between them; one produced a play for the Earl of Pembroke's servants—the other for the Lord Chamberlain's servants, out of some older play, much of which was probably improvisated by the Clowns, and whose main action, the discipline of the Shrew, would be irresistibly attractive to a rough audience, without the pompous declamation of the one remodeller, or the natural poetry and rich humour of the other. Whether the author or improver of the play printed in 1594 be Marlowe or Greene, there can be little question as to the characteristic superiority of Shakspere's work. His was, perhaps, a more careful re-modelling or re-creation. In 'The Taming of a Shrew' it is not difficult to detect, especially in Sly and Sander, coarser things than belong either to Greene or Marlowe.

But there is a third theory—that of Tieck—that 'The Taming of a Shrew' was a youthful work of Shakspere himself. We leave this for the investigation of our readers. To our minds the old play is totally different from the imagery and the versification of Shakspere.

We have to observe, in concluding this notice of the chronology of Shakspere's Taming of the Shrew, that the names of Petrucio and Licio are found in George Gascoigne's prose comedy, 'The Supposes,' which was first acted in 1566. Farmer considered that Shakspere borrowed from this source that part of the plot in which the Pedant personates Vincentio. Gascoigne's collected works were printed in 1587. We have also to mention, as we did in the Introductory Notice to Hamlet, that in Henslowe's accounts, found at Dulwich College, we have an entry on the 11th June, 1594, of the performance at the theatre at Newington Butts of 'the taminge of a shrewe.' Malone considered this to be the old play. But it must be observed that the old play had been acted (as the title to the first edition expresses it, in that very year) by "the Earl of Pembroke, his servants." From the 3d June, 1594, Henslowe's accounts are headed as receipts at performances by "my lord admirell men and my lord chamberlen men." The "lord admirell" was the Earl of Nottingham; "the lord chamberlen men" were the players of Shakspere's own company; and their occupation of the theatre at Newington Butts was temporary, while the Globe Theatre was being erected. The Earl of Pembroke's servants were an entirely distinct company. This entry

INTRODUCTORY NOTICE.

of 'the taminge of a shrewe' immediately follows that of Hamlet; and we see nothing to shake our belief that both these were Shakspere's plays (Hamlet, of course, only the original sketch) performed by the Lord Chamberlain's servants.

PERIOD OF THE ACTION, AND MANNERS.

The Italy of Shakspere's own time is intended to be presented in this play. So thoroughly are the manners Italian, that a belief, and not an unreasonable one, has grown up, that Shakspere visited Italy before its composition. To a highly-valued friend, who had recently returned from Italy, we were much indebted for some interesting local illustrations, which greatly strengthen the conjecture that our poet had founded his accurate allusions in this play to Italian scenes and customs upon personal observation. These illustrations accompany Acts I., II., IV., and V., and are distinguished by the initial (M).

It is scarcely necessary for us here to add many remarks to these illustrations. Mr. Brown[*] has strenuously maintained the opinion that Shakspere did visit Italy, before the composition of the Taming of the Shrew, the Merchant of Venice, and Othello. Nothing was more common in the time of Elizabeth than such a journey; and to "swim in a gondola" was as familiar a thing then, to those of the upper ranks, as to eat an ice at Tortoni's now. Nor were the needier men of letters always debarred by their circumstances from acquiring that experience of Italian manners, which, while it enlarged their stores of knowledge, had not an equally favourable effect upon their morals. In 'The Repentance of Robert Greene,' which was published by Cuthbert Burby, in 1592, after Greene's death—which rare tract Mr. Dyce believes to be genuine—we have the following passage:—
'For being at the University of Cambridge, I light amongst wags as bad as myself, with whom I consumed the flower of my youth, who drew me to travel into Italy and Spain, in which places I saw and practised such villainy as is abominable to declare." Shakspere, we now know, must have been comparatively wealthy before he was thirty, and fully able, as far as the expense was concerned, to have made the journey to Italy. He was acquainted, moreover, with "divers of worship," to whom his companionship in such a journey would have been a delight. That he took the journey is perhaps more than can be proved; that his description of Italian scenes and manners are more minute and accurate than if he had derived his information wholly from books, we have no doubt. This subject may, however, be better discussed when we have gone through all his Italian plays; and may more properly find a place in his Life.

[*] Shakspere's Autobiographical Poems.

[King James I., and Attendants hawking.]

TAMING OF THE SHREW.

Costume.

It is singular enough that the Induction to this comedy affords us the only opportunity of presenting our readers with the costume of England during the life of the Poet himself. Even in this instance the scene of the comedy itself lies in Padua and its neighbourhood; in illustration of the costume of which famous city we give the figure of a lady from the pages of J. Wiegel, and that of a Paduan bride, from Vecellio's work, so often quoted.* The principal characteristic of the latter is the hair hanging down the back in natural profusion; a fashion in bridal array very prevalent throughout Europe during the middle ages. The Induction, we repeat, enables us to introduce an English nobleman of Shakspere's day in his hunting garb, with his attendants, from 'The Noble Art of Venerie,' printed in 1611; an English lady of the same date, from a painting by Mark Gerrard; James the First, and attendants, hawking, from 'A Jewell for Gentrie,' 1614; and a country ale-wife, from Strutt's 'Dress and Habits,' the badges of whose calling were a white apron and a scarlet petticoat.

* The male costume of Padua, given by Vecellio, is only that of official personages: but the trunk-hose, long-bellied doublet, short cloak, precise ruff, and sugarloaf cap or high velvet bonnet, appear to have been worn throughout Lombardy and the northern Italian states at this period. *Vide* Merchant of Venice, Othello, &c.

[English Lady and Hostess.]

[Wincot.]

INDUCTION.

PERSONS REPRESENTED.

A LORD.
CHRISTOPHER SLY, *a drunken Tinker.*
Hostess, Page, Players, Huntsmen, and other Servants.

¹SCENE I.—*Before an Alehouse on a Heath.*

Enter HOSTESS *and* SLY.

Sly. I 'll pheese[a] you, in faith.
Host. A pair of stocks, you rogue!
Sly. Y' are a baggage; the Slys[b] are no rogues: Look in the chronicles, we came in with Richard Conqueror.[c] Therefore, *paucas pallabris*;[d] let the world slide: *Sessa!*

Host. You will not pay for the glasses you have burst![a]
Sly. No, not a denier: Go by, S. Jeronimy, —Go to thy cold bed, and warm thee.[b]
Host. I know my remedy, I must go fetch the thirdborough.[c] [*Exit.*

---

[a] *Pheese.* Johnson says, "To pheese, or feaze, is to separate a twist into single threads." He derived this explanation of the word from Sir T Smith, who, in his book 'De Sermone Anglico,' says, "To feize means *in fila deducere.*" Gifford affirms that it is a common word in the west of England, meaning to *beat,* to *chastise,* to *humble.* In the latter sense Shakspere uses it in Troilus and Cressida: "An be be proud with me, I 'll pheese his pride." Shakspere found the word in the old 'Taming of a Shrew.'

[b] *Slys.* This is ordinarily printed *Slies;* but such a change of the plural of a proper name is clearly wrong.

[c] The tinker was right in boasting of the antiquity of his family, though he has no precise recollection of the name of the Conqueror. *Sly* and *sleigh* are the same, corresponding with *sleight.* The *Slys* or *Sleighs* were skilful men—cunning of hand. We are informed that Sly was anciently a common name in Shakspere's own town.

[d] *Paucas pallabris—pocas pallabras—few words,* as they have it in Spain. *Sessa,* in the same way, is the *cessa* of the Spaniards—*be quiet.*

[a] *Burst*—broken. John of Gaunt "*burst* Shallow's head for crowding in among the marshal's men."

[b] This sentence is generally printed, "Go by, says Jeronimy;—Go to thy cold bed," &c. Theobald pointed out that in the old play of *Hieronymo* there is the expression "*Go by, go by;*" and that the speech of Sly was in ridicule of the passage. Mason, to confirm this, altered the "Go by S. Jeronimie" of the original copy to "Go by, says Jeronimy." The Cambridge editors suggest that the reading is "Go by, Jeronimy," the S. having been mistaken for a note of exclamation. It is usually printed as a note of interrogation.

[c] *Thirdborough.* In the original folio, this is, by mistake, printed *headborough,* by which the humour of Sly's answer is lost. The *thirdborough* was a petty constable; and, from the following passage in 'The Constable's Guide,' 1771, the name appears, in recent times, to have been peculiar to Warwickshire: "There are in several counties of this realm other officers; that is, by other titles but not much inferior to our constables; as, in Warwickshire, a *thirdborough.*"

S'y. Third, or fourth, or fifth borough. I'll answer him by law: I'll not budge an inch, boy; let him come, and kindly.

[*Lies down on the ground, and falls asleep.*

Wind horns. Enter a LORD *from hunting, with his Train.*

Lord. Huntsman, I charge thee, tender well my hounds:
Brach[a] Merriman,—the poor cur is emboss'd;
And couple Clowder with the deep-mouth'd Brach.
Saw'st thou not, boy, how Silver made it good
At the hedge corner, in the coldest fault?
I would not lose the dog for twenty pound.

1 Hun. Why, Belman is as good as he, my lord;
He cried upon it at the merest loss,
And twice to-day pick'd out the dullest scent:
Trust me, I take him for the better dog.

Lord. Thou art a fool; if Echo were as fleet,
I would esteem him worth a dozen such.
But sup them well, and look unto them all;
To-morrow I intend to hunt again.

1 Hun. I will, my lord.

Lord. What's here? one dead, or drunk? See, doth he breathe?

2 Hun. He breathes, my lord: Were he not warm'd with ale,
This were a bed but cold to sleep so soundly.

Lord. O monstrous beast! how like a swine he lies!
Grim death, how foul and loathsome is thine image!
Sirs, I will practise on this drunken man.
What think you, if he were convey'd to bed,
Wrapp'd in sweet clothes, rings put upon his fingers,
A most delicious banquet by his bed,
And brave attendants near him when he wakes,
Would not the beggar then forget himself?

1 Hun. Believe me, lord, I think he cannot choose.

2 Hun. It would seem strange unto him when he wak'd.

Lord. Even as a flattering dream, or worthless fancy.
Then take him up, and manage well the jest:
Carry him gently to my fairest chamber,
And hang it round with all my wanton pictures
Balm his foul head in warm distilled waters,
And burn sweet wood to make the lodging sweet:
Procure me music ready when he wakes,
To make a dulcet and a heavenly sound;
And if he chance to speak, be ready straight,
And, with a low submissive reverence,
Say,—What is it your honour will command?
Let one attend him with a silver bason,
Full of rose water, and bestrew'd with flowers;
Another bear the ewer, the third a diaper,
And say,—Will 't please your lordship cool your hands?
Some one be ready with a costly suit,
And ask him what apparel he will wear;
Another tell him of his hounds and horse,
And that his lady mourns at his disease:
Persuade him that he hath been lunatic;
And, when he says he is—,[a] say, that he dreams,
For he is nothing but a mighty lord.
This do, and do it kindly,[b] gentle sirs;
It will be pastime passing excellent,
If it be husbanded with modesty.

1 Hun. My lord, I warrant you, we'll play our part,
As he shall think, by our true diligence,
He is no less than what we say he is.

Lord. Take him up gently and to bed with him;
And each one to his office, when he wakes.

[*Some bear out* SLY. *A trumpet sounds.*

Sirrah, go see what trumpet 't is that sounds:

[*Exit* Servant.

Belike, some noble gentleman, that means,
Travelling some journey, to repose him here.

Re-enter a Servant.

How now? who is it?

Serv. An it please your honour,
Players that offer service to your lordship.

Lord. Bid them come near:

Enter Players.

Now, fellows, you are welcome.

Players. We thank your honour.

Lord. Do you intend to stay with me to-night?

2 Play. So please your lordship to accept our duty.

---

[a] *Brach.* In one instance (*Lear*, Act III. Sc. v.), Shakspere uses this word as indicating a dog of a particular species:—

"Mastiff, greyhound, mongrel grim,
Hound or spaniel, brach or lym."

But he in other places employs it in the way indicated in an old book on sports,—"The Gentleman's Recreation."—"A *brach* is a *manscript-name* for all hound bitches." We should have thought that the meaning of this passage could not have been mistaken. The lord is pointing out one of his pack:—"Brach Merriman,"—adding, "the poor cur is *emboss'd*,"—that is, swollen by hard running. Ritson, however, would read—"*Bathe* Merriman,"—and Hanmer, "*Leech* Merriman."

[a] *And when he says he is—.* The dash is probably intended to indicate a *blank*. It is as if the lord had said, "And when he says he is *So and So*," when he tells his name. Steevens would read, "And when he says he's *poor*;" Johnson, "And when he says he's Sly."

[b] *Kindly*, naturally.

Lord. With all my heart.—This fellow I remember,
Since once he play'd a farmer's eldest son;—
'Twas where you woo'd the gentlewoman so well:
I have forgot your name; but, sure, that part
Was aptly fitted, and naturally perform'd.

1 Play.[a] I think, 't was Soto that your honour means.

Lord. 'T is very true;—thou didst it excellent.—
Well, you are come to me in happy time;
The rather for I have some sport in hand,
Wherein your cunning can assist me much.
There is a lord will hear you play to-night:
But I am doubtful of your modesties;
Lest, over-eyeing of his odd behaviour,
(For yet his honour never heard a play,)
You break into some merry passion,
And so offend him; for I tell you, sirs,
If you should smile, he grows impatient.

1 Play. Fear not, my lord; we can contain ourselves,
Were he the veriest antic in the world.

Lord. Go, sirrah, take them to the buttery,
And give them friendly welcome every one:
Let them want nothing that my house affords.—
[*Exeunt* Servant *and* Players.
Sirrah, go you to Bartholomew my page,
[*To a* Servant.
And see him dress'd in all suits like a lady:
That done, conduct him to the drunkard's chamber,
And call him madam, do him obeisance.
Tell him from me, as he will win my love,
He bear himself with honourable action,
Such as he hath observ'd in noble ladies
Unto their lords, by them accomplished:
Such duty to the drunkard let him do,
With soft low tongue, and lowly courtesy;
And say,—What is 't your honour will command,
Wherein your lady, and your humble wife,
May show her duty, and make known her love?
And then, with kind embracements, tempting kisses,
And with declining head into his bosom,
Bid him shed tears, as being overjoy'd
To see her noble lord restored to health,
Who, for this seven years, hath esteemed him
No better than a poor and loathsome beggar:

[a] *1 Play.* In the original this line is given to *Sincklo*. This was the name of a player of inferior parts in Shakspere's company. The same performer is also mentioned in the quarto edition of Henry IV., Part II., as also in Henry VI. Sode in the name of a character in Beaumont and Fletcher's 'Woman Pleased;' but it is very questionable whether Shakspere alluded to this play.

And if the boy have not a woman's gift,
To rain a shower of commanded tears,
An onion will do well for such a shift;
Which in a napkin being close convey'd,
Shall in despite enforce a watery eye.
See this despatch'd with all the haste thou canst;
Anon I'll give thee more instructions.
[*Exit* Servant.
I know the boy will well usurp the grace,
Voice, gait, and action of a gentlewoman:
I long to hear him call the drunkard husband;
And how my men will stay themselves from laughter,
When they do homage to this simple peasant.
I'll in to counsel them: haply, my presence
May well abate the over-merry spleen,
Which otherwise would grow into extremes.
[*Exeunt.*

SCENE II.—*A Bedchamber in the* LORD'S *House.*

SLY *is discovered in a rich night-gown, with Attendants; some with apparel, others with bason, ewer, and other appurtenances. Enter* LORD, *dressed like a servant.*

Sly. For God's sake, a pot of small ale.

1 Serv. Will 't please your lordship drink a cup of sack?

2 Serv. Will 't please your honour taste of these conserves?

3 Serv. What raiment will your honour wear to-day?

Sly. I am Christophero Sly. Call not me—honour, nor lordship: I never drank sack in my life; and if you give me any conserves, give me conserves of beef: Ne'er ask me what raiment I'll wear: for I have no more doublets than backs, no more stockings than legs, nor no more shoes than feet; nay, sometime, more feet than shoes, or such shoes as my toes look through the overleather.

Lord. Heaven cease this idle humour in your honour!
O, that a mighty man of such descent,
Of such possessions, and so high esteem,
Should be infused with so foul a spirit!

Sly. What! would you make me mad? Am not I Christopher Sly, old Sly's son of Burtonheath;[2] by birth a pedlar, by education a cardmaker, by transmutation a bear-herd, and now by present profession a tinker? Ask Marian Hacket, the fat alewife of Wincot,[4] if she know me not: if she say I am not fourteen pence on the score for sheer ale, score me up for the lyingest knave in Christendom. What! I am not bestraught:* Here's—

1 *Serv.* O, this it is that makes your lady mourn.

2 *Serv.* O, this it is that makes your servants droop.

Lord. Hence comes it that your kindred shun your house,
As beaten hence by your strange lunacy.
O, noble lord, bethink thee of thy birth;
Call home thy ancient thoughts from banishment,
And banish hence these abject lowly dreams.
Look how thy servants do attend on thee,
Each in his office ready at thy beck.
Wilt thou have music? hark! Apollo plays,
[*Music.*
And twenty caged nightingales do sing:
Or wilt thou sleep? we'll have thee to a couch,
Softer and sweeter than the lustful bed
On purpose trimm'd up for Semiramis.
Say, thou wilt walk; we will bestrew the ground:
Or wilt thou ride? thy horses shall be trapp'd,
Their harness studded all with gold and pearl.
Dost thou love hawking? thou hast hawks will soar
Above the morning lark: Or wilt thou hunt?
Thy hounds shall make the welkin answer them,
And fetch shrill echoes from the hollow earth.

1 *Serv.* Say, thou wilt course; thy greyhounds are as swift
As breathed stags, ay, fleeter than the roe.

2 *Serv.* Dost thou love pictures? we will fetch thee straight
Adonis, painted by a running brook;
And Cytherea all in sedges hid,
Which seem to move and wanton with her breath,
Even as the waving sedges play with wind.

Lord. We'll show thee Io, as she was a maid;
And how she was beguiled and surpris'd,
As lively painted as the deed was done.

3 *Serv.* Or Daphne, roaming through a thorny wood;
Scratching her legs that one shall swear she bleeds:
And at that sight shall sad Apollo weep,
So workmanly the blood and tears are drawn.

Lord. Thou art a lord, and nothing but a lord:
Thou hast a lady far more beautiful
Than any woman in this waning age.

1 *Serv.* And, till the tears that she hath shed for thee,
Like envious floods o'er-ran her lovely face,

* *Bestraught*, synonymous with *distraught*, distracted.
274

She was the fairest creature in the world;
And yet she is inferior to none.

Sly. Am I a lord? and have I such a lady?
Or do I dream, or have I dream'd till now?
I do not sleep: I see, I hear, I speak;
I smell sweet savours, and I feel soft things:—
Upon my life, I am a lord, indeed;
And not a tinker, nor Christopher Sly.
Well, bring our lady hither to our sight;
And once again, a pot o' the smallest ale.

2 *Serv.* Will't please your mightiness to wash your hands?
[*Servants present an ewer, bason, and napkin.*

O, how we joy to see your wit restor'd!
O, that once more you know but what you are!
These fifteen years you have been in a dream;
Or, when you wak'd, so wak'd as if you slept.

Sly. These fifteen years? by my fay, a goodly nap.
But did I never speak of all that time?

1 *Serv.* O yes, my lord; but very idle words:—
For though you lay here in this goodly chamber,
Yet would you say ye were beaten out of door;
And rail upon the hostess of the house;
And say, you would present her at the leet,
Because she brought stone jugs and no seal'd quarts:*
Sometimes you would call out for Cicely Hacket.

Sly. Ay, the woman's maid of the house.

3 *Serv.* Why, sir, you know no house, nor no such maid;
Nor no such men, as you have reckon'd up,—
As Stephen Sly, and old John Naps of Greece,
And Peter Turf, and Henry Pimpernell;
And twenty more such names and men as these,
Which never were, nor no man ever saw.

Sly. Now, Lord be thanked for my good amends!

All. Amen.

Sly. I thank thee; thou shalt not lose by it.

Enter the Page, *as a lady, with* Attendants.

Page. How fares my noble lord?

Sly. Marry, I fare well; for here is cheer enough.
Where is my wife?

Page. Here, noble lord. What is thy will with her?

Sly. Are you my wife, and will not call me husband?

* At the *leet*, or *court-leet*, of a manor, the jury presented those who used false weights and measures; and, amongst others, those who, like the "fat alewife of Wincot," used jugs of irregular capacity instead of the *sealed* or licensed quart.

My men should call me lord; I am your good-
    man.
  Page. My husband and my lord, my lord and
    husband;
I am your wife in all obedience.
  Sly. I know it well: What must I call her?
  Lord. Madam.
  Sly. Al'ce madam, or Joan madam?
  Lord Madam, and nothing else; so lords call
    ladies.
  Sly. Madam wife, they say that I have
    dream'd,
And slept above some fifteen year or more.
  Page. Ay, and the time seems thirty unto me;
Being all this time abandon'd from your bed.
  Sly. 'Tis much. Servants, leave me and her
    alone.
Madam, undress you, and come now to bed.
  Page. Thrice noble lord, let me entreat of you
To pardon me yet for a night or two;
Or, if not so, until the sun be set:
For your physicians have expressly charg'd,
In peril to incur your former malady,
That I should yet absent me from your bed:
I hope, this reason stands for my excuse.
  Sly. Ay, it stands so, that I may hardly tarry
so long. But I would be loath to fall into my
dreams again. I will therefore tarry, in despite
of the flesh and the blood.

    Enter a Servant.

  Serv. Your honour's players, hearing your
    amendment,
Are come to play a pleasant comedy,
For so your doctors hold it very meet:
Seeing too much sadness hath congeal'd your
    blood,
And melancholy is the nurse of frenzy,
Therefore, they thought it good you hear a play,
And frame your mind to mirth and merriment,
Which bars a thousand harms, and lengthens
    life.
  Sly. Marry, I will let them play: Is it not a
commonty, a Christmas gambol, or a tumbling-
trick?
  Page. No, my good lord: it is more pleasing
    stuff.
  Sly. What, household stuff?
  Page. It is a kind of history.
  Sly. Well, we'll see't: Come, madam wife,
sit by my side, and let the world slip; we shall
ne'er be younger.   [*They sit down.*

'Barton-on-the-Heath.'

ILLUSTRATIONS OF THE INDUCTION.

¹ Scene 1.—"*Before an Alehouse on a Heath.*"

In the old play of the 'Taming of a Shrew,' of which we have presented an analysis in the Introductory Notice, we find the outline of Shakspere's most spirited Induction. There are few things in our poet which more decidedly bear the stamp of his peculiar genius than this fragment of a comedy, if we may so call it; and his marvellous superiority over other writers is by nothing more distinctly exhibited than by a comparison of this with the parallel Induction in the old play. It must be observed, that this old play is by no means an ordinary performance. It is evidently the work of a very ambitious poet. The passage, for example, in which the lord directs his servants how to effect the transformation of Sly is by no means deficient in force or harmony. But compare it with the similar passage of Shakspere, beginning—

"Sirs, I will practise on this drunken man,"

and we at once see the power which he possessed of adorning and elevating all that he touched. It will be necessary for us to furnish several examples of the old play; and it will be more convenient, therefore, to the reader, if we give them in the Illustrations, instead of the Introductory Notice. We first select the opening scene:—

Enter a Tapster, *beating out of his doors* Slie, *drunken*.

Tap. You whoreson drunken slave, you had best be gone
And empty your drunken paunch somewhere else,
For in this house thou shalt not rest to-night. [*Exit* Tapster.

Slie. Tilly vally, by crisee, Tapster, I'll fese you anon.
Fill's the t' other pot, and all's paid for, look you.
I do drink it of mine own instigation: [*Omne bene.*
Here I'll lie a while: why, Tapster, I say,
Fill's a fresh cushen here:
Heigh ho, here's good warm lying. [*He falls asleep.*

276

TAMING OF THE SHREW.

Enter a Nobleman and his Men from hunting

Lord. Now that the gloomy shadow of the night,
Longing to view Orion's drisling looks
Leaps from th' antarctic world unto the sky,
And dims the welkin with her pitchy breath,
And darksome night o'ershades the crystal heavens,
Here break we off our hunting for to night.
Couple up the hounds, let us hie us home,
And bid the huntsman see them mealed well,
For they have all deserv'd it well to-day.
But soft, what sleepy fellow is this lies here?
Or is he dead, see one what he doth lack?
  Serv. My lord, 'tis nothing but a drunken sleep
His head is too heavy for his body,
And he hath drunk so much that he can go no further.
  Lord. Fye, how the slavish villain stinks of drink!
Ho, sirrah, arise. What! so sound asleep?
Go, take him up, and bear him to my house,
And bear him easily for fear he wake,
And in my fairest chamber make a fire,
And set a sumptuous banquet on the board,
And put my richest garments on his back,
Then set him at the table in a chair.
When that is done, against he shall awake,
Let heavenly music play about him still.
Go two of you away, and bear him hence.
And then I'll tell you what I have devised;
But see in any case you wake him not. [*Exeunt two with* SLIE.
Now take my cloak, and give me one of yours.
All fellows now, and see you take me so:
For we will wait upon this drunken man,
To see his countenance when he doth awake,
And find himself clothed in such attire,
With heavenly music sounding in his ears,
And such a banquet set before his eyes,
The fellow sure will think he is in heaven:
But we will [be] about him when he wakes,
And see you call him lord at every word,
And offer thou him his horse to ride abroad,
And thou his hawks, and hounds to hunt the deer,
And I will ask what suits he means to wear,
And whatsoe'er he saith, see you do not laugh,
But still persuade him that he is a lord.

The players then enter, and *Sander*, a clown, is the principal speaker. The scene, when *Slie* awakes in his lordly guise, succeeds. Compare it with the rich poetry and the even richer humour of Sly (reminding us, as Hazlitt well observes, of Sancho Panza). The *Slie* of the old play is but a vulgar tinker, the lord and attendants somewhat fustian ranters:—

Enter two with a table and a banquet on it, and two others with SLIE *asleep in a chair, richly apparelled, and the music playing.*

  One. So, sirrah, now go call my lord,
And tell him that all things are ready as he will'd it.
  Another. Set thou some wine upon the board,
And then I'll go fetch my lord presently. [*Exit.*

Enter the Lord *and his Men.*

  Lord. How now! what! is all things ready?
  One. Yea, my lord.
  Lord. Then sound the music, and I'll wake him straight,
And see you do as erst I gave in charge.
My lord, my lord, he sleeps soundly, my lord.
  Sly. Tapster, give 's a little small ale: heigh-ho.
  Lord. Here's wine, my lord, the purest of the grape.
  Sly. For which lord?
  Lord. For your honour, my lord.

  Sli. Who, I? Am I a lord? Jesus, what fine apparel he. I got!
  Lord. More richer far your honour hath to wear,
And if it please you I will fetch them straight,
  Wil. And if your honour please to ride abroad,
I'll fetch you lusty steeds more swift of pace
Than winged Pegasus in all his pride,
That ran so swiftly over Persian plains.
  Tom. And if your honour please to hunt the deer,
Your hounds stand ready coupled at the door,
Who in running will o'ertake the roe,
And make the long-breath'd tiger broken-winded.
  Sly. By the mass, I think I am a lord indeed.
What's thy name?
  Lord. Simon, an if it please your honour.
  Sly. Sim, that's much to say Simion, or Simon,
Put forth thy hand and fill the pot.
Give me thy hand, Sim; am I a lord indeed?
  Lord. Ay, my gracious lord, and your lovely lady
Long time hath mourned for your absence here,
And now with joy behold where she doth come
To gratulate your honour's safe return.

² SCENE I.—"*What think you, if he were convey'd to bed.*"

The story upon which this Induction is founded in all probability had an Eastern origin. 'The Sleeper Awakened,' of the Thousand and One Nights, is conjectured by Mr. Lane, in the notes to his admirable translation, not to be a genuine tale, its chief and best portion being "an historical anecdote related as a fact." Mr. Lane adds,—" The author by whom I have found the chief portion of this tale related as an historical anecdote is El-Is-hakee, who finished his history shortly before the close of the reign of the 'Osmánlee Sultán Mustafa apparently in the year of the Flight 1032 (A. D. 1623). He does not mention his authority; and whether it is related by an older *historian*, I do not know; but perhaps it is founded upon fact."

Our readers will be gratified by a few extracts from Mr. Lane's version of the "historical anecdote," which he has blended with portions of the tale as given in the Breslau edition of the Thousand and One Nights. Aboo-l-Hasan, who had spent one-half of his property amongst boon-companions, resolved to associate no longer with ungrateful familiars, but to entertain a stranger for one night only, and then afterwards to refuse to recognise him. In pursuance of this resolution he one night entertained the Khaleefeh.—" And they drank and caroused until midnight."

"After this, the Khaleefeh said to his host, O Abu-l-Hasan, is there any service that thou wouldst have performed, or any desire that thou wouldst have accomplished? And Aboo-l Hasan answered, In our neighbourhood is a mosque, to which belong an Imám and four sheykhs, and whenever they hear music or any sport they incite the Wálees against me, and impose fines upon me, and trouble my life, so that I suffer torment from them. If I had them in my power, therefore, I would give each of them a thousand lashes, that I might be relieved from their excessive annoyance.

"Er-Rasheed replied, May Allah grant thee the accomplishment of thy wish! And without his being aware of it, he put into a cup a lozenge of benj

277

and handed it to him; and as soon as it had settled in his stomach, he fell asleep immediately. Er-Rasheed then arose and went to the door, where he found his young men waiting for him, and he ordered them to convey Abu-l-Hasan upon a mule, and returned to the palace; Abu-l-Hasan being intoxicated and insensible. And when the Khaleefeh had rested himself in the palace, he called for his Weezeer Jaafar, and 'Abd Allah the son of Tahir, the Walee of Baghdad, and certain of his chief attendants, and said to them all, In the morning, when ye see this young man (pointing to Abu-l-Hasan) seated on the royal couch, pay obedience to him, and salute him as Khaleefeh, and whatsoever he commandeth you, do it. Then going in to his female slaves, he directed them to wait upon Abu-l-Hasan, and to address him as Prince of the Faithful; after which he entered a private closet, and, having let down a curtain over the entrance, slept.

"So when Abu-l-Hasan awoke, he found himself upon the royal couch, with the attendants standing around, and kissing the ground before him; and a maid said to him, O our lord, it is the time for morning-prayer. Upon which he laughed, and, looking round about him, he beheld a pavilion whose walls were adorned with gold and ultramarine, and the roof bespotted with red gold, surrounded by chambers with curtains of embroidered silk hanging before their doors; and he saw vessels of gold and China-ware and crystal, and furniture and carpets spread, and lighted lamps, and female slaves and eunuchs, and other attendants; whereat he was perplexed in his mind, and said, By Allah, either I am dreaming, or this is Paradise, and the Abode of Peace. And he closed his eyes. So a eunuch said to him, O my lord, this is not thy usual custom, O Prince of the Faithful! And he was perplexed at his case, and put his head into his bosom, and then began to open his eyes by little and little, laughing, and saying, What is this state in which I find myself? And he bit his finger; and when he found that the bite pained him, he cried, Ah!—and was angry. Then raising his head, he called one of the female slaves, who answered him, At thy service, O Prince of the Faithful! And he said to her, What is thy name? She answered, Shejeret ed-Durr. And he said, Knowest thou in what place I am, and who I am?—Thou art the Prince of the Faithful, she answered, sitting in thy palace, upon the royal couch. He replied, I am perplexed at my case, my reason hath departed, and it seemeth that I am asleep; but what shall I say of my yesterday's guest? I imagine nothing but that he is a devil or an enchanter, who hath sported with my reason.

"All this time, the Khaleefeh was observing him, from a place where Abu-l-Hasan could not see him.—And Abu-l-Hasan looked towards the chief eunuch, and called to him. So he came, and kissed the ground before him, saying to him, Yes, O Prince of the Faithful. And Abu-l-Hasan said to him, Who is the Prince of the Faithful?—Thou, he answered. Abu-l-Hasan replied, Thou liest. And addressing another eunuch, he said to him, O my chief, as thou hopest for Allah's protection, tell me, am I the Prince of the Faithful?—Yes, by Allah, answered the eunuch: thou art at this present time the Prince of the Faithful, and the Khaleefeh of the Lord of all creatures. And Abu-l-Hasan, perplexed at all that he beheld, said, In one night do I become Prince of the Faithful? Was I not yesterday Abu-l-Hasan; and to-day am I Prince of the Faithful?—He remained perplexed and confounded until the morning, when a eunuch advanced to him and said to him, May Allah grant a happy morning to the Prince of the Faithful! And he handed to him a pair of shoes of gold stuff, reticulated with precious stones and rubies; and Abu-l-Hasan took them, and after examining them a long time, put them into his sleeve. So the eunuch said to him, These are shoes, to walk in. Abu-l-Hasan replied, Thou hast spoken truth. I put them into my sleeve but in my fear lest they should be soiled.—He therefore took them forth, and put them on his feet. And shortly after, the female slaves brought him a basin of gold and a ewer of silver, and poured the water upon his hands; and when he had performed the ablution, they spread for him a prayer-carpet; and he prayed; but knew not how to do so. He continued his inclinations and prostrations until he had performed twenty rek'ahs; meditating and saying within himself, By Allah, I am none other than the Prince of the Faithful, in truth; or else this is a dream, and all these things occur not in a dream. He therefore convinced himself and determined in his mind, that he was the Prince of the Faithful; and he pronounced the salutations, and finished his prayers. They then brought him a magnificent dress, and, looking at himself, as he sat upon the couch, he retracted, and said, All this is an illusion, and a machination of the Ján.

"And while he was in this state, lo, one of the memlooks came in and said to him, O Prince of the Faithful, the chamberlain is at the door, requesting permission to enter.—Let him enter, replied Abu-l-Hasan. So he came in, and, having kissed the ground before him, said, Peace be on thee, O Prince of the Faithful! And Abu-l-Hasan rose, and descended from the couch to the floor; whereupon the chamberlain exclaimed, Allah! Allah! O Prince of the Faithful! Knowest thou not that all men are thy servants, and under thy authority, and that it is not proper for the Prince of the Faithful to rise to any one?—Abu-l-Hasan was then told that Jaafar el-Barmekee, and 'Abd Allah the son of Tahir, and the chiefs of the memlooks, begged permission to enter. And he gave them permission. So they entered, and kissed the ground before him, each of them addressing him as Prince of the Faithful. And he was delighted at this, and returned their salutation; after which, he called the Walee, who approached him, and said, At thy service, O Prince of the Faithful! And Abu-l-Hasan said to him, Repair immediately to such a street, and give a hundred pieces of gold to the mother of Abu-l-Hasan the Wag, with my salutation: then take the Imám of the mosque, and the four sheykhs, inflict upon each of them a thousand lashes; and when thou hast done that, write a bond against them, confirmed by oath, that they shall not reside in the street, after thou shalt have paraded them through the city, mounted on beasts, with their faces to the tails, and hast proclaimed before them, This is the recompense of those who annoy their neighbours!—And beware of neglecting that which I have commanded thee to do.—So the Wálee did as he was ordered. And when Abu-l-Hasan had exercised his authority until the close of the day, he looked towards the chamberlain and the rest of the attendants, and said to them, Depart.

"He then called for a eunuch who was near at hand, and said to him, I am hungry, and desire something to eat. And he replied, I hear and obey:—and led him by the hand into the eating-chamber, where the attendants placed before him a table of rich viands; and ten slave girls, high-bosomed virgins, stood behind his head. Abu-l-Hasan, looking at one of these, said to her, What is thy name? She answered Kádeeb el-Bán. And he said to her, O Kádeeb el-Bán, who am I?—Thou art the Prince of the Faithful, she answered. But he replied, Thou liest, by Allah, thou slut! Ye girls are laughing at me.—So she said, Fear Allah, O Prince of the Faithful; this is thy palace, and the female slaves are thine. And upon this he said within himself, It is no great matter to be effected by God, to whom be ascribed might and glory! Then the slave-girls led him by the hand to the drinking-chamber, where he saw what astonished the mind; and he continued to say within himself, No doubt these are of the Ján, and this person who was my guest is one of the Kings of the Ján, who saw no way of requiting and compensating me for my kindness to him but by ordering his 'O'us to address me as Prince of the Faithful. All these are of the Ján. May Allah then deliver me from them happily!—And while he was thus talking to himself, lo, one of the slave-girls filled for him a cup of wine; and he took it from her hand and drank it; after which, the slave-girls plied him with wine in abundance; and one of them threw into his cup a lozenge of benj; and when it had settled in his stomach, he fell down senseless.

"Er-Rasheed then gave orders to convey him to his house; and the servants did so, and laid him on his bed, still in a state of insensibility."

The parallel here ends between Abu-l-Hasan and Christopher Sly; and it is unnecessary for us to follow the fortunes of "the Wag."

The following story, which has been extracted by Malone from Goulart's 'Admirable and Memorable Histories,' translated by E. Grimestone, 1607, is to be found in Heuterus, Rerum Burgund. lib. iv. Malone thinks that it had appeared in English before the old 'Taming of a Shrew;'—

"Philip, called the Good, Duke of Burgundy, in the memory of our ancestors, being at Bruxelles with his Court, and walking one night after supper through the streets, accompanied with some of his favourites, he found lying upon the stones a certain artisan that was very drunk, and that slept soundly. It pleased the prince, in this artisan, to make trial of the vanity of our life, whereof he had before discoursed with his familiar friends. He, therefore, caused this sleeper to be taken up, and carried into his palace; he commands him to be laid in one of the richest beds; a rich night-cap to be given him; his foul shirt to be taken off, and to have another put on him of fine holland. When as this drunkard had digested his wine, and began to awake, behold there comes about his bed pages and grooms of the Duke's chamber, who draw the curtains, and make many courtesies, and, being bareheaded, ask him if it please him to rise, and what apparel it would please him to put on that day.—They bring him rich apparel. This new *Monsieur*, amazed at such courtesy, and doubting whether he dreamed or waked, suffered himself to be dressed, and led out of the chamber. There came noblemen which saluted him with all honour, and conduct him to the mass, where with great ceremony they gave him the book of the Gospel, and Pixe to kiss, as they did usually to the Duke. From the mass, they bring him back unto the palace; he washes his hands, and sits down at the table well furnished. After dinner, the Great Chamberlain commands cards to be brought, with a great sum of money. This Duke in imagination plays with the chief of the court. Then they carry him to walk in the garden, and to hunt the hare, and to hawk. They bring him back unto the palace, where he sups in state. Candles being lighted, the musicians begin to play; and, the tables taken away, the gentlemen and gentlewomen fell to dancing. Then they played a pleasant Comedy, after which followed a banquet, whereat they had presently store of Ipocras and precious wine, with all sorts of confitures, to this prince of the new impression, so as he was drunk, and fell soundly asleep. Thereupon the Duke commanded that he should be disrobed of all his rich attire. He was put into his old rags, and carried into the same place where he had been found the night before; where he spent that night. Being awake in the morning, he began to remember what had happened before;—he knew not whether it were true indeed, or a dream that had troubled his brain. But in the end, after many discourses, he concludes that all was but a dream that had happened unto him; and so entertained his wife, his children, and his neighbours, without any other apprehension."

³ SCENE II.—"*Old Sly's son of Burton-heath.*"

Barton-on-the-Heath is a small village on the borders of Warwickshire and Oxfordshire. In Domesday-Book, according to Dugdale, it is written *Bertone*,—so that the Burton of the text may be correct. It consists of some twenty or thirty cottages, intermixed with a few small farm-houses, making together one short irregular street. The church is small, and peculiar in its architectural arrangements; an old mansion near it of the Elizabethan era is the rectory. The village is situated two miles from Long Compton on the road to Stratford from Oxford, and the approaches on all sides are by lonely lanes, and in its general aspect it is solitary and neglected. Of the "heath," however, from which it partly takes its name, no traces remain, the land being wholly enclosed.

⁴ SCENE II.—"*The fat ale-wife of Wincot.*"

Wincot is the name of a hamlet farm situated about four miles from Stratford on the road to Cheltenham. Wincot is a substantial stone build-

ILLUSTRATIONS OF THE INDUCTION.

ing of the Elizabethan period, and was probably at its first erection a manorial residence, but at no period in the memory of the neighbourhood has it ever been used as an alehouse. The house of the "fat ale-wife of Wincot" is not therefore here to be found; but its site may perhaps be indicated by a few square patches of rank dark-coloured grass, which, at the distance of a quarter of a mile from the farm, and near the road-side, are all that remain to corroborate the memories of the villagers of Clifford, (the parish in which the hamlet stands,) who say that "a house once stood there." Wincot is a wild place, in which sword-dances are still prevalent, and annual fights continue to be held to adjust the quarrels of the year.

We believe, however, that in this passage, as in Henry IV., Part II., the place to which Shakspere alludes is the hamlet of *Wilmecote*, anciently Wylmyncote, about three miles to the north of Stratford, in the parish of Aston-Cantlow. Here lived Robert Arden, our poet's maternal grandfather; and his youngest daughter, the mother of Shakspere, inherited a house and lands here situate. It is most probable, therefore, that this hamlet, which Malone says (though he gives no authority) was also called *Wyncote*, was in Shakspere's thoughts. The matter is of little consequence here; and in our life of Shakspere we shall present a view of Wilmecote, a straggling village with a few old houses, amongst whose secluded fields our poet no doubt passed many of his boyish hours.

[Abu l-Hasan awakening in the Palace.]

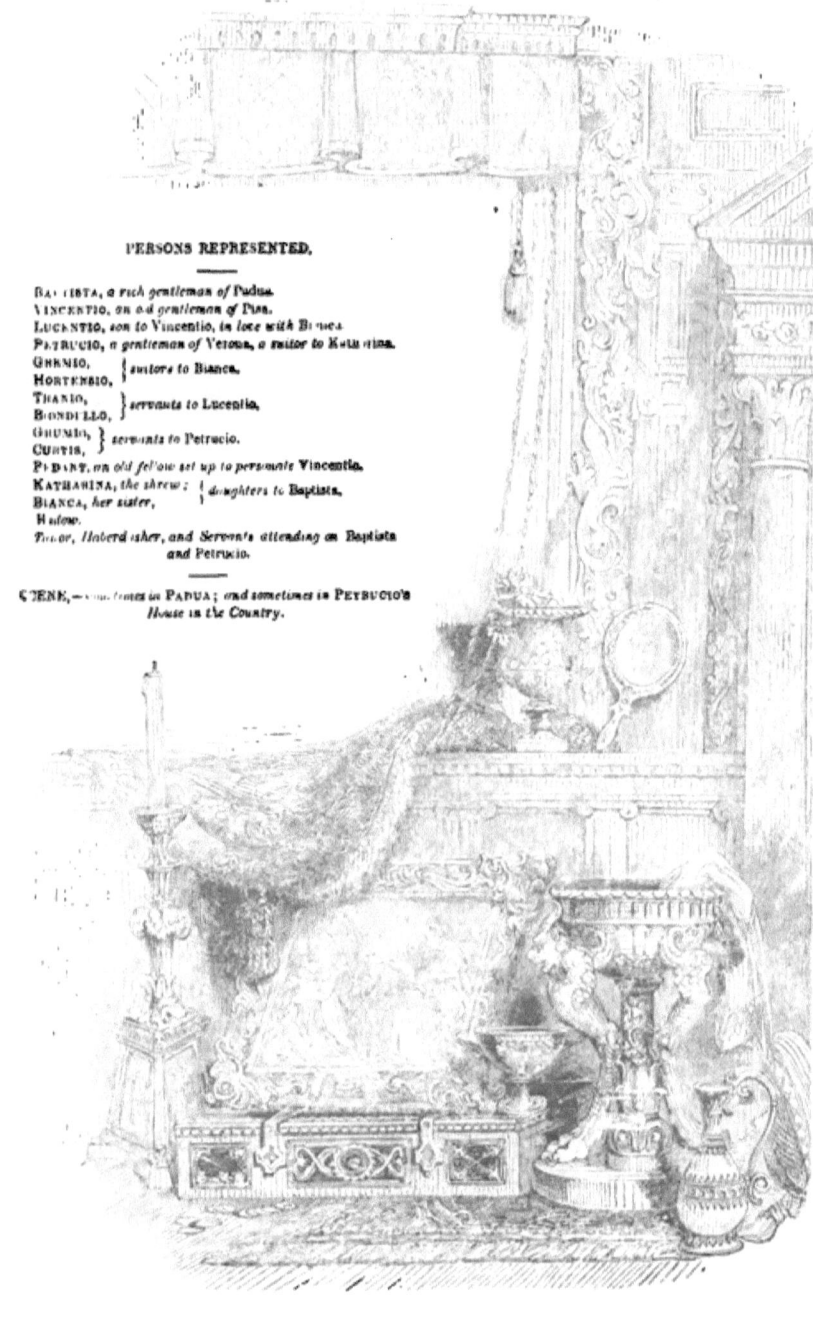

PERSONS REPRESENTED.

BAPTISTA, *a rich gentleman of Padua.*
VINCENTIO, *an old gentleman of Pisa.*
LUCENTIO, *son to Vincentio, in love with Bianca.*
PETRUCIO, *a gentleman of Verona, a suitor to Katharina.*
GREMIO, } *suitors to Bianca.*
HORTENSIO,
TRANIO, } *servants to Lucentio.*
BIONDELLO,
GRUMIO, } *servants to Petrucio.*
CURTIS,
PEDANT, *an old fellow set up to personate* VINCENTIO.
KATHARINA, *the shrew;* } *daughters to Baptista.*
BIANCA, *her sister,*
Widow.
Tailor, Haberdasher, and Servants attending on Baptista and Petrucio.

SCENE.—*Sometimes in* PADUA; *and sometimes in* PETRUCIO'S *House in the Country.*

[Town-house, Padua.]

ACT I.

SCENE I.—Padua. *A public Place.*

Enter LUCENTIO *and* TRANIO.

Luc. Tranio, since for the great desire I had
To see fair Padua, nursery of arts,[1]
I am arriv'd for fruitful Lombardy,
The pleasant garden of great Italy;[2]
And, by my father's love and leave, am arm'd
With his good will, and thy good company,
My[a] trusty servant, well approv'd in all;
Here let us breathe, and haply institute
A course of learning, and ingenious studies.
Pisa, renowned for grave citizens,
Gave me my being, and my father first,
A merchant of great traffic through the world,
Vincentio, come of the Bentivolii.
Vincentio's son, brought up in Florence,
It shall become, to serve all hopes conceiv'd,
To deck his fortune with his virtuous deeds:[b]
And therefore, Tranio, for the time I study,
Virtue, and that part of philosophy
Will I apply, that treats of happiness
By virtue 'specially to be achiev'd.
Tell me thy mind: for I have Pisa left,

And am to Padua come, as he that leaves
A shallow plash, to plunge him in the deep,
And with satiety seeks to quench his thirst.
  Tra. Mi perdonate, gentle master mine,
I am in all affected as yourself;
Glad that you thus continue your resolve,
To suck the sweets of sweet philosophy.
Only, good master, while we do admire
This virtue, and this moral discipline,
Let 's be no stoics, nor no stocks, I pray;
Or so devote to Aristotle's checks,[a]
As Ovid be an outcast quite abjur'd:
Balk[b] logic with acquaintance that you have,
And practise rhetoric in your common talk:
Music and poesy use to quicken you;
The mathematics, and the metaphysics,
Fall to them, as you find your stomach serves
  you:
No profit grows where is no pleasure ta'en:—
In brief, sir, study what you most affect.
  Luc. Gramercies, Tranio, well dost thou advise

---

[a] *My.* So the folio. The word has been changed by the modern editors to *most*.
[b] This passage has been a source of perplexity to the commentators; but it appears to us sufficiently clear: Pisa gave me my being, and also first gave my father being—that father was Vincentio, &c. It shall become Vincentio's son, that he may fulfil the hopes conceived of him, to deck his fortune with his virtuous deeds.

[a] *Checks.* Sir W. Blackstone proposes to read *ethicks.* In Ben Jonson's 'Silent Woman' we have "Aristotle's *ethicks.*" Aristotle's "checks" are his ethical principles, as opposed to the excitements of Ovid. (*White.*)
[b] *Balk.* This word of the original has been changed into *talk,* "corrected by Mr. Rowe." By this correction the meaning of the passage has been destroyed. Tranio draws a distinction between the dry and the agreeable of the liberal sciences. *Balk* logic—pass over logic—with your acquaintance, but practise rhetoric in your common *talk;*—see 'in the legitimate sense of resorting to *frequently*) music and poetry to quicken you, but fall to mathematics and metaphysics as you find your inclination serves.

283

If, Biondello, thou wert come ashore,
We could at once put us in readiness;
And take a lodging, fit to entertain
Such friends as time in Padua shall beget.
But stay awhile: What company is this?
   Tra. Master, some show, to welcome us to
      town.

Enter BAPTISTA, KATHARINA, BIANCA, GREMIO,
and HORTENSIO. LUCENTIO *and* TRANIO *stand
aside.*

  Bap. Gentlemen, importune me no farther,
For how I firmly am resolv'd you know:
That is, not to bestow my youngest daughter,
Before I have a husband for the elder:
If either of you both love Katharina,
Because I know you well, and love you well,
Leave shall you have to court her at your pleasure.
  Gre. To cart her rather: She's too rough for
    me:
There, there, Hortensio, will you any wife?
  Kath. I pray you, sir, [*to* BAP.] is it your will
To make a stale of me amongst these mates?*
  Hor. Mates, maid! how mean you that? no
    mates for you,
Unless you were of gentler, milder mould.
  Kath. I' faith, sir, you shall never need to fear:
I wis, it is not half way to her heart:
But, if it were, doubt not her care should be
To comb your noddle with a three-legg'd stool,
And paint your face, and use you like a fool.
  Hor. From all such devils, good Lord, deliver
    us!
  Gre. And me too, good Lord!
  Tra. Hush, master! here is some good pastime
    toward;
That wench is stark mad, or wonderful froward.
  Luc. But in the other's silence do I see
Maids' mild behaviour and sobriety.
Peace, Tranio.
  Tra. Well said, master; mum! and gaze your
    fill.
  Bap. Gentlemen, that I may soon make good
What I have said, Bianca, get you in:
And let it not displease thee, good Bianca;
For I will love thee ne'er the less, my girl.
  Kath. A pretty peat;[b] 't is best
Put finger in the eye—an she knew why.

  Bian. Sister, content you in my discontent.
Sir, to your pleasure humbly I subscribe:
My books and instruments shall be my company,
On them to look, and practise by myself.
  Luc. Hark, Tranio! thou may'st hear Minerva
    speak.   [*Aside.*
  Hor. Signior Baptista, will you be so strange?
Sorry am I that our good will effects
Bianca's grief.
  Gre.   Why, will you mew her,
Signior Baptista, for this fiend of hell,
And make her bear the penance of her tongue?
  Bap. Gentlemen, content ye; I am resolv'd:
Go in, Bianca.   [*Exit* BIANCA.
And, for I know she taketh most delight
In music, instruments, and poetry,
Schoolmasters will I keep within my house,
Fit to instruct her youth. If you, Hortensio,
Or Signior Gremio, you, know any such,
Prefer them hither; for to cunning* men
I will be very kind, and liberal
To mine own children in good bringing-up;
And so farewell. Katharina you may stay;
For I have more to commune with Bianca. [*Exit.*
  Kath. Why, and I trust I may go too. May
    I not?
What, shall I be appointed hours; as though,
    belike,
I knew not what to take, and what to leave! Ha!
                                   [*Exit.*
  Gre. You may go to the devil's dam; your
gifts are so good here is none will hold you.
Their love[b] is not so great, Hortensio, but we
may blow our nails together, and fast it fairly
out; our cake's dough on both sides. Farewell:—Yet, for the love I bear my sweet Bianca,
if I can by any means light on a fit man to teach
her that wherein she delights, I will wish him[c]
to her father.
  Hor. So will I, signior Gremio: But a word,
I pray. Though the nature of our quarrel yet

---

* *Cunning*—knowing—learned. **Cunning**, *cunning*, was originally knowledge, skill; and is so used in our translation of the Bible. Shakspere, in general, uses *cunning* in the modern sense, as in Lear:—
"Time shall unfold what plaited *cunning* hides."
But in this play the adjective is used in two other instances in the same way as in the passage before us: (See Act ii. Sc 1.)
"*Cunning* in music and the mathematics."
"*Cunning* in Greek, Latin, and other languages."

[b] *Their love.* Mason would read *our love*; Malone, *your love*. *Their love*, it appears to us, refers to the affection between Katharine and her father, who have been *jarring* throughout the scene. Baptista has resolved that Bianca shall not wed till he has found a husband for his elder daughter. Gremio and Hortensio, who aspire to Bianca, think their love is so little love between the Shrew and her father, that his resolve will change, while they blow their nails together—while they submit to some delay.

[c] *Wish him*—commend him.

---

* Douce says that this expression seems to have been suggested by the obvious term of *stale-mate*. Surely the occurrence of *mates* and *stale* in the same line does not warrant his assertion. A *stale* is a thing *stalled*—exposed for common sale. Baptista, somewhat coarsely, has offered Katharine to Gremio and Hortensio, "either of you;" and Katharine is justly indignant at being set up for the bidding of these companions.

[b] *Peat*—pet—spoiled child.

Pet. Will it not be?
Faith, sirrah, an you'll not knock, I'll wring it;
I'll try how you can *sol, fa,* and sing it.
[*He wrings* GRUMIO *by the ears.*
Gru. Help, masters, help! my master is mad.
Pet. Now, knock when I bid you: sirrah! villain!

Enter HORTENSIO.

Hor. How now? what's the matter?—My old friend Grumio! and my good friend Petrucio!—How do you all at Verona?
Pet. Signior Hortensio, come you to part the fray?
Con tutto il core bene trovato, may I say.
*Hor. Alla nostra casa bene venuto,
Molto honorato signor mio Petrucio.*
Rise, Grumio, rise; we will compound this quarrel.
Gru. Nay, 't is no matter, what he 'leges[a] in Latin.—If this be not a lawful cause for me to leave his service,—Look you, sir,—he bid me knock him, and rap him soundly, sir: Well, was it fit for a servant to use his master so; being, perhaps (for aught I see,) two and thirty,—a pip out?
Whom, 'would to God, I had well knocked at first,
Then bad not Grumio come by the worst.
Pet. A senseless villain!—Good Hortensio,
I bade the rascal knock upon your gate,
And could not get him for my heart to do it.
Gru. Knock at the gate?—O heavens!
Spake you not these words plain,—'Sirrah, knock me here,
Rap me here, knock me well, and knock me soundly?'
And come you now with—knocking at the gate?
Pet. Sirrah, be gone, or talk not, I advise you.
Hor. Petrucio, patience; I am Grumio's pledge:
Why, this a heavy chance 'twixt him and you;
Your ancient, trusty, pleasant servant, Grumio.
And tell me now, sweet friend,—what happy gale
Blows you to Padua here, from old Verona?
Pet. Such wind as scatters young men through the world,
To seek their fortunes farther than at home,
Where small experience grows. But, in a few,
Signior Hortensio, thus it stands with me:—
Antonio, my father, is deceas'd;
And I have thrust myself into this maze,
Haply to wive, and thrive, as best I may:

[a] 'Leges—alleges.

Crowns in my purse I have, and goods at home,
And so am come abroad to see the world.
Hor. Petrucio, shall I then come roundly to thee,
And wish thee to a shrew'd ill-favour'd wife?
Thou'dst thank me but a little for my counsel:
And yet I'll promise thee she shall be rich,
And very rich:—but thou 'rt too much my friend,
And I'll not wish thee to her.
Pet. Signior Hortensio, 'twixt such friends as we
Few words suffice: and, therefore, if thou know
One rich enough to be Petrucio's wife,
(As wealth is burden of my wooing dance,)
Be she as foul as was Florentius' love,
As old as Sibyl, and as curst and shrewd
As Socrates' Xantippe, or a worse,
She moves me not, or not removes, at least,
Affection's edge in me. Were she as rough
As are the swelling Adriatic seas;
I come to wive it wealthily in Padua;
If wealthily, then happily in Padua.
Gru. Nay, look you, sir, he tells you flatly what his mind is: Why, give him gold enough and marry him to a puppet, or an aglet-baby;[a] or an old trot with ne'er a tooth in her head, though she have as many diseases as two and fifty horses: why, nothing comes amiss, so money comes withal.
Hor. Petrucio, since we are stept thus far in,
I will continue that I broach'd in jest.
I can, Petrucio, help thee to a wife
With wealth enough, and young, and beauteous;
Brought up as best becomes a gentlewoman:
Her only fault (and that is faults enough,)
Is,—that she is intolerable curst,
And shrewd, and froward: so beyond all measure,
That, were my state far worser than it is,
I would not wed her for a mine of gold.
Pet. Hortensio, peace; thou know'st not gold's effect:
Tell me her father's name, and 't is enough;
For I will board her, though she chide as loud
As thunder, when the clouds in autumn crack.
Hor. Her father is Baptista Minola,
An affable and courteous gentleman:
Her name is Katharina Minola,
Renown'd in Padua for her scolding tongue.
Pet. I know her father, though I know not her;
And he knew my deceased father well:
I will not sleep, Hortensio, till I see her;

[a] *Aglet-baby.* Aglet is *aiguillette*—a point. The *baby* was a small carving on the point which carried the lace.

And therefore let me be thus bold with you,
To give you over at this first encounter,
Unless you will accompany me thither.

Gru. I pray you, sir, let him go while the humour lasts. O' my word, an she knew him as well as I do, she would think scolding would do little good upon him: She may, perhaps, call him half a score knaves, or so: why, that's nothing; an he begin once, he'll rail in his rope-tricks.[a] I'll tell you what, sir,—an she stand him but a little, he will throw a figure in her face, and so disfigure her with it, that she shall have no more eyes to see withal than a cat:[b] you know him not, sir.

Hor. Tarry, Petrucio, I must go with thee;
For in Baptista's keep my treasure is:
He hath the jewel of my life in hold,
His youngest daughter, beautiful Bianca;
And her withholds from me, and other more
Suitors to her, and rivals in my love:
Supposing it a thing impossible,
(For those defects I have before rehears'd,)
That ever Katharina will he woo'd,
Therefore this order hath Baptista ta'en,
That none shall have access unto Bianca,
Till Katharine the curst have got a husband.

Gru. Katharine the curst!
A title for a maid of all titles the worst.

Hor. Now shall my friend Petrucio do me grace;
And offer me, disguis'd in sober robes,
To old Baptista as a schoolmaster
Well seen in music[c], to instruct Bianca:
That so I may by this device, at least,
Have leave and leisure to make love to her,
And, unsuspected, court her by herself.

Enter GREMIO; *with him* LUCENTIO *disguised, with books under his arm.*

Gru. Here's no knavery! See; to beguile the old folks, how the young folks lay their heads together! Master, master, look about you: Who goes there? ha!

Hor. Peace, Grumio; 't is the rival of my love:—Petrucio, stand by a while.

Gru. A proper stripling, and an amorous!
[*They retire*

Gre. O, very well: I have perus'd the note.
Hark you, sir; I'll have them very fairly bound
All books of love, see that at any hand;
And see you read no other lectures to her:
You understand me:—Over and beside
Signior Baptista's liberality,
I'll mend it with a largess:—Take your papers too,
And let me have them very well perfum'd;
For she is sweeter than perfume itself,
To whom they go. What will you read to her?

Luc. Whate'er I read to her, I'll plead for you,
As for my patron, (stand you so assur'd,)
As firmly as yourself were still in place:
Yea, and perhaps with more successful words
Than you, unless you were a scholar, sir.

Gre. O this learning! what a thing it is!
Gru. O this woodcock! what an ass it is!
Pet. Peace, sirrah.
Hor. Grumio, mum!—God save you, signior Gremio!
Gre. And you're well met, signior Hortensio.
Trow you,
Whither I am going?—To Baptista Minola.
I promis'd to inquire carefully
About a schoolmaster for the fair Bianca:
And, by good fortune, I have lighted well
On this young man; for learning, and behaviour,
Fit for her turn; well read in poetry
And other books,—good ones, I warrant ye.

Hor. 'T is well: and I have met a gentleman,
Hath promis'd me to help me to another,
A fine musician to instruct our mistress;
So shall I no whit be behind in duty
To fair Bianca, so belov'd of me.

Gre. Belov'd of me,—and that my deeds shall prove:
Gru. And that his bags shall prove. [*Aside.*
Hor. Gremio, 't is now no time to vent our love;
Listen to me, and if you speak me fair,
I'll tell you news indifferent good for either.
Here is a gentleman, whom by chance I met,
Upon agreement from us to his liking,
Will undertake to woo curst Katharine;
Yea, and to marry her, if her dowry please.

Gre. So said, so done, is well:—
Hortensio, have you told him all her faults?
Pet. I know she is an irksome brawling scold;
If that be all, masters, I hear no harm.

---

[a] *Rope-tricks.* Sir T. Hanmer would read *rhetoric!* In Romeo and Juliet, we have *ropery.*

[b] Steevens cannot understand this: "This animal is remarkable for the keenness of its sight." Johnson thus assists him: "He shall swell up her eyes with blows, till she seem to peep with a contracted pupil, like a cat in the dark." Grumio was not a person to be very correct in his similes. If Shakspere had anywhere made a clown say, "as sick as a horse," we should have been informed by the commentators that horses, being temperate animals, are not subject to sickness, and yet this simile is daily used by persons of Grumio's character.

[c] *Well seen in music*—Well versed. Thus, in Spenser, (Fairy Queen, b. iv., c. 2,)—
"Well seen in every science that mote be."

Gre. No, say'st me so, friend? What countryman?

Pet. Born in Verona, old Antonio's son:
My father dead, my fortune lives for me;
And I do hope good days, and long, to see.

   Gre. O, sir, such a life, with such a wife,
were strange:
But if you have a stomach, to 't o' God's name;
You shall have me assisting you in all.
But, will you woo this wild cat?

   Pet.   Will I live?

   Gru. Will he woo her? ay, or I'll hang her.
                                     [*Aside.*

   Pet. Why came I hither, but to that intent?
Think you, a little din can daunt mine ears?
Have I not in my time heard lions roar?
Have I not heard the sea, puff'd up with winds,
Rage like an angry boar, chafed with sweat?
Have I not heard great ordnance in the field,
And heaven's artillery thunder in the skies?
Have I not in a pitched battle heard
Loud 'larums, neighing steeds, and trumpets'
clang?
And do you tell me of a woman's tongue;
That gives not half so great a blow to hear,[b]
As will a chestnut in a farmer's fire?
Tush! tush! fear boys with bugs.[b]

   Gru.   For he fears none.
                                       [*Aside.*

   Gre. Hortensio, hark!
This gentleman is happily arriv'd,
My mind presumes, for his own good, and
yours.

   Hor. I promis'd, we would be contributors,
And bear his charge of wooing, whatsoe'er.

   Gre. And so we will, provided that he win
her.

   Gru. I would, I were as sure of a good
dinner.   [*Aside.*

Enter TRANIO, *bravely apparelled;* and BIONDELLO.

   Tra. Gentlemen, God save you! If I may be
bold,
Tell me, I beseech you, which is the readiest
way
To the house of Signior Baptista Minola?

   Bion. He that has the two fair daughters:—
is 't he you mean?[c]

   Tra. Even he, Biondello.

   Gre. Hark you, sir; you mean not her to——

   Tra. Perhaps, him and her, sir. What have
you to do?

   Pet. Not her that chides, sir, at any hand, I
pray.

   Tra. I love no chiders, sir.—Biondello, let 's
away.

   Luc. Well begun, Tranio.   [*Aside.*

   Hor. Sir, a word ere you go;—
Are you a suitor to the maid you talk of, yea, or
no?

   Tra. An if I be, sir, is it any offence?

   Gre. No; if, without more words, you will
get you hence.

   Tra. Why, sir, I pray, are not the streets as
free
For me, as for you?

   Gre.   But so is not she.

   Tra. For what reason, I beseech you?

   Gre. For this reason, if you 'll know,
That she 's the choice love of signior Gremio.

   Hor. That she 's the chosen of signior Hortensio.

   Tra. Softly, my masters! if you be gentlemen,
Do me this right,—hear me with patience.
Baptista is a noble gentleman,
To whom my father is not all unknown;
And, were his daughter fairer than she is,
She may more suitors have, and me for one
Fair Leda's daughter had a thousand wooers;
Then well one more may fair Bianca have:
And so she shall; Lucentio shall make one,
Though Paris came, in hope to speed alone.

   Gre. What! this gentleman will out-talk us
all.

   Luc. Sir, give him head; I know, he 'll prove
a jade.

   Pet. Hortensio, to what end are all these
words?

   Hor. Sir, let me be so bold as ask you,
Did you yet ever see Baptista's daughter?

   Tra. No, sir; but hear I do, that he hath
two;
The one as famous for a scolding tongue,
As is the other for beauteous modesty.

   Pet. Sir, sir, the first 's for me; let her go by.

   Gre. Yea, leave that labour to great Hercules;
And let it be more than Alcides' twelve.

   Pet. Sir, understand you this of me, in
sooth;—
The youngest daughter, whom you hearken for,

---

[a] *To hear.* So the folio. The ordinary reading (Hanmer's) is *to the ear.* This is, perhaps, to be preferred.

[b] *Fear boys with bugs*—frighten boys with hobgoblins. Douce has given us a curious passage from Mathew's Bible, Psalm xci. v. 5: "Thou shalt not nede to be afraied for any *bugs* by night." The English name of the *puss-ce* was not applied till late in the seventeenth century, and is evidently metaphorical.

[c] This line, upon a suggestion of Tyrwhitt, has been usually given to Gremio. It seems quite unnecessary to disturb the original copy.

Her father keeps from all access of suitors,
And will not promise her to any man,
Until the elder sister first be wed;
The younger then is free, and not before.

 Tra. If it be so, sir, that you are the man
Must stead us all, and me among the rest;
An if you break the ice, and do this feat,—
Achieve the elder, set the younger free
For our access,—whose hap shall be to have her,
Will not so graceless be to be ingrate.

 Hor. Sir, you say well, and well you do conceive;
And since you do profess to be a suitor,
You must, as we do, gratify this gentleman,
To whom we all rest generally beholden.

 Tra. Sir, I shall not be slack: in sign whereof,
Please ye we may contrive this afternoon,*
And quaff carouses to our mistress' health;
And do as adversaries do in law,—
Strive mightily, but eat and drink as friends.

 Gru. Bion. O excellent motion! Fellows, let's begone.

 Hor. The motion's good indeed, and be it so;—
Petrucio, I shall be your *ben venuto.* [*Exeunt.*

* *Contrive this afternoon.*—wear away the afternoon. It is here used in the original Latin sense, as in Terence: "Totum hanc contrivi diem."

[Ladies of Padua.]

ILLUSTRATIONS OF ACT I.

¹ SCENE I.—" *Fair Padua, nursery of arts.*"

DURING the ages when books were scarce and seminaries of learning few, men of accomplishment in literature, science, and art, crowded into cities which were graced by universities. Nothing could be more natural and probable than that a tutor, like Licio, should repair to Padua from Mantua;

" His name is Licio, born in Mantua;"

or a student, like Lucentio, from Pisa,

" As he that leaves
shallow plash, to plunge him in the deep;"

or "a pedant," (Act IV. Sc. II.) turning aside from the road to Rome and Tripoli, to spend "a week or two" in the great "nursery of arts" of the Italian peninsula. The university of Padua was in all its glory in Shakspere's day; and it is difficult to those who have explored the city to resist the persuasion that the poet himself had been one of the travellers who had come from afar to look upon its seats of learning, if not to partake of its "ingenious studies." There is a pure Paduan atmosphere hanging about this play; and the visitor of to-day sees other Lucentios and Tranios in the knots of students who meet and accost in the "public places," and the servants who buy in the market; while there may be many an accomplished Bianca among the citizens' daughters who take their walks along the arcades of the venerable streets. Influences of learning, love, and mirth, are still abroad in the place, breathing as they do from the play.

The university of Padua was founded by Frederick Barbarossa, early in the thirteenth century, and was, for several hundred years, a favourite resort of learned men. Among other great personages, Petrarch, Galileo, and Christopher Columbus studied there. The number of students was once (we believe in Shakspere's age) eighteen thousand. Now that universities have multiplied, none are so thronged; but that of Padua still numbers from fifteen hundred to twenty-three hundred. Most of the educated youth of Lombardy pursue their studies there, and numbers from a greater distance. "The mathematics" are still a favourite branch of learning, with some "Greek, Latin, and other languages;" also natural philosophy and medicine. History and morals, and consequently politics, seem to be discouraged, if not omitted. The aspect of the university of Padua is now somewhat forlorn, though its halls are respectably tenanted by students. Its mouldering courts and dim staircases are thickly hung with the heraldic blazonry of the pious benefactors of the institution. The number of these coats-of-arms is so vast as to convey a strong impression of what the splendour of this seat of learning must once have been.—(M.)

² SCENE I.—" *fruitful Lombardy,
The pleasant garden of great Italy.*"

The rich plain of Lombardy is still like "a pleasant garden," and appears as if it must ever continue to be so, sheltered as it is by the vast barrier of the Alps, and fertilized by the streams which descend from their glaciers. From the walls of the Lombard cities, which are usually reared on rising grounds, the prospects are enchanting, presenting a fertile expanse, rarely disfigured by fences intersected by the great Via Æmilia—one long avenue of mulberry trees; gleaming here and there with transparent lakes, and adorned with scattered towns, villas, and churches, rising from among the vines. Corn, oil, and wine, are everywhere ripening together; and not a speck of barrenness is visible, from the northern Alps and eastern Adriatic, to the unobstructed southern horizon, where the plain melts away in sunshine.—(M.)

³ SCENE I.—" *O yes, I saw sweet beauty in her face,
Such as the daughter of Agenor had,*" &c.

There are in this play a few delicate touches of mythological images, as in the passage before us. But the old 'Tauing of a Shrew' is crammed full of the learning of a university student, paraded with an ostentation totally inconsistent with dramatic propriety. The classical allusions introduced by Shakspere in this and other comedies are just such as a gentleman might use without pedantry. But the following passage from the old play (and there are many of a similar character) is as far removed from the language of nature as it is from that of high scholarship. It is nothing beyond a school-boy's exercise:—

" *Philema.* Not for great Neptune, no, nor Jove himself
Will Philema leave Aurelius' love:
Could he instal me empress of the world,
Or make me queen and guidress of the heaven,
Yet would I not exchange my love for his:
Thy company is poor Philema's heaven,
And without thee heaven were hell to me.

ILLUSTRATIONS OF ACT I.

Emelia. And should my love, as erst did Hercules,
Attempt the burning vaults of hell,
I would, with piteous looks and pleasing words,
As once did Orpheus with his harmony,
And ravishing sound of his melodious harp,
Entreat grim Pluto, and of him obtain
That thou might'st go, and safe return again.
   Philema. And should my love, as erst Leander did,
Attempt to swim the boiling Hellespont
For Hero's love, no towers of brass should hold,
But I would follow thee through those raging floods,
With locks dishever'd, and my breast all bare:
With bended knees upon Abidae's shore,
I would, with smoky sighs and brinish tears,
Importune Neptune and the watery gods,
To send a guard of silver-scaled dolphins,
With sounding Tritons, to be our convoy,
And to transport us safe unto the shore,
Whilst I would hang about thy lovely neck,
Redoubling kiss on kiss upon thy cheeks,
And with our pastime still the swelling waves.
   Eme. Should Polidor, as Achilles did,
Only employ himself to follow arms,
Like to the warlike Amazonian queen,
Penthesilea, Hector's paramour,
Who foil'd the bloody Pyrrhus, murd'rous Greek,
I 'll thrust myself amongst the thickest throngs,
And with my utmost force assist my love."

'Scene I.—"*The presenters above speak.*"

In the second scene of the Induction, the original stage-direction is "Enter aloft the drunkard with attendants," &c. In the same way, in the parting scene of Romeo and Juliet, we have a similar direction,—"Enter Romeo and Juliet aloft." In the Illustrations of the third Act of Romeo and Juliet will be given a description and representation of the construction of the balcony, or upper stage, of our old theatres, to which these directions refer.

'Scene II.—"*Nay, 't is no matter, what he 'leges in Latin.*"

"Petrucio," says Steevens, "has been just speaking Italian to Hortensio, which Grumio mistakes for the other language." Monck Mason has a delicious remark on this:—"Mr Steevens appears to have been a little absent when he wrote his note. He forgot that Italian was Grumio's native language, and that therefore he could not possibly mistake it for Latin." To this Steevens rejoins, " I was well aware that Italian was Grumio's native language, but was not, nor am now, certain of our author's attention to this circumstance, because his Italians necessarily speak English throughout the play, with the exception of a few colloquial sentences." But if our author did attend " to this circumstance," he could not have made Grumio blunder more naturally. The "Italians *necessarily* speak English throughout the play;"—and when they speak "a few colloquial sentences" of Italian, they speak them as an Englishman would speak that or any other foreign language. To make the citizens and scholars of Padua speak English at all is—to test poetry by laws which do not apply to it—a violation of propriety. But that violation admitted, the mistake of Grumio is perfectly in keeping.

⁶ Scene II.—" *Be she as foul as was Florentius' love.*"

In Gower, 'De Confessione Amantis,' we have the description of a deformed hag whom *Florent*, a young knight, had bound himself to marry, provided she gave him the key to a riddle, upon the solution of which his life depended.

⁷ Scene II.—" *Were she as rough
As are the swelling Adriatic seas.*"

The Adriatic, though well land-locked, and in summer often as still as a mirror, is subject to severe and sudden storms. Shakspere, we have no doubt, found the image in Horace, Ode ix. Book iii. of whose odes there was no translation in the sixteenth century. Herrick has a neat translation of the ode, ' Douec gratus eram tibi, which thus concludes:

   " *Rough as the Adriatic sea, yet I
Will live with thee, or else for thee will die.*"

[Pisa.]

ACT II.

SCENE I.—*The same. A Room in Baptista's House.*

Enter KATHARINA *and* BIANCA.

Bian. Good sister, wrong me not, nor wrong yourself,
To make a bondmaid and a slave of me;
That I disdain: But for these other gawds,[a]
Unbind my hands, I'll pull them off myself,
Yea, all my raiment, to my petticoat;
Or, what you will command me, will I do,
So well I know my duty to my elders.

Kath. Of all thy suitors, here I charge thee, tell
Whom thou lov'st best: see thou dissemble not.

Bian. Believe me, sister, of all the men alive,
I never yet beheld that special face
Which I could fancy more than any other.

Kath. Minion, thou liest: Is 't not Hortensio?

Bian. If you affect him, sister, here I swear,
I'll plead for you myself but you shall have him.

Kath. O then, belike, you fancy riches more;
You will have Gremio to keep you fair.

Bian. Is it for him you do envy me so?

---
[a] *Gawds.*—The original reads *goods.* The correction was made by Theobald.

Nay, then you jest; and now I well perceive,
You have but jested with me all this while:
I prithee, sister Kate, untie my hands.

Kath. If that be jest, then all the rest was so.
[*Strikes her.*

Enter BAPTISTA.

Bap. Why, how now, dame! whence grows this insolence?
Bianca stand aside;—poor girl! she weeps:—
Go ply thy needle; meddle not with her
For shame, thou hilding,[a] of a devilish spirit,
Why dost thou wrong her that did ne'er wrong thee?

Kath. Her silence flouts me, and I'll be reveng'd. [*Flies after* BIANCA.

Bap. What, in my sight?—Bianca, get thee in. [*Exit* BIANCA.

Kath. What, will you not suffer me? Nay, now I see
She is your treasure, she must have a husband,
I must dance bare-foot on her wedding-day,
And, for your love to her, lead apes in hell.[b]

---
[a] *Hilding*—a mean-spirited person. See note on Henry IV. Part II. Act I. Sc. I. Capulet applies the term to Juliet (Romeo and Juliet, Act III. Sc. v.)
[b] A proverbial expression, applied to the ill-used class of old maids

Talk not to me. I will go sit and weep,
Till I can find occasion of revenge.
[*Exit* KATHARINA.
Bap. Was ever gentleman thus griev'd as I?
But who comes here?

Enter GREMIO, *with* LUCENTIO *in the habit of a mean man*; PETRUCIO, *with* HORTENSIO *as a musician; and* TRANIO, *with* BIONDELLO *bearing a lute and books.*

Gre. Good-morrow, neighbour Baptista.
Bap. Good-morrow, neighbour Gremio: God save you, gentlemen!
Pet. And you, good sir! Pray, have you not a daughter
Call'd Katharina, fair, and virtuous?
Bap. I have a daughter, sir, call'd Katharina.
Gre. You are too blunt, go to it orderly.
Pet. You wrong me, signior Gremio; give me leave.
I am a gentleman of Verona, sir,
That, hearing of her beauty, and her wit,
Her affability, and bashful modesty,
Her wondrous qualities, and mild behaviour,
Am bold to show myself a forward guest
Within your house, to make mine eye the witness
Of that report which I so oft have heard.
And, for an entrance to my entertainment,
I do present you with a man of mine,
[*Presenting* HORTENSIO.
Cunning in music, and the mathematics,
To instruct her fully in those sciences,
Whereof, I know, she is not ignorant:
Accept of him or else you do me wrong;
His name is Licio, born in Mantua.
Bap. You're welcome, sir; and he for your good sake:
But for my daughter Katharine, this I know,
She is not for your turn, the more my grief.
Pet. I see you do not mean to part with her;
Or else you like not of my company.
Bap. Mistake me not, I speak but as I find.
Whence are you, sir? what may I call your name?
Pet. Petrucio is my name; Antonio's son,
A man well known throughout all Italy.
Bap. I know him well: you are welcome for his sake.
Gre. Saving your tale, Petrucio, I pray,
Let us, that are poor petitioners, speak too:
Baccare![a] you are marvellous forward.

Pet. O, pardon me, signior Gremio; I would fain be doing.
Gre. I doubt it not, sir; but you will curse your wooing.
Neighbour, this is a gift very grateful, I am sure of it. To express the like kindness myself, that have been more kindly beholden to you than any, I freely give unto you this young scholar, [*presenting* LUCENTIO] that hath been long studying at Rheims; as cunning in Greek, Latin, and other languages, as the other in music and mathematics: his name is Cambio; pray accept his service.
Bap. A thousand thanks, signior Gremio: welcome, good Cambio.—But, gentle sir, [*to* TRANIO] methinks, you walk like a stranger. May I be so bold to know the cause of your coming?
Tra. Pardon me, sir, the boldness is mine own;
That, being a stranger in this city here,
Do make myself a suitor to your daughter,
Unto Bianca, fair, and virtuous.
Nor is your firm resolve unknown to me
In the preferment of the eldest sister:
This liberty is all that I request,—
That upon knowledge of my parentage,
I may have welcome 'moungst the rest that woo,
And free access and favour as the rest.
And, toward the education of your daughters,
I here bestow a simple instrument,
And this small packet of Greek and Latin books:[1]
If you accept them, then their worth is great.
Bap. Lucentio is your name? of whence, I pray?
Tra. Of Pisa, sir; son to Vincentio.
Bap. A mighty man of Pisa: by report I know him well: you are very welcome, sir.
Take you [*to* HOR.] the lute, and you [*to* LUC.] the set of books,
You shall go see your pupils presently.
Holla, within!

Enter a Servant.

Sirrah, lead
These gentlemen to my daughters; and tell them both,
These are their tutors; bid them use them well.
[*Exit* Servant, *with* HORTENSIO, LUCENTIO, *and* BIONDELLO.
We will go walk a little in the orchard,
And then to dinner: You are passing welcome,
And so I pray you all to think yourselves.

---

[a] *Baccare*—a word once in common use, meaning *go back.* "*Backare*, quoth Mortimer to his sow," was a proverbial expression before the time of Shakspere. It occurs in 'Ralph Roister Doister;' and John Heywood gives it in his 'Proverbs,' (1516). *Back* is Anglo-Saxon, in the usual sense of the word; and *are, ar,* or *aer,* is an ancient word common to the Greek and Gothic language, meaning *to go.*

We shall be able to furnish our readers with a more complete exposition of the elements of this word *baccare*, when we have occasion to speak of *aroint* in Macbeth.

ACT II.   TAMING OF THE SHREW.   [SCENE

Pet. Signior Baptista, my business asketh haste,
And every day I cannot come to woo.[a]
You knew my father well; and in him, me,
Left solely heir to all his lands and goods,
Which I have better'd rather than decreas'd:
Then tell me,—If I get your daughter's love,
What dowry shall I have with her to wife?

Bap. After my death, the one half of my lands:
And, in possession, twenty thousand crowns.

Pet. And, for that dowry, I'll assure her of
Her widowhood,[b]—be it that she survive me,—
In all my lands and leases whatsoever:
Let specialties be therefore drawn between us,
That covenants may be kept on either hand.

Bap. Ay, when the special thing is well obtain'd,
That is,—her love: for that is all in all.

Pet. Why, that is nothing; for I tell you, father,
I am as peremptory as she proud-minded;
And where two raging fires meet together,
They do consume the thing that feeds their fury:
Though little fire grows great with little wind,
Yet extreme gusts will blow out fire and all:
So I to her, and so she yields to me;
For I am rough, and woo not like a babe.

Bap. Well may'st thou woo, and happy be thy speed!
But be thou arm'd for some unhappy words.

Pet. Ay, to the proof; as mountains are for winds,
That shake not, though they blow perpetually.

Re-enter HORTENSIO, *with his head broken.*

Bap. How now, my friend? why dost thou look so pale?

Hor. For fear, I promise you, if I look pale.

Bap. What, will my daughter prove a good musician?

Hor. I think, she'll sooner prove a soldier;
Iron may hold with her, but never lutes.

Bap. Why, then thou canst not break her to the lute?

Hor. Why, no; for she hath broke the lute to me.
I did but tell her she mistook her frets,[c]
And bow'd her hand to teach her fingering;
When, with a most impatient devilish spirit,

'Frets, call you these?' quoth she: 'I'll fume with them:'
And, with that word, she struck me on the head,
And through the instrument my pate made way;
And there I stood amazed for a while,
As on a pillory, looking through the lute;
While she did call me,—rascal fiddler,
And twangling Jack; with twenty such vile terms,
As she had studied to misuse me so.

Pet. Now, by the world, it is a lusty wench;
I love her ten times more than e'er I did:
O, how I long to have some chat with her!

Bap. Well, go with me, and be not so discomfited:
Proceed in practice with my younger daughter;
She's apt to learn, and thankful for good turns.
Signior Petrucio, will you go with us:
Or shall I send my daughter Kate to you?

Pet. I pray you do; I will attend her here,—
[*Exeunt* BAPTISTA, GREMIO, TRANIO, *and* HORTENSIO.
And woo her with some spirit when she comes.
Say, that she rail; why, then I'll tell her plain
She sings as sweetly as a nightingale:
Say, that she frown; I'll say, she looks as clear
As morning roses newly wash'd with dew:[a]
Say, she be mute, and will not speak a word;
Then I'll commend her volubility,
And say she uttereth piercing eloquence:
If she do bid me pack, I'll give her thanks
As though she bid me stay by her a week;
If she deny to wed, I'll crave the day
When I shall ask the banns, and when be married:—
But here she comes; and now, Petrucio, speak.

Enter KATHARINA.

Good-morrow, Kate; for that's your name, I hear.

Kath. Well have you heard, but something hard of hearing;
They call me—Katharine, that do talk of me.

Pet. You lie, in faith; for you are call'd plain Kate,
And bonny Kate, and sometimes Kate the curst:
But Kate, the prettiest Kate in Christendom,
Kate of Kate-Hall, my super-dainty Kate,
For dainties are all cates; and therefore, Kate,
Take this of me, Kate of my consolation;—
Hearing thy mildness prais'd in every town,
Thy virtues spoke of, and thy beauty sounded,

---

[a] The burthen of an old ballad called 'The Ingenious Braggadocio,' was

"And I cannot come every day to woo."

[b] *Her widowhood. Widowhood* must here mean, not the condition of a widow, but the property to which the widow would be entitled. Petrucio would assure Katharine of a widow's full provision in all his "lands and leases." He would not "bar dower,"—by fine and recovery.

[c] See Hamlet, Act III. Sc. II.

---

[a] Shakspere had a portion of this beautiful image from the old play:—

"As glorious as the morning wash'd with dew."

Milton has transferred the idea of our poet to his L'Allegro:—

"There, on beds of violets blue,
And fresh-blown roses wash'd in dew."

TAMING OF THE SHREW.

(Yet not so deeply as to thee belongs,)
Myself am mov'd to woo thee for my wife.
Kath. Mov'd! in good time: let him that
    mov'd you hither
Remove you hence: I knew you at the first,
You were a moveable.
Pet.   Why, what's a moveable?
Kath. A joint-stool.
Pet   Thou hast hit it: come, sit on me.
Kath. Asses are made to bear, and so are you.
Pet. Women are made to bear, and so are you.
Kath. No such jade as you, if me you mean.
Pet. Alas, good Kate! I will not burden thee:
For, knowing thee to be but young and light,—
Kath. Too light for such a swain as you to
    catch;
And yet as heavy as my weight should be.
Pet. Should be? should° buz!ᵃ
Kath.   Well ta'en, and like a buzzard.
Pet. O, slow-wing'd turtle! shall a buzzard
    take thee?
Kath. Ay, for a turtle; as he takes a buzzard.
Pet. Come, come, you wasp; i' faith, you are
    too angry.
Kath. If I be waspish, best beware my sting.
Pet. My remedy is then, to pluck it out.
Kath. Ay, if the fool could find it where it lies.
Pet. Who knows not where a wasp does wear
    his sting?
In his tail.
Kath.   In his tongue.
Pet.   Whose tongue?
Kath. Yours, if you talk of tails; and so fare-
    well.
Pet. What, with my tongue in your tail? nay,
    come again,
Good Kate; I am a gentleman.
Kath.   That I'll try.
                      [*Striking him.*
Pet. I swear I'll cuff you, if you strike again.
Kath. So may you lose your arms:
If you strike me you are no gentleman;
And if no gentleman, why, then no arms.
Pet. A herald, Kate? O, put me in thy books.
Kath. What is your crest? a coxcomb?
Pet. A combless cock, so Kate will be my hen.
Kath. No cock of mine, you crow too like a
    craven.ᵇ

Pet. Nay, come, Kate, come; you must not
    look so sour.
Kath. It is my fashion, when I see a crab.
Pet. Why, here's no crab; and therefore look
    not sour.
Kath. There is, there is.
Pet. Then show it me.
Kath.   Had I a glass, I would.
Pet. What, you mean my face?
Kath.   Well aim'd of such a young one.
Pet. Now, by Saint George, I am too young
    for you.
Kath. Yet you are withered.
Pet.   'Tis with cares.
Kath.   I care not.
Pet. Nay, hear you, Kate: in sooth, you
    'scape not so.
Kath. I chafe you, if I tarry; let me go.
Pet. No, not a whit. I find you passing gentle.
'Twas told me, you were rough, and coy, and
    sullen,
And now I find report a very liar;
For thou art pleasant, gamesome, passing cour-
    teous,
But slow in speech, yet sweet as spring-time
    flowers:
Thou canst not frown, thou canst not look
    askance,
Nor bite the lip, as angry wenches will;
Nor hast thou pleasure to be cross in talk;
But thou with mildness entertain'st thy wooers,
With gentle conference, soft and affable.
Why does the world report that Kate doth limp?
O slanderous world! Kate, like the hazel-twig,
Is straight, and slender; and as brown in hue,
As hazel-nuts, and sweeter than the kernels.
O, let me see thee walk: thou dost not halt.
Kath. Go, fool, and whom thou keep'st com-
    mand.
Pet. Did ever Dian so become a grove,
As Kate this chamber with her princely gait?
O, be thou Dian, and let her be Kate,
And then let Kate be chaste, and Dian sportful.
Kath. Where did you study all this goodly
    speech?
Pet. It is extempore, from my mother-wit.
Kath. A witty mother! witless else her son.
Pet. Am I not wise?
Kath.   Yes; keep you warm.
Pet. Marry, so I mean, sweet Katharine, in
    thy bed:

ᵃ This is ordinarily printed
    "Should be? Should buz."
We follow the original, which is clearly right. *Buz* is an interjection of ridicule, as in Hamlet:—
    "*Pol.* The actors are come hither, my lord.
    Ham. Buz, buz!"
ᵇ *Craven.*—A craven cock, and a craven knight, were each contemptible. The knight who had craven, or craved, life from an antagonist, was branded with the name which

he had uttered in preferring safety to honour. The terms of chivalry and cock-fighting were synonymous in the feudal times, as those of the cock-pit and the boxing-ring are equivalent now. To show *a white feather* is now a term of pugilism, derived from the ruffled plumes of the frightened bird.

And therefore, setting all this chat aside,—
Thus in plain terms:—Your father hath consented
That you shall be my wife; your dowry 'greed on;
And, will you, nill you, I will marry you.
Now, Kate, I am a husband for your turn;
For, by this light, whereby I see thy beauty,
(Thy beauty that doth make me like thee well,)
Thou must be married to no man but me;
For I am he am born to tame you, Kate;
And bring you from a wild Kate* to a Kate
Conformable, as other household Kates.
Here comes your father; never make denial,
I must and will have Katharine to my wife.

Re-enter BAPTISTA, GREMIO, *and* TRANIO.

Bap. Now, Signior Petrucio: How speed you with my daughter?
Pet. How but well, sir? how but well?
It were impossible I should speed amiss.
Bap. Why, how now, daughter Katharine? in your dumps?
Kath. Call you me daughter? now I promise you,
You have show'd a tender fatherly regard,
To wish me wed to one half lunatic,
A mad-cap ruffian, and a swearing Jack,
That thinks with oaths to face the matter out.
Pet. Father, 't is thus,—yourself and all the world,
That talk'd of her, have talk'd amiss of her;
If she be curst, it is for policy:
For she 's not froward, but modest as the dove;
She is not hot, but temperate as the morn;
For patience she will prove a second Grissel;
And Roman Lucrece for her chastity:
And to conclude,—we have 'greed so well together,
That upon Sunday is the wedding-day.
Kath. I 'll see thee hang'd on Sunday first.
Gre. Hark, Petrucio! she says she 'll see thee hang'd first.
Tra. Is this your speeding? nay, then, good night our part!
Pet. Be patient, gentlemen; I choose her for myself;
If she and I be pleas'd, what 's that to you?
'T is bargain'd 'twixt us twain, being alone,
That she shall still be curst in company.
I tell you, 't is incredible to believe
How much she loves me: O, the kindest Kate!
She hung about my neck; and kiss on kiss
She vied so fast, protesting oath on oath,
That in a twink she won me to her love.

* *Kate* in the first folio, *Kat* in the second.

O, you are novices! 't is a world to see,
How tame, when men and women are alone,
A meacock wretch can make the curstest shrew.
Give me thy hand, Kate: I will unto Venice,
To buy apparel 'gainst the wedding-day:*
Provide the feast, father, and bid the guests;
I will be sure my Katharine shall be fine.
Bap. I know not what to say: but give me your hands;
God send you joy, Petrucio! 't is a match.
Gre. Tra. Amen, say we; we will be witnesses.
Pet. Father, and wife, and gentlemen, adieu;
I will to Venice; Sunday comes apace:
We will have rings, and things, and fine array;
And kiss me, Kate, we will be married o' Sunday.
[*Exeunt* PETRUCIO *and* KATHARINA *severally.*
Gre. Was ever match clapp'd up so suddenly?
Bap. Faith, gentlemen, now I play a merchant's part,
And venture madly on a desperate mart.
Tra. 'T was a commodity lay fretting by you;
'T will bring you gain, or perish on the seas.
Bap. The gain I seek is—quiet in the match.
Gre. No doubt, but he hath got a quiet catch.
But now, Baptista, to your younger daughter;
Now is the day we long have looked for;
I am your neighbour, and was suitor first.
Tra. And I am one that love Bianca more
Than words can witness, or your thoughts can guess.
Gre. Youngling! thou canst not love so dear as I.
Tra. Grey-beard! thy love doth freeze.
Gre. But thine doth fry.
Skipper, stand back; 't is age that nourisheth.
Tra. But youth, in ladies' eyes that flourisheth.
Bap. Content you, gentlemen; I will compound this strife:
'T is deeds must win the prize; and he, of both,
That can assure my daughter greatest dower,
Shall have my Bianca's love.
Say, signior Gremio, what can you assure her?
Gre. First, as you know, my house within the city
Is richly furnished with plate and gold;
Basins, and ewers, to lave her dainty hands;
My hangings all of Tyrian tapestry:
In ivory coffers I have stuff'd my crowns;
In cypress chests my arras, counterpoints,*
Costly apparel, tents and canopies,

* *Counterpoints* and *counterpanes* are the same. These coverlets were composed of counter panes or points, of various colours, contrasting with each other.

Fine linen, Turkey cushions boss'd with pearl,
Valance of Venice gold in needle-work,
Pewter and brass, and all things that belong
To house, or housekeeping: then, at my farm,
I have a hundred milch-kine to the pail,
Sixscore fat oxen standing in my stalls,
And all things answerable to this portion.
Myself am struck in years, I must confess;
And, if I die to-morrow, this is hers,
If, whilst I live, she will be only mine.
   Tra. That, only, came well in. Sir, list to
    me:
I am my father's heir, and only son;
If I may have your daughter to my wife,
I'll leave her houses three or four as good,
Within rich Pisa walls, as any one
Old signior Gremio has in Padua,
Besides two thousand ducats by the year,
Of fruitful land, all which shall be her jointure.
What! have I pinch'd you, signior Gremio?
   Gre. Two thousand ducats by the year of
    land!
My land amounts not to so much in all:
That she shall have; besides an argosy
That now is lying in Marseilles' road.[a]
What! have I chok'd you with an argosy?
   Tra. Gremio, 'tis known my father hath no
    less
Than three great argosies; besides two galliasses,[b]
And twelve tight galleys: these I will assure her,
And twice as much, whate'er thou offer'st next.
   Gre. Nay, I have offer'd all, I have no more;
And she can have no more than all I have.
If you like me, she shall have me and mine.

  [a] Gremio's land was not worth "two thousand ducats by
the year:" but he made up the deficiency by "an argosy."
Du Cange says that *argosy* is derived from *Argo*, the fabulous
name of the first ship.
  [b] *Galliass*—galley, galleon, galleot, were vessels of burthen, navigated both with sails and oars.

   Tra. Why, then the maid is mine from all
    the world,
By your firm promise. Gremio is outvied.
   Bap. I must confess your offer is the best;
And, let your father make her the assurance,
She is your own; else, you must pardon me:
If you should die before him, where's her dower?
   Tra. That's but a cavil: he is old, I young.
   Gre. And may not young men die, as well as
    old?
   Bap. Well, gentlemen,
I am thus resolv'd:—On Sunday next you know
My daughter Katharine is to be married:
Now, on the Sunday following, shall Bianca
Be bride to you, if you make this assurance;
If not, to signior Gremio:
And so I take my leave, and thank you both.
                                           [*Exit.*
   Gre. Adieu, good neighbour.—Now I fear
    thee not;
Sirrah, young gamester, your father were a fool
To give thee all, and, in his waning age,
Set foot under thy table: Tut! a toy!
An old Italian fox is not so kind, my boy.
                                           [*Exit.*
   Tra. A vengeance on your crafty wither'd
    hide!
Yet I have faced it with a card of ten.[a]
'Tis in my head to do my master good:—
I see no reason, but suppos'd Lucentio
Must get a father call'd—suppos'd Vincentio,
And that's a wonder: fathers, commonly,
Do get their children; but, in this case of wooing,
A child shall get a sire, if I fail not of my cunning.
                                           [*Exit.*

  [a] *Card of ten*—a proverbial expression, as old as Skelton:—
"First pick a quarrel, and fall out with him then,
And so outface him with *a card of ten.*"

RECENT NEW READING.

Sc. I. p. 29d.—"She is not hot, but temperate as the morn."

"She is not hot, but temperate as the *moon*."—*Collier.*
Mr. Collier says *moon*, "in reference to the chaste coldness of the moon, was doubtless the true word." But if authority were necessary for the retention of *moon* in connection with *temperate*, Shakspere might furnish it:—
"Modest as morning, when she coldly eyes
The youthful Phœbus."
       'TROILUS AND CRESSIDA' Act I. Sc. III.

ILLUSTRATIONS OF ACT II.

¹ SCENE I.—"*And this small packet of Greek and Latin books.*"

It is not to be supposed that the daughters of Baptista were more learned than other ladies of their city and their time.

Under the walls of universities, then the only centres of intellectual light, knowledge was shed abroad like sunshine at noon, and was naturally more or less enjoyed by all. At the time when Shakspere and the university of Padua flourished, the higher classes of women were not deemed unfitted for a learned education. Queen Elizabeth, Lady Jane Grey, the daughters of Sir Thomas More, and others, will at once occur to the reader's recollection in proof of this. "Greek, Latin, and other languages," "the mathematics," and "to read philosophy," then came as naturally as "music" within the scope of female education. Any association of pedantry with the training of the young ladies of this play is in the prejudices of the reader, not in the mind of the poet.—(M.)

² SCENE I.—"*Good morrow, Kate.*"

The first scene between Petrucio and Kate is founded upon a similar scene in 'The Taming of a Shrew.' Our readers may amuse themselves by a comparison of Shakspere and his predecessor:—

"*Alf.* Ha, Kate, come hither, wench, and list to me:
Use this gentleman friendly as thou canst.
Fer. Twenty good morrows to my lovely Kate.
Kate. You jest, I am sure; is she yours already?
Fer. I tell thee, Kate, I know thou lov'st me well.
Kate. The devil you do! who told you so?
Fer. My mind, sweet Kate, doth say I am the man,
Must wed, and bed, and marry bonny Kate.
Kate. Was ever seen so gross an ass as this?
Fer. Ay, to stand so long, and never get a kiss.
Kate. Hands off, I say, and get you from this place;
Or I will set my ten commandments in your face.
Fer. I prithee do, Kate; they say thou art a shrew,
And I like thee the better, for I would have thee so.
Kate. Let go my hand for fear it reach your ear.
Fer. No, Kate, this hand is mine, and I thy love.
Kate. I'faith, sir, no, the woodcock wants his tail.
Fer. But yet his bill will serve if the other fail.
Alf. How now, Ferando? what, my daughter?
Fer. She's willing, sir, and loves me as her life.
Kate. 'Tis for your skin, then, but not to be your wife.
Alf. Come hither, Kate, and let me give thy hand
To him that I have chosen for thy love,
And thou to-morrow shalt be wed to him.
Kate. Why, father, what do you mean to do with me,
To give me thus unto this brainsick man,
That in his mood cares not to murder me?
                    [*She turns aside and speaks.*
And yet I will consent and marry him,
(For I, methinks, have liv'd too long a maid,)
And match him too, or else his manhood's good.
Alf. Give me thy hand; Ferando loves thee well,
And will with wealth and ease maintain thy state.

Here, Ferando, take her for thy wife,
And Sunday next shall be our wedding-day.
Fer. Why so, did I not tell thee I should be the man?
Father, I leave my lovely Kate with you,
Provide yourselves against our marriage-day,
For I must hie me to my country house
In haste, to see provision may be made
To entertain my Kate when she doth come.
Alf. Do so; come, Kate, why dost thou look
So sad? Be merry, wench, thy wedding-day's at hand;
Son, fare you well, and see you keep your promise.
                    [*Exit ALFONSO and KATE.*'

³ SCENE I.—"*I will unto Venice,
To buy apparel 'gainst the wedding-day.*"

. . . . . .

"*My house within the city
Is richly furnished with plate and gold,*" &c.

If Shakspere had not seen the interior of Italian houses when he wrote this play, he must have possessed some effectual means of knowing and realising in his imagination the particulars of such an interior. Every educated man might be aware that the extensive commerce of Venice must bring within the reach of the neighbouring cities a multitude of articles of foreign production and taste. But there is a particularity in his mention of these articles, which strongly indicates the experience of an eye-witness. The "cypress chests," and "ivory coffers," rich in antique carving, are still existing, with some remnants of "Tyrian tapestry," to carry back the imagination of the traveller to the days of the glory of the republic. The "plate and gold" are, for the most part, gone, to supply the needs of the impoverished aristocracy, who (to their credit) will part with everything sooner than their pictures. The "tents and canopies," and "Turkey cushions 'bossed with pearl," now no longer seen, were appropriate to the days when Cyprus, Candia, and the Morea were dependencies of Venice, scattering their productions through the eastern cities of Italy, and actually establishing many of their customs in the singular capital of the Venetian dominion. After Venice, Padua was naturally first served with importations of luxury.

Venice was, and is still, remarkable for its jewellery, especially its fine works in gold. "Venice gold" was wrought into "valance"—tapestry—by the needle, and was used for every variety of ornament, from chains as fine as if made of woven hair, to the most massive form in which gold can be worn. At the present day, the traveller who walks round the Piazza of St. Mark's is surprised at the large proportion of jewellers' shops, and at the variety and elegance of the ornaments they contain,—the shell necklaces, the jewelled rings and tiaras, and the profusion of gold chains —(M.)

[Church of St. Giustina, Padua.]

ACT III.

SCENE I.—*A Room in* Baptista's *House.*

Enter LUCENTIO, HORTENSIO, *and* BIANCA.

Luc. Fiddler, forbear; you grow too forward, sir:
Have you so soon forgot the entertainment
Her sister Katharine welcom'd you withal?
  Hor. But, wrangling pedant, this is
The patroness of heavenly harmony:
Then give me leave to have prerogative;
And when in music we have spent an hour,
Your lecture shall have leisure for as much.
  Luc. Preposterous ass! that never read so far
To know the cause why music was ordain'd!
Was it not, to refresh the mind of man,
After his studies, or his usual pain?
Then give me leave to read philosophy,
And, while I pause, serve in your harmony.
  Hor. Sirrah, I will not bear these braves of thine.
  Bian. Why, gentlemen, you do me double wrong,
To strive for that which resteth in my choice:
I am no breeching scholar in the schools;
I'll not be tied to hours, nor 'pointed times,
But learn my lessons as I please myself.
And, to cut off all strife, here sit we down:

Take you your instrument, play you the whiles;
His lecture will be done ere you have tun'd.
  Hor. You'll leave his lecture when I am in tune?
                      [*To* BIANCA.—HORTENSIO *retires.*
  Luc. That will be never;—tune your instrument.
  Bian. Where left we last?
  Luc. Here, madam:—
*Hac ibat Simois; hic est Sigeia tellus;
Hic steterat Priami regia celsa senis.*
  Bian. Conster them.
  Luc. Hac ibat, as I told you before,—*Simois,*
I am Lucentio,—*hic est,* son unto Vincentio of
Pisa,—*Sigeia tellus,* disguised thus to get your
love;—*Hic steterat,* and that Lucentio that
comes a wooing,—*Priami,* is my man Tranio,
—*regia,* bearing my port,—*celsa senis,* that we
might beguile the old pantaloon.
  Hor. Madam, my instrument's in tune.
                                   [*Returning*
  Bian. Let's hear;—   [HORTENSIO *plays.*
O fye! the treble jars.
  Luc. Spit in the hole, man, and tune again.
  Bian. Now let me see if I can construe it:
Hac ibat Simois, I know you not;—*hic est Sigeia
tellus,* I trust you not;—*Hic steterat Priami,*

LUCENTIO AND BIANCA.

Bianca. "Where left we last?
Lucentio. Here, Madam.—
*Hic ibat Simois; hic est Sigeia tellus;
Hic steterat Priami regia celsa senis.*
Bianca. Construe them.
Lucentio. Hic ibat, as I told you before—*Simois,* I am Lucentio,—
hic est, son unto Vincentio of Pisa,—*Sigeia tellus,* disguised thus to get
your love;—*Hic steterat,* and that Lucentio that comes a wooing —
Priami, is my man Tranio,—*regia,* bearing my port,—*celsa senis,* that
we might beguile the old pantaloon."

Taming of the Shrew. Act iii. s. 1.

take heed he hear us not ;—*regia*, presume not ; *celsa senis*, despair not.
Hor. Madam, 't is now in tune.
Luc. All but the base.
Hor. The base is right; 't is the base knave that jars.
How fiery and forward our pedant is!
Now, for my life, the knave doth court my love:
Pedascule, I 'll watch you better yet,
Bian. In time I may believe, yet I mistrust.
Luc. Mistrust it not ; for, sure, Æacides
Was Ajax,—call'd so from his grandfather.
Bian. I must believe my master; else, I promise you,
I should be arguing still upon that doubt:
But let it rest.—Now, Licio, to you:—
Good masters, take it not unkindly, pray,
That I have been thus pleasant with you both.
Hor. You may go walk, [*to* LUCENTIO] and give me leave awhile;
My lessons make no music in three parts.
Luc. Are you so formal, sir? well, I must wait,
And watch withal; for, but I be deceiv'd,[a]
Our fine musician groweth amorous. [*Aside.*
Hor. Madam, before you touch the instrument,
To learn the order of my fingering,
I must begin with rudiments of art ;
To teach you gamut in a briefer sort,
More pleasant, pithy, and effectual,
Than hath been taught by any of my trade :
And there it is in writing, fairly drawn.
Bian. Why, I am past my gamut long ago.
Hor. Yet read the gamut of Hortensio.
Bian. [*Reads.*] Gamut *I am, the ground of all accord,*
A re, *to plead Hortensio's passion;*
B mi, *Bianca,* take him for thy lord,
C fa ut, *that loves with all affection :*
D sol re, *one cliff, two notes have I ;*
E la mi, *show pity, or I die.*[b]
Call you this gamut ? tut ! I like it not :
Old fashions please me best ; I am not so nice,
To change true rules for odd inventions.[b]

Enter a Servant.

Serv. Mistress, your father prays you leave your books,

[a] But I be deceiv'd—unless I be deceived.
[b] The original reads,—
"To change true rules for *old* inventions."
These alterations, which were made by **the Editor of the** second folio, and by Theobald, are not violent, **and belong to** the class of typographical corrections.

And help to dress your sister's chamber up ;
You know, to-morrow is the wedding-day.
Bian. Farewell, sweet masters, both ; I must be gone.
[*Exeunt* BIANCA *and* Serv.
Luc. 'Faith, mistress, then I have no cause to stay. [*Exit.*
Hor. But I have cause to pry into this pedant;
Methinks, he looks as though he were in love:
Yet if thy thoughts, Bianca, be so humble,
To cast thy wand'ring eyes on every stale,
Seize thee that list : If once I find thee ranging,
Hortensio will be quit with thee by changing.
[*Exit.*

SCENE II.—*The same. Before* Baptista's *House.*

Enter BAPTISTA, TRANIO, KATHARINA, BIANCA, LUCENTIO, *and* Attendants.

Bap. Signior Lucentio, [*to* TRANIO] this is the 'pointed day
That Katharine and Petrucio should be married,
And yet we hear not of our son-in-law :
What will he said ? what mockery will it be,
To want the bridegroom, when the priest attends
To speak the ceremonial rites of marriage ?
What says Lucentio to this shame of ours ?
Kath. No shame but mine : I must, forsooth, be forc'd
To give my hand, oppos'd against my heart,
Unto a mad-brain rudesby, full of spleen ;
Who woo'd in haste, and means to wed at leisure.
I told you, I, he was a frantic fool,
Hiding his bitter jests in blunt behaviour :
And, to be noted for a merry man,
He 'll woo a thousand, 'point the day of marriage,
Make friends, invite them, and proclaim the banns ;
Yet never means to wed where he hath woo'd.
Now must the world point at poor Katharine,
And say,—' Lo, there is mad Petrucio's wife,
If it would please him come and marry her.'
Tra. Patience good Katharine, and Baptista too;
Upon my life, Petrucio means but well,
Whatever fortune stays him from his word :
Though he be blunt, I know him passing wise ;
Though he be merry, yet withal he 's honest.
Kath. 'Would Katharine had never seen him, though !
[*Exit, weeping, followed by* BIANCA, *and others.*
Bap. Go, girl ; I cannot blame thee now to weep ;
For such an injury would vex a saint,
Much more a shrew of thy impatient humour.

Enter BIONDELLO.

Bion. Master, master! news, old news,[a] and such news as you never heard of!

Bap. Is it new and old too? how may that be?

Bion. Why, is it not news, to hear of Petrucio's coming?

Bap. Is he come?

Bion. Why, no, sir.

Bap. What then?

Bion. He is coming.

Bap. When will he be here?

Bion. When he stands where I am, and sees you there.

Tra. But, say, what:—To thine old news.

Bion. Why, Petrucio is coming, in a new hat and an old jerkin; a pair of old breeches, thrice turned; a pair of boots that have been candle-cases, one buckled, another laced; an old rusty sword ta'en out of the town armoury, with a broken hilt, and chapeless; with two broken points:[b] His horse hipped with an old mothy saddle, and stirrups of no kindred: besides, possessed with the glanders, and like to mose in the chine; troubled with the lampass, infected with the fashions,[c] full of wind-galls, sped with spavins, raied with the yellows, past cure of the fives, stark spoiled with the staggers, begnawn with the bots; swayed in the back, and shoulder-shotten; ne'er legg'd before; and with a half-checked bit, and a head-stall of sheep's leather, which, being restrained to keep him from stumbling, hath been often burst, and now repaired with knots; one girth six times pieced, and a woman's crupper of velure,[d] which hath two letters for her name, fairly set down in studs, and here and there pieced with packthread.[e]

Bap. Who comes with him?

Bion. O, Sir, his lackey, for all the world caparisoned like the horse; with a linen stock[e] on one leg, and a kersey boot-hose on the other, gartered with a red and blue list; an old hat, and *The humour of forty fancies* pricked in't for a feather:[f] a monster, a very monster in apparel;

and not like a Christian footboy, or a gentleman's lackey.

Tra. 'T is some odd humour pricks him to this fashion;
Yet oftentimes he goes but mean apparel'd.

Bap. I am glad he is come, howsoe'er he comes.

Bion. Why, sir, he comes not.

Bap. Didst thou not say, he comes?

Bion. Who? that Petrucio came?

Bap. Ay, that Petrucio came.

Bion. No, sir; I say, his horse comes with him on his back.

Bap. Why, that's all one.

Bion. Nay, by Saint Jamy, I hold you a penny,
A horse and a man is more than one, and yet not many.

Enter PETRUCIO *and* GRUMIO.

Pet. Come, where be these gallants? who's at home?

Bap. You are welcome, sir.

Pet. And yet I come not well.

Bap. And yet you halt not.

Tra. Not so well apparel'd
As I wish you were.

Pet. Were it better I should rush in thus.
But where is Kate? where is my lovely bride?
How does my father?—Gentles, methinks you frown:
And wherefore gaze this goodly company;
As if they saw some wondrous monument,
Some comet, or unusual prodigy?

Bap. Why, sir, you know, this is your wedding-day:
First we were sad, fearing you would not come;
Now sadder, that you come so unprovided.
Fye! doff this habit, shame to your estate,
An eye-sore to our solemn festival.

Tra. And tell us, what occasion of import
Hath all so long detain'd you from your wife,
And sent you hither so unlike yourself?

Pet. Tedious it were to tell, and harsh to hear:
Sufficeth, I am come to keep my word,
Though in some part enforced to digress;
Which, at more leisure, I will so excuse
As you shall well be satisfied withal.
But, where is Kate? I stay too long from her;
The morning wears, 't is time we were at church.

Tra. See not your bride in these unreverent robes;
Go to my chamber, put on clothes of mine.

Pet. Not I, believe me; thus I'll visit her.

Bap. But thus I trust, you will not marry her

---

[a] *Old news—tare news.* The words, however, are not in the original, being added by Rowe. But they are necessary for the context.

[b] *Two broken points.* Johnson says, "How a sword should have two broken points I cannot tell." The *points* were amongst the most costly and elegant parts of the dress of Elizabeth's time; and to have *two broken* was certainly indicative of more than ordinary slovenliness.

[c] *Fashions*—the farcins, or farcy. In Greene's 'Looking-glass for London and England,' we have mentioned, amongst the "outward diseases" of a horse, "the *spavin*, splent, ringbone, windgall, and *fashion*."

[d] *Velure*—velvet.

[e] *Stock*—stocking.

[f] *The humour of forty fancies* was, it is conjectured by Warburton, a slight collection of ballads, or short poems, which Petrucio's lackey pricked in his hat for a feather.

302

Pet. Good sooth, even thus; therefore ha'
 done with words;
To me she's married, not unto my clothes:
Could I repair what she will wear in me,
As I can change these poor accoutrements,
'T were well for Kate, and better for myself.
But what a fool am I, to chat with you,
When I should bid good-morrow to my bride,
And seal the title with a lovely kiss!
 [*Exeunt* PETRUCIO, GRUMIO, *and* BIONDELLO.
 Tra. He hath some meaning in his mad attire:
We will persuade him, be it possible,
To put on better ere he go to church.
 Bap. I'll after him, and see the event of this.
 [*Exit.*
 Tra. But, sir, to love* concerneth us to add
Her father's liking: Which to bring to pass,
As I before imparted to your worship,
I am to get a man,—whate'er he be,
It skills not much; we'll fit him to our turn,—
And he shall be Vincentio of Pisa;
And make assurance, here in Padua,
Of greater sums than I have promised.
So shall you quietly enjoy your hope,
And marry sweet Bianca with consent.
 Luc. Were it not that my fellow schoolmaster
Doth watch Bianca's steps so narrowly,
'T were good, methinks, to steal our marriage;
Which once perform'd, let all the world say—
 no,
I'll keep mine own, despite of all the world.
 Tra. That by degrees we mean to look into,
And watch our vantage in this business:
We'll over-reach the greybeard, Gremio,
The narrow-prying father, Minola,
The quaint musician, amorous Licio;
All for my master's sake, Lucentio.
 Enter GREMIO.

Signior Gremio! came you from the church?
 Gre. As willingly as e'er I came from school.
 Tra. And is the bride and bridegroom coming
 home?
 Gre. A bridegroom, say you? 't is a groom
 indeed,
A grumbling groom, and that the girl shall find.
 Tra. Curster than she? why, 't is impossible.
 Gre. Why he's a devil, a devil, a very fiend.
 Tra. Why, she's a devil, a devil, the devil's
 dam.
 Gre. Tut! she's a lamb, a dove, a fool to him.
I'll tell you, sir Lucentio; When the priest
Should ask—if Katharine should be his wife,

---
* To love.—The word *to* is omitted in the folio. Malone added *her* as well as *to*, which appears unnecessary.

'Ay, by gogs-wouns,' quoth he; and swore so
 loud
That, all amaz'd, the priest let fall the book:
And, as he stoop'd again to take it up,
This mad-brain'd bridegroom took him such a
 cuff,
That down fell priest and book, and book and
 priest;
'Now take them up,' quoth he, 'if any list.'
 Tra. What said the wench, when he arose
 again?
 Gre. Trembled and shook; for why, he
 stamp'd, and swore,
As if the vicar meant to cozen him.
But after many ceremonies done,
He calls for wine:—'A health,' quoth he,* as if
He had been aboard, carousing to his mates
After a storm:—Quaff'd off the muscadel,
And threw the sops all in the sexton's face;
Having no other reason,—
But that his beard grew thin and hungerly,
And seem'd to ask him sops as he was drinking.
This done, he took the bride about the neck,
And kiss'd her lips with such a clamorous smack,
That, at the parting, all the church did echo.
And I, seeing this, came thence for very shame;
And after me, I know, the rout is coming:
Such a mad marriage never was before.
Hark, hark! I hear the minstrels play.
 [*Music.*

Enter PETRUCIO, KATHARINA, BIANCA, BAPTISTA, HORTENSIO, GRUMIO, *and Train.*

 Pet. Gentlemen and friends, I thank you for
 your pains:
I know, you think to dine with me to-day,
And have prepar'd great store of wedding cheer;
But so it is, my haste doth call me hence,
And therefore here I mean to take my leave.
 Bap. Is 't possible you will away to-night?
 Pet. I must away to-day, before night come:
Make it no wonder; if you knew my business,
You would entreat me rather go than stay.
And, honest company, I thank you all,
That have beheld me give away myself
To this most patient, sweet, and virtuous wife.
Dine with my father, drink a health to me;
For I must hence, and farewell to you all.
 Tra. Let us entreat you stay till after dinner.
 Pet. It may not be.
 Gre.   Let me entreat you.
 Pet. It cannot be.
 Kath.   Let me entreat you.
 Pet. I am content.
 Kath.   Are you content to stay?

[Act III.] TAMING OF THE SHREW. [Scene II.

Pet. I am content you shall entreat me stay;
But yet not stay, entreat me how you can.
  Kath. Now, if you love me, stay.
  Pet.   Grumio, my horse.[a]
  Gru. Ay, sir, they be ready; the oats have eaten the horses.
  Kath. Nay, then,
Do what thou canst, I will not go to-day;
No, nor to-morrow, nor till I please myself.
The door is open, sir, there lies your way,
You may be jogging whiles your boots are green;
For me, I'll not be gone, till I please myself:
'T is like, you 'll prove a jolly surly groom,
That take it on you at the first so roundly.
  Pet. O Kate, content thee; prithee be not angry.
  Kath. I will be angry. What hast thou to do?
Father, be quiet: he shall stay my leisure.
  Gre. Ay, marry, sir: now it begins to work.
  Kath. Gentlemen, forward to the bridal dinner:
I see, a woman may be made a fool,
If she had not a spirit to resist.
  Pet. They shall go forward, Kate, at thy command:
Obey the bride, you that attend on her:
Go to the feast, revel and domineer,
Carouse full measure to her maidenhead,
Be mad and merry,—or go hang yourselves;
But for my bonny Kate, she must with me.
Nay, look not big, nor stamp, nor stare, nor fret;
I will be master of what is mine own:

  [a] *Horse* is here used in the plural.

She is my goods, my chattels; she is my house,
My household-stuff, my field, my barn,
My horse, my ox, my ass, my any thing;
And here she stands, touch her whoever dare;
I'll bring mine action on the proudest he
That stops my way in Padua. Grumio,
Draw forth thy weapon, we are beset with thieves;
Rescue thy mistress, if thou be a man:—
Fear not, sweet wench, they shall not touch thee, Kate;
I'll buckler thee against a million.
  [*Exeunt* PETRUCIO, KATHARINA, *and* GRUMIO.
  Bap. Nay, let them go, a couple of quiet ones.
  Gre. Went they not quickly I should die with laughing.
  Tra. Of all mad matches, never was the like!
  Luc. Mistress, what's your opinion of your sister?
  Bian. That, being mad herself, she's madly mated.
  Gre. I warrant him, Petrucio is Kated.
  Bap. Neighbours and friends, though bride and bridegroom wants
For to supply the places at the table,
You know there wants no junkets at the feast;
Lucentio, you shall supply the bridegroom's place;
And let Bianca take her sister's room.
  Tra. Shall sweet Bianca practise how to bride it?
  Bap. She shall, Lucentio.—Come, gentlemen, let's go. [*Exeunt.*

[Hark, hark! I hear the minstrels play.]

ILLUSTRATIONS OF ACT III.

¹ Scene I.—"*Gamut I am, the ground of all accord,*" &c.

GAMUT, or, more correctly, *Gammut*, is, in the sense here intended, the lowest note of the musical scale, established in the eleventh century by a Benedictine monk, Guido, of Arezzo in Tuscany. To this sound (a, the first line in the base,) he gave the name of the third letter in the Greek alphabet, Γ *(Gamma)*, cutting off the final vowel, and affixing the syllable *ut*. This, and the other syllables, *re, mi, fa,* &c., names assigned by Guido to the notes of the diatonic scale, were suggested to him by the following verses, which form the first stanza of a hymn, by Paulus Diaconus, to St. John the Baptist :—

Ut queant laxis *re*sonare fibris,
*Mi*ra gestorum *fa*muli tuorum
*Sol*ve polluti *la*bii reatum,
Sancte Joannes!

The tune to which this hymn was anciently sung in the Catholic church, ascends by the Diatonic intervals C, A, B, C, D, and E, at the syllables here printed in italics.

² Scene II.—"*His horse hipped,*" &c.

Shakspere describes the imperfections and unsoundness of a horse with as much precision as if he had been bred in a farrier's shop. In the same way, in the Venus and Adonis, he is equally circumstantial in summing up the qualities of a noble courser :—

"Round hoof'd, short jointed, fetlocks shag and long,
Broad breast, full eye, small head, and nostrils wide,
High crest, short ears, straight legs and passing strong,
Thin mane, thick tail, broad buttock, tender hide."

³ Scene II.—"*A health, quoth &c.*"

It was the universal custom, in our poet's time, at the marriage of the humblest as well as the highest, for a *bride-cup*, sometimes called "a *knitting-cup*" to be quaffed in church. At the marriage of Philip and Mary, in Winchester cathedral, in 1554, this part of the ceremony is thus described :—"The trumpets sounded, and they both returned to their traverses in the quire, and there remained until mass was done; at which time *wine and sops* were hallow'd and delivered to them both" *(Leland's Collectanea).* In Laneham's Letter (1575), describing the entertainments at Kenilworth, we have an account of a real rustic wedding, in which there was borne before the bride, "The bride-cup, formed of a sweet sucket barrel, a fair-turned post set to it, all seemingly besilvered and parcel-gilt." Laneham adds that "the busy flies flocked about the bride-cup for the sweetness of the sucket that it savoured on."

⁴ Scene II.—"*I must away to-day,*" &c.

We subjoin the parallel scene in the other play :—

Fer. Father, farewell, my Kate and I must home.
Sirrah, go make ready my horse presently.
Alf. Your horse! what, son, I hope you do but jest;
I am sure you will not go so suddenly.
Kate. Let him go or tarry, I am resolved to stay,
And not to travel on my wedding-day.
Fer. Tut, Kate, I tell thee we must needs go home.
Villain, hast thou saddled my horse?
San. Which horse—your curtall?
Fer. Zounds! you slave, stand you prating here!
Saddle the bay gelding for your mistress.
Kate. Not for me, for I will not go.
San. The ostler will not let me have him; you owe ten-pence
For his meat, and sixpence for stuffing my mistress' saddle.
Fer. Here, villain, go pay him straight.
San. Shall I give them another peck of lavender?
Fer. Out, slave! and bring them presently to the door.
Alf. Why, son, I hope at least you'll dine with us.
San. I pray you, master, let's stay till dinner be done.
Fer. Zounds, villain, art thou here yet? [*Exit* SANDER.
Come, Kate, our dinner is provided at home.
Kate. But not for me, for here I mean to dine:
I'll have my will in this as well as you;
Though you in madding mood would leave your friends,
Despite of you I'll tarry with them still.
Fer. Ay, Kate, so thou shalt, but at some other time:
When as thy sisters here shall be espoused,
Then thou and I will keep our wedding-day
In better sort than now we can provide;
For here I promise thee before them all,
We will ere long return to them again.
Come, Kate, stand not on terms, we will away:
This is my day, to-morrow thou shalt rule,
And I will do whatever thou command'st.
Gentlemen, farewell, we'll take our leaves,
It will be late before that we come home.
[*Exeunt* FERANDO *and* KATE.

[Prato della Valle, Padua.]

ACT IV.

SCENE I.—*A Hall in Petruchio's Country House.*

Enter GRUMIO.

Gru. Fye, fye, on all tired jades! on all mad masters! and all foul ways! Was ever man so beaten? was ever man so rayed?[a] was ever man so weary? I am sent before to make a fire, and they are coming after to warm them. Now, were not I a little pot, and soon hot, my very lips might freeze to my teeth, my tongue to the roof of my mouth, my heart in my belly, ere I should come by a fire to thaw me:—But, I, with blowing the fire, shall warm myself; for, considering the weather, a taller man than I will take cold. Holla, hoa! Curtis!

Enter CURTIS.

Curt. Who is that calls so coldly?
Gru. A piece of ice! If thou doubt it, thou may'st slide from my shoulder to my heel, with no greater a run but my head and my neck. A fire, good Curtis.

[a] *Rayed*—covered with mire—sullied. As in Spenser (Fairy Queen, b. vi. c. 5):—

"From his soft eyes the tears he wiped away
And from his face the filth that did it ray"

Curt. Is my master and his wife coming, Grumio?
Gru. O, ay, Curtis, ay: and therefore fire, fire; cast on no water.
Curt. Is she so hot a shrew as she's reported?
Gru. She was, good Curtis, before this frost: but, thou know'st, winter tames man, woman, and beast; for it hath tamed my old master, and my new mistress, and myself,[a] fellow Curtis.
Curt. Away, you three inch fool! I am no beast.
Gru. Am I but three inches? why, thy horn is a foot; and so long am I, at the least. But wilt thou make a fire, or shall I complain on thee to our mistress, whose hand (she being now at hand,) thou shalt soon feel, to thy cold comfort, for being slow in thy hot office?
Curt. I prithee, good Grumio, tell me, How goes the world?
Gru. A cold world, Curtis, in every office but thine; and, therefore, fire: Do thy duty, and have thy duty; for my master and mistress are almost frozen to death.

[a] *Myself.* Some would read *thyself*, because Curtis says, "I am no beast." But Grumio, calling himself a beast, has also called Curtis *fellow*—hence the offence

Curt. There's fire ready; And, therefore, good Grumio, the news?

Gru. Why, Jack, boy! ho, boy! and as much news as thou wilt.

Curt. Come, you are so full of conycatching.

Gru. Why, therefore, fire; for I have caught extreme cold. Where's the cook? is supper ready, the house trimmed, rushes strewed, cobwebs swept; the serving-men in their new fustian, the white stockings, and every officer his wedding garment on? Be the jacks fair within, 'the jills fair without,' the carpets laid,' and every thing in order?

Curt. All ready. And, therefore, I pray thee, news?

Gru. First, know, my horse is tired; my master and mistress fallen out.

Curt. How?

Gru. Out of their saddles into the dirt. And thereby hangs a tale.

Curt. Let's ha't, good Grumio.

Gru. Lend thine ear.

Curt. Here.

Gru. There. [*Striking him.*

Curt. This 'tis to feel a tale, not to hear a tale.

Gru. And therefore 't is called, a sensible tale: and this cuff was but to knock at your ear, and beseech listening. Now I begin: *Imprimis*, we came down a foul hill, my master riding behind my mistress:—

Curt. Both on one horse?

Gru. What's that to thee?

Curt. Why, a horse.

Gru. Tell thou the tale:—But had'st thou not crossed me, thou should'st have heard how her horse fell, and she under her horse; thou should'st have heard, in how miry a place: how she was bemoiled; how he left her with the horse upon her; how he beat me because her horse stumbled; how she waded through the dirt to pluck him off me; how he swore; how she prayed, that never pray'd before; how I cried; how the horses ran away; how her bridle was burst; how I lost my crupper; with many things of worthy memory, which now shall die in oblivion, and thou return unexperienced to thy grave.

Curt. By this reckoning, he is more shrew than she.

Gru. Ay, and that thou and the proudest of you all shall find, when he comes home. But what talk I of this?—Call forth Nathaniel, Joseph, Nicholas, Philip, Walter, Sugarsop, and the rest. Let their heads be sleekly combed, their blue coats brushed, and their garters of an indifferent knit: let them curtsey with their left legs; and not presume to touch a hair of my master's horse-tail, till they kiss their hands. Are they all ready?

Curt. They are.

Gru. Call them forth.

Curt. Do you hear, ho? you must meet my master, to countenance my mistress.

Gru. Why, she hath a face of her own.

Curt. Who knows not that?

Gru. Thou, it seems, that callest for company to countenance her.

Curt. I call them forth to credit her.

Gru. Why, she comes to borrow nothing of them.

Enter several Servants.

Nath. Welcome home, Grumio.

Phil. How now, Grumio?

Jos. What, Grumio!

Nich. Fellow Grumio!

Nath. How now, old lad?

Gru. Welcome, you;—how now, you;—what, you;—fellow, you;—and thus much for greeting. Now, my spruce companions, is all ready, and all things neat?

Nath. All things is ready: how near is our master?

Gru. E'en at hand, alighted by this: and therefore be not,—Cock's passion, silence!—I hear my master.

Enter PETRUCIO *and* KATHARINA.

Pet. Where be these knaves? What, no man at door,
To hold my stirrup, nor to take my horse?
Where is Nathaniel, Gregory, Philip?

All Serv. Here, here, sir; here, sir.

Pet. Here, sir! here, sir! here, sir! here, sir!
You logger-headed and unpolish'd grooms!
What, no attendance? no regard? no duty?
Where is the foolish knave I sent before?

Gru. Here, sir; as foolish as I was before.

Pet. You peasant swain! you whoreson malt-horse drudge!
Did I not bid thee meet me in the park,
And bring along these rascal knaves with thee?

---

* *Jacks* were leathern drinking vessels—*Jills*, cups or measures of metal. The leathern jugs were to be kept clean within—the pewter ones bright without. But Grumio is quibbling upon the application of *Jills* to maids, and *Jacks* to men.

b *Carpets laid*—to cover the tables. The floors were strewed with rushes.

c *Bemoiled*—bemired.

* *Indifferent knit.* Malone conjectures that parti-coloured garters are here meant.

Gru. Nathaniel's coat, sir, was not fully made,
And Gabriel's pumps were all unpink'd i' the heel;
There was no link to colour Peter's hat,
And Walter's dagger was not come from sheathing:
There were none fine but Adam, Ralph, and Gregory;
The rest were ragged, old, and beggarly;
Yet, as they are, here are they come to meet you.

Pet. Go, rascals, go, and fetch my supper in.— [*Exeunt some of the Servants.*
Where is the life that late 1 led—[a]   [*Sings.*
Where are those——Sit down, Kate, and welcome.
Soud, soud, soud, soud![b]

 Re-enter Servants, *with Supper.*

Why, when, I say?—Nay, good sweet Kate, be merry.
Off with my boots, you rogues, you villains; When?
    It was the friar of orders grey,   [*Sings.*
    As he forth walked on his way:—
Out, out you rogue! you pluck my foot awry;
Take that, and mend the plucking of the other.— [*Strikes him.*
Be merry, Kate:—Some water here; what, ho!
Where 's my spaniel Troilus?—Sirrah, get you hence,
And bid my cousin Ferdinand come hither; [*Exit Servant.*
One, Kate, that you must kiss, and be acquainted with.
Where are my slippers?—Shall I have some water? [*A basin is presented to him.*
Come, Kate, and wash, and welcome heartily:— [*Servant lets the ewer fall.*
You whoreson villain! will you let it fall? [*Strikes him.*

Kath. Patience, I pray you; 't was a fault unwilling.

Pet. A whoreson, beetle-headed, flap-ear'd knave!
Come, Kate, sit down; I know you have a stomach.
Will you give thanks, sweet Kate, or else shall I?—
What is this? mutton?

1 Serv.   Ay.

Pet.   Who brought it?

---

[a] In 'A Handeful of Pleasant Delites,' 1584, this is the title of a "new Sonet."
[b] Malone thinks these words are meant to express the noise made by a person heated and fatigued.

308

1 Serv.   I.

Pet. 'T is burnt; and so is all the meat:
What dogs are these?—Where is the rascal cook?
How durst you, villains, bring it from the dresser,
And serve it thus to me that love it not?
There, take it to you, trenchers, cups, and all: [*Throws the meat, &c. about the stage.*
You heedless jolthcads, and unmanner'd slaves!
What, do you grumble? I 'll be with you straigat.

Kat. I pray you, husband, be not so disquiet;
The meat was well, if you were so contented.

Pet. I tell thee, Kate, 't was burnt and dried away;
And I expressly am forbid to touch it,
For it engenders choler, planteth anger;
And better 't were that both of us did fast,
Since, of ourselves, ourselves are choleric,
Than feed it with such over-roasted flesh.
Be patient; to-morrow it shall be mended,
And, for this night, we 'll fast for company:
Come, I will bring thee to thy bridal chamber: [*Exeunt* PETRUCIO, KATHARINA, *and* CURTIS.

Nath. [*Advancing.*] Peter, didst ever see the like?

Peter. He kills her in her own humour.

 Re-enter CURTIS.

Gru. Where is he?

Curt. In her chamber,
Making a sermon of continency to her:
And rails, and swears, and rates; that she, poor soul,
Knows not which way to stand, to look, to speak;
And sits as one new-risen from a dream.
Away, away! for he is coming hither. [*Exeunt.*

 Re-enter PETRUCIO.

Pet. Thus have I politicly begun my reign,
And 't is my hope to end successfully:
My falcon now is sharp, and passing empty;
And, till she stoop, she must not be full-gorg'd,
For then she never looks upon her lure.
Another way I have to man my haggard,[a]
To make her come, and know her keeper's call,
That is, to watch her, as we watch these kites,
That bate, and beat, and will not be obedient.
She eat no meat to-day, nor none shall eat;
Last night she slept not, nor to-night she shall not;
As with the meat, some undeserved fault

---

[a] *To man my haggard*—to tame my wild hawk.

I'll find about the making of the bed;
And here I'll fling the pillow, there the bolster,
This way the coverlet, another way the sheets:—
Ay, and amid this hurly, I intend,
That all is done in reverend care of her;
And, in conclusion, she shall watch all night:
And, if she chance to nod, I'll rail and brawl,
And with the clamour keep her still awake.
This is a way to kill a wife with kindness;
And thus I'll curb her mad and headstrong humour:
He that knows better how to tame a shrew,
Now let him speak; 't is charity to show. *Exit.*

SCENE II.—Padua. *Before Baptista's House.*

Enter TRANIO *and* HORTENSIO.

Tra. Is't possible, friend Licio, that mistress Bianca
Doth fancy any other but Lucentio?
I tell you, sir, she bears me fair in hand.
Hor. Sir, to satisfy you in what I have said,
Stand by, and mark the manner of his teaching.
[*They stand aside.*

Enter BIANCA *and* LUCENTIO.

Luc. Now, mistress, profit you in what you read?
Bian. What, master, read you? first resolve me that.
Luc. I read that I profess, the art to love.
Bian. And may you prove, sir, master of your art!
Luc. While you, sweet dear, prove mistress of my heart. [*They retire.*
Hor. Quick proceeders, marry! Now, tell me, I pray,
You that durst swear that your mistress Bianca
Lov'd none in the world so well as Lucentio.
Tra. O despiteful love! unconstant womankind!
I tell thee, Licio, this is wonderful.
Hor. Mistake no more: I am not Licio,
Nor a musician, as I seem to be;
But one that scorn to live in this disguise,
For such a one as leaves a gentleman,
And makes a god of such a cullion:
Know, sir, that I am called Hortensio.
Tra. Signior Hortensio, I have often heard
Of your entire affection to Bianca;
And since mine eyes are witness of her lightness,
I will with you,—if you be so contented,—
Forswear Bianca, and her love for ever.
Hor. See, how they kiss and court! Signior Lucentio,
Here is my hand, and here I firmly vow
Never to woo her more; but do forswear her,
As one unworthy all the former favours
That I have fondly flatter'd her withal.
Tra. And here I take the like unfeigned oath,
Never to marry with her though she would entreat:
Fye on her! see, how beastly she doth court him.
Hor. 'Would all the world, but he, had quite forsworn!
For me, that I may surely keep mine oath,
I will be married to a wealthy widow
Ere three days pass; which hath as long lov'd me,
As I have lov'd this proud disdainful haggard:
And so farewell, signior Lucentio.
Kindness in women, not their beauteous looks,
Shall win my love: and so I take my leave,
In resolution as I swore before.
[*Exit* HORTENSIO.—LUCENTIO *and* BIANCA *advance.*

Tra. Mistress Bianca, bless you with such grace
As 'longeth to a lover's blessed case!
Nay, I have ta'en you napping, gentle love;
And have forsworn you with Hortensio.
Bian. Tranio, you jest. But have you both forsworn me?
Tra. Mistress, we have.
Luc. Then we are rid of Licio.
Tra. I' faith, he'll have a lusty widow now,
That shall be woo'd and wedded in a day.
Bian. God give him joy!
Tra. Ay, and he'll tame her.
Bian. He says so, Tranio.
Tra. 'Faith, he is gone unto the taming-school.
Bian. The taming-school! what, is there such a place?
Tra. Ay, mistress, and Petrucio is the master;
That teacheth tricks eleven and twenty long,
To tame a shrew, and charm her chattering tongue.

Enter BIONDELLO, *running.*

Bion. O master, master, I have watch'd so long
That I'm dog-weary; but at last I spied
An ancient engle* coming down the hill,
Will serve the turn.

* *Engle.* The original copy, as well as modern editions, read *angel.* But Theobald and others suggested that the word should be *engle,*—a gull. Tranio intends to deceive the Pedant, "if he be credulous." Ben Jonson several times uses *engle* in this sense; and Gifford has no doubt that the same wo d is meant in the passage before us. Mr. Dyce somewhat inclines to the original reading of *angel,* citing a passage from Cotgrave's Dictionary, "*Angelot a la grosse escaille,* an *old angel,* and by metaphor, a fellow of the old, sound, honest, and worthie stamp." Tranio requires a respectable looking man to pass for Vincentio.

Tra. What is he, Biondello?
Bion. Master, a mercatante, or a pedant,
I know not what; but formal in apparel,
In gait and countenance surely like a father.
Luc. And what of him, Tranio?
Tra. If he be credulous, and trust my tale,
I'll make him glad to seem Vincentio;
And give assurance to Baptista Minola,
As if he were the right Vincentio.
Take in your love, and then let me alone.
   [*Exeunt* LUCENTIO *and* BIANCA.

   Enter a PEDANT.

Ped. God save you, sir!
Tra.   And you, sir! you are welcome.
Travel you far on, or are you at the farthest?
Ped. Sir, at the farthest for a week or two;
But then up farther; and as far as Rome;
And so to Tripoli, if God lend me life.
Tra. What countryman, I pray?
Ped.   Of Mantua.
Tra. Of Mantua, sir?—marry, God forbid!
And come to Padua, careless of your life?
Ped. My life, sir! how, I pray? for that goes hard.
Tra. 'Tis death for any one in Mantua
To come to Padua. Know you not the cause?
Your ships are staid at Venice; and the duke
(For private quarrel 'twixt your duke and him,)
Hath publish'd and proclaim'd it openly:
'Tis marvel; but that you are but newly come,
You might have heard it else proclaim'd about.
Ped. Alas, sir, it is worse for me than so;
For I have bills for money by exchange
From Florence, and must here deliver them.
Tra. Well, sir, to do you courtesy,
This will I do, and this I will advise you:
First, tell me, have you ever been at Pisa?
Ped. Ay, sir, in Pisa have I often been;
Pisa, renowned for grave citizens.
Tra. Among them, know you one Vincentio?
Ped. I know him not, but I have heard of him;
A merchant of incomparable wealth.
Tra. He is my father, sir; and, sooth to say,
In countenance somewhat doth resemble you.
Bion. As much as an apple doth an oyster, and all one.   [*Aside.*
Tra. To save your life in this extremity,
This favour will I do you for his sake;
And think it not the worst of all your fortunes,
That you are like to sir Vincentio.
His name and credit shall you undertake,
And in my house you shall be friendly lodg'd.
Look, that you take upon you as you should;
You understand me, sir;—so shall you stay
Till you have done your business in the city
If this be courtesy, sir, accept of it.
Ped. O, sir, I do; and will repute you ever
The patron of my life and liberty.
Tra. Then go with me, to make the matter good.
This, by the way, I let you understand;
My father is here look'd for every day,
To pass assurance of a dower in marriage
'Twixt me and one Baptista's daughter here:
In all these circumstances I'll instruct you:
Go with me, sir, to clothe you as becomes you.
   [*Exeunt.*

SCENE III.—*A Room in* Petrucio's *House.*

   Enter KATHARINA *and* GRUMIO.

Gru. No, no; forsooth, I dare not, for my life.*
Kath. The more my wrong, the more his spite appears:
What, did he marry me to famish me?
Beggars that come unto my father's door,
Upon entreaty, have a present alms;
If not, elsewhere they meet with charity:
But I, who never knew how to entreat,
Nor never needed that I should entreat,*
Am starv'd for meat, giddy for lack of sleep;
With oaths kept waking, and with brawling fed;
And that which spites me more than all these wants,
He does it under name of perfect love;
As who should say, if I should sleep, or eat,
'Twere deadly sickness, or else present death.
I prithee go, and get me some repast;
I care not what, so it be wholesome food.
Gru. What say you to a neat's foot?
Kath. 'Tis passing good; I prithee let me have it.
Gru. I fear, it is too choleric a meat:
How say you to a fat tripe, finely broil'd?
Kath. I like it well; good Grumio, fetch it me.

---

* This line was omitted in *every* edition of Shakspere of the present century, when our 'Pictorial' was originally published. We had taken some pains to trace the origin of this typographical blunder, and found that the line was first left out in Reed's edition of 1803. This, being the standard edition, has furnished the text of every succeeding one. In the same manner, of the well-known lines in Hamlet—
   "Thy knotted and combined locks to part,
   And each particular hair to stand on end,
   Like quills upon the fretful porcupine,"
the middle line is omitted in Reed's edition, and the blunder is copied in Chalmers'. No book was more incorrectly printed than the booksellers' stereotype edition of Shakspere in one volume. In this very play we had *abroad* for *aboard*—*fee for to*—*forward* for *froward*—besides errors of punctuation in abundance. And yet the typographical errors of the first folio, printed from a manuscript, are always visited by some commentators with the severest reprehension.

Gru. I cannot tell; I fear, 't is choleric.
What say you to a piece of beef, and mustard?
Kath. A dish that I do love to feed upon.
Gru. Ay, but the mustard is too hot a little.
Kath. Why, then the beef, and let the mustard rest.
Gru. Nay, then I will not; you shall have the mustard,
Or else you get no beef of Grumio.
Kath. Then both, or one, or any thing thou wilt.
Gru. Why, then the mustard without the beef.
Kath. Go, get thee gone, thou false deluding slave, [*Beats him.*
That feed'st me with the very name of meat:
Sorrow on thee, and all the pack of you,
That triumph thus upon my misery!
Go, get thee gone, I say.

Enter PETRUCIO, *with a dish of meat; and* HORTENSIO.

Pet. How fares my Kate? What, sweeting, all amort?[a]
Hor. Mistress, what cheer?
Kath.   'Faith, as cold as can be.
Pet. Pluck up thy spirits, look cheerfully upon me.
Here, love; thou see'st how diligent I am,
To dress thy meat myself, and bring it thee:
                    [*Sets the dish on a table.*
I am sure, sweet Kate, this kindness merits thanks.
What, not a word? Nay, then thou lov'st it not;
And all my pains is sorted to no proof:
Here, take away this dish.
Kath.   I pray you, let it stand.
Pet. The poorest service is repaid with thanks;
And so shall mine, before you touch the meat.
Kath. I thank you, sir.
Hor. Signior Petrucio, fye! you are to blame!
Come, mistress Kate, I'll bear you company.
Pet. Eat it up all, Hortensio, if thou lov'st me.
                              [*Aside.*
Much good do it unto thy gentle heart!
Kate, eat apace;—And now my honey love,
Will we return unto thy father's house;
And revel it as bravely as the best,
With silken coats, and caps, and golden rings,
With ruffs, and cuffs, and farthingales, and things;[b]

With scarfs, and fans, and double change of bravery,
With amber bracelets, beads, and all this knavery.
What, hast thou din'd? The tailor stays thy leisure,
To deck thy body with his ruffling[a] treasure.

Enter Tailor.

Come, tailor, let us see these ornaments;[a]

Enter Haberdasher.

Lay forth the gown.—What news with you, sir?
Hab. Here is the cap your worship did bespeak.
Pet. Why, this was moulded on a porringer,
A velvet dish;—fye, fye! 't is lewd and filthy:
Why, 't is a cockle, or a walnutshell,
A knack, a toy, a trick, a baby's cap;
Away with it, come, let me have a bigger.
Kath. I'll have no bigger; this doth fit the time,
And gentlewomen wear such caps as these.
Pet. When you are gentle, you shall have one too,
And not till then.
Hor.   That will not be in haste. [*Aside.*
Kath. Why, sir, I trust, I may have leave to speak;
And speak I will. I am no child, no babe:
Your betters have endur'd me say my mind;
And, if you cannot, best you stop your ears.
My tongue will tell the anger of my heart;
Or else my heart, concealing it, will break;
And rather than it shall, I will be free
Even to the uttermost, as I please, in words.
Pet. Why, thou say'st true; it is a paltry cap,
A custard coffin,[b] a bauble, a silken pie:
I love thee well, in that thou lik'st it not.
Kath. Love me, or love me not, I like the cap;
And it I will have, or I will have none.
Pet. Thy gown? why, ay.—Come, tailor, let us see 't.
O mercy, God! what masking stuff is here!
What 's this? a sleeve? 't is like a demi-cannon:
What! up and down, carv'd like an apple tart?
Here 's snip, and nip, and cut, and slish, and slash,
Like to a censer in a barber's shop:

---

[a] *All amort*—dispirited. The expression is common in the old dramatists.
[b] *Things.* Johnson says, "Though *things* is a poor word, yet I have no better; and perhaps the author had not another that would rhyme." It is marvellous that the lexicographer did not see how characteristic the word is of Petrucio's bold and half-satirical humour. He has used it before:—
"We will have rings and *things*, and fine array."

[a] *Ruffling.* Pope changed this to *rustling*. The word was familiar to the Elizabethan literature. In Lyly's "Euphues" we have, "Shall I *ruffle* in new devices, with chains, with bracelets, with rings, with robes?" In Ben Jonson's "Cynthia's Revels," we find, "Lady, I cannot *ruffle* it in red and yellow."
[b] *Custard-coffin.* The crust of a pie was called the coffin

Why, what, o' devil's name, tailor, call'st thou
   this?
Hor. I see, she's like to have neither cap nor
   gown. [*Aside.*
Tai. You bid me make it orderly and well,
According to the fashion and the time.
   Pet. Marry, and did; but if you be remem-
      ber'd,
I did not bid you mar it to the time.
Go, hop me over every kennel home,
For you shall hop without my custom, sir:
I'll none of it; hence, make your best of it.
   Kath. I never saw a better fashion'd gown,
More quaint, more pleasing, nor more commend-
   able:
Belike, you mean to make a puppet of me.
   Pet. Why, true; he means to make a puppet
      of thee.
   Tai. She says, your worship means to make a
puppet of her.
   Pet. O monstrous arrogance! Thou liest,
      thou thread,
Thou thimble,
Thou yard, three-quarters, half-yard, quarter,
   nail,
Thou flea, thou nit, thou winter cricket thou:
Brav'd in mine own house with a skein of
   thread!
Away, thou rag, thou quantity, thou remnant;
Or I shall so be-mete thee with thy yard,
As thou shalt think on prating whilst thou liv'st!
I tell thee, I, that thou hast marr'd her gown.
   Tai. Your worship is deceived; the gown is
      made
Just as my master had direction:
Grumio gave order how it should be done.
   Gru. I gave him no order; I gave him the
      stuff.
   Tai. But how did you desire it should be
      made?
   Gru. Marry, sir, with needle and thread.
   Tai. But did you not request to have it cut?
   Gru. Thou hast faced[a] many things.
   Tai. I have.
   Gru. Face not me: thou hast braved[b] many
men; brave not me. I will neither be faced nor
braved. I say unto thee—I bid thy master cut
out the gown; but I did not bid him cut it to
pieces: *ergo*, thou liest.
   Tai. Why, here is the note of the fashion to
testify.
   Pet. Read it.

[a] *Faced*—made facings.
[b] *Braved*—made fine. In the old stage directions the
word is commonly used in this sense. In this play we find,
"Enter Tranio, *brave*."

312

   Gru. The note lies in 's throat, if he say I
said so.
   Tai. Imprimis, a loose-bodied gown:
   Gru. Master, if ever I said loose-bodied gown,
sew me in the skirts of it, and beat me to death
with a bottom of brown thread: I said, a gown.
   Pet. Proceed.
   Tai. With a small compassed cape;
   Gru. I confess the cape.
   Tai. With a trunk sleeve;
   Gru. I confess two sleeves.
   Tai. The sleeves curiously cut.
   Pet. Ay, there's the villainy.
   Gru. Error i' the bill, sir; error i' the bill. I
commanded the sleeves should be cut out, and
sewed up again: and that I'll prove upon thee,
though thy little finger be armed in a thimble.
   Tai. This is true, that I say; an I had thee
in place where thou should'st know it.
   Gru. I am for thee straight: take thou the
bill, give me thy mete-yard, and spare not me.
   Hor. God-a-mercy, Grumio! then he shall
have no odds.
   Pet. Well, sir, in brief, the gown is not for me.
   Gru. You are i' the right, sir; 't is for my mis-
tress.
   Pet. Go, take it up unto thy master's use.
   Gru. Villain, not for thy life: Take up my
mistress' gown for thy master's use!
   Pet. Why, sir, what's your conceit in that?
   Gru. O, sir, the conceit is deeper than you
think for:
Take up my mistress' gown to his master's use!
O, fye, fye, fye!
   Pet. Hortensio, say thou wilt see the tailor
      paid:— [*Aside.*
Go, take it hence; begone, and say no more.
   Hor. Tailor, I'll pay thee for thy gown to-
morrow.
Take no unkindness of his hasty words:
Away, I say; commend me to thy master.
      [*Exit Tailor.*
   Pet. Well, come, my Kate; we will unto
      your father's,
Even in these honest mean habiliments;
Our purses shall be proud, our garments poor:
For 't is the mind that makes the body rich;
And as the sun breaks through the darkest clouds,
So honour peereth in the meanest habit.
What, is the jay more precious than the lark,
Because his feathers are more beautiful?
Or is the adder better than the eel,
Because his painted skin contents the eye?
O, no, good Kate; neither art thou the worse
For this poor furniture and mean array.

If thou account'st it shame, lay it on me:
And therefore, frolic; we will hence forthwith,
To feast and sport us at thy father's house.
Go, call my men, and let us straight to him;
And bring our horses unto Long-lane end,
There will we mount, and thither walk on foot.
Let 's see; I think, 't is now some seven o'clock,
And well we may come there by dinner-time.

Kath. I dare assure you, sir, 't is almost two;
And 'twill be supper-time ere you come there.

Pet. It shall be seven, ere I go to horse:
Look, what I speak, or do, or think to do,
You are still crossing it.—Sirs, let 't alone:
I will not go to-day; and ere I do,
It shall be what o'clock I say it is.

Hor. Why, so! this gallant will command the sun. [*Exeunt.*

SCENE IV.—Padua. *Before* Baptista's *House.*

Enter TRANIO, *and the* PEDANT *dressed like* VINCENTIO.

Tra. Sir, this is the house. Please it you, that I call?

Ped. Ay, what else? and, but I be deceived,
Signior Baptista may remember me,
Near twenty years ago, in Genoa,
Where we were lodgers at the Pegasus.

Tra. 'T is well; and hold your own, in any case,
With such austerity as 'longeth to a father.

Enter BIONDELLO.

Ped. I warrant you: But, sir, here comes your boy;
'T were good he were school'd.

Tra. Fear you not him. Sirrah Biondello,
Now do your duty throughly, I advise you;
Imagine 't were the right Vincentio.

Bion. Tut! fear not me.

Tra. But hast thou done thy errand to Baptista?

Bion. I told him, that your father was at Venice;
And that you look'd for him this day in Padua.

Tra. Thou 'rt a tall fellow; hold thee that to drink.
Here comes Baptista:—set your countenance, sir.

Enter BAPTISTA *and* LUCENTIO.

Signior Baptista, you are happily met:—
Sir, [*to the* Pedant]
This is the gentleman I told you of:

I pray you, stand good father to me now,
Give me Bianca for my patrimony.

Ped. Soft, son!
Sir, by your leave, having come to Padua
To gather in some debts, my son Lucentio
Made me acquainted with a weighty cause
Of love between your daughter and himself:
And,—for the good report I hear of you;
And for the love he beareth to your daughter
And she to him,—to stay him not too long,
I am content, in a good father's care,
To have him match'd; and,—if you pleas'd to like
No worse than I, sir—upon some agreement,
Me shall you find ready and willing[a]
With one consent to have her so bestow'd;
For curious[b] I cannot be with you,
Signior Baptista, of whom I hear so well.

Bap. Sir, pardon me in what I have to say;—
Your plainness and your shortness please me well.
Right true it is, your son Lucentio here
Doth love my daughter, and she loveth him,
Or both dissemble deeply their affections:
And, therefore, if you say no more than this,
That like a father you will deal with him,
And pass my daughter a sufficient dower,
The match is made, and all is done:[c]
Your son shall have my daughter with consent.

Tra. I thank you, sir. Where then do you know best,
We be affied; and such assurance ta'en,
As shall with either part's agreement stand?

Bap. Not in my house, Lucentio; for, you know,
Pitchers have ears, and I have many servants:
Besides, old Gremio is heark'ning still;
And, happily, we might be interrupted.

Tra. Then at my lodging, an it like you:
There doth my father lie; and there, this night,
We 'll pass the business privately and well:
Send for your daughter by your servant here,
My boy shall fetch the scrivener presently.
The worst is this, that, at so slender warning,
You 're like to have a thin and slender pittance.

Bap. It likes me well: Cambio, hie you home,
And bid Bianca make her ready straight;

---
[a] We print this line as in the old copy. It was changed by Hanmer to—
"Me shall you find *most* ready *and most* willing."
In this play we have many examples of short lines; and certainly Shakspere would not have resorted to these feeble expletives to make out ten syllables.
[b] Curious—scrupulous.
[c] Again, we print this line as in the folio. Hanmer changed it to—
"The match is made, and all is *fully* done."

And, if you will, tell what hath happened:
Lucentio's father is arrived in Padua,
And how she's like to be Lucentio's wife!
   Luc. I pray the gods she may, with all my heart!
   Tra. Dally not with the gods, but get thee gone.
Signior Baptista, shall I lead the way?
Welcome! one mess is like to be your cheer;
Come, sir; we will better it in Pisa.
   Bap.   I follow you.
            [*Exeunt* TRANIO, PEDANT, *and* BAPTISTA.
   Bion. Cambio.
   Luc.   What say'st thou, Biondello?
   Bion. You saw my master wink and laugh upon you?
   Luc. Biondello, what of that?
   Bion. 'Faith nothing; but he has left me here behind, to expound the meaning or moral of his signs and tokens.
   Luc. I pray thee, moralize them.
   Bion. Then thus. Baptista is safe, talking with the deceiving father of a deceitful son.
   Luc. And what of him?
   Bion. His daughter is to be brought by you to the supper.
   Luc. And then?
   Bion. The old priest at Saint Luke's church is at your command at all hours.
   Luc. And what of all this?
   Bion. I cannot tell; expect* they are busied about a counterfeit assurance: Take you assurance of her, *cum privilegio ad imprimendum solùm:* to the church;—take the priest, clerk, and some sufficient honest witnesses:
If this be not that you look for, I have no more to say,
But bid Bianca farewell for ever and a day.
                                  [*Going.*
   Luc. Hear'st thou, Biondello?
   Bion. I cannot tarry: I knew a wench married in an afternoon as she went to the garden for parsley to stuff a rabbit; and so may you, sir; and so adieu, sir. My master hath appointed me to go to Saint Luke's, to bid the priest be ready to come against you come with your appendix.   [*Exit.*
   Luc. I may, and will, if she be so contented:
She will be pleas'd, then wherefore should I doubt?
Hap what hap may, I'll roundly go about her;
It shall go hard, if Cambio go without her.
                                    [*Exit.*

---

* *Expect.* This is generally printed *except.* Biondello means to say, believe—think—they are busied, &c.

SCENE V.—*A public Road.*

Enter PETRUCIO, KATHARINA, *and* HORTENSIO.

   Pet. Come on, o' God's name; once more toward our father's.
Good Lord, how bright and goodly shines the moon!
   Kath. The moon! the sun; it is not moonlight now.
   Pet. I say, it is the moon that shines so bright.
   Kath. I know, it is the sun that shines so bright.
   Pet. Now, by my mother's son, and that's myself,
It shall be moon, or star, or what I list,
Or ere I journey to your father's house:
Go one, and fetch our horses back again.
Evermore cross'd and cross'd: nothing but cross'd!
   Hor. Say as he says, or we shall never go.
   Kath. Forward, I pray, since we have come so far,
And be it moon, or sun, or what you please:
And if you please to call it a rush candle,
Henceforth I vow it shall be so for me.
   Pet. I say, it is the moon.
   Kath.   I know it is the moon.
   Pet. Nay, then you lie; it is the blessed sun.
   Kath. Then, God be bless'd, it is the blessed sun:
But sun it is not, when you say it is not;
And the moon changes, even as your mind.
What you will have it nam'd, even that it is;
And so it shall be so for Katharine.
   Hor. Petrucio, go thy ways; the field is won.
   Pet. Well, forward, forward: thus the bowl should run,
And not unluckily against the bias.
But soft; what company is coming here?

Enter VINCENTIO, *in a travelling dress.*

Good morrow, gentle mistress: Where away?
                                  [*To* VINCENTIO.
Tell me, sweet Kate, and tell me truly too,
Hast thou beheld a fresher gentlewoman?
Such war of white and red within her cheeks?
What stars do spangle heaven with such beauty,
As those two eyes become that heavenly face?
Fair lovely maid, once more good day to thee;
Sweet Kate, embrace her for her beauty's sake.

---

* The repetition by Katharine, "I know it is *the moon,*" is most characteristic of her humbled deportment. Steevens strikes out "*the moon,*" with, "the old copy redundantly reads," &c.

Hor. 'A will make the man mad, to make a woman of him.

Kath. Young budding virgin, fair, and fresh, and sweet,
Whither away; or where is thy abode?
Happy the parents of so fair a child;
Happier the man, whom favourable stars
Allot thee for his lovely bed-fellow!

Pet. Why, how now, Kate? I hope thou art not mad:
This is a man, old, wrinkled, faded, wither'd;
And not a maiden, as thou say'st he is.

Kath. Pardon, old father, my mistaking eyes,
That have been so bedazzled with the sun,
That everything I look on seemeth green:
Now I perceive thou art a reverend father;
Pardon, I pray thee, for my mad mistaking.

Pet. Do, good old grandsire; and, withal, make known
Which way thou travellest: if along with us,
We shall be joyful of thy company.

Vin. Fair sir, and you my merry mistress,
That with your strange encounter much amaz'd me,
My name is called Vincentio: my dwelling Pisa;
And bound I am to Padua; there to visit
A son of mine, which long I have not seen.

Pet. What is his name?

Vin. Lucentio, gentle sir.

Pet. Happily met; the happier for thy son.
And now by law, as well as reverend age,
I may entitle thee my loving father;
The sister to my wife, this gentlewoman,
Thy son by this hath married: Wonder not,
Nor be not griev'd; she is of good esteem,
Her dowry wealthy, and of worthy birth;
Beside, so qualified as may beseem
The spouse of any noble gentleman.
Let me embrace with old Vincentio:
And wander we to see thy honest son,
Who will of thy arrival be full joyous.

Vin. But is this true? or is it else your pleasure,
Like pleasant travellers, to break a jest
Upon the company you overtake?

Hor. I do assure thee, father, so it is.

Pet. Come, go along, and see the truth hereof;
For our first merriment hath made thee jealous.
[*Exeunt* PETRUCIO, KATHARINA, *and* VINCENTIO.

Hor. Well, Petrucio, this hath put me in heart.
Have to my widow; and if she be froward,
Then hast thou taught Hortensio to be untoward.
[*Exit*

[Scene V.—' A public road.']

ILLUSTRATIONS OF ACT IV.

¹ SCENE I.—"*Curt. Who is that calls so coldly?* *Gru. A piece of ice?*"

At Venice, surrounded by the sea, the temperature is rarely below 6° Reaumur—18° Fahrenheit; but the cold is much greater on the mainland, even at its nearest points; and at Padua, from which Petrucio's country-house was obviously not very distant, it is frequently so extreme as to justify all Grumio's lamentations. During a considerable period of last winter, nearly 200 men were daily employed in breaking up the ice on the Brenta for the passage of boats to Venice; and piles of ice, of great height, might be seen till spring.—(M.)

² SCENE I.—"*Jack, boy! ho, boy!*"

The first words of a *Round* for four voices, printed, in 1609, in a musical work, now become exceedingly rare, entitled '*Pammelia, Musickes Miscellanie; or Mixed Varietie of Pleasant Roundelayes and delightful Catches,*' &c.

Malone gives a rather inaccurate copy of this, and in the enigmatic form which it takes in *Pammelia*, without seeming to be aware that it is printed in that work, for he cites Sir John Hawkins as his authority, in whose 'History of Music,' however, it not only does not appear, but is not even alluded to. We here insert it as it would have been shaped by the composer himself in the present day, merely changing the tenor clef into the treble, and adding, as the correction of what most likely is a clerical error, a sharp to the c in the third staff.

³ SCENE I.—"*Where be these knaves*," &c.

This scene is one of the most spirited and characteristic in the play; and we see a joyous, revelling spirit shining through Petrucio's affected violence. The *Ferando* of the old 'Taming of a Shrew' is a coarse bully, without the fine animal spirits and the real self-command of our Petrucio. The following is the parallel scene in that play; and it is remarkable how closely Shakspere copies the incidents :—

Enter FERANDO *and* KATE.

Fer. Now welcome, Kate, Where's these villains
Here? What, not supper yet upon the board,
Nor table spread, nor nothing done at all!
Where's that villain that I sent before?
Sun. Now, adsum, sir.

TAMING OF THE SHREW.

Fer. Come hither, you villain, I'll cut your nose.
You rogue, help me off with my boots; will 't please
You to lay the cloth? Zounds! the villain
Hurts my foot. pull easily, I say, yet again!
                                    [*He beats them all.*
       [*They cover the board, and fetch in the meat.*
Zounds, burnt and scorch'd! Who dress'd this meat?
  Wil. Forsooth, John Cook.
           [*He throws down the table, and meat, and all, and beats them all.*
  Fer. Go, you villains, bring me such meat!
Out of my sight, I say, and bear it hence:
Come, Kate, we'll have other meat provided.
Is there a fire in my chamber, sir?
  San. Ay, forsooth.   [*Exeunt* FERANDO *and* KATE.
      [*Manent* Serving-men, *and eat up all the meat.*
  Tom. Zounds! I think of my conscience my master's
mad since he was married.
  Wil. I laughed, what a box he gave Sander for pulling
off his boots.

         Enter FERANDO *again.*

  San. I hurt his foot for the nonce, man.
  Fer. Did you so, you damned villain?
                  [*He beats them all out again.*
This humour must I hold me to awhile,
To bridle and hold back my headstrong wife,
With curbs of hunger, ease, and want of sleep,
Nor sleep, nor meat, shall she enjoy to-night.
I'll mew her up as men do mew their hawks,
And make her gently come unto the lure.
Were she as stubborn, or as full of strength,
As was the Thracian horse Alcides tamed,
That king Egeus fed with flesh of men,
Yet would I pull her down, and make her come,
As hungry hawks do fly unto their lure.   [*Exit.*

'SCENE I.—"*It was the friar of orders grey,*" &c.

Percy's poem, 'The Friar of Orders Grey,' which is partly made up of fragments of ballads found in Shakspere, begins thus:—

      "It was a friar of orders grey
      Walk'd forth to tell his beads."

'SCENE III.—"*No, no; forsooth, I dare not for my life.*"

We subjoin the parallel scene from the other play:—

     Enter SANDER *and his Mistress.*

  San. Come, mistress.
  Kate. Sander, I prithee help me to some meat,
I am so faint that I can scarcely stand.
  San. Ay, marry, mistress, but you know my master has given me a charge that you must eat nothing, but that which he himself giveth you.
  Kate. Why, man, thy master needs never know it.
  San. You say true, indeed. Why look you, mistress, what say you to a piece of beef and mustard now?
  Kate. Why, I say 'tis excellent meat; canst thou help me to some?
  San. Ay, I could help you to some, but that I doubt the mustard is too choleric for you. But what say you to a sheep's head and garlic?
  Kate. Why, anything, I care not what it be.
  San. Ay, but the garlic I doubt will make your breath stink, and then my master will curse me for letting you eat it. But what say you to a fat capon?
  Kate. That's meat for a king, sweet Sander, help me to some of it.

  San. Nay, by'r lady! then 'tis too dear for us; we must not meddle with the king's meat.
  Kate. Out, villain! dost thou mock me?
Take that for thy sauciness.   [*She beats him.*

Grey has been hastily betrayed into a remark upon this scene in Shakspere, which is singularly opposed to his usual accuracy:—"This seems to be borrowed from Cervantes' account of Sancho Panza's treatment by his physician, when sham governor of the island of Barataria." The first part of 'Don Quixote' was not published till 1605; and the scene is found in the old 'Taming of a Shrew,' which was published in 1594.

'SCENE III.—"*Come, tailor, let us see these ornaments,*" &c.

The resemblance of this scene to the scene in the other play, in which the Shrew is tried to the utmost by her husband's interference with her dress, is closer than in almost any other part. The "face not me," and "brave not me," of Grumio, are literally the same jokes. In the speech of Petrucio, after the tailor is driven out, we have three lines which are the same, with the slightest alteration:—

  "Come, Kate, we now will go see thy father's house,
  Even in these honest, mean habiliments;
  Our purses shall be rich, our garments plain."

And yet the differences in spirit and taste are as remarkable as the resemblances.

    Enter FERANDO *and* KATE, *and* SANDER.

  San. Master, the haberdasher has brought my mistress home her cap here.
  Fer. Come hither, sirrah: what have you there?
  Haberdasher. A velvet cap, sir, an it please you.
  Fer. Who spoke for it? didst thou, Kate?
  Kate. What if I did? Come hither, sirrah, give me the cap; I'll see if it will fit me.   [*She sets it on her head.*
  Fer. O monstrous! why, it becomes thee not:
Let me see it, Kate. Here, sirrah, take it hence,
This cap is out of fashion quite.
  Kate. The fashion is good enough; belike you mean to make a fool of me.
  Fer. Why, true, he means to make a fool of thee
To have thee put on such a curtail'd cap.
Sirrah, begone with it.

    Enter the Tailor with a Gown.

  San. Here is the tailor, too, with my mistress' gown.
  Fer. Let me see it, tailor: what, with cuts and jags?
Zounds, thou villain, thou hast spoiled the gown!
  Tailor. Why, sir, I made it as your man gave me direction. You may read the note here.
  Fer. Come hither, sirrah. Tailor, read the note.
  Tailor. Item, a fair round compassed cape.
  San. Ay, that's true.
  Tailor. And a large trunk sleeve.
  San. That's a lie, master, I said two trunk sleeves.
  Fer. Well, sir, go forward.
  Tailor. Item, a loose-bodied gown.
  San. Master, if ever I said loose bodied gown, sew me in a seam, and beat me to death with a bottom of brown thread.
  Tailor. I made it as the note bade me.
  San. I say the note lies in his throat, and thou too an thou sayest it.
  Tailor. Nay, nay, ne'er be so hot, sirrah, for I fear you not.

ILLUSTRATIONS OF ACT IV.

Son. Dost thou hear, Tailor, thou hast braved many men: brave not me. Thou hast faced many men—
Tailor. Well, sir?
San. Face not me: I 'll neither be faced nor braved at thy hands. I can tell thee.
Kate. Come, come, I like the fashion of it well enough; Here 's more ado than needs; I 'll have it, ay, And if you do not like it, hide your eyes; I think I shall have nothing by your will.

SCENE V.—*" Good Lord, how bright and goodly shines the moon !" &c.*

We trespass once more upon the indulgence of our readers while we give the parallel scene from the other play. The incidents are the same in both.

Fer. Come, Kate, the moon shines clear to night, methinks.
Kate. The moon! why, husband, you are deceiv'd, It is the sun.
Fer. Yet again, come back again, it shall be The moon ere we come at your father's.
Kate. Why, I'll say as you say; it is the moon.
Fer. Jesus, save the glorious moon!
Kate. Jesus, save the glorious moon!
Fer. I am glad, Kate, your stomach is come down; I know it well thou know'st it is the sun, But I did try to see if thou wouldst speak, And cross me now as thou hast done before;

And trust me, Kate, hadst thou not named the moon, We had gone back again as sure as death. But soft, who 's this that 's coming here?

Enter the Duke *of* Cestus, *alone*.

Duke. Thus all alone from Cestus am I come, And left my princely court and noble train, To come to Athens, and in this disguise, To see what course my son Aurelius takes. But stay, here 's some, it may be, travels thither; Good sir, can you direct me the way to Athens?
Fer. [*speaks to the old man.*] Fair, lovely maiden, young and affable,
More clear of hue, and far **more beautiful**
Than precious sardonix or purple **rocks**
Of amethysts or glittering hyacinth,
More amiable far than is the plain,
Where glittering Cepherus in silver bowers
Gazeth upon the Giant, Andromede
Sweet Kate, entertain this lovely woman.
Duke. I think the man is mad; he calls me a woman.
Kate. Fair, lovely lady, bright and crystalline,
Beauteous and stately as the eye-train'd bird,
As glorious as the morning washed with dew,
Within whose eyes she takes her dawning beams
And golden summer sleeps upon thy cheeks,
Wrap up thy radiations in some cloud,
Lest that thy beauty make this stately town
Inhabitable like the burning zone,
With sweet reflections of thy lovely face.

(Gymnasium, Padua.)

ACT V.

SCENE I.—Padua.   Before Lucentio's House.

Enter on one side BIONDELLO, LUCENTIO, *and* BIANCA: GREMIO *walking on the other side.*

Bion. Softly and swiftly, sir; for the priest is ready.

Luc. I fly, Biondello: but they may chance to need thee at home, therefore leave us.

Bion. Nay, faith, I'll see the church o' your back; and then come back to my master as soon as I can.

[*Exeunt* LUCENTIO, BIANCA, *and* BIONDELLO.

Gre. I marvel Cambio comes not all this while.

Enter PETRUCIO, KATHARINA, VINCENTIO, *and Attendants.*

Pet. Sir, here's the door, this is Lucentio's house,
My father's bears more toward the market place;
Thither must I, and here I leave you, sir.

Vin. You shall not choose but drink before you go;
I think I shall command your welcome here,
And by all likelihood, some cheer is toward.
[*Knocks.*

Gre. They're busy within, you were best knock louder.

Enter PEDANT *above at a window.*

Ped. What's he that knocks as he would beat down the gate?

Vin. Is signior Lucentio within, sir?

Ped. He's within, sir, but not to be spoken withal.

Vin. What if a man bring him a hundred pound or two to make merry withal?

Ped. Keep your hundred pounds to yourself; he shall need none, so long as I live.

Pet. Nay, I told you your son was well beloved in Padua.—Do you hear, sir?—to leave frivolous circumstances,—I pray you, tell Signior Lucentio, that his father is come from Pisa, and is here at the door to speak with him.

Ped. Thou liest; his father is come from Pisa, and is here looking out at the window.

Vin. Art thou his father?

Ped. Ay, sir; so his mother says, if I may believe her.

Pet. Why, how now, gentleman! [*To* VINCEN.] why, this is flat knavery, to take upon you another man's name.

Ped. Lay hands on the villain. I believe 'a means to cozen somebody in this city under my countenance.

Re-enter BIONDELLO.

Bion. I have seen them in the church to-

ACT V.] TAMING OF THE SHREW. [SCENE I.

gether; God send 'em good shipping!—But who is here? mine old master, Vincentio? Now, we are undone, and brought to nothing.

Vin. Come hither, crack-hemp.   [*Seeing* BIONDELLO.

Bion. I hope I may choose, sir.

Vin. Come hither, you rogue. What, have you forgot me?

Bion. Forgot you? no, sir: I could not forget you, for I never saw you before in all my life.

Vin. What, you notorious villain, didst thou never see thy master's father, Vincentio?

Bion. What, my old, worshipful old master? Yes, marry, sir; see where he looks out of the window.

Vin. Is't so, indeed?   [*Beats* BIONDELLO.

Bion. Help, help, help! here's a madman will murder me.   [*Exit.*

Ped. Help, son! help, signior Baptista!   [*Exit from the window.*

Pet. Prithee, Kate, let's stand aside, and see the end of this controversy.   [*They retire.*

Re-enter PEDANT *below;* BAPTISTA, TRANIO, *and Servants.*

Tra. Sir, what are you that offer to beat my servant?

Vin. What am I, sir? nay, what are you, sir? —O immortal gods! O fine villain! A silken doublet! a velvet hose! a scarlet cloak! and a copataiu hat![a]—O, I am undone, I am undone! While I play the good husband at home, my son and my servant spend all at the university.

Tra. How now? what's the matter?

Bap. What, is the man lunatic?

Tra. Sir, you seem a sober ancient gentleman by your habit, but your words show you a madman. Why, sir, what cerns[b] it you if I wear pearl and gold? I thank my good father, I am able to maintain it.

Vin. Thy father? O villain! he is a sail-maker in Bergamo.[1]

Bap. You mistake, sir; you mistake, sir: Pray, what do you think is his name?

Vin. His name? as if I knew not his name: I have brought him up ever since he was three years old, and his name is Tranio.

Ped. Away, away, mad ass! His name is Lu-

centio; and he is mine only son, and heir to the lands of me, signior Vincentio.

Vin. Lucentio! O, he hath murdered his master! lay hold on him, I charge you, in the duke's name: O, my son, my son!—tell me, thou villain, where is my son, Lucentio.

Tra. Call forth an officer: [*Enter one with an Officer.*] Carry this mad knave to the gaol:—Father Baptista, I charge you see that he be forthcoming.

Vin. Carry me to the gaol!

Gre. Stay, officer; he shall not go to prison.

Bap. Talk not, signior Gremio. I say he shall go to prison.

Gre. Take heed, signior Baptista, lest you be coney-catched in this business. I dare swear this is the right Vincentio.

Ped. Swear, if thou darest.

Gre. Nay, I dare not swear it.

Tra. Then thou wert best say that I am not Lucentio.

Gre. Yes, I know thee to be signior Lucentio.

Bap. Away with the dotard: to the gaol with him.

Vin. Thus strangers may be haled and abus'd. O monstrous villain!

Re-enter BIONDELLO. *with* LUCENTIO *and* BIANCA.

Bion. O, we are spoiled, and—Yonder he is; deny him, forswear him, or else we are all undone.

Luc. Pardon, sweet father.   [*Kneeling.*

Vin.   Lives my sweet son?
   [BIONDELLO, TRANIO, *and* PEDANT *run out.*

Bian. Pardon, dear father.   [*Kneeling.*

Bap.   How hast thou offended? Where is Lucentio?

Luc.   Here's Lucentio,
Right son unto the right Vincentio;
That have by marriage made thy daughter mine,
While counterfeit supposes blear'd thine eyne.

Gre. Here's packing with a witness, to deceive us all!

Vin. Where is that damned villain, Tranio, That fac'd and brav'd me in this matter so?

Bap. Why, tell me, is not this my Cambio?

Bian. Cambio is chang'd into Lucentio.

Luc. Love wrought these miracles. Bianca's love
Made me exchange my state with Tranio,
While he did bear my countenance in the town;
And happily I have arrived at last
Unto the wished haven of my bliss:
What Tranio did, myself enforc'd him to:
Then pardon him, sweet father, for my sake.

---

[a] *Copataiu hat*—high crowned hat. *Cop* is the top. The copataiu hat was probably that described by Stubbe's, 'Anatomie of Abuses,' 1595:—"Sometimes they use them sharp on the crown, peaking up like the spear or shaft of a steeple, standing a quarter of a yard above the crown of their heads."

[b] *Cerns.* So the original. It means, and is usually printed, *concerns.* Perhaps Tranio uses the word as an abbreviation; for we know no instance in which *cern* (*cernere*), is used without a prefix, such as *con, dis, de*

320

Act V.] TAMING OF THE SHREW. [Scene II.

Vin. I'll slit the villain's nose, that would have sent me to the gaol.
Bap. But do you hear, sir? [*To* Lucentio.] Have you married my daughter without asking my good-will?
Vin. Fear not, Baptista; we will content you: go to:
But I will in, to be revenged for this villany. [*Exit.*
Bap. And I, to sound the depth of this knavery. [*Exit.*
Luc. Look not pale, Bianca; thy father will not frown. [*Exeunt* Luc. *and* Bian.
Gre. My cake is dough:* But I'll in among the rest;
Out of hope of all,—but my share of the feast. [*Exit.*

Petrucio *and* Katharina *advance.*

Kath. Husband, let's follow, to see the end of this ado.
Pet. First kiss me, Kate, and we will.
Kath. What, in the midst of the street?
Pet. What, art thou ashamed of me?
Kath. No, sir; God forbid:—but ashamed to kiss.
Pet. Why, then, let's home again:—Come, sirrah, let's away.
Kath. Nay, I will give thee a kiss: now pray thee, love, stay.
Pet. Is not this well?—Come, my sweet Kate; Better once than never, for never too late. [*Exeunt.*

SCENE II.—*A Room in* Lucentio's *House.*

A banquet set out. Enter Baptista, Vincentio, Gremio, *the* Pedant, Lucentio, Bianca, Petrucio, Katharina, Hortensio, *and* Widow. Tranio, Biondello, Grumio, *and others, attending.*

Luc. At last, though long, our jarring notes agree;
And time it is, when raging war is done,
To smile at 'scapes and perils overblown.
My fair Bianca, bid my father welcome,
While I with self-same kindness welcome thine:
Brother Petrucio,—sister Katharina,—
And thou, Hortensio, with thy loving widow,—
Feast with the best, and welcome to my house.
My banquet is to close our stomachs up,

After our great good cheer: Pray you, sit down: For now we sit to chat, as well as eat. [*They sit at table.*
Pet. Nothing but sit and sit, and eat and eat.
Bap. Padua affords this kindness, son Petrucio.
Pet. Padua affords nothing but what is kind.
Hor. For both our sakes, I would that word were true.
Pet. Now, for my life, Hortensio fears his widow.
Wid. Then never trust me if I be afeard.*
Pet. You are very sensible, and yet you miss my sense;
I mean, Hortensio is afeard of you.
Wid. He that is giddy thinks the world turns round.
Pet. Roundly replied.
Kath. Mistress, how mean you that?
Wid. Thus I conceive by him.
Pet. Conceives by me!—How likes Hortensio that?
Hor. My widow says, thus she conceives her tale.
Pet. Very well mended: Kiss him for that, good widow.
Kath. He that is giddy thinks the world turns round:—
I pray you, tell me what you meant by that.
Wid. Your husband, being troubled with a shrew,
Measures my husband's sorrow by his woe:
And now you know my meaning.
Kath. A very mean meaning.
Wid. Right, I mean you.
Kath. And I am mean, indeed, respecting you.
Pet. To her, Kate!
Hor. To her, widow!
Pet. A hundred marks, my Kate does put her down.
Hor. That's my office.
Pet. Spoke like an officer:—Ha' to thee, lad. [*Drinks to* Hortensio.
Bap. How likes Gremio these quick-witted folks?
Gre. Believe me, sir, they butt together well.
Bian. Head, and butt? an hasty witted body
Would say your head and butt were head and horn.
Vin. Ay, mistress bride, hath that awaken'd you?
Bian. Ay, but not frighted me; therefore I'll sleep again.

---
* *My cake is dough.* This proverbial expression is used in Howell's Letters, to express the disappointment of the heir-presumptive of France when Louis XIV. was born: "So that now Monsieur's cake is dough."

* The use of *fear* in the active and passive sense is here exemplified.

Pet. Nay, that you shall not; since you have begun,
Have at you for a bitter jest or two.*
　Bian. Am I your bird? I mean to shift my bush,
And then pursue me as you draw your bow:—
You are welcome all.
　　[*Exeunt* BIANCA, KATHARINA, *and* Widow.
　Pet. She hath prevented me.—Here, signior Tranio,
This bird you aim'd at, though you hit her not;
Therefore, a health to all that shot and miss'd.
　Tra. O, sir, Lucentio slipp'd me like his greyhound,
Which runs himself, and catches for his master.
　Pet. A good swift simile, but something currish.
　Tra. 'Tis well, sir, that you hunted for yourself;
'T is thought, your deer does hold you at a bay.
　Bap. O ho, Petrucio, Tranio hits you now.
　Luc. I thank thee for that gird, good Tranio.
　Hor. Confess, confess, hath he not hit you here?
　Pet. 'A has a little gall'd me, I confess;
And, as the jest did glance away from me,
'T is ten to one it maim'd you two outright.
　Bap. Now, in good sadness, son Petrucio,
I think thou hast the veriest shrew of all.
　Pet. Well, I say—no: and therefore, for assurance,
Let 's each one send unto his wife;
And he, whose wife is most obedient
To come at first when he doth send for her,
Shall win the wager which we will propose.
　Hor. Content: What is the wager?
　Luc. 　　　　　　　Twenty crowns.
　Pet. Twenty crowns!
I 'll venture so much on my hawk, or hound,
But twenty times so much upon my wife.
　Luc. A hundred then.
　Hor.　.　　　　Content.
　Pet.　　　　　　　A match; 't is done.
　Hor. Who shall begin?
　Luc. That will I.
Go, Biondello, bid your mistress come to me.
　Bion. I go.　　　　　　　[*Exit.*
　Bap. Son, I will be your half, Bianca comes.
　Luc. I 'll have no halves; I 'll bear it all myself.

　　Re-enter BIONDELLO.

How now! what news?

　* *Bitter.* The original reads *better.* We adopt the correction of Capell.

　Bion. Sir, my mistress sends you word
That she is busy, and she cannot come.
　Pet. How! she is busy, and she cannot come!
Is that an answer?
　Gre. 　　　Ay, and a kind one too:
Pray God, sir, your wife send you not a worse.
　Pet. I hope, better.
　Hor. Sirrah Biondello, go, and entreat my wife
To come to me forthwith.　　[*Exit* BIONDELLO.
　Pet. 　　　　　O, ho! entreat her!
Nay, then she must needs come.
　Hor. 　　　　　I am afraid, sir,
Do what you can, yours will not be entreated.

　　Re-enter BIONDELLO.

Now where 's my wife?
　Bion. She says, you have some goodly jest in hand;
She will not come; she bids you come to her.
　Pet. Worse and worse; she will not come! O vile,
Intolerable, not to be endur'd!
Sirrah, Grumio, go to your mistress;
Say I command her come to me.
　　　　　　　　　　　[*Exit* GRUMIO.
　Hor. I know her answer.
　Pet. 　　　　　　What?
　Hor. 　　　　　　　　She will not.
　Pet. The fouler fortune mine, and there an end.

　　Enter KATHARINA.

　Bap. Now, by my holidame, here comes Katharina!
　Kath. What is your will, sir, that you send for me?
　Pet. Where is your sister, and Hortensio's wife?
　Kath. They sit conferring by the parlour fire.
　Pet. Go, fetch them hither; if they deny to come,
Swinge me them soundly forth unto their husbands:
Away, I say, and bring them hither straight.
　　　　　　　　　　　[*Exit* KATHARINA.
　Luc. Here is a wonder, if you talk of a wonder.
　Hor. And so it is; I wonder what it bodes.
　Pet. Marry, peace it bodes, and love, and quiet life,
An awful rule, and right supremacy;
And, to be short, what not, that 's sweet and happy.
　Bap. Now fair befal thee, good Petrucio!

The wager thou hast won; and I will add
Unto their losses twenty thousand crowns!
Another dowry to another daughter,
For she is chang'd, as she had never been.
　Pet. Nay, I will win my wager better yet;
And show more sign of her obedience,
Her new-built virtue and obedience.

Re-enter KATHARINA, *with* BIANCA *and* Widow.

See, where she comes; and brings your froward wives
As prisoners to her womanly persuasion.
Katharine, that cap of yours becomes you not;
Off with that bauble, throw it under foot.

　　　[KATHARINA *pulls off her cap, and throws
　　　　it down.*

　Wid. Lord, let me never have a cause to sigh,
Till I be brought to such a silly pass!
　Bian. Fye! what a foolish duty call you this?
　Luc. I would, your duty were as foolish too:
The wisdom of your duty, fair Bianca,
Hath cost me an hundred crowns since supper-time.
　Bian. The more fool you, for laying on my duty.
　Pet. Katharine, I charge thee, tell these headstrong women
What duty they do owe their lords and husbands.
　Wid. Come, come, you're mocking; we will have no telling.
　Pet. Come on, I say; and first begin with her.
　Wid. She shall not.
　Pet. I say, she shall;—and first begin with her.
　Kath. Fye, fye! unknit that threat'ning unkind brow;
And dart not scornful glances from those eyes,
To wound thy lord, thy king, thy governor:
It blots thy beauty, as frosts do bite the meads;
Confounds thy fame, as whirlwinds shake fair buds;
And in no sense is meet or amiable.
A woman mov'd is like a fountain troubled,[2]
Muddy, ill-seeming, thick, bereft of beauty;
And, while it is so, none so dry or thirsty
Will deign to sip, or touch one drop of it.
Thy husband is thy lord, thy life, thy keeper,
Thy head, thy sovereign; one that cares for thee,
And for thy maintenance; commits his body
To painful labour, both by sea and land;
To watch the night in storms, the day in cold,
While thou liest warm at home, secure and safe;

And craves no other tribute at thy hands,
But love, fair looks, and true obedience,—
Too little payment for so great a debt.
Such duty as the subject owes the prince,
Even such a woman oweth to her husband:
And when she's froward, peevish, sullen, sour,
And not obedient to his honest will,
What is she, but a foul contending rebel,
And graceless traitor to her loving lord?
I am asham'd, that women are so simple
To offer war, where they should kneel for peace;
Or seek for rule, supremacy, and sway,
When they are bound to serve, love, and obey.
Why are our bodies soft, and weak, and smooth,
Unapt to toil, and trouble in the world,
But that our soft conditions, and our hearts,
Should well agree with our external parts?
Come, come, you froward and unable worms!
My mind hath been as big as one of yours,
My heart as great; my reason, haply, more,
To bandy word for word, and frown for frown;
But now, I see our lances are but straws;
Our strength as weak, our weakness past compare,—
That seeming to be most, which we indeed least are.
Then vail your stomachs, for it is no boot;
And place your hands below your husbands' foot:
In token of which duty, if he please,
My hand is ready, may it do him ease!
　Pet. Why, there's a wench!—Come on, and kiss me, Kate.
　Luc. Well, go thy ways, old lad; for thou shalt ha't.
　Vin. 'Tis a good hearing, when children are toward.
　Luc. But a harsh hearing, when women are froward.
　Pet. Come, Kate, we'll to bed:
We three are married, but you two are sped.
'Twas I won the wager, though you hit the white;[a]　　　　　　　　[*To* LUCENTIO.
And, being a winner, God give you good night!
　　　　　　　[*Exeunt* PETRUCIO *and* KATH.
　Hor. Now go thy ways, thou hast tam'd a curst shrew.[b]
　Luc. 'Tis a wonder, by your leave, she will be tam'd so.　　　　　　　[*Exeunt.*

---

[a] *Hit the white*—a term in archery.
[b] *Shrew.* It would appear from this couplet, and another in this scene, where *shrew* rhymes to *woe*, that *shrow* was the old pronunciation.

ILLUSTRATIONS OF ACT V.

¹ Scene I.—"*A sail-maker in Bergamo.*"

It seems rather odd to select sail-making as the occupation of a resident in a town so far from the sea as Bergamo. It is possible, however, that the sails required for the navigation of the Lakes Lecco and Garda might have been made in the intermediate town of Bergamo. I looked through the place for a sail-maker; but the nearest approach I could find to one was a maker of awnings, &c. (M.)

² Scene II.—"*A woman moved is like a fountain troubled.*"

The fountain is the favourite of the many ornaments of the court of an Italian palazzo. It is important for its utility during the heats of summer; and such arts are lavished upon this species of erection as make it commonly a very beautiful object. It is worth the trouble of ascending a campanile in an Italian city in summer, merely to look down into the shady courts of the surrounding houses, where, if such houses be of the better sort, the fountains in the centre of the courts may be seen brimming and spouting, so as to refresh the gazer through the imagination. The birds that come to the basin to drink, and the servants of the house to draw water, form pictures which are a perpetual gratification to the eye. The clearness of the pool is the first requisite to the enjoyment of the fountain, without which, however elegant may be its form, it is "ill-seeming—bereft of beauty."—(M.)

³ Scene II.—"*Exeunt.*"

Shakspere's play terminates without disposing of Christopher Sly. The actors probably dealt with him as they pleased after his most characteristic speech at the end of the second scene of Act I. The old 'Taming of a Shrew' concludes as follows :—

Then enter two bearing of SLIE *in his own apparel again, and leave him where they found him, and then go out: then enters the* TAPSTER.

Tap. Now that the darksome night is overpast,
And dawning day appears in crystal sky,
Now must I haste abroad: but soft, who's this?
What, Slie? O wondrous! hath he lain here all night?
I'll wake him; I think he's starved by this,
But that his belly was so stuff'd with ale.
What, now, Slie, awake, for shame.
Slie. Sim, give's some more wine: what, all the players gone? Am not I a lord?
Tap. A lord with a murrain: come, art thou drunken still?
Slie. Who's this? Tapster! O Lord, sirrah, I have had the bravest dream to-night that ever thou heardst in all thy life.
Tap. Yea, marry, but you had best get you home,
For your wife will curse you for dreaming here to-night.
Slie. Will she? I know now how to tame a shrew;
I dreamt upon it all this night till now,
And thou hast waked me out of the best dream
That ever I had in my life: but I'll to my wife presently,
And tame her too if she anger me.
Tap. Nay, tarry, Slie, for I'll go home with thee,
And hear the rest that thou hast dreamt to-night.

[*Exeunt omnes.*

[Sly at the Alehouse door.]

[Itinerant Players in a Country Hall.]

SUPPLEMENTARY NOTICE.

This play was produced in a "taming" age. Men tamed each other by the axe and the fagot; parents tamed their children by the rod and the ferrule, as they stood or knelt in trembling silence before those who had given them life; and, although England was then called the "paradise of women," and, as opposed to the treatment of horses, they were treated "obsequiously," husbands thought that "taming," after the manner of Petrucio, by oaths and starvation, was a commendable fashion. Fletcher was somewhat heretical upon this point; for he wrote a play called 'The Tamer Tamed; or the Taming of the Tamer,' in which Petrucio, having married a second wife, was subjected to the same process by which he conquered "Katharine the curst." The discipline appeared to be considered necessary for more than a century afterwards; for we find in the 'Tatler' a story told as new and original, of a gentleman in Lincolnshire who had four daughters, one of whom was of "so imperious a temper (usually called a high spirit), that it continually made great uneasiness in the family," but who was entirely reclaimed by the Petrucio recipe of "taking a woman down in her wedding shoes."

We are—the happier our fortune—living in an age when this practice of Petrucio is not universally considered orthodox; and we owe a great deal to him who has exhibited the secrets of the "taming school" with so much spirit in this comedy, for the better belief of our age, that violence is not to be subdued by violence. It was *he* who said, when the satirist cried out—

"Give me leave
To speak my mind, and I will through and through
Cleanse the foul body of the infected world"—

SUPPLEMENTARY NOTICE.

It was *he* who said, in his own proper spirit of gentleness and truth,

"Fie on thee, I can tell what thou would'st do—
"Most mischievous foul sin in chiding sin."

It was *he* who found "a soul of goodness in things evil,"—who taught us, in the same delicious reflection of his own nature, the real secret of conquering opposition:—

"Your *gentleness* shall force,
More than your *force* move us to gentleness."*

Pardon be for him, if, treading in the footsteps of a predecessor whose sympathies with the peaceful and the beautiful were immeasurably inferior to his own, and sacrificing something to the popular appetite, he should have made the husband of a froward woman "kill her in her own humour," and bring her upon her knees to the abject obedience of a revolted, but penitent slave:—

"A foul contending rebel,
And graceless traitor to her loving lord."

Pardon for *him!* If there be one reader of Shakspere, and especially if that reader be a female, who cherishes unmixed indignation when Petrucio, in his triumph, exclaims—

"He that knows better how to tame a shrew,
Now let him speak,'—

we would say,—the indignation which you feel, and in which thousands sympathise, belongs to the age in which you live; but the principle of justice, and of justice to women above all, from which it springs, has been established, more than by any other lessons of human origin, by him who has now moved your anger. It is to him that woman owes, more than to any other human authority, the popular elevation of the feminine character, by the most matchless delineations of its purity, its faith, its disinterestedness, its tenderness, its heroism, its union of intellect and sensibility. It is he that, as long as the power of influencing mankind by high thoughts, clothed in the most exquisite language, shall endure, will preserve the ideal elevation of women pure and unassailable from the attacks of coarseness or libertinism,—ay, and even from the degradation of the example of the crafty and worldly-minded of their own sex;—for it is he that has delineated the ingenuous and trusting Imogen, the guileless Perdita, the impassioned Juliet, the heart-stricken but loving Desdemona, the generous and courageous Portia, the unconquerable Isabella, the playful Rosalind, the world-unknowing Miranda. Shakspere may have exhibited one froward woman wrongly tamed; but who can estimate the number of those from whom his all-penetrating influence has averted the curse of being froward?

If Shakspere requires any apology for the Taming of the Shrew, it is for having adopted the subject at all,—not for his treatment of it. The Kate that he found ready to his hand was a thoroughly unfeminine person, coarse and obstreperous, without the humour which shines through the violence of his Katharine. He describes his Shrew

"Young and beauteous;
Brought up as best becomes a gentlewoman."

She has "a scolding tongue," "her only fault." Her temper, as Shakspere has delineated it, is the result of her pride and her love of domination. She is captious to her father; she tyrannizes over her younger sister; she is jealous of the attractions of that sister's gentleness. This is a temper that perhaps could not be subdued by kindness, except after Petrucio's fashion of "killing a wife with kindness." At any rate, it could not be so subdued, except by a long course of patient discipline, quite incompatible with the hurried movement of a dramatic action. In the scene where Katharine strikes Bianca her temper has been exhibited at the worst. It is bad enough; but not quite so bad as appears from the following description of a French commentator:—"Catherine bat sa sœur par fantaisie et pour passer le temps, malgré les prières et les larmes de Bianca, qui ne se défend que par la douceur. Baptista accourt, et met Bianca en sureté dans sa chambre. Catherine sort, enragée de n'avoir plus personne à battre."† It is in her worst humour that Petrucio woos her; and surely nothing can be more animated than the wooing:—

"For you are call'd plain Kate,
And bonny Kate, and sometimes Kate the curst;
But Kate, the prettiest Kate in Christendom,
Kate of Kate-Hall, my super-dainty Kate,
For dainties are all cates; and therefore, Kate,
Take this of me, Kate of my consolation;—

* As You Like It.   † Paul Duport, Essais Littéraires, tom. ii. p. 2 [?].

TAMING OF THE SHREW.

> Hearing thy mildness prais'd in every town,
> Thy virtues spoke of, and thy beauty sounded,
> (Yet not so deeply as to thee belongs,)
> Myself am mov'd to woo thee for my wife."

Mr. Brown* has very judiciously pointed out the conduct of this scene, as an example of Shakspere's intimate knowledge of Italian manners. The conclusion of it is in reality a betrothment; of which circumstance no indication is given in the older play. The imperturbable spirit of Petrucio, and the daring mixture of reality and jest in his deportment, subdued Katharine at the first interview:—

> " Setting all this chat aside,
> Thus in plain terms :—Your father hath consented
> That you shall be my wife;—your dowry 'greed on;
> And will you, nill you, I will marry you."

Katharine denounces him as,—

> " A madcap ruffian, and a swearing Jack;"

Petrucio heeds it not :—

> " We have 'greed so well together,
> That upon Sunday is the wedding-day."

Katharine rejoinds,—

> " I'll see thee hang'd on Sunday first;"

but, nevertheless, the betrothment proceeds :—

> " Give me thy hand, Kate : I will unto Venice,
> To buy apparel 'gainst the wedding-day :—
> Provide the feast, father, and bid the guests;
> I will be sure, my Katharine shall be fine.
> *Bap.* I know not what to say : but give me your hands,
> God send you joy, Petrucio ! 't is a match.
> *Gre. Tra.* Amen, say we; we will be witnesses."

" Father and wife," says Petrucio. The betrothment is complete; and Katharine acknowledges it when Petrucio does not come to his appointment :—

> " Now must the world point at poor Katharine,
> And say—Lo ! there is mad Petrucio's wife,
> If it would please him come and marry her."

The " taming " has begun; her pride is touched in a right direction. But Petrucio *does* come. What passes in the church is matter of description, but the description is Shakspere all over. When we compare the freedom and facility which our poet has thrown into these scenes, with the drawling course of his predecessor, we are amazed that any one should have a difficulty in distinctly tracing his "fine Roman hand." Nor are the scenes of the under-plot in our opinion less certainly his. Who but Shakspere could have written these lines ?—

> " Tranio, I saw her coral lips to move,
> And with her breath she did perfume the air;
> Sacred and sweet was all I saw in her."

Compare this exquisite simplicity, this tender and unpretending harmony, with the bombastic images, and the formal rhythm, of the old play; the following passage for example :—

> " Come fair Emelia, my lovely love,
> Brighter than the burnish'd palace of the Sun,
> The eyesight of the glorious firmament,
> In whose bright looks sparkles the radiant fire
> Wily Prometheus slily stole from Jove."

And who but Shakspere could have created Grumio out of the stupid *Sander* of his predecessor ! That

> " Ancient, trusty, pleasant, servant Grumio,"

is one of those incomparable characters who drove the old clowns and fools off the stage, and trampled their wooden daggers and coxcombs for ever under foot. He is one of that numerous train that Shakspere called up, of whom Shadwell said, that " they had more wit than any of the wits and critics of his time." When Grumio comes with Petrucio to wed, he says not a word; but who has not pictured him " with a linen stock on one leg, and a kersey boot-hose on the other—a very monster in apparel, and not like a Christian foot-boy or a gentleman's lackey ?" We imagine him, like Sancho or Ralpho, somewhat under-sized. His profound remark, " considering the weather, a taller man than I would take cold," is indicative equally of his stature and and his wit. His scene with Curtis, in the fourth Act, is almost as good as Launce and Touchstone.

* Shakspeare's Autobiographical Poems.

SUPPLEMENTARY NOTICE.

But we are digressing from Petrucio, the soul of this drama. Hazlitt's character of him is very just:—" Petrucio is a madman in his senses; a very honest fellow, who hardly speaks a word of truth, and succeeds in all his tricks and impostures. He acts his assumed character to the life, with the most fantastical extravagance, with complete presence of mind, with untired animal spirits, and without a particle of ill humour from beginning to end." The great skill which Shakspere has shown in the management of this comedy, is established in the conviction that he produces all along that Petrucio's character is *assumed*. Whatever he may say, whatever he may do, we are satisfied that he has a real fund of good humour at the bottom of all the outbreaks of his inordinate self-will. We know that if he succeeds in subduing the violence of his wife by a much higher extravagance of violence, he will be prepared not only to return her affection, but to evoke it, in all the strength and purity of woman's love, out of the pride and obstinacy in which it has been buried. His concluding line,

" Why, there 's a wench!—Come on, and kiss me, Kate,"

is in earnest of his happiness.

Of the 'Induction' we scarcely know how to speak without appearing hyperbolical in our praise. It is to us one of the most precious gems in Shakspere's casket. The elegance, the truth, the high poetry, the consummate humour, of this fragment, are so remarkable, that if we apply ourselves to compare it carefully, with the earlier Induction upon which Shakspere formed it, and with the best of the dramatic poetry of his contemporaries, we shall in some degree obtain a conception, not only of the qualities in which he equalled and excelled the highest things of other men, and in which he could be measured with them,—but of those wonderful endowments in which he differed from all other men, and to which no standard of comparison can be applied. Schlegel says, " The last half of this prelude, that in which the tinker in his new state again drinks himself out of his senses, and is transformed in his sleep into his former condition, from some accident or other is lost." We doubt whether it was ever produced; and whether Shakspere did not exhibit his usual judgment in letting the curtain drop upon honest Christopher, when his wish was accomplished at the close of the comedy which he had expressed very early in its progress:—

" 'T is a very excellent piece of work. madam lady; 'Would 't were done!'"

Had Shakspere brought him again upon the scene, in all the richness of his first exhibition, perhaps the impatience of the audience would never have allowed them to sit through the lessons of "the taming-school." We have had farces enough *founded* upon the legend of Christopher Sly, but no one has ventured to *continue* him. Neither this fragment, nor that of 'Cambuscan bold,' could be made perfect, unless we could

" Call up him that left half-told
The story."

[' The pleasant garden of great Italy.']

['Hippolyta, I woo'd thee with my sword.']

INTRODUCTORY NOTICE.

State of the Text, and Chronology, of A Midsummer-Night's Dream.

A MIDSUMMER-NIGHT'S DREAM was first printed in 1600. In that year there appeared two editions of the play;—the one published by Thomas Fisher, a bookseller; the other by James Roberts, a printer. The differences between these two editions are very slight. Steevens, in his collection of twenty plays, has reprinted that by Roberts, giving the variations of the edition by Fisher. It is difficult to say whether both of these were printed with the consent of the author, or whether one was genuine and the other pirated. If the entries at Stationers' Hall may be taken as evidence of a proprietary right, the edition by Fisher is the genuine one, "A booke called A Mydsomer Nyghte Dreame" having been entered by him Oct. 8, 1600. One thing is perfectly clear to us—that the original of these editions, whichever it might be, was printed from a genuine copy, and carefully superintended through the press. The text appears to us as perfect as it is possible to be, considering the state of typography in that day. There is one remarkable evidence of this. The prologue to the interlude of the Clowns, in the fifth act, is purposely made inaccurate in its punctuation throughout. The speaker "does not stand upon points." It was impossible to have effected the object better than by the punctuation of Roberts' edition; and this is precisely one of those matters of nicety in which a printer would have failed, unless he had followed an extremely clear copy, or his proofs had been corrected by an author or an editor. The play was not reprinted after 1600, till it was collected into the folio of 1623; and the text in that edition differs in very few instances, and those very slight ones, from that of the preceding quartos.

Malone has assigned the composition of A Midsummer-Night's Dream to the year 1594. We are not disposed to object to this,—indeed we are inclined to believe that he has pretty exactly indicated the precise year, as far as it can be proved by one or two allusions which the play contains. But we entirely object to the reasons upon which Malone attempts to show that it was one of our author's "*earliest* attempts in comedy." He derives the proof of this from "the poetry of this piece, glowing with all the warmth of a youthful and lively imagination, the many scenes which it contains of almost continual rhyme, the poverty of the fable, and want of discrimination among the higher personages." Malone would place A Midsummer-Night's Dream in the same rank as The Two Gentlemen of Verona, Love's Labour's Lost, and The Comedy of Errors; and he supposes all of them written within a year or two of each other. We have no objection to believe that our poet wrote A Midsummer-Night's Dream when he was thirty years of age, that is in 1594. But it so far exceeds the three other comedies in all the higher attributes of poetry, that we cannot avoid repeating here the opinion which we have so often expressed, that he had written these for the stage before his twenty-fifth year, when he was a considerable share holder in the Blackfriars' company, some of them, perhaps, as early as 1585, at which period the vulgar tradition assigns to Shakspere—a husband, a father, and a man conscious of the possession of the very highest order of talent—the dignified office of holding horses at the theatre door. The year 1594 is, as nearly as possible, the period where we would place A Midsummer-Night's Dream, with reference to our strong belief that Shakspere's earliest plays must be assigned to the commencement of his dramatic career; and that two or three even of his great works had then been given to the world in an unformed shape, subsequently worked up to completeness and perfection.

INTRODUCTORY NOTICE.

But it appears to us a misapplication of the received meaning of words, to talk of "the warmth of a youthful and lively imagination" with reference to A Midsummer-Night's Dream, and the Shakspere of thirty. We can understand these terms to apply to the unpruned luxuriance of the Venus and Adonis; but the poetry of this piece—the almost continual rhyme—and even the poverty of the fable, are to us evidences of the very highest art having obtained a perfect mastery of its materials after years of patient study. Of all the dramas of Shakspere there is none more entirely harmonious than A Midsummer-Night's Dream. All the incidents, all the characters, are in perfect subordination to the will of the poet. "Throughout the whole piece," says Malone, "the more exalted characters are subservient to the interests of those beneath them." Precisely so. An unpractised author—one who had not in command "a youthful and lively imagination"—when he had got hold of the Theseus and Hippolyta of the heroic ages, would have made them ultra-heroical. They would have commanded events, instead of moving with the supernatural influence around them in perfect harmony and proportion. "Theseus, the associate of Hercules, is not engaged in any adventure worthy of his rank or reputation, nor is he in reality an agent throughout the play." Precisely so. An immature poet, again, if the marvellous creation of Oberon and Titania and Puck could have entered into such a mind, would have laboured to make the power of the fairies produce some strange and striking events. But the exquisite beauty of Shakspere's conception is, that, under the supernatural influence, "the human mortals" move precisely according to their respective natures and habits. Demetrius and Lysander are impatient and revengeful;—Helena is dignified and affectionate, with a spice of female error;—Hermia is somewhat vain and shrewish. And then Bottom! Who but the most skilful artist could have given us such a character? Of him Malone says, "Shakspeare would naturally copy those manners first, with which he was first acquainted. The ambition of a theatrical candidate for applause he has happily ridiculed in Bottom the weaver." A theatrical candidate for applause! Why, Bottom the weaver is the representative of the whole human race. His confidence in his own power is equally profound, whether he exclaims, "Let me play the lion too;" or whether he sings alone, "that they shall hear I am not afraid;" or whether, conscious that he is surrounded with spirits, he cries out, with his voice of authority, "Where's Peas-blossom?" In every situation Bottom is the same,—the same personification of that self-love which the simple cannot conceal, and the wise can with difficulty suppress. Malone thus concludes his analysis of the internal evidence of the chronology of A Midsummer-Night's Dream:—"That a drama, of which the principal personages are thus insignificant, and the fable thus meagre and uninteresting, was one of our author's earliest compositions, does not, therefore, seem a very improbable conjecture; nor are the beauties with which it is embellished inconsistent with this supposition." The beauties with which it is embellished include, of course, the whole rhythmical structure of the versification. The poet has here put forth all his strength. We venture to offer an opinion that if any single composition were required to exhibit the power of the English language for purposes of poetry, that composition would be the Midsummer-Night's Dream. This wonderful model which, at the time it appeared, must have been the commencement of a great poetical revolution,—and which has never ceased to influence our higher poetry, from Fletcher to Shelley—was, according to Malone, the work of "the genius of Shakspeare, even *in its minority*."

Mr. Hallam has, as might be expected, taken a much more correct view of this question than Malone. He places A Midsummer-Night's Dream *among* the early plays; but having mentioned The Comedy of Errors, The Two Gentlemen of Verona, Love's Labour's Lost, and The Taming of the Shrew, he adds, "its superiority to those we have already mentioned affords some presumption that it was written after them." *

A Midsummer-Night's Dream is mentioned by Francis Meres in 1598. The date of the first publication of the play, therefore, in 1600, does not tend to fix its chronology. Nor is it very material to ascertain whether it preceded 1598 by three, or four, or five years. The state of the weather in 1593 and 1594, when England was visited with peculiarly ungenial seasons, may have suggested Titania's beautiful description in Act II. Scene II. (See Illustrations.) The allusion of two lines in Act IV. is by no means so clear:—

> "The thrice three muses mourning for the death
> Of learning, late deceas'd in beggary."

This passage was once thought to allude to the death of Spenser. But the misfortunes and the death of Spenser did not take place till 1599. Even if the allusion were inserted between the first

* Literature of Europe, vol. II, p. 387.

production of the piece, and its publication in 1600, it is difficult to understand how an elegy on the great poet could have been called—
"Some satire keen and critical."

T. Warton suggested "that Shakspeare here, perhaps, alluded to Spenser's poem, entitled 'The Tears of the Muses, on the Neglect and Contempt of Learning.' This piece first appeared in quarto, with others, 1591." We greatly doubt the propriety of this conjecture, which Malone has adopted. Spenser's poem is certainly a satire in one sense of the word; for it makes the Muses lament that all the glorious productions of men that proceeded from their influence had vanished from the earth. All that—

" ——was wont to work delight
Through the divine infusion of their skill,
And all that els seemd fair and fresh in sight,
So made by nature for to serve their will,
Was turned now to dismall heavinesse,
Was turned now to dreadful uglinesse."

Clio complains that mighty peers "only boast of arms and ancestry;" Melpomene that "all man's life me seems a tragedy;" Thalia is "made the servant of the many;" Euterpe weeps that "now no pastoral is to be heard;" and so on. These laments do not seem to be identical with the

"mourning for the death
Of learning, late deceas'd in beggary."

These expressions are too precise and limited to refer to the tears of the Muses for the decay of knowledge and art. We cannot divest ourselves of the belief that some real person, and some real death, was alluded to. May we hazard a conjecture?—Greene, a man of learning, and one whom Shakspere in the generosity of his nature might wish to point at kindly, died in 1592, in a condition that might truly be called beggary. But how was his death, any more than that of Spenser, to be the occasion of "some satire keen and critical?" Every student of our literary history will remember the famous controversy of Nash and Gabriel Harvey, which was begun by Harvey's publication, in 1592, of 'Four Letters, and certain Sonnets, especially touching Robert Greene, and other parties by him abused.' Robert Greene was dead; but Harvey came forward, in revenge of an incautious attack of the unhappy poet, to satirize him in his grave—to hold up his vices and his misfortunes to the public scorn—to be "keen and critical" upon "learning, late deceas'd in beggary." The conjecture which we offer may have little weight, and the point is certainly of very small consequence.

COSTUME.

For the costume of the Greeks in the heroical ages we must look to the frieze of the Parthenon. It has been justly remarked ('Elgin Marbles,' p. 165), that we are not to consider the figures of the Parthenon frieze as affording us "a close representation of the national costume," harmony of

INTRODUCTORY NOTICE.

composition having been the principal object of the sculptors. But, nevertheless, although not one figure in all the groups may be represented as fully attired according to the custom of the country, nearly all the component parts of the ancient Greek dress are to be found in the frieze. Horsemen are certainly represented with no garment but the chlamys, according to the practice of the sculptors of that age; but the tunic which was worn beneath it is seen upon others, as well as the cothurnus, or buskin, and the petasus, or Thessalian hat, which all together completed the male attire of that period. On other figures may be observed the Greek crested helmet and cuirass; the closer skull-cap, made of leather, and the large circular shield, &c. The Greeks of the heroic ages wore the sword under the left arm-pit, so that the pommel touched the nipple of the breast. It hung almost horizontally in a belt which passed over the right shoulder. It was straight, intended for cutting and thrusting, with a leaf-shaped blade, and not above twenty inches long. It had no guard, but a cross bar, which, with the scabbard, was beautifully ornamented. The hilts of the Greek swords were sometimes of ivory and gold. The Greek bow was made of two long goat's horns fastened into a handle. The original bow-strings were thongs of leather, but afterwards horse-hair was substituted. The knocks were generally of gold, whilst metal and silver also ornamented the bows on other parts. The arrow-heads were sometimes pyramidal, and the

A MIDSUMMER-NIGHT'S DREAM.

shafts were furnished with feathers. They were carried in quivers, which, with the bow, was slung behind the shoulders. Some of these were square, others round, with covers to protect the arrows from dust and rain. Several which appear on fictile vases seem to have been lined with skins. The spear was generally of ash, with a leaf-shaped head of metal, and furnished with a pointed ferule at the butt, with which it was stuck in the ground—a method used, according to Homer, when the troops rested on their arms, or slept upon their shields. The hunting-spear (in Xenophon and Pollux) had two salient parts, sometimes three crescents, to prevent the advance of the wounded animal. On the coins of Ætolia is an undoubted hunting-spear.

The female dress consisted of the long sleeveless tunic (stola or calasiris), or a tunic with shoulder-flaps almost to the elbow, and fastened by one or more buttons down the arm (axillaris). Both descriptions hung in folds to the feet, which were protected by a very simple sandal (solea or crepida). Over the tunic was worn the peplum, a square cloth or veil fastened to the shoulders and hanging over the bosom as low as the zone (tænia or strophium), which confined the tunic just beneath the bust. Athenian women of high rank wore hair-pins (one ornamented with a cicada, or grasshopper, is engraved in Hope's 'Costume of the Ancients,' plate 138), ribands or fillets, wreaths of flowers, &c. The hair of both sexes was worn in long, formal ringlets, either of a flat and zigzagged or of a round and corkscrew shape.

The lower orders of Greeks were clad in a short tunic of coarse materials, over which slaves wore a sort of leathern jacket, called diphthera: slaves were also distinguished from freemen by their hair being closely shorn.

The Amazons are generally represented on the Etruscan vases in short embroidered tunics with sleeves to the wrist, (the peculiar distinction of Asiatic or barbaric nations,) pantaloons, ornamented with stars and flowers to correspond with the tunic, the chlamys, or short military cloak, and the Phrygian cap or bonnet. Hippolyta is seen so attired on horseback contending with Theseus. Vide Hope's 'Costumes.'

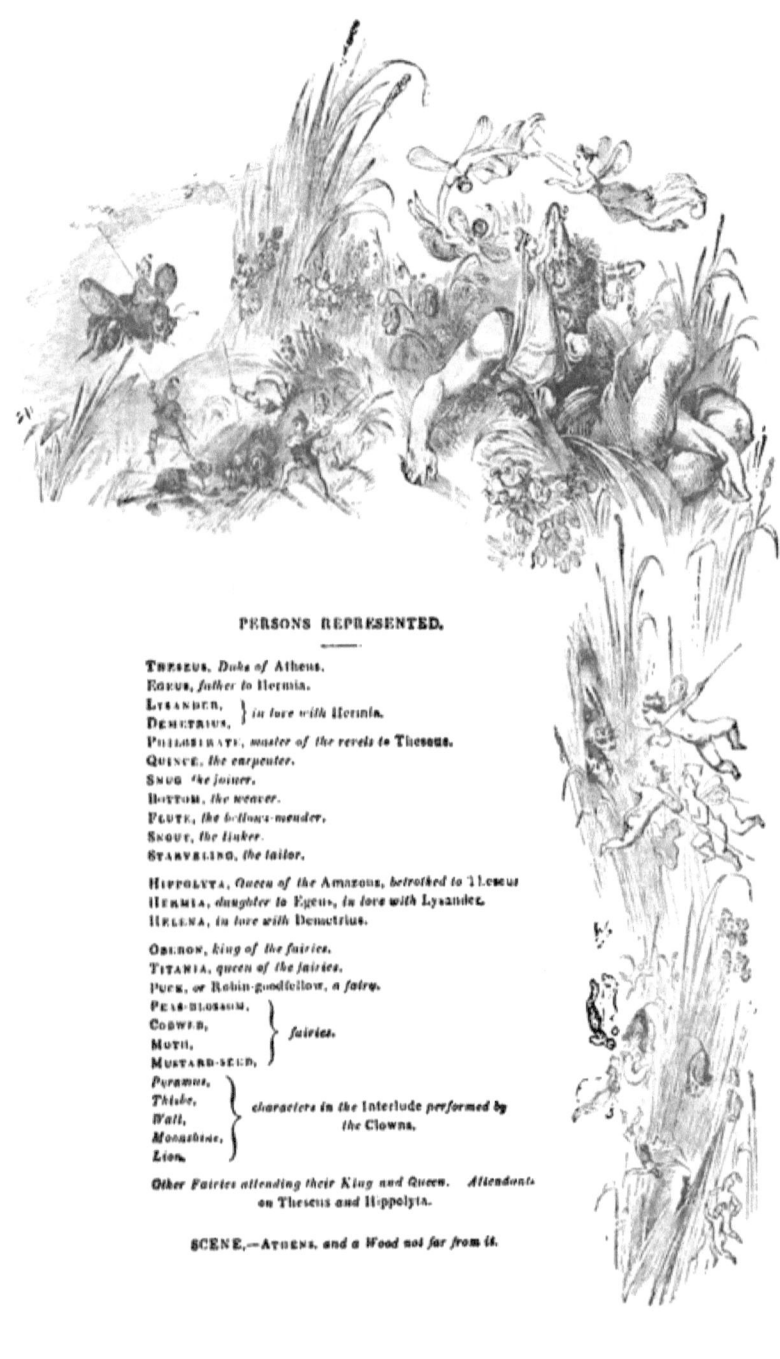

PERSONS REPRESENTED.

THESEUS, *Duke of Athens.*
EGEUS, *father to Hermia.*
LYSANDER, } *in love with Hermia.*
DEMETRIUS,
PHILOSTRATE, *master of the revels to* THESEUS.
QUINCE, *the carpenter.*
SNUG, *the joiner.*
BOTTOM, *the weaver.*
FLUTE, *the bellows-mender.*
SNOUT, *the tinker.*
STARVELING, *the tailor.*

HIPPOLYTA, *Queen of the Amazons, betrothed to* THESEUS.
HERMIA, *daughter to Egeus, in love with Lysander.*
HELENA, *in love with Demetrius.*

OBERON, *king of the fairies.*
TITANIA, *queen of the fairies.*
PUCK, *or Robin-goodfellow, a fairy.*
PEAS-BLOSSOM,
COBWEB,   } *fairies.*
MOTH,
MUSTARD-SEED,
Pyramus,
Thisbe,   } *characters in the Interlude performed by*
Wall,   *the Clowns.*
Moonshine,
Lion.

Other Fairies attending their King and Queen.   Attendants on Theseus and Hippolyta.

SCENE.—ATHENS, *and a Wood not far from it.*

("And in the wood, where often you and I
Upon faint primrose beds were wont to lie.")

ACT I.

SCENE I.—Athens. *A Room in the Palace of Theseus.*

Enter THESEUS, HIPPOLYTA, PHILOSTRATE, *and Attendants.*

The. Now, fair Hippolyta, our nuptial hour
Draws on apace; four happy days bring in
Another moon: but, oh, methinks, how slow
This old moon wanes! she lingers my desires,
Like to a step-dame, or a dowager,
Long withering out a young man's revenue.
 Hip. Four days will quickly steep themselves
    in nights;
Four nights will quickly dream away the time;
And then the moon, like to a silver bow
New bent[a] in heaven, shall behold the night
Of our solemnities.

[a] *New bent.* The two quartos of 1600, and the folio of 1623, read "now bent." *New* was supplied by Rowe. We believe

The. Go, Philostrate,
Stir up the Athenian youth to merriments;
Awake the pert and nimble spirit of mirth;
Turn melancholy forth to funerals,
The pale companion is not for our pomp.
 [*Exit* PHILOSTRATE.
Hippolyta, I woo'd thee with my sword,[1]
And won thy love, doing thee injuries;
But I will wed thee in another key,
With pomp, with triumph, and with revelling.[a]

that *now* was the original word, but used in the sense of *new*, both the words having an etymological affinity. In the same manner, we have, in All's Well that Ends Well, Act ii. Sc. iii.—

"—— whose ceremony
Shall seem expedient on the now-born brief."

This, in many editions, has been changed to "new-born brief," certainly without necessity. In the present case, the corrected reading must, we apprehend, be received; for *now* could not be restored without producing an ambiguity.

[a] See Two Gentlemen of Verona, Illustrations of Act V.

ACT I.] A MIDSUMMER-NIGHT'S DREAM. [SCENE I

Enter EGEUS, HERMIA, LYSANDER, *and* DEMETRIUS.

Ege. Happy be Theseus, our renowned duke![a]
The. Thanks, good Egeus: What's the news with thee?
Ege. Full of vexation come I, with complaint
Against my child, my daughter Hermia.
Stand forth, Demetrius: My noble lord,
This man hath my consent to marry her.—
Stand forth, Lysander:—and, my gracious duke,
This man[b] hath bewitch'd the bosom of my child:
Thou, thou, Lysander, thou hast given her rhymes,
And interchang'd love-tokens with my child:
Thou hast by moon-light at her window sung,
With feigning voice, verses of feigning love;
And stol'n the impression of her fantasy
With bracelets of thy hair, rings, gawds, conceits,
Knacks, trifles, nosegays, sweet-meats; messengers
Of strong prevailment in unharden'd youth:
With cunning hast thou filch'd my daughter's heart;
Turn'd her obedience, which is due to me,
To stubborn harshness:—And, my gracious duke,
Be it so she will not here before your grace
Consent to marry with Demetrius,
I beg the ancient privilege of Athens;
As she is mine, I may dispose of her:
Which shall be either to this gentleman,
Or to her death; according to our law,
Immediately provided in that case.
The. What say you, Hermia? Be advis'd, fair maid:
To you your father should be as a god;
One that compos'd your beauties; yea, and one
To whom you are but as a form in wax,
By him imprinted, and within his power
To leave the figure, or disfigure it.
Demetrius is a worthy gentleman.
Her. So is Lysander.
The. In himself he is:
But, in this kind, wanting your father's voice,
The other must be held the worthier.
Her. I would my father look'd but with my eyes.

The. Rather your eyes must with his judgment look.
Her. I do entreat your grace to pardon me.
I know not by what power I am made bold,
Nor how it may concern my modesty,
In such a presence here, to plead my thoughts:
But I beseech your grace that I may know
The worst that may befal me in this case,
If I refuse to wed Demetrius.
The. Either to die the death, or to abjure
For ever the society of men.
Therefore, fair Hermia, question your desires,
Know of your youth, examine well your blood,
Whether, if you yield not to your father's choice,
You can endure the livery of a nun;
For aye to be in shady cloister mew'd,
To live a barren sister all your life,
Chanting faint hymns to the cold fruitless moon.
Thrice blessed they that master so their blood,
To undergo such maiden pilgrimage:
But earthly happier[a] is the rose distill'd,
Than that, which, withering on the virgin thorn,
Grows, lives, and dies, in single blessedness.
Her. So will I grow, so live, so die, my lord,
Ere I will yield my virgin patent up
Unto his lordship,[b] whose unwished yoke
My soul consents not to give sovereignty.[c]
The. Take time to pause; and, by the next new moon,
(The sealing-day betwixt my love and me,
For everlasting bond of fellowship,)
Upon that day either prepare to die,
For disobedience to your father's will;
Or else, to wed Demetrius, as he would;
Or on Diana's altar to protest,
For aye, austerity and single life.

---

[a] *Earthly happier*—more happy in an earthly sense. The reading of all the old copies is *earthlier happy*, and this has been generally followed, although Pope and Johnson proposed *earlier happy*, and Steevens *earthly happy*. We have no doubt that Capell's reading, which we have adopted, is the true one; and that the old reading arose out of one of the commonest of typographical errors, the orthography of the folio is *earthlier happie*;—if the comparative had not been used, it would have been *earthlie happie*; and it is easy to see, therefore, that the r has been transposed.

[b] *Lordship*—authority. The word *dominion* in our present translation of the Bible (Romans, ch. vi.) is *lordship* in Wickliffe's translation.

[c] This is one of those elliptical expressions which frequently occur in our poet. The editor of the second folio, who was not scrupulous in adapting Shakspere's language to the changes of a quarter of a century, printed the lines—

"Unto his lordship, *to* whose unwish'd yoke," &c.

The *to* must be understood after *sovereignty*. In the same manner, the particle *as* must be understood in a passage in Cymbeline:—

"Whom heavens, in justice, (both on her and hers,) Have laid most heavy hand." (as.)

The same elliptical construction occurs in Othello's speech to the Senate:—

"What conjurations and what mighty magic I won his daughter." (*with*.)

---

[a] *Our renowned duke*. In a note upon the first chapter of the first book of Chronicles, where we find a list of "*the dukes of Edom*," the editor of the Pictorial Bible says, "Duke is rather an awkward title to assign to the chiefs of E'om. The original word is *aluph*, which would perhaps be best rendered by the general and indefinite title 'prince.'" At the time of the translation of the Bible *duke* was used in this general and indefinite sense. The word, as pointed out by Gibbon, was a corruption of the Latin *dux*, which was indiscriminately applied to any military chief. Chaucer has *duke* Theseus,—Gower, *duke* Spartacus,—Stonyhurst, *duke* Æneas. The "awkward title" was a word in general use; and therefore Steevens is not justified in calling it "a misapplication of a modern title."

[b] *This man*. So the old copies. In modern editions *man* is omitted; and the emphatic repetition of Egeus is in consequence destroyed.

Dem. Relent, sweet Hermia:—And, Lysander, yield
Thy crazed title to my certain right.
Lys. You have her father's love, Demetrius;
Let me have Hermia's: Do you marry him.
Ege. Scornful Lysander! true he hath my love;
And what is mine my love shall render him;
And she is mine; and all my right of her
I do estate unto Demetrius.
Lys. I am, my lord, as well deriv'd as he,
As well possess'd; my love is more than his;
My fortunes every way as fairly rank'd,
If not with vantage, as Demetrius';
And, which is more than all these boasts can be,
I am belov'd of beauteous Hermia:
Why should not I then prosecute my right?
Demetrius, I'll avouch it to his head,
Made love to Nedar's daughter, Helena,
And won her soul; and she, sweet lady, dotes,
Devoutly dotes, dotes in idolatry,
Upon this spotted[a] and inconstant man.
The. I must confess that I have heard so much,
And with Demetrius thought to have spoke thereof;
But, being over-full of self-affairs,
My mind did lose it.—But, Demetrius, come;
And come, Egeus; you shall go with me,
I have some private schooling for you both.
For you, fair Hermia, look you arm yourself
To fit your fancies to your father's will;
Or else the law of Athens yields you up
(Which by no means we may extenuate,)
To death, or to a vow of single life.
Come, my Hippolyta: What cheer, my love?
Demetrius, and Egeus, go along:
I must employ you in some business
Against our nuptial; and confer with you
Of something nearly that concerns yourselves.
Ege. With duty and desire, we follow you.

[*Exeunt* THES. HIP. EGE. DEM. *and train.*

Lys. How now, my love? why is your cheek so pale?
How chance the roses there do fade so fast?
Her. Belike for want of rain; which I could well
Beteem[b] them from the tempest of mine eyes.
Lys. Ah me! for aught that ever I could read,[c]
Could ever hear by tale or history,
The course of true love never did run smooth:
But, either it was different in blood;—
Her. O cross! too high to be enthrall'd to low![c]

[a] *Spotted*—stained, impure; the opposite of *spotless*.
[b] *Beteem*—pour forth.
[c] The quartos and the folio, read—

"O cross! too high to be enthrall'd to *love*."

Theobald altered *love* to *low*; and the antithesis, which is

Lys. Or else misgraffed, in respect of years;—
Her. O spite! too old to be engag'd to young!
Lys. Or else it stood upon the choice of friends;[a]—
Her. O hell! to choose love by another's eye!
Lys. Or, if there were a sympathy in choice,
War, death, or sickness did lay siege to it;
Making it momentany[b] as a sound,
Swift as a shadow, short as any dream,
Brief as the lightning in the collied[c] night,
That, in a spleen,[d] unfolds both heaven and earth,
And ere a man hath power to say,—Behold!
The jaws of darkness do devour it up:
So quick bright things come to confusion.
Her. If then true lovers have been ever cross'd,
It stands as an edict in destiny:
Then let us teach our trial patience,
Because it is a customary cross;
As due to love as thoughts, and dreams, and sighs,
Wishes, and tears, poor fancy's[e] followers.
Lys. A good persuasion; therefore, hear me, Hermia.
I have a widow aunt, a dowager
Of great revenue, and she hath no child;
From Athens is her house remov'd[f] seven leagues;
And she respects me as her only son.
There, gentle Hermia, may I marry thee;

kept up through the subsequent lines, justifies the change:—
high—low; old—young.

[a] *Friends*—so the quartos. In the folio we find—
"Or else it stood upon the choice of *merit*."

The alteration in the folio was certainly not an accidental one; but we hesitate to adopt the reading, the meaning of which is more reconcile than that of *friends*. The "choice of merit" is opposed to the "sympathy in choice;"—the merit of the suitor recommends itself to "another's eye," but not to the person beloved.

[b] *Momentany*. So the folio of 1623; the quartos read *momentany*, which Johnson says is the old and proper word. *Momentany* has certainly a more antique sound than *momentary*; but they were each indifferently used by the writers of Shakspere's time. We prefer the reading of the folio, because *momentany* occurs in four other passages in our poet's dramas; and this is a solitary example of the use of *momentany*, and that only in the quartos. The reading of the folio is invariably *momentary*.

[c] *Collied*—black, smutted. This is a word still in use in the Staffordshire collieries. Shakspere found it there, and transplanted it into the region of poetry.

[d] *In a spleen*—in a sudden fit of passion or caprice.

[e] *Fancy's followers*—the followers of Love. *Fancy* is here used in the same sense as in the exquisite song in the Merchant of Venice:—

"Tell me where is *fancy* bred."

The word is repeated with the same meaning three times in this play: in Act II. Sc. II.—

"In maiden meditation, *fancy-free*;"—

in Act III. Sc. II.—

"All *fancy-sick* she is, and pale of cheer;"—

and in Act IV. Sc. I.,

"Fair Helena in *fancy* following me."

[f] *Remov'd*—the reading of the folio. In the quartos we find *remote*. The reading of the folio is supported by several parallel passages; as in Hamlet,—

"It wafts you to a more *removed* ground;"

and in As You Like It—"Your accent is somewhat finer than you could purchase in so *removed* a dwelling."

And to that place the sharp Athenian law
Cannot pursue us: If thou lov'st me then,
Steal forth thy father's house to-morrow night;
And in the wood, a league without the town,
Where I did meet thee once with Helena,
To do observance to a morn of May,[2]
There will I stay for thee.
   Her.   My good Lysander!
I swear to thee by Cupid's strongest bow;
By his best arrow with the golden head;
By the simplicity of Venus' doves;
By that which knitteth souls, and prospers loves;
And by that fire which burn'd the Carthage queen,
When the false Trojan under sail was seen;
By all the vows that ever men have broke,
In number more than ever women spoke;
In that same place thou hast appointed me,
To-morrow truly will I meet with thee.
  Lys. Keep promise, love: Look, here comes
      Helena.

Enter HELENA.

  Her. God speed fair Helena! Whither away?
  Hel. Call you me fair? that fair again unsay.
Demetrius loves your fair:[a] O happy fair!
Your eyes are load-stars;[4] and your tongue's
      sweet air
More tunable than lark to shepherd's ear,
When wheat is green, when hawthorn buds
      appear.
Sickness is catching; O, were favour[b] so,
Your's would I catch,[c] fair Hermia, ere I go;
My ear should catch your voice, my eye your eye,
My tongue should catch your tongue's sweet
      melody.
Were the world mine, Demetrius being bated,
The rest I'll give to be to you translated.
O, teach me how you look; and with what art
You sway the motion of Demetrius' heart.

  Her. I frown upon him, yet he loves me still.
  Hel. O, that your frowns would teach my
      smiles such skill!
  Her. I give him curses, yet he gives me love.
  Hel. O, that my prayers could such affection
      move!
  Her. The more I hate, the more he follows me.
  Hel. The more I love, the more he hateth me.
  Her. His folly, Helena, is no fault of mine.[a]
  Hel. None. But your beauty; would that
      fault were mine!
  Her. Take comfort; he no more shall see my
      face;
Lysander and myself will fly this place.
Before the time I did Lysander see,
Seem'd Athens like a paradise to me:
O then, what graces in my love do dwell,
That he hath turn'd a heaven unto a hell!
  Lys. Helen, to you our minds we will unfold:
To-morrow night, when Phœbe doth behold
Her silver visage in the wat'ry glass,
Decking with liquid pearl the bladed grass,
(A time that lovers' flights doth still conceal,)
Through Athens' gates have we devis'd to steal.
  Her. And in the wood, where often you and I
Upon faint primrose beds were wont to lie,
Emptying our bosoms of their counsel sweet,
There my Lysander and myself shall meet:
And thence, from Athens, turn away our eyes,
To seek new friends and stranger companies.[b]
Farewell, sweet playfellow; pray thou for us,
And good luck grant thee thy Demetrius!—
Keep word, Lysander: We must starve our sight
From lovers' food, till morrow deep midnight.
                                [*Exit* HERMIA.
  Lys. I will, my Hermia.—Helena, adieu:
As you on him, Demetrius dote on you!
                                [*Exit* LYSANDER.
  Hel. How happy some o'er other some can be!
Through Athens I am thought as fair as she.
But what of that? Demetrius thinks not so;
He will not know what all but he do know.
And as he errs, doting on Hermia's eyes,
So I, admiring of his qualities.

---

[a] *Fair*—used as a substantive for *beauty*. As in the Comedy of Errors,—
        "My decayed *fair*
  A sunny look of his would soon repair."
This is the reading of the quartos. In the folio we have "*you fair*."

[b] *Favour*—features—appearance—outward qualities. In Cymbeline we find—
        "I have surely seen him;
  His *favour* is familiar to me;"
In Measure for Measure, "Surely, sir, a good *favour* you have;" and in Hamlet, "Tell her, let her paint an inch thick, to this *favour* she must come."

[c] *Your's would I catch.* The reading of all the old editions is, *Your words I catch*. The substitution was made by Hanmer. We leave the text as in most modern editions, but if the passage be pointed thus, we have an intelligible meaning in the original text:—
      "Sickness is catching; O, were favour so,
    (Your words I catch, fair Hermia,) ere I go,
    My ear should catch your voice," &c.
It is in the repetition of the word *fair* that Helena catches the words of Hermia; but she would also catch her voice, her intonation, and her expression, as well as her words.

---

[a] This is the reading of the quarto printed by Fisher. That by Roberts, and the folio, read,—
    "His folly, Helena, is none of *mine*."

[b] In the original editions we have the following reading:—
    "And in the wood, where often you and I
    Upon faint primrose beds were wont to lie,
    Emptying our bosoms of their counsel *swell'd*,
    There my Lysander and myself shall meet,
    And thence from Athens turn away our eyes
    To seek new friends and *strange companions*."
It will be observed that the whole scene is in rhyme; and the introduction, therefore, of four lines of blank verse has a harsh effect. The emendations were made by Theobald; and they are certainly ingenious and unforced. *Companies* for *companions* has an example in Henry V.:—
    "His *companies* unletter'd, rude, and shallow."

Things base and vild,[a] holding no quantity,
Love can transpose to form and dignity.
Love looks not with the eyes, but with the mind;
And therefore is wing'd Cupid painted blind.
Nor hath love's mind of any judgment taste;
Wings, and no eyes, figure unheedy haste:
And therefore is love said to be a child,
Because in choice he is so oft beguil'd.
As waggish boys in game themselves forswear,
So the boy love is perjur'd every where:
For ere Demetrius look'd on Hermia's eyne,
He hail'd down oaths, that he was only mine;
And when this hail some heat from Hermia felt,
So he dissolv'd, and showers of oaths did melt.
I will go tell him of fair Hermia's flight:
Then to the wood will he, to-morrow night,
Pursue her; and for this intelligence
If I have thanks, it is a dear expense:
But herein mean I to enrich my pain,
To have his sight thither and back again. [*Exit*.

SCENE II.—*The same. A Room in a Cottage.*

Enter SNUG, BOTTOM, FLUTE, SNOUT, QUINCE,
and STARVELING.

Quin. Is all our company here?

Bot. You were best to call them generally,
man by man, according to the scrip.[b]

Quin. Here is the scroll of every man's name,
which is thought fit, through all Athens, to play
in our interlude before the duke and the duchess, on his wedding-day at night.

Bot. First, good Peter Quince, say what the
play treats on; then read the names of the
actors; and so grow on to a point.

Quin. Marry, our play is—The most lamentable comedy, and most cruel death of Pyramus
and Thisby.

Bot. A very good piece of work, I assure you,[c]
and a merry.—Now, good Peter Quince, call
forth your actors by the scroll: Masters, spread
yourselves.

Quin. Answer, as I call you.—Nick Bottom,
the weaver.

Bot. Ready. Name what part I am for, and
proceed.

Quin. You, Nick Bottom, are set down for
Pyramus.

Bot. What is Pyramus? a lover, or a tyrant?

Quin. A lover, that kills himself most gallantly for love.

Bot. That will ask some tears in the true performing of it: If I do it, let the audience look
to their eyes; I will move storms, I will condole
in some measure. To the rest:—Yet my chief
humour is for a tyrant: I could play Ercles
rarely, or a part to tear a cat in, to make all split.

'The raging rocks,
'And shivering shocks,
'Shall break the locks
'Of prison gates:
'And Phibbus' car
'Shall shine from far,
'And make and mar
'The foolish fates.'

This was lofty!—Now name the rest of the
players.—This is Ercles' vein,[a] a tyrant's vein; a
lover is more condoling.

Quin. Francis Flute, the bellows-mender.

Flu. Here, Peter Quince.

Quin. You must take Thisby on you.

Flu. What is Thisby? a wandering knight?

Quin. It is the lady that Pyramus must love.

Flu. Nay, faith, let not me play a woman; I
have a beard coming.

Quin. That's all one; you shall play it in a
mask,[b] and you may speak as small as you will.

Bot. An I may hide my face, let me play
Thisby, too: I 'll speak in a monstrous little
voice;—'Thisne, Thisne,—Ah, Pyramus, my
lover dear; thy Thisby dear! and lady dear!'

Quin. No, no, you must play Pyramus; and,
Flute, you Thisby.

Bot. Well, proceed.

Quin. Robin Starveling, the tailor.

Star. Here, Peter Quince.

Quin. Robin Starveling, you must play
Thisby's mother.—Tom Snout, the tinker.

Snout. Here, Peter Quince.

Quin. You, Pyramus's father; myself, Thisby's
father;—Snug, the joiner, you, the lion's part:
—and, I hope, here is a play fitted.

Snug. Have you the lion's part written? pray
you, if it be, give it me, for I am slow of study.

Quin. You may do it extempore, for it is
nothing but roaring.

Bot. Let me play the lion too: I will roar,
that I will do any man's heart good to hear me;
I will roar, that I will make the duke say, 'Let
him roar again, let him roar again.'

Quin. An you should do it too terribly, you
would fright the duchess and the ladies, that

---

[a] *Vild*—vile. The word repeatedly occurs in Shakspere, as in Spenser; and when it does so occur we are scarcely justified in substituting the vile of the modern editors.
[b] *Scrip*—script—a written paper. Bills of exchange are called by Locke "*scrips* of paper;" and the term is still known upon the Stock Exchange.
[c] Bottom and Sly both speak of a theatrical representation as they would of a piece of cloth or a pair of shoes. Sly says of the play, "'Tis a very excellent piece of work."

[a] *Ercles*—Hercules—was one of the roaring heroes of the rude drama which preceded Shakspere. In Greene's 'Groat's-worth of Wit,' (1592,) a player says, "The twelve labours of Hercules have I terribly thundered on the stage."

they would shriek; and that were enough to hang us all.

All. That would hang us every mother's son.

Bot. I grant you, friends, if that you should fright the ladies out of their wits, they would have no more discretion but to hang us; but I will aggravate my voice so, that I will roar you as gently as any sucking dove; I will roar you an 't were any nightingale.

Quin. You can play no part but Pyramus: for Pyramus is a sweet-faced man; a proper man as one shall see in a summer's day; a most lovely, gentleman-like man; therefore you must needs play Pyramus.

Bot. Well, I will undertake it. What beard were I best to play it in?

Quin. Why, what you will.

Bot. I will discharge it in either your straw-coloured beard, your orange-tawny beard, your purple-in-grain beard, or your French-crown-coloured beard, your perfect yellow.

Quin. Some of your French crowns have no hair at all, and then you will play bare-faced.—But, masters, here are your parts: and I am to entreat you, request you, and desire you, to con them by to-morrow night; and meet me in the palace wood, a mile without the town, by moonlight; there we will rehearse: for if we meet in the city we shall be dog'd with company, and our devices known. In the mean time I will draw a bill of properties,[a] such as our play wants. I pray you fail me not.

Bot. We will meet; and there we may rehearse more obscenely and courageously. Take pains; be perfect; adieu.

Quin. At the duke's oak we meet.

Bot. Enough. Hold, or cut bow-strings.[b]

[*Exeunt.*

---

[a] *Properties.* The technicalities of the theatre are very unchanging. The person who has charge of the wooden swords, and pasteboard shields, and other trumpery required for the business of the stage, is still called the *property-man*. In the 'Antipodes,' by R. Brome, 1640, (quoted by Mr. Collier,) we have the following ludicrous account of the "properties," which form as curious an assemblage as in Hogarth's Strollers:—

"He has got into our tiring-house amongst us,
And ta'en a strict survey of all our properties;
Our statues and our images of gods,
Our planets and our constellations,
Our giants, monsters, furies, beasts, and bugbears,
Our helmets, shields and vizors, hairs and beards,
Our pasteboard marchpanes, and our wooden pies."

[b] Capell says, this is a proverbial expression derived from the days of archery:—"When a party was made at butts, assurance of meeting was given in the words of that phrase."

["I will roar you an't were any nightingale."]

ILLUSTRATIONS OF ACT I.

¹ SCENE I.—"*Hippolyta, I woo'd thee with my sword.*"

THE very ingenious writer of 'A Letter on Shakspere's Authorship of The Two Noble Kinsmen,' (1833,) remarks, that "the characters in A Midsummer-Night's Dream are classical, but the costume is strictly Gothic, and shows that it was through the medium of romance that he drew the knowledge of them." It was in Chaucer's Knight's Tale that our poet found the Duke of Athens, and Hippolyta, and Philostrate; in the same way that the author of 'The Two Noble Kinsmen,' and subsequently Dryden, found there the story of Palamon and Arcite. Hercules and Theseus have been called by Godwin, "the knight-errants of antiquity;"* and truly the mode in which the fabulous histories of the ancient world blended themselves with the literature of the chivalrous ages fully justifies this seemingly anomalous designation. It is not difficult to trace Shakspere in passages of the Knight's Tale. The opening lines of that beautiful poem offer an example:—

"Whilom, as olde stories tellen us,
Ther was a duk that highte Theseus.
Of Athenes he was lord and governour,
And in his time swiche a conquerour,
That greter was ther non under the sonne.
Ful many a riche contree had he wonne.
What with his wisdom and his chevalrie,
He conquerd all the regne of Feminie,
That whilom was ycleped Scythia;
And wedded the fresshe quene Ipolita,
And brought hire home with him to his contree
With mochel glorie and gret solempnitee,
And eke hire yonge suster Emelie,
And thus with victorie and with melodie
Let I this worthy duk to Athenes ride,
And all his host, in armes him beside.
   And certes, if it n'ere to long to here,
I wolde have tolde you fully the manere,
How wonnen was the regne of Feminie,
By Theseus, and by his chevalrie:
And of the grete bataille for the nons
Betwix Athenes and the Amazones:
And how assieged was Ipolita
The faire hardy quene of Scythia;
And of the feste, that was at hire wedding,
And of the temple at hire home coming,
But all this thing I moste as now forbere
I have, God wot, a large field to ere."

* *Life of Chaucer*, vol. i. p. 30.

² SCENE I.—"*Ah me! for aught that ever I could read,*" &c.

The passage in Paradise Lost, in which Milton has imitated this famous passage of Shakspere, is conceived in a very different spirit. Lysander and Hermia lament over the evils by which

"—— true lovers have been ever cross'd,"

as "an edict in destiny," to which they must both submit with patience and mutual forbearance. The Adam of Milton reproaches Eve with the

"——innumerable
Disturbances on earth through female snares,"

as a trial of which lordly man has alone a right to complain:

"—— for either
He never shall find out fit mate, but such
As some misfortune brings him, or mistake;
Or whom he wishes most shall seldom gain
Through her perverseness, but shall see her gain'd
By a far worse, or if she love, withheld
By parents; or his happiest choice too late
Shall meet, already link'd and wedlock-bound
To a fell adversary, his hate or shame:
Which infinite calamity shall cause
To human life, and household peace confound."
(*Par. Lost*, book x. v. 895.)

Adam had certainly cause to be angry when he uttered these reproaches; and therefore Milton has dramatically forgotten that man is not the only sufferer in such "disturbances on earth."

³ SCENE I.—"*To do observance to a morn of May.*"

The very expression, "*to do observance,*" in connexion with the rites of May, occurs twice in Chaucer's Knight's Tale:—

"Thus passeth yere by yere, and day by day,
Till it fell ones in a morwe of May
That Emelie, that fayrer was to sene
Than is the lilie upon his stalke grene,
And fresher than the May with floures newe,
(For with the rose colour strof hire hewe;
I n'ot which was the finer of hem two,)
Er it was day, as she was wont to do,
She was arisen, and all redy dight,
For May wol have no slogardie a-night.
The seson pricketh every gentil herte,
And maketh him out of his slepe to sterte,
And sayth, arise, and *do this observance.*"

ILLUSTRATIONS OF ACT I

Again:—

"Arcite, that is in the court real
With Theseus the squier principal,
Is risen, and loketh on the mery day
And for to don his observance to May."

The "observance," in the days of Chaucer, as in those of Shakspere, was a tribute from the city and the town to the freshness of a beautiful world; and our ancestors, as Stow has described, went out "into the sweet meadows and green woods, there to rejoice their spirits with the beauty and savour of sweet flowers, and with the harmony of birds praising God in their kind." Stubbs, however, in his 'Anatomie of Abuses,' first printed in 1585—at the very period when Shakspere was laying up in his native fields those stores of high and pleasant thoughts which show his love for the country and for country delights —has, while he describes the "observance" of May, denounced it as being under the superintendence of "Sathan." This passage of the inflexible Puritan is curious and interesting:—

"Against May, Whitsunday, or some other time of the year, every parish, town, and village assemble themselves together, both men, women, and children, old and young, even all indifferently; and either going all together, or dividing themselves into companies, they go some to the woods and groves, some to the hills and mountains, some to one place, some to another, where they spend all the night in pleasant pastimes, and in the morning they return, bringing with them birch boughs, and branches of trees, to deck their assemblies withal. And no marvel, for there is a great lord present amongst them, as superintendent and lord over their pastimes and sports, namely Sathan, Prince of Hell. But their chiefest jewel they bring from thence is their Maypole, which they bring home with great veneration, as thus: they have twenty or forty yoke of oxen, every ox having a sweet nosegay of flowers tied on the tip of his horns, and these oxen draw home this Maypole (this stinking idol rather), which is covered all over with flowers and herbs, bound round about with strings, from the top to the bottom, and sometime painted with variable colours, with two or three hundred men, women, and children, following it with great devotion. And thus being reared up, with handkerchiefs, and flags streaming on the top, they strew the ground about it, bind green boughs and arbours hard by it; and then fall they to banquet and feast, to leap and dance about it, as the heathen people did at the dedication of their idols, whereof this is a perfect pattern, or rather the thing itself."

The old spirit of joy was not put down when Herrick wrote sixty years afterwards—the spirit in which Chaucer sung—

"O Maye, with all thy floures and thy crene,
Right welcome be thou, faire fresshe Maye!"

The spirit, indeed, was too deeply implanted in "Merry England" to be easily put down; and the young, at any rate, were for the most part ready to exclaim with Herrick,—

"Come, let us go, while we are in our prime,
And take the harmless folly of the time."

[Bringing in the May-pole.]

A MIDSUMMER-NIGHT'S DREAM.

SCENE I.—"*Your eyes are load-stars.*"

The *load-star* is the north star, by which sailors steered their course in the early days of navigation. Chaucer used the term in this sense; and Spenser also:—

"Like as a ship who, *load-star* suddenly
Cover'd with clouds, her pilot hath dismay'd."

It was under this guiding star that danger was avoided, and the haven reached. Thus, Sidney in his 'Arcadia,' says, "Be not, most excellent lady—you, that nature has made to be the *load-star* of comfort—be not the rock of shipwreck." The *load-star* of Shakspere and the *cynosure* of Milton are the same in their metaphorical use:—

"Towers and battlements it sees
Bosom'd high in tufted trees,
Where perhaps some Beauty lies,
The *cynosure* of neighb'ring eyes."—*L'Allegro.*

In the 'Spanish Tragedy' we have the same application of the image:

"Led by the *load-star* of her heavenly looks."

SCENE II.—"*You shall play it in a mask.*"

Coryat, describing the theatres of Venice in 1608, writes,"—I observed certain things that I never saw before; for I saw women act,—a thing that I never saw before." Prynne, in his Histrio-Mastix, (1633,) after denouncing women-actors in the most furious terms, speaks of them as recently introduced upon the English stage:—"as they have now their female-players in Italy, and other foreign parts; and as they had such *French women-actors* in a play not long since personated in Blackfriars play-house, to which there was great resort." In a note he explains "not long since" as "Michaelmas Term, 1629." We therefore can have no doubt that in Shakspere's time the parts of women were personated by men and boys; and, indeed, Prynne denounces this as a more pernicious custom than the acting of women. The objection of Flute that he had "a beard coming," was doubtless a common objection; and the remedy was equally common—"You shall play it in a mask." Quince, instructing his

"Hard-handed men, that work in Athens here,"

reminds us of the celebrated picture, found at Pompeii, of the Choragus giving directions to the actors. The travesti would probably have been as just two thousand years ago as in the days of Shakspere.

[Choragus instructing the Actors.]

[Scenes I and II.]

ACT II.

SCENE I.—*A Wood near* Athens.

Enter a Fairy *on one side, and* PUCK *on the other.*

Puck. How now, spirit! whither wander you?

Fai. Over hill, over dale,
    Thorough bush, thorough briar,
Over park, over pale,
    Thorough flood, thorough fire,
I do wander everywhere
Swifter than the moon's sphere;
And I serve the fairy queen,
To dew her orbs[a] upon the green:
The cowslips tall her pensioners[a] be;
In their gold coats spots you see;
Those be rubies, fairy favours,
In those freckles live their savours:
I must go seek some dew-drops here,
And hang a pearl in every cowslip's ear.
Farewell, thou lob[b] of spirits, I'll be gone;
Our queen and all her elves come here anon.

Puck. The king doth keep his revels here to-night;
Take heed, the queen come not within his sight.

---

[a] *Orbs.* The *fairy rings,* as they are popularly called; which, however explained by philosophy, will always have a poetical charm connected with the beautiful superstition that the night-tripping fairies have, on these verdant circles, danced their merry roundels. It was Puck's office to dew these orbs, which had been parched under the fairy-feet in the moonlight revels.

[a] *Pensioners.* These courtiers, whom Mrs Quickly put above earls, (Merry Wives of Windsor, Act II. Sc. II.,) were Queen Elizabeth's favourite attendants. They were the handsomest men of the first families,—tall, as the cowslip was to the fairy, and shining in their spotted gold coats like that flower under an April sun.

[b] *Lob*—looby, lubber, lubbard.

A MIDSUMMER-NIGHT'S DREAM.

For Oberon is passing fell and wrath,
Because that she, as her attendant, hath
A lovely boy stol'n from an Indian king;
She never had so sweet a changeling:
And jealous Oberon would have the child
Knight of his train, to trace the forests wild:
But she, perforce, withholds the loved boy,
Crowns him with flowers, and makes him all her
  joy:
And now they never meet in grove, or green,
By fountain clear, or spangled star-light sheen,
But they do square;[b] that all their elves, for fear,
Creep into acorn cups, and hide them there.
  Fai. Either I mistake your shape and making
    quite,
Or else you are that shrewd and knavish sprite,
Call'd Robin Goodfellow:[2] are you not he,
T. at frights the maidens of the villagery;
Skim milk; and sometimes labour in the quern;[c]
And bootless make the breathless housewife
    churn;
And sometime make the drink to bear no barm;[d]
Mislead night-wanderers, laughing at their harm?
Those that Hobgoblin call you, and sweet Puck,
You do their work, and they shall have good
    luck:
Are not you he?
  Puck.   Thou speak'st aright;
I am that merry wanderer of the night.
I jest to Oberon, and make him smile,
When I a fat and bean-fed horse beguile,
Neighing in likeness of a filly foal:
And sometime lurk I in a gossip's bowl,
In very likeness of a roasted crab;
And, when she drinks, against her lips I bob,
And on her wither'd dewlap pour the ale,
The wisest aunt, telling the saddest tale,
Sometime for three-foot stool mistaketh me;
Then slip I from her bum, down topples she,
And *tailor* cries, and falls into a cough;
And then the whole quire hold their hips and
    loffe,
And waxen in their mirth, and neeze and swear
A merrier hour was never wasted there.—

But room, Faery, here comes Oberon.
  Fai. And here my mistress:—Would that he
    were gone!

SCENE II.—*Enter* OBERON, *on one side, with
his train, and* TITANIA, *on the other, with hers.*

  Obe. Ill met by moon-light, proud Titania.[2]
  Tita. What, jealous Oberon? Fairies, skip
    hence;
I have forsworn his bed and company.
  Obe. Tarry, rash wanton. Am not I thy lord?
  Tita. Then I must be thy lady: But I know
When thou hast stolen away from fairy land,
And in the shape of Corin sat all day,
Playing on pipes of corn,[c] and versing love
To amorous Phillida. Why art thou here,
Come from the farthest steep of India?
But that, forsooth, the bouncing Amazon,
Your buskin'd mistress, and your warrior love,
To Theseus must he wedded; and you come
To give their bed joy and prosperity.
  Obe. How canst thou thus, for shame, Titania,
Glance at my credit with Hippolyta,
Knowing I know thy love to Theseus?
Didst thou not lead him through the glimmering
    night
From Perigenia, whom he ravished?
And make him with fair Æglé break his faith,
With Ariadne, and Antiopa?
  Tita. These are the forgeries of jealousy:
And never, since the middle summer's spring,[a]
Met we on hill, in dale, forest, or mead,
By paved fountain,[b] or by rushy brook,
Or in the beached margent of the sea,
To dance our ringlets to the whistling wind,
But with thy brawls thou hast disturb'd our sport.
Therefore, the winds, piping to us in vain,[c]
As in revenge, have suck'd up from the sea
Contagious fogs; which, falling in the land,
Have every pelting[e] river made so proud,
That they have overborne their continents:[d]
The ox hath therefore stretch'd his yoke in vain,
The ploughman lost his sweat; and the green
    corn
Hath rotted, ere his youth attain'd a beard:
The fold stands empty in the drowned field,

---

[a] *Changeling*—a child procured in exchange.
[b] *Square*—to quarrel. It is difficult to understand how to *square*, which, in the ordinary sense, is to agree, should mean to disagree. And yet there is no doubt that the word was used in this sense. Holinshed has " Falling *at square* with her husband." In Much Ado about Nothing, Beatrice says, " Is there *no* young *squarer* now, that will make a voyage with him to the devil?" Mr. Richardson, after explaining the usual meaning of this verb, adds, " To *square* is also, consequently, to broaden: to set out broadly, in a position or attitude of offence or defence—(or *quarrel*)." The word is thus used in the language of pugilism. There is more of our old dialect in *such* terms than is generally supposed.
[c] *Quern*—a handmill; from the Anglo Saxon, *cwyrn*.
[d] *Barm*—yeast. Holland, in his translation of Pliny, speaks of "the froth, or *barm*, that riseth from these ales or beers."

[a] *Middle summer's spring*. The *spring* is the beginning—as the *spring of the day*, a common expression in our early writers. The *middle summer* is the *midsummer*.
[b] *Paved fountain*—a fountain, or clear stream, rushing over pebble.—certainly not an artificially paved fountain, as Johnson has supposed. The *paved fountain* is contrasted with the *rushy brook*. The epithet *paved* is used in the same sense as in the "pearl-paved ford" of Drayton, the "pebble-paved channel" of Marlow, and the "coral-paven bed" of Milton.
[c] *Pelting*—petty, contemptible. See note on "pelting farm," in Richard II. Act. II Sc. 1.
[d] *Continents*—banks. A *continent* is that which contains.

347

And crows are fatted with the murrion flock,
The nine men's morris is fill'd up with mud; [b]
And the quaint mazes in the wanton green,
For lack of tread, are undistinguishable;
The human mortals[a] want; their winter here,[b]
No night is now with hymn or carol blest:—
Therefore, the moon, the governess of floods,
Pale in her anger, washes all the air,
That rheumatic diseases do abound:
And thorough this distemperature, we see
The seasons alter: hoary-headed frosts
Fall in the fresh lap of the crimson rose;
And on old Hyems' thin and icy crown,
An odorous chaplet of sweet summer buds
Is, as in mockery, set: The spring, the summer,
The childing[c] autumn, angry winter, change
Their wonted liveries; and the mazed wor'd,
By their increase,[d] now knows not which is
    which:
And this same progeny of evils comes
From our debate, from our dissension;
We are their parents and original.

Obe. Do you amend it then: it lies in you:
Why should Titania cross her Oberon?
I do but beg a little changeling boy,
To be my henchman.[e]

[a] *Human mortals.* This beautiful expression has been supposed to indicate the difference between mankind and fairy-kind in the following manner—that they were each mortal, but that the less spiritual beings were distinguished as human. Upon this assertion of Steevens, Ritson and Reed enter into fierce controversy. Chapman, in his Homer, has an inversion of the phrase, "mortal humans;" and we suppose that, in the same way, whether Titania were, or were not, subject to death, she employed the language of poetry in speaking of "human mortals," without reference to the conditions of fairy existence.

[b] *Their winter here.* The emendation proposed by Theobald, *their winter cheer,* is very plausible. The original reading is—
  "The humane mortals want their winter *heere.*"
Johnson says *here* means, in this country, and their *winter* signifies their winter evening sports. The ingenious author of a pamphlet, 'Explanations and Emendations,' &c. (Edinburgh, 1814,) would read—
  "The human mortals want; their winter here,
  No night is now with hymn or carol blest."
The writer does not support his emendation by any argument; but we believe that he is right. The swollen rivers have rotted the corn, the fold stands empty, the flocks are murrain, the sports of summer are at an end, the human mortals *want.* This is the climax. Their winter is *here—* is come—although the season is the latter summer, or autumn; and in consequence the hymns and carols which gladdened the nights of a seasonable winter are wanting to this premature one. The "*therefore,*" which follows, introduces another clause in the catalogue of evils produced by the "brawls" of Oberon and Titania; as in the case of the preceding use of the same emphatic word in two instances:—
  "*Therefore,* the winds, piping to us in vain," &c.,
and—
  "The ox hath *therefore* stretch'd his yoke in vain," &c.

[c] *Childing*—producing. "The childing autumn" is "the teeming autumn" of our poet's 97th sonnet.

[d] *Increase*—produce.

[e] *Henchman*—a page—originally a horseman. In Chaucer we find—
  "And every knight had after him riding
  Three *henchmen,* on him awaiting."

Tita.   Set your heart at rest,
The fairy land buys not the child of me.
His mother was a vot'ress of my order:
And, in the spiced Indian air, by night,
Full often hath she gossip'd by my side;
And sat with me on Neptune's yellow sands,
Marking the embarked traders on the flood;
When we have laugh'd to see the sails conceive,
And grow big-bellied, with the wanton wind:
Which she, with pretty and with swimming gait,
Following (her womb then rich with my young
    squire,)
Would imitate: and sail upon the land,
To fetch me trifles, and return again,
As from a voyage, rich with merchandize.
But she, being mortal, of that boy did die;
And, for her sake, I do rear up her boy;
And, for her sake, I will not part with him.

Obe. How long within this wood intend you
    stay?

Tita. Perchance, till after Theseus' wedding-
    day.
If you will patiently dance in our round,
And see our moonlight revels, go with us;
If not, shun me, and I will spare your haunts.

Obe. Give me that boy, and I will go with thee.

Tita. Not for thy fairy[a] kingdom. Fairies
    away:
We shall chide downright, if I longer stay.
        [*Exeunt* TITANIA *and her train.*

Obe. Well, go thy way: thou shalt not from
    this grove,
Till I torment thee for this injury.
My gentle Puck, come hither: Thou remember'st[f]
Since once I sat upon a promontory,
And heard a mermaid, on a dolphin's back,
Uttering such dulcet and harmonious breath,
That the rude sea grew civil at her song;
And certain stars shot madly from their spheres,
To hear the sea-maid's music.

Puck.   I remember.

Obe. That very time I saw, (but thou could'st
    not,)
Flying between the cold moon and the earth,
Cupid all arm'd:[b] a certain aim he took

It has been conjectured that *henchman* is *haunchman—*one that follows a chief or lord at his *haunch.* The derivation from the Anglo-Saxon *hengst,* a horse, seems more probable.

[f] *Fairy.* This epithet is not found in modern editions, being rejected by Steevens—"By the advice of Dr. Farmer I have omitted the useless adjective, *fairy,* as it spoils the metre." Steevens scarcely wanted the advice of another as presumptuous as himself to perpetrate these atrocities.

[b] *All arm'd.* One of the commentators turned this epithet into "alarm'd." The original requires no explanation beyond the recollection of the Cupid of the poets:—
  "He doth bear a golden bow,
  And a quiver hanging low,
  Full of arrows that outbrave
  Dian's shafts."—(BEN JONSON.)

At a fair vestal, throned by the west;
And loos'd his love-shaft smartly from his bow,
As it should pierce a hundred thousand hearts:
But I might see young Cupid's fiery shaft
Quench'd in the chaste beams of the watery
　　moon;
And the imperial votaress passed on,
In maiden meditation, fancy-free.
Yet mark'd I where the bolt of Cupid fell:
It fell upon a little western flower,—
Before, milk-white, now purple with love's
　　wound,—
And maidens call it love-in-idleness.
Fetch me that flower; the herb I show'd thee
　　once;
The juice of it on sleeping eyelids laid,
Will make or man or woman madly dote
Upon the next live creature that it sees.
Fetch me this herb: and be thou here again,
Ere the leviathan can swim a league.

Puck. I'll put a girdle round about the earth
In forty minutes.ᵃ　　　　　　　[*Exit* PUCK.

Obe. Having once this juice,
I'll watch Titania when she is asleep,
And drop the liquor of it in her eyes:
The next thing then she waking looks upon,
(Be it on lion, bear, or wolf, or bull,
On meddling monkey, or on busy ape,)
She shall pursue it with the soul of love.
And ere I take this charm from off her sight,
(As I can take it, with another herb,)
I'll make her render up her page to me.
But who comes here? I am invisible;
And I will over-hear their conference.

　Enter DEMETRIUS, HELENA *following him.*

Dem. I love thee not, therefore pursue me not.
Where is Lysander, and fair Hermia?
The one I'll stay, the other stayeth me.ᵇ
Thou told'st me, they were stol'n into this
　　wood.
And here am I, and woodᶜ within this wood,

ᵃ This is the reading of Fisher's quarto. That of Roberts, and the folio, omit *round*, printing the passage as one line:—
　"I'll put a girdle about the earth in forty minutes."
ᵇ This is the invariable reading of the old copies. Theobald, upon the suggestion of Dr. Thirlby, changed it to—
　"The one I'll slay, the other stayeth me."
But it is surely unnecessary to assign to Demetrius any such murderous intents. He seus has betrayed her friend:—
　"I will go tell him of fair Hermia's flight;
　Then to the wood will he, to-morrow night,
　Pursue her."
He is pursuing her, when he exclaims—
　"The one I'll slay, the other stayeth me."
He will slay—stop—Hermia; Lysander stayeth—hindereth—him.
ᶜ *Wood*,—mad, from the Anglo-Saxon *wod*. Chaucer uses it in the form of *wode*, and it is still in common use in Scotland as *wud*.

Because I cannot meet myᵃ Hermia.
Hence, get thee gone, and follow me no more.
　Hel. You draw me, you hard-hearted ada-
　　mant;
But yet you draw not iron, for my heart
Is true as steel: Leave you your power to draw,
And I shall have no power to follow you.
　Dem. Do I entice you? Do I speak you fair?
Or, rather, do I not in plainest truth
Tell you—I do not, nor I cannot love you?
　Hel. And even for that do I love you the more.
I am your spaniel; and, Demetrius,
The more you beat me, I will fawn on you:
Use me but as your spaniel, spurn me, strike me,
Neglect me, lose me; only give me leave,
Unworthy as I am, to follow you.
What worser place can I beg in your love,
(And yet a place of high respect with me,)
Than to be used as you do use your dog?
　Dem. Tempt not too much the hatred of my
　　spirit;
For I am sick when I do look on thee.
　Hel. And I am sick when I look not on you.
　Dem. You do impeach your modesty too
　　much,
To leave the city, and commit yourself
Into the hands of one that loves you not;
To trust the opportunity of night,
And the ill counsel of a desert place,
With the rich worth of your virginity.
　Hel. Your virtue is my privilege for that.
It is not night, when I do see your face,
Therefore I think I am not in the night:
Nor doth this wood lack worlds of company;
For you, in my respect, are all the world:
Then how can it be said, I am alone,
When all the world is here to look on me?
　Dem. I'll run from thee, and hide me in the
　　brakes,
And leave thee to the mercy of wild beasts.
　Hel. The wildest hath not such a heart as you.
Run when you will, the story shall be chang'd:
Apollo flies, and Daphne holds the chase;
The dove pursues the griffin; the mild hind
Makes speed to catch the tiger: Bootless speed!
When cowardice pursues, and valour flies.
　Dem. I will no stay thy questions; let me go:
Or, if thou follow me, do not believe
But I shall do thee mischief in the wood.
　Hel. Ay, in the temple, in the town, and field,
You do me mischief. Fye, Demetrius!
Your wrongs do set a scandal on my sex:

ᵃ *My Hermia.* This has been enfeebled by some editor who has been followed without apology by others, into
　"Because I cannot meet *with* Hermia."

We cannot fight for love, as men may do:
We should be woo'd, and were not made to woo.
I'll follow thee, and make a heaven of hell,
To die upon the hand I love so well.
                      [*Exeunt* DEM. *and* HEL.
  Obe. Fare thee well, nymph: ere he do leave
      this grove,
Thou shalt fly him, and he shall seek thy love.

Re-enter PUCK.

Hast thou the flower there, welcome wanderer?
  Puck. Ay, there it is.
  Obe.   I pray thee, give it me.
I know a bank where the wild thyme blows,^a
Where ox-lips and the nodding violet grows;
Quite over-canopied with luscious woodbine,^b
With sweet musk-roses, and with eglantine:
There sleeps Titania, sometime of the night,
Lull'd in these flowers with dances and delight;
And there the snake throws her enamell'd skin,
Weed wide enough to wrap a fairy in :
And with the juice of this I'll streak her eyes,
And make her full of hateful fantasies.
Take thou some of it, and seek through this grove:
A sweet Athenian lady is in love
With a disdainful youth: anoint his eyes;
But do it when the next thing he espies
May be the lady: Thou shalt know the man
By the Athenian garments he hath on.
Effect it with some care; that he may prove
More fond on her, than ene upon her love:
And look thou meet me ere the first cock crow.
  Puck. Fear not, my lord, your servant shall
      do so.   [*Exeunt.*

SCENE III.—*Another part of the Wood.*

Enter TITANIA *with her train.*

  Tita. Come, now a roundel, and a fairy song;
Then, for the third part of a minute, hence;
Some, to kill cankers in the musk-rose buds;
Some, war with rear-mice^c for their leathern
    wings,
To make my small elves coats; and some, keep
    back

---

    ^a So all the old copies. Steevens, who hated **variety in** rhythm, as he gloated on a *double-entendre*, gives us—
      "I know a bank whereon the wild thyme blows."
    ^b For the same love of counting syllables upon the fingers, **the** *luscious* woodbine of the old copies is changed into *lush* woodbine: Farmer, who knew as little about the melody of verse as Steevens, would read—
      "O'er-canopied with luscious woodbine."
  Mr. Collier's Corrector of the folio **of 1632, would read,**
      "Quite over-canopied with *lush* woodbine."
and
      "Lull'd in these *bowers* with dances and delight."
  ^c *Rear-mice*—bats.

The clamorous owl, that nightly hoots and
    wonders
At our quaint spirits: Sing me now asleep;
Then to your offices, and let me rest.

SONG.

I.

1 *Fai.* You spotted snakes,* with double tongue,
      Thorny hedge-hogs, be not seen;
    Newts, and blind-worms, do no wrong;
      Come not near our fairy queen:

CHORUS.

Philomel, with melody
  Sing in our sweet lullaby;
Lulla, lulla, lullaby; lulla, lulla, lullaby;
  Never harm, nor spell nor charm,
  Come our lovely lady nigh;
So, good night, with lullaby.

II.

2 *Fai.* Weaving spiders, come not here:
    Hence, you long-legg'd spinners, hence:
    Beetles black, approach not near;
    Worm, nor snail, do no offence.

CHORUS.

Philomel, with melody, &c.

2 *Fai.* Hence, away; now all is well:
One, aloof, stand sentinel.
         [*Exeunt* Fairies. TITANIA *sleeps.*

Enter OBERON.

  Obe. What thou seest, when thou dost wake,
      [*Squeezes the flower on* TITANIA'S *eyelids.*
Do it for thy true-love take;
Love and languish for his sake;
Be it ounce, or cat, or bear,
Pard, or boar with bristled hair,
In thy eye that shall appear
When thou wak'st, it is thy dear;
Wake, when some vile thing is near.   [*Exit.*

Enter LYSANDER *and* HERMIA.

  Lys. Fair love, you faint with wandering in
      the wood;
And, to speak troth, I have forgot our way;
We'll rest us, Hermia, if you think it good,
And tarry for the comfort of the day.
  Her. Be it so, Lysander, find you out a bed,
For I upon this bank will rest my head.
  Lys. One turf shall serve as pillow for us both;
One heart, one bed, two bosoms and one troth.

Her. Nay, good Lysander; for my sake, my dear,
Lie further off yet, do not lie so near.
  Lys. O, take the sense, sweet, of my innocence;
Love takes the meaning, in love's conference.
I mean, that my heart unto yours is knit;
So that but one heart can you make of it:
Two bosoms interchained[a] with an oath;
So then, two bosoms, and a single troth.
Then, by your side no bed-room me deny;
For, lying so, Hermia, I do not lie.
  Her. Lysander riddles very prettily:—
Now much beshrew my manners and my pride,
If Hermia meant to say, Lysander lied.
But, gentle friend, for love and courtesy
Lie further off; in human modesty
Such separation, as, may well be said,
Becomes a virtuous bachelor and a maid:
So far be distant; and good night, sweet friend:
Thy love ne'er alter, till thy sweet life end!
  Lys. Amen, Amen, to that fair prayer say I;
And then end life, when I end loyalty!
Here is my bed: Sleep give thee all his rest!
  Her. With half that wish the wisher's eyes be press'd!   [*They sleep.*

Enter PUCK.

  Puck. Through the forest have I gone,
But Athenian find[b] I none,
On whose eyes I might approve
This flower's force in stirring love.
Night and silence! who is here?
Weeds of Athens he doth wear:
This is he my master said
Despised the Athenian maid;
And here the maiden, sleeping sound,
On the dank and dirty ground.
Pretty soul! she durst not lie
Near this lack-love, this kill-courtesy.[c]
Churl, upon thy eyes I throw
All the power this charm doth owe:
When thou wak'st, let love forbid
Sleep his seat on thy eye-lid.
So awake, when I am gone;
For I must now to Oberon.   [*Exit.*

Enter DEMETRIUS *and* HELENA, *running.*

  Hel. Stay, though thou kill me, sweet Demetrius.
  Dem. I charge thee, hence, and do not haunt me thus.
  Hel. O, wilt thou darkling leave me? do not so.
  Dem. Stay, on thy peril; I alone will go.
                                 [*Exit* DEMETRIUS.
  Hel. O, I am out of breath in this fond chase!
The more my prayer, the lesser is my grace.
Happy is Hermia, wheresoe'er she lies;
For she hath blessed and attractive eyes
How came her eyes so bright? Not with salt tears:
If so, my eyes are oftener wash'd than hers.
No, no, I am as ugly as a bear;
For beasts that meet me run away for fear.
Therefore, no marvel, though Demetrius
Do, as a monster, fly my presence thus.
What wicked and dissembling glass of mine
Made me compare with Hermia's sphery eyne?
But who is here?—Lysander! on the ground!
Dead? or asleep? I see no blood, no wound!
Lysander, if you live, good sir, awake.
  Lys. And run through fire I will, for thy sweet sake.   [*Waking*
Transparent Helena! Nature shows her art,[*]
That through thy bosom makes me see thy heart.
Where is Demetrius? O, how fit a word
Is that vile name to perish on my sword?
  Hel. Do not say so, Lysander; say not so:
What though he love your Hermia? Lord, what though?
Yet Hermia still loves you: then be content.
  Lys. Content with Hermia? No: I do repent
The tedious minutes I with her have spent.
Not Hermia, but Helena now I love:
Who will not change a raven for a dove?
The will of man is by his reason sway'd:
And reason says you are the worthier maid.
Things growing are not ripe until their season
So I, being young, till now ripe not to reason
And touching now the point of human skill
Reason becomes the marshal to my will,
And leads me to your eyes; where I o'erlook
Love's stories, written in love's richest book.
  Hel. Wherefore was I to this keen mockery born?
When, at your hands, did I deserve this scorn?

---

[a] *Interchained*—is the reading of the quartos. The folio has *interchanged.*
[b] *Find*—is the reading of the folio, and of one of the quartos. The other quarto has *found.*
[c] This is the reading of the old copies. It is evidently intended for a long line amidst those of seven or eight syllables.

[*] *Nature shows her art.* The quartos read, "Nature shows art;" the folio, "Nature here shows art;" this is clearly a typographical error; and we agree, with Malone, that "Nature shows her art" is more probably a genuine reading than "Nature here shows art," which is the received one.

Is 't not enough, is 't not enough, young man,
That I did never, no, nor never can,
Deserve a sweet look from Demetrius' eye,
But you must flout my insufficiency?
Good troth, you do me wrong, good sooth, you do,
In such disdainful manner me to woo.
But fare you well: perforce I must confess,
I thought you lord of more true gentleness.
O, that a lady of one man refus'd
Should of another therefore be abus'd! [Exit.
 Lys. She sees not Hermia:—Hermia, sleep thou there;
And never may'st thou come Lysander near!
For, as a surfeit of the sweetest things
The deepest loathing to the stomach brings;
Or, as the heresies that men do leave
Are hated most of those they did deceive;
So thou, my surfeit, and my heresy,
Of all be hated; but the most of me!
And all my powers address your love and might
To honour Helen, and to be her knight. [Exit.
 Her. [starting.] Help me, Lysander, help me!
To pluck this crawling serpent from my breast!
Ah me, for pity!—what a dream was here!
Lysander, look how I do quake with fear!
Methought a serpent ate my heart away,
And you sat smiling at his cruel prey:
Lysander! what, remov'd? Lysander! lord!
What, out of hearing? gone? no sound, no word?
Alack, where are you? speak, an if you hear;
Speak, of all loves;* I swoon almost with fear.
No? then I well perceive you are not nigh:
Either death, or you, I 'll find immediately.
[Exit.

* *Of all loves.* We have this phrase in the Merry Wives of Windsor, and in Othello.

[' What thou seest, when thou dost wake,
Do it for thy true love take.']

ILLUSTRATIONS OF ACT II.

¹ Scene I.—" *Over hill, over dale,
Thorough bush, thorough briar,*" &c.

Theobald printed this passage as it appears in the folio and in one of the quartos—

"Through bush, through briar."

Coleridge is rather hard upon him:—" What a noble pair of ears this worthy Theobald must have had!" He took the passage as he found it. It is remarkable that the reading was corrupted in the folio; for Drayton, in his imitation in the 'Nymphidia,' which was published a few years before the folio, exhibits the value of the word " *thorough :*"—

"Thorough brake, thorough briar,
Thorough muck, thorough mire,
Thorough water, thorough fire."

On the other hand, Steevens had not the justification of any text when he gave us—

" Swifter than the moones sphere."

Mr. Guest, in his 'History of English Rhythm,' (a work of great research, but which belongs to a disciple of the school of Pope, rather than of one nurtured by our elder poet,) observes upon the passage as we print it,—

" Swifter than the moon's sphere."—

"The flow of Shakspere's line is quite in keeping with the peculiar rhythm which he has devoted to his fairies." This rhythm, Mr. Guest, in another place, describes as consisting of "abrupt verses of two, three, or four accents."

² Scene I. ——" *that shrewd and knavish sprite,
Call'd Robin Goodfellow.*"

There can be no doubt that the attributes of Puck, or Robin Goodfellow, as described by Shakspere, were collected from the popular superstitions of his own day. In Harsnet's 'Declaration of Egregious Popish Impostures,' (1603,) he is mixed up as a delinquent with the friars :—" And if that the bowle of curds and creame were not duly set ont for Robin Goodfellow, the frier, and Sisse the dairy-maid, why then either the pottage was burnt to next day in the pot, or the cheeses would not curdle, or the butter would not come, or the ale in the fat [vat] never would have good head." Again, in Scot's 'Discoverie of Witchcraft,' (1584,) we have, " Your grandames' maids were wont to set a bowl of milk for him, for his pains in grinding malt and mustard, and sweeping the house at midnight—this white bread, and bread and milk, was his standing fee." But Robin Goodfellow, does not find a place in English poetry before the time of Shakspere. He is Puck's poetical creator. The poets who have followed in his train have endeavoured to vary the character of the "shrewd and meddling elf;" but he is nevertheless essentially the same. Drayton thus describes him in the 'Nymphidia :'—

"This Puck seems but a dreaming dolt,
Still walking like a ragged colt,
And oft out of a bush doth bolt,
  Of purpose to deceive us;
And leading us, makes us to stray,
Long winter nights, out of the way,
And when we stick in mire and clay,
  He doth with laughter leave us."

In the song of Robin Goodfellow printed in 'Percy's Reliques,' (which has been attributed to Ben Jonson,) we have the same copy of the original features :—

"Yet now and then, the maids to please,
At midnight I card up their wool;
And while they sleep, and take their ease,
With wheel to threads their flax I pull.
  I grind at mill
    Their malt up still;
  I dress their hemp, I spin their tow.
    If any wake,
    And would me take,
  I wend me, laughing, ho, ho, ho!"

The "lubbar-fiend" of Milton is the "lob of spirits" of Shakspere. The hind, "by friar's lanthorn led,"

"Tells how the drudging Goblin sweat,
To earn his cream-bowl duly set,
When in one night, ere glimpse of morn,
His shadowy flail hath thresh'd the corn,
That ten day-lab'rers could not end;
Then lies him down the lubbar-fiend,
And, stretch'd out all the chimney's length,
Basks at the fire his hairy strength,
And crop-full out of door he flings,
Ere the first cock his matin rings."—(*L'Allegro.*)

³ Scene II.—" *Ill met by moonlight, proud
Titania,*" &c.

The name of "Oberon, King of Fairies," is found in Greene's 'James the IVth.' Greene died in

ILLUSTRATIONS OF ACT II.

1592. But the name was long familiar in Lord Berners' translation of the French romance of 'Sir Hugh of Bordeaux.' It is probable that Shakspere was indebted for the name to this source. Tyrwhitt has given his opinion that the Pluto and Proserpina of Chaucer's 'Marchantes Tale' were the true progenitors of Oberon and Titania. Chaucer calls Pluto the "King of Faerie," and Proserpina is "Queen of Faerie;" and they take a solicitude in the affairs of mortals. But beyond this they have little in common with Oberon and Titania. In the 'Wife of Bathes Tale,' however, Shakspere found the popular superstition presented in that spirit of gladsome revelry which it was reserved for him to work out in this matchless drama:—

"In olde dayes of the King Artour,
Of which that Bretons speken gret honour,
All was this land fulfilled of faerie,
The elfe-queene with her joly compagnie,
Danced ful oft in many a grene mede."

⁴ SCENE II.—"*Playing on pipes of corn.*"

"Pipes made of grene corne" were amongst the rustic music described by Chaucer. Sidney's 'Arcadia,' at the time when Shakspere wrote his Midsummer-Night's Dream, had made pastoral images familiar to all. It is pleasant to imagine that our poet had the following beautiful passage in his thoughts:—"There were hills which garnished their proud heights with stately trees; humble valleys, whose base estate seemed comforted with the refreshing of silver rivers; meadows, enamelled with all sorts of eye-pleasing flowers; thickets, which being lined with most pleasant shade were witnessed so too by the cheerful disposition of many well-tuned birds: each pasture stored with sheep, feeding with sober security, while the pretty lambs with bleating oratory craved the dam's comfort: here a shepherd's boy piping, as though he should never be old; there a young shepherdess knitting, and withal singing, and it seemed that her voice comforted her hands to work, and her hands kept time to her voice-music."

⁵ SCENE II.—"*Therefore, the winds, piping to us in vain,*" &c.

In Churchyard's 'Charitie,' a poem published in 1595, the "distemperature" of that year is thus described:—

"A colder time in world was never seen:
The skies do lower, the sun and moon wax dim,
Summer scarce known but that the leaves are green.
The winter's waste drives water o'er the brim;
Upon the land great floats of wood may swim.
Nature thinks scorn to do her duty right,
Because we have displeased the Lord of Light."

This "progeny of evils" has been recorded by the theologians as well as the poets. In Strype's Annals, we have an extract from a lecture preached by Dr. J. King, at York, in which are enumerated the signs of divine wrath with which England was visited in 1593 and 1594. The lecturer says:—"Remember that the spring" (that year when the plague broke out) "was very unkind, by means of the abundance of rains that fell. Our July hath been like to a February; our June even as an April; so that the air must needs be infected.".... Then, having spoken of three successive years of scarcity, he adds,—"And see, whether the Lord doth not threaten us much more, by sending such unseasonable weather, and storms of rain among us; which if we will observe, and compare it with that which is past, we may say that the course of nature is very much inverted. Our years are turned upside down. Our summers are no summers—our harvests are no harvests: our seed-times are no seed-times. For a great space of time, scant any day hath been seen that it hath not rained upon us."

⁶ SCENE II.—"*The nine men's morris is filled up with mud.*"

Upon the green turf of their spacious commons the shepherds and ploughmen of England were wont to cut a rude series of squares, and other right lines, upon which they arranged eighteen stones, divided between two players, who moved them alternately, as at chess or draughts, till the game was finished by one of the players having all his pieces taken or impounded. This was the *nine men's morris*. It is affirmed that the game was brought hither by the Norman conquerors, under the name of *merelles;* and that this name, which signifies *counters*, was subsequently corrupted into *morals* and *morris*. In a wet season the lines upon which the *nine* men moved were "filled up with mud;" and "the quaint mazes," which the more active of the youths and maidens in propitious seasons trod "in the wanton green," were obliterated.

⁷ SCENE II.—"*My gentle Puck, come hither,*" &c.

The most remarkable of the shows of Kenilworth, when Elizabeth was the guest of Leicester, were associated with the mythology and the romance of lakes and seas. "Triton, in likeness of a mermaid, came towards the Queen's Majesty." "Arion appeared sitting on a dolphin's back." So George Gascoigne, in his 'Brief Rehearsal,' or rather a true copy of as much as was presented before her Majesty at Kenilworth.' But Laneham describes a song of Arion with an ecstasy which may justify the belief that the "dulcet and harmonious breath" of "the sea-maid's music" might be the echo of melodies heard by the young Shakspere as he stood by the lake of Kenilworth. If Elizabeth be the "fair vestal throned by the west," of which there can be no reasonable doubt, the most appropriate scene of the mermaid's song would be Kenilworth, and "that very time" the summer of 1575.

⁸ SCENE III.—"*You spotted snakes,*" &c.

Fletcher's 'Faithful Shepherdess' has passages which strongly remind us of the Midsummer-Night's Dream.

["I will walk up and down here, and I will sing, that they shall hear I am not afraid."]

ACT III.

SCENE I.—*The Wood. The Queen of Fairies lying asleep.*

Enter QUINCE, SNUG, BOTTOM, FLUTE, SNOUT, *and* STARVELING.

Bot. Are we all met?

Quin. Pat, pat; and here's a marvellous convenient place for our rehearsal: This green plot shall be our stage, this hawthorn brake our tyring-house; and we will do it in action, as we will do it before the duke.

Bot. Peter Quince,—

Quin. What say'st thou, bully Bottom?

Bot. There are things in this comedy of *Pyramus and Thisby* that will never please. First, Pyramus must draw a sword to kill himself; which the ladies cannot abide. How answer you that?

Snout. By'rlakin,[a] a parlous[b] fear.

Star. I believe we must leave the killing out, when all is done.

Bot. Not a whit; I have a device to make all well. Write me a prologue: and let the prologue seem to say, we will do no harm with our swords; and that Pyramus is not killed indeed: and, for the more better assurance, tell them, that I Pyramus am not Pyramus, but Bottom the weaver: This will put them out of fear.

Quin. Well, we will have such a prologue; and it shall be written in eight and six.[c]

Bot. No, make it two more; let it be written in eight and eight.

Snout. Will not the ladies be afeard of the lion?

Star. I fear it, I promise you.

Bot. Masters, you ought to consider with yourselves: to bring in, God shield us! a lion among ladies, is a most dreadful thing:[1] for there is not

---

[a] *By'rlakin.*—Ly our ladykin—our little lady
[b] *Parlous,*—perilous.
[c] *Eight and six*—alternate verses of eight and six syllables.

a more fearful wild-fowl than your lion, living; and we ought to look to it.

Snout. Therefore, another prologue must tell he is not a lion.

Bot. Nay, you must name his name, and half his face must be seen through the lion's neck; and he himself must speak through, saying thus, or to the same defect,—Ladies, or fair ladies, I would wish you, or, I would request you, or I would entreat you, not to fear, not to tremble: my life for yours. If you think I come hither as a lion, it were pity of my life: No, I am no such thing; I am a man as other men are: and there, indeed, let him name his name; and tell them plainly he is Snug the joiner.

Quin. Well, it shall be so. But there is two hard things; that is, to bring the moon-light into a chamber: for you know, Pyramus and Thisby meet by moon-light.

Snug. Doth the moon shine that night we play our play?

Bot. A calendar, a calendar! look in the almanac; find out moon-shine, find out moon-shine.

Quin. Yes, it doth shine that night.

Bot. Why, then may you leave a casement of the great chamber-window, where we play, open; and the moon may shine in at the casement.

Quin. Ay; or else one must come in with a bush of thorns and a lantern, and say, he comes to disfigure, or to present, the person of moon-shine. Then there is another thing: we must have a wall in the great chamber; for Pyramus and Thisby, says the story, did talk through the chink of a wall.

Snug. You can never bring in a wall.—What say you, Bottom?

Bot. Some man or other must present wall: and let him have some plaster, or some lome, or some rough-cast about him, to signify wall; and let him hold his fingers thus, and through that cranny shall Pyramus and Thisby whisper.

Quin. If that may be, then all is well. Come, sit down, every mother's son, and rehearse your parts. Pyramus, you begin: when you have spoken your speech, enter into that brake; and so every one according to his cue.

Enter PUCK *behind.*

Puck. What hempen home-spuns have we swaggering here,
So near the cradle of the fairy queen?
What, a play toward? I'll be an auditor;
An actor too, perhaps, if I see cause.

Quin. Speak, Pyramus:—Thisby, stand forth.

'*Pyr.* Thisby, the flowers of odious savours sweet.'

Quin. Odours, odours.

'*Pyr.* —— odours savours sweet:
So hath thy breath, my dearest Thisby dear.
But, hark, a voice! stay thou but here a while,
And by and by I will to thee appear.' [*Exit.*

Puck. A stranger Pyramus than e'er play'd here! [*Aside.—Exit.*

This. Must I speak now?

Quin. Ay, marry, must you: for you must understand, he goes but to see a noise* that he heard, and is to come again.

'*This.* Most radiant Pyramus, most lily white of hue,
Of colour like the red rose on triumphant brier,
Most brisky juvenal, and eke most lovely Jew,
As true as truest horse that yet would never tire,
I'll meet thee, Pyramus at Ninny's tomb.'

Quin. Ninus' tomb, man. Why you must not speak that yet; that you answer to Pyramus: you speak all your part at once, cues and all.—Pyramus enter; your cue is past; it is, *never tire.*

Re-enter PUCK, *and* BOTTOM *with an ass's head.*

'*This.* O,—As true as truest horse, that yet would never tire.
Pyr. If I were fair, Thisby, I were only thine:'—

Quin. O monstrous! O strange! we are haunted. Pray, masters! fly, masters! help!
[*Exeunt Clowns.*

Puck. I'll follow you, I'll lead you about a round,
Through bog, through bush, through brake, through brier;
Sometime a horse I'll be, sometime a hound,
A hog, a headless bear, sometime a fire;
And neigh, and bark, and grunt, and roar, and burn,
Like horse, hound, hog, bear, fire, at every turn.
[*Exit.*

Bot. Why do they run away? this is a knavery of them, to make me afeard.

Re-enter SNOUT.

Snout. O Bottom, thou art changed! what do I see on thee?

Bot. What do you see? you see an ass-head of your own; Do you?

Re-enter QUINCE.

Quin. Bless thee, Bottom! bless thee! thou art translated. [*Exit.*

Bot. I see their knavery: this is to make an ass of me; to fright me, if they could. But I will not stir from this place, do what they can:

---

* Quince's description of Bottom going "to see a noise," is akin to Sir Toby Belch's notion of "to hear by the nose." (*Twelfth Night*, Act II. Sc. III.)

I will walk up and down here, and I will sing,
that they shall hear I am not afraid.   [*Sings*.
    The woosel-cock, so black of hue,
      With orange-tawny bill,[a]
    The throstle with his note so true,
    The wren with little quill;
  Tita. What angel wakes me from my flowery
    bed?   [*Waking*.
  Bot. The finch, the sparrow, and the lark,
    The plain-song cuckoo gray,
    Whose note full many a man doth mark,
    And dares not answer, nay—
tor, indeed, who would set his wit to so foolish a
bird? who would give a bird the lie, though he
cry *cuckoo* never so?

  Tita. I pray thee, gentle mortal, sing again:
Mine ear is much enamour'd of thy note,
So is mine eye enthralled to thy shape;
And thy fair virtue's force perforce doth move
    me,
On the first view, to say, to swear, I love thee.[a]

  Bot. Methinks, mistress, you should have
little reason for that: And yet, to say the truth,
reason and love keep little company together
now-a-days: The more the pity, that some honest neighbours will not make them friends.
Nay, I can gleek[b] upon occasion.

  Tita. Thou art as wise as thou art beautiful.

  Bot. Not so, neither: but if I had wit enough
to get out of this wood, I have enough to serve
mine own turn.

  Tita. Out of this wood do not desire to go;
Thou shalt remain here, whether thou wilt or no.
I am a spirit, of no common rate;
The summer still doth tend upon my state,
And I do love thee: therefore, go with me;
I'll give thee fairies to attend on thee;
And they shall fetch thee jewels from the deep,
And sing, while thou on pressed flowers dost
    sleep:
And I will purge thy mortal grossness so,
That thou shalt like an airy spirit go.—
Peas-blossom! Cobweb! Moth! and Mustard-
    seed!

        Enter four Fairies.

1 *Fai.* Ready.
2 *Fai.*   And I.
3 *Fai.*   And I.
4 *Fai.*   And I.

[a] This is the reading of the preceding five lines in the quarto printed by Fisher. In that by Roberts, and in the folio, two of the lines, namely, the third and fourth of Titania's speech, are transposed.
[b] *Gleek.* This verb is generally used in the sense of to *scoff*: but we apprehend Bottom only means to say that he can *joke*.

  All. Where shall we go?[a]
  Tita. Be kind and courteous to this gen-
    tleman;
Hop in his walks, and gambol in his eyes;
Feed him with apricocks, and dewberries;[b]
With purple grapes, green figs, and mulberries;
The honey bags steal from the humble-bees,
And, for night tapers, crop their waxen thighs,
And light them at the fiery glow-worm's eyes,
To have my love to bed, and to arise;
And pluck the wings from painted butterflies,
To fan the moon-beams from his sleeping eyes:
Nod to him, elves, and do him courtesies.

  1 *Fai.* Hail, mortal!
  2 *Fai.* Hail!
  3 *Fai.* Hail!
  4 *Fai.* Hail!

  Bot. I cry your worship's mercy, heartily.—I
beseech your worship's name.

  Cob. Cobweb.

  Bot. I shall desire you of more acquaintance,
good master Cobweb: If I cut my finger, I shall
make bold with you.—Your name, honest gentleman?

  Peas. Peas-blossom.

  Bot. I pray you, commend me to mistress
Squash, your mother, and to master Peas-cod,
your father. Good master Peas-blossom, I shall
desire you of more acquaintance too.—Your
name, I beseech you, sir?

  Mus. Mustard-seed.

  Bot. Good master Mustard-seed, I know your
patience[c] well: that same cowardly, giant-like
ox-beef hath devoured many a gentleman of
your house: I promise you, your kindred hath
made my eyes water ere now. I desire you
more acquaintance, good master Mustard-seed.

  Tita. Come, wait upon him; lead him to my
    bower.
The moon, methinks, looks with a watery eye;
And when she weeps, weeps every little flower,
Lamenting some enforced chastity,
Tie up my love's tongue, bring him silently.
                        [*Exeunt*.

[a] Steevens omitted the "And I" of the fourth Fairy, and gave her the "Where shall we go?" which the original copies assigned to *all*; and this he calls getting rid of "a useless repetition."
[b] *Dewberries.* This delicate wild-fruit is perfectly well known to all who have lived in the country; but one of the commentators tells us dewberries are gooseberries, and another raspberries.
[c] The *patience* of the family of Mustard in being devoured by the ox-beef is one of those brief touches of wit, so common in Shakspere, which take him far out of the range of ordinary writers. But his critics see common-place; and therefore Hanmer would read *parentage*,—Farmer, *passions*,—and Mason, *passing*. Reed then solemnly pronounces "no change is necessary;" and so half a page of the variorum Shakspere is filled.

SCENE II.—*Another part of the Wood.*

Enter OBERON.

Obe. I wonder, if Titania be awak'd;
Then, what it was that next came in her eye,
Which she must dote on in extremity.

Enter PUCK.

Here comes my messenger.—How now, mad
   spirit?
What night-rule[a] now about this haunted grove?
  Puck. My mistress with a monster is in love.
Near to a close and consecrated bower,
While she was in her dull and sleeping hour,
A crew of patches, rude mechanicals,
That work for bread upon Athenian stalls,
Were met together to rehearse a play,
Intended for great Theseus' nuptial day.
The shallowest thick-skin of that barren sort,
Who Pyramus presented, in their sport
Forsook his scene, and enter'd in a brake:
When I did him at this advantage take,
An ass's nowl[b] I fixed on his head;
Anon, his Thisbe must be answered,
And forth my mimic[c] comes: When they him
   spy,
As wild geese that the creeping fowler eye,
Or russet-pated choughs, many in sort,
Rising and cawing at the gun's report,
Sever themselves, and madly sweep the sky;
So at his sight away his fellows fly:
And, at our stamp, here o'er and o'er one falls;
He murder cries, and help from Athens calls.
Their sense thus weak, lost with their fears thus
   strong,
Made senseless things begin to do them wrong:
For briers and thorns at their apparel snatch;
Some, sleeves; some, hats; from yielders all
   things catch.
I led them on in this distracted fear,
And left sweet Pyramus translated there:
When in that moment (so it came to pass,)
Titania wak'd, and straightway lov'd an ass.
  Obe. This falls out better than I could devise.
But hast thou yet latch'd[d] the Athenian's eyes
With the love-juice, as I did bid thee do?
  Puck. I took him sleeping,—that is finish'd
   too,—
And the Athenian woman by his side;
That when he wak'd of force she must be ey'd.

[a] *Night rule*—night-revel. The old spelling of *revel* became *rule*; and by this corruption we obtained, says Douce, "the lord of mis-rule."
[b] *Nowl*—noll—head.
[c] *Mimic*—actor. *Mimmick* is the reading of the folio; *minnock*, and *minnick*, are found in the quartos.
[d] *Latch'd*—fastened, according to Hanmer.

Enter DEMETRIUS *and* HERMIA.

  Obe. Stand close; this is the same Athenian.
  Puck. This is the woman, but not this the
   man.
  Dem. O, why rebuke you him that loves you
   so?
Lay breath so bitter on your bitter foe.
  Her. Now I but chide, but I should use thee
   worse;
For thou, I fear, hast given me cause to curse.
If thou hast slain Lysander in his sleep,
Being o'er shoes in blood, plunge in knee-deep,[e]
And kill me too.
The sun was not so true unto the day,
As he to me: Would he have stol'n away
From sleeping Hermia? I'll believe as soon,
This whole earth may be bor'd; and that the
   moon
May through the centre creep, and so displease
Her brother's noontide with the Antipodes.
It cannot be, but thou hast murder'd him;
So should a murderer look; so dead, so grim.
  Dem. So should the murder'd look; and so
   should I,
Pierc'd through the heart with your stern cruelty:
Yet you, the murderer, look as bright, as clear,
As yonder Venus in her glimmering sphere.
  Her. What's this to my Lysander? where is
   he?
Ah, good Demetrius, wilt thou give him me?
  Dem. I had rather give his carcase to my
   hounds.
  Her. Out, dog! out, cur! thou driv'st me
   past the bounds
Of maiden's patience. Hast thou slain him then?
Henceforth be never number'd among men!
Oh! once tell true, tell true, even for my sake;
Durst thou have look'd upon him, being awake,
And hast thou kill'd him sleeping? O brave
   touch!
Could not a worm, an adder, do so much?
An adder did it; for with doubler tongue
Than thine, thou serpent, never adder stung.
  Dem. You spend your passion on a mispris'd
   mood:
I am not guilty of Lysander's blood;
Nor is he dead, for aught that I can tell.
  Her. I pray thee, tell me then that he is well.
  Dem. An if I could, what should I get
   therefore?
  Her. A privilege never to see me more.—
And from thy hated presence part I so;
See me no more, whether he be dead or no. [*Exit.*

[e] *Knee-deep*, suggested by W. S. Walker in the place of *the deep*.

Dem. There is no following her in this fierce vein:
Here, therefore, for a while I will remain.
So sorrow's heaviness doth heavier grow
For debt that bankrout sleep doth sorrow owe;
Which now, in some slight measure, it will pay,
If for his tender here I make some stay.
    [*Lies down.*

Obe. What hast thou done? thou hast mistaken quite,
And laid the love-juice on some true-love's sight:
Of thy misprision must perforce ensue
Some true-love turn'd, and not a false turn'd true.

Puck. Then fate o'er-rules; that one man holding troth,
A million fail, confounding oath on oath.

Obe. About the wood go swifter than the wind,
And Helena of Athens look thou find:
All fancy-sick she is, and pale of cheer*
With sighs of love, that cost the fresh blood dear.
By some illusion see thou bring her here;
I'll charm his eyes against she doth appear.

Puck. I go, I go; look, how I go;
Swifter than arrow from the Tartar's bow.
    [*Exit.*

Obe. Flower of this purple die,
Hit with Cupid's archery,
Sink in apple of his eye!
When his love he doth espy
Let her shine as gloriously
As the Venus of the sky.
When thou wak'st, if she be by
Beg of her for remedy.

    Re-enter PUCK.

Puck. Captain of our fairy band,
Helena is here at hand,
And the youth, mistook by me,
Pleading for a lover's fee;
Shall we their fond pageant see?
Lord, what fools these mortals be!

Obe. Stand aside: the noise they make,
Will cause Demetrius to awake.

Puck. Then will two at once woo one—
That must needs be sport alone;
And those things do best please me,
That befal preposterously.

    Enter LYSANDER *and* HELENA.

Lys. Why should you think that I should woo in scorn?
Scorn and derision never come in tears.
Look, when I vow, I weep; and vows so born,
In their nativity all truth appears.

* *Cheer—face.* From the old French *chère.*

How can these things in me seem scorn to you,
Bearing the badge of faith, to prove them true?

Hel. You do advance your cunning more and more.
When truth kills truth, O devilish-holy fray!
These vows are Hermia's; Will you give her o'er?
Weigh oath with oath, and you will nothing weigh:
Your vows to her and me, put in two scales,
Will even weigh; and both as light as tales.

Lys. I had no judgment, when to her I swore.

Hel. Nor none, in my mind, now you give her o'er.

Lys. Demetrius loves her, and he loves not you.

Dem. [*awaking.*] O Helen, goddess, nymph, perfect, divine!
To what, my love, shall I compare thine eyne?
Crystal is muddy. O, how ripe in show
Thy lips, those kissing cherries, tempting grow!
That pure congealed white, high Taurus' snow,
Fann'd with the eastern wind, turns to a crow,
When thou hold'st up thy hand: O let me kiss
This princess of pure white, this seal of bliss!

Hel. O spite! O hell! I see you all are bent
To set against me, for your merriment.
If you were civil and knew courtesy,
You would not do me thus much injury.
Can you not hate me, as I know you do,
But you must join, in souls, to mock me too?
If you were men, as men you are in show,
You would not use a gentle lady so.
To vow, and swear, and superpraise my parts,
When, I am sure, you hate me with your hearts.
You both are rivals, and love Hermia;
And now both rivals, to mock Helena:
A trim exploit, a manly enterprize,
To conjure tears up in a poor maid's eyes,
With your derision! none of noble sort
Would so offend a virgin; and extort
A poor soul's patience, all to make you sport.

Lys. You are unkind, Demetrius; be not so;
For you love Hermia: this, you know, I know:
And here, with all good will, with all my heart,
In Hermia's love I yield you up my part;
And yours of Helena to me bequeath,
Whom I do love, and will do to my death.

Hel. Never did mockers waste more idle breath.

Dem. Lysander, keep thy Hermia; I will none:
If e'er I lov'd her, all that love is gone.

My heart with her but as guest-wise sojourn'd;
And now to Helen it is home return'd,
There to remain.
Lys.   Helen, it is not so.
Dem. Disparage not the faith thou dost not know,
Lest, to thy peril, thou aby it dear.—
Look, where thy love comes; yonder is thy dear.

Enter HERMIA.

Her. Dark night, that from the eye his function takes,
The ear more quick of apprehension makes;
Wherein it doth impair the seeing sense,
It pays the hearing double recompense:
Thou art not by mine eye, Lysander, found;
Mine ear, I thank it, brought me to thy sound.
But why unkindly didst thou leave me so?
  Lys. Why should he stay whom love doth press to go?
  Her. What love could press Lysander from my side?
  Lys. Lysander's love, that would not let him hide;
Fair Helena; who more engilds the night
Than all you fiery oes[a] and eyes of light.
Why seek'st thou me? could not this make thee know,
The hate I bare thee made me leave thee so?
  Her. You speak not as you think; it cannot be.
  Hel. Lo, she is one of this confederacy!
Now I perceive they have conjoin'd, all three,
To fashion this false sport in spite of me.
Injurious Hermia! most ungrateful maid!
Have you conspir'd, have you with these contriv'd
To bait me with this foul derision?
Is all the counsel that we two have shar'd,
The sisters' vows, the hours that we have spent,
When we have chid the hasty-footed time
For parting us,—O, and is all forgot?
All school-days' friendship, childhood innocence?
We, Hermia, like two artificial gods,
Have with our needles[b] created both one flower,
Both on one sampler, sitting on one cushion,
Both warbling of one song, both in one key;
As if our hands, our sides, voices, and minds,
Had been incorporate. So we grew together,
Like to a double cherry, seeming parted;
But yet a union in partition,
Two lovely berries moulded on one stem:

So, with two seeming bodies, but one heart;
Two of the first, like coats in heraldry,
Due but to one, and crowned with one crest.
And will you rent our ancient love asunder,
To join with men in scorning your poor friend?
It is not friendly, 't is not maidenly:
Our sex, as well as I, may chide you for it;
Though I alone do feel the injury.
  Her. I am amazed at your passionate words:
I scorn you not; it seems that you scorn me.
  Hel. Have you not set Lysander, as in scorn,
To follow me, and praise my eyes and face?
And made your other love, Demetrius,
(Who even but now did spurn me with his foot,)
To call me goddess, nymph, divine, and rare,
Precious, celestial? Wherefore speaks he this
To her he hates? and wherefore doth Lysander
Deny your love, so rich within his soul,
And tender me, forsooth, affection;
But by your setting on, by your consent?
What though I be not so in grace as you,
So hung upon with love, so fortunate;
But miserable most, to love unlov'd!
This you should pity, rather than despise.
  Her. I understand not what you mean by this?
  Hel. Ay, do, persever, counterfeit sad looks,
Make mouths upon me when I turn my back;
Wink each at other; hold the sweet jest up:
This sport, well carried, shall be chronicled.
If you have any pity, grace, or manners,
You would not make me such an argument.
But, fare ye well: 't is partly mine own fault;
Which death, or absence, soon shall remedy.
  Lys. Stay, gentle Helena; hear my excuse;
My love, my life, my soul, fair Helena!
  Hel. O excellent!
  Her.   Sweet, do not scorn her so.
  Dem. If she cannot entreat, I can compel.
  Lys. Thou canst compel no more than she entreat;
Thy threats have no more strength, than her weak prayers.[a]—
Helen, I love thee; by my life I do;
I swear by that which I will lose for thee,
To prove him false that says I love thee not.
  Dem. I say, I love thee more than he can do.
  Lys. If thou say so, withdraw, and prove it too.
  Dem. Quick, come,—
  Her.   Lysander, whereto tends all this?
  Lys. Away, you Ethiope!
  Dem.   No, no, sir:—

---
[a] *Oes*—circles.
[b] *Needds* in the old copies.

[a] *Prayers*—in the old copies, *praise*.

Seem to break loose; take on as you would follow;
But yet come not: You are a tame man, go!
Lys. Hang off, thou cat, thou burr: vile thing, let loose;
Or I will shake thee from me, like a serpent.
Her. Why are you grown so rude? what change is this,
Sweet love?
Lys. Thy love? out, tawny Tartar, out!
Out, loathed medicine! hated poison, hence!
Her. Do you not jest?
Hel. Yes, 'sooth; and so do you.
Lys. Demetrius, I will keep my word with thee.
Dem. I would I had your bond; for I perceive
A weak bond holds you; I'll not trust your word.
Lys. What, should I hurt her, strike her, kill her dead?
Although I hate her, I'll not harm her so.
Her. What, can you do me greater harm than hate?
Hate me! wherefore? O me! what news, my love?
Am not I Hermia? Are not you, Lysander?
I am as fair now as I was erewhile.
Since night you lov'd me; yet, since night you left me:
Why then you left me,—O, the gods forbid!—
In earnest, shall I say?
Lys. Ay, by my life;
And never did desire to see thee more.
Therefore, be out of hope, of question, of doubt,
Be certain, nothing truer, 't is no jest,
That I do hate thee, and love Helena.
Her. O me! you juggler! you canker-blossom!
You thief of love! what, have you come by night,
And stol'n my love's heart from him?
Hel. Fine, i' faith!
Have you no modesty, no maiden shame,
No touch of bashfulness? What, will you tear
Impatient answers from my gentle tongue?
Fie, fie! you counterfeit, you puppet, you!
Her. Puppet! why so? Ay, that way goes the game.
Now I perceive that she hath made compare
Between our statures, she hath urg'd her height;
And with her personage, her tall personage,
Her height, forsooth, she hath prevail'd with him.
And are you grown so high in his esteem,
Because I am so dwarfish, and so low?

How low am I, thou painted maypole? speak;
How low am I? I am not yet so low,
But that my nails can reach unto thine eyes.
Hel. I pray you, though you mock me, gentlemen,
Let her not hurt me: I was never curst;[a]
I have no gift at all in shrewishness;
I am a right maid for my cowardice;
Let her not strike me: You, perhaps, may think,
Because she's something lower than myself,
That I can match her.
Her. Lower! hark, again.
Hel. Good Hermia, do not be so bitter with me.
I evermore did love you, Hermia,
Did ever keep your counsels, never wrong'd you;
Save that, in love unto Demetrius,
I told him of your stealth unto this wood:
He follow'd you; for love, I follow'd him.
But he hath chid me hence; and threaten'd me
To strike me, spurn me, nay, to kill me too:
And now, so you will let me quiet go,
To Athens will I bear my folly back,
And follow you no further: Let me go:
You see how simple and how fond I am.
Her. Why, get you gone: Who is't that hinders you?
Hel. A foolish heart that I leave here behind.
Her. What, with Lysander?
Hel. With Demetrius.
Lys. Be not afraid: she shall not harm thee, Helena.
Dem. No, sir; she shall not, though you take her part.
Hel. O, when she's angry, she is keen and shrewd;
She was a vixen, when she went to school;
And, though she be but little, she is fierce.
Her. Little again? nothing but low and little?
Why will you suffer her to flout me thus?
Let me come to her.
Lys. Get you gone, you dwarf;
You minimus, of hind'ring knot-grass[b] made;
You bend, you acorn.
Dem. You are too officious
In her behalf that scorns your services.
Let her alone; speak not of Helena;
Take not her part: for if thou dost intend[c]
Never so little show of love to her,
Thou shalt aby[d] it

---
[a] *Curst*—shrewish.
[b] *Knot-grass*—"a low reptant herb," according to **Rlenars** Tomlinson, a botanical apothecary of the seventeenth century.
[c] *Intend.* Steevens explains this word by *pretend.* That is scarcely the meaning, which is rather to *direct.*
[d] *Aby it*—suffer for it. Thus, in Beaumont and Fletcher:—
"Fool-hardy knight, full *a* on thou shalt *aby*
This fond reproach."

Lys.   Now she holds me not;
Now follow, if thou dar'st, to try whose right,
Or thine or mine, is most in Helena.
   Dem. Follow? nay, I'll go with thee, cheek
         by jole.   [*Exeunt* LYS. *and* DEM.
   Her. You, mistress, all this coil is long of you:
Nay, go not back.
   Hel.   I will not trust you, I ;
Nor longer stay in your curst company.
Your hands than mine are quicker for a fray ;
My legs are longer though, to run away. [*Exit.*
   Her. I am amaz'd, and know not what to say.ᵃ
                     [*Exit, pursuing* HELENA.
   Obe. This is thy negligence: still thou mis-
         tak'st,
Or else committ'st thy knaveries willingly.ᵇ
   Puck. Believe me king of shadows, I mistook.
Did not you tell me, I should know the man
By the Athenian garments he had on ?
Aud so far blameless proves my enterprize,
That I have 'nointed an Athenian's eyes :
And so far am I glad it so did sort,
As this their jangling I esteem a sport.
   Obe. Thou seest, these lovers seek a place to
         fight :
Hie therefore, Robin, overcast the night ;
The starry welkin cover thou anon
With drooping fog, as black as Acheron ;
And lead these testy rivals so astray,
As one come not within another's way.
Like to Lysander sometime frame thy tongue,
Then stir Demetrius up with bitter wrong ;
And sometime rail thou like Demetrius ;
And from each other look thou lead them thus,
Till o'er their brows death-counterfeiting sleep
With leaden legs and batty wings doth creep
Then crush this herb into Lysander's eye,
Whose liquor hath this virtuous property,
To take from thence all error, with his might,
And make his eye-balls roll with wonted sight.
When they next wake, all this derision
Shall seem a dream, and fruitless vision ;⁹
And back to Athens shall the lovers wend,
With league, whose date till death shall never end.
Whiles I in this affair do thee employ,
I'll to my queen, and beg her Indian boy ;
And then I will her charmed eye release
From monster's view, and all things shall be
         peace.
   Puck. My fairy lord, this must be done with
         haste ;
For night's swift dragons cut the clouds full fast,¹⁰
And yonder shines Aurora's harbinger ;

ᵃ This line is not found in the folio of 1623, but is in the
previous quartos.
ᵇ *Willingly*, in the folio; *wilfully*, in the quartos.

At whose approach, ghosts, wandering here and
         there,
Troop home to church-yards : damned spirits all,
That in cross-ways and floods have burial,
Already to their wormy beds are gone ;
For fear lest day should look their shames upon,
They wilfully themselves exile from light,
And must for aye consort with black-brow'd night
   Obe. But we are spirits of another sort :
I with the morning's love have oft made sport ;¹¹
And, like a forester, the groves may tread,
Even till the eastern gate, all fiery-red,
Opening on Neptune with fair blessed beams,
Turns into yellow gold his salt-green streams.¹²
But, notwithstanding, haste ; make no delay :
We may effect this business yet ere day.
                              [*Exit* OBERON.
   Puck. Up and down, up and down ;
      I will lead them up and down :
      I am fear'd in field and town ;
      Goblin, lead them up and down.
Here comes one.

            Enter LYSANDER.

   Lys. Where art thou, proud Demetrius?
         speak thou now.
   Puck. Here, villain ; drawn and ready. Where
         art thou ?
   Lys. I will be with thee straight.
   Puck.   Follow me then
To plainer ground.
            [*Exit* LYS. *as following the voice.*

            Enter DEMETRIUS.

   Dem.   Lysander ! speak again.
Thou runaway, thou coward, art thou fled ?
Speak. In some bush ? Where dost thou hide
         thy head ?
   Puck. Thou coward, art thou bragging to the
         stars,
Telling the bushes that thou look'st for wars,
And wilt not come ? Come, recreant ; come,
         thou child ;
I'll whip thee with a rod : He is defil'd
That draws a sword on thee.
   Dem.   Yea ; art thou there ?
   Puck. Follow my voice ; we'll try no manhood
         here.   [*Exeunt.*

            Re-enter LYSANDER.

   Lys. He goes before me, and still dares me on ;
When I come where he calls then he is gone
The villain is much lighter heel'd than I :
I follow'd fast, but faster he did fly ;
That fallen am I in dark uneven way,
And here will rest me. Come, thou gentle day !
                              [*Lies down.*

For if but once thou show me thy grey light,
I'll find Demetrius, and revenge this spite.
                              [*Sleeps.*

        Re-enter PUCK *and* DEMETRIUS.

Puck. Ho, ho! ho, ho![13] Coward, why com'st
  thou not?
Dem. Abide me, if thou dar'st; for well I wot,
Thou runn'st before me, shifting every place;
And dar'st not stand, nor look me in the face.
Where art thou now?
  Puck.   Come hither; I am here.
  Dem. Nay, then, thou mock'st me. Thou
  shalt buy[a] this dear,
If ever I thy face by daylight see:
Now, go thy way. Faintness constraineth me
To measure out my length on this cold bed.
By day's approach look to be visited.
                    [*Lies down and sleeps.*

           Enter HELENA.

Hel. O weary night, O long and tedious night,
  Abate thy hours: shine, comforts, from the
  east,
That I may back to Athens, by daylight,
  From these that my poor company detest:—
And, sleep, that sometimes shuts up sorrow's eye,
Steal me awhile from mine own company.
                             [*Sleeps.*

  Puck. Yet but three? Come one more;
Two of both kinds makes up four.

[a] *Buy*—so the old copies; *buy it dear* is still a familiar expression.

Here she comes, curst and sad:
Cupid is a knavish lad,
Thus to make poor females mad.

           Enter HERMIA.

Her. Never so weary, never so in woe,
  Bedabbled with the dew, and torn with
  briers;
I can no further crawl, no further go;
  My legs can keep no pace with my desires.
Here will I rest me, till the break of day.
Heavens shield Lysander, if they mean a fray!
                                [*Lies down.*

  Puck. On the ground
     Sleep sound:
     I'll apply
     To your eye,
  Gentle lover, remedy.
        [*Squeezing the juice on* LYS.'*s eye.*
     When thou wak'st,
     Thou tak'st[14]
     True delight
     In the sight
  Of thy former lady's eye:
  And the country proverb known,
  That every man should take his own,
  In your waking shall be shown:
     Jack shall have Jill;
     Nought shall go ill;
The man shall have his mare again, and all shall
  be well.
             [*Exit* PUCK.—DEM. HEL. &c. *sleep.*

['Up and down, up and down;
I will lead them up and down.']

[¹ The ouzel-cock, so black of hue.]

ILLUSTRATIONS OF ACT III.

¹ SCENE I.—"*A lion among ladies is a most dreadful thing.*"

THERE was an account published in 1594 of the ceremonies observed at the baptism of Henry, the eldest son of the King of Scotland. A triumphal chariot, according to this account, was drawn in by a "black-moor." The writer adds—"This chariot should have been drawn in by a lion, but because his presence might have brought *some fear* to the nearest, or that the sight of the lighted torches might have commoved his tameness, it was thought meet that the moor should supply that room." It is not improbable that Shakspere meant to ridicule this incident, in—"there is not a more fearful wild-fowl than your lion, living."

² SCENE I.—"*Let him name his name; and tell them plainly he is Snug the joiner.*"

This passage will suggest to our readers Sir Walter Scott's description of the pageant at Kenilworth, when Lambourne, not knowing his part, tore off his vizard and swore, "Cogs-bones! he was none of Arion or Orion either, but honest Mike Lambourne, that had been drinking her Majesty's health from morning till midnight, and was come to bid her heartily welcome to Kenilworth Castle." But a circumstance of this nature actually happened upon the Queen's visit to Kenilworth, in 1575; and is recorded in the 'Merry Passages and Jests,' compiled by Sir Nicholas Lestrange, which is published by the Camden Society from the Harleian MS.—"There was a spectacle presented to Queen Elizabeth upon the water, and, amongst others, Harry Goldingham was to represent Arion upon the dolphin's back, but finding his voice to be very hoarse and unpleasant when he came to perform it, he tears off his disguise and swears he was none of Arion not he, but e'en honest Harry Goldingham; which blunt discovery pleased the Queen better than if it had gone through in the right way; yet he could order his voice to an instrument exceeding well." It is by no means improbable that Shakspere was familiar with this local anecdote, and has applied it in the case of Snug the joiner. Bottom, and Quince, and the other "hard-handed men," must also have been exceedingly like the citizens of Coventry, who played their Hock play before the Queen, on the memorable occasion of her visit to their neighbourhood.

A MIDSUMMER-NIGHT'S DREAM.

¹ SCENE I.—" *Look in the almanac; find out moonshine.*"

The popular almanac of Shakspere's time was that of Leonard Digges, the worthy precursor of the Moores and Murphys. He had a higher ambition than these his degenerate descendants; for, while they prophecy only by the day and the week, he prognosticated for ever, as his title-page shows: —' A Prognostication *everlastinge* of right good effect, fruictfully augmented by the auctour, contayning plain, briefe, pleasaunte, chosen rules to iudge the Weather by the Sunne, Moone, Starres, Cometes, Rainebow, Thunder, Cloudes, with other extraordinarye tokens, not omitting the Aspects of the Planets, with a briefe iudgement *for euer,* of Plenty, Lucke, Sickenes, Dearth, Warres, &c., opening also many natural causes worthy to be knowen,' (1575).

² SCENE I.—" *The woosel-cock, so black of hue, With orange-tawny bill.*"

Although Bottom has here described the blackbird with zoological precision, there are some commentators hardly enough to deny his scientific pretensions, maintaining that the woosel or ousel is something else. It is sufficient for us to show that this name expressed the blackbird in Shakspere's day. It is used by Drayton as synonymous with the *merle* (about which there can be no doubt) in his description of the "rough woodlands" of the Warwickshire Arden, where both he and his friend Shakspere studied the book of nature:—

" The throstel, with shrill sharps; as purposely he song
T' wake the lustlesse sun, or chiding that so long
He was in coming forth, that should the thickets thrill;
The woosel near at hand, that hath a golden bill;
As nature him had mark'd of purpose, t' let us see
That from all other birds his tunes should different be:
For, with their vocal sounds, they sing to pleasant May;
Upon his dulcet pipe the merle doth only play."
(*Poly-Olbion,* 13th Song.)

³ SCENE I.—" *And light them at the fiery glow-worm's eyes.*"

Shakspere was certainly a much truer lover of nature, and therefore a much better naturalist, than Dr. Johnson, who indeed professed to despise such studies; but the critic has, nevertheless, ventured in this instance to be severe upon the poet:—" I know not how Shakspeare, who commonly derived his knowledge of nature from his own observation, happened to place the glow-worm's light in his eyes, which is only in his tail." Well, then, let us correct the poet, and make Titania describe the glow-worm with a hatred of all metaphor:—

" And light them at the fiery glow-worm's tail."

We fear this will not do. It reminds us of the attempt of a very eminent naturalist to unite science and poetry in verses which he called the 'Pleasures of Ornithology,' of which union the following is a specimen:—

" The morning wakes, as from the lofty elm
The cuckoo sends the monotone. Yet he,
Polygamous, ne'er knows what pleasures wait
On pure monogamy."

We may be wrong, but we would rather have Bottom's

" ——plain-song cuckoo gray."

than these hard words.

⁴ SCENE II.—" *Thy lips, those kissing cherries,*" &c.

The " kissing cherries" of Shakspere gave Herrick a stock in trade for half-a-dozen poems. We would quote the ' Cherry ripe,' had it not passed into that extreme popularity which almost renders a beautiful thing vulgar. The following is little known:—

" I saw a cherry weep, and why?
Why wept it? but for shame;
Because my Julia's lip was by,
And did out-red the same.
But, pretty fondling, let not fall
A tear at all for that;
Which rubies, corals, scarlets, all,
For tincture, wonder at."

Of " high Taurus' snow" we have no illustration to offer, besides an engraving of the mountain.

⁵ SCENE II.—" *O, and is all forgot?*" &c.

Gibbon compares this beautiful passage with some lines of a poem of Gregory Nazianzen on his own life.

⁶ SCENE II.—" *Two of the first, like coats in heraldry,*" &c.

Mr. Monck Mason's explanation of this passage seems the most intelligible:—" Every branch of a family is called a house; and none but the first of the first house can bear the arms of the family without some distinction; two of the first, therefore, means two coats of the first house, which are properly due but to one."

⁷ SCENE II.—" *Shall seem a dream, and fruitless vision.*"

Mr. Guest classes this line in the division of " sectional rhyme"—an ancient form of emphatically marking a portion of a verse. We have it in the Taming of the Shrew:—

" With cuffs and ruffs; and farthingales, and things."

and, in Love's Labour's Lost:—

" Or groan for Joan, or spend a minute's time."

⁸ SCENE II.—" *For night's swift dragons cut the clouds full fast.*"

The chariot of night was drawn by dragons, on account of their watchfulness. They were the serpents, " whose eyes were never shut." In Milton' Il Penseroso:—

" Cynthia checks her dragon yoke."

ILLUSTRATIONS OF ACT III.

[11] SCENE II.—"*I with the morning's love have oft made sport.*"

Whether Oberon meant to laugh at Tithonus, the old husband of Aurora, or sport "like a forester" with young Cephalus, the morning's love, is matter of controversy.

[12] SCENE II.—"*Even till the eastern gate,*" &c.

This splendid passage was perhaps suggested by some lines in Chaucer's 'Knight's Tale:'—

"The besy larke, the messager of day,
Salewith in hire song the morwe gray;
And firy Phebus riseth up so bright,
That all the orient laugheth of the sight,
And with his stremes drieth in the greves
The silver dropes, hanging on the leves."

[13] SCENE II.—"*Ho, ho, ho!*"

The devil of the old mysteries was as well known by his Ho, ho! as Henry VIII. by his Ha, ha! Robin Goodfellow succeeded to the pass-word of the ancient devil. Of the old song which we quoted in Act II., each stanza ends with "ho, ho, ho!"

[14] SCENE II.—"*When thou wak'st,
Thou tak'st.*"

The second line is generally corrupted into—

"*See* thou tak'st."

The structure of the verse is precisely the same as in the previous lines—

"On the ground
Sleep sound."

Mount Taurus.

["When in a wood of Crete they bay'd the bear."]

ACT IV.

SCENE I.—*The Wood.*

Enter TITANIA *and* BOTTOM, *Fairies attending;* OBERON *behind unseen.*

Tita. Come, sit thee down upon this flowery bed,
While I thy amiable cheeks do coy,
And stick musk-roses in thy sleek smooth head,
And kiss thy fair large ears, my gentle joy.
Bot. Where 's Peas-blossom?
Peas. Ready.
Bot. Scratch my head, Peas-blossom.—Where 's monsieur Cobweb?[a]

Cob. Ready.
Bot. Monsieur Cobweb; good monsieur, get your weapons in your hand, and kill me a red-hipped humble-bee on the top of a thistle; and, good monsieur, bring me the honey-bag. Do not fret yourself too much in the action, monsieur; and, good monsieur, have a care the honey-bag break not; I would be loth to have you overflown[b] with a honey-bag, signior.—Where 's monsieur Mustard-seed?
Must. Ready.

[a] *Monsieur.* Throughout the folio and quartos (as pointed out by Mr. White) Bottom characteristically uses *Mounseur.*

[b] *Overflown*—flooded—drowned. The sense in which this word is here used may explain a passage in Milton, which has been thought corrupt:—

"Then wander forth the sons
Of Belial, flown with insolence and wine."
(*Paradise Lost,* book 1.)

367

[ACT IV.] A MIDSUMMER-NIGHT'S DREAM. [SCENE I.

Bot. Give me your neif,[a] monsieur Mustard-seed. Pray you, leave your courtesy, good monsieur.

Must. What's your will?

Bot. Nothing, good monsieur, but to help cavalery Cobweb[b] to scratch. I must to the barber's, monsieur; for, methinks, I am marvellous hairy about the face; and I am such a tender ass, if my hair do but tickle me I must scratch.

Tita. What, wilt thou hear some music, my sweet love?

Bot. I have a reasonable good ear in music: let us have the tongs and the bones.[c]

Tita. Or say, sweet love, what thou desir'st to eat.

Bot. Truly, a peck of provender: I could munch your good dry oats. Methinks I have a great desire to a bottle of hay: good hay, sweet hay, hath no fellow.

Tita. I have a venturous fairy that shall seek The squirrel's hoard, and fetch thee new nuts.

Bot. I had rather have a handful, or two, of dried peas. But, I pray you, let none of your people stir me; I have an exposition of sleep come upon me.

Tita. Sleep thou, and I will wind thee in my arms.
Fairies, be gone, and be all ways away.
So doth the woodbine the sweet honeysuckle
Gently entwist; the female ivy so
Enrings the barky fingers of the elm.[d]
O, how I love thee! how I dote on thee!
    [*They sleep.*

---
[a] *Neif*—fist. Thus in Henry IV., Part II., Act II., Sc. IV.—"Sweet knight, I kiss thy neif."
[b] *Cobweb.* This is probably a misprint for *Peas-blossom*. Cobweb has been sent after the "red-hipped humble-bee;" and Peas-blossom has already been appointed to the honoured office in which *Mustard-seed* is now called to assist him.
[c] The folio has here a stage-direction:—"Music. Tongs; Rural music."
[d] According to Steevens, "the sweet honeysuckle" is an explanation of what the poet means by "the woodbine," which name was sometimes applied to the ivy. "The honey-suckle" doth entwist—"the female ivy" enrings—"the barky fingers of the elm." Upon this interpretation the lines would be thus printed:—

"So doth the woodbine, the sweet honeysuckle,
Gently entwist,—the female ivy so
Enrings,—the barky fingers of the elm."

This is certainly very different from the usual Shaksperian construction. Nor is our poet fond of expletives. If the "elm" is the only plant entwisted and enringed, we have only one image. But if the "woodbine" is not meant to be identical with the "honeysuckle," we have two images, each distinct and each beautiful. Gifford pointed out the true meaning of the passage, in his note upon a parallel passage in Ben Jonson:—

"—— behold
How the blue bindweed doth itself enfold
With honeysuckle, and both these intwine
Themselves with bryony and jessamine."

"In many of our counties," says Gifford, "the woodbine is still the name for the great convolvulus."

OBERON *advances.* *Enter* PUCK.

Obe. Welcome, good Robin. See'st thou this sweet sight?
Her dotage now I do begin to pity.
For meeting her of late, behind the wood,
Seeking sweet favours for this hateful fool,
I did upbraid her and fall out with her:
For she his hairy temples then had rounded
With coronet of fresh and fragrant flowers;
And that same dew, which some time on the buds
Was wont to swell like round and orient pearls,
Stood now within the pretty flow'rets' eyes,
Like tears that did their own disgrace bewail.
When I had, at my pleasure, taunted her,
And she, in mild terms, begg'd my patience,
I then did ask of her her changeling child;
Which straight she gave me, and her fairies sent
To bear him to my bower in fairy land.
And now I have the boy, I will undo
This hateful imperfection of her eyes.
And, gentle Puck, take this transformed scalp
From off the head of this Athenian swain;
That he awaking when the other do,
May all to Athens back again repair;
And think no more of this night's accidents,
But as the fierce vexation of a dream.
But first I will release the fairy queen.
    Be, as thou was wont to be;
    [*Touching her eyes with an herb.*
    See, as thou was wont to see:
Dian's bud o'er Cupid's flower
Hath such force and blessed power.
Now, my Titania, wake you, my sweet queen.

Tita. My Oberon! what visions have I seen!
Methought I was enamour'd of an ass.

Obe. There lies your love.

Tita.   How came these things to pass?
O, how mine eyes do loath his visage now!

Obe. Silence a while.—Robin, take off this head.—
Titania, music call; and strike more dead
Than common sleep, of all these five the sense.

Tita. Music, ho! music; such as charmeth sleep.

Puck. Now, when thou wak'st, with thine own fool's eyes peep.[a]

Obe. Sound, music. [*Still music.*] Come, my queen, take hands with me,

---
[a] *Now,* at the beginning of the line, is found in Fisher's edition.

And rock the ground whereon these sleepers be.
Now thou and I are new in amity;
And will, to-morrow midnight, solemnly,
Dance in Duke Theseus' house triumphantly,
And bless it to all fair posterity:
There shall the pairs of faithful lovers be
Wedded, with Theseus, all in jollity.
  Puck. Fairy king, attend, and mark;
    I do hear the morning lark.
  Obe. Then, my queen, in silence sad,
    Trip we after the night's shade:
    We the globe can compass soon,
    Swifter than the wand'ring moon.
  Tita. Come, my lord; and in our flight,
    Tell me how it came this night,
    That I sleeping here was found,
    With these mortals on the ground. [*Exeunt.*
              [*Horns sound within.*

Enter THESEUS, HIPPOLYTA, EGEUS, *and train.*

  The. Go one of you, find out the forester;[1]
For now our observation is perform'd;
And since we have the vaward of the day,
My love shall hear the music of my hounds.
Uncouple in the western valley; let them go:
Despatch, I say, and find the forester.
We will, fair queen, up to the mountain's top,
And mark the musical confusion
Of hounds and echo in conjunction.
  Hip. I was with Hercules and Cadmus once,
When in a wood of Crete they bay'd the bear
With hounds of Sparta: never did I hear
Such gallant chiding; for, besides the groves,
The skies, the fountains, every region near
Seem'd all one mutual cry: I never heard
So musical a discord, such sweet thunder.
  The. My hounds are bred out of the Spartan kind,
So flew'd, so sanded; and their heads are hung
With ears that sweep away the morning dew;
Crook-knee'd and dew-lap'd like Thessalian bulls;
Slow in pursuit, but match'd in mouth like bells,
Each under each. A cry more tuneable
Was never holla'd to, nor cheer'd with horn,
In Crete, in Sparta, nor in Thessaly:
Judge, when you hear.—But, soft; what nymphs are these?
  Ege. My lord, this is my daughter here asleep;
And this Lysander; this Demetrius is;
This Helena, old Nedar's Helena:
I wonder of their being here together.

  The. No doubt they rose up early, to observe
The rite of May; and, hearing our intent,
Came here in grace of our solemnity.
But, speak, Egeus; is not this the day
That Hermia should give answer of her choice?
  Ege. It is, my lord.
  The. Go, bid the huntsmen wake them with their horns.

Horns, and shout within. DEMETRIUS, LYSANDER, HERMIA, *and* HELENA, *wake, and start up.*

  The. Good morrow, friends. Saint Valentine is past;
Begin these wood-birds but to couple now?
  Lys. Pardon, my lord.
              [*He and the rest kneel to* THESEUS.
  The.   I pray you all, stand up.
I know you two are rival enemies;
How comes this gentle concord in the world,
That hatred is so far from jealousy,
To sleep by hate, and fear no enmity?
  Lys. My lord, I shall reply amazedly,
Half 'sleep, half waking: But as yet, I swear,
I cannot truly say how I came here:
But, as I think, (for truly would I speak,—
And now I do bethink me, so it is;)
I came with Hermia hither: our intent
Was to be gone from Athens, where we might be
Without the peril of the Athenian law.
  Ege. Enough, enough, my lord; you have enough:
I beg the law, the law, upon his head.
They would have stol'n away, they would, Demetrius,
Thereby to have defeated you and me;
You of your wife, and me of my consent,—
Of my consent that she should be your wife.
  Dem. My lord, fair Helen told me of their stealth,
Of this their purpose hither, to this wood;
And I in fury hither follow'd them;
Fair Helena in fancy following me.
But, my good lord, I wot not by what power,
(But, by some power it is,) my love to Hermia,
Melted as the snow, seems to me now
As the remembrance of an idle gaud,
Which in my childhood I did dote upon:
And all the faith, the virtue of my heart,
The object, and the pleasure of mine eye,
Is only Helena. To her, my lord,
Was I betroth'd ere I saw Hermia:
But, like in sickness, did I loath this food;
But, as in health, come to my natural taste,

Now do I wish it, love it, long for it,
And will for evermore be true to it.
  The. Fair lovers, you are fortunately met:
Of this discourse we will hear more anon.
Egeus, I will overbear your will;
For in the temple, by and by with us,
These couples shall eternally be knit.
And, for the morning now is something worn,
Our purpos'd hunting shall be set aside.
Away, with us, to Athens: Three and three,
We'll hold a feast in great solemnity.
Come, Hippolyta.
  [*Exeunt* THESEUS, HIPPOLYTA, EGEUS, *and train.*
  Dem. These things seem small and undistinguishable,
Like far-off mountains turned into clouds.
  Her. Methinks I see these things with parted eye,
When every thing seems double.
  Hel.   So, methinks:
And I have found Demetrius like a jewel,[a]
Mine own, and not mine own.
  Dem.   It seems to me,
That yet we sleep, we dream.—Do not you think,
The duke was here, and bid us follow him?
  Her. Yea, and my father.
  Hel.   And Hippolyta.
  Lys. And he did bid us follow to the temple.
  Dem. Why then, we are awake: let's follow him;
And, by the way, let us recount our dreams.
                                          [*Exeunt.*

          As they go out, BOTTOM *awakes.*

  Bot. When my cue comes, call me, and I will answer:—my next is, 'Most fair Pyramus.'—Hey, ho!—Peter Quince! Flute, the bellows-mender! Snout, the tinker! Starveling! God's my life! stolen hence, and left me asleep! I have had a most rare vision. I have had a dream,—past the wit of man to say what dream it was:—Man is but an ass if he go about to expound this dream. Methought I was—there is no man can tell what. Methought I was, and methought I had.—But man is but a patched fool[b] if he will offer to say what methought I had. The eye of man hath not heard, the ear of man hath not seen, man's hand is not able to taste, his tongue to conceive, nor his heart to

report, what my dream was. I will get Peter Quince to write a ballad of this dream: it shall be called Bottom's Dream, because it hath no bottom; and I will sing it in the latter end of our play, before the duke: Peradventure, to make it the more gracious, I shall sing it at her death.[a]   [*Exit*

SCENE II.—Athens. *A Room in* Quince's *House.*

Enter QUINCE, FLUTE, SNOUT, *and* STARVELING

  Quin. Have you sent to Bottom's house? is he come home yet?
  Star. He cannot be heard of. Out of, doubt, he is transported.
  Flu. If he come not, then the play is marred; It goes not forward, doth it?
  Quin. It is not possible: you have not a man in all Athens able to discharge Pyramus, but he.
  Flu. No; he hath simply the best wit of any handicraft man in Athens.
  Quin. Yea, and the best person too: and he is a very paramour for a sweet voice.
  Flu. You must say, paragon: a paramour is, God bless us, a thing of naught.

                    Enter SNUG.

  Snug. Masters, the duke is coming from the temple, and there is two or three lords and ladies more married: if our sport had gone forward we had all been made men.
  Flu. O sweet Bully Bottom! Thus hath he lost sixpence a-day during his life; he could not have 'scaped sixpence a-day: an the duke had not given him sixpence a-day for playing Pyramus, I'll be hanged; he would have deserved it: sixpence a-day, in Pyramus, or nothing.

                  Enter BOTTOM.

  Bot. Where are these lads? where are these hearts?
  Quin. Bottom!—O most courageous day! O most happy hour!
  Bot. Masters, I am to discourse wonders: but ask me not what; for if I tell you I am no true Athenian. I will tell you every thing, right as it fell out.
  Quin. Let us hear, sweet Bottom.
  Bot. Not a word of me. All that I will tell

---

[a] She has found Demetrius, as a person picks up a jewel—for the moment it is his own, but its value may cause it to be reclaimed. She feels insecure in the possession of her treasure.

[b] *Patched fool*—a fool in a parti-coloured coat.

[a] Probably, at the death of Thisbe. Theobald would read "*after death,*"—that is, after Bottom had been killed in the part of Pyramus.

Act IV.] A MIDSUMMER-NIGHT'S DREAM. [Scene II.

you is, that the duke hath dined: Get your apparel together; good strings to your beards,[a] new ribbons to your pumps; meet presently at the palace; every man look o'er his part; for, the short and the long is, our play is preferred.[b] In any case, let Thisby have clean linen; and let not him that plays the lion pare his nails, for they shall hang out for the lion's claws. And, most dear actors, eat no onions, nor garlic, for we are to utter sweet breath; and I do not doubt but to hear them say it is a sweet comedy. No more words; away; go, away. [*Exeunt.*

[a] *Preferred*—not in the sense of chosen in preference—but offered—as a suit is preferred.

[Bottom awaking.]

ILLUSTRATIONS OF ACT IV.

¹ Scene I.—*"Go one of you, find out the forester."*

The Theseus of Chaucer was a mighty hunter:—

> "This mene I now by mighty Theseus
> That for to hunten is so desirous,
> And namely at the grete hart in May,
> That in his bed ther daweth him no day
> That he n'is clad, and redy for to ride
> With hunte and horne, and houndes him beside.
> For in his hunting hath he swiche delite,
> That it is all his joye and appetite
> To ben himself the grete hartes bane,
> For after Mars he serveth now Diane."
>
> (*The Knightes Tale.*)

² Scene II.—*"Good strings to your beards."*

In the first Act, Bottom has told us that he will "discharge" the part of Pyramus, "in either your straw-coloured beard, your orange-tawny beard, your purple-in-grain beard, or your French-crown-coloured beard, your perfect yellow." He is now solicitous that the strings by which the artificial beards were to be fastened should be in good order. The custom of wearing coloured beards was not confined to the stage. In the comedy of 'Ram-alley,' (1611,) we have:—

> "What colour'd beard comes next by the window?"
> "A black man's, I think."
> "I think, a red; for that is most in fashion."

In the 'Alchymist' we find, "he had dyed his beard, and all." Stubbes, the great dissector of "Abuses," gives us nothing about the coloured beards of men; but he is very minute about the solicitude of the ladies to procure false hair, and to dye their hair. We dare say the anxiety was not confined to one sex:—

"If curling and laying out their own natural hair were all, (which is impious, and at no hand lawful, being, as it is, an ensign of pride, and the stern of wantonness to all that behold it,) it were the less matter; but they are not simply content with their own hair, but buy other hair, either of horses, mares, or any other strange beasts, dyeing it of what colour they list themselves. And if there be any poor woman (as now and then, we see, God doth bless them with beauty as well as the rich) that have fair hair, these nice dames will not rest till they have bought it. Or if any children have fair hair, they will entice them into a secret place, and for a penny or two they will cut off their hair; as I heard that one did in the city of Londinum of late, who, meeting a little child with very fair hair, inveigled her into a house, promised her a penny, and so cut off her hair. And this they wear in the same order, as you have heard, as though it were their own natural hair; and upon the other side, if any have hair of her own natural growing, which is not fair enough, then will they dye it in divers colours, almost changing the substance into accidents by their devilish, and more than these cursed, devices."

("Now, until the break of day,
Through this house each fairy stray.")

ACT V.

SCENE I.—*Athens. An Apartment in the Palace of* Theseus.

Enter THESEUS, HIPPOLYTA, PHILOSTRATE, Lords *and* Attendants.

Hip. 'T is strange, my Theseus, that these lovers speak of.
The. More strange than true. I never may believe
These antique fables, nor these fairy toys.
Lovers and madmen have such seething brains,
Such shaping fantasies, that apprehend
More than cool reason ever comprehends.
The lunatic, the lover, and the poet,
Are of imagination all compact:
One sees more devils than vast hell can hold—
That is the madman: the lover, all as frantic,
Sees Helen's beauty in a brow of Egypt:
The poet's eye, in a fine frenzy rolling,
Doth glance from heaven to earth, from earth to heaven,
And, as imagination bodies forth
The forms of things unknown, the poet's pen
Turns them to shapes, and gives to airy nothing
A local habitation and a name.
Such tricks hath strong imagination;
That, if it would but apprehend some joy,
It comprehends some bringer of that joy;
Or, in the night, imagining some fear,
How easy is a bush suppos'd a bear?
Hip. But all the story of the night told over
And all their minds transfigur'd so together,

ACT V.] A MIDSUMMER-NIGHT'S DREAM. [SCENE I.

More witnesseth than fancy's images,
And grows to something of great constancy;
But, howsoever, strange, and admirable.

Enter LYSANDER, DEMETRIUS, HERMIA, *and*
HELENA.

The. Here come the lovers, full of joy and mirth.
Joy, gentle friends! joy, and fresh days of love,
Accompany your hearts!
  Lys. More than to us
Wait in your royal walks, your board, your bed!
  The. Come now; what masks, what dances shall we have,
To wear away this long age of three hours,
Between our after-supper and bed-time?
Where is our usual manager of mirth?
What revels are in hand? Is there no play,
To ease the anguish of a torturing hour?
Call Philostrate.
  Philost. Here, mighty Theseus.
  The. Say, what abridgment ᵃ have you for this evening?
What mask, what music? How shall we beguile
The lazy time, if not with some delight?
  Philost. There is a brief, how many sports are rife;ᵇ
Make choice of which your highness will see first.
                          [*Giving a paper.*
  Lys. [*reads.*ᶜ] 'The battle with the Centaurs, to be sung,
By an Athenian eunuch to the harp.'
  The. We'll none of that: that have I told my love,
In glory of my kinsman Hercules.
  Lys. 'The riot of the tipsy Bacchanals,
Tearing the Thracian singer in their rage.'
  The. That is an old device, and it was play'd
When I from Thebes came last a conqueror.
  Lys. 'The thrice three Muses mourning for the death
Of learning, late deceas'd in beggary.'
  The. That is some satire, keen, and critical,
Not sorting with a nuptial ceremony.
  Lys. 'A tedious brief scene of young Pyramus,
And his love Thisbe; very tragical mirth.'
  The. Merry and tragical? Tedious and brief?

That is, hot ice, and wondrous strange snow ᵃ
How shall we find the concord of this discord?
  Philost. A play there is, my lord, some ten words long;
Which is as brief as I have known a play;
But by ten words, my lord, it is too long,
Which makes it tedious: for in all the play
There is not one word apt, one player fitted.
And tragical, my noble lord, it is;
For Pyramus therein doth kill himself.
Which when I saw rehears'd, I must confess,
Made mine eyes water; but more merry tears
The passion of loud laughter never shed.
  The. What are they that do play it?
  Philost. Hard-handed men, that work in Athens here,
Which never labour'd in their minds till now;
And now have toil'd their unbreath'd memories
With this same play, against your nuptial.
  The. And we will hear it.
  Philost. No, my noble lord,
It is not for you: I have heard it over,
And it is nothing, nothing in the world,
(Unless you can find sport in their intents,)ᵇ
Extremely stretch'd and conn'd with cruel pain
To do you service.
  The. I will hear that play;
For never any thing can be amiss
When simpleness and duty tender it.
Go, bring them in: and take your places, ladies.
                         [*Exeunt* PHILOSTRATE.
  Hip. I love not to see wretchedness o'ercharg'd,
And duty in his service perishing.
  The. Why, gentle sweet, you shall see no such thing.
  Hip. He says, they can do nothing in this kind.
  The. The kinder we, to give them thanks for nothing.
Our sport shall be, to take what they mistake:
And what poor duty cannot do,
Noble respect takes it in might,ᶜ not merit.
Where I have come, great clerks have purposed
To greet me with premeditated welcomes;
Where I have seen them shiver and look pale,

ᵃ *Wondrous strange snow.* This has sorely puzzled the commentators. They want an antithesis for *snow*, as *hot* is for *ice*. Upton, therefore, reads, "*black* snow;" Hanmer, "*scorching* snow," and Mason, "*strong* snow." Surely, snow is a common thing; and, therefore, "wondrous strange" is sufficiently antithetical—hot ice, and snow as strange.

ᵇ This line is parenthetical, and we print it so. Johnson says he does not know what it is to *stretch* and *con* an *intent*. It is the *play* which Philostrate has heard over, so *stretch'd* and *conn'd*.

ᶜ *Might.* This is not used to express *power*, but *will—what one mayeth—*the *will* for the *deed*. See Tooke's 'Diversions of Purley,' Part II., c. v.)

ᵃ *Abridgment—pastime—*something that may *abridge* "the lazy time."

ᵇ *Rife—*so the folio. One of the quartos, *ripe*.

ᶜ In the quartos, *Theseus* reads the "brief," and makes the remarks u: on each item;—in the folio, *Lysander* reads the list. The lines are generally printed as in the quartos; but the division of so long a passage is clearly better, and is perfectly natural and proper.

ACT V.] A MIDSUMMER-NIGHT'S DREAM. [SCENE I.

Make periods in the midst of sentences,
Throttle their practis'd accent in their fears,
And, in conclusion, dumbly have broke off,
Not paying me a welcome : Trust me, sweet,
Out of this silence yet I pick'd a welcome ;
And in the modesty of fearful duty
I read as much, as from the rattling tongue
Of saucy and audacious eloquence.
Love, therefore, and tongue-tied simplicity,
In least speak most, to my capacity.

Enter PHILOSTRATE.

Philost. So please your grace, the prologue is addrest.[a]

The. Let him approach.
[*Flourish of trumpets.*

Enter Prologue.

Prol. 'If we offend, it is with our good will.
'That you should think we come not to offend,
But with good will. To show our simple skill,
'That is the true beginning of our end.
'Consider then, we come but in despite.
'We do not come as minding to content you,
Our true intent is. All for your delight,
'We are not here. That you should here repent you,
'The actors are at hand ; and, by their show,
You shall know all that you are like to know.'

The. This fellow doth not stand upon points.[b]
Lys. He hath rid his prologue like a rough colt ; he knows not the stop. A good moral, my lord : It is not enough to speak, but to speak true.
Hip. Indeed he hath played on his prologue like a child on a recorder ; a sound, but not in government.
The. His speech was like a tangled chain ; nothing impaired, but all disordered. Who is next ?

Enter PYRAMUS *and* THISBE, Wall, Moonshine, *and* Lion, *as in dumb show.*

Prol. ' Gentles, perchance you wonder at this show ;
' But wonder on, till truth make all things plain.
This man is Pyramus, if you would know ;
' This beauteous lady Thisby is, certain.

---

[a] *Addrest*—ready.
[b] The Prologue is very carefully mis-pointed in the original editions—" a tangled chain: nothing impaired, but all disordered." Had the fellow stood " upon points" it would have read thus :—

" If we offend, it is with our good will
That you should think we come not to offend ;
But with good will to show our simple skill.
That is the true beginning of our end.
Consider then. We come : but in despite
We do not come. As, minding to content you,
Our true intent is all for your delight.
We are not here that you should here repent you.
The actors are at hand ; and, by their show,
You shall know all that you are like to know."

We fear that we have taken longer to puzzle out this enigma, than the poet did to produce it.

'This man, with lime and rough-cast, doth present
'Wall, that vile wall which did these lovers sunder :
'And through-wall's chink, poor souls, they are content
'To whisper, at the which let no man wonder.
'This man, with lantern, dog, and bush of thorn,
'Presenteth moonshine: for, if you will know,
'By moonshine did these lovers think no scorn
'To meet at Ninus' tomb, there, there to woo.
'This grisly beast, which by name lion hight,
'The trusty Thisby, coming first by night,
'Did scare away, or rather did affright :
'And, as she fled, her mantle she did fall ;[a]
'Which lion vile with bloody mouth did stain :
'Anon comes Pyramus, sweet youth and tall,
'And finds his trusty Thisby's mantle slain :
'Whereat with blade, with bloody blameful blade,
'He bravely broach'd his boiling bloody breast ;
'And, Thisby tarrying in mulberry shade,
'His dagger drew, and died. For all the rest,
'Let lion, moon-shine, wall, and lovers twain,
'At large discourse, while here they do remain.'
[*Exeunt* Prol. THISBE, Lion, *and* Moonshine

The. I wonder, if the lion be to speak.
Dem. No wonder, my lord : one lion may when many asses do.
Wall. 'In this same interlude, it doth befall,
'That I, one Snout by name, present a wall :
'And such a wall as I would have you think,
'That had in it a cranny'd hole, or chink,
'Through which the lovers, Pyramus and Thisby,
'Did whisper often very secretly.
'This loam, this rough-cast, and this stone doth show
'That I am that same wall ; the truth is so :
'And this the cranny is, right and sinister,
'Through which the fearful lovers are to whisper.

The. Would you desire lime and hair to speak better ?
Dem. It is the wittiest partition that ever I heard discourse, my lord.
The. Pyramus draws near the wall : silence

Enter PYRAMUS.

Pyr. 'O grim-look'd night ! O night with hue so black !
'O night, which ever art when day is not !
'O night, O night, alack, alack, alack,
'I fear my Thisby's promise is forgot !
'And thou, O wall, thou sweet and lovely wall,
'That stands between her father's ground and mine ;
'Thou wall, O wall, O sweet and lovely wall,
'Shew me thy chink, to blink through with mine eyne.
[*Wall holds up his fingers.*
'Thanks, courteous wall : Jove shield thee well for this !
'But what see I? No Thisby do I see.
'O wicked wall, through whom I see no bliss ;
'Curst be thy stones for thus deceiving me !'

The. The wall, methinks, being sensible, should curse again.
Bot. No, in truth, sir, he should not. ' Deceiving me,' is Thisby's cue : she is to enter now, and I am to spy her through the wall. You shall see, it will fall pat as I told you :—Yonder she comes.

---

[a] *fall*—used actively.

875

Enter THISBE.

This. 'O wall, full often hast thou heard my moans,
'For parting my fair Pyramus and me:
My cherry lips have often kiss'd thy stones;
'Thy stones with lime and hair knit up in thee.'
Pyr. 'I see a voice: now will I to the chink,
'To spy an I can hear my Thisby's face.
Thisby!'
This. 'My love! thou art my love, I think.'
Pyr. 'Think what thou wilt, I am thy lover's grace;
And like Limander am I trusty still.'
This. 'And I like Helen, till the fates me kill.'
Pyr. 'Not Shafalus to Procrus was so true.'
This. 'As Shafalus to Procrus, I to you.'
Pyr. 'O, kiss me through the hole of this vile wall.'
This. 'I kiss the wall's hole, not your lips at all.'
Pyr. 'Wilt thou at Ninny's tomb meet me straightway?'
This. 'Tide life, 'tide death, I come without delay.'
Wall. 'Thus have I, wall, my part discharged so;
And, being done, thus wall away doth go.'
            [*Exeunt* Wall, PYRAMUS, *and* THISBE.

The. Now is the mural down between the two neighbours.

Dem. No remedy, my lord, when walls are so wilful to hear without warning.

Hip. This is the silliest stuff that e'er I heard.

The. The best in this kind are but shadows; and the worst are no worse, if imagination amend them.

Hip. It must be your imagination then, and not theirs.

The. If we imagine no worse of them than they of themselves, they may pass for excellent men. Here come two noble beasts in, a man and a lion.

Enter Lion *and* Moonshine.

Lion. 'You, ladies, you, whose gentle hearts do fear
'The smallest monstrous mouse that creeps on floor,
May now, perchance, both quake and tremble here,
'When lion rough in wildest rage doth roar.
Then know that I, one Snug the joiner, am
A lion's fell, nor else no lion's dam:
For if I should as lion come in strife
'Into this place, 'twere pity of my life.'

The. A very gentle beast, and of a good conscience.

Dem. The very best at a beast, my lord, that e'er I saw.

Lys. This lion is a very fox for his valour.

The. True; and a goose for his discretion.

Dem. Not so, my lord; for his valour cannot carry his discretion; and the fox carries the goose.

The. His discretion, I am sure, cannot carry his valour; for the goose carries not the fox. It is well: leave it to his discretion, and let us hearken to the moon.

Moon. 'This lantern doth the horned moon present.'

Dem. He should have worn the horns on his head.

The. He is no crescent, and his horns are invisible within the circumference.

Moon. 'This lantern doth the horned moon present;
'Myself the man i' th' moon do seem to be.'?

The. This is the greatest error of all the rest: the man should be put into the lantern: How is it else the man i' the moon?

Dem. He dares not come there for the candle: for, you see, it is already in snuff.

Hip. I am weary of this moon: Would he would change.

The. It appears, by his small light of discretion, that he is in the wane: but yet, in courtesy, in all reason, we must stay the time.

Lys. Proceed, moon.

Moon. 'All that I have to say is, to tell you, that the lantern is the moon; I, the man in the moon; this thorn-bush my thorn-bush; and this dog my dog.'

Dem. Why, all these should be in the lantern; for they are in the moon. But, silence; here comes Thisbe.

Enter THISBE.

This. 'This is old Ninny's tomb: Where is my love?'
Lion. 'Oh—.'
            [*The* Lion *roars.—*THISBE *runs off.*

Dem. Well roared, lion.
The. Well run, Thisbe.
Hip. Well shone, moon. Truly, the moon shines with a good grace.
The. Well moused, lion.
            [*The* Lion *tears* THISBE's *mantle, and exit.*
Dem. And then came Pyramus.
Lys. And so the lion vanished.ᵃ

Enter PYRAMUS.

Pyr. 'Sweet moon, I thank thee for thy sunny beams
'I thank thee, moon, for shining now so bright;
'For, by thy gracious, golden, glittering gleams,ᵇ
'I trust to taste of truest Thisby's sight.
        'But stay;—O spite!
        'But mark;—Poor knight,
    'What dreadful dole is here!
        'Eyes, do you see!
        'How can it be?
    'O dainty duck! O dear!
        'Thy mantle good,
        'What, stain'd with blood?
    'Approach, ye furies fell!
        'O fates! come, come;
        'Cut thread and thrum;
    'Quail, crush, conclude, and quell!'

ᵃ This passage, according to an emendation of the old copies by Dr. Farmer, is always printed—

    "And as comes Pyramus,
    And then the moon vanishes."

Farmer makes the correction, because, in this mock-play, the moon vanishes after Pyramus dies. But Demetrius and Lysander do not profess to have any knowledge of the play; it is Philostrate who has "heard it over." They are thinking of the classical story; and, like Hamlet, they are each "a good chorus."

ᵇ *Gleams.* The word in the original copies is *beams*, which is clearly an error. The editor of the second folio altered it to *streams*. I suggested *gleams*, as the ridicule of excessive alliteration would then have been carried further.

The. This passion, and the death of a dear friend, would go near to make a man look sad.
Hip. Beshrew my heart, but I pity the man.

Pyr. 'O, wherefore, nature, didst thou lions frame!
'Since lion vile hath here deflour'd my dear:
'Which is—no, no—which was the fairest dame,
That liv'd, that lov'd, that lik'd, that look'd with cheer.
    'Come, tears, confound;
    'Out, sword, and wound
  'The pap of Pyramus:
    'Ay, that left pap
    'Where heart doth hop:—
  'Thus die I, thus, thus, thus.
    'Now am I dead,
    'Now am I fled;
  'My soul is in the sky:
    'Tongue, lose thy light!
    'Moon, take thy flight!
  'Now die, die, die, die, die.'
                [*Dies.—Exit* Moonshine.

Dem. No die, but an ace, for him; for he is but one.
Lys. Less than an ace, man; for he is dead; he is nothing.
The. With the help of a surgeon, he might yet recover, and prove an ass.
Hip. How chance moonshine is gone, before Thisbe comes back and finds her lover?
The. She will find him by starlight.—Here she comes; and her passion ends the play.

Enter THISBE.

Hip. Methinks, she should not use a long one for such a Pyramus: I hope she will be brief.
Dem. A mote will turn the balance, which Pyramus, which Thisbe, is the better.
Lys. She hath spied him already with those sweet eyes.
Dem. And thus she moans, *videlicet.*

This. 'Asleep, my love!
    'What, dead, my dove?
  'O Pyramus, arise,
    'Speak, speak. Quite dumb?
    'Dead, dead! A tomb
  'Must cover thy sweet eyes.
    'These lily lips,ᵃ
    'This cherry nose,
  'These yellow cowslip cheeks,
    'Are gone, are gone!
    'Lovers, make moan!
  'His eyes were green as leeks.
    'O sisters three
    'Come, come to me,
  'With hands as pale as milk;
    'Lay them in gore,
    'Since you have shore
  'With shears his thread of silk.
    'Tongue, not a word:
    'Come, trusty sword;
  'Come, blade, my breast imbrue;
    'And farewell, friends;
    'Thus Thisbe ends;
  'Adieu, adieu, adieu.'   [*Dies.*

ᵃ *Lips*—in the original copies, which Theobald changed to *brows.*

The. Moonshine and lion are left to bury the dead.
Dem. Ay, and wall too.
Bot. No, I assure you; the wall is down that parted their fathers. Will it please you to see the epilogue, or to hear a Bergomaskᵃ dance, between two of our company.
The. No epilogue, I pray you; for your play needs no excuse. Never excuse; for when the players are all dead, there need none to be blamed. Marry, if he that writ it had played Pyramus, and hanged himself in Thisbe's garter, it would have been a fine tragedy: and so it is truly; and very notably discharged. But come, your Bergomask: let your epilogue alone.
          [*Here a dance of* Clowns.
The iron tongue of midnight hath told twelve:—
Lovers to bed; 'tis almost fairy time.
I fear we shall outsleep the coming morn,
As much as we this night have over-watch'd.
This palpable-gross playᵃ hath well beguil'd
The heavy gait of night.—Sweet friends, to bed.—
A fortnight hold we this solemnity,
In nightly revels, and new jollity.   [*Exeunt.*

SCENE II.

Enter PUCK.

Puck. Now the hungry lion roars,ᵃ
   And the wolf behowlsᵇ the moon;
Whilst the heavy ploughman snores,
   All with weary task fordone
Now the wasted brands do glow,
   Whilst the scritch-owl, scritching loud,
Puts the wretch, that lies in woe,
   In remembrance of a shroud.
Now it is the time of night,
   That the graves, all gaping wide,
Every one lets forth his sprite,
   In the church-way paths to glide:
And we fairies, that do run
   By the triple Hecate'sᶜ team,
From the presence of the sun,
   Following darkness like a dream,
Now are frolic; not a mouse
Shall disturb this hallow'd house:
I am sent, with broom, before,
To sweep the dust behind the door.

ᵃ An Italian dance, after the manner of the peasants of Bergomasco.
ᵇ *Behowls.* This is *beholds* in the original text, but clearly an error. In *As You Like It,* we have—"'T is like the howling of Irish wolves against the moon. The image is familiar to poetry, from Shakspere to Pope—

"Silence, ye wolves, while Ralph to Cynthia howls."

ᶜ Marlowe, Middleton, and Golding, also use *Hecate* as dissyllable. In Spenser and Jonson we find *Hecaté.*

ACT V] A MIDSUMMER-NIGHT'S DREAM. [SCENE II.

Enter OBERON *and* TITANIA, *with their train.*

Obe. Through[a] the house give glimmering light,
  By the dead and drowsy fire:
Every elf, and fairy sprite,
  Hop as light as bird from brier;
And this ditty, after me,
Sing, and dance it trippingly.[b]

Tita. First, rehearse this song by rote
  To each word a warbling note,
Hand in hand, with fairy grace,
Will we sing, and bless this place.

SONG, AND DANCE.

Obe. Now, until the break of day,
  Through this house each fairy stray.
To the best bride-bed will we,[b]
  Which by us shall blessed be:
And the issue there create,
  Ever shall be fortunate.
So shall all the couples three
  Ever true in loving be;
And the blots of nature's hand
  Shall not in their issue stand;
Never mole, hare-lip, nor scar,
  Nor mark prodigious, such as are
Despised in nativity,
  Shall upon their children be.

[a] *Though*—Mr. White's suggestion instead of *through*.

With this field-dew consecrate,
Every fairy take his gait;
And each several chamber bless,
Through this palace with sweet peace;
Ever shall in safety rest,
And the owner of it blest.[a]
  Trip away;
  Make no stay:
Meet me all by break of day.

[*Exeunt* OBERON, TITANIA, *and train.*

Puck. If we shadows have offended,
  Think but this, (and all is mended,)
That you have but slumber'd here,
  While these visions did appear.
And this weak and idle theme,
  No more yielding but a dream,
Gentles, do not reprehend;
  If you pardon, we will mend.
And, as I am an honest Puck,
  If we have unearned luck
Now to 'scape the serpent's tongue,
  We will make amends, ere long:
Else the Puck a liar call.
  So, good night unto you all.
Give me your hands, if we be friends,
  And Robin shall restore amends.

[*Exit.*

[a] It has been suggested that these two lines should be transposed.

"I am sent, with broom, before,
  To sweep the dust behind the door."

[Theseus and the Centaur.]

ILLUSTRATIONS OF ACT V.

¹ SCENE I.—"*The battle with the Centaurs.*"

THESEUS has told his love the story of the battle with the Centaurs—

"In glory of my kinsman Hercules."

Shakspere has given to Theseus the attributes of a real hero, amongst which modesty is included. He has attributed the glory to his "kinsman Hercules." The poets and sculptors of antiquity have made Theseus himself the great object of their glorification. The Elgin Marbles and Shakspere have made the glories of Theseus familiar to the modern world.

² SCENE I.—"*Myself the man i' th' moon do seem to be.*"

The "man in the moon" was a considerable personage in Shakspere's day. He not only walked in the moon, ("his lantern,") with his "thorn-bush" and his "dog," but he did sundry other odd things, such as the man in the moon has ceased to do in these our unimaginative days. There is an old black-letter ballad of the time of James II, preserved in the British Museum, entitled 'The Man in the Moon drinks Claret,' adorned with a woodcut of this remarkable tippler.

³ SCENE I.—"*This palpable-gross play.*"

There is a general opinion, and probably a correct one, that the state of the early stage is shadowed in the 'Pyramus and Thisbe.' We believe that the resemblance is intended to be general, rather than pointed at any particular example of the rudeness of the ancient drama. The description by Quince of his play—'The most lamentable Comedy,' is considered by Steevens to be a burlesque of the title-page of Cambyses, 'A lamentable Tragedie, mixed full of pleasant mirth.' Capell thinks that " in the Clowns' Interlude you have some particular burlesques of passages in 'Sir Clyomon and Sir Chlamydes,' and in 'Damon and Pithias.'"—

"O sisters three
Come, come to me,"

certainly resembles the following in 'Damon and Pithias:'—

'Gripe me, you greedy griefs,
And present pangs of death,
You sisters three, with cruel hands,
With speed now stop my breath.'

We incline to think that the Interlude is intended as a burlesque on 'The Art of Sinking,' whether in dramatic or other poetry. In Clement Robinson's 'Handefull of Pleasant Delites,' (1584,) we have a 'Tale of Pyramus and Thisbe' which well deserves the honour of a travestie:—

"A NEW SONET OF PYRAMUS AND THISBIE.

"You dames (I say) that climbe the mount
Of Helicon,
Come on with me, and give account
What hath been don.
Come tell the chaunce, ye Muses all,
And doleful newes,
Which on these lovers did befall,
Which I accuse.

ILLUSTRATIONS OF ACT V.

In Babilon, not long agone,
    A noble Prince did dwell,
Whose daughter bright, dimd ech ones sight,
    So farre she did excel.

" Another lord of high renowne,
    Who had a sonne ;
And dwelling there within the towne,
    Great love begunne ;
Pyramus, this noble knight,
    (I tel you true,)
Who with the love of Thisbie bright,
    Did cares renue.
It came to passe, their secrets was
    Be knowne unto them both :
And then in minute, they place do finde,
    Where they their love unclothe

" This love they use long tract of time ;
    Till it befell,
At last they promised to meet at prime,
    By Ninus Well ;
Where they might lovingly imbrace,
    In loves delight :
That he might see his Thisbies face,
    And she his sight.
In joyful case, she approcht the place
    Where she her Pyramus
Had thought to viewd ; but was renewd
    To them most dolorous.

" Thus, while she staies for Pyramus,
    There did proceed
Out of the wood a lion fierce,
    Made Thisbie dreed :
And, as in haste she fled awaie,
    Her mantle fine
The lion tare, in stead of praie ;
    Till that the time
That Pyramus proceeded thus,
    And see how lion tare
The mantle this, of Thisbie his,
    He desperately doth fare.

" For why ! he thought the lion had
    Faire Thisbie slaine.
And then the beast, with his bright blade
    He slew certaine.
Then made he mone, and said ' Alas !
    O wretched wight !
Now art thou in woful case
    For Thisbie bright :
Oh ! gods above, my faithful love
    Shal never faile this need ;
For this my breath, by fatall death,
    Shal weave Atropos threed.'

" Then from his sheath he drew his blade,
    And to his hart
He thrust the point, and life did war'z,
    With painfull smart :

Then Thisbie she from cabin came,
    With pleasure great ;
And to the Well spane she ran,
    There for to treat.
And to discusse to Pyramus,
    Of all her former feares ;
And when slaine she found him, truly
    She shed forth bitter teares.

' when sorrow great that she had made,
    She took in hand
The bloudie knife, to end her life
    By fatall hand.
You ladies all, peruse and see
    The faithfulnesse,
How these two lovers did agree
    To die in distresse.
You muses waile, and do not faile
    But still do you lament
These lovers twaine, who with such paine
    Did die so well content."

¹ SCENE II.—" *Now the hungry lion roars*," &c.

" Very Anacreon," says Coleridge, " in perfectness, proportion, grace, and spontaneity. So far it is Greek ; but then add, O ! what wealth, what wild ranging, and yet what compression and condensation of English fancy. In truth, there is nothing in Anacreon more perfect than these thirty lines, or half so rich and imaginative. They form a speckless diamond."—(Literary Remains, vol. ii. p. 114).

² SCENE II.—" *Sing, and dance it trippingly.*"

The *trip* was the fairy pace : in the Tempest we have—
    " Each one *tripping* on his toe,
    Will be here with mop and moe."
In the Venus and Adonis—
    " Or, like a fairy *trip* upon the green."
In the Merry Wives of Windsor—
    " About him, fairies, sing a scornful rhyme,
    And as you *trip* still pinch him to your time.

³ SCENE II.—" *To the best bride-bed will we*," &c.

" The ceremony of blessing the bed," says Douce, " was used at all marriages." Those who desire to consult the original form of blessing, illustrated by a copy of a hideous ancient woodcut, may find very full details in Douce, vol. ii. p. 199.

[Love in Idleness.]

SUPPLEMENTARY NOTICE

"THIS is the silliest stuff that ever I heard," says Hippolyta, when Wall has "discharged" his part. The answer of Theseus is full of instruction :—"The best in this kind are but shadows; and the worst are no worse if imagination amend them." It was in this humble spirit that the great poet judged of his own matchless performances. He felt the utter inadequacy of his art, and indeed of any art, to produce its due effect upon the mind unless the imagination, to which it addressed itself, was ready to convert the shadows which it presented into living forms of truth and beauty. "I am convinced," says Coleridge, "that Shakspeare availed himself of the title of this play in his own mind, and worked upon it as a dream throughout." The poet says so, in express words :—

"If we shadows have offended,
Think but this, (and all is mended,)
That you have but slumber'd here,
While these visions did appear.
And this weak and idle theme,
No more yielding but a dream,
Gentles, do not reprehend."

But to understand this dream—to have all its gay, and soft, and harmonious colours impressed upon the vision—to hear all the golden cadences of its poesy—to feel the perfect congruity of all its parts, and thus to receive it as a truth—we must not suppose that it will enter the mind amidst the lethargic slumbers of the imagination. We must receive it—

"As youthful poets dream
On summer eves by haunted stream."

Let no one expect that the beautiful influences of this drama can be truly felt when he is under the subjection of the literal and prosaic parts of our nature; or, if he habitually refuses to believe that there are higher and purer regions of thought than are supplied by the physical realities of the world. In these cases he will have a false standard by which to judge of this, and of all other high poetry— such a standard as that possessed by a critic—acute, learned, in many respects wise—Dr. Johnson

SUPPLEMENTARY NOTICE.

who lived in a prosaic age, and fostered in this particular the real ignorance by which he was surrounded. He sums up the merits of A Midsummer-Night's Dream, after this extraordinary fashion:—" Wild and fantastical as this play is, all the parts in their various modes are well written, and give the kind of pleasure which the author designed. Fairies, in his time, were much in fashion: common tradition had made them familiar, and Spenser's poem had made them great." It is perfectly useless to attempt to dissect such criticism: let it be a beacon to warn us, and not a "load-star" to guide us.

Mr. Hallam accounts A Midsummer-Night's Dream poetical, more than dramatic; "yet rather so, because the indescribable profusion of imaginative poetry in this play overpowers our senses, till we can hardly observe anything else, than from any deficiency of **dramatic excellence**. For, in reality, the structure of the fable, consisting as it does of three **if not four actions, very distinct in their subjects and personages, yet wrought into each other without effort or confusion,** displays the skill, or rather instinctive felicity, of Shakspeare, as much as in any play he has written." Yet, certainly, with all its harmony of dramatic arrangement, this play is not for the stage—at least not for the modern stage. It may reasonably be doubted whether it was ever eminently successful **in performance**. The tone of the epilogue is decidedly apologetic, and "the best of **this kind** are but **shadows**," is in the same spirit. Hazlitt has admirably described its failure as an acting drama **in his own day** :—

"The Midsummer-Night's Dream, when acted, is converted from **a delightful fiction into a dull pantomime. All that is finest** in the play is lost in the representation. The spectacle was grand; but the spirit was evaporated, the genius was fled. Poetry and the stage do not agree well together. The attempt to reconcile them in this instance fails not only of effect, but of decorum. The *ideal* can have no place upon the stage, which is a picture without perspective: everything there is in the foreground. That which was merely an airy shape, a dream, a passing thought, immediately becomes an unmanageable reality. Where all is left to the imagination (as is the case in reading), every circumstance, near or remote, has an equal chance of being kept in mind, and tells accordingly to the mixed impression of all that has been suggested. But the imagination cannot sufficiently qualify the actual impressions of the senses. Any offence given to the eye is not to be got rid of by explanation. Thus Bottom's head in the play is a fantastic illusion, produced by magic spells; on the stage it is an ass's head, and nothing more; certainly a very strange costume for a gentleman to appear in. Fancy cannot be embodied any more than a simile can be painted; and it is as idle to attempt it as to personate *Wall* or *Moonshine*."

And yet, just and philosophical as are these remarks, they offer no objection to the opinion of Mr. Hallam, that in this play there is **no deficiency of** dramatic excellence. We can conceive that, with scarcely what can be called **a model before him,** Shakspere's early dramatic attempts must have been a series of experiments to establish a standard by which he should regulate what he addressed to a mixed audience. The **plays** of his middle and **mature** life, with scarcely an exception, are acting plays; and they **are so, not** from the absence of the higher poetry, **but from the predominance** of character **and passion in** association **with it. But even in** those plays **which call for a considerable exercise of the unassisted** imaginative **faculty in an** audience, such **as the Tempest, and A Midsummer-Night's Dream,** where **the passions are** not powerfully **roused, and the senses are not** held **enchained** by the interests of **a plot, he is** still essentially **dramatic. What has been called** of late **years the** dramatic poem—that **something** between **the epic and the dramatic, which is held to form an apology for** whatever **of episodical or incongruous the author may choose to** introduce—was unattempted **by him. The 'Faithful Shepherdess' of Fletcher—a poet who knew how to accommodate himself to the taste of a mixed audience more readily than** Shakspere—was **condemned on the first night of** its **appearance.** Seward, one of **his** editors, **calls this the scandal of our nation. And yet it is extremely difficult to understand how the event should have been otherwise; for the 'Faithful Shepherdess' is essentially undramatic. Its exquisite poetry was therefore thrown away upon** an impatient **audience—its occasional indelicacy could not propitiate them.** Milton's **'Comus'** is in the same **way essentially undramatic; and** none but **such a refined audience as that at** Ludlow Castle **could have endured its** representation. **But the Midsummer-Night's Dream is** composed **altogether upon a different principle. It exhibits all that congruity of parts—that natural** progression of scenes—**that subordination of action and character to one leading design—that ultimate harmony evolved out of seeming confusion—which constitute the dramatic spirit. With "audience fit, though few,"—with a stage not encumbered with**

A MIDSUMMER-NIGHTS DREAM.

decorations,—with actors approaching (if it were so possible) to the idea of grace and aeolness which belong to the fairy troop—the subtle and evanescent beauties of this drama might not be wholly lost in the representation. But under the most favourable circumstances much would be sacrificed. It is in the closet that we must not only suffer our senses to be overpowered by its "indescribable profusion of imaginative poetry," but trace the instinctive felicity of Shakspere in the "structure of the fable." If the Midsummer-Night's Dream could be acted, there can be no doubt how well it would act. Our imagination must amend what is wanting.

Schlegel has happily remarked upon this drama, that "the most extraordinary combination of the most dissimilar ingredients seems to have arisen without effort by some ingenious and lucky accident; and the colours are of such clear transparency, that we think the whole of the variegated fabric may be blown away with a breath." It is not till after we have attentively studied this wonderful production that we understand how solidly the foundations of the fabric are laid. Theseus and Hippolyta move with a stately pace as their nuptial hour draws on. Hermia takes time to pause, before she submits—

"To death, or to a vow of single life,"—

secretly resolving "through Athens' gates to steal." Helena, in the selfishness of her own love, resolves to betray her friend. Bottom the weaver, and Quince the carpenter, and Snug the joiner, and Flute the bellows-mender, and Snout the tinker, and Starveling the tailor, are "thought fit through all Athens to play in the interlude before the Duke and Duchess on his wedding-day, at night." Here are, indeed, "dissimilar ingredients." They appear to have no aptitude for combination. The artists are not yet upon the scene, who are to make a mosaic out of these singular materials. We are only presented in the first act with the extremes of high and low—with the slayer of the Centaurs, and the weaver, who "will roar you an 't were any nightingale,"—with the lofty Amazon, who appears elevated above woman's hopes and fears, and the pretty and satirical Hermia, who swears—

"By all the vows that ever men have broke,
In number more than ever woman spoke."

"The course of true love" does not at all "run smooth" in these opening scenes. We have the love that is crossed, and the love that is unrequited; and worse than all, the unhappiness of Helena makes her treacherous to her friend. We have little doubt that all this will be set straight in the progress of the drama; but what Quince and his company will have to do with the untying of this knot is a mystery.

To offer an analysis of this subtle and ethereal drama would, we believe, be as unsatisfactory as the attempts to associate it with the realities of the stage. With scarcely an exception, the proper understanding of the other plays of Shakspere may be assisted by connecting the apparently separate parts of the action, and by developing and reconciling what seems obscure and anomalous in the features of the characters. But to follow out the caprices and allusions of the loves of Demetrius and Lysander,—of Helena and Hermia;—to reduce to prosaic description the consequence of the jealousies of Oberon and Titania;—to trace the Fairy Queen under the most fantastic of deceptions, where grace and vulgarity blend together like the Cupids and Chimeras of Raphael's Arabesques; and, finally, to go along with the scene till the illusions disappear—till the lovers are happy, and "sweet bully Bottom" is reduced to an ass of human dimensions;—such an attempt as this would be worse even than unreverential criticism. No,—the Midsummer Night's Dream must be left to its own influences.

"It is probable," says Steevens, "that the hint of this play was received from Chaucer's 'Knight's Tale.'" We agree with this opinion, and have noticed some similarities in our Illustrations. Malone has, with great hardihood, asserted that the part of the fable which relates to the quarrels of Oberon and Titania was "not of our author's invention." He has nothing to shew in support of this, but the opinion of Tyrwhitt, that Pluto and Proserpina, in Chaucer's 'Merchant's Tale,' were the true progenitors of Oberon and Titania; that Robert Greene boasts of having performed the King of the Fairies, and that Greene has introduced Oberon in his play of 'James IV.' (See Illustrations of Act II.) Malone's assertion, and the mode altogether in which he speaks of this drama, furnish a decisive proof of his incompetence to judge of the higher poetry of Shakspere. Because the names of Oberon and Titania existed before Shakspere, he did not invent his Oberon

SUPPLEMENTARY NOTICE.

and Titania! The opinion of Mr. Hallam may correct some of the errors which the commentators have laboured to propagate. "The Midsummer-Night's Dream is, I believe, altogether original in one of the most beautiful conceptions that ever visited the mind of a poet, the fairy machinery. A few before him had dealt in a vulgar and clumsy manner with popular superstitions; but the sportive, beneficent, invisible population of the air and earth, long since established in the creed of childhood, and of those simple as children, had never for a moment been blended with 'human mortals' among the personages of the drama. Lyly's 'Maid's Metamorphosis' is probably later than this play of Shakspeare, and was not published till 1600. It is unnecessary to observe that the fairies of Spenser, as he has dealt with them, are wholly of a different race."* Of these imaginary beings Gervinus says,—

"Separated from their external actions and their reference to human kind, it is marvellous how Shakspere has made their inner character correspond with their outward occupations. He has represented them as beings without any delicate feelings and without morals—as in a dream we receive no shock to our sympathies and are without any moral rules or apprehensions. They carelessly, and without convenience, mislead human creatures to faithlessness; the effects of the changes which they cause make no impressions upon their minds; they take no part in the inward torment of the lovers, but only sport and wonder at their apparent errors, and the folly of their behaviour. . . . These little deities are depicted as natural souls without the higher capabilities of the human spirit; lords, not of the realms of reason and morals, but of material ideas and the charms of imagination; and therefore equally the creatures of the fancy which works in dreams and the illusions of love. Their notions thus go not beyond the corporeal. They lead a luxurious and cheerful natural and sensual life; they possess a knowledge of the secrets of nature, the powers of flowers and plants. To sleep in blossoms, lulled by song and dance, guarded from the moonbeams, fanned by the wings of butterflies, is their delight; attire of flowers with pearls of dew their pride; if Titania desires to tempt her new love she proffers him honey, apricots, grapes, and a dance. This simple and sensual life is mingled, by the power of fancy, with a delight in, and a desire for, whatever is choicest, beautiful, and agreeable. With butterflies and nightingales they sympathize; they make war on all ugly animals, hedgehogs, spiders, and bats; dance, sport, and song are their highest enjoyments; they steal beautiful children and substitute changelings; deformed old age, toothless gossips, 'wisest aunts,' the clumsy associates in the play of Pyramus and Thisbe, they annoy; while they love and reward cleanliness and kindness. This accords with the popular belief. . . . Their sense of the beautiful is perhaps the only superiority they have, not only over the mere animal, but over the low human creatures utterly destitute of any appreciation of the fanciful or beautiful. Thus to the notions of the fairies, whose sense of the fitting and agreeable have been so finely developed, it must have been doubly comic that the elegant Titania should have become enamoured of an ass's head."

* Literature of Europe, vol. ii. p. 388.

[Group of Fairies.]

[Venice. From the Lagunes.]

INTRODUCTORY NOTICE.

STATE OF THE TEXT, AND CHRONOLOGY, OF THE MERCHANT OF VENICE.

THE MERCHANT OF VENICE, like A Midsummer-Night's Dream, was first printed in 1600; and it had a further similarity to that play from the circumstance of two editions appearing in the same year—the one bearing the name of a publisher, Thomas Heyes, the other that of a printer, J. Roberts. The edition of Heyes is printed by J. Roberts; and it is probable that he, the printer, obtained the first copy. On the 22nd of July, 1598, the following entry was made in the books of the Stationers' Company:—"James Robertes. A booke of the Marchaunt of Venyce, or otherwise called the Jewe of Venyce. Provided that yt bee not prynted by the said James Robertes or anye other whatsoever, without lycence first had of the right honourable the Lord Chamberlen." The title of Roberts' edition is very circumstantial:—"The excellent History of the Merchant of Venice. With the extreme cruelty of Shylocke the Jew towards the said Merchant, in cutting a just pound of his flesh. And the obtaining of Portia by the choyce of three Caskets. Written by W. Shakespeare." On the 28th of October, 1600, Thomas Haies enters at Stationers' Hall, "The book of the Merchant of Venyce." The edition of Heyes is by no means identical with that of Roberts; but the differences are not many. In the title page of that edition we have added:— "As it hath beene divers times acted by the Lord Chamberlaine his Servants." The play was not reprinted till it appeared in the folio of 1623. In that edition there are a few variations from the quartos, which we have indicated in our notes. All these editions present the internal evidence of having been printed from correct copies.

The Merchant of Venice is one of the plays of Shakspere mentioned by Francis Meres in 1598, and it is the last mentioned in his list. From the original entry at Stationers' Hall, in 1598, providing that it be not printed without licence first had of the Lord Chamberlain, it may be assumed that it had not then been acted by the Lord Chamberlain's servants. We know, however, so little about the formalities of licence that we cannot regard this point as certain. Malone considers that a play called the 'Venesyan Comedy,' which it appears from Henslowe's Manuscripts was acted in 1594, was The

INTRODUCTORY NOTICE.

Merchant of Venice; and he has therefore assigned it to 1594. He supports this by one military conjecture. In Act III. Portia exclaims:—

"He may win;
And what is music then? then music is
Even as the flourish when true subjects bow
To a new-crowned monarch."

Malone considers that this alludes to the coronation of Henry IV. of France, in 1594. Chalmers would fix it in 1597, because, when Antonio says,—

"Nor is my whole estate
Upon the fortune of this present year,"—

he alludes to 1597, which was a year of calamity to merchants. Surely this is laborious trifling. We know absolutely nothing of the date of The Merchant of Venice beyond what is furnished by the entry at Stationers' Hall, and the notice by Meres.

SUPPOSED SOURCE OF THE PLOT.

STEPHEN GOSSON, who, in 1579, was moved to publish a tract, called 'The School of Abuse, containing a pleasant invective against poets, pipers, players, jesters, and such like caterpillars of the commonwealth,' thus describes a play of his time:—"The Jew, shewn at the Bull, representing the greedyness of worldly choosers, and the bloody minds of usurers." Mr. Skottowe somewhat leaps to a conclusion that this play contains the same plot as The Merchant of Venice:—"The loss of this performance is justly a subject of regret, for, as it combined within its plot the two incidents of the bond and the caskets, it would, in all probability, have thrown much additional light on Shakspeare's progress in the composition of his highly-finished comedy."* As all we know of this play is told us by Gosson, it is rather bold to assume that it combined the two incidents of the bond and the caskets. The combination of these incidents is perhaps one of the most remarkable examples of Shakspere's dramatic skill. "In the management of the plot," says Mr. Hallam, "which is sufficiently complex without the slightest confusion or incoherence, I do not conceive that it has been surpassed in the annals of any theatre." The rude dramatists of 1579 were not remarkable for the combination of incidents. It was probably reserved for the skill of Shakspere to bring the caskets and the bond in juxtaposition. He found the incidents far apart, but it was for him to fuse them together. We cannot absolutely deny Mr. Douce's conjecture that the play mentioned by Gosson *might* have furnished our poet with the whole of the plot; but it is certainly an abuse of language to say that it *did* furnish him, because the Jew shewn at the Bull deals with "worldly choosers," and the "bloody minds of usurers." We admit that the coincidence is curious.

Whatever might have been the plot of the 'Jew' mentioned by Gosson, the story of the bond was ready to Shakspere's hand, in a ballad to which Warton first drew attention. He considers that the ballad was written before The Merchant of Venice, for reasons which we shall subsequently point out. In the mean time we reprint this curious production from the copy in Percy's 'Reliques:'—

A NEW SONG.

SHEWING THE CRUELTIE OF GERNUTUS, A JEWE, WHO, LENDING TO A MERCHANT AN HONDRED CROWNS, WOULD HAVE A POUND OF HIS FLESHE, BECAUSE HE COULD NOT PAY HIM AT THE TIME APPOINTED.

To the Tune of 'Blacks and Yellow.'

THE FIRST PART.

In Venice towne not long agoe
A cruel Jew did dwell,
Which lived all on usurie,
As Italian writers tell.

Gernutus called was the Jew,
Which never thought to dye;
Nor ever yet did any good
To them in streets that lie.

His life was like a barrow hogge,
That liveth many a day,
Yet never once doth any good,
Until men will him slay.

Or like a filthy heap of dung,
That lyeth in a whoard;
Which never can do any good,
Till it be spread abroad.

* Life of Shakspeare, vol. i. p. 336.

INTRODUCTORY NOTICE.

So farae it with the usurer,
  He cannot sleep in rest,
For feare the thiefe will him pursue
  To plucke him from his nest.

His heart doth thinke on many a wile,
  How to deceive the poore:
His mouth is almost ful of mucke,
  Yet still he gapes for more.

His wife must lend a shilling,
  For every weeke a penny,
Yet bring a pledge, that is double worth,
  If that you will have any.

And see, likewise, you keepe your day
  Or else you loose it all:
This was the living of the wife,
  Her cow she did it call.

Within that citie dwelt that time
  A marchant of great fame,
Which, being distressed in his need,
  Unto Gernutus came:

Desiring him to stand his friend
  For twelve month and a day,
To lend to h m an hundred crownes:
  And he for it would pay

Whatsoever he would demand of him,
  And pledges he should have.
No, (quoth the Jew, with fleuring lookes,)
  Sir, aske what you will have.

No penny for the loane of it
  For one year you shall pay;
You may doe me as good a turne,
  Before my dying day.

But we will have a merry feast,
  For to be talked long:
You shall make me a bond, quoth he,
  That shall be large and strong:

And this shall be the forfeyture
  Of your own fleshe a pound.
If you agree, make you the bond,
  And here is a hundred crownes.

With right good will! the marchant says:
  And so the bond was made.
When twelve month and a day drew on
  That backe it should be payd,

The marchant's ships were all at sea,
  And money came not in;
Which way to take, or what to don,
  To think he doth begin;

And to Gernutus strait he comes
  With cap and bended knee,
And sayde to him, Of curtesie
  I pray you beare with mee.

My day is come, and I have not
  The money for to pay:
And little good the forfeyture
  Will doe you, I dare say.

With all my heart, Gernutus sayd,
  Commaund it to your minde:
In things of bigger waight then this
  You shall me ready finde.

He goes his way; the day once past,
  Gernutus doth not slacke
To get a sergiant presently;
  And clapt him on the backe:

And layd him into prison strong,
  And sued his bond withall;
And when the judgement day was come,
  For judgement he did call.

The marchant's friends came thither fast,
  With many a weeping eye,
For other meanes they could not find,
  But he that day must dye.

THE SECOND PART.

OF THE JEW'S CRUELTIE; SETTING FORTH THE MERCIFULNESSE OF THE JUDGE TOWARDS THE MARCHANT

To the Tune of 'Blacke and Yellow.'

Some offered for his hundred crownes
  Five hundred for to pay;
And some a thousand, two, or three,
  Yet still he did denay.

And at the last ten thousand crownes
  They offered, him to save.
Gernutus sayd, I will no gold:
  My forfeite I will have.

A pound of fleshe is my demand,
  And that shall be my hire.
Then sayd the Judge, Yet, good, my friend,
  Let me of you desire

To take the fleshe from such a place,
  As yet you let him live:
Do so, and lo! an hundred crownes
  To thee here will I give.

No; no; quoth he; no; judgement here
  For this it shall be tride,
For I will have my pound of fleshe
  From under his right side.

It grieved all the companie
  His crueltie to see,
For neither friend nor foe could helpe,
  But he must spoyled bee.

The bloudie Jew now ready is
  With whetted blade in hand,
To spoyle the bloud of innocent,
  By forfeite of his bond.

And as he was about to strike
  In him the deadly blow,
Stay (quoth the judge) thy crueltie;
  I charge thee to do so.

Sith needs thou wilt thy forfeite have,
  Which is of fleshe a pound,
See that thou shed no drop of bloud,
  Nor yet the man confound.

For if thou doe, like murderer,
  Thou here shalt hanged be:
Likewise of flesh see that thou cut
  No more than 'longes to thee:

THE MERCHANT OF VENICE

For if thou take either more or lesse
 To the value of a mite,
Thou shalt be hanged presently,
 As is both law and right.

Gernutus now waxt frantic mad,
 And woies not what to say;
Quoth he at last, Ten thousand crownes
 I will that he shall pay;

And so I graunt to let him free.
 The judge doth answere make:
You shall not have a penny given;
 Your forfeyture now take.

At the last he doth demaund
 But for to have his owne.
No, quoth the judge, doe as you list,
 Thy judgement shall be showne.

Either take your pound of flesh, quoth he,
 Or cancell me your bond.

O cruell judge, then quoth the Jew,
 That doth against me stand!

And so with gripìng grieved mind
 He biddeth them fare-well.
Then all the people pray'd the Lord,
 That ever this heard tell.

Good people, that doe heare this song,
 For trueth I dare well say,
That many a wretch as ill as hee
 Doth live now at this day;

That seeketh nothing but the spoyle
 Of many a wealthey man,
And for to trap the innocent
 Deviseth what they can.

From whome the Lord deliver me,
 And every Christian too,
And send to them like sentence eke
 That meaneth so to do.

Warton's opinion of the priority of this ballad to The Merchant of Venice is thus expressed:—" It may be objected, that this ballad might have been written after, and copied from Shakespeare's play. But if that had been the case, it is most likely that the author would have preserved Shakespeare's name of Shylock for the Jew; and nothing is more likely than that Shakespeare, in copying from this ballad, should alter the name from Gernutus to one more Jewish . . . Our ballad has the air of a narrative written before Shakespeare's play; I mean, that if it had been written after the play, it would have been much more full and circumstantial. At present, it has too much the nakedness of an original."* The reasoning of Warton is scarcely borne out by a new fact, for which we are indebted to the indefatigable researches of Mr. Collier. Thomas Jordan, in 1664, printed a ballad or romance, called, 'The Forfeiture;' and Mr. Collier says:—"So much does Shakespeare's production seem to have been forgotten in 1664, that Thomas Jordan made a ballad of it, and printed it as an original story (at least without any acknowledgment), in his *Royal Arbor of Loyal Poesie*, in that year. In the same scarce little volume he also uses the plot of the serious part of Much Ado About Nothing, and of The Winter's Tale, both of which had been similarly laid by for a series of years, partly, perhaps, on account of the silencing of the theatres from and after 1642. The circumstance has hitherto escaped observation; and Jordan felt authorized to take such liberties with the story of The Merchant of Venice, that he has represented the Jew's daughter, instead of Portia, as assuming the office of assessor to the Duke of Venice in the trial-scene, for the sake of saving the life of the Merchant, with whom she was in love."† Now, it is remarkable that this ballad by Jordan, which was unquestionably written *after* the play, is much less full and circumstantial than the old ballad of 'Gernutus;' so that Warton's argument, as a general principle, will not hold. It appears to us that 'Gernutus' is, in reality, very full and circumstantial; and that some of the circumstances are identical with those of the play. Compare, for example,—

 "Go with me to a notary, seal me there
 Your single bond; and in *a merry sport*," &c.

with,—

 "But we will have *a merry feast*,
 For to be talked on,
 You shall make me a bond, quoth he
 That shall be large and strong."

And, again, compare

with

 "Why dost thou whet thy knife so earnestly?"

 "The bloudie Jew now ready is
 With whetted blade in hand."

It will be observed, however, that the ballad of 'Gernutus' wants that remarkable feature of the play, the intervention of Portia to save the life of the Merchant; and this, to our minds, is the

* 'Observations on The Fairy Queen,' 1807, vol. i. p. 182.
† 'New Particulars regarding the Works of Shakspeare,' p. 96.

INTRODUCTORY NOTICE.

strongest confirmation that the ballad *preceded* the comedy. Shakspere found that incident in the source from which the ballad-writer professed to derive his history:—

"In Venice towne not long agoe,
A cruel Jew did dwell,
Which lived all on usurie,
As *Italian writers* tell."

It was from an Italian writer, Ser Giovanni, the author of a collection of tales, called, *Il Pecorone*, written in the fourteenth century, and first published at Milan in 1558, that Shakspere unquestionably derived some of the incidents of his story, although he might be familiar with another version of the same tale. An abstract of this chapter of the *Pecorone* may be found in Mr. Dunlop's 'History of Fiction;' and a much fuller epitome of a scarce translation of the tale, printed in 1755, was first given in Johnson's edition of Shakspere, and is reprinted in all the variorum editions. In this story we have a rich lady *at Belmont*, who is to be won upon certain conditions; and she is finally the prize of a young merchant, whose friend, having become surety for him to a Jew, under the same penalty as in the play, is rescued from the forfeiture by the adroitness of the married lady, who is disguised as a lawyer. The pretended judge receives, as in the comedy, her marriage ring as a gratuity; and afterwards banters her husband, in the same way, upon the loss of it.

Some of the stories of *Il Pecorone*, as indeed of Boccaccio, and other early Italian writers, appear to have been the common property of Europe, derived from some Oriental origin. Mr. Douce has given an extremely curious extract from the English *Gesta Romanorum*,—"A Manuscript, preserved in the Harleian Collection, No. 7333, written in the reign of Henry the Sixth," in which the daughter of "Selestinus, a wise emperor in Rome," exacts somewhat similar conditions, from a knight who loved her, as the lady in the *Pecorone*. Being reduced to poverty by a compliance with these conditions, he applies to a merchant to lend him money; and the loan is granted under the following covenant:—" And the covenaunt shalle be this, that thou make to me a charter of thine owne blood, in condicion that yf thowe kepe not thi day of payment, hit shalle be lefulle to me for to draw awey alle the flesh of thy body froo the bone with a sharp swerde, and yf thow wolt assent hereto, I shalle fulfille thi wille." In this ancient story, the borrower of the money makes himself subject to the penalty without the intervention of a friend; and, having forgotten the day of payment, is authorised by his wife to give any sum which is demanded. The money is refused by the merchant, and the charter of blood exacted. Judgment was given against the knight; but, "the damysell, his love, whenne she harde tell that the lawe passid agenst him, she kytte of al the long her of hir hede, and cladde hir in precious clothing like to a man, and yede to the palys." The scene that ensues in the *Gesta Romanorum* has certainly more resemblance to the conduct of the incident in Shakspere than the similar one in the *Pecorone*. Having given a specimen of the *language* of the manuscript of Henry the Sixth's time, which Mr. Douce thinks was of the same period as the writing, we shall continue the story in orthography which will present fewer difficulties to many of our readers, and which will allow them to feel the beautiful simplicity of this ancient romance. We have no doubt that Shakspere was familiar with this part of the *Gesta Romanorum*, as well as of that portion from which he derived the story of the caskets, to which we shall presently advert:—" Now in all this time, the damsel his love, had sent knights for to espy and inquire how the law was pursued against him. And when she heard tell that the law passed against him, she cut off all the long hair of her head, and clad her in precious clothing like to a man, and went to the palace where her leman was to be judged, and saluted the justice, and all trowed that she had been a knight. And the judge inquired of what country she was, and what she had to do there. She said, I am a knight, and come of far country; and bear tidings that there is a knight among you that should be judged to death, for an obligation that he made to a merchant, and therefore I am come to deliver him. Then the judge said, It is law of the emperor, that whosoever bindeth him with his own proper will and consent without any constraining, he should be served so again. When the damsel heard this, she turned to the merchant, and said, Dear friend, what profit is it to thee that this knight, that standeth here redy to the doom, be slain? It were better to thee to have money than to have him slain. Thou speakest all in vain, quoth the merchant; for, without doubt, I will have the law, since he bound himself so freely; and therefore he shall have none other grace than law will, for he came to me, and I not to him. I desire him not thereto against his will. Then said she, I pray thee how much shall I give to have my petition? I shall give thee thy money double; and if that be not pleasing to thee, ask of me what thou wilt, and thou shalt have. Then said he, Thou heardest me never say but that I would have my covenant kept. Truly, said she; and I say before you, Sir Judge, and before you all, thou shalt believe me with a right knowledge of that I shall say to you. Ye have heard how much I have proffered this merchant for the life of this knight, and he forsaketh oil and asketh for more, and that liketh me much. And, therefore, lordings that be here, hear me what I shall say. Ye know well, that the knight bound him by letter that the merchant should have power to cut his flesh from the bones, but there was no covenant made of shedding of blood. Thereof was nothing spoken; and, therefore, let him set hand on him anon; and if he shed any blood with his shaving of the flesh, forsooth, then shall the king have good law upon him. And when the merchant heard this, he said, Give me my money, and I forgive my action. Forsooth. quoth she, thou shalt not have one penny. for before all this company I proffered to thee all that I might, and thou forsook it, and saidst loudly, I shall have my covenant; and therefore do thy best with him, but look that thou shed no blood I charge thee, for it is not thine, and no covenant was thereof. Then the merchant seeing this, went away confounded; and so was the knight's life saved, and no penny paid."

In 'The Orator,' translated from the French of Alexander Silvayn, printed in 1596, the arguments urged by a Jew and a Christian, under similar circumstances, are set forth at great length. It has been generally asserted that Shakspere borrowed from this source; but the similarity appears to us exceedingly small. The arguments, or declamations, as they are called, are given at length in the variorum editions.

"It is well known," says Mrs. Jameson, "that The Merchant of Venice is founded on two different tales; and in weaving together his double plot in so masterly a manner, Shakspere has rejected altogether the character of the astutious lady of Belmont, with her magic potions, who figures in the Italian novel. With yet more refinement, he has thrown out all the licentious part of the story, which some of his cotemporary dramatists would have seized on with avidity, and made the best or the worst of it possible; and he has substituted the trial of the caskets from another source."* That source is the *Gesta Romanorum*. In Mr. Douce's elaborate treatise upon this most singular collection of ancient stories, we have the following analysis of the ninety-ninth chapter of the English *Gesta*; which, Mr. Douce says, " is obviously the story which supplied the caskets of The Merchant of Venice." .... " A marriage was proposed between the son of Anselmus, emperor of Rome, and the daughter of the king of Apulia. The young lady in her voyage was shipwrecked and swallowed by a whale. In this situation she contrived to make a fire and to wound the animal with a knife, so that he was driven towards the shore, and slain of an earl named Pirius, who delivered the princess and took her under his protection. On relating her story she was conveyed to the emperor. In order to prove whether she was worthy to receive the hand of his son, he placed before her three vessels. The first was of gold, and filled with dead men's bones; on it was this inscription—' *Who chuses me shall find what he deserves.*' The second was of silver, filled with earth, and thus inscribed—' *Who chuses me shall find what nature covets.*' The third vessel was of lead, but filled with precious stones; it had this inscription—' *Who chuses me shall find what God hath placed.*' The emperor then commanded her to chuse one of the vessels, informing her that if she made choice of that which should profit herself and others, she would obtain his son; if of what should profit neither herself nor others, she would lose him. The princess, after praying to God for assistance, preferred the leaden vessel. The emperor informed her that she had chosen as he wished, and immediately united her with his son."

In dealing with the truly dramatic subject of the forfeiture of the bond, Shakspere had to choose between one of two courses that lay open before him. The *Gesta Romanorum* did not surround the debtor and the creditor with any prejudices. We hear nothing of one being a Jew, the other a Christian. There is a remarkable story told by Gregorio Leti, in his Life of Pope Sixtus the Fifth, in which the debtor and creditor of The Merchant of Venice change places. The debtor is the Jew,— the revengeful creditor the Christian; and this incident is said to have happened at Rome in the time of Sir Francis Drake. This, no doubt, was a pure fiction of Leti, whose narratives are by no means to

---

* 'Characteristics of Women,' vol. I. p. 72.

INTRODUCTORY NOTICE

be received as authorities; but it shows that he felt the intolerance of the old story, and endeavoured to correct it, though in a very inartificial manner. Shakspere took the story as he found it in those narratives which represented the popular prejudice. If he had not before him the ballad of 'Gernutus,' (upon which point it is difficult to decide,) he had certainly access to the tale of the *Pecorone.* If he had made the contest connected with the story of the bond between two of the same faith, he would have lost the most powerful hold which the subject possessed upon the feelings of an audience, two centuries and a half ago. If he had gone directly counter to those feelings, (supposing that the story which Leti tells had been known to him, as some have supposed,) his comedy would have been hooted from the stage. The ballad of 'Gernutus' has the following amongst its concluding stanzas:—

> " Good people, that doe heare this song
> For trueth I dare well say,
> That many a wretch as ill as hee
> Doth live now at this day:
>
> That seeketh nothing but the spoyle
> Of many a wealthey man,
> And for to trap the innocent
> Deviseth what they can."

It is probable that, although the Jews had been under an edict of banishment from England from the time of Edward I., they had crept into the country after the Reformation. Lord Bacon says that the objectors against usury maintained " That usurers should have orange-tawny bonnets, because they do judaize." The orange-tawny bonnet was the descendant of the *badge of yellow felt*, of the length of six inches, and of the breadth of three inches, to be worn by each Jew after he shall be seven years old, upon his outer garment. *(Stat. de Jeuerie.)* The persecuted race settled again openly in England after the Restoration; and the pious wish, with which Thomas Jordan's ballad concludes, has evidently reference to this circumstance :—

> " I wish such Jews may never come
> To England, nor to London."

The 'Prioress's Tale' of Chaucer belonged to the period when the Jews were robbed, maimed, banished, and most foully vilified, with the universal consent of the powerful and the lowly, the learned and the ignorant :—

> " There was in Asie, In a gret citee,
> Amonges Cristen folk a Jewerie,
> Susteined by a lord of that contree,
> For foul usure, and lucre of vilanie,
> Hateful to Crist, and to his compagnie."

It was scarcely to be avoided in those times, that even Chaucer, the most genuine and natural of poets, should lend his great powers to the support of the popular belief, that Jews ought to be proscribed as—

> Hateful to Crist, and to his compagnie."

But we ought to expect better things when we reach the times in which the principles of religious liberty were at least germinated. And yet what a play is Marlowe's 'Jew of Malta,'—undoubtedly one of the most popular plays even of Shakspere's day, judging as we may from the number of performances recorded in Henslowe's papers! That drama, as compared with The Merchant of Venice, has been described by Charles Lamb, with his usual felicity :—" Marlowe's Jew does not approach so near to Shakspere's as his Edward II. Shylock, in the midst of his savage purpose, is a man. His motives, feelings, resentments, have something human in them. 'If you wrong us, shall we not revenge?' Barabas is a mere monster, brought in with a large painted nose, to please the rabble. He kills in sport—poisons whole nunneries—invents infernal machines. He is just such an exhibition as a century or two earlier might have been played before the Londoners, *by the Royal command*, when a general pillage and massacre of the Hebrews had been previously resolved on in the cabinet." 'The Jew of Malta' was written essentially upon an intolerant principle. The Merchant of Venice, whilst it seized upon the prejudices of the multitude, and dealt with them as a foregone conclusion by which the whole dramatic action was to be governed, had the intention of making those prejudices as hateful as the reaction of cruelty and revenge of which they are the cause. We shall endeavour to work out this position in our Supplementary Notice.

THE MERCHANT OF VENICE.

PERIOD OF THE ACTION, AND MANNERS.

THE Venice of Shakspere's own time, and the manners of that city, are delineated with matchless accuracy in this drama. To the same friend who furnished us with some local illustrations of The Taming of the Shrew, we are indebted for some equally interesting notices of similar passages in this play. They go far to prove that Shakspere had visited Italy. Mr. Brown has justly observed, " The Merchant of Venice is a merchant of no other place in the world."

[Costume of the Doge of Venice.]

COSTUME.

THE dresses of the most civilised nations of Europe have at all periods borne a strong resemblance to each other: the various fashions have been generally invented amongst the southern, and gradually adopted by the northern, ones. Some slight distinctions, however, have always remained to characterise, more or less particularly, the country of which the wearer was a native; and the Republic of Venice, perhaps, differed more than any other State in the habits of its nobles, magistrates, and merchants, from the universal fashion of that quarter of the globe in which it was situate.

To commence with the chief officer of the Republic :—The Doge, like the Pope, appears to have worn different habits on different occasions. Cæsar Vecellio describes at some length the alterations made in the ducal dress by several princes, from the close of the twelfth century down to that of the sixteenth, the period of the action of the play before us; at which time the materials of which it was usually composed were cloth of silver, cloth of gold, and crimson velvet, the cap always corresponding in colour with the robe and mantle. On the days sacred to the Holy Virgin the Doge always appeared entirely in white. Coryat, who travelled in 1608, says, in his 'Crudities,' "The fifth day of August, being Friday . . . I saw the Duke in some of his richest ornaments. . . . He himself then wore two very rich robes, or long garments, whereof the uppermost was white cloth of silver, with great massy buttons of gold; the other cloth of silver also, but adorned with many curious works made in colours with needlework." Howell, in his 'Survey of the Signorie of Venice,' Lond. 1651, after telling us that the Duke "always goes clad in silk and

INTRODUCTORY NOTICE.

purple," observes, that "sometimes he shows himself to the public in a robe of cloth of gold, and a white mantle; he hath his head covered with a thin coif, and on his forehead he wears a crimson kind of mitre, with a gold border, and, behind, it turns up in form of a horn: on his shoulders he carries ermine skins to the middle, which is still a badge of the Consul's habit; on his feet he wears embroidered sandals,* tied with gold buttons, and about his middle a most rich belt, embroidered with costly jewels, in so much, that the habit of the Duke, when at festivals he shows himself in the highest state, is valued at about 100,000 crowns."†

The chiefs of the Council of Ten, who were three in number, wore "red gowns with long sleeves, either of cloth, camlet, or damask, according to the weather, with a flap of the same colour over their left shoulders, red stockings, and slippers." The rest of the Ten, according to Coryat, were black camlet gowns with marvellous long sleeves, that reach almost down to the ground.

[Costume of 'the Clarissimoes.']

The "clarissimoes" generally wore gowns of black cloth faced with black taffata, with a flap of black cloth, edged with taffata, over the left shoulder;‡ and "all these gowned men," says the same author, "do wear marvellous little black caps of felt, without any brims at all, and very diminutive falling bands, no ruffs at all, which are so shallow, that I have seen many of them not above a little inch deep." The colour of their under garments was also generally black, and consisted of "a slender doublet made close to the body, without much quilting or bombast, and long hose plain, without those new-fangled curiosities and ridiculous superfluities of panes, plaits, and other light toys used with us Englishmen. Yet," he continues, "they make it of costly stuff, well beseeming gentlemen and eminent persons of their places, as of the best taffatas and satins that Christendom doth yield, which are fairly garnished also with lace of the best sort. The Knights of St. Mark, or of the Order of the Glorious Virgin, &c., were distinguished by wearing red apparel under their black gowns." "Young lovers," says Vecellio, "wear generally a doublet and breeches of satin, tabby, or other silk, cut or slashed in the form of crosses or stars, through which slashes is seen the lining of coloured taffata: gold buttons, a lace ruff, a bonnet of rich velvet or silk with an ornamental band, a silk cloak, and silk stockings, Spanish morocco shoes, a flower in one hand, and their gloves and handkerchief in the other." This habit, he tells us,

---

* C. Vecellio, a much better authority, says slippers. "Porta in piedi le piandelle più del medesimo usasi anche da cavalieri nobili di Venetia."
† In the collection at Goodrich Court is the walking-staff of a Doge of Venice of the sixteenth century.
‡ Garzas.

THE MERCHANT OF VENICE.

was worn by many of the nobility, as well of Venice as of other Italian cities, especially by the young men before they put on the gown with the sleeves, "a comito," which was generally in their eighteenth or twentieth year.

[Costume of the 'young lover.']

Vecellio also furnishes us with the dress of a doctor of laws, the habit in which Portia defends Antonio. The upper robe was of black damask cloth, velvet, or silk according to the weather. The under one of black silk with a silk sash, the ends of which hang down to the middle of the leg; the stockings of black cloth or velvet; the cap of rich velvet or silk.

[Costume of a Doctor of Laws.]

INTRODUCTORY NOTICE

And now to speak of the dress of the principal character of this play. Great difference of opinion has existed, and much ink been shed, upon this subject, as it seems to us very needlessly. If a work, written and published by Venetians in their own city, at the particular period when this play was composed, is not sufficient authority, we know not what can be considered such. Vecellio expressly informs us that the Jews differed in nothing, as far as regarded dress, from Venetians of the same professions, whether merchants, artisans, &c.,* with the exception of a *yellow bonnet*, which they were *compelled to wear by order of the government*.† Can anything be more distinct and satisfactory? In opposition to this positive assertion of a Venetian writing upon the actual subject of dress, we have the statement of Saint Didier, who, in his 'Histoire de Venise,' says that the Jews of Venice wore *scarlet hats lined with black taffata*, and a notification in Hakluyt's 'Voyages' (p. 179, edit. 1598), that in the year 1581 the Jews wore *red caps* for distinction's sake. We remember also to have met somewhere with a story, apparently in confirmation of this latter statement, that the colour was changed from *red* to *yellow*, in consequence of a Jew having been accidentally taken for a cardinal! But besides that neither of the two last-mentioned works are to be compared with Vecellio's, in respect of authority for what may be termed Venetian costume, it is not likely that scarlet, a sacred colour among Catholics generally, and appropriated particularly by the Venetian knights and principal magistrates, would be selected for a badge of degradation, or rather infamous distinction. Now yellow, on the contrary, has always been in Europe a mark of disgrace. Tenne (i. e orange) was considered by many heralds as *stainant*. The Jews, in England, wore yellow caps of a peculiar shape as early as the reign of Richard I.; and Lord Verulam, in his 'Essay on Usury,' speaking of the witty invectives that men have made against usury, states one of them to be that "usurers should have *orange-tawny bonnets*, because they do *Judaize*."

As late, also, as the year 1825, an order was issued by the Pope that "the Jews should wear a *yellow* covering on their hats, and the women a *yellow* riband on their breast, under the pain of severe penalties."—Vide *Examiner*, Sunday Newspaper, Nov. 20th, 1825. The which order there can be little doubt, from the evidence before us, was the re-enforcement of the old edict, latterly disregarded by the Jews of Italy. It is not impossible that "the orange-tawny bonnet" might have been worn of so deep a colour by some of the Hebrew population as to have been described as red by a careless observer, or that some Venetian Jews, in fact, did venture to wear red caps or bonnets in defiance of the statute, and thereby misled the traveller or the historian. We cannot, however imagine that a doubt can exist of the propriety of Shylock wearing a yellow, or, at all events, an orange-coloured, cap of the same form as the black one of the Christian Venetian merchants. Shakspere makes Shylock speak of "his Jewish gaberdine;" but, independently of Vecellio's assurance, that no difference existed between the dress of the Jewish and Christian merchants save the yellow bonnet, aforesaid, the word gaberdine conveys to us no precise form of garment, its description being different in nearly every dictionary, foreign or English. In German it is called a rock or frock, a mantle, coat, petticoat, gown, or cloak. In Italian, "*palandrano*," or "great-coat," and "*gavardina*, a peasant's jacket." The French have only "*gaban*" and "*gabardine*,"—cloaks for rainy weather. In Spanish, "*gubardina*" is rendered a sort of cassock with close-buttoned sleeves. In English, a shepherd's coarse frock or coat.

Speaking of the ladies of Venice, Coryat says, "Most of these women, when they walk abroad, especially to church, are veiled with long veils, whereof some do reach almost to the ground behind. These veils are either black, or white, or yellowish. The black, either wives or widows do wear; the white, maids, and so the yellowish also, but they wear more white than yellowish. It is the custom of these maids, when they walk the streets, to cover their faces with their veils, the stuff being so thin and slight, that they may easily look through it, for it is made of a pretty slender silk, and very finely curled. . . . Now, whereas I said that only maids do wear white veils, I mean these white silk curled veils, which (as they told me) none do wear but maids. But other white veils wives do much wear, such as are made in Holland, whereof the greatest part is handsomely edged with great and very fair bonelace."

The account in Howell's 'Survey' differs slightly from Coryat's, but Vecellio confirms the latter and states that courtezans wore black veils, in imitation of women of character.

---

* "Imitano gli altri mercanti e artigiani di questa litta." Edit. 1590
† "Portano per commandamento publico la berretta gialla." Ibid

397

THE MERCHANT OF VENICE.

Jewish females, Vecellio says, were distinguished from Christian women by their being "highly *painted*," and wearing *yellow* veils, but that in other respects their dresses were perfectly similar.* We must not forget to mention that singular portion of a Venetian lady's costume at this period, "the chioppine;" but, as we have already described and given an engraving of several varieties of this monstrosity in our Illustrations of the second Act of Hamlet, we refer the reader to page 126 of that tragedy.

* Edit. 1590.

[Costume of a Lady of Venice.]

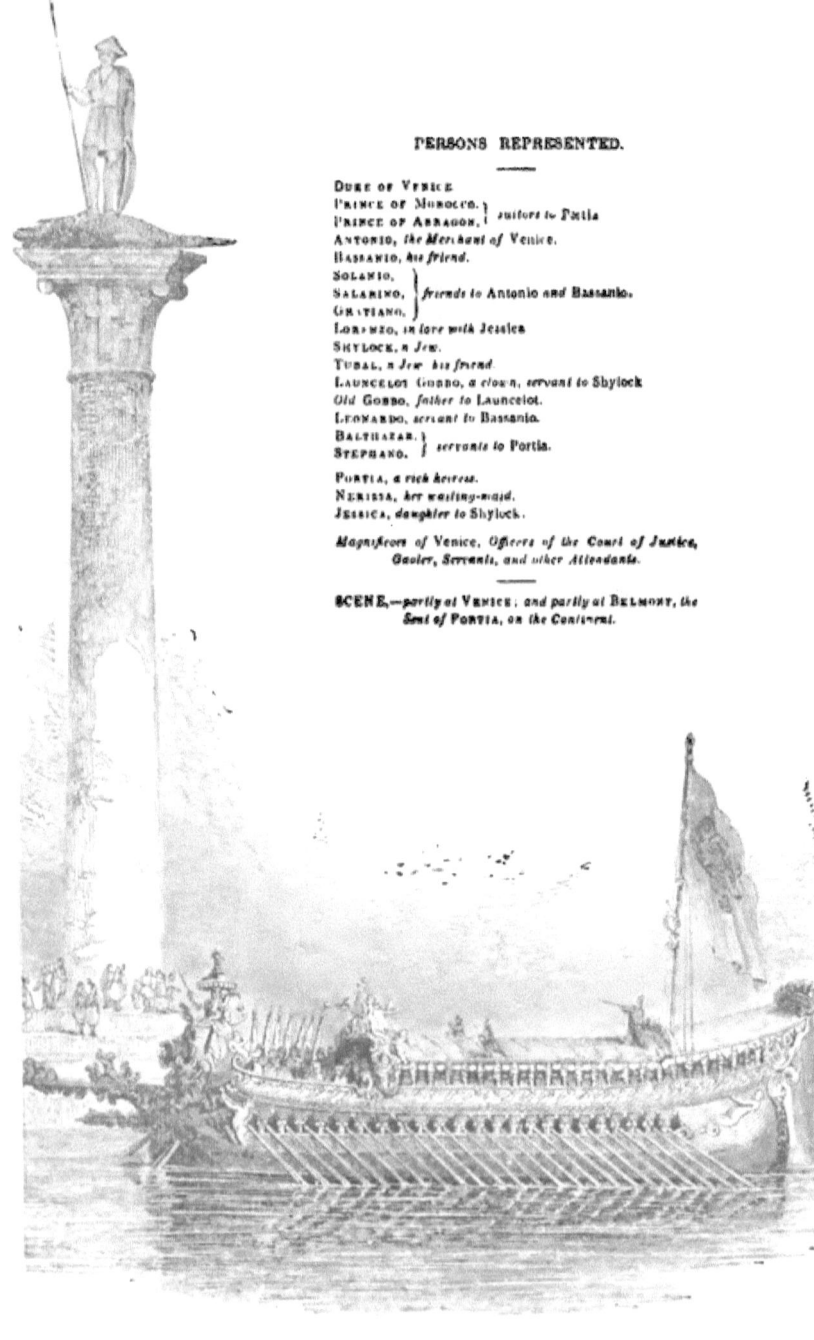

PERSONS REPRESENTED.

DUKE OF VENICE.
PRINCE OF MOROCCO,
PRINCE OF ARRAGON, } *suitors to Portia.*
ANTONIO, *the Merchant of Venice.*
BASSANIO, *his friend.*
SOLANIO,
SALARINO, } *friends to Antonio and Bassanio.*
GRATIANO,
LORENZO, *in love with Jessica.*
SHYLOCK, *a Jew.*
TUBAL, *a Jew, his friend.*
LAUNCELOT GOBBO, *a clown, servant to Shylock.*
Old GOBBO, *father to Launcelot.*
LEONARDO, *servant to Bassanio.*
BALTHAZAR,
STEPHANO, } *servants to Portia.*

PORTIA, *a rich heiress.*
NERISSA, *her waiting-maid.*
JESSICA, *daughter to Shylock.*

Magnificoes of Venice, Officers of the Court of Justice, Gaoler, Servants, and other Attendants.

SCENE,—*partly at* VENICE, *and partly at* BELMONT, *the Seat of* PORTIA, *on the Continent.*

[Saint Mark's Place.]

ACT I.

SCENE I.—Venice. *A Street.*

Enter ANTONIO, SALARINO,[a] *and* SOLANIO.

Ant. In sooth, I know not why I am so sad;
It wearies me; you say, it wearies you;
But how I caught it, found it, or came by it,
What stuff 'tis made of, whereof it is born,
I am to learn;
And such a want-wit sadness makes of me,
That I have much ado to know myself.

Salar. Your mind is tossing on the ocean;
There, where your argosies with portly sail,[a]
Like signiors and rich burghers on the flood,
Or, as it were, the pageants of the sea,
Do overpeer the petty traffickers,
That curt'sy to them, do them reverence,
As they fly by them wi'h their woven wings.

Solan. Believe me, sir, had I such venture forth,
The better part of my affections would
Be with my hopes abroad. I should be still
Plucking the grass, to know where sits the wind;
Peering in maps, for ports, and piers, and roads;
And every object that might make me fear
Misfortune to my ventures, out of doubt,
Would make me sad.—

Salar. My wind, cooling my broth,
Would blow me to an ague, when I thought
What harm a wind too great might do at sea.
I should not see the sandy hour-glass run,
But I should think of shallows and of flats;
And see my wealthy Andrew[a] dock'd in sand,
Vailing her high-top[b] lower than her ribs,

---

[a] *Salarino.* Nothing can be more confused than the manner in which the names of *Salarino* and *Solanio* are indicated in the folio of 1623. Neither in that edition, nor in the quartos, is there any enumeration of characters. In the text of the folio we find *Salarino* and *Slarino*; *Salanio*, *Solanio*, and *Solina*. Further, in the third act we have a *Salarino*, who has been raised to the dignity of a distinct character by Steevens. *Gratiano* calls this *Salerio* "my old Venetian friend;" and there is no reason whatever for not receiving the name as a misprint of *Solanio*, or *Salanio*. But if there be confusion even in these names when given at length in the text, the abbreviations prefixed to the speeches are "confusion worse confounded." *Solanio* begins with being *Sal.*, but he immediately turns into *Sol.*, and afterwards to *Sol.*; *Salarino* is at first *Salar.*, then *Sola.*, and finally *Sal.* We have adopted the distinction which Capell recommended to prevent the mistake of one abbreviation for another—*Solan.* and *Salar.*; and we have in some instances deviated from the usual assignment of the speeches to each of these characters, following for the most part the quarto, which in this particular is much less perplexed than the folio copy. Some early editors appear to have exercised only their caprice in this matter; and thus they have given *Salarino* and *Salanio* alternate speeches, after the fashion of Tityrus and Meliboeus; whereas *Salarino* is decidedly meant for the liveliest and the greatest talker.

[a] *Wealthy Andrew.* Johnson explains this (which is scarcely necessary) as "the name of the ship;" but he does not point out the propriety of the name for a ship, in association with the great naval commander, Andrea Doria, famous through all Italy.

[b] *Vailing her high-top.* To vail is to let down: the high-top was shattered—fallen—when the Andrew was on the shallows.

To kiss her burial. Should I go to church,
And see the holy edifice of stone,
And not bethink me straight of dangerous rocks,
Which, touching but my gentle vessel's side,
Would scatter all her spices on the stream;
Enrobe the roaring waters with my silks;
And, in a word, but even now worth this,
And now worth nothing? Shall I have the
    thought
To think on this; and shall I lack the thought
That such a thing, bechanc'd, would make me
    sad?
But tell not me; I know Antonio
Is sad to think upon his merchandize.
  Ant. Believe me, no: I thank my fortune
    for it,
My ventures are not in one bottom trusted,
Nor to one place; nor is my whole estate
Upon the fortune of this present year;
Therefore, my merchandize makes me not sad.
  Salar. Why then you are in love.
  Ant.   Fye, fye!
  Salar. Not in love neither? Then let us say,
    you are sad
Because you are not merry; an 'twere as easy
For you to laugh, and leap, and say you are
    merry,
Because you are not sad. Now, by two-headed
    Janus,[3]
Nature hath fram'd strange fellows in her time:
Some that will evermore peep through their eyes,
And laugh, like parrots, at a bagpiper:
And other of such vinegar aspect,
That they'll not show their teeth in way of
    smile,
Though Nestor swear the jest be laughable.

Enter BASSANIO, LORENZO, *and* GRATIANO.

  Solan. Here comes Bassanio, your most noble
    kinsman,
Gratiano, and Lorenzo: Fare you well;
We leave you now with better company.
  Salar. I would have staid till I had made you
    merry,
If worthier friends had not prevented me.
  Ant. Your worth is very dear in my regard.
I take it, your own business calls on you,
And you embrace the occasion to depart.
  Salar. Good-morrow, my good lords.
  Bass. Good signiors both, when shall we
    laugh? Say, when?
You grow exceeding strange: Must it be so?

  Salar. We'll make our leisures to attend on
    yours.
             [*Exeunt* SALARINO *and* SOLANIO.
  Lor. My lord Bassanio, since you have found
    Antonio,
We two will leave you; but at dinner-time
I pray you have in mind where we must meet.
  Bass. I will not fail you.
  Gra. You look not well, signior Antonio;
You have too much respect upon the world:
They lose it that do buy it with much care.
Believe me, you are marvellously chang'd.
  Ant. I hold the world but as the world,
    Gratiano;
A stage, where every man must play a part,
And mine a sad one.
  Gra.   Let me play the Fool:[a]
With mirth and laughter let old wrinkles come;
And let my liver rather heat with wine,
Than my heart cool with mortifying groans.
Why should a man whose blood is warm
    within
Sit like his grandsire cut in alabaster?
Sleep when he wakes? and creep into the
    jaundice
By being peevish? I tell thee what, Antonio,—
I love thee, and it is my love that speaks;—
There are a sort of men, whose visages
Do cream and mantle like a standing pond;
And do a wilful stillness entertain,[a]
With purpose to be dress'd in an opinion
Of wisdom, gravity, profound conceit;
As who should say, 'I am Sir Oracle,[b]
And when I ope my lips let no dog bark!'
O, my Antonio, I do know of these,
That therefore only are reputed wise
For saying nothing; who, I am very sure,
If they should speak, would almost damn those
    ears
Which, hearing them, would call their brothers
    fools.
I'll tell thee more of this another time:
But fish not with this melancholy bait,
For this fool gudgeon, this opinion.
Come, good Lorenzo:—Fare ye well, a while;
I'll end my exhortation after dinner.
  Lor. Well, we will leave you then till dinner-
    time:
I must be one of these same dumb wise men,
For Gratiano never lets me speak.

---

[a] *And do a wilful stillness, &c.* So Pope, addressing *Silence:*—
  "With thee, in private, modest Dulness lies,
  And in thy bosom lurks, in thought's disguise,
  Thou vanisher of fools, and cheat of all the wise."
[b] *Sir Oracle.* So the quartos of 1600.

---

[a] *My ventures, &c.* This was no doubt proverbial—something more elegant than "all the eggs in one basket." Sir Thomas More, in his 'History of Richard III.,' has:—"For what wise merchant adventureth all his good in one ship?"

402

Gra. Well, keep me company but two years more,
Thou shalt not know the sound of thine own tongue.
Ant. Farewell: I'll grow a talker for this gear.[a]
Gra. Thanks, i' faith; for silence is only commendable
In a neat's tongue dried, and a maid not vendible.
　　　　[*Exeunt* GRATIANO *and* LORENZO.
Ant. Is that any thing now?
Bass. Gratiano speaks an infinite deal of nothing, more than any man in all Venice: His reasons are two grains of wheat[b] hid in two bushels of chaff; you shall seek all day ere you find them; and when you have them they are not worth the search.
Ant. Well; tell me now, what lady is the same
To whom you swore a secret pilgrimage,
That you to-day promis'd to tell me of?
Bass. 'Tis not unknown to you, Antonio,
How much I have disabled mine estate,
By something showing a more swelling port[c]
Than my faint means would grant continuance:
Nor do I now make moan to be abridg'd
From such a noble rate; but my chief care
Is to come fairly off from the great debts
Wherein my time, something too prodigal,
Hath left me gaged: To you, Antonio,
I owe the most in money and in love;
And from your love I have a warranty
To unburthen all my plots and purposes,
How to get clear of all the debts I owe.
Ant. I pray you, good Bassanio, let me know it;
And, if it stand, as you yourself still do,
Within the eye of honour, be assur'd
My purse, my person, my extremest means,
Lie all unlock'd to your occasions.
Bass. In my school-days, when I had lost one shaft
I shot his fellow of the self-same flight
The self-same way, with more advised watch
To find the other forth; and by adventuring both
I oft found both: I urge this childhood proof,
Because what follows is pure innocence.
I owe you much; and, like a wilful youth,
That which I owe is lost: but if you please
To shoot another arrow that self way
Which you did shoot the first, I do not doubt,

As I will watch the aim, or to find both
Or bring your latter hazard back again,
And thankfully rest debtor for the first.
Ant. You know me well; and herein spend but time,
To wind about my love with circumstance;
And, out of doubt, you do me now more wrong
In making question of my uttermost,
Than if you had made waste of all I have.
Then do but say to me what I should do,
That in your knowledge may by me be done,
And I am prest[a] unto it: therefore speak.
Bass. In Belmont is a lady richly left,
And she is fair, and, fairer than that word,
Of wond'rous virtues. Sometimes[b] from her eyes
I did receive fair speechless messages:
Her name is Portia; nothing undervalued
To Cato's daughter, Brutus' Portia.
Nor is the wide world ignorant of her worth;
For the four winds blow in from every coast
Renowned suitors: and her sunny locks
Hang on her temples like a golden fleece;
Which makes her seat of Belmont, Colchos' strand,
And many Jasons come in quest of her.
O, my Antonio! had I but the means
To hold a rival place with one of them,
I have a mind presages me such thrift,
That I should questionless be fortunate.
Ant. Thou know'st that all my fortunes are at sea;
Neither have I money, nor commodity
To raise a present sum: therefore go forth,
Try what my credit can in Venice do;
That shall be rack'd, even to the uttermost,
To furnish thee to Belmont, to fair Portia.
Go, presently inquire, and so will I,
Where money is; and I no question make,
To have it of my trust, or for my sake.
　　　　　　　　　　　　　　[*Exeunt.*

SCENE II.—Belmont. *A Room in* Portia's *House.*

Enter PORTIA *and* NERISSA.

Por. By my troth, Nerissa, my little body is a-weary of this great world.
Ner. You would be, sweet madam, if your miseries were in the same abundance as your good fortunes are: And yet, for aught I see, they are as sick that surfeit with too much, as they that starve with nothing: It is no small happiness, therefore, to be seated in the mean: superfluity comes sooner by white hairs, but competency lives longer.

---

[a] *For this gear*—a colloquial expression, meaning, *for this matter.* The Anglo-Saxon *gearwian* is to *prepare—gear* is the thing prepared, in hand—the business or subject in question.
[b] *Two grains of wheat.* The ordinary reading, that of the quartos, is, as two grains, &c. The folio omits *as*.
[c] *Port*—appearance, carriage.

[a] *Prest*—ready.　　[b] *Sometimes*—formerly.

Por. Good sentences, and well pronounced.

Ner. They would be better, if well followed.

Por. If to do were as easy as to know what were good to do, chapels had been churches, and poor men's cottages princes' palaces. It is a good divine that follows his own instructions: I can easier teach twenty what were good to be done, than be one of the twenty to follow mine own teaching. The brain may devise laws for the blood; but a hot temper leaps o'er a cold decree: such a hare is madness the youth, to skip o'er the meshes of good council the cripple. But this reasoning is not in the fashion to choose me a husband:—O me, the word choose! I may neither choose whom I would, nor refuse whom I dislike; so is the will of a living daughter curb'd by the will of a dead father:—Is it not hard, Nerissa, that I cannot choose one, nor refuse none?

Ner. Your father was ever virtuous; and holy men at their death have good inspirations; therefore, the lottery that he hath devised in these three chests, of gold, silver, and lead, (whereof who chooses his meaning chooses you,) will, no doubt, never be chosen by any rightly, but one who you shall rightly love. But what warmth is there in your affection towards any of these princely suitors that are already come?

Por. I pray thee, over-name them; and as thou namest them I will describe them; and according to my description level at my affection.

Ner. First, there is the Neapolitan prince.

Por. Ay, that's a colt, indeed, for he doth nothing but talk of his horse; and he makes it a great appropriation to his own good parts that he can shoe him himself: I am much afraid my lady his mother played false with a smith.

Ner. Then, is there the county Palatine.

Por. He doth nothing but frown; as who should say, ' An you will not have me, choose : ' he hears merry tales, and smiles not : I fear he will prove the weeping philosopher when he grows old, being so full of unmannerly sadness in his youth. I had rather to be married to a death's head with a bone in his mouth, than to either of these. God defend me from these two!

Ner. How say you by the French lord, Monsieur Le Bon?

Por. God made him, and therefore let him pass for a man. In truth, I know it is a sin to be a mocker. But, he! why, he hath a horse better than the Neapolitan's ; a better had habit of frowning than the count Palatine : he is every man in no man : if a throstle sing he falls straight a capering ; he will fence with his own shadow : if I should marry him I should marry twenty husbands : If he would despise me I would forgive him ; for if he love me to madness I shall never requite him.

Ner. What say you then to Faulconbridge, the young baron of England?

Por. You know I say nothing to him ; for he understands not me, nor I him : he hath neither Latin, French, nor Italian ; and you will come into the court and swear that I have a poor pennyworth in the English. He is a proper man's picture. But, alas! who can converse with a dumb show? How oddly he is suited! I think he bought his doublet in Italy, his round hose in France, his bonnet in Germany, and his behaviour every where.

Ner. What think you of the Scottish lord,[a] his neighbour?

Por. That he hath a neighbourly charity in him ; for he borrowed a box of the ear of the Englishman, and swore he would pay him again when he was able : I think the Frenchman became his surety, and sealed under for another.

Ner. How like you the young German, the duke of Saxony's nephew?

Por. Very vilely in the morning, when he is sober ; and most vilely in the afternoon, when he is drunk : when he is best he is a little worse than a man ; and when he is worst he is little better than a beast : an the worst fall that ever fell, I hope I shall make shift to go without him.

Ner. If he should offer to choose, and choose the right casket, you should refuse to perform your father's will if you should refuse to accept him.

Por. Therefore, for fear of the worst, I pray thee set a deep glass of Rhenish wine on the contrary casket : for, if the devil be within, and that temptation without, I know he will choose it. I will do any thing, Nerissa, ere I will be married to a sponge.

Ner. You need not fear, lady, the having any of these lords ; they have acquainted me with their determinations ; which is, indeed, to return to their home and to trouble you with no more suit ; unless you may be won by some other sort than your father's imposition, depending on the caskets.

---

[a] *Scottish lord*—the folio reads *other* lord. The quartos of 1600, *Scottish*. The sarcasm against the political conduct of Scotland was suppressed upon the accession of James.

Por. If I live to be as old as Sibylla I will die as chaste as Diana, unless I be obtained by the manner of my father's will: I am glad this parcel of wooers are so reasonable; for there is not one among them but I dote on his very absence, and I wish them a fair departure.

Ner. Do you not remember, lady, in your father's time, a Venetian, a scholar, and a soldier, that came hither in company of the Marquis of Montferrat?

Por. Yes, yes, it was Bassanio; as I think so was he called.

Ner. True, madam; he, of all the men that ever my foolish eyes looked upon was the best deserving a fair lady.

Por. I remember him well; and I remember him worthy of thy praise.ᵃ

Enter a Servant.

Serv. The four strangers seek you, madam, to take their leave: and there is a fore-runner come from a fifth, the prince of Morocco; who brings word the prince, his master, will be here to-night.

Por. If I could bid the fifth welcome with so good heart as I can bid the other four farewell, I should be glad of his approach: if he have the condition of a saint, and the complexion of a devil, I had rather he should shrive me than wive me.

Come, Nerissa. Sirrah, go before. Whiles we shut the gate upon one wooer, another knocks at the door.ᵇ [*Exeunt.*

SCENE III.—*Venice. A public Place.*ᵃ

Enter BASSANIO *and* SHYLOCK.ᵇ

Shy. Three thousand ducats,—well.

Bass. Ay, sir, for three months.

Shy. For three months,—well.

Bass. For the which, as I told you, Antonio shall be bound.

Shy. Antonio shall become bound,—well.

Bass. May you stead me? Will you pleasure me? Shall I know your answer?

Shy. Three thousand ducats, for three months, and Antonio bound.

Bass. Your answer to that.

Shy. Antonio is a good man.

Bass. Have you heard any imputation to the contrary?

Shy. Oh no, no, no, no;—my meaning in saying he is a good man is, to have you understand me that he is sufficient: yet his means are in supposition: he hath an argosy bound to Tripolis, another to the Indies; I understand moreover upon the Rialto, he hath a third at Mexico, a fourth for England; and other ventures he hath, squander'd abroad.ᵃ But ships are but boards, sailors but men: there be landrats and water-rats, water-thieves and landthieves; I mean, pirates; and then, there is the peril of waters, winds, and rocks: The man is, notwithstanding, sufficient;—three thousand ducats;—I think I may take his bond.

Bass. Be assured you may.

Shy. I will be assured I may; and that I may be assured I will bethink me: May I speak with Antonio?

Bass. If it please you to dine with us.

Shy. Yes, to smell pork; to eat of the habitation which your prophet, the Nazarite, conjured the devil into! I will buy with you, sell with you, talk with you, walk with you, and so following; but I will not eat with you, drink with you, nor pray with you.—What news on the Rialto?ᵃ—Who is he comes here?

Enter ANTONIO.

Bass. This is signior Antonio.

Shy. [*Aside.*] How like a fawning publican he looks!
I hate him for he is a Christian:
But more, for that, in low simplicity,
He lends out money gratis, and brings down
The rate of usance here with us in Venice.ᵃ
If I can catch him once upon the hip,ᵇ
I will feed fat the ancient grudge I bear him.
He hates our sacred nation; and he rails,
Even there where merchants most do congregate,
On me, my bargains, and my well-won thrift,
Which he calls interest: Cursed be my tribe
If I forgive him!

ᵃ *Squander'd abroad.* In a letter published by Mr. Waldron, in Woodfall's 'Theatrical Repertory,' 1801, it is stated that "Macklin, mistakenly, spoke the word with a tone of reprobation, implying that Antonio had, as we say of prodigals, unthriftly squander'd his wealth." The meaning is simply, *scatter'd*; of which Mr. Waldron gives an example from Howell's Letters: "The Jews, once an elect people, but now grown contemptible, and strangely *squander'd* up and down the world." In Dryden's 'Annus Mirabilis' we have the same expression applied to ships:—

"They drive, they *squander,* the huge Belgian fleet."

ᵇ *Upon the hip.* We have the same expression in Othello:—

"I 'll have our Michael Cassio on the hip."

Johnson says the expression is taken from the practice of wrestling.

ᵃ *Worthy of thy praise.* In the folio the sentence here concludes. In the quartos, Portia, addressing the servant, says, "How now! what news?" The question may well be spared, for it does not belong to Portia's calm and dignified character.

ᵇ We have printed the conclusion of this scene as verse. The doggrel line is not inconsistent with the playfulness of the preceding dialogue.

405

Bass. Shylock, do you hear?
Shy. I am debating of my present store:
And, by the near guess of my memory,
I cannot instantly raise up the gross
Of full three thousand ducats: What of that?
Tubal, a wealthy Hebrew of my tribe,
Will furnish me: But soft: How many months
Do you desire?—Rest you fair, good signior:
                                [*To* ANTONIO.
Your worship was the last man in our mouths.
  Ant. Shylock, albeit I neither lend nor borrow,
By taking, nor by giving of excess,
Yet, to supply the ripe wants of my friend,
I'll break a custom:—Is he yet possess'd*
How much you would?
  Shy.   Ay, ay, three thousand ducats.
  Ant. And for three months.
  Shy. I had forgot,—three months, you told me so.
Well then, your bond; and, let me see. But hear you:
Methought you said, you neither lend nor borrow,
Upon advantage.
  Ant.   I do never use it.
  Shy. When Jacob graz'd his uncle Laban's sheep,
This Jacob from our holy Abraham was
(As his wise mother wrought in his behalf)
The third possessor; ay, he was the third.
  Ant. And what of him? did he take interest?
  Shy. No, not take interest; not, as you would say,
Directly interest: mark what Jacob did.
When Laban and himself were compromis'd
That all the eanlings⁰ which were streak'd and pied
Should fall, as Jacob's hire; the ewes, being rank,
In end of autumn turned to the rams:
And when the work of generation was
Between these woolly breeders in the act,
The skilful shepherd pill'd ᶜ me certain wands,
And, in the doing of the deed of kind,
He stuck them up before the fulsome ewes;
Who then conceiving, did in eaning-time
Fall ᵇ particolour'd lambs, and those were Jacob's.
This was a way to thrive, and he was blest;
And thrift is blessing, if men steal it not.

  Ant. This was a venture, sir, that Jacob serv'd for;
A thing not in his power to bring to pass,
But sway'd and fashion'd by the hand of heaven.
Was this inserted to make interest good?
Or is your gold and silver ewes and rams?
  Shy. I cannot tell; I make it breed as fast:
But note me, signior.
  Ant.   Mark you this, Bassanio,
The devil can cite scripture for his purpose.
An evil soul producing holy witness
Is like a villain with a smiling cheek;
A goodly apple rotten at the heart,
O, what a goodly outside falsehood hath!
  Shy. Three thousand ducats,—'tis a good round sum.
Three months from twelve, then let me see the rate.
  Ant. Well, Shylock, shall we be beholden to you?
  Shy. Signior Antonio, many a time and oft
In the Rialto you have rated me
About my monies, and my usances: ¹⁰
Still have I borne it with a patient shrug;
For sufferance is the badge of all our tribe:
You call me misbeliever, cut-throat dog,
And spet* upon my Jewish gaberdine,
And all for use of that which is mine own.
Well then, it now appears you need my help:
Go to then; you come to me, and you say,
' Shylock, we would have monies;' You say so;
You, that did void your rheum upon my beard
And foot me, as you spurn a stranger cur
Over your threshold; monies is your suit.
What should I say to you? Should I not say,
' Hath a dog money? is it possible
A cur can lend three thousand ducats?' or
Shall I bend low, and in a bondman's key,
With 'bated breath, and whispering humbleness,
Say this,—
' Fair sir, you spet on me on Wednesday last;
You spurn'd me such a day; another time
You call'd me dog; and for these courtesies
I'll lend you thus much monies?'
  Ant. I am as like to call thee so again,
To spet on thee again, to spurn thee too.
If thou wilt lend this money, lend it not
As to thy friends; (for when did friendship take
A breed of barren metal of his friend?)
But lend it rather to thine enemy;
Who, if he break, thou may'st with better face
Exact the penalties.

ᵃ *Possess'd*—informed.
ᵇ *Eanlings*—lambs just dropped.
ᶜ *Pill'd.* This is usually printed peel'd. The words are synonymous; but in the old and the present translations of the Bible we find pill'd, in the passage of Genesis to which Shylock alludes.
ᵈ *Fall*—to let fall.

* *Spet*—was the more received orthography in Shakspere's time; and it was used by Milton:—
    " The womb
Of Stygian darkness spets her thickest gloom."

Shy.   Why, look you, how you storm!
I would be friends with you, and have your love;
Forget the shames that you have stain'd me with;
Supply your present wants, and take no doit
Of usance for my monies, and you'll not hear
            me :
This is kind I offer.
    Bass.   This were kindness.
    Shy. This kindness will I show :
Go with me to a notary : seal me there
Your single bond; and, in a merry sport,
If you repay me not on such a day,
In such a place, such sum, or sums, as are
Express'd in the condition, let the forfeit
Be nominated for an equal pound
Of your fair flesh, to be cut off and taken
In what part of your body pleaseth me.
    Ant. Content, in faith; I'll seal to such a bond,
And say there is much kindness in the Jew.
    Bass. You shall not seal to such a bond for me;
I'll rather dwell* in my necessity.
    Ant. Why, fear not, man; I will not forfeit it;
Within these two months, that's a month before
This bond expires, I do expect return
Of thrice three times the value of this bond.

<small>* *Dwell*—continue.</small>

Shy. O father Abraham, what these Christians
            are,
Whose own hard dealings teaches them suspect
The thoughts of others! Pray you, tell me this;
If he should break his day, what should I gain
By the exaction of the forfeiture ?
A pound of man's flesh, taken from a man,
Is not so estimable, profitable neither,
As flesh of muttons, beefs, or goats. I say,
To buy his favour I extend this friendship;
If he will take it, so; if not, adieu ;
And, for my love, I pray you wrong me not.
    Ant. Yes, Shylock, I will seal unto this bond.
    Shy. Then meet me forthwith at the notary's,
Give him direction for this merry bond,
And I will go and purse the ducats straight;
See to my house, left in the fearful guard *
Of an unthrifty knave ; and presently
I will be with you.   [*Exit*
    Ant.   Hie thee, gentle Jew.
This Hebrew will turn Christian; he grows kind.
    Bass. I like not fair terms and a villain's mind.
    Ant. Come on ; in this there can be no dismay,
My ships come home a month before the day.
                                                    [*Exeunt*

<small>* *Fearful guard*—a guard that is the cause of fear.</small>

[Argosies with portly sail.]

ILLUSTRATIONS OF ACT I.

¹ SCENE I.—"*Argosies with portly sail.*"

THE largest vessels now used, and supposed to have been ever employed in Venetian commerce, are of two hundred tons. Fleets of such made up the ancient "argosies with portly sail." The smallest trading vessels,—coasters, "petty traffickers,"—are brigs and brigantines, which may be seen daily hovering, "with their woven wings," around the Island City.

The most splendid "pageants of the sea" ever beheld, were perhaps some that put forth from Venice in the days of her glory. Cleopatra's barge itself could not surpass the Buciutoro, with its exterior of scarlet and gold, its burnished oars, its inlaid deck and seats, its canopy and throne. The galleys of many of the wealthier citizens almost equalled this state vessel in splendour, to judge by the keels and other remains of ancient vessels which are preserved at the arsenal.—(M.)

² SCENE I.—"*Plucking the grass to know where sits the wind.*"

Though sea-weed is much more common than grass in Venice, there is enough land-vegetation in the gardens belonging to some of the palazzi to furnish the means of Solanio's experiment.—(M.)

³ SCENE I.—"*Now, by two-headed Janus,*" &c.

Warburton, upon this passage, justly and sensibly says, "Here Shakspeare shows his knowledge in the antique. By *two-headed* Janus is meant those antique bifrontine heads, which generally represent a young and smiling face, together with an old and wrinkled one, being of Pan and Bacchus, of Saturn and Apollo, &c. These are not uncommon in collections of antiques, and in the books of the antiquaries, as Montfaucon, Spanheim, &c. Farmer upon this displays his unfairness and impertinence very strikingly:—"In the Merchant of Venice we have an oath, 'By two-headed Janus;' and here, says Dr Warburton, Shakspeare shows his knowledge in the antique: and so, again does the Water-poet, who describes Fortune—

'Like a Janus with a double face.'"

Farmer had just told us that "honest John Taylor, the Water poet, declares that he never learned his Accidence, and that Latin and French were to him Heathen Greek." Now, Warburton's remark does not apply to the simple use by Shakspere of the term "two headed Janus," but to the propriety of its use in association with the image which was passing in Salarino's mind, of one set of heads that would "laugh, like parrots,"—and others of "vinegar aspect"—the open-mouth'd and clos'd mouth'd—"strange fellows,"—as different as the Janus looking to the east, and the Janus looking to the west.

⁴ SCENE I.—"*Let me play the Fool.*"

The part of the Fool, running over with "mirth and laughter," was opposed to the "sad" part which Antonio played. The Fool which Shakspere found in possession of the "stage" was a rude copy of the domestic fool—licentious, if not witty. Our great poet, in clothing him with wit, hid half his grossness. In the time of Middleton (Charles I.), when the domestic Fool was extinct, and the Fool of the stage nearly so, he is thus described retrospectively:—

"Oh, the clowns that I have seen in my time!
The very passing out of one of them would have

THE MERCHANT OF VENICE.

Made a young heir laugh though his father lay a-dying;
A man undone in law the day before
(The saddest case that can be) might for his second
Have burst himself with laughing, and ended all
His miseries. Here was a merry world, my masters."
                                    Mayor of Quinborough.

⁵ Scene II.—"*He hath neither Latin, French, nor Italian.*"

"A satire," says Warburton, "on the ignorance of the young English travellers in our author's time." Authors are not much in the habit of satirizing themselves; and yet, according to Farmer and his school, Shakspere knew "neither Latin, French, nor Italian."

⁶ Scene III.—"*Venice. A public Place.*"

Though there are three hundred and six canals in Venice, serving for thoroughfares, there is no lack also of streets and public places. The streets are probably the narrowest in Europe, from the value of ground in this City of the Sea. The public places (excepting the great squares before St Mark's and the Ducal Palace) are small open spaces in front of the churches, or formed by the intersection of streets, or by four ways meeting, or a bridge. These resound with a bubbub of voices, from the multitude of conferences perpetually going on; thus forming a remarkable contrast with the neighbouring canals, where the plash of the oar, and its echo from the high walls of the houses, is usually all that is heard. As conferences cannot well take place on these watery ways, and the inhabitants had, a few years ago, nowhere else to meet, all out-door conversation must take place in the alleys and on the bridges; and it is probable that a greater amount of discourse goes up from the streets of Venice than from any other equal space of ground in Europe. There must, however, be less now than there was, since Napoleon conferred on the Venetians the inestimable boon of the public gardens, where thousands of the inhabitants can now converse while pacing the grass, (that rare luxury to a Venetian,) under the shade of a grove of acacias.—(M.)

⁷ Scene III.—"*Shylock.*"

Farmer asserts that Shakspere took the name of his Jew from a pamphlet, entitled 'Caleb Shillocke his prophesie, or the Jew's prediction.' Boswell, who had seen a copy of this pamphlet, says its date was 1607. Farmer's theory is therefore worthless. *Scialac* was the name of "a Maronite of Mount Libanus," as we learn from 'An Account of Manuscripts in the Library of the King of France,' 1739.

⁸ Scene III.—"*What news on the Rialto?*"

The Rialto spoken of throughout this play is, in all probability, not the bridge to which belong our English associations with the name. The bridge was built in 1591, by A. da Ponte, under the Doge Pascul Cicogna.
The Rialto of ancient commerce is an island,—one of the largest of those on which Venice is built. Its name is derived from *riva alta*,—high shore,—and its being larger and somewhat more elevated than the others accounts for its being the first inhabited. The most ancient church of the city is there; and there were erected the buildings for the magistracy and commerce of the infant settlement. The arcades used for these purposes were burned down in the great fire of 1513, and rebuilt on the same spot in 1555, as they now stand. Rialto Island is situated at the head of the Grand Canal, by which it is bounded on two sides, while the Rio della Beccarie and another small canal bound it on the other two. There is a vegetable market there daily; and, though the great squares by St Mark's are now the places "where merchants most do congregate," the old rendezvous is still so thronged, and has yet so much the character of a "mart," as to justify now, as formerly, the question, "What news on the Rialto?"—(M.)

⁹ Scene III.

"*He lends out money gratis, and brings down
The rate of usance here with us in Venice.*"

When the commerce of Venice extended over the whole civilized world, and Cyprus, Candia, and the Morea were her dependencies (which was the case during a part of Shakspere's century), the city was not only the resort of strangers from all lands, but the place of residence of merchants of every nation, to whom it was the policy of the state to afford every encouragement and "commodity." Much of this convenience consisted in the lending of capital, which was done by the Jews, to the satisfaction of the government. These Jews were naturally feared and disliked by their merchant debtors; but while they were essential to these very parties, and countenanced by the ruling powers, they throve, to the degree declared by Thomas, in his 'History of Italy,' published in 1561,—ten years before the republic lost Cyprus.

"It is almost incredyble what gaine the Venetians receive by the usurie of the Jewes, both privately and in common. For in everie citie the Jewes kepe open shops of usurie, taking gaiges of ordinarie for xv in the hundred by the yere; and if, at the yere's end, the gaige be not redeemed, it is forfeite, or at least dozen away to a great disadvantage, by reason whereof the Jewes are out of measure **wealthie** in those parts."—(M.)

¹⁰ Scene III. ———"*you have rated me
About my monies, and my usances.*'

Upon this passage Douce observes,—" Mr. Steevens asserts that *use* and *usance* anciently signified *usury*, but both his quotations show the contrary." Ritson and Malone both state that *usance* signifies *interest of money*. And so *usury* formerly did. When *interest* was legalized, *usury* came to signify *excessive interest*. It is evident, from Bacon's masterly 'Essay on Usury,' in which he has anticipated all that modern political economy has given us on the subject, that *usury* meant *interest at any rate*. One of the objections, he says, which is urged against usury is, "that it is against nature for money to beget money."

[" The villain Jew with outcries rais'd the duke;
Who went with him to search Bassanio's ship.']

ACT II.

SCENE I.—Belmont. *A Room in* Portia's *House.*

Flourish of Cornets. Enter the Prince of Morocco, *and his Train;* Portia, Nerissa, *and other of her* Attendants.[1]

Mor. Mislike me not for my complexion,
The shadow'd livery of the burnish'd sun,
To whom I am a neighbour, and near bred.
Bring me the fairest creature northward born,
Where Phœbus' fire scarce thaws the icicles,
And let us make incision for your love,
To prove whose blood is reddest, his, or mine.
I tell thee, lady, this aspect of mine
Hath fear'd the valiant; by my love, I swear,
The best-regarded virgins of our clime
Have lov'd it too: I would not change this hue,
Except to steal your thoughts, my gentle queen.

Por. In terms of choice I am not solely led
By nice direction of a maiden's eyes:
Besides, the lottery of my destiny
Bars me the right of voluntary choosing.
But, if my father had not scanted me,
And hedg'd me by his wit,[a] to yield myself
His wife who wins me by that means I told you,
Yourself, renowned prince, then stood as fair
As any comer I have look'd on yet,
For my affection.

Mor.   Even for that I thank you;
Therefore, I pray you, lead me to the caskets,
To try my fortune. By this scimitar,
That slew the Sophy, and a Persian prince
That won three fields of Sultan Solyman,
I would o'er-stare[b] the sternest eyes that look,
Out-brave the heart most daring on the earth,
Pluck the young sucking cubs from the she bear,

---

a *Wit.* The word is here used in its ancient sense of mental power in general. To *wit*, from the Anglo-Saxon *witan*, is *to know.*

b *O'er-stare.* So the folio and one of the quartos; the ordinary reading, which is of the other quarto, is *out-stare*

Yea, mock the lion when he roars for prey,
To win thee, lady But, alas the while!
If Hercules and Lichas play at dice
Which is the better man, the greater throw
May turn by fortune from the weaker hand:
So is Alcides beaten by his page;[a]
And so may I, blind fortune leading me,
Miss that which one unworthier may attain,
And die with grieving.

Por. You must take your chance;
And either not attempt to choose at all,
Or swear, before you choose,—if you choose wrong.
Never to speak to lady afterward
In way of marriage; therefore be advis'd.

Mor. Nor will not; come, bring me unto my chance.

Por. First, forward to the temple; after dinner
Your hazard shall be made.

Mor. Good fortune then! [*Cornets.*
To make me blest or cursed'st among men.
[*Exeunt.*

SCENE II.—Venice. *A Street.*

Enter LAUNCELOT GOBBO.[b]

Laun. Certainly my conscience will serve me to run from this Jew, my master: The fiend is at mine elbow, and tempts me; saying to me,—Gobbo, Launcelot Gobbo, good Launcelot, or good Gobbo, or good Launcelot Gobbo, use your legs, take the start, run away:—My conscience says,—no; take heed, honest Launcelot; take heed, honest Gobbo; or (as aforesaid) honest Launcelot Gobbo; do not run: scorn running with thy heels:[c] Well, the most courageous fiend bids me pack. Via! says the fiend; away! says the fiend, for the heavens;[d] rouse up a brave mind, says the fiend, and run. Well, my conscience, hanging about the neck of my heart, says very wisely to me,—my honest friend, Launcelot, being an honest man's son, or rather an honest woman's son;—for, indeed, my father did something smack, something grow to, he had a kind of taste;—well, my conscience says,

Launcelot, budge not: budge, says the fiend; budge not, says my conscience: Conscience, say I, you counsel well; fiend, say I, you counsel well: to be ruled by my conscience I should stay with the Jew my master, who (God bless the mark!) is a kind of devil; and to run away from the Jew I should be ruled by the fiend, who, saving your reverence, is the devil himself: Certainly, the Jew is the very devil incarnation: and, in my conscience, my conscience is a kind of hard conscience, to offer to counsel me to stay with the Jew: The fiend gives the more friendly counsel: I will run, fiend; my heels are at your commandment, I will run.

Enter Old GOBBO, *with a basket.*

Gob. Master, young man, you, I pray you; which is the way to master Jew's?

Laun. [*Aside.*] O heavens, this is my true-begotten father! who, being more than sand-blind,[a] high-gravel blind, knows me not: I will try conclusions with him.

Gob. Master young gentleman, I pray you which is the way to master Jew's?[b]

Laun. Turn upon your right hand at the next turning, but, at the next turning of all, on your left; marry, at the very next turning, turn of no hand, but turn down indirectly to the Jew's house.

Gob. By God's sonties, 'twill be a hard way to hit. Can you tell me whether one Launcelot that dwells with him dwell with him, or no?

Laun. Talk you of young master Launcelot?—Mark me now—[*aside.*] now will I raise the waters:—Talk you of young master Launcelot?

Gob. No master, sir, but a poor man's son: his father, though I say it, is an honest exceeding poor man, and, God be thanked, well to live.

Laun. Well, let his father be what a will, we talk of young master Launcelot.

Gob. Your worship's friend, and Launcelot.[b]

Laun. But I pray you *ergo*, old man, *ergo*, I beseech you, talk you of young master Launcelot.[c]

Gob. Of Launcelot, an't please your mastership.

---

[a] *Page.* All the old copies read *rage.* But there can be no doubt that Lichas, the unhappy servant of Hercules, was thus designated. The correction was made by Theobald.

[b] The original stage direction is, "*Enter the clown,*" by which name Launcelot is invariably distinguished.

[c] When Pistol says, "He hears with ears," Sir Hugh Evans calls the phrase "affectations." Perhaps Launcelot uses "*scorn running with thy heels*" in the same affected fashion. Steevens, however, suggests the following marvellous emendation: "Do not run; scorn running; *withe* thy heels; *i. e.* connect them with a *withe* (a band made of osiers), as the legs of cattle are hampered in some countries."

[d] *For the heavens.* This expression is simply, as Gifford states, "a petty oath." It occurs in Ben Jonson and Dekker.

[a] *Sand-blind*—having an imperfect sight, as if there were sand in the eye. *Gravel-blind,* a coinage of Launcelot's, is the exaggeration of *sand-blind. Pur-blind,* or pore-blind, if we may judge from a sentence in Latimer is something less than *sand-blind:*—"They be pur-blind and sand-blind."

[b] The same form of expression occurs in Love's Labour's Lost—"Your servant, and Costard." It would seem, from the context, that the old man's name was Launcelot:—"I beseech you, talk you of *young master* Launcelot," says the clown, when the old man has named himself.

[c] This sentence is usually put interrogatively, contrary to the punctuation of all the old copies; which is not to be so utterly despised as the modern editors would pretend. The Cambridge editors say the sign was often omitted, and that Mr. Dyce remarks that it is a repetition inconclusive.

411

Laun. Ergo, master Launcelot; talk not of master Launcelot, father; for the young gentleman (according to fates and destinies, and such odd sayings, the sisters three, and such branches of learning,) is, indeed, deceased; or, as you would say in plain terms, gone to heaven.

Gob. Marry, God forbid! the boy was the very staff of my age, my very prop.

Laun. Do I look like a cudgel, or a hovel-post, a staff, or a prop?—Do you know me, father?

Gob. Alack the day, I know you not, young gentleman: but, I pray you tell me, is my boy (God rest his soul!) alive or dead?

Laun. Do you not know me, father?

Gob. Alack, sir, I am sand-blind, I know you not.

Laun. Nay, indeed, if you had your eyes you might fail of the knowing me: it is a wise father that knows his own child. Well, old man, I will tell you news of your son: Give me your blessing: truth will come to light; murder cannot be hid long; a man's son may; but, in the end, truth will out.

Gob. Pray you, sir, stand up; I am sure you are not Launcelot, my boy.

Laun. Pray you, let's have no more fooling about it, but give me your blessing; I am Launcelot, your boy that was, your son that is, your child that shall be.

Gob. I cannot think you are my son.

Laun. I know not what I shall think of that: but I am Launcelot, the Jew's man; and I am sure Margery, your wife, is my mother.

Gob. Her name is Margery, indeed: I'll be sworn if thou be Launcelot, thou art mine own flesh and blood. Lord, worshipp'd might he be! what a beard hast thou got! thou hast got more hair on thy chin than Dobbin my phill-horse[a] has on his tail.

Laun. It should seem then that Dobbin's tail grows backward; I am sure he had more hair of his tail than I have of my face, when I last saw him.

Gob. Lord, how art thou changed! How dost thou and thy master agree? I have brought him a present. How 'gree you now?

Laun. Well, well; but for mine own part, as I have set up my rest to run away, so I will not rest till I have run some ground. My master's a very Jew. Give him a present! give him a halter: I am famish'd in his service; you may tell every finger I have with my ribs. Father, I am glad you are come: give me your present to one master Bassanio, who, indeed, gives rare new liveries; if I serve not him, I will run as far as God has any ground.—O rare fortune! here comes the man;—to him, father; for I am a Jew if I serve the Jew any longer.

Enter BASSANIO, *with* LEONARDO, *and other Followers.*

Bass. You may do so:—but let it be so hasted that supper be ready at the farthest by five of the clock: See these letters deliver'd; put the liveries to making; and desire Gratiano to come anon to my lodging. [*Exit a* Servant.

Laun. To him, father.

Gob. God bless your worship!

Bass. Gramercy! Would'st thou aught with me?

Gob. Here's my son, sir, a poor boy,—

Laun. Not a poor boy, sir, but the rich Jew's man; that would, sir, as my father shall specify,—

Gob. He hath a great infection, sir, as one would say, to serve,—

Laun. Indeed, the short and the long is, I serve the Jew, and have a desire, as my father shall specify,—

Gob. His master and he (saving your worship's reverence) are scarce cater-cousins:

Laun. To be brief, the very truth is, that the Jew having done me wrong, doth cause me, as my father, being I hope an old man, shall frutify unto you,—

Gob. I have here a dish of doves,[b] that I would bestow upon your worship; and my suit is,—

Laun. In very brief, the suit is impertinent[c] to myself, as your worship shall know by this honest old man; and, though I say it, though old man, yet, poor man, my father.

Bass. One speak for both:—What would you?

Laun. Serve you, sir.

Gob. That is the very defect of the matter, sir.

Bass. I know thee well, thou hast obtain'd thy suit:

Shylock, thy master, spoke with me this day,
And hath preferr'd thee, if it be preferment,
To leave a rich Jew's service, to become
The follower of so poor a gentleman.

Laun. The old proverb is very well parted

---

[a] *Phill-horse.* The word is so spelt in all the old copies. It is the same as *thill-horse*—the horse in the shafts—and is the word best understood in the midland counties.

[c] *Impertinent.* Launcelot is a blunderer as well as one who "can play upon a word;" here he means *pertinent*.

between my master Shylock and you, sir; you have the grace of God, sir, and he hath enough.
  Bass. Thou speak'st it well. Go, father, with thy son:—
Take leave of thy old master, and inquire
My lodging out:— give him a livery
                             [*To his followers.*
More guarded [a] than his fellows': See it done.
  Laun. Father, in:—I cannot get a service, no!
—I have ne'er a tongue in my head!— Well; [*looking on his palm*] if any man in Italy have a fairer table; which doth offer to swear upon a hook I shall have good fortune! Go to, here's a simple line of life! [b] here's a small trifle of wives: Alas, fifteen wives is nothing; eleven widows and nine maids, is a simple coming in for one man: and then, to 'scape drowning thrice; and to be in peril of my life with the edge of a feather-bed; here are simple 'scapes! Well, if fortune be a woman, she's a good wench for this gear.—Father, come. I'll take my leave of the Jew in the twinkling of an eye.
            [*Exeunt* LAUNCELOT *and Old* GOBBO.
  Bass. I pray thee, good Leonardo, think on this;
These things being bought, and orderly bestow'd,
Return in haste, for I do feast to-night
My best-esteem'd acquaintance: hie thee, go.
  Leon. My best endeavours shall be done herein.

            Enter GRATIANO.

  Gra. Where is your master?
  Leon.   Yonder, sir, he walks.
                             [*Exit* LEONARDO.
  Gra. Signior Bassanio,—
  Bass. Gratiano!
  Gra. I have a suit to you.
  Bass.   You have obtain'd it.
  Gra. You must not deny me: I must go with you to Belmont.
  Bass. Why, then you must.—But hear thee, Gratiano;
Thou art too wild, too rude, and bold of voice;
Parts, that become thee happily enough,
And in such eyes as ours appear not faults;
But where they are not known, why, there they show

Something too liberal:—pray thee take pain
To allay with some cold drops of modesty
Thy skipping spirit; lest, through thy wild behaviour,
I be misconstrued in the place I go to,
And lose my hopes.
  Gra.   Signior Bassanio, hear me:
If I do not put on a sober habit,
Talk with respect, and swear but now and then,
Wear prayer-books in my pocket, look demurely;
Nay more, while grace is saying, hood mine eyes
Thus with my hat, and sigh, and say amen;
Use all the observance of civility,
Like one well studied in a sad ostent [a]
To please his grandam,—never trust me more.
  Bass. Well, we shall see your bearing.
  Gra. Nay, but I bar to-night; you shall not gage me
By what we do to-night.
  Bass.   No, that were pity;
I would entreat you rather to put on
Your boldest suit of mirth, for we have friends
That purpose merriment: But fare you well,
I have some business.
  Gra. And I must to Lorenzo and the rest;
But we will visit you at supper-time.
                             [*Exeunt.*

SCENE III.—Venice. *A Room in Shylock's House.*

            Enter JESSICA *and* LAUNCELOT.

  Jes. I am sorry thou wilt leave my father so;
Our house is hell, and thou, a merry devil,
Didst rob it of some taste of tediousness:
But fare thee well: there is a ducat for thee:
And, Launcelot, soon at supper shalt thou see
Lorenzo, who is thy new master's guest:
Give him this letter; do it secretly,
And so farewell; I would not have my father
See me in talk [b] with thee.
  Laun. Adieu!— tears exhibit my tongue. Most beautiful pagan,—most sweet Jew! If a Christian did not play the knave and get thee, I am much deceived: [c] But, adieu! these foolish drops do somewhat drown my manly spirit: adieu!   [*Exit.*

---

[a] *More guarded*—more ornamented, laced, fringed.
[b] This passage is ordinarily pointed thus—"Well; if any man in Italy have a fairer table, which doth offer to swear upon a book.—I shall have good fortune." The punctuation which we have adopted was suggested by Tyrwhitt, and indeed it is borne out by the original punctuation. The table (palm) which doth offer to swear upon a book is not very different from other palms: but the palm which doth offer to swear *that* the owner shall have good fortune is a fair table to be proud of. (See Illustration.)

[a] *Ostent*—display.
[b] *In talk.* We prefer this reading of the quartos. That of the folio is, *see me talk with thee.*
[c] We follow, for once, the reading of the second folio. The quartos, and the folio of 1623, read, ' If a Christian do not play the knave and get thee, I am much deceived.' The matter is hardly worth the fierce controversy which Steevens and Malone had upon the subject.

Jes. Farewell, good Launcelot.
Alack, what heinous sin is it in me,
To be asham'd to be my father's child!
But though I am a daughter to his blood,
I am not to his manners: O Lorenzo,
If thou keep promise, I shall end this strife;
Become a Christian, and thy loving wife.
[*Exit.*

SCENE IV.—Venice. *A Street.*

Enter GRATIANO, LORENZO, SALARINO, *and* SOLANIO.

Lor. Nay, we will slink away in supper-time;
Disguise us at my lodging, and return
All in an hour.
Gra. We have not made good preparation.
Salar. We have not spoke us yet of torch-bearers.
Solan. 'Tis vile, unless it may be quaintly order'd;
And better, in my mind, not undertook.
Lor. 'Tis now but four o'clock; we have two hours
To furnish us.—

Enter LAUNCELOT, *with a letter.*

Friend Launcelot, what's the news?
Laun. An it shall please you to break up* this, it shall seem to signify.
Lor. I know the hand: In faith, 'tis a fair hand;
And whiter than the paper it writ on
Is the fair hand that writ.
Gra. Love-news, in faith.
Laun. By your leave, sir.
Lor. Whither goest thou?
Laun. Marry, sir, to bid my old master the Jew to sup to-night with my new master the Christian.
Lor. Hold here, take this:—tell gentle Jessica,
I will not fail her;—speak it privately: go.
Gentlemen, [*Exit* LAUNCELOT.
Will you prepare you for this masque to-night?
I am provided of a torch-bearer.
Salar. Ay, marry, I'll be gone about it straight.
Solan. And so will I.
Lor. Meet me and Gratiano
At Gratiano's lodging some hour hence.
Salar. 'Tis good we do so.
[*Exeunt* SALAR. *and* SOLAN.

Gra. Was not that letter from fair Jessica?
Lor. I must needs tell thee all: She hath directed
How I shall take her from her father's house;
What gold and jewels she is furnish'd with;
What page's suit she hath in readiness.
If e'er the Jew her father come to heaven,
It will be for his gentle daughter's sake:
And never dare misfortune cross her foot,
Unless she do it under this excuse,—
That she is issue to a faithless Jew.
Come, go with me; peruse this as thou goest:
Fair Jessica shall be my torch-bearer.
[*Exeunt.*

SCENE V.—Venice. *Before* Shylock's *House.*

Enter SHYLOCK *and* LAUNCELOT.

Shy. Well, thou shalt see, thy eyes shall be thy judge,
The difference of old Shylock and Bassanio:
What, Jessica!—thou shalt not gormandize,[6]
As thou hast done with me;—What, Jessica!—
And sleep and snore, and rend apparel out;—
Why, Jessica, I say!
Laun. Why, Jessica!
Shy. Who bids thee call? I do not bid thee call.
Laun. Your worship was wont to tell me I could do nothing without bidding.

Enter JESSICA.

Jes. Call you? What is your will?
Shy. I am bid forth to supper, Jessica;
There are my keys:—But wherefore should I go?
I am not bid for love; they flatter me:
But yet I'll go in hate, to feed upon
The prodigal Christian.—Jessica, my girl,
Look to my house:—I am right loath to go;
There is some ill a brewing towards my rest,
For I did dream of money-bags to-night.
Laun. I beseech you, sir, go; my young master doth expect your reproach.
Shy. So do I his.
Laun. And they have conspired together,—
I will not say, you shall see a masque; but if you do, then it was not for nothing that my nose fell a bleeding on Black-Monday[7] last, at six o'clock i' the morning, falling out that year on Ash-Wednesday was four year in the afternoon.
Shy. What! are there masques? Hear you me, Jessica;
Lock up my doors; and when you hear the drum

---

* *To break up this.* It would scarcely require an explanation, that, to break up, was to open, unless Steevens had explained that, to break up, is a term of carving. In the Winter's Tale we have, "*break up the seals,* and read."

And the vile squealing^a of the wry-neck'd fife,^a
Clamber not you up to the casements then,
Nor thrust your head into the public street,
To gaze on Christian fools with varnish'd faces:
But stop my house's ears, I mean my case-
   ments;
Let not the sound of shallow foppery enter
My sober house.—By Jacob's staff I swear,
I have no mind of feasting forth to-night:
But I will go.—Go you before me, sirrah;
Say, I will come.
  Laun.   I will go before, sir.—
Mistress, look out at window, for all this;
  There will come a Christian by,
  Will be worth a Jewess' eye.^a
                                  [*Exit* LAUN.
  Shy. What says that fool of Hagar's off-
   spring, ha?
  Jes. His words were, Farewell, mistress;
   nothing else.
  Shy. The patch^b is kind enough; but a huge
   feeder,
Snail-slow in profit, and he sleeps by day
More than the wild cat: drones hive not with
   me,
Therefore I part with him; and part with him
To one that I would have him help to waste
His borrow'd purse.—Well, Jessica, go in;
Perhaps, I will return immediately;
Do as I bid you,
Shut doors after you: Fast bind, fast find;
A proverb never stale in thrifty mind. [*Exit.*
  Jes. Farewell; and if my fortune be not cross'd,
I have a father, you a daughter, lost. [*Exit.*

SCENE VI.—*The same.*

Enter GRATIANO *and* SALARINO, *masqued.*

  Gra. This is the pent-house, under which
   Lorenzo
Desir'd us to make stand.
  Salar.   His hour is almost past.
  Gra. And it is marvel he out-dwells his hour,
For lovers ever run before the clock.
  Salar. O, ten times faster Venus' pigeons fly
To seal love's bonds new made, than they are
   wont
To keep obliged faith unforfeited!

  Gra. That ever holds: who riseth from a
   feast,
With that keen appetite that he sits down?
Where is the horse that doth untread again
His tedious measures with the unbated fire
That he did pace them first? All things that are,
Are with more spirit chased than enjoy'd.
How like a younger,^a or a prodigal,
The scarfed^b bark puts from her native bay,
Hugg'd and embraced by the strumpet wind!
How like a prodigal doth she return,
With over-weather'd ribs, and ragged sails,
Lean, rent, and beggar'd by the strumpet wind!

Enter LORENZO.

  Salar. Here comes Lorenzo;—more of this
   hereafter.
  Lor. Sweet friends, your patience for my long
   abode;
Not I, but my affairs, have made you wait:
When you shall please to play the thieves for
   wives,
I'll watch as long for you then.—Approach;
Here dwells my father Jew:—Ho! who's
   within?

Enter JESSICA, *above, in boy's clothes.*

  Jes. Who are you? Tell me, for more cer-
   tainty,
Albeit I'll swear that I do know your tongue.
  Lor. Lorenzo, and thy love.
  Jes. Lorenzo, certain; and my love, indeed;
For who love I so much? and now who knows
But you, Lorenzo, whether I am yours?
  Lor. Heaven, and thy thoughts, are witness
   that thou art.
  Jes. Here, catch this casket; it is worth the
   pains.
I am glad 'tis night, you do not look on me,
For I am much asham'd of my exchange:
But love is blind, and lovers cannot see
The pretty follies that themselves commit;
For if they could, Cupid himself would blush
To see me thus transformed to a boy.
  Lor. Descend, for you must be my torch-
   bearer.
  Jes. What, must I hold a candle to my
   shames?
They in themselves, good sooth, are too too light.
Why, 'tis an office of discovery, love;
And I should be obscur'd.
  Lor.   So are you, sweet,
Even in the lovely garnish of a boy

---

^a *Squealing.* So the folio and one of the quartos; the other quarto, which is usually followed, has *squeaking*.
^b *Patch.* The domestic fool was sometimes called a patch; and it is probable that this class was thus named from the patched dress of their vocation. The usurper in Hamlet, the "vice of kings," was "a king of shreds and patches." It is probable that in this way the word patch came to be an expression of contempt, as, in A Midsummer Night's Dream—
  "A crew of patches, rude mechanicals."
Shylock here uses the word in this sense; just as we say still, *cross-patch.*

^a *Younger.* So all the old copies. It is the same word as *younker* and *youngling.*
^b *Scarfed bark*—the vessel gay with streamers.

But come at once;
For the close night doth play the runaway,
And we are staid for at Bassanio's feast.
  Jes. I will make fast the doors, and gild myself
With some more ducats, and be with you straight. [*Exit, from above.*
  Gra. Now, by my hood, a Gentile and no Jew.
  Lor. Beshrew me, but I love her heartily:
For she is wise, if I can judge of her;
And fair she is, if that mine eyes be true;
And true she is, as she hath prov'd herself;
And therefore, like herself, wise, fair, and true,
Shall she be placed in my constant soul.

Enter JESSICA, *below.*

What, art thou come?—On, gentlemen, away;
Our masquing mates by this time for us stay.
  [*Exit, with* JESSICA *and* SALARINO.

Enter ANTONIO.

  Ant. Who's there?
  Gra. Signior Antonio?
  Ant. Fye, fye, Gratiano! where are all the rest?
'Tis nine o'clock: our friends all stay for you:
No masque to-night; the wind is come about;
Bassanio presently will go aboard:
I have sent twenty out to seek for you.
  Gra. I am glad on't; I desire no more delight
Than to be under sail and gone to-night.
  [*Exeunt.*

SCENE VII.—Belmont. *A Room in Portia's House.*

Flourish of Cornets. Enter PORTIA, *with the* PRINCE OF MOROCCO, *and both their Trains.*

  Por. Go, draw aside the curtains, and discover
The several caskets to this noble prince:—
Now make your choice.
  Mor. The first, of gold, who this inscription hears:
    'Who chooseth me shall gain what many men desire.'
The second, silver, which this promise carries:
    'Who chooseth me shall get as much as he deserves.'
This third, dull lead, with warning all as blunt:
    'Who chooseth me must give and hazard all he hath.'
How shall I know if I do choose the right?
  Por. The one of them contains my picture, prince;
If you choose that, then I am yours withal.

  Mor. Some god direct my judgment! Let me see.
I will survey the inscriptions back again:
What says this leaden casket?
    'Who chooseth me must give and hazard all he hath'
Must give—For what? for lead? hazard for lead?
This casket threatens: Men that hazard all
Do it in hope of fair advantages:
A golden mind stoops not to shows of dross;
I'll then nor give, nor hazard, aught for lead.
What says the silver, with her virgin hue?
    'Who chooseth me shall get as much as he deserves.'
As much as he deserves?—Pause there, Morocco,
And weigh thy value with an even hand:
If thou be'st rated by thy estimation,
Thou dost deserve enough; and yet enough
May not extend so far as to the lady:
And yet to be afeard of my deserving
Were but a weak disabling of myself.
As much as I deserve!—Why, that's the lady:
I do in birth deserve her, and in fortunes,
In graces, and in qualities of breeding;
But more than these, in love I do deserve.
What if I stray'd no further, but chose here?—
Let's see once more this saying grav'd in gold:—
    'Who chooseth me shall gain what many men desire.'

Why, that's the lady: all the world desires her·
From the four corners of the earth they come,
To kiss this shrine, this mortal breathing saint.
The Hyrcanian deserts, and the vasty wilds
Of wide Arabia, are as through-fares now,
For princes to come view fair Portia:
The watery kingdom, whose ambitious head
Spits in the face of heaven, is no bar
To stop the foreign spirits; but they come,
As o'er a brook, to see fair Portia.
One of these three contains her heavenly picture.
Is't like that lead contains her? 'Twere damnation
To think so base a thought: it were too gross
To rib her cerecloth in the obscure grave.
Or shall I think in silver she's immur'd,
Being ten times undervalued to tried gold?
O sinful thought! Never so rich a gem
Was set in worse than gold. They have in England
A coin that bears the figure of an angel [10]
Stamped in gold; but that's insculp'd upon;
But here an angel in a golden bed
Lies all within.—Deliver me the key;
Here do I choose, and thrive I as I may!

Por. There, take it, prince, and if my form
  lie there,
Then I am yours.
                    [*He unlocks the golden casket.*
Mor. O hell! what have we here?
A carrion death, within whose empty eye
There is a written scroll? I'll read the writing.

 ' All that glisters is not gold,
  Often have you heard that told:
  Many a man his life hath sold
  But my outside to behold:
  Gilded tombs a do worms infold.
  Had you been as wise as bold,
  Young in limbs, in judgment old,
  Your answer had not been inscroll'd:
  Fare you well; your suit is cold.'

Cold, indeed; and labour lost:
Then, farewell heat; and welcome frost.—
Portia, adieu! I have too griev'd a heart
To take a tedious leave: thus losers part.
                                     [*Exit.*
Por. A gentle riddance:—Draw the curtains,
  go;—
Let all of his complexion choose me so.
                                   [*Exeunt.*

SCENE VIII.—Venice. *A Street.*

Enter SALARINO *and* SOLANIO.

Salar. Why man, I saw Bassanio under sail;
With him is Gratiano gone along;
And in their ship, I am sure, Lorenzo is not.
Solan. The villain Jew with outcries rais'd the
  duke;
Who went with him to search Bassanio's ship.
Salar. He came too late, the ship was under
  sail:
But there the duke was given to understand,
That in a gondola were seen together [11]
Lorenzo and his amorous Jessica;
Besides, Antonio certified the duke,
They were not with Bassanio in his ship.
Solan. I never heard a passion so confus'd,

So strange, outrageous, and so variable,
As the dog Jew did utter in the streets:
' My daughter!—O my ducats!—O my daugh-
  ter!
Fled with a Christian?—O my christian ducats!—
Justice! the law! my ducats, and my daughter!
A sealed bag, two sealed bags of ducats,
Of double ducats, stol'n from me by my daugh-
  ter!
And jewels; two stones, two rich and precious
  stones,
Stol'n by my daughter!—Justice! find the
  girl!
She hath the stones upon her, and the ducats!'
Salar. Why, all the boys in Venice follow
  him,
Crying,—his stones, his daughter, and his
  ducats.
Solan. Let good Antonio look he keep his day,
Or he shall pay for this.
Salar.   Marry, well remember'd:
I reason'd a with a Frenchman yesterday,
Who told me,—in the narrow seas that part
The French and English, there miscarried
A vessel of our country, richly fraught:
I thought upon Antonio when he told me,
And wish'd in silence that it were not his.
Solan. You were best to tell Antonio what
  you hear;
Yet do not suddenly, for it may grieve him.
Salar. A kinder gentleman treads not the
  earth.
I saw Bassanio and Antonio part:
Bassanio told him, he would make some speed
Of his return; he answer'd—' Do not so,
Slubber not business for my sake, Bassanio,
But stay the very riping of the time;
And for the Jew's bond, which he hath of me,
Let it not enter in your mind of love:
Be merry; and employ your chiefest thoughts
To courtship, and such fair ostents of love
As shall conveniently become you there:'
And even there, his eye being big with tears,
Turning his face, he put his hand behind him,
And with affection wondrous sensible
He wrung Bassanio's hand, and so they parted.
Solan. I think he only loves the world for
  him.
I pray thee, let us go and find him out,
And quicken his embraced heaviness
With some delight or other.
Salar.   Do we so. [*Exeunt.*

---

a *Gilded tombs.* The reading of all the old editions is " gilded timber." The critics of the Augustan age could not understand that timber, a word of common acceptation and in some uses technical, could belong to poetry. Rowe, therefore, turned timber into wood. Johnson converted the timber and the wood into tombs. We are disposed to agree with Douce that timber is possibly the right reading. But we think that Malone's interpretation of this reading may be questioned—" Worms do unfold gilded timber." To this Steevens replies—"How 's it possible for worms that have bred within timber to infold it?" It is somewhat strange that neither Malone nor Steevens saw that, without any violation of grammatical propriety, timber might be used as a plural noun. Gilded timber—timbers—engilt—do infold worms, not worms the timber. In the same manner, the golden casket which Morocco unlocked contained "a carrion death." Still, the original reading is harsh and startling; and Johnson very justly observes that the old mode of writing tombes might be easily mistaken for timber.

a *Reason'd* is here used for *discours'd*. We have the same employment of the word in Beaumont and Fletcher—
  "There is no end of women's *reasoning.*"

SCENE IX.—Belmont. *A Room in* Portia's
                    House.

Enter NERISSA, *with a* Servant.

Ner. Quick, quick, I pray thee, draw the
                    curtain straight;
The prince of Arragon hath ta'en his oath,
And comes to his election presently.

Flourish of Cornets. Enter the PRINCE OF ARRA-
GON, PORTIA, *and their Trains.*

Por. Behold, there stand the caskets, noble
    prince;
If you choose that wherein I am contain'd,
Straight shall our nuptial rites be solemniz'd;
But if you fail, without more speech, my lord,
You must be gone from hence immediately.
    Ar. I am enjoin'd by oath to observe three
    things:
First, never to unfold to any one
Which casket 'twas I chose; next, if I fail
Of the right casket, never in my life
To woo a maid in way of marriage; lastly,
If I do fail in fortune of my choice,
Immediately to leave you and be gone.
    Por. To these injunctions every one doth swear
That comes to hazard for my worthless self.
    Ar. And so have I address'd me: Fortune now
To my heart's hope!—Gold, silver, and base lead.

'Who chooseth me must give and hazard all he hath:'

You shall look fairer, ere I give, or hazard.
What says the golden chest? ha! let me see:

'Who chooseth me shall gain what many men desire.'

What many men desire.—That many may be
    meant
By the fool multitude, that choose by show,
Not learning more than the fond eye doth teach,
Which pries not to the interior, but, like the
    martlet,
Builds in the weather on the outward wall,
Even in the force and road of casualty.
I will not choose what many men desire,
Because I will not jump with common spirits,
And rank me with the barbarous multitudes.
Why, then to thee, thou silver treasure-house;
Tell me once more what title thou dost bear:

'Who chooseth me shall get as much as he deserves:'

And well said too. For who shall go about
To cozen fortune, and be honourable
Without the stamp of merit! Let none presume
To wear an undeserved dignity.
O, that estates, degrees, and offices,
Were not deriv'd corruptly! and that clear
    honour

Were purchas'd by the merit of the wearer!
How many then should cover that stand bare!
How many be commanded that command!
How much low peasantry would then be glean'd
From the true seed of honour! and how much
    honour
Pick'd from the chaff and ruin of the times,
To be new varnish'd! Well, but to my choice:

'Who chooseth me shall get as much as he deserves:'

I will assume desert:—Give me a key for this,
And instantly unlock my fortunes here.
    Por. Too long a pause for that which you find
        there.
    Ar. What's here? the portrait of a blinking
        idiot,
Presenting me a schedule? I will read it.
How much unlike art thou to Portia?
How much unlike my hopes and my deservings?

'Who chooseth me shall have as much as he deserves.'

Did I deserve no more than a fool's head?
Is that my prize? are my deserts no better?
    Por. To offend, and judge, are distinct offices,
And of opposed natures.
    Ar.   What is here?

    'The fire seven times tried this;
    Seven times tried that judgment is
    That did never choose amiss.
    Some there be that shadows kiss;
    Such have but a shadow's bliss.
    There be fools alive, I wis,
    Silver'd o'er; and so was this.
    Take what wife you will to bed,
    I will ever be your head:
    So begone; you are sped.'*

Still more fool I shall appear
By the time I linger here:
With one fool's head I came to woo,
But I go away with two.
Sweet, adieu! I'll keep my oath,
Patiently to bear my wroth.
            [*Exeunt* ARRAGON *and Train.*
    Por. Thus hath the candle sing'd the moth.
O these deliberate fools! when they do choose,
They have the wisdom by their wit to lose.
    Ner. The ancient saying is no heresy;—
Hanging and wiving goes by destiny.
    Por. Come, draw the curtain, Nerissa.

Enter a Servant.

    Serv. Where is my lady?
    Por.   Here; what would my lord?
    Serv. Madam, there is alighted at your gate
A young Venetian, one that comes before

* This line is usually corrupted into—
    "So begone, sir, you are sped"—
for the sake of the metre, as the syllable-counters say.

To signify the approaching of his lord:
From whom he bringeth sensible regreets;[a]
To wit, besides commends and courteous breath,
Gifts of rich value; yet I have not seen
So likely an ambassador of love:
A day in April never came so sweet,
To show how costly summer was at hand,
As this fore-spurrer comes before his lord.

  [a] *Regreets*—salutations.

Por. No more, I pray thee; I am half
    afeard,
Thou wilt say anon he is some kin to thee,
Thou spend'st such high-day wit in praising
    him.
Come, come, Nerissa; for I long to see
Quick Cupid's post that comes so mannerly.
  Ner. Bassanio, lord love if thy will it be!
                                    [*Exeunt*

['In a gondola were seen together.']

ILLUSTRATIONS OF ACT II.

¹ Scene I.

THE stage direction of the quartos is curious, as exhibiting a proof that some attention to costume prevailed in the ancient theatres:—"Enter Morochus, a tawny Moore all in white, and three or foure followers accordingly, with Portia, Nerissa, and their traius."

² Scene II.—" *Which is the way to master Jew's ?*"

It does not appear that the Jews (hardly used everywhere) had more need of patience in Venice than in other states. The same traditional reports against them exist there as elsewhere, testifying to the popular hatred and prejudice : but they were too valuable a part of a commercial population not to be more or less considered and taken care of. An island was appropriated to them ; but they long ago overflowed into other parts of the city. Many who have grown extremely rich by money-lending have their fine palaces in various quarters ; and of these, some are among the most respectable and enlightened of the citizens. The Jews who people their quarter are such as are unable to rise out of it. Its buildings are ancient and lofty, but ugly and sordid. " Our synagogue" is, of course, there. Judging by the commotion among its inhabitants when the writer traversed it, it would seem that strangers rarely enter the quarter. It is situated on the canal which leads to Mestre. There are houses old enough to have been Shylock's, with balconies from which Jessica might have talked ; and ground enough beneath, between the house and the water, for her lover to stand, hidden in the shadow, or under "a pent-house." Hence, too, her gondola might at once start for the mainland, without having to traverse any part of the city.—(M.)

³ Scene II.—" *I will run as far as God has any ground.*"

A characteristic speech in the mouth of a Venetian. Ground to run upon being a scarce convenience in Venice, its lower orders of inhabitants regard the great expanse of the mainland with feelings of admiration which can be little entered into by those who have been able, all their days, to walk where they would.—(M.)

⁴ Scene II.—" *I have here a dish of doves.*"

Mr. Brown, as we have noticed in The Taming of the Shrew, has expressed his decided conviction that some of the dramas of Shakspere exhibit the most striking proofs that our poet had visited Italy. The passage before us is cited by Mr. Brown as one of these proofs :—" Where did he obtain his numerous graphic touches of national manners? where did he learn of an old villager's coming into the city with ' a dish of doves' as a present to his son's master ? A present thus given, and in our days too, and of doves, is not uncommon in Italy. I myself have partaken there, with due relish, in memory of poor old Gobbo, of a dish of doves, presented by the father of a servant."—(*Autobiographical Poems.*)

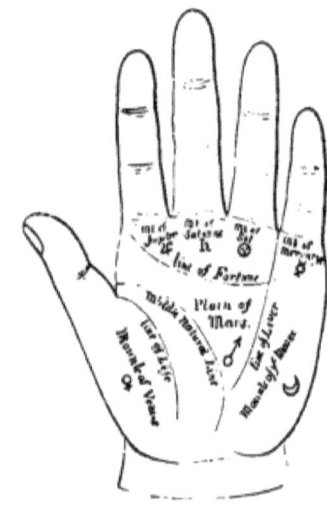

⁵ Scene II.—" *Go to, here's a simple line of life !*"

Palmistry, or chiromancy, had once its learned professors as well as astrology. The printing-press consigned the delusion to the gypsies. Chiromancy and physiognomy were once kindred sciences. The one has passed away amongst other credulities belonging to ages which we call ignorant and superstitious. The other, although fashionable half a century ago, is professed by none, but, more or less, has its influence upon all. The wood-cut which we prefix is copied from a little book with which Shakspere must have been familiar :—' Briefe introductions, both natural, pleasaunte, and also delectable, unto the Art of Chiromancy, or manual divination, and Phisiognomy: with circumstances upon the faces of the Signes. Also certain Canons or Rules upon Diseases and Sicknesses, &c. Written in yᵉ Latin tongue by Jhon Indagine, Prieste, and now lately translated into Englishe, by Fabian Withers. For Richard Jugge, 1558.' Launcelot, as well as his betters, were diligent students of the mysteries interpreted by John Indagine, Priest; and a simple or complex line of life were indications that made even some of the wise exult or tremble. Launcelot's "small trifle of wives" was, however, hardly compatible with the *simple* line of life. There must have been too many *crosses* in such a destiny.

⁶ SCENE V.—" *Thou shalt not gormandize.*"

The word *gormandize*, which is equivalent to the French *gourmander*, is generally considered to be of uncertain origin. Zachary Grey, however, in his ' Notes on Shakspeare,' quotes a curious story from Webb's ' Vindication of Stone-Heng restored' (1665), which at any rate will amuse, if it does not convince, our readers :—" During the stay of the Danes in Wiltshire they consumed their time in profuseness and belly cheer, in idleness and sloth. Insomuch that, as from their laziness in general, we even to this day call them Lur-Danes; so, from the licentiousness of *Gurmond* and his army in particular, we brand all luxurious and profuse people by the name of *Gurmandizers*. And this luxury and this laziness are the sole monuments, the only memorials, by which the Danes have made themselves notorious to posterity, by lying encamped in Wiltshire."

⁷ SCENE V.—" *Black Monday.*"

Stow, the Chronicler, thus describes the origin of this name :—" Black-Monday is Easter-Monday, and was so called on this occasion: in the 34th of Edward III. (1360), the 14th of April, and the morrow after Easter-day, King Edward, with his host, lay before the city of Paris: which day was full dark of mist and hail, and so bitter cold, that many men died on their horses' backs with the cold. Wherefore unto this day it hath been called Black-Monday."

⁸ SCENE V.—" *The wry-neck'd fife.*"

There is some doubt whether *the fife* is here the instrument or the musician. Boswell has given a quotation from Barnaby Rich's Aphorisms, 1618, which is very much in point :—" *A fife is a wry-neckt musician*, for he always looks away from his instrument." And yet we are inclined to think that Shakspere intended the instrument. We are of this opinion principally from the circumstance that the passage is an imitation of Horace, in which the instrument is decidedly meant :—

" Primâ nocte domum claude; neque in vias.
Sub cantu querulae despice tibiae."—(*Carm*. l. iii. 7.)

(By the way, Farmer has not told us from what source, except the original, Shakspere derived this idea; nor could Farmer, for there was no English translation of any of the Odes of Horace in Shakspere's time.) But, independent of the internal evidence derived from the imitation, the form of the old English flute—the fife being a small flute—justifies, we think, the epithet *wry-neck'd*. This flute was called the *flute à bec*, the upper part or mouth-piece resembling the beak of a bird. And this form was as old as the Pan of antiquity. The terminal figure of Pan in the Townly Gallery exhibits it :—

⁹ SCENE V.—" *Will be worth a Jewess' eye.*"

The play upon the word alludes to the common proverbial expression, " worth a Jew's eye." That worth was the price which the persecuted Jews paid for the immunity from mutilation and death. When our rapacious King John extorted an enormous sum from the Jew of Bristol by drawing his teeth, the threat of putting out an eye would have the like effect upon other Jews. The former prevalence of the saying is proved from the fact that we still retain it, although its meaning is now little known.

¹⁰ SCENE VII.—"*A coin that bears the figure of an angel.*"

Verstegan, in his 'Restitution of Decayed Intelligence,' gives the following account of the origin of the practice amongst the English monarchs of insculping an angel upon their coin :—

"To come now unto the cause of the general calling of our ancestors by the name of Englishmen, and our country consequently by the name of England, it is to be noted, that the seven petty kingdoms aforenamed, of Kent, South-Saxons, East-English, West-Saxons, East-Saxons, Northumbers, and Mercians, came in fine one after another by means of the West-Saxons, who subdued and got the sovereignty of all the rest, to be all brought into one monarchy under King Egbert, king of the said West-Saxons. This king then considering that so many different names as the distinct kingdoms before had caused, was now no more necessary, and that as the people were all originally of one nation, so was it fit they should again be brought under one name; and although they had had the general name of Saxons, as unto this day they are of the Welch and Irish called, yet did he rather choose and ordain that they should be all called English-men, as but a part of them before were called; and that the country should be called England. To the affectation of which name of English-men, it should seem he was chiefly moved in respect of Pope Gregory, his alluding the name of *Engelisce* unto Angel-like. The name of *Engel* is yet at this present in all the Teutonick tongues to wit, the high and low Dutch, &c., as much to say, as Angel, and if a Dutch-man be asked how he would in his language call an Angel-like-man, he would answer, *ein English-man;* and being asked how in his own language he would or doth call an English-man, he can give no other name for him, but even the very same that he gave before for an Angel-like-man, that is, as before is said, *ein English-man, Engel* being in their tongue an Angel, and English, which they write *Englische,* Angel-like. And such reason and consideration may have moved our former kings, upon their best coin of pure and fine gold, to set the image of an angel, which, may be supposed, hath as well been used before the Norman conquest, as since"

We subjoin the angel of Elizabeth.

¹¹ SCENE VIII.—"*That in a gondola were seen together.*"

The only way of reaching the mainland was in a gondola. But to be "seen" was altogether a matter of choice,—the gondola being the most private mode of conveyance in the world, (not excepting the Turkish palanquin,) and the fittest for an elopement.

[Angel of Queen Elizabeth.]

[Rialto Bridge]

ACT III.

SCENE I.—Venice. *A Street.*

Enter SOLANIO *and* SALARINO.

Solan. Now, what news on the Rialto?

Salar. Why, yet it lives there unchcck'd, that Antonio hath a ship of rich lading wracked on the narrow seas,—the Goodwins, I think they call the place;[1] a very dangerous flat and fatal, where the carcases of many a tall ship lie buried, as they say, if my gossip report be an honest woman of her word.

Solan. I would she were as lying a gossip in that, as ever knapp'd ginger, or made her neighbours believe she wept for the death of a third husband: But it is true,—without any slips of prolixity, or crossing the plain high-way of talk, —that the good Antonio, the honest Antonio,— O that I had a title good enough to keep his name company!—

Salar. Come, the full stop.

Solan. Ha,—what say'st thou?—Why the end is, he hath lost a ship.

Salar. I would it might prove the end of his losses!

Solan. Let me say amen betimes, lest the devil cross my prayer; for here he comes in the likeness of a Jew.

Enter SHYLOCK.

How now, Shylock? wnat news among the merchants?

Shy. You knew, none so well, none so well as you, of my daughter's flight.

Salar. That's certain. I, for my part, knew the tailor that made the wings she flew withal.

Solan. And Shylock, for his own part, knew the bird was fledg'd; and then it is the complexion of them all to leave the dam.

Shy. She is damn'd for it.

Salar. That's certain, if the devil may be her judge.

Shy. My own flesh and blood to rebel!

Solan. Out upon it, old carrion! rebels it at these years?

Shy. I say, my daughter is my flesh and blood.

Salar. There is more difference between thy flesh and hers, than between jet and ivory; more between your bloods, than there is between red wine and rhenish:—But tell us, do you hear whether Antonio have had any loss at sea or no?

Shy. There I have another bad match: a bankrout, a prodigal, who dare scarce show his head on the Rialto; a beggar, that was used to come so smug upon the mart.—Let him look to his bond: he was wont to call me usurer;—let him look to his bond: he was wont to lend money for a Christian courtesy;—let him look to his bond.

Salar. Why, I am sure, if he forfeit, thou wilt not take his flesh? What's that good for?

Shy. To bait fish withal: if it will feed nothing else it will feed my revenge. He hath disgraced me, and hindered me half a million; laughed at my losses, mocked at my gains, scorned my nation, thwarted my bargains, cooled my friends, heated mine enemies; and what's his reason? I am a Jew: Hath not a Jew eyes? hath not a Jew hands, organs, dimensions, senses, affections, passions? fed with the same food, hurt with the same weapons, subject to the same diseases, healed by the same means, warmed and cooled by the same winter and summer, as a Christian is? If you prick us, do we not bleed? if you tickle us, do we not laugh? if you poison us, do we not die? and if you wrong us, shall we not revenge? If we are like you in the rest, we will resemble you in that. If a Jew wrong a Christian, what is his humility? revenge: If a Christian wrong a Jew, what should his sufferance be by Christian example? why, revenge. The villainy you teach me I will execute; and it shall go hard but I will better the instruction.

Enter a Servant.

Serv. Gentlemen, my master Antonio is at his house, and desires to speak with you both.

Salar. We have been up and down to seek him.

Enter TUBAL.

Solan. Here comes another of the tribe; a third cannot be matched, unless the devil himself turn Jew.

[*Exeunt* SOLAN. SALAR. *and* Servant.

Shy. How now, Tubal, what news from Genoa? hast thou found my daughter?

Tub. I often came where I did hear of her, but cannot find her.

Shy. Why there, there, there, there! a diamond gone, cost me two thousand ducats in Frankfort! The curse never fell upon our nation till now; I never felt it till now:—two thousand

ducats in that; and other precious, precious jewels.—I would my daughter were dead at my foot, and the jewels in her ear! 'would she were hears'd at my foot, and the ducats in her coffin! No news of them?—Why, so:—and I know not how much is* spent in the search: Why, thou loss upon loss! the thief gone with so much, and so much to find the thief; and no satisfaction, no revenge: nor no ill luck stirring but what lights o' my shoulders; no sighs but o' my breathing; no tears but o' my shedding.

Tub. Yes, other men have ill luck too. Antonio, as I heard in Genoa,—

Shy. What, what, what? ill luck, ill luck?

Tub.—hath an argosy cast away, coming from Tripolis.

Shy. I thank God, I thank God:—Is it true? is it true?

Tub. I spoke with some of the sailors that escaped the wrack.

Shy. I thank thee, good Tubal;—Good news, good news: ha! ha!—Where? in Genoa?

Tub. Your daughter spent in Genoa, as I heard, one night, fourscore ducats!

Shy. Thou stick'st a dagger in me:—I shall never see my gold again: Fourscore ducats at a sitting! fourscore ducats!

Tub. There came divers of Antonio's creditors in my company to Venice, that swear he cannot choose but break.

Shy. I am very glad of it: I'll plague him; I'll torture him; I am glad of it.

Tub. One of them showed me a ring, that he had of your daughter for a monkey.

Shy. Out upon her! Thou torturest me, Tubal: it was my turquoise; I had it of Leah, when I was a bachelor: I would not have given it for a wilderness of monkeys.

Tub. But Antonio is certainly undone.

Shy. Nay, that's true, that's very true: Go, Tubal, fee me an officer, bespeak him a fortnight before: I will have the heart of him, if he forfeit; for were he out of Venice, I can make what merchandize I will: Go, Tubal, and meet me at our synagogue; go, good Tubal; at our synagogue, Tubal. [*Exeunt*

SCENE II.—Belmont. *A Room in* Portia's *House.*

Enter BASSANIO, PORTIA, GRATIANO, NERISSA, *and* Attendants. *The caskets are set out.*

Por. I pray you, tarry; pause a day or two, Before you hazard; for, in choosing wrong

* *How much is*—So the folio. The quartos, *what's*

I lose your company; therefore, forbear a while:
There's something tells me, (but it is not love,)
I would not lose you; and you know yourself,
Hate councils not in such a quality:
But lest you should not understand me well,
(And yet a maiden hath no tongue but thought,)
I would detain you here some month or two,
Before you venture for me. I could teach you
How to choose right, but then I am forsworn;
So will I never be: so may you miss me;
But if you do, you'll make me wish a sin,
That I had been forsworn. Beshrew your eyes,
They have o'er-look'd[a] me, and divided me;
One half of me is yours, the other half yours,—
Mine own, I would say; but if mine, then yours,
And so all yours: O! these naughty times
Put bars between the owners and their rights;
And so, though yours, not yours.—Prove it so,
Let fortune go to hell for it,—not I.
I speak too long; but 'tis to peize[b] the time;
To eke it, and to draw it out in length,
To stay you from election.
  Bass.   Let me choose;
For, as I am, I live upon the rack.
  Por. Upon the rack, Bassanio? then confess
What treason there is mingled with your love.
  Bass. None, but that ugly treason of mistrust,
Which makes me fear the enjoying of my love:
There may as well be amity and life
'Tween snow and fire, as treason and my love.
  Por. Ay, but I fear you speak upon the rack,
Where men enforced do speak any thing.
  Bass. Promise me life, and I'll confess the truth.
  Por. Well, then, confess and live.
  Bass.   Confess, and love,
Had been the very sum of my confession:
O happy torment, when my torturer
Doth teach me answers for deliverance!
But let me to my fortune and the caskets.
  Por. Away then: I am lock'd in one of them;
If you do love me, you will find me out.
Nerissa, and the rest, stand all aloof.
Let music sound, while he doth make his choice;
Then, if he lose, he makes a swan-like end,
Fading in music: that the comparison
May stand more proper, my eye shall be the stream,
And watery death-bed for him: He may win;

And what is music then? then music is
Even as the flourish when true subjects bow
To a new-crowned monarch: such it is,
As are those dulcet sounds in break of day,
That creep into the dreaming bridegroom's ear,
And summon him to marriage. Now he goes,
With no less presence, but with much more love,
Than young Alcides, when he did redeem
The virgin tribute paid by howling Troy
To the sea-monster: I stand for sacrifice
The rest aloof are the Dardanian wives,
With bleared visages, come forth to view
The issue of the exploit. Go, Hercules!
Live thou, I live:—With much much more dismay
I view the fight, than thou that mak'st the fray.

  Music, whilst BASSANIO *comments on the caskets to himself.*

SONG.

1. Tell me where is fancy bred,
   Or in the heart, or in the head?
   How begot, how nourished?
   Reply, reply.[a]

2. It is engender'd in the eyes,
   With gazing fed; and fancy dies
   In the cradle where it lies:
   Let us all ring fancy's knell;
   I'll begin it,—Ding, dong, bell.
   All.   Ding, dong, bell.

  Bass. So may the outward shows be least themselves;[b]
The world is still deceiv'd with ornament.
In law, what plea so tainted and corrupt,
But, being season'd with a gracious voice,
Obscures the show of evil? In religion,
What damned error, but some sober brow
Will bless it, and approve it with a text,
Hiding the grossness with fair ornament?
There is no vice so simple, but assumes
Some mark of virtue on his outward parts.
How many cowards, whose hearts are all as false
As stayers of sand,[c] wear yet upon their chins

---

[a] These words "*Reply, reply.*" which are unquestionably part of the song, were considered by Johnson to stand in the old copies as a marginal direction; and thus, from Johnson's time, in many editions in which his authority is admitted, the line has been suppressed. In all the old copies the passage is printed thus, in italic type:—
" *How begot, how nourished. Replie, replie.*"
The reply is then made; and, probably, by a second voice. The mutilation of the song, in the belief that the words were a stage direction, is certainly one of the most tasteless corruptions of the many for which the editors of Shakspere are answerable.

[b] The old stage direction for the conduct of this scene has been retained in the modern editions:—" *Music, whilst Bassanio comments on the caskets to himself.*" He has made up his mind whilst the music has proceeded, and then follows out the course of his thoughts in words.

[c] *Stayers of sand.* This is ordinarily printed *stairs of sand;* and no explanation is given by the commentators. In the first folio the word is printed, as we print it—*stayers*

---

[a] *O'erlook'd.* In the Merry Wives of Windsor we have
" Vild worm, thou wast o'erlook'd even in thy birth."
The word is here used in the same sense; which is derived from the popular superstition of the influence of fairies and witches. The eyes of Bassanio have o'erlook'd Portia, and she yields to the enchantment.

[b] *Peize. Poise* and *Peize* are the same words. To weigh the *time*, is, to keep it in suspense,—upon the balance.

The beards of Hercules and frowning Mars,
Who, inward search'd, have livers white as milk;
And these assume but valour's excrement,
To render them redoubted! Look on beauty,
And you shall see 'tis purchas'd by the weight;
Which therein works a miracle in nature,
Making them lightest that wear most of it:
So are those crisped snaky golden locks,
Which make such wanton gambols with the wind,
Upon supposed fairness, often known
To be the dowry of a second head,
The scull that bred them in the sepulchre.'
Thus ornament is but the guiled ᵃ shore
To a most dangerous sea; the beauteous scarf
Veiling an Indian beauty; in a word,
The seeming truth which cunning times put on
To entrap the wisest. Therefore, thou gaudy
    gold,
Hard food for Midas, I will none of thee;
Nor none of thee, thou pale and common drudge
'Tween man and man. But thou, thou meagre
    lead,
Which rather threat'nest than dost promise
    aught,
Thy paleness ᵇ moves me more than eloquence,
And here choose I. Joy be the consequence!

Por. How all the other passions fleet to air,
As doubtful thoughts, and rash-embrac'd despair,
And shudd'ring fear, and green-ey'd jealousy.
O love, be moderate, allay thy ecstacy,
In measure rain thy joy,ᶜ scant this excess;
I feel too much thy blessing, make it less,
For fear I surfeit!

Bass.   What find I here?
            [*Opening the leaden casket.*

Fair Portia's counterfeit? What demi-god
Hath come so near creation? Move these eyes?
Or whether, riding on the balls of mine,
Seem they in motion? Here are sever'd lips,
Parted with sugar breath; so sweet a bar
Should sunder such sweet friends: Here in her
    hairs
The painter plays the spider; and hath woven
A golden mesh to entrap the hearts of men,
Faster than gnats in cobwebs: But her eyes,—
How could he see to do them? having made one,
Methinks it should have power to steal both his,
And leave itself unfurnish'd:ᵃ Yet look, how far
The substance of my praise doth wrong this
    shadow
In underprising it, so far this shadow
Doth limp behind the substance.—Here's the
    scroll,
The continent and summary of my fortune.

  ' You that choose not by the view,
    Chance as fair, and choose as true!
    Since this fortune falls to you,
    Be content, and seek no new.
    If you be well pleas'd with this,
    And hold your fortune for your bliss,
    Turn you where your lady is,
    And claim her with a loving kiss.'

A gentle scroll.—Fair lady, by your leave:
                        [*Kissing her.*
I come by note, to give and to receive.
Like one of two contending in a prize,
That thinks he hath done well in people's eyes,
Hearing applause and universal shout,
Giddy in spirit, still gazing in a doubt
Whether those peals of praise be his or no;
So, thrice fair lady, stand I, even so;
As doubtful whether what I see be true,
Until confirm'd, sign'd, ratified by you.

Por. You see me, lord Bassanio, where I
    stand,ᵇ
Such as I am: though, for myself alone,
I would not be ambitious in my wish,
To wish myself much better; yet, for you,
I would be trebled twenty times myself;
A thousand times more fair, ten thousand times
More rich;
That only to stand high in your account,
I might in virtues, beauties, livings, friends,

In the same edition we have, in *As You Like It,* "In these
degrees have they made a *paires of staires* to marriage." We
have no great reliance upon the orthography of any of the
old editions; but the distinction between *stayers* and *staires*
is here remarkable. Further, the propriety of the image
appears to us to justify the restoration of the original word
in this passage. Cowards in their falseness—their assumption of appearances without realities—may be compared to
stairs of sand, which betray the feet of those who trust to
them; but *we* have here cowards appearing ready to face an
enemy with—
   "The beards of Hercules and frowning Mars:"
they are false as *stayers* of sand—banks, bulwarks of sand,
—that the least opposition will throw down—vain defences
—feeble ramparts. We derive the word *stair* from the
Anglo-Saxon *stigan, to ascend;*—*staig*—and thence *stayer*—
from the Teutonic *staen* or *stehen, to stand.*

ᵃ *Guiled,*—deceiving. The active and passive participles
are often substituted each for the other by Shakspere, and
the other Elizabethan poets.

ᵇ *Paleness.* So all the old copies. But it is ordinarily printed
plainness, upon a suggestion of Warburton. It appeared to
him that, because silver was called "thou pale and common
drudge," lead ought to be distinguished by some other
quality. Malone has justly observed that if the emphasis
is placed on *thy,* Warburton's objection is obviated.

ᶜ *Rain the joy.* Some would read *rein* thy joy. To *rain*
is here to pour down. Lord Lansdowne, who in 1701 had
the temerity to produce an improved version of *The Merchant* of Venice, modernizes the passage into—
        "In measure *pour* thy joy."

ᵃ *Unfurnish'd*—unsurrounded by the other features. The
poetic conceit of this passage is supposed by Steevens to
have been founded upon a description in Greene's 'History
of fair Bellora.' But it is by no means certain that the tract
was written by Greene, or that it was published before The
Merchant of Venice. The passage, however, illustrates the
text,—" If Apelles had been tasked to have drawn her counterfeit, her two bright burning lamps would have so dazzled
his quick-seeing senses, that, quite despairing to express
with his cunning pencil so admirable a work of nature, he
had been inforced to have stayed his hand, and left this
earthly Venus *unfinished.*"

Exceed account: but the full sum of me
Is sum of nothing;* which, to term in gross,
Is an unlesson'd girl, unschool'd, unpractis'd:
Happy in this, she is not yet so old
But she may learn; happier than this,
She is not bred so dull but she can learn;
Happiest of all, is, that her gentle spirit
Commits itself to yours to be directed,
As from her lord, her governor, her king.
Myself, and what is mine, to you and yours
Is now converted: but now I was the lord
Of this fair mansion, master of my servants,
Queen o'er myself; and even now, but now,
This house, these servants, and this same myself,
Are yours, my lord,—I give them with this
    ring;
Which when you part from, lose, or give away,
Let it presage the ruin of your love,
And be my vantage to exclaim on you.
    Bass. Madam, you have bereft me of all
      words,
Only my blood speaks to you in my veins:
And there is such confusion in my powers,
As, after some oration fairly spoke
By a beloved prince, there doth appear
Among the buzzing pleased multitude;
Where every something, being blent together,
Turns to a wild of nothing, save of joy,
Express'd, and not express'd: But when this
    ring
Parts from this finger, then parts life from
    hence;
O, then be bold to say, Bassanio's dead.
    Ner. My lord and lady, it is now our time,
That have stood by and seen our wishes
    prosper,
To cry, good joy; Good joy, my lord and lady!
    Gra. My lord Bassanio, and my gentle lady,
I wish you all the joy that you can wish;
For I am sure you can wish none from me:
And, when your honours mean to solemnize
The bargain of your faith, I do beseech you,
Even at that time I may be married too.
    Bass. With all my heart, so thou canst get a
      wife.
    Gra. I thank your lordship; you have got
      me one.
My eyes, my lord, can look as swift as yours:
You saw the mistress, I beheld the maid;
You lov'd, I lov'd; for intermission
No more pertains to me, my lord, than you.
Your fortune stood upon the caskets there;

* *Sum of nothing.* So the folio, and one of the quartos. The quarto printed by Roberts reads *sum of something*; which is the ordinary text. We agree with Monck Mason in preferring the reading of the folio. "as it is Portia's intention in this speech to undervalue herself."

And so did mine too, as the matter falls:
For wooing here, until I sweat again,
And swearing, till my very roof was dry
With oaths of love, at last,—if promise last,—
I got a promise of this fair one here,
To have her love, provided that your fortune
Achiev'd her mistress.
    Por.   Is this true, Nerissa?
    Ner. Madam, it is, so you stand pleas'd
        withal.
    Bass. And do you, Gratiano, mean good
      faith?
    Gra. Yes, faith, my lord.
    Bass. Our feast shall be much honour'd in
      your marriage.
    Gra. We'll play with them, the first boy for
a thousand ducats.
    Ner. What, and stake down?
    Gra. No; we shall ne'er win at that sport,
        and stake down.
But who comes here? Lorenzo, and his infidel?
What, and my old Venetian friend, Solanio?*

    Enter LORENZO, JESSICA, *and* SOLANIO.

    Bass. Lorenzo, and Solanio, welcome hither;
If that the youth of my new interest here
Have power to bid you welcome:—By your
    leave,
I bid my very friends and countrymen,
Sweet Portia, welcome.
    Por.   So do I, my lord;
They are entirely welcome.
    Lor. I thank your honour:—For my part, my
        lord,
My purpose was not to have seen you here;
But meeting with Solanio by the way,
He did entreat me, past all saying nay,
To come with him along.
    Solan.   I did, my lord,
And I have reason for it. Signior Antonio
Commends him to you.
        [*Gives* BASSANIO *a letter.*

* *Solanio.* For the reasons assigned in the first note to this play, we have dispensed with the character of Salerio, and have substituted Solanio in the present scene. It appears to us not only that there is no necessity for introducing a new character, Salerio, in addition to Solanio and Salarino, but that the dramatic propriety is violated by this introduction. In the first scene of this act the servant of Antonio thus addresses Solanio and Salarino:—" Gentlemen, my master Antonio is at his house, and desires to speak with you both." To the unfortunate Antonio, then, these friends repair. What can be more natural than that, after the conference, the one should be despatched to Bassanio, and the other remain with him whose " creditors grow cruel!" We accordingly find in the third scene of this Act, that one of them accompanies Antonio when he is in custody of the gaoler. In the confusion in which the names are printed, it is difficult to say which goes to Belmont, and which remains at Venice. We have determined the matter by the metre of this line, and of the subsequent lines in which the name is mentioned.

THE MERCHANT OF VENICE.

Bass.   Ere I ope his letter,
I pray you tell me how my good friend doth.
  Solan. Not sick, my lord, unless it be in mind;
Nor well, unless in mind: his letter there
Will show you his estate.
  Gra. Nerissa, cheer yon stranger: bid her
    welcome.
Your hand, Solanio. What's the news from
    Venice?
How doth that royal merchant, good Antonio?
I know he will be glad of our success;
We are the Jasons, we have won the fleece.
  Solan. I would you had won the fleece that he
    hath lost!
  Por. There are some shrewd contents in yon
    same paper,
That steal the colour from Bassanio's cheek;
Some dear friend dead; else nothing in the
    world
Could turn so much the constitution
Of any constant man. What, worse and worse?—
With leave, Bassanio; I am half yourself,
And I must freely have the half of anything
That this same paper brings you.
  Bass.   O sweet Portia,
Here are a few of the unpleasant'st words
That ever blotted paper! Gentle lady,
When I did first impart my love to you,
I freely told you, all the wealth I had
Ran in my veins,—I was a gentleman;
And then I told you true: and yet, dear lady,
Rating myself at nothing, you shall see
How much I was a braggart: When I told you
My state was nothing, I should then have told
    you
That I was worse than nothing; for, indeed,
I have engag'd myself to a dear friend,
Engag'd my friend to his mere enemy,
To feed my means. Here is a letter, lady;
The paper as the body of my friend,
And every word in it a gaping wound,
Issuing life-blood. But is it true, Solanio?
Have all his ventures fail'd? What, not one hit?
From Tripolis, from Mexico, and England,
From Lisbon, Barbary, and India?
And not one vessel 'scape the dreadful touch
Of merchant-marring rocks?
  Solan.   Not one, my lord.
Besides, it should appear, that if he had
The present money to discharge the Jew,
He would not take it: Never did I know
A creature that did bear the shape of man,
So keen and greedy to confound a man:
He plies the duke at morning, and at night;
And doth impeach the freedom of the state

If they deny him justice: twenty merchants,
The duke himself, and the magnificoes
Of greatest port, have all persuaded with him;
But none can drive him from the envious plea
Of forfeiture, of justice, and his bond.
  Jes. When I was with him, I have heard him
    swear
To Tubal, and to Chus, his countrymen,
That he would rather have Antonio's flesh
Than twenty times the value of the sum
That he did owe him; and I know, my lord,
If law, authority, and power deny not,
It will go hard with poor Antonio.
  Por. Is it your dear friend that is thus in
    trouble?
  Bass. The dearest friend to me, the kindest
    man,
The best condition'd and unwearied spirit
In doing courtesies; and one in whom
The ancient Roman honour more appears,
Than any that draws breath in Italy.
  Por. What sum owes he the Jew?
  Bass. For me, three thousand ducats.
  Por.   What, no more?
Pay him six thousand, and deface the bond;
Double six thousand, and then treble that,
Before a friend of this description
Shall lose a hair through Bassanio's fault.
First, go with me to church, and call me wife:
And then away to Venice to your friend;
For never shall you lie by Portia's side
With an unquiet soul. You shall have gold
To pay the petty debt twenty times over;
When it is paid, bring your true friend along:
My maid Nerissa, and myself, mean time,
Will live as maids and widows. Come, away;
For you shall hence upon your wedding-day:
Bid your friends welcome, show a merry
    cheer:
Since you are dear bought, I will love you dear.
But let me hear the letter of your friend.
  Bass. [*Reads.*]
  'Sweet Bassanio, my ships have all miscarried, my creditors grow cruel, my estate is very low, my bond to the Jew is forfeit: and since, in paying it, it is impossible I should live, all debts are cleared between you and I, if I might but see you at my death: notwithstanding, use your pleasure: if your love do not persuade you to come, let not my letter.'
  Por. O love, despatch all business, and be
    gone.
  Bass. Since I have your good leave to go
    away,
I will make haste: but till I come again,
No bed shall e'er be guilty of my stay,
Nor rest be interposer 'twixt us twain.
                                [*Exeunt.*

SCENE III.—Venice. *A Street.*

Enter SHYLOCK, SALARINO, ANTONIO, *and* Gaoler.

Shy. Gaoler, look to him. Tell not me of mercy;—
This is the fool that lends out money gratis;—
Gaoler, look to him.
  Ant.   Hear me yet, good Shylock.
  Shy. I'll have my bond; speak not against my bond;
I have sworn an oath that I will have my bond:
Thou call'dst me dog, before thou hadst a cause:
But, since I am a dog, beware my fangs:
The duke shall grant me justice.—I do wonder,
Thou naughty gaoler, that thou art so fond [a]
To come abroad with him at his request.
  Ant. I pray thee, hear me speak.
  Shy. I'll have my bond; I will not hear thee speak:
I'll have my bond; and therefore speak no more.
I'll not be made a soft and dull-ey'd fool,
To shake the head, relent, and sigh, and yield
To Christian intercessors. Follow not;
I'll have no speaking; I will have my bond.
                           [*Exit* SHYLOCK.
  Salar. It is the most impenetrable cur
That ever kept with men.
  Ant.   Let him alone;
I'll follow him no more with bootless prayers.
He seeks my life; his reason well I know;
I oft deliver'd from his forfeitures
Many that have at times made moan to me;
Therefore he hates me.
  Salar.   I am sure the duke
Will never grant this forfeiture to hold.
  Ant. The duke cannot deny the course of law,
For the commodity that strangers have
With us in Venice; if it be denied,
'Twill much impeach the justice of the state; [b]

---

[a] *Fond.* This is generally explained as *foolish*—one of the senses in which Shakspere very often uses the word. We are inclined to think that it here means *indulgent*, tender, weakly compassionate.
[b] The construction of this passage, as it stands in all the old copies, is exceedingly difficult; and the paraphrases of Warburton and Malone do not remove the difficulty. Their reading, which is ordinarily followed, is:—
  "The Duke cannot deny the course of law;
  For the commodity that strangers have
  With us in Venice, if it be denied,
  Will much impeach the justice of the state."
Here *commodity* governs *impeach.* But *commodity* is used in the sense of traffic—commercial intercourse; and although the traffickers might impeach the justice of the state, the traffic cannot. Capell, neglected and despised by all the commentators, has, with the very slightest change of the

Since that the trade and profit of the city
Consisteth of all nations. Therefore, go:
These griefs and losses have so 'bated me,
That I shall hardly spare a pound of flesh
To-morrow to my bloody creditor.
Well, gaoler, on:—Pray God, Bassanio come
To see me pay his debt, and then I care not!
                           [*Exeunt.*

SCENE IV.—Belmont. *A Room in* Portia's *House.*

Enter PORTIA, NERISSA, LORENZO, JESSICA, *and* BALTHAZAR.

  Lor. Madam, although I speak it in your presence,
You have a noble and a true conceit
Of god-like amity; which appears most strongly
In bearing thus the absence of your lord.
But, if you knew to whom you show this honour,
How true a gentleman you send relief,
How dear a lover of my lord your husband,
I know you would be prouder of the work,
Than customary bounty can enforce you.
  Por. I never did repent for doing good,
Nor shall not now: for in companions
That do converse and waste the time together
Whose souls do bear an equal yoke of love,
There must be needs a like proportion
Of lineaments, of manners, and of spirit;
Which makes me think, that this Antonio,
Being the bosom lover of my lord,
Must needs be like my lord: If it be so,
How little is the cost I have bestow'd,
In purchasing the semblance of my soul
From out the state of hellish cruelty!
This comes too near the praising of myself;
Therefore, no more of it: hear other things.
Lorenzo, I commit into your hands
The husbandry and manage of my house,
Until my lord's return: for mine own part,
I have toward heaven breath'd a secret vow,
To live in prayer and contemplation,
Only attended by Nerissa here,
Until her husband and my lord's return:
There is a monastery two miles off,
And there we will abide. I do desire you
Not to deny this imposition;
To which my love, and some necessity,
Now lays upon you.

---

original, supplied a text which has a clear and precise meaning; and this we have followed:—The Duke cannot deny the course of law *on account of* the interchange which strangers have with us in Venice; if it be denied, 'twill much impeach the justice of the state.

Lor. Madam, with all my heart,
I shall obey you in all fair commands.
Por. My people do already know my mind,
And will acknowledge you and Jessica
In place of lord Bassanio and myself.
So fare you well, till we shall meet again.
   Lor. Fair thoughts and happy hours attend
      on you!
   Jes. I wish your ladyship all heart's content.
   Por. I thank you for your wish, and am well
      pleas'd
To wish it back on you: fare you well, Jessica.
      [*Exeunt* JESSICA *and* LORENZO.
Now, Balthazar,
As I have ever found thee honest, true,
So let me find thee still: Take this same letter,
And use thou all the endeavour of a man
In speed to Padua;[a] see thou render this
Into my cousin's hand, doctor Bellario;
And, look, what notes and garments he doth
      give thee
Bring them, I pray thee, with imagin'd speed
Unto the traneect,[b] to the common ferry
Which trades to Venice:[c]—waste no time in
      words,
But get thee gone; I shall be there before thee.
   Balth. Madam, I go with all convenient speed.
      [*Exit.*
   Por. Come on, Nerissa; I have work in hand,
That you yet know not of: we'll see our hus-
      bands
Before they think of us.
   Ner. Shall they see us?
   Por. They shall, Nerissa; but in such a habit,
That they shall think we are accomplished
With that we lack. I'll hold thee any wager,
When we are both accouter'd like young men,
I'll prove the prettier fellow of the two,
And wear my dagger with the braver grace;
And speak, between the change of man and boy,
With a reed voice; and turn two mincing steps
Into a manly stride; and speak of frays,
Like a fine bragging youth: and tell quaint lies,
How honourable ladies sought my love,
Which I denying they fell sick and died;
I could not do withal.[c] then I'll repent,
And wish, for all that, that I had not kill'd them:

And twenty of these puny lies I'll tell,
That men shall swear I have discontinued school
Above a twelvemonth:—I have within my mind
A thousand raw tricks of these bragging Jacks,
Which I will practise.
   Ner. Why, shall we turn to men?
   Por. Fye! what a question's that,
If thou wert near a lewd interpreter!
But come, I'll tell thee all my whole device
When I am in my coach, which stays for us
At the park gate; and therefore haste away,
For we must measure twenty miles to-day.
      [*Exeunt.*

      SCENE V.—*The same. A Garden.*

      Enter LAUNCELOT *and* JESSICA.

   Laun. Yes, truly;—for, look you, the sins of
the father are to be laid upon the children;
therefore, I promise you I fear you. I was always plain with you, and so now I speak my
agitation of the matter: Therefore, be of good
cheer; for, truly, I think, you are damn'd.
There is but one hope in it that can do you any
good; and that is but a kind of bastard hope
neither.
   Jes. And what hope is that, I pray thee?
   Laun. Marry, you may partly hope that your
father got you not, that you are not the Jew's
daughter.
   Jes. That were a kind of bastard hope, indeed; so the sins of my mother should be visited
upon me.
   Laun. Truly then I fear you are damned both
by father and mother: thus when I shun Scylla,
your father, I fall into Charybdis, your mother;
well, you are gone both ways.
   Jes. I shall be saved by my husband; he
hath made me a Christian.
   Laun. Truly, the more to blame he: we were
Christians enough before; e'en as many as could
well live, one by another: This making of Christians will raise the price of hogs; if we grow
all to be pork-eaters we shall not shortly have
a rasher on the coals for money.

      Enter LORENZO.

   Jes. I'll tell my husband, Launcelot, what
you say; here he comes.
   Lor. I shall grow jealous of you shortly,
Launcelot, if you thus get my wife into corners

---

a *Padua.* The old copies read Mantua—evidently a mistake: as we have in the fourth Act:—

  "Came you from Padua, from Bellario?"

b *Tranect.* No other example is found of the use of this word in English, and yet there is little doubt that the word is correct. *Tranare,* and *trainare,* are interpreted by Florio not only as *to draw,* which is the common acceptation, but as *to pass or swim over.* Thus the *tranect* was most probably the *tow-boat* of the ferry.

c *I could not do withal.* Gifford is very properly indignant at the mode in which a corruption of this reading

—*I could not do with all*—has been commented upon by Steevens, under the name of Collins. He says:—"The phrase, so shamelessly misinterpreted, is in itself perfectly innocent, and means neither more nor less than, *I could not help it.*"—*Notes on 'The Silent Woman.'*

Jes. Nay, you need not fear us, Lorenzo. Launcelot and I are out; he tells me flatly, there is no mercy for me in heaven, because I am a Jew's daughter: and he says, you are no good member of the commonwealth; for, in converting Jews to Christians, you raise the price of pork.

Lor. I shall answer that better to the commonwealth, than you can the getting up of the negro's belly; the Moor is with child by you, Launcelot.

Laun. It is much, that the Moor should be more than reason: but if she be less than an honest woman, she is, indeed, more than I took her for.

Lor. How every fool can play upon the word! I think, the best grace of wit will shortly turn into silence; and discourse grow commendable in none only but parrots.—Go in, sirrah; bid them prepare for dinner.

Laun. That is done, sir; they have all stomachs.

Lor. Goodly lord, what a wit-snapper are you! then bid them prepare dinner.

Laun. That is done, too, sir; only, cover is the word.

Lor. Will you cover then, sir?

Laun. Not so, sir, neither; I know my duty.

Lor. Yet more quarrelling with occasion! Wilt thou show the whole wealth of thy wit in an instant? I pray thee, understand a plain man in his plain meaning; go to thy fellows; bid them cover the table, serve in the meat, and we will come in to dinner.

Laun. For the table, sir, it shall be served in; for the meat, sir, it shall be covered; for your coming in to dinner, sir, why, let it be as humours and conceits shall govern.

[*Exit* LAUNCELOT.

Lor. O dear discretion, how his words are suited!
The fool hath planted in his memory
An army of good words; and I do know
A many fools, that stand in better place,
Garnish'd like him, that for a tricksy word
Defy the matter. How cheer'st thou, Jessica?
And now, good sweet, say thy opinion;—
How dost thou like the lord Bassanio's wife?

Jes. Past all expressing: It is very meet,
The lord Bassanio live an upright life;
For, having such a blessing in his lady,
He finds the joys of heaven here on earth;
And, if on earth he do not mean it, it
Is reason he should never come to heaven.
Why, if two gods should play some heavenly match,
And on the wager lay two earthly women,
And Portia one, there must be something else
Pawn'd with the other; for the poor rude world
Hath not her fellow.

Lor. Even such a husband
Hast thou of me, as she is for a wife.

Jes. Nay, but ask my opinion too of that.

Lor. I will anon; first, let us go to dinner.

Jes. Nay, let me praise you, while I have a stomach.

Lor. No, pray thee, let it serve for table-talk;
Then, howsoe'er thou speak'st, 'mong other things
I shall digest it.

Jes. Well, I'll set you forth. [*Exeunt*

('The Goodwins.' From an original Sketch.)

ILLUSTRATIONS OF ACT III.

'SCENE I.—"*The Goodwins, I think they call the place.*"

THE popular notion of the Goodwin Sand was, not only that it was "a very dangerous flat and fatal," but that it possessed a "voracious and ingurgitating property; so that should a ship of the largest size strike on it, in a few days it would be so wholly swallowed up by these quicksands, that no part of it would be left to be seen." It is to this belief that Shakspere most probably alludes when he describes the place as one "where the carcases of many a tall ship lie buried." It has, however, been ascertained that the sands of the opposite shore are of the same quality as that which tradition reports to have once formed the island property of Goodwin, Earl of Kent.

² SCENE I.—"*It was my turquoise.*"

The turquoise, turkise, or Turkey-stone, was supposed to have a marvellous property, thus described in Fenton's ' Secret Wonders of Nature,' 1569:—"The turkeys doth move when there is any peril prepared to him that weareth it." Ben Jonson and Drayton refer to the same superstition. But the Jew, who had "affections, senses, passions," values his turquoise for something more than its commercial worth or its imaginary virtue. "I had it of Leah, when I was a bachelor: I would not have given it for a wilderness of monkeys."

"One touch of nature makes the whole world kin;" and Shakspere here, with marvellous art, shows us the betrayed and persecuted Shylock, at the moment when he is raving at the desertion of his daughter, and panting for a wild revenge, as looking back upon the days when the fierce passions had probably no place in his heart—"I had it of Leah, when I was a bachelor."

³ SCENE II.—"*The scull that bred them in the sepulchre.*"

Shakspere appears to have had as great an antipathy to false hair as old Stubbes himself; from whose ' Anatomy of Abuses' we gave a quotation upon this subject in 'A Midsummer-Night's Dream' (Illustrations of Act IV.). Timon of Athens says:—

—— " thatch your poor thin roofs
With burdens of the dead."

In the passage before us the idea is more elaborated, and so it is also in the 68th Sonnet:—

"Thus in his cheek the map of days outworn,
When beauty liv'd and died as flowers do now,
Before these bastard signs of fair were borne,
Or durst inhabit on a living brow

THE MERCHANT OF VENICE

> Before the golden tresses of the dead,
> The right of sepulchres, were shorn away,
> To live a second life on second head,
> Ere beauty's dead fleece made another gay ·
> In him those holy antique hours are seen,
> Without all ornament, itself, and true,
> Making no summer of another's green,
> Robbing no old to dress his beauty new.

The "holy antique hours" appear to allude to a state of society in which the fashion, thus placed under its most revolting aspect, did not exist. Stow says—" Women's periwigs were first brought into England about the time of the massacre of Paris" (1572). Barnaby Rich, in 1615, speaking of the periwig-sellers, tells us—" These attire-makers within these forty years were not known by that name." And he adds—"But now they are not ashamed to set them forth upon their stalls—such monstrous moppoles of hair—so proportioned and deformed that but within these twenty or thirty years would have drawn the passers by to stand and gaze, and to wonder at them."

'SCENE IV.—"*Unto the tranect, to the common ferry Which trades to Venice.*

If Shakspere had been at Venice, (which, from the extraordinary keeping of the play, appears the most natural supposition,) he must surely have had some situation in his eye for Belmont. There is "a common ferry" at two places,—Fusina and Mestre. The Fusina ferry would be the one if Portia lived in perhaps the most striking situation, under the Euganean Hills. But the Mestre ferry is the most convenient medium between Padua and Venice. There is a large collection of canal-craft there. It is eighteen English miles from Padua, and five from Venice. Supposing Belmont to lie in the plain N.W. from Venice, Balthazar might cut across the country to Padua, and meet Portia at Mestre, while she travelled thither at a lady's speed.—(M.)

(Court of the Ducal Palace.)

ACT IV.

SCENE I.—Venice. *A Court of Justice.*

Enter the DUKE, *the* Magnificoes;[a] ANTONIO, BASSANIO, GRATIANO, SALARINO, SOLANIO, *and others.*

Duke. What, is Antonio here?

Ant. Ready, so please your grace.

Duke. I am sorry for thee; thou art come to answer
A stony adversary, an inhuman wretch
Uncapable of pity, void and empty
From any dram of mercy.

Ant. I have heard
Your grace hath ta'en great pains to qualify
His rigorous course; but since he stands obdurate,
And that no lawful means can carry me
Out of his envy's reach,[b] I do oppose
My patience to his fury; and am arm'd
To suffer, with a quietness of spirit,
The very tyranny and rage of his.

Duke. Go one, and call the Jew into the court.

Solan. He's ready at the door: he comes, my lord.

Enter SHYLOCK.

Duke. Make room, and let him stand before our face.
Shylock, the world thinks, and I think so too,
That thou but lead'st this fashion of thy malice
To the last hour of act; and then, 'tis thought
Thou'lt show thy mercy and remorse, more strange
Than is thy strange apparent cruelty:
And where thou now exact'st the penalty,
(Which is a pound of this poor merchant's flesh,)
Thou wilt not only lose the forfeiture,[a]
But touch'd with human gentleness and love,
Forgive a moiety of the principal;
Glancing an eye of pity on his losses,
That have of late so huddled on his back,
Enough to press a royal merchant[b] down,
And pluck commiseration of his state
From brassy bosoms, and rough hearts of flint,
From stubborn Turks and Tartars, never train'd
To offices of tender courtesy.
We all expect a gentle answer, Jew.

---

[a] *Magnificoes.*—So the old copies. Coryat calls the nobles of Venice, *Clarissimors.*

[b] *Envy's reach.* Envy is here used in the sense of *malice, hatred;* as in the translation of the Bible (Mark xv. 10.)—"For he knew that the chief priests had delivered him for envy."

[a] Mr. White prints *loose,* understanding by it the release of the forfeiture.

[b] *Royal merchant.* Warburton says that *royal* is not a mere sounding epithet, but was peculiarly applicable to the old Venetian merchants, who were rulers of principalities in the Archipelago. He adds that the title was given them generally throughout Europe.

Shy. I have possess'd your grace of what I
  purpose:
And by our holy Sabbath have I sworn,
To have the due and forfeit of my bond:
If you deny it, let the danger light
Upon your charter, and your city's freedom.
You'll ask me, why I rather choose to have
A weight of carrion flesh, than to receive
Three thousand ducats: I'll not answer that:
But, say, it is my humour: Is it answer'd?
What if my house be troubled with a rat,
And I be pleas'd to give ten thousand ducats
To have it ban'd? What, are you answer'd yet?
Some men there are love not a gaping pig;[a]
Some, that are mad if they behold a cat;
And others, when the bagpipe sings i' the nose,
Cannot contain their urine: for affection,
Master of passion, sways it to the mood[b]
Of what it likes, or loaths: ¹ Now, for your answer.
As there is no firm reason to be render'd,
Why he cannot abide a gaping pig;
Why he, a harmless necessary cat;
Why he, a woollen[c] bagpipe,²—but of force

Must yield to such inevitable shame,
As to offend himself, being offended;
So can I give no reason, nor I will not.
More than a lodg'd hate, and a certain loathing,
I bear Antonio, that I follow thus
A losing suit against him. Are you answer'd?
  Bass. This is no answer, thou unfeeling man,
To excuse the current of thy cruelty.
  Shy. I am not bound to please thee with my
    answer.
  Bass. Do all men kill the things they do not
    love?
  Shy. Hates any man the thing he would not
    kill?
  Bass. Every offence is not a hate at first.
  Shy. What, would'st thou have a serpent sting
    thee twice?
  Ant. I pray you, think you question with the
    Jew.*
You may as well go stand upon the beach,
And bid the main flood bate his usual height;
You may as well use question with the wolf,
Why he hath made the ewe bleat for the lamb;
You may as well forbid the mountain pines
To wag their high tops, and to make no noise,
When they are fretted with the gusts of heaven;
You may as well do any thing most hard,
As seek to soften that (than which what's
    harder?)
His Jewish heart:—Therefore, I do beseech
    you,
Make no more offers, use no further means,
But, with all brief and plain conveniency,
Let me have judgment, and the Jew his will.
  Bass. For thy three thousand ducats here is
    six.
  Shy. If every ducat in six thousand ducats
Were in six parts, and every part a ducat,
I would not draw them,—I would have my
    bond.
  Duke. How shalt thou hope for mercy, ren-
    d'ring none?
  Shy. What judgment shall I dread, doing no
    wrong?
You have among you many a purchas'd slave,
Which, like your asses, and your dogs, and
    mules,
You use in abject and in slavish parts,
Because you bought them:—Shall I say to
    you,
Let them be free, marry them to your heirs?
Why sweat they under burthens? let their beds

---

[a] *A gaping pig.* In Henry VIII. (Act v., Sc. III.) the porter at the Palace Yard thus addresses the mob:—"You'll leave your *noise* anon, ye rascals, ye rude slaves: leave your *gaping*." Here *to gape* is to *bawl*—a sense in which Littleton gives the word in his Dictionary. But, in Webster we have "*a pig's head gaping*;" and in Fletcher, "*gaping like a roasted pig.*" We are inclined to think that Shylock alludes to the squeaking of the living animal. He is particularizing the objects of offence to other men; and he would scarcely repeat his own dislike to pork, so strongly expressed in the first Act.

[b] Shylock himself, in a previous scene, has distinguished between *affection* and *passion*:—"Hath not a Jew hands, organs, dimensions, senses, *affections, passions*?" The distinction, indeed, is a very marked one, in the original use of the words. *Affection* is that state of the mind, whether pleasant or disagreeable, which is produced by some *external* object or quality. *Passion* is something higher and stronger—the *suggestive* state of the mind—going to a point by the force of its own will. The distinction is very happily preserved in an old play, Never too Late:—"His heart was fuller *of passions* than his eyes of *affections*." Keeping in view this distinction, we have a key to this very difficult passage. In the original the period is closed at *affection;* and the line which follows, after a full point, is—

"*Masters of passion* sways it to the mood," &c.

Steevens would read, upon an ingenious suggestion of Mr. Waldron,—" *Mistress* of passion;"—supposing that *mistress* was originally written *maistress*, and thence corrupted into *masters*. But it appears to us a less violent change to read *master*. The meaning then is, that *affection*, either for love or dislike—sympathy or antipathy—being the *master of passion*,—sways it (passion) to the mood of what it (affection) likes or loaths. If we were to adopt the reading which Malone prefers,—

"*Masters* of passion *sway it* to the mood
Of what it *likes or* loaths,"

the second *it* would be inconsistent with the sense. The *masters* (if *masters* should be the word) govern the *sense*, not allowing it to judge of what it likes or loaths; and we ought in that case to read—of what *they* like or loath.

[c] *Woollen.* So the old copies. It is ordinarily written *swollen bagpipe*, upon the suggestion of Sir John Hawkins. Dr. Johnson would read *wooden*. Douce very properly desires to adhere to the old reading, having the testimony of Dr. Leyden in his edition of 'The Complaynt of Scotland,' who informs us that the Lowland bagpipe commonly had the bag or sack covered with *woollen cloth*, of a green colour, a practice which, he adds, prevailed in the northern counties of England.

* We believe that this line should be understood thus:—
"I pray you think [consider that] you question with the Jew."
The sentence ends, and Antonio goes on to show the hardness of the Jew-ish heart.

Be made as soft as yours, and let their palates
Be seasou'd with such viands? You will answer,
The slaves are ours :—So do I answer you.
The pound of flesh, which I demand of him,
Is dearly bought; 'tis mine, and I will have it:
If you deny me, fye upon your law!
There is no force in the decrees of Venice:
I stand for judgment: answer; shall I have it?
   Duke. Upon my power, I may dismiss this
     court,
Unless Bellario, a learned doctor,
Whom I have sent for to determine this,
Come here to-day.
   Solan.   My lord, here stays without
A messenger with letters from the doctor,
New come from Padua.
   Duke. Bring us the letters; Call the mes-
     senger.
   Bass. Good cheer, Antonio! What, man!
     courage yet!
The Jew shall have my flesh, blood, bones, and
    all,
Ere thou shalt lose for me one drop of blood.
   Ant. I am a tainted wether of the flock,
Meetest for death; the weakest kind of fruit
Drops earliest to the ground, and so let me:
You cannot better be employ'd, Bassanio,
Than to live still, and write mine epitaph.

Enter NERISSA, *dressed like a lawyer's clerk.*

   Duke. Came you from Padua, from Bellario?
   Ner. From both, my lord: Bellario greets
     your grace.   [*Presents a letter.*
   Bass. Why dost thou whet thy knife so ear-
     nestly?
   Shy. To cut the forfeiture from that bankrout
     there.
   Gra. Not on thy sole, but on thy soul, harsh
     Jew,
Thou mak'st thy knife keen;[a] but no metal can,
No, not the hangman's axe, bear half the keen-
    ness
Of thy sharp envy. Can no prayers pierce
    thee?
   Shy. No, none that thou hast wit enough to
     make.
   Gra. O, be thou damn'd, inexecrable[b] dog!
And for thy life let justice be accus'd.
Thou almost mak'st me waver in my faith,
To hold opinion with Pythagoras,

---
[a] A passage in Henry IV., Part II., will explain this :—
    "Thou bid'st a thousand daggers in thy thoughts;
    Which thou hast whetted on thy stony heart,
    To stab at half an hour of my life."
[b] *Inexecrable.*—So the old copies. The ordinary reading is *inexorable.* Malone thinks that *in* is used as an augmentative particle, the sense being *most execrable.*

That souls of animals infuse themselves
Into the trunks of men: thy currish spirit
Govern'd a wolf, who, hang'd for human slaugh-
    ter
Even from the gallows did his fell soul fleet,
And, whilst thou lay'st in thy unhallow'd dam,
Infus'd itself in thee; for thy desires
Are wolfish, bloody, sterv'd,[c] and ravenous.
   Shy. Till thou can'st rail the seal from off my
     bond,
Thou but offend'st thy lungs to speak so loud:
Repair thy wit, good youth; or it will fall
To cureless ruin.—I stand here for law.
   Duke. This letter from Bellario doth com-
     mend
A young and learned doctor to our court :—
Where is he?
   Ner.   He attendeth here hard by,
To know your answer, whether you'll admit him.
   Duke. With all my heart:—some three or
     four of you
Go give him courteous conduct to this place.—
Meantime, the court shall hear Bellario's letter.

   [*Clerk reads.*] 'Your grace shall understand, that, at the receipt of your letter, I am very sick; but in the instant that your messenger came, in loving visitation was with me a young doctor of Rome; his name is Balthazar: I acquainted him with the cause in controversy between the Jew and Antonio the merchant: we turned o'er many books together; he is furnish'd with my opinion; which, better'd with his own learning, (the greatness whereof I cannot enough commend,) comes with him, at my importunity, to fill up your grace's request in my stead. I beseech you, let his lack of years be no impediment to let him lack a reverend estimation; for I never knew so young a body with so old a head. I leave him to your gracious acceptance, whose trial shall better publish his commendation.'

   Duke. You hear the learned Bellario, what he
     writes:
And here, I take it, is the doctor come.—

Enter PORTIA, *dressed like a doctor of laws.*

Give me your hand: Came you from old Bel-
     lario?
   Por. I did, my lord.
   Duke.   You are welcome: take your place.
Are you acquainted with the difference
That holds this present question in the court?
   Por. I am informed throughly of the cause.
Which is the merchant here, and which the Jew?
   Duke. Antonio and old Shylock, both stand
     forth.
   Por. Is your name Shylock?
   Shy.   Shylock is my name.
   Por. Of a strange nature is the suit you follow;
Yet in such rule that the Venetian law

---
[c] *Sterv'd*—synonymous with *starved*, and used by Spenser and the elder poets.

Cannot impugn you, as you do proceed.—
You stand within his danger,[a] do you not?
[*To* ANTONIO.
Ant. Ay, so he says.
Por. Do you confess the bond?
Ant. I do.
Por. Then must the Jew be merciful.
Shy. On what compulsion must I? tell me that.
Por. The quality of mercy is not strain'd;[3]
It droppeth, as the gentle rain from heaven
Upon the place beneath: it is twice bless'd;
It blesseth him that gives, and him that takes:
'Tis mightiest in the mightiest; it becomes
The throned monarch better than his crown;
His sceptre shows the force of temporal power,
The attribute to awe and majesty,
Wherein doth sit the dread and fear of kings;
But mercy is above this sceptred sway,
It is enthroned in the hearts of kings,
It is an attribute to God himself;
And earthly power doth then show likest God's
When mercy seasons justice. Therefore, Jew,
Though justice be thy plea, consider this—
That in the course of justice, none of us
Should see salvation: we do pray for mercy;
And that same prayer doth teach us all to render
The deeds of mercy. I have spoke thus much,
To mitigate the justice of thy plea;
Which if thou follow, this strict court of Venice
Must needs give sentence 'gainst the merchant
there.
Shy. My deeds upon my head! I crave the law,
The penalty and forfeit of my bond.
Por. Is he not able to discharge the money?
Bass. Yes, here I tender it for him in the court;
Yea, twice the sum: if that will not suffice,
I will be bound to pay it ten times o'er,
On forfeit of my hands, my head, my heart:
If this will not suffice, it must appear
That malice bears down truth.[b] And I beseech you,
Wrest once the law to your authority:
To do a great right do a little wrong;
And curb this cruel devil of his will.
Por. It must not be; there is no power in Venice

Can alter a decree established:
'Twill be recorded for a precedent;
And many an error, by the same example,
Will rush into the state: it cannot be.
Shy. A Daniel come to judgment! yea, a Daniel!
O wise young judge, how do I honour thee!
Por. I pray you, let me look upon the bond.
Shy. Here 'tis, most reverend doctor, here it is.
Por. Shylock, there's thrice thy money offer'd thee.
Shy. An oath, an oath, I have an oath in heaven:
Shall I lay perjury upon my soul?
No, not for Venice.
Por. Why, this bond is forfeit;
And lawfully by this the Jew may claim
A pound of flesh, to be by him cut off
Nearest the merchant's heart:—Be merciful;
Take thrice thy money; bid me tear the bond.
Shy. When it is paid according to the tenour.
It doth appear you are a worthy judge;
You know the law, your exposition
Hath been most sound: I charge you by the law,
Whereof you are a well-deserving pillar,
Proceed to judgment: by my soul I swear,
There is no power in the tongue of man
To alter me: I stay here on my bond.
Ant. Most heartily I do beseech the court
To give the judgment.
Por. Why then, thus it is:
You must prepare your bosom for his knife.
Shy. O noble judge! O excellent young man!
Por. For the intent and purpose of the law
Hath full relation to the penalty,
Which here appeareth due upon the bond.
Shy. 'Tis very true: O wise and upright judge!
How much more elder art thou than thy looks!
Por. Therefore, lay bare your bosom.
Shy. Ay, his breast:
So says the bond;—Doth it not, noble judge?—
Nearest his heart, those are the very words.
Por. It is so. Are there balance here, to weigh the flesh?
Shy. I have them ready.
Por. Have by some surgeon, Shylock, on your charge,
To stop his wounds, lest he should bleed to death.
Shy. Is it so nominated in the bond?
Por. It is not so express'd; But what of that?
'Twere good you do so much for charity.
Shy. I cannot find it; 'tis not in the bond.
Por. Come, merchant, have you any thing to say?

---

[a] Dr. Jamieson says, '*In his dawnger, under his dawneer,* in his power as a captive. The old French *danger* frequently occurs as signifying *power, dominion.*" Steevens quotes from Harl. MS. (1013):—

"Two detters some tyme there were
Oughten money to an usurere,
The one was in his dawngere,
Fyve hundred poundes tolde."

But the phrase is not used by Portia in the limited and secondary sense of being in debt.
[b] *Truth*, is here used in the sense of *honesty*.

Ant. But little; I am arm'd, and well prepar'd.—
Give me your hand, Bassanio; fare you well!
Grieve not that I am fallen to this for you;
For herein fortune shows herself more kind
Than is her custom: it is still her use,
To let the wretched man outlive his wealth,
To view with hollow eye, and wrinkled brow,
An age of poverty; from which lingering penance
Of such a misery doth she cut me off.
Commend me to your honourable wife:
Tell her the process of Antonio's end,
Say, how I lov'd you, speak me fair in death;
And, when the tale is told, bid her be judge
Whether Bassanio had not once a love.
Repent not you that you shall lose your friend,
And he repents not that he pays your debt;
For, if the Jew do cut but deep enough,
I'll pay it instantly with all my heart.
 Bass. Antonio, I am married to a wife,
Which is as dear to me as life itself;
But life itself, my wife, and all the world,
Are not with me esteem'd above thy life;
I would lose all, ay, sacrifice them all
Here to this devil, to deliver you.
 Por. Your wife would give you little thanks for that,
If she were by, to hear you make the offer.
 Gra. I have a wife, whom I protest I love;
I would she were in heaven, so she could
Entreat some power to change this currish Jew.
 Ner. 'Tis well you offer it behind her back;
The wish would make else an unquiet house.
 Shy. These be the Christian husbands: I have a daughter;
Would any of the stock of Barrabas.
Had been her husband, rather than a Christian! [*Aside.*
We trifle time; I pray thee pursue sentence.
 Por. A pound of that same merchant's flesh is thine;
The court awards it, and the law doth give it.
 Shy. Most rightful judge!
 Por. And you must cut this flesh from off his breast;
The law allows it, and the court awards it.
 Shy. Most learned judge!—A sentence; come, prepare.
 Por. Tarry a little;—there is something else.—
This bond doth give thee here no jot of blood;
The words expressly are a pound of flesh:
Then take thy bond, take thou thy pound of flesh;*

* The quartos have *take then,* instead of *then take.*
438

But, in the cutting it, if thou dost shed
One drop of Christian blood, thy lands and goods
Are, by the laws of Venice, confiscate
Unto the state of Venice.
 Gra. O upright judge!—Mark, Jew!—O learned judge!
 Shy. Is that the law?
 Por. Thyself shall see the act:
For, as thou urgest justice, be assur'd
Thou shalt have justice, more than thou desirest.
 Gra. O learned judge!—Mark, Jew;—a learned judge!
 Shy. I take this offer then,—pay the bond thrice,
And let the Christian go.
 Bass. Here is the money.
 Por. Soft.
The Jew shall have all justice;—soft;—no haste;—
He shall have nothing but the penalty.
 Gra. O Jew! an upright judge, a learned judge!
 Por. Therefore, prepare thee to cut off the flesh.
Shed thou no blood; nor cut thou less, nor more,
But just a pound of flesh: if thou tak'st more,
Or less, than just a pound,—be it but so much
As makes it light, or heavy, in the substance,
Or the division of the twentieth part
Of one poor scruple,—nay, if the scale do turn
But in the estimation of a hair,—
Thou diest, and all thy goods are confiscate.
 Gra. A second Daniel, a Daniel, Jew!
Now, infidel, I have thee on the hip.
 Por. Why doth the Jew pause? take thy forfeiture.
 Shy. Give me my principal, and let me go.
 Bass. I have it ready for thee; here it is.
 Por. He hath refus'd it in the open court;
He shall have merely justice, and his bond.
 Gra. A Daniel, still say I; a second Daniel!—
I thank thee, Jew, for teaching me that word.
 Shy. Shall I not have barely my principal?
 Por. Thou shalt have nothing but the forfeiture,
To be so taken at thy peril, Jew.
 Shy. Why then the devil give him good of it!
I'll stay no longer question.
 Por. Tarry, Jew;
The law hath yet another hold on you.
It is enacted in the laws of Venice,—
If it be proved against an alien,
That by direct or indirect attempts
He seek the life of any citizen,

The party 'gainst the which he doth contrive
Shall seize one half his goods; the other half
Comes to the privy coffer of the state;
And the offender's life lies in the mercy
Of the duke only, 'gainst all other voice.
In which predicament, I say, thou stand'st:
For it appears by manifest proceeding,
That, indirectly, and directly too,
Thou hast contriv'd against the very life
Of the defendant; and thou hast incurr'd
The danger formerly by me rehears'd.
Down therefore, and beg mercy of the duke.
   Gra. Beg that thou may'st have leave to hang
      thyself:
And yet, thy wealth being forfeit to the state,
Thou hast not left the value of a cord;
Therefore, thou must be hang'd at the state's
      charge.
   Duke. That thou shalt see the difference of
      our spirit,
I pardon thee thy life before thou ask it:
For half thy wealth, it is Antonio's;
The other half comes to the general state,
Which humbleness may drive unto a fine.
   Por. Ay, for the state; not for Antonio.
   Shy. Nay, take my life and all, pardon not that:
You take my house, when you do take the prop
That doth sustain my house; you take my life,
When you do take the means whereby I live.
   Por. What mercy can you render him, Antonio?
   Gra. A halter gratis; nothing else, for God's
      sake.
   Ant. So please my lord the duke, and all the
      court,
To quit the fine for one half of his goods;
I am content, so he will let me have
The other half in use,* to render it,
Upon his death, unto the gentleman
That lately stole his daughter;
Two things provided more,—That for this favour,
He presently become a Christian;
The other, that he do record a gift,
Here in the court, of all he dies possess'd,
Unto his son Lorenzo and his daughter.
   Duke. He shall do this; or else I do recant
The pardon that I late pronounced here.
   Por. Art thou contented, Jew; what dost
      thou say?
   Shy. I am content.
   Por.   Clerk, draw a deed of gift.
   Shy. I pray you give me leave to go from hence:

* *In use.* Mr. Staunton says *in use* here, is *in trust* for Shylock; that "this is a conveyance to uses," and that here Shakspere has "the strictness of a technical conveyancer."

   I am not well: send the deed after me,
And I will sign it.
   Duke.   Get thee gone, but do it.
   Gra. In christening, thou shalt have two god
      fathers;
Had I been judge, thou should'st have had ten
      more,*
To bring thee to the gallows, not the font.
                      [*Exit* SHYLOCK.
   Duke. Sir, I entreat you with me home to
      dinner.
   Por. I humbly do desire your grace of
      pardon.
I must away this night toward Padua;
And it is meet I presently set forth.
   Duke. I am sorry that your leisure serves you
      not.
Antonio, gratify this gentleman;
For, in my mind, you are much bound to him.
            [*Exeunt* DUKE, *Magnificoes, and Train.*
   Bass. Most worthy gentleman, I and my
      friend.
Have by your wisdom been this day acquitted
Of grievous penalties; in lieu whereof,
Three thousand ducats, due unto the Jew,
We freely cope your courteous pains withal.
   Ant. And stand indebted, over and above,
In love and service to you evermore.
   Por. He is well paid that is well satisfied;
And I, delivering you, am satisfied,
And therein do account myself well paid;
My mind was never yet more mercenary.
I pray you know me, when we meet again;
I wish you well, and so I take my leave.
   Bass. Dear sir, of force I must attempt you
      further;
Take some remembrance of us, as a tribute,
Not as a fee: grant me two things, I pray you,
Not to deny me, and to pardon me.
   Por. You press me far, and therefore I will
      yield.
Give me your gloves, I'll wear them for your
      sake;
And, for your love, I'll take this ring from
      you:—
Do not draw back your hand; I'll take no more;
And you in love shall not deny me this.
   Bass. This ring, good sir,—alas, it is a trifle;
I will not shame myself to give you this.
   Por. I will have nothing else but only this;
And now, methinks, I have a mind to it.
   Bass. There's more depends on this than on
      the value.

* *Ten more.* Jurymen were jestingly called godfathers— "Godfathers in law," as Ben Jonson has it.

The dearest ring in Venice will I give you,
And find it out by proclamation;
Only for this I pray you pardon me.
  Por. I see, sir, you are liberal in offers:
You taught me first to beg; and now, methinks,
You teach me how a beggar should be answer'd.
  Bass. Good sir, this ring was given me by my
    wife;
And, when she put it on, she made me vow
That I should neither sell, nor give, nor lose it.
  Por. That 'scuse serves many men to save
    their gifts.
An if your wife be not a mad woman,
And know how well I have deserv'd this ring,
She would not hold out enemy for ever,
For giving it to me. Well, peace be with you!
      [*Exeunt* PORTIA *and* NERISSA.
  Ant. My lord Bassanio, let him have the
    ring;
Let his deservings, and my love withal,
Be valued 'gainst your wife's commandment.
  Bass. Go, Gratiano, run and overtake him;
Give him the ring; and bring him, if thou
    can'st,
Unto Antonio's house:—away, make haste.
      [*Exit* GRATIANO.
Come, you and I will thither presently;
And in the morning early will we both
Fly toward Belmont: Come, Antonio.
      [*Exeunt.*

SCENE II.—*Venice. A Street.*

Enter PORTIA *and* NERISSA.

  Por. Inquire the Jew's house out, give him
    this deed,
And let him sign it; we'll away to-night,
And be a day before our husbands home:
This deed will be well welcome to Lorenzo.

Enter GRATIANO.

  Gra. Fair sir, you are well o'erta'en:
My lord Bassanio, upon more advice,
Hath sent you here this ring; and doth entreat
Your company at dinner.
  Por.   That cannot be:
His ring I do accept most thankfully,
And so, I pray you, tell him: Furthermore,
I pray you, show my youth old Shylock's house.
  Gra. That will I do.
  Ner.   Sir, I would speak with you:—
I'll see if I can get my husband's ring.
                    [*To* PORTIA.
Which I did make him swear to keep for ever.
  Por. Thou may'st, I warrant. We shall have
    old swearing,
That they did give the rings away to men;
But we'll outface them, and outswear them too.
Away, make haste; thou know'st where I will
    tarry.
  Ner. Come, good sir, will you show me to
    this house?   [*Exeunt.*

Street in Venice.

ILLUSTRATIONS OF ACT IV.

Scene I.—"*Some men there are,*" &c.

There is a passage in Donne's 'Devotions,' (1626), in which the doctrine of antipathies is put in a somewhat similar manner:—"A man that is not afraid of a lion is afraid of a cat; not afraid of starving, and yet is afraid of some joint of meat at the table, presented to feed him; not afraid of the sound of drums and trumpets and shot, and those which they seek to drown, the last cries of men, and is afraid of some particular harmonious instrument; so much afraid, as that with any of these the enemy might drive this man, otherwise valiant enough, out of the field."

² Scene I.—"*Bagpipe.*"

We extract the following notice of this instrument (which we apprehend is not the "particular harmonious instrument" alluded to by Donne) from the 'English Cyclopedia:'—" The bagpipe, or something nearly similar to it, was in use among the ancients. Blanchinus gives a figure of it, under the name of *tibia utricularis*, though this is not precisely the same as the modern instrument. Luscinius, in his 'Musurgia' (1536) has a woodcut of it, whence it appears that the bagpipe in his time was in all respects the same as ours. Indeed, it is mentioned, though not described, by Chaucer, who says of his miller—

'A baggepipe wel coude he blowe and sonne;'

and this, we are told in the same prologue, was the music to which the Canterbury pilgrims performed their journey." The following engraving is copied from a carving in the church of Cirencester, which is supposed to be of the period of Henry VII.

³ Scene I.

"*The quality of mercy is not strain'd,*" &c.

Douce has pointed to the following verse in Ecclesiasticus (xxxv. 20) as having suggested the beautiful image of the rain from heaven:—"Mercy is seasonable in the time of affliction, as clouds of rain in the time of drought." The subsequent passage, when Portia says, "we do pray for mercy," is considered by Sir William Blackstone to be out of character as addressed to a Jew. Shakspere had probably the Lord's Prayer immediately in his mind; but the sentiment is also found in Ecclesiasticus, ch. xxviii.

("Sit, Jessica.")

ACT V.

SCENE I.—Belmont. *Avenue to Portia's House.*

Enter LORENZO *and* JESSICA.

Lor. The moon shines bright :—In such a
  night as this,
When the sweet wind did gently kiss the trees,
And they did make no noise,—in such a night,
Troilus, methinks, mounted the Trojan walls,
And sigh'd his soul toward the Grecian tents,
Where Cressid lay that night.
  Jes.   In such a night,
Did Thisbe fearfully o'ertrip the dew;
And saw the lion's shadow ere himself,
And ran dismay'd away.
  Lor.   In such a night,
Stood Dido with a willow in her hand²
Upon the wild sea-banks, and waft her love
To come again to Carthage.
  Jes.   In such a night,
Medea gather'd the enchanted herbs³
That did renew old Æson.

  Lor.   In such a night,
Did Jessica steal from the wealthy Jew;
And with an unthrift love did run from Venice
As far as Belmont.
  Jes.   In such a night,
Did young Lorenzo swear he lov'd her well;
Stealing her soul with many vows of faith,
And ne'er a true one.
  Lor.   In such a night,
Did pretty Jessica, like a little shrew,
Slander her love, and he forgave it her.
  Jes. I would out-night you, did no body come.
But, hark, I hear the footing of a man.

Enter STEPHANO.

  Lor. Who comes so fast in silence of the
    night?
  Steph. A friend.
  Lor. A friend? what friend? your name, I
    pray you, friend.
  Steph. Stephano is my name; and I bring
    word,

ACT V.] THE MERCHANT OF VENICE. [SCENE I.

My mistress will before the break of day
Be here at Belmont; she doth stray about
By holy crosses,⁴ where she kneels and prays
For happy wedlock hours.
   Lor.   Who comes with her?
   Steph. None, but a holy hermit, and her
     maid.
I pray you, is my master yet return'd?
   Lor. He is not, nor we have not heard from
     him.—
But go we in, I pray thee, Jessica,
And ceremoniously let us prepare
Some welcome for the mistress of the house.

            Enter LAUNCELOT.

   Laun. Sola, sola, wo ha, ho, sola, sola!
   Lor. Who calls?
   Laun. Sola! Did you see master Lorenzo,
and mistress Lorenzo? sola, sola!
   Lor. Leave hollaing, man; here.
   Laun. Sola! where? where?
   Lor. Here.
   Laun. Tell him, there's a post come from my
master, with his horn full of good news; my
master will be here ere morning.   [*Exit.*
   Lor. Sweet soul, let's in, and there expect
their coming.
And yet no matter;—Why should we go in?
My friend Stephano, signify, I pray you,
Within the house, your mistress is at hand;
And bring your music forth into the air.
                       [*Exit* STEPHANO.
How sweet the moon-light sleeps upon this
    bank!ᵃ
Here will we sit, and let the sounds of music
Creep in our ears; soft stillness, and the night,
Become the touches of sweet harmony.
Sit, Jessica.ᶜ Look how the floor of heaven
Is thick inlaid with patines ᵃ of bright gold.
There's not the smallest orb which thou be-
    hold'st
But in his motion like an angel sings,
Still quiring to the young-eyed cherubins;ᵇ
Such harmony is in immortal souls;
But whilst this muddy vesture of decay
Doth grossly close it in, we cannot hear it.—

   ᵃ *Patines.* The word in the folio is spelt *patens.* A *paten*
is the small flat dish or plate used in the service of the altar.
Archbishop Laud bequeaths to the Duke of Buckingham
his "chalice and *potts* of gold."
   ᵇ *Cherubins.* We follow the orthography of the old
editions, though *cherubim* may be more correct. Spenser
uses *cherubins* as the plural of cherubin; Milton, more
learnedly, *cherubim.*
   ᶜ *Close it in.* In one of the quartos, and the folio, this is
printed *close in it;* the verb in this case being probably compound—*close-in.* *Close us in,* has crept into some texts,—
for which there is no authority.

           Enter Musicians.

Come, ho, and wake Diana with a hymn;
With sweetest touches pierce your mistress'
    ear,
And draw her home with music.
   Jes. I am never merry when I hear sweet
     music.   [*Music.*
   Lor. The reason is your spirits are attentive:
For do but note a wild and wanton herd,
Or race of youthful and unhandled colts,
Fetching mad bounds, bellowing, and neighing
    loud,
Which is the hot condition of their blood;
If they but hear perchance a trumpet sound,
Or any air of music touch their ears,
You shall perceive them make a mutual stand,
Their savage eyes turn'd to a modest gaze,
By the sweet power of music: Therefore, the
    poet
Did feign that Orpheus drew trees, stones, and
    floods;
Since nought so stockish, hard, full of rage,
But music for the time doth change his nature:
The man that hath no music in himself,⁷
Nor is not mov'd with concord of sweet sounds,
Is fit for treasons, stratagems, and spoils;
The motions of his spirit are dull as night,
And his affections dark as Erebus:
Let no such man be trusted.—Mark the music.

   Enter PORTIA *and* NERISSA, *at a distance.*

   Por. That light we see is burning in my
     hall.
How far that little candle throws his beams!
So shines a good deed in a naughty world.
   Ner. When the moon shone we did not see
     the candle.
   Por. So doth the greater glory dim the less:
A substitute shines brightly as a king,
Until a king be by; and then his state
Empties itself, as doth an inland brook
Into the main of waters. Music! hark!
   Ner. It is your music, madam, of the house.
   Por. Nothing is good, I see, without respect;
Methinks it sounds much sweeter than by day.
   Ner. Silence bestows that virtue on it,
     madam.
   Por. The crow doth sing as sweetly as the
     lark,⁵
When neither is attended; and, I think,
The nightingale, if she should sing by day,
When every goose is cackling, would be thought
No better a musician than the wren.
How many things by season season'd are
To their right praise, and true perfection:—

ACT V.]   THE MERCHANT OF VENICE.   [SCENE I.

Peace! How the moon* sleeps with Endymion,
And would not be awak'd!   [*Music ceases.*
  Lor.   That is the voice,
Or I am much deceiv'd, of Portia.
  Por. He knows me, as the blind man knows
         the cuckoo,
By the bad voice.
  Lor.   Dear lady, welcome home.
  Por. We have been praying for our hus-
         bands' welfare,
Which speed, we hope, the better for our words.
Are they return'd?
  Lor.   Madam, they are not yet;
But there is come a messenger before,
To signify their coming.
  Por.   Go in, Nerissa;
Give order to my servants, that they take
No note at all of our being absent hence;
Nor you, Lorenzo;—Jessica, nor you.
                       [*A tucket sounds.*
  Lor. Your husband is at hand; I hear his
         trumpet:
We are no tell-tales, madam; fear you not.
  Por. This night, methinks, is but the day-
         light sick.
It looks a little paler; 'tis a day
Such as the day is when the sun is hid.

Enter BASSANIO, ANTONIO, GRATIANO, *and their
         Followers.*

  Bass. We should hold day with the Antipodes,
If you would walk in absence of the sun.
  Por. Let me give light, but let me not be
         light;
For a light wife doth make a heavy husband,
And never be Bassanio so for me;
But God sort all!—You are welcome home, my
         lord.
  Bass. I thank you, madam: give welcome to
         my friend.—
This is the man, this is Antonio,
To whom I am so infinitely bound.
  Por. You should in all sense be much bound
         to him,

For, as I hear, he was much bound for you.
  Ant. No more than I am well acquitted of.
  Por. Sir, you are very welcome to our house
It must appear in other ways than words,
Therefore, I scant this breathing courtesy.
       [GRATIANO *and* NERISSA *seem to talk apart.*
  Gra. By yonder moon, I swear you do me
         wrong;
In faith, I gave it to the judge's clerk:
Would he were gelt that had it, for my part,
Since you do take it, love, so much at heart.
  Por. A quarrel, ho, already? what's the
         matter?
  Gra. About a hoop of gold, a paltry ring
That she did give me; whose poesy was
For all the world, like cutler's poetry
Upon a knife, ' Love me, and leave me not.'
  Ner. What talk you of the poesy, or the
         value?
You swore to me, when I did give it you,
That you would wear it till the hour of death;
And that it should lie with you in your grave:
Though not for me, yet for your vehement
         oaths,
You should have been respective,* and have
         kept it.
Gave it a judge's clerk!—but well I know,
The clerk will ne'er wear hair on's face that
         had it.
  Gra. He will, an if he live to be a man.
  Ner. Ay, if a woman live to be a man.
  Gra. Now, by this hand, I gave it to a
         youth,—
A kind of boy; a little scrubbed* boy,
No higher than thyself, the judge's clerk;
A prating boy, that begg'd it as a fee;
I could not for my heart deny it him.
  Por. You were to blame, I must be plain with
         you,
To part so slightly with your wife's first gift;
A thing stuck on with oaths upon your finger,
And so riveted with faith unto your flesh.
I gave my love a ring, and made him swear
Never to part with it; and here he stands,—
I dare be sworn for him, he would not leave it,
Nor pluck it from his finger, for the wealth
That the world masters. Now, in faith, Gratiano,
You give your wife too unkind a cause of grief;
An 'twere to me, I should be mad at it.
  Bass. Why, I were best to cut my left hand off,
And swear, I lost the ring defending it. [*Aside.*
  Gra. My lord Bassanio gave his ring away

---

^a *Peace! How the moon, &c.* So all the old copies. Malone substituted, *Peace! Ho! The moon.* There are certainly examples in Shakspere of the union of these interjectional words; as in Romeo and Juliet—*Peace! Ho! For shame!* In this, and in other instances, they express a violent interposition. Malone thinks that Portia uses the words as commanding the music to cease. This would be a singularly unlady-like act of Portia. In reality, as well as in expression. We apprehend that, having been talking somewhat loudly to Nerissa as she approached the house, she checks herself as she comes close to it, with the interjection—*Peace!*—equivalent to *hush!* and then gives the poetical reason for being silent.—

"How the moon sleeps with Endymion,
  And would not be awak'd."

The stage direction, *Music ceases*, is a coincidence with Portia's *Peace!* but not a consequence of it.

444

^a *Respective,*—regardful.
^b *Scrubbed.* Warton would read *stubbed*, in the sense of *stunted.*

Unto the judge that begg'd it, and, indeed,
Deserv'd it too; and then the boy, his clerk,
That took some pains in writing, he begg'd mine:
And neither man, nor master, would take aught
But the two rings.

Por. What ring gave you, my lord?
Not that, I hope, which you receiv'd of me.

Bass. If I could add a lie unto a fault,
I would deny it; but you see, my finger
Hath not the ring upon it, it is gone.

Por. Even so void is your false heart of truth.
By heaven, I will ne'er come in your bed
Until I see the ring.

Ner. Nor I in yours,
Till I again see mine.

Bass. Sweet Portia,
If you did know to whom I gave the ring,
If you did know for whom I gave the ring,
And would conceive for what I gave the ring,
And how unwillingly I left the ring,
When nought would be accepted but the ring,
You would abate the strength of your displeasure.

Por. If you had known the virtue of the ring,
Or half her worthiness that gave the ring,
Or your own honour to contain* the ring,
You would not then have parted with the ring.
What man is there so much unreasonable,
If you had pleas'd to have defended it
With any terms of zeal, wanted the modesty
To urge the thing held as a ceremony?
Nerissa teaches me what to believe;
I'll die for't, but some woman had the ring.

Bass. No, by mine honour, madam, by my soul,
No woman had it, but a civil doctor,
Which did refuse three thousand ducats of me,
And begg'd the ring; the which I did deny him,
And suffer'd him to go displeas'd away;
Even he that had held up the very life
Of my dear friend. What should I say, sweet
lady?
I was enforc'd to send it after him;
I was beset with shame and courtesy;
My honour would not let ingratitude
So much besmear it: Pardon me, good lady;
For, by these blessed candles of the night,
Had you been there, I think, you would have
begg'd
The ring of me to give the worthy doctor.

Por. Let not that doctor e'er come near my
house:
Since he hath got the jewel that I lov'd,
And that which you did swear to keep for me,
I will become as liberal as you;
I'll not deny him any thing I have,

* *Contain,* and *retain,* are here synonymous.

No, not my body, nor my husband's bed:
Know him I shall, I am well sure of it:
Lie not a night from home; watch me, like
Argus;
If you do not, if I be left alone,
Now, by mine honour, which is yet mine own,
I'll have that doctor for my bedfellow.

Ner. And I his clerk; therefore be well advis'd,
How you do leave me to mine own protection.

Gra. Well, do you so: let not me take him
then;
For, if I do, I'll mar the young clerk's pen.

Ant. I am the unhappy subject of these
quarrels.

Por. Sir, grieve not you; you are welcome
notwithstanding.

Bass. Portia, forgive me this enforced wrong;
And, in the hearing of these many friends,
I swear to thee, even by thine own fair eyes,
Wherein I see myself,—

Por. Mark you but that!
In both my eyes he doubly sees himself:
In each eye one:—swear by your double self,
And there's an oath of credit.

Bass. Nay, but hear me;
Pardon this fault, and by my soul I swear,
I never more will break an oath with thee.

Ant. I once did lend my body for his wealth;
Which, but for him that had your husband's ring,
[*To* PORTIA.
Had quite miscarried: I dare be bound again,
My soul upon the forfeit, that your lord
Will never more break faith advisedly.

Por. Then you shall be his surety: Give him
this;
And bid him keep it better than the other.

Ant. Here, lord Bassanio; swear to keep this
ring.

Bass. By heaven, it is the same I gave the
doctor!

Por. I had it of him: pardon me, Bassanio;
For by this ring the doctor lay with me.

Ner. And pardon me, my gentle Gratiano;
For that same scrubbed boy, the doctor's clerk,
In lieu of this last night did lie with me.

Gra. Why, this is like the mending of high-
ways
In summer, where the ways are fair enough:
What! are we cuckolds, ere we have deserv'd it?

Por. Speak not so grossly.—You are all
amaz'd:
Here is a letter, read it at your leisure;
It comes from Padua, from Bellario:
There you shall find, that Portia was the doctor;

Nerissa there, her clerk: Lorenzo here
Shall witness, I set forth as soon as you,
And but e'en now return'd; I have not yet
Enter'd my house.—Antonio, you are welcome;
And I have better news in store for you
Than you expect: unseal this letter soon;
There you shall find, three of your argosies
Are richly come to harbour suddenly:
You shall not know by what strange accident
I chanced on this letter.
   Ant.   I am dumb.
   Bass. Were you the doctor, and I knew you not?
   Gra. Were you the clerk, that is to make me cuckold?
   Ner. Ay; but the clerk that never means to do it,
Unless he live until he be a man.
   Bass. Sweet doctor, you shall be my bed-fellow;
When I am absent then lie with my wife.
   Ant. Sweet lady, you have given me life, and living;
For here I read for certain, that my ships
Are safely come to road.

   Por.   How now, Lorenzo?
My clerk hath some good comforts too for you.
   Ner. Ay, and I'll give them him without a fee.—
There do I give to you and Jessica,
From the rich Jew, a special deed of gift,
After his death, of all he dies possess'd of.
   Lor. Fair ladies, you drop manna in the way
Of starved people.
   Por.   It is almost morning,
And yet, I am sure, you are not satisfied
Of these events at full: Let us go in;
And charge us there upon inter'ga'ories,[a]
And we will answer all things faithfully.
   Gra. Let it be so; The first in ter'gatory,
That my Nerissa shall be sworn on, is,
Whether till the next night she had rather stay,
Or go to bed now, being two hours to-day:
But were the day come, I should wish it dark,
Till I were couching with the doctor's clerk.
Well, while I live, I'll fear no other thing
So sore,[b] as keeping safe Nerissa's ring.
                                                  [*Exeunt.*

[a] Inter'gatories. Ben Jonson several times uses this elision.
[b] *Sore*—excessively—extremely—much.

[Italian Villa by Moonlight.]

ILLUSTRATIONS OF ACT V.

¹ SCENE I.—"*Troilus, methinks, mounted the Trojan walls.*"

OUR poet had Chaucer in his mind :—

"The dale goth fast, and after that came eve,
And yet came not to Troilus Cresseide.
He looketh forth, by hedge, by tre, by greve,
And ferre his heade ovir the walle he lelde."

² SCENE I.— "*In such a night,
Stood Dido with a willow in her hand.*"

"This passage," says Steevens, "contains a small instance out of many that might be brought to prove that Shakspeare was no reader of the classics." And why?—because the Dido of the classics is never represented with a willow! Shakspere was not, like many of Steevens' day who had made great reputations with slender means, a mere transcriber of the thoughts of other men. He has here given us a picture of the forsaken Dido, which was perfectly intelligible to the popular mind. Those who remember Desdemona's willow-song in Othello need no laboured comment to show them that the willow was emblematic of the misery that Dido had to bear.

³ SCENE I.— "*In such a night,
Medea gather'd the enchanted herbs,*" &c.

The picture of the similar scene in Gower (*Confessio Amantis*) is exceedingly beautiful :—

"Thus it befell upon a night
Whann there was nought but sterre light,
She was vanished right as hir list,
That no wight but herself wist ;
And that was at midnight tide,
The world was still on every side."

⁴ SCENE I.— ——" *she doth stray about
By holy crosses.*"

These holy crosses still, as of old, bristle the land in Italy, and sanctify the sea. Besides those contained in churches, they mark the spots where heroes were born, where saints rested, where travellers died. They rise on the summits of hills, and at the intersection of roads; and there is now a shrine of the Madonna del Mare in the midst of the sea between Mestre and Venice, and another between Venice and Palestrina, where the gondolier and the mariner cross themselves in passing, and whose lamp nightly gleams over the waters in moonlight or storm. The days are past when pilgrims of all ranks, from the queen to the beggar-maid, might be seen kneeling and praying "for happy wedlock hours," or for whatever else lay nearest their hearts; and the reverence of the passing traveller is now nearly all the homage that is paid at these shrines.—(M.)

⁵ SCENE I.—"*How sweet the moonlight sleeps upon this bank.*"

One characteristic of an Italian garden is that its trees and shrubs are grown in avenues and gathered into thickets, while the grass-plots and turfy banks are studded with parterres of roses and other flowers, which lie open to the sunshine and the dews. The moonlight thus *sleeps* upon such lawns and banks, instead of being disturbed by the flickering of overshadowing trees.—(M.)

⁶ SCENE I.—"*Sit, Jessica,*" &c.

Mr. Hallam, in his very interesting account of the philosophy of Campanella, thus paraphrases one of the most imaginative passages of the Dominican friar :—" The sky and stars are endowed with the keenest sensibility ; nor is it unreasonable to suppose that they signify their mutual thoughts to each other by the transference of light, and that their sensibility is full of pleasure. The blessed spirits, that inform such living and bright mansions, behold all things in nature, and in the divine ideas; they have also a more glorious light than their own, through which they are elevated to a supernatural beatific vision." Mr. Hallam adds : " We can hardly read this, without recollecting the most sublime passage perhaps in Shakspeare ;" and he then quotes the following lines, which our readers will thank us for offering to them apart from the general text :—

"Sit, Jessica. Look how the floor of heaven
Is thick inlaid with patines of bright gold.
There's not the smallest orb which thou behold'st
But in his motion like an angel sings,
Still quiring to the young-eyed cherubins :
Such harmony is in immortal souls;
But whilst this muddy vesture of decay
Doth grossly close it in, we cannot hear it."*

Campanella was of a later period than Shakspere, who probably found the idea in some of the Platonic works of which his writings unquestionably show that he was a student. In his hands it has

* Literature of Europe, vol. iii. p. 147. Mr. Hallam has quoted from memory; having put "vault" for "floor," with two or three minor variations.

447

ILLUSTRATIONS OF ACT V.

reached its utmost perfection of beauty. After those glorious lines, the parallel passage in Milton's 'Arcades,' fine as it is, appears to us less perfect in sentiment and harmony:—

> "In deep of night when drowsiness
> Hath lock'd up mortal sense, then listen I
> To the celestial Sirens' harmony,
> That sit upon the nine infolded spheres,
> And sing to those that hold the vital shears,
> And turn the adamantine spindle round,
> On which the fate of gods and men is wound.
> Such sweet compulsion doth in music lie,
> To lull the daughter of Necessity,
> And keep unsteady Nature to her law,
> And the low world in measur'd motion draw
> After the heavenly tune, which none can hear
> Of human mould, with gross unpurged ear."

Coleridge has approached the subject in lines which are worthy to stand by the side of those of Shakspere and Milton:—

> "Soul of Alvar!
> Hear our soft suit, and heed my milder spell;—
> So may the gates of Paradise, unbarr'd,
> Cease thy swift toils! Since haply thou art one
> Of that innumerable company
> Who in broad circle, lovelier than the rainbow,
> Girdle this round earth in a dizzy motion,
> With noise too vast and constant to be heard;—
> Fitliest unheard! For oh, ye numberless
> And rapid travellers! what ear unstunn'd,
> What sense unmadden'd, might bear up against
> The rushing of your congregated wings?"
>
> (*Remorse*, Act III., Sc. I.)

¹ SCENE I.—"*The man that hath no music in himself.*"

There is a great controversy amongst the commentators upon the moral fitness of this passage; and those who are curious in such matters may turn to the variorum edition, for a long and perilous attack upon Shakspere's opinions by Steevens, and to a defence of them, in their separate works, by Douce and Monck Mason. The interest of the dispute wholly consists in the solemn stupidity with which it is conducted. The summing-up of Steevens is unequalled:—"Let not this capricious sentiment of Shakspeare descend to posterity unattended by the opinion of the late Lord Chesterfield upon the same subject;" and then he quotes one of his Lordship's letters, containing an insolent attack upon "fiddlers."

² SCENE I.—"*The crow doth sing as sweetly as the lark,*" &c.

The animals mentioned in this play are all proper to the country, and to that part of it, to which the play relates. The wren is uncommon; but its note is occasionally heard. The crow, lark, jay, cuckoo, nightingale, goose, and eel, are all common in Lombardy.—(M.)

³ SCENE I.—"*This night, methinks, is but the daylight sick.*"

The light of moon and stars in Italy is almost as yellow as sunlight in England. The planets burn like golden lamps above the pinnacles and pillared statues of the city and the tree-tops of the plain, with a brilliancy which cannot be imagined by those who have dwelt only in a northern climate. The infant may there hold out its hands, not only for the full moon, but for "the old moon sitting in the young moon's lap,"—an appearance there as obvious to the eye as any constellation. Two hours after sunset, on the night of new moon, we have seen so far over the lagunes, that the night seemed indeed only a paler day,—"a little paler."—(M.)

[The Caskets.]

SUPPLEMENTARY NOTICE.

Mrs. Inchbald, in her edition of the Acted Drama, thus describes Lord Lausdown's *arrangement, with variations*, of The Merchant of Venice:—"The Jew of Venice, by Lord Lansdown, is an alteration of this play, and was acted in 1701. The noble author made some *emendations* in the work; but having made *the Jew a comic character*, as such he caused *more laughter than detestation*, which wholly *destroyed the moral* designed by the original author." A *comic* Shylock is certainly the masterpiece of the improvements upon Shakspere. We have reached a period when it is scarcely necessary to discuss whether this *emendation* of Shakspere were right or wrong; nor, indeed, whether Mrs. Inchbald herself be perfectly correct in assuming that, if the trial scene were now brought upon the stage for the first time, "the company in the side-boxes would faint or withdraw." The Merchant of Venice of the stage is, in many respects, the play of Shakspere. Macklin put down Lord Lansdown. But it is, with green-room propriety, accommodated to the taste of "the company in the side-boxes," by the omission of a great deal of what is highest in its poetry, and by the substitution, in some cases, of the actor's verses for Shakspere's. It is scarcely worth while to enter into details upon matters which, with regard to Shakspere in a large sense, are so intrinsically worthless; but we will furnish our readers with one parallel between the uncorrupted text and the text of the "prompt-book," to justify an opinion, which we venture to express with becoming diffidence,—that the sooner the prompt-books of Shakspere are burnt, the more creditable it will be to all those who interpret Shakspere to the public ear. Our specimen will simply consist of a lyric, which has been cast out of the prompt-book, as compared with one which has found its way into it. We may add that all the editions of this Acted Drama contain several other specimens of composition, equally worthy of being compared with the "old and antique song" of Voltaire's "barbarian."

SUPPLEMENTARY NOTICE.

A DUET BY SHAKSPERE, *not found in the Prompt-Book*.
"Tell me where is fancy bred,
Or in the heart, or in the head?
How begot, how nourished?
    Reply, reply.

It is engender'd in the eyes,
With gazing fed; and fancy dies
In the cradle where it lies:
    Let us all ring fancy's knell;
    I'll begin it,—Ding, dong, bell.
    All. Ding, dong, bell."
    (Act III., Edit. of 1623.)

A DUET FROM THE PROMPT-BOOK, *not found in Shakspere*.
Lorenzo.
"For thee, my gentle Jessy,
What labour would seem hard!
Jessica.
For thee, each task how easy
Thy love the sweet reward.
Lorenzo and Jessica.
The bee thus, uncomplaining,
Esteems no toil severe,
The sweet reward obtaining,
Of honey all the year."
    (Act v. of the Acted Drama.)

Passing from such truly insignificant matters, (but which, insignificant as they are, occasionally demand a slight observation,) we come to an opinion in which Mrs. Inchbald is by no means singular—that *detestation* of the Jew is "*the moral designed* by the original author." It is probable that, even in Shakspere's time, this was the popular notion. In an anonymous MS. 'Elegy on Burbage,' "one of the characters he is represented to have filled is that of Shylock, who is called 'the red-hair'd Jew.' This establishes that the part was dressed in an artificial red beard and wig, in order to render it more odious and objectionable to the audience."* This circumstance, however, is by no means a proof to us that Shakspere intended the Jew to move the audience to unmitigated odium. The players might have thought, indeed, that he was not odious enough for the popular appetite, and in consequence made him "more odious and objectionable." The question may be better understood as we proceed in an analysis of the characters and incidents of this drama.

A contemporary German critic, Dr. Ulrici†, has presented to us the entire plot of The Merchant of Venice under a very original aspect. His object has been to discover—what he maintains had not been previously discovered—the fundamental idea of the drama—the link which holds together all its apparently heterogeneous parts. We are scarcely yet accustomed to the profound views which the philosophical critics of Germany are disposed to take of the higher works of art, and of the creations of Shakspere especially. We are more familiar with the common opinion that genius works upon no very settled principles, and produces the finest combinations by some happy accident. It is thus that some of us are disposed to reject the opposite doctrines as mystical and paradoxical; and that nearly all of us are inclined to agree that "'twere to consider too curiously to consider so" as Tieck, and Ulrici, and others of their school consider. We, of England, however—strong as our determination may be to cling to what we call the common-sense view of a subject—are learning to receive with respect, at least for their ingenuity, those criticisms which look beyond the external forms of poetry; and for this reason we do not hesitate to offer to our readers a rapid notice of Dr. Ulrici's judgment upon the drama before us. The critic first passes the several characters in review. Antonio is the noble and great hearted, yielding to a passive melancholy, produced by the weight of a too agitating life of action; Bassanio, somewhat inconsiderate, but generous and sensible, is the genuine Italian gentleman, in the best sense of the word; Portia is most amiable, and intellectually rich (*geistreich*); Jessica is a child of nature, lost in an oriental love enthusiasm. The critic presents these characteristics in a very few words; but his portrait of Shylock is more elaborate. He is the well-struck image of the Jewish character in general—of the fallen member of a race dispersed over the whole earth, and enduring long centuries of persecution. Their firmness had become obstinacy; their quickness of intellect, craft; their love of possessions, a revolting avarice. "Nothing," says Dr. Ulrici, "had kept its rank in their universal decay, but the unconquerable constancy, the dry mummy-like tenacity of the Jewish nature. So appears Shylock—a pitiable ruin of a great and significant by-past time—the glimmering ash-spark of a faded splendour which can no longer warm or preserve, but can yet burn or destroy. We are as little able to deny him our compassion, as we can withhold our disgust against his modes of thinking and acting."

Dr. Ulrici next proceeds to notice Shakspere's mastership in the composition, uniting, and unfolding of the intricate plot. "We have three curious, and in themselves very complicated,

---

* Collier's 'New Particulars,' &c.
† 'Ueber Shakspeare's dramatische Kunst und sein Verhältniss zu Calderon un Göthe.

THE MERCHANT OF VENICE.

knots wound into each other:—first, the process between Antonio and Shylock; next, the marriages of Bassanio and Portia, of Gratiano and Nerissa; and, lastly, the elopement of Jessica, and her love's history with Lorenzo. These various interests, actions, and adventures are disposed with such a clearness and fixedness—one so develops itself out of and with the others,—that we never lose the thread that everywhere reveals an animated and harmoniously-framed principle." The critic then proceeds to say, that, although an *external* union of the chief elements is clearly enough supported, the whole seems in truth to be inevitably falling asunder; and that " we have now to inquire where lies the *internal* spiritual unity which will justify the combination of such heterogeneous elements in one drama."

Throughout many of Shakspere's plays, according to Dr Ulrici, the leading fundamental idea, concentrated in itself, is so intentionally hidden—the *single* makes itself so decidedly important, and comes before us so free, and self-sustained, and complete,—that the entire work is occasionally exposed to the ungrounded reproach of looseness of plan and want of coherency. On the other hand, there are sufficient intimations of the meaning of the whole scattered throughout; so that whoever has in some degree penetrated into the depths of the Shaksperian art cannot well go wrong. The sense and significancy of the process between Antonio and the Jew rest clearly upon the old juridical precept, *Summum jus, summa injuria*—(the highest law, the highest injustice.) Shylock has, clearly, all that is material, except justice, on his side; but while he seizes and follows his right to the letter, he falls through it into the deepest and most criminal injustice; and the same injustice, through the internal necessity which belongs to the nature of sin, falls back destructively on his own head. The same aspect in which this principle is presented to us in its extremest harshness, in the case of Shylock, shows itself in various outbursts of light and shadow throughout all the remaining elements of this drama. The arbitrary will of her father, which fetters Portia's inclination, and robs her of all participation in the choice of a husband, rests certainly upon paternal right; but even this right, when carried to an extreme, becomes the highest injustice. The injustice which lies in the enforcement of this paternal right would have fallen with tragical weight, if chance had not conducted it to a fortunate issue. The flight and marriage of Jessica, against her father's will, comprehends a manifest injustice. Nevertheless, who will condemn her for having withdrawn herself from the power of such a father? In the sentence laid upon the Jew, by which he is compelled to recognise the marriage of his daughter, is again reflected the precept—*Summum jus, summa injuria;* right and unright are here so closely driven up into the same limit, that they are no longer separated, but immediately pass over one to the other. Thus we see that the different, and apparently heterogeneous, events unite themselves in the whole into one point. They are only variations of the same theme. All human life is a great lawsuit; where right is received as the centre and basis of our being. From this point of view proceeds the drama But the more this basis is built upon, the more insecure does it exhibit itself. Unquestionably, right and law ought to uphold and strengthen human life. But they are not its basis and true centre. In them the whole truth of human existence does not lie enclosed. In their one-sidedness right becomes unright, and unright becomes right. Law and right have their legality and truth, not through and in themselves; but they rest upon the higher principles of the true morality, from which they issue only as single rays. Man has in and for himself no rights, but only duties. But, at the same time, against others his duties are rights; and there is no true living right that does not include, and may be itself indeed, a duty. Not upon right, then, but upon the heavenly grace rests the human being and life. The union of the human with the Divine will is the true animating morality of mankind—through which right and unright first receive their value and significancy. Shakspere indicates this in the following beautiful verses:—

> " The quality of mercy is not strain'd;
> It droppeth, as the gentle rain from heaven
> Upon the place beneath: it is twice bless'd;
> It blesseth him that gives, and him that takes:
> 'Tis mightiest in the mightiest; it becomes
> The throned monarch better than his crown:
> His sceptre shows the force of temporal power,
> The attribute to awe and majesty,
> Wherein doth sit the dread and fear of kings.
> But mercy is above this sceptred sway,

SUPPLEMENTARY NOTICE.

> It is enthroned in the hearts of kings,
> It is an attribute to God himself;
> And earthly power doth then show likest **God's**
> When mercy seasons justice. Therefore, **Jew**,
> Though justice be thy plea, consider this—
> That, in the course of justice, none of us
> Should see salvation: we do pray for mercy;
> And that same prayer doth teach us all to render
> The deeds of mercy."

We have thus very briefly, and, therefore, somewhat imperfectly, exhibited the views of Dr. Ulrici, with reference to the idea in which this drama is conceived. They belong to that philosophy which, whether for praise or for blame, has been called transcendental. We cannot avoid expressing our opinion that, although Shakspere might not have proposed to himself so *systematic* a display of the contest that is unremittingly going forward in the world between our conventional and our natural being, he did intend to represent the anomalies that have always existed between the circumstances by which human agents are surrounded, and the higher motives by which they should act. And this idea, as it appears to us, is the basis of the large toleration which belongs to this drama, amidst its seeming intolerance. Men are to be judged upon a higher principle than belongs to mere edicts,—by and through all the associations amidst which they have been nurtured, and by which they have been impelled. We will take a case or two in point.

Antonio is one of the most beautiful of Shakspere's characters. He does not take a very prominent part in the drama: he is a sufferer rather than an actor. We view him, in the outset, rich, liberal, surrounded with friends; yet he is unhappy. He has higher aspirations than those which ordinarily belong to one dependent upon the chances of commerce; and this uncertainty, as we think, produces his unhappiness. He will not acknowledge the forebodings of evil which come across his mind. Ulrici says " It was the over-great magnitude of his earthly riches, which, although his heart was by no means dependent upon their amount, unconsciously confined the free flight of his soul." We doubt if Shakspere meant this. He has addressed the reproof of that state of mind to Portia, from the lips of Nerissa:—

"*Por.* By my troth, Nerissa, my little body is a-weary of this great world.

"*Ner.* You would be, sweet madam, if your miseries were in the same abundance as your good fortunes are: And yet, for aught I see, they are as sick that surfeit with too much, as they that starve with nothing."

Antonio may say—

"In sooth, I know not why I am so sad;"

but his reasoning denial of the cause of his sadness is a proof to us that the foreboding of losses—

"Enough to press a royal merchant down,—"

is at the bottom of his sadness. It appears to us as a self-delusion, which his secret nature rejects, that he says,—

> "My ventures are not in one bottom trusted.
> Nor to one place ; nor is my whole estate
> Upon the fortune of this present year;
> Therefore, my merchandize makes me not sad.'

When he has given the fatal bond, he has a sort of desperate confidence, which to us looks very unlike assured belief:—

> "Why, fear not, man; I will not forfeit it;
> Within these two months, that's a month before
> This bond expires, I do expect return
> Of thrice three times the value of this bond."

And, finally, when his calamity has become a real thing, and not a shadowy notion, his deportment shows that his mind has been long familiar with images of ruin:—

> "Give me your hand, Bassanio; fare you well!
> Grieve not that I am fallen to this for you;
> For herein fortune shows herself more kind
> Than is her custom: It is still her use,
> To let the wretched man outlive his wealth,
> To view, with hollow eye and wrinkled brow,
> An age of poverty; from which lingering penance
> Of such a misery doth she cut me off."

THE MERCHANT OF VENICE.

The generosity of Antonio's nature unfitted him for a contest with the circumstances amid which his lot was cast. The Jew says:—

> "In low simplicity,
> He lends out money gratis."

He himself says:—

> 'I oft deliver'd from his forfeitures
> Many that have at times made moan to me."

Bassanio describes him, as:—

> "The kindest man,
> The best condition'd and unwearied spirit
> In doing courtesies."

To such a spirit, whose "means are in supposition"—whose ventures are "squander'd abroad"—the curse of the Jew must have sometimes presented itself to his own prophetic mind:—

> "This is the fool that lends out money gratis."

Antonio and his position are not in harmony. But there is something else discordant in Antonio's mind. This kind friend—this generous benefactor—this gentle spirit—this man "unwearied in doing courtesies"—can outrage and insult a fellow-creature, because he is of another creed:—

> *Shy.* "Fair sir, you spet on me on Wednesday last;
> You spurn'd me such a day; another time
> You call'd me dog; and for these courtesies
> I'll lend you thus much monies.
> *Ant.* I am as like to call thee so again,
> To spet on thee again, to spurn thee too."

Was it without an object that Shakspere made this man, so entitled to command our affections and our sympathy, act so unworthy a part, and not be ashamed of the act? Most assuredly the poet did not intend to justify the indignities which were heaped upon Shylock; for in the very strongest way he has made the Jew remember the insult in the progress of his wild revenge:—

> "Thou call'dst me dog, before thou had'st a cause;
> But, since I am a dog, beware my fangs."

Here, to our minds, is the first of the lessons of charity which this play teaches. Antonio is as much to be pitied for his prejudices as the Jew for his. They had both been nurtured in evil opinions. They had both been surrounded by influences which more or less held in subjection their better natures. The honoured Christian is as intolerant as the despised Jew. The one habitually pursues with injustice the subjected man that he has been taught to loath; the other, in the depths of his subtle obstinacy, seizes upon the occasion to destroy the powerful man that he has been compelled to fear. The companions of Antonio exhibit, more or less, the same reflexion of the prejudices which have become to them a second nature. They are not so gross in their prejudices as Launcelot, to whom "the Jew is the very devil incarnation." But to Lorenzo, who is about to marry his daughter, Shylock is a "faithless Jew." When the unhappy father is bereft of all that constituted the solace of his home, and before he has manifested that spirit of revenge which might well call for indignation and contempt, he is to the gentlemanly Solanio "the villain Jew," and "the dog Jew." When the unhappy man speaks of his daughter's flight, he is met with a brutal jest on the part of Salarino, who, within his own circle, is the pleasantest of men:—"I, for my part, knew the tailor that made the wings she flew withal." We can understand the reproaches that are heaped upon Shylock in the trial scene, as something that might come out of the depths of any passion-stirred nature; but the habitual contempt with which he is treated by men who in every other respect are gentle and good-humoured and benevolent, is a proof to us that Shakspere meant to represent the struggle that must inevitably ensue, in a condition of society where the innate sense of justice is deadened in the powerful by those hereditary prejudices which make cruelty virtue; and where the powerless, invested by accident with the means of revenge, say with Shylock, "The villainy you teach me I will execute; and it shall go hard but I will better the instruction." The climax of this subjection of our higher and better natures to conventional circumstances is to be found in the character of the Jew's daughter. Young, agreeable, intelligent, formed for happiness, she is shut up by her father in a dreary solitude. One opposed to her in creed gains her affections; and the ties which bind the father and the child are broken for ever. But they are not broken without compunction:—

SUPPLEMENTARY NOTICE.

> "Alack! what heinous sin is it in me
> To be asham'd to be my father's child."

This is nature. But when she has fled from him—robbed him—spent fourscore ducats in one night—given his turquoise for a monkey—and, finally, revealed his secrets, with an evasion of the ties that bound them, which makes one's flesh creep,—

> "When I was with him,"—

we see the poor girl plunged into the most wretched contest between her duties and her pleasures by the force of external circumstances. We grant, then, to all these our compassion; for they commit injustice ignorantly, and through a force which they cannot withstand. Is the Jew himself not to be measured by the same rule? We believe that it was Shakspere's intention so to measure him.

When Pope exclaimed of Macklin's performance of Shylock, —

> "This is the Jew
> That Shakspere drew!"

the higher philosophy of Shakspere was little appreciated. Macklin was, no doubt, from all traditionary report of him, perfectly capable of representing the subtlety of the Jew's malice and the energy of his revenge. But it is a question with us, whether he perceived, or indeed if any actor ever efficiently represented, the more delicate traits of character that lie beneath these two great passions of the Jew's heart. Look, for example, at the extraordinary mixture of the personal and the national in his dislike of Antonio. He hates him for his gentle manners :—

> "How like a fawning publican he looks!"

He hates him, "for he is a Christian;"—he hates him, for that "he lends out money gratis;"—but he hates him more than all, because

> "He hates our sacred nation."

It is this national feeling which, when carried in a right direction, makes a patriot and a hero, that assumes in Shylock the aspect of a grovelling and fierce personal revenge. He has borne insult and injury "with a patient shrug;" but ever in small matters he has been seeking retribution :—

> "I am not bid for love, they flatter me:
> But yet I'll go in hate, to feed upon
> The prodigal Christian."

The mask is at length thrown off—he has the Christian in his power; and his desire of revenge, mean and ferocious as it is, rises into sublimity, through the unconquerable energy of the oppressed man's wilfulness. "I am a Jew: Hath not a Jew eyes? hath not a Jew hands, organs, dimensions, senses, affections, passions? fed with the same food, hurt with the same weapons, subject to the same diseases, healed by the same means, warmed and cooled by the same winter and summer, as a Christian is? If you prick us, do we not bleed? if you tickle us, do we not laugh? if you poison us, do we not die? and if you wrong us, shall we not revenge? If we are like you in the rest, we will resemble you in that." It is impossible, after this exposition of his feelings, that we should not feel that he has properly cast the greater portion of the odium which belongs to his actions upon the social circumstances by which he has been hunted into madness. He has been made the thing he is by society. In the extreme wildness of his anger, when he utters the harrowing imprecation,—"I would my daughter were dead at my foot, and the jewels in her ear! would she were hearsed at my foot, and the ducats in her coffin;" the tenderness that belongs to our common humanity, even in its most passionate forgetfulness of the dearest ties, comes across him in the remembrance of the mother of that execrated child :—"Out upon her! Thou torturest me, Tubal: it was my turquoise; I had it of Leah when I was a bachelor."

It is in the conduct of the trial scene that, as it appears to us, is to be sought the concentration of Shakspere's leading idea in the composition of this drama. The merchant stands before the Jew a better and a wiser man than when he called him "dog :"—

> "I do oppose
> My patience to his fury, and am arm'd
> To suffer, with a quietness of spirit,
> The very tyranny and rage of his."

THE MERCHANT OF VENICE.

Misfortune has corrected the influences which, in happier moments, allowed him to forget the gentleness of his nature, and to heap unmerited abuse upon him whose badge was sufferance. The Jew is unchanged. But if Shakspere in the early scenes made us entertain some compassion for his wrongs, he has now left him to bear all the indignation which we ought to feel against one "uncapable of pity." But we cannot despise the Jew. His intellectual vigour rises supreme over the mere reasonings by which he is opposed. He defends his own injustice by the example of as great an injustice of everyday occurrence—and no one ventures to answer him :—

> You have among you many a purchas'd slave,
> Which, like your asses, and your dogs, and mules,
> You use in abject and in slavish parts,
> Because you bought them :—Shall I say to you,
> Let them be free, marry them to your heirs?
> Why sweat they under burdens? let their beds
> Be made as soft as yours, and let their palates
> Be season'd with such viands? You will answer,
> The slaves are ours :—So do I answer you.
> The pound of flesh, which I demand of him,
> Is dearly bought; 'tis mine, and I will have it:
> If you deny me, fye upon your law!"

It would have been exceedingly difficult for the merchant to have escaped from the power of the obdurate man, so strong in the letter of the law, and so resolute to carry it out by the example of his judges in other matters, had not the law been found here, as in most other cases, capable of being bent to the will of its administrators. Had it been the inflexible thing which Shylock required it to be, a greater injustice would have been committed than the Jew had finally himself to suffer. Mrs. Jameson has very justly and ingeniously described the struggle which Portia had, in abandoning the high ground which she took in her great address to the Jew :—"She maintains at first a calm self-command, as one sure of carrying her point in the end; yet the painful heart-thrilling uncertainty in which she keeps the whole court, until suspense verges upon agony, is not contrived for effect merely; it is necessary and inevitable. She has two objects in view : to deliver her husband's friend, and to maintain her husband's honour by the discharge of his just debt, though paid out of her own wealth ten times over. It is evident that she would rather owe the safety of Antonio to anything rather than the legal quibble with which her cousin Bellario has armed her, and which she reserves as a last resource. Thus all the speeches addressed to Shylock, in the first instance, are either direct or indirect experiments on his temper and feelings. She must be understood from the beginning to the end, as examining with intense anxiety the effect of her own words on his mind and countenance; as watching for that relenting spirit which she hopes to awaken either by reason or persuasion "*

Had Shylock relented after that most beautiful appeal to his mercy, which Shakspere has here placed as the exponent of the higher principle upon which all law and right are essentially dependent, the real moral of the drama would have been destroyed. The weight of injuries transmitted to Shylock from his forefathers, and still heaped upon him even by the best of those by whom he was surrounded, was not so easily to become light, and to cease to exasperate his nature. Nor would it have been a true picture of society in the sixteenth century had the poet shown the judges of the Jew wholly magnanimous in granting him the mercy which he denied to the Christian. We certainly do not agree with the Duke, in his address to Shylock, that the conditions upon which his life is spared are imposed—

> "That thou shalt see the difference of our spirit."

Nor do we think that Shakspere meant to hold up these conditions as anything better than examples of the mode in which the strong are accustomed to deal with the weak. There is still something discordant in this, the real catastrophe of the drama. It could not be otherwise, and yet be true to nature.

But how artistically has the poet restored the balance of pleasurable sensations! Throughout the whole conduct of the play, what may be called its tragic portion has been relieved by the romance which belongs to the personal fate of Portia. But after the great business of the drama is wound up, we fall back upon a repose which is truly refreshing and harmonious. From the lips of Lorenzo and

---

* 'Characteristics of Women,' vol. i. p. 75.

SUPPLEMENTARY NOTICE.

Jessica, as they sit in the "paler day" of an Italian moon, are breathed the lighter strains of the most playful poetry, mingled with the highest flights of the most elevated. Music and the odours of sweet flowers are around them. Happiness is in their hearts. Their thoughts are lifted by the beauties of the earth above the earth. This delicious scene belongs to what is universal and eternal, and takes us far away from those bitter strifes of our social state which are essentially narrow and temporary. And then come the affectionate welcomes, the pretty, pouting contests, and the happy explanations of Portia and Nerissa with Bassanio and Gratiano. Here again we are removed into a sphere where the calamities of fortune, and the injustice of man warring against man, may be forgotten. The poor Merchant is once more happy. The "gentle spirit" of Portia is perhaps the happiest, for she has triumphantly concluded a work as religious as her pretended pilgrimage "by holy crosses." To use the words of Dr. Ulrici, "the sharp contrarieties of right and unright are played out."

www.ingramcontent.com/pod-product-compliance
Lightning Source LLC
Chambersburg PA
CBHW022108300426
44117CB00007B/628